Clare McGrath-Merkle

BÉRULLE'S SPIRITUAL THEOLOGY OF PRIESTHOOD

A Study in Speculative Mysticism and Applied Metaphysics

Aschendorff
Verlag

Münster
2018

© 2018 ASCHENDORFF VERLAG GMBH & CO. KG, MÜNSTER
www.aschendorff-buchverlag.de

Printed in Germany
Gedruckt auf säurefreiem, alterungsbeständigem Papier ∞
ISBN: 978-3-402-11910-5
ISBN (E-book-PDF): 978-3-402-11911-2

In Memoriam

Reverend Father John Lubey
thaumaturge, ecstatic, friend of Jesus

Le bon Dieu est dans le détail.

Gustave Flaubert

Table of Contents

Acknowledgments

My sincerest gratitude to Dr. Raymond Studzinki, O.S.B., my mentor and advisor at The Catholic University of America's School of Theology and Religious Studies, without whose unparalleled combined expertise in spiritual theology and identity studies, as well as gracious encouragement, I would not have been prepared to attempt this study.

My thanks to the late Dr. Jacques Gres-Gayer for his bibliographic assistance on the topic of Jansenism. Thanks also to Dr. John F. Wippel for providing bibliographic assistance on the topic of essentialism in the Christology of the sixteenth century. Many thanks to Rev. David Thayer, S.S. for fruitful conversations regarding the French School and for the loan of books, without which this study could not have proceeded. Special thanks to Dr. Peter B. Merkle for his suggestion on the use of concept mapping.

Thanks, especially, to Mary Ann Parks for her suggestion at the beginning of my doctoral studies to follow a course of study on the influences of Jansenism and essentialism on the priesthood. Thanks to Dr. Wilfrid Dubé, who graciously provided me a copy of his dissertation, recommendations on the authenticity of certain texts, notably regarding the vows of servitude, and his views regarding the absence of nominalism in Bérulle's thought. A special word of gratitude to all the staff members of the Knott Library at St. Mary's Seminary and University in Baltimore. Thanks to the Sulpician family who permitted me the use of this excellent library collection. Special thanks to the student assistants of the University of Augsburg for providing copies of works not available in the U.S., as well as scholars and librarians in Europe who also procured copies.

My heartfelt thanks to my benefactors without whom this study would not have been possible: Jack Ames for his support, Dr. Leon Podles and The Crossland Foundation for travel and book purchase support; Beth Hungerford for travel support; the Parks family for financial support; and Katherine Fisher for the gift of frequent flyer miles. Special thanks to Mary Agnes Merkle for her gifts of encouragement and humor.

Thanks to all my other friends, relatives, colleagues, and advisors, especially Father John Dillon Ph.D., Arlene Spadone and fellow students Dr. Jeanne Kamat, O.C.D.S. and Rev. Dr. Beverly Goines for their encouragement; Stella Davis and members of CWIA for their spiritual support; the secular Carmelites of St. Joseph's Secular Carmel of Port Tobacco for their prayers and support; Susie Flaherty for her doses of Irish grit; Kathleen O'Connor for formatting assistance; Mary Ann Parks for copyediting and Jean Ferrante-Burke for proofreading assistance; Dr. Nathalie Davis-Haslbeck and Anne-Elisabeth Giuliani for the review of French quotations; Dr. Jennifer Ottman for review, final proofreading, and technical assistance with German, Greek, and Latin quotations; and Greg, Stephen, and Chips Merkle for their generosity.

My sincerest thanks to Prof. Dr. Uwe Voigt and Prof. Dr. Freimut Löser as members of my dissertation committee. Most importantly, my deepest gratitude to Prof. Dr. Thomas Schärtl for his direction of my study of the Trinity in relation to Calvinism, his ultimate taking on of the direction of my thesis at the University of Augsburg, and his scholarly support and encouragement. His tutelage on the metaphysics of eternal generation was crucial in determining my course of research.

Finally, I dedicate this work to Our Lady, Undoer of Knots.

List of Abbreviations

Bérulle's Works

OC, Bourgoing ed.	*Les Œuvres de l'éminentissime et révérendissime Pierre cardinal de Bérulle…augmentées de divers opuscules de controverse et de piété, avec plusieurs lettres: et enrichies de sommaires et de tables*, ed. François Bourgoing (Paris: Paris: Antoine Estienne, 1644).
OC, Migne ed.	*Œuvres complètes de Bérulle, cardinal de l'Église Romaine, fondateur et premier supérieur de l'Oratoire* (Paris: M. Migne, 1856).
OC, Montsoult ed.	*Œuvres complètes du cardinal de Bérulle* (Montsoult: Maison d'institution de l'Oratoire, 1960) (Photographic reproduction).
OC, title and date	*Œuvres complètes* (Paris: Oratoire de Jésus, 1995–2011).
CB	*Correspondance du cardinal Pierre de Bérulle*, 3 volumes (Paris: Desclée de Brouwer, 1937–39).
Grandeurs	*Discours de l'état et des grandeurs de Jésus par l'union ineffable de la divinité avec l'humanité, et de la dépendance et servitude qui lui est due et à sa très sainte Mère en suite de cet état admirable*, various editions.
Mémorial	*Mémorial de quelques points servans a la direction des Supérieurs en la Congrégation de l'Oratoire de Iesus.*
OC	*Œuvres complètes*, various editions.
OP	*Œuvres de piété*, various editions.

OR   Texts related to the Oratory as included in Michel Dupuy and Pierre de Bérulle, *Bérulle et le sacerdoce: étude historique et doctrinale: Textes inédits* (Paris: Lethielleux, 1969).

BLS   Michel Dupuy and Pierre de Bérulle, *Bérulle et le sacerdoce: étude historique et doctrinale: Textes inédits* (Paris: Lethielleux, 1969).

Collationes   *Collationes congregationis nostrae*

Other Works

AS   J. Huijben, "Aux sources de la spiritualité française du XVIIe siècle," *Supplément à la Vie spirituelle* 25 (December 1930): 113–39; 26 (January 1931): 17–46; 26 (February 1931): 75–111; 27 (April 1931): 20–42; and 27 (May 1931): 94–122.

BSA   Michel Dupuy, *Bérulle: une spiritualité de l'adoration* (Tournai, Belgium: Desclée & Co., 1964).

CD   Pseudo-Dionysius, Beate Regina Suchla, Günter Heil, and Adolf Martin Ritter, *Corpus Dionysiacum* (Berlin: de Gruyter, 1990).

CO   John Calvin, *Corpus Reformatorum* (Brunswick: C. A. Schwetschke, 1863–1900).

DSAM   Marcel Viller, Charles Baumgartner, and André Rayez, *Dictionnaire de spiritualité: ascétique et mystique, doctrine et histoire* (Paris: G. Beauchesne et ses fils, 1932).

DTC   Alfred Vacant, E. Mangenot, and Emile Amann, *Dictionnaire de théologie catholique, contenant l'exposé des doctrines de la théologie catholique, leurs preuves et leur histoire* (Paris: Letouzey et Ané, 1899).

État	Guillén F. Preckler, *"État" chez le cardinal de Bérulle: théologie et spiritualité des états bérulliens* (Rome: Università Gregoriana, 1974).
Institutes	John Calvin, *Institutes of the Christian Religion*, various editions.
Institution	Jean Calvin and J. D. Benoit, *Institution de la religion chrestienne.* (Paris: Vrin, 1957–60).
Le mystère	G. Yelle, *Le mystère de la sainteté du Christ selon le cardinal Pierre de Bérulle* (Montréal: Université de Montréal, 1938).
LS	Lawrence Terrien, "Living Sacraments: Some Reflections on Priesthood in Light of the French School and Documents of the Magisterium," *Bulletin de Saint-Sulpice* 31 (2005): 243–59.
LW	Martin Luther, Jaroslav Pelikan, Helmut T. Lehmann, and Christopher Boyd Brown, *Luther's Works*, 75 vols. (Philadelphia and St. Louis: Fortress Press, 1955–).
PDV	Catholic Church and John Paul II, *Post-synodal Apostolic Exhortation <u>Pastores Dabo Vobis</u> of His Holiness John Paul II: To the Bishops, Clergy and Faithful on the Formation of Priests in the Circumstances of the Present Day* (Vatican City: Libreria Editrice Vaticana, 1992).
SM	Jean-Michel Le Lannou, "Le 'sacrifice du moi' selon Bérulle," *Revue des sciences religieuses* 78, no. 2 (2004): 205–30.
Subsistence	Charles A. Whannou, *Subsistence chez Bérulle: essai historique et doctrinale sur la place et l'importance de la notion de "subsistence" dans la spiritualité bérullienne de la divinisation* (Porto-Novo,

République du Bénin: Imprimerie Notre-Dame, 1993).

TG   Mary Jane McKay, "A Theology of Grace in the Works of Cardinal Pierre de Bérulle (1575–1629)" (PhD diss., South Bend, IN: University of Notre Dame, 1992).

TM   Henri Bremond, *A Literary History of Religious Thought in France from the Wars of Religion Down to Our Own Times*, vol. 3, *The Triumph of Mysticism*, trans. K. L. Montgomery (London: Society for Promoting Christian Knowledge, 1928–36). The 1936 edition has been cited in this study. Originally published as *Histoire littéraire du sentiment religieux en France depuis la fin de guerres de religion jusqu'a nos jours*, vol. 3, *La conquête mystique: l'École française* (Paris: Bloud et Gay, 1921).

UC   Dennis E. Tamburello, *Union with Christ: John Calvin and the Mysticism of St. Bernard* (Louisville, KY: Westminster John Knox Press, 1994).

WA   Martin Luther, *Luthers Werke: Kritische Gesammtausgabe*, Weimar: Hermann Böhlau, 1883–.

Introduction

Purpose of This Study

Pope Saint John Paul II's apostolic exhortation on the formation of seminarians, *Pastores Dabo Vobis (PDV)*,[1] has been called the "magna carta" of the theology of priesthood.[2] Donovan noted that the image of the priest set forth in the document follows that of the French School of spirituality.[3] Cardinal Pierre de Bérulle (1575–1629) is considered the founder of the French School, also known as Berullism.[4] Although this spirituality perdured at least until the advent of the Second Vatican Council and is now experiencing a renewed interest, a critical appraisal of Bérulle's ideals and his possible influence on the development of the theology of priesthood has not been conducted. The purpose of this study is to explore and appraise Bérulle's spiritual theology of priesthood.

Thesis

Cardinal, diplomat, statesman, and controversialist, Bérulle saw France as having been destroyed by heresy, and so founded the Congregation of the Oratory of Jesus and Mary Immaculate in 1611 for the formation of secular priests. His purpose was to purify Catholicism by a return to primitive Christianity.[5] The Council of Trent had urged bishops to found seminaries as part of its efforts at

---

[1] Catholic Church and John Paul II, *Post-synodal Apostolic Exhortation Pastores Dabo Vobis of His Holiness John Paul II: To the Bishops, Clergy and Faithful on the Formation of Priests in the Circumstances of the Present Day* (Vatican City: Libreria Editrice Vaticana, 1992), hereafter *PDV*.

[2] Thomas McGovern, *Priestly Identity: A Study in the Theology of Priesthood* (Dublin: Four Courts Press, 2002), 68–83.

[3] Daniel Donovan, *What Are They Saying About the Ministerial Priesthood?* (New York, NY, and Mahwah, NJ: Paulist Press, 1992), 30.

[4] Yves Krumenacker, "Qu'est-ce qu'une école de spiritualité?," in *Port-Royal et l'école française de spiritualité: actes du colloque organisé par la société des amis de Port-Royal* (Paris: Bibliothèque Mazarine, 2007), 11–23.

[5] Charles E. Williams, *The French Oratorians and Absolutism, 1611–1641* (New York: Peter Lang, 1989), xi.

reform,[6] and in France, these efforts flourished.[7] Bérulle began what ultimately grew into the seminary movement of the Society of Saint-Sulpice, founded by Jean-Jacques Olier, another clerical leader of the French School and the inheritor of his ideals on the priesthood.

The thesis of this study is that Bérulle's spiritual theology of priesthood created a sea change in the Church's theology of priesthood. Principally by means of oral conferences presented to his Oratorians and other pieces related to the Oratory, Bérulle created a highly complex and syncretistic spiritual theology of priesthood by means of a polemicized positive theological method, incorporating ideas from the realms of speculative mysticism and applied metaphysics.

Scope

This work explores Bérulle's spiritual theology of priesthood in relation to the complex debates of the Reformation and Counter-Reformation insofar as key polemical themes may have influenced his project and, so, the development of the theology of priesthood in general. While this study is not unconcerned with authoritative sources in regard to the theology of priesthood, it mainly explores Bérulle's spiritual theology of priesthood, constructed with ideas he appropriated from the positive theologies of his era and from a long tradition dealing with speculative mysticism, that is, philosophical speculation regarding mystical experience, and shaped into an applied metaphysic. Key themes related to theology, philosophy, and spirituality present in tradition, as well as those leading up to and including the Reformation and Counter-Reformation eras, will be explored in tandem with societal, ecclesial, and cultural influences which may have had a bearing on Bérulle's spirituality and theologizing.

This analysis will highlight especially those aspects, many of which scholars of the French School have already signaled, that may be vitiated by some central error and which may have survived even until the present in some form, although a comparison with current ideas surrounding the priesthood is beyond the scope of this study.

---

[6]   Yves Krumenacker, "Du prêtre tridentine au 'bon prêtre'," in *L'image du prêtre dans la littérature classique, XVIIe–XVIIIe siècles*, ed. Danielle Fister (Frankfurt: Peter Lang, 2001), 125.

[7]   Gustave Martelet, *Deux mille ans d'Église en question: théologie du sacerdoce*, vol. 3, *Du schisme d'Occident à Vatican II* (Paris: Éditions du Cerf, 1990), 158–61.

Setting the Stage

This introduction will now highlight certain challenges associated with the study of speculative mysticism and give an overview of the discipline known as spiritual theology, the chosen specialized focus of this study. Following will be a discussion of the characteristics of Baroque theological method in general and Bérulle's in particular. Next will be a review of various textual and linguistic issues associated with the French School and Bérulle's work, as well as a commentary on the texts under consideration. Last will be a discussion of detailed aspects of the priesthood to be studied in this analysis in relation to Bérulle's spiritual theology in light of what scholars have indicated are French School concepts known to be influences on those of the Second Vatican Council as well as *Pastores Dabo Vobis*.

Speculative Mysticism, the Discipline of Spiritual Theology, and the Limits of this Study

Rahner wrote, "There is generally no received theology of mysticism within the body of Christian theology."[8] "*Mystical theology*… must on its own principles be only a part of dogmatic theology."[9] Importantly, Rahner noted a problem for mystical theology in the relationship between nature and grace.[10] So, too, for this study of concepts related to Bérulle's spiritual theology, in which the nature and grace debates influenced theorizing about the relationship between configuration and conformity in terms of sacerdotal character and sacerdotal grace, as well as both the practice of theology in relation to the priesthood and the formation of priests for centuries to come.

The problem of the relationship of grace and nature in mystical theology dogged the era of the Counter-Reformation in particular, in certain treatises on the priesthood written by "moralists," who at the time focused these clerical formation manuals on ideals related to sacerdotal spirituality and mores. In fact, implicit and explicit concepts pertaining to both theology and philosophy were integral to texts such as these. Generally overlooked in these works have been the dynamic between systematic, mystical, ascetical, and moral theologies and their

---

[8]   Karl Rahner, *The Practice of the Faith: A Handbook of Contemporary Spirituality* (New York: Crossroad Publishing Company, 1983), 70. Originally published as *Praxis des Glaubens: geistliches Lesebuch*, ed. Karl Lehmann and Albert Raffelt (Zürich: Benziger, 1982).

[9]   Ibid., 73.

[10]   Ibid., 74–75.

possible influence on the theology of priesthood, notably due to theologians' dismissal of the quality and pertinence of these works.

Similarly, Bérulle's ideas, presented mainly in the form of oral conferences for his Oratorians and pieces related to the Oratory, have also been dismissed and not understood in terms of their possible influence—thus the impetus for this study.

Rahner wrote, "A true theologian ought to prove his education also by planning within five or ten years to acquire an idea of the history of spirituality…"[11] In fact, theologians in the twentieth century have returned to a more expanded notion of theological inquiry to include spirituality studies. This *ressourcement* began at a time when, according to Dryer and Burrows, the study of dogmatic or systematic theology had become "divorced from what became ascetic or mystical theology." The latter was relegated to a lesser status, focusing on piety, the pursuit of perfection or everyday practices. This recent renewed interest in spirituality has encouraged its status as an academic discipline,[12] referred to as "spiritual theology."[13]

One challenge, however, still facing the integration of spiritual theology into theological research, according to Burton-Christie, has been the failure of theology to "pay sufficient attention to the ground of experience that informs meaningful theological discourse."[14] This study seeks to meet this challenge with an in-depth study of the spiritual theology of priesthood of Bérulle, which became a major influence on the theology of priesthood through the influence of the French School.

The Practice of Baroque Theology

The Catholic Reformation spanned three periods during the transition between the Reform and the Enlightenment: the Renaissance, the Baroque, and the

---

[11] Rahner, *The Practice of the Faith*, 56, quoted in Pierre de Bérulle and William Thompson, *Bérulle and the French School: Selected Writings* (New York, NY, and Mahwah, NJ: Paulist Press, 1989), 83.

[12] This brief overview is taken from Douglas Burton-Christie, "Introduction: Beginnings," in *Minding the Spirit: The Study of Christian Spirituality*, ed. Elizabeth Dreyer and Mark S. Burrows (Baltimore, MD: Johns Hopkins University Press, 2005), xxi–xxvii. It is not clear whether Dreyer and Burrows combine the two fields of mystical theology and ascetical theology.

[13] Bernard McGinn, "The Letter and the Spirit: Spirituality as an Academic Discipline," in *Minding the Spirit: The Study of Christian Spirituality*, ed. Elizabeth Dreyer and Mark S. Burrows (Baltimore, MD: Johns Hopkins University Press, 2005), 30.

[14] Burton-Christie, "Introduction," xxiv.

Rococo, according to Pereira and Fastiggi. The Baroque era was characterized by the desire for structure, the formulation of laws, and the reduction of phenomena to comprehensibility, as well as the themes of counterpoint and antithesis,[15] all characteristics shared by Bérulle.

One aim of Pereira and Fastiggi was to "present Baroque mysticism in the context of the age's total theological achievement."[16] At the climax of Baroque Scholasticism, Suárez, for example, created the integration of two systems, that of philosophy and theology, into one "super system" (the latter based on the former).[17] The authors wrote, "The blessed rage for system, endemic in baroque theology, affected spirituality also."[18]

Baroque positive theology was concerned with doctrine as determined by sources in Catholic theology, the scriptures, and tradition. It took three forms, those of biblical exegesis, ecclesiological history, and notably, patristics. The goal of theology was not simply to instruct but to persuade and move to action.[19]

Bérulle's complex notions surrounding the spiritual theology of priesthood became just such a super system, with an emphasis on patristics and couched in the high rhetoric of the day.

Bérulle's Theologizing

Certain spiritual writers in the sixteenth century turned to Thomas Aquinas and to theology to attempt to analyze mystical experience, according to Le Brun. An evolution was occurring in terminology. "Mystical theology," which had signified mystical experience and the *science des saints*, grew to designate the systematization of mystical experience by theological reflection—and with serious consequences, as it suffered from imprecision.[20] Bérulle's work falls firmly within this trend.

In fact, a wide diversity of thought and a lack of doctrinal clarity was already reflected, according to McGrath, in a theology of religious orders which had begun in thirteenth-century Paris with the assigning of particular academic chairs to religious orders, following various thinkers such as Aquinas, Duns Scot,

---

[15] José Pereira and Robert Fastiggi, *The Mystical Theology of the Catholic Reformation: An Overview of Baroque Spirituality* (Lanham, MD: University Press of America, 2006), ix.

[16] Ibid., 2.

[17] Ibid., 23.

[18] Ibid., 34.

[19] Ibid., 45.

[20] Jacques Le Brun, "Le grand siècle de la spiritualité française et ses lendemains," in *Histoire spirituelle de la France: spiritualité du catholicisme en France et dans les pays de langue française, des origines à 1914* (Paris: Beauchesne, 1964), 236–38.

Bonaventure, and Giles of Rome. This diversity continued into the sixteenth century.[21]

Bérulle's own affective and Platonic theology, couched in Thomistic terms, was an effort especially to reconcile the thought of Aquinas and Duns Scot and their successors.

Janz noted also that Thomism was a major influence in Luther's world as well, and Luther admitted to having studied the best of its literature. He came to see Thomism as antithetical to the scriptures, and Thomists led the attack against him, including Cajetan.[22]

Yelle, in reviewing briefly key figures who had commented on Bérulle's work, highlighted Prat's observation of Bérulle's tendency to *singularité*.[23] Important to this study, the singularity of Bérulle's work merited accusations of heresy in his day and the suppression of key texts, contributing to a general under-reading of his work, and a misappraisal of the character and influence of his work on the theology of priesthood.

Carraud, a contemporary philosopher, has written on Bérulle's philosophical ideals.[24] He noted that Bérulle neither claimed to be a philosopher, nor is his work considered a typical philosophical work. In fact, Bérulle's enterprise was explicitly anti-philosophical, following St. Paul's invective against empty philosophizing. His was a rejection of Scholasticism and its philosophical love of self, as he held that human philosophy could not arrive at true knowledge of the self, which he understood to be a *néant* in relation to God, as we will explore.[25]

[21] Alister E. McGrath, *The Intellectual Origins of the European Reformation*, 2nd ed. (Malden, MA: Blackwell Publishing, 2004), 7–19.

[22] Denis R. Janz, "Thomism," in *Oxford Encyclopedia of the Reformation*, vol. 4 (New York and Oxford: Oxford University Press, 1996), 151–54.

[23] Jean-Marie Prat, *Recherches historiques et critiques sur la Compagnie de Jésus en France au temps du Coton*, vol. 2 (Lyon, 1876), bk. 12, ch. 5, 378, quoted. Also cited in G. Yelle, *Le mystère de la sainteté du Christ selon le cardinal Pierre de Bérulle* (Montréal: Université de Montréal, 1938), 22.

[24] Vincent Carraud, "De l'état de néant à l'état anéanti: le système du néant de Bérulle," *Cahiers de philosophie de l'Université de Caen*, no. 43 (2007): 211–47. Carraud utilized the Montsoult, Migne, and 1995–2011 editions of the *Œuvres completes*, as indicated.

[25] Ibid., 212–15. See also Mary Jane McKay, "A Theology of Grace in the Works of Cardinal Pierre de Bérulle (1575–1629)" (PhD diss., South Bend, IN: University of Notre Dame, 1992), 153, hereafter cited as TG. McKay clarified Bérulle's notion of *néant* as signifying nothingness. McKay wrote, "This non-being which is otherness relative to God is central to the meaning of the term *néant* which passed from Pseudo-Dionysius into Rheno-Flemish spiritual theology. It is possible that Bérulle retained this concept because it was key to one of his expressions of the movement toward unity...However, Bérulle did not simply adopt the term *néant* as it came to him from the Rheno-Flemish masters. Because

Bourgoing, an early companion and, later, third superior general of the Oratory, hailed Bérulle as a master of positive, Scholastic, and mystical theologies, who revealed the last as a purer theology, into which everything was reduced.[26]

This reduction or reframing of positive theology and Scholastic concepts into a mystical schema can be found throughout Bérulle's work. His theology was more than the blend of these three theologies, however. As Congar asserted, "the Reformation…brought to life a new activity of defense which, under the name of 'polemics' or 'controversy,' was quickly constituted a separate branch of theology…" Its creation and development, according to Congar, "influence(d) the very conception of theology."[27]

This study will demonstrate that Bérulle's polemicized positive spiritual theology of priesthood influenced the Church's conception of the theology of priesthood itself.

Lastly, referencing Étienne's analysis, de Certeau pinpointed a key influence in the era of the "modern" Augustinianism of Jean Driedo in promoting a theological method that always had as reference the movements of the soul.[28] This could certainly be applied to any reading of Bérulle, but most notably in his spiritual conferences for members of his Oratory.

The Issues of Mysticism and Mystical Language in Bérulle's Work

According to Le Brun, in the midst of a mysticism vs. anti-mysticism debate in the seventeenth century, and influenced, in part, by a religious classicism in decline, spirituality had a central question regarding mysticism, its nature, and

---

he sees the human being as primarily weak and unfulfilled, Bérulle assimilates 'emptiness' and 'indigence' to *néant*."

[26] Jean Galy, *Le sacrifice dans l'école française* (Paris: Nouvelles Éditions Latines, 1951), 25n17. Galy loosely quoted François Bourgoing, "Préface," in Pierre de Bérulle and J.-P. Migne, *Œuvres complètes de Bérulle, cardinal de l'Église romaine, fondateur et premier supérieur de l'Oratoire, augmentées de plusieurs opuscules inédits et d'un grand nombre de pièces recueillies dans divers ouvrages, disposés dans un ordre logique* (Paris: Ateliers catholiques Migne, 1856), 83–84, hereafter *OC*, Migne ed.

[27] Yves M.-J. Congar, *A History of Theology*, trans. and ed. Hunter Guthrie (Garden City, NY: Doubleday & Company, Inc., 1968), 175. Based on the article "Théologie" in *Dictionnaire de théologie catholique*, hereafter referred to as *DTC*, vol. 15, pt. 1 (1946): 341–502.

[28] Michel de Certeau, "La réforme dans le catholicisme," in *Histoire spirituelle de la France: spiritualité du catholicisme en France et dans les pays de langue française, des origines à 1914* (Paris: Beauchesne, 1964), 202. See J. Étienne, *Spiritualisme érasmien et théologiens louvanistes: un changement de problématique au début du XVIe siècle* (Louvain: Publications universitaires de Louvain, 1956), 160.

its role in spirituality: is spirituality about extraordinary states or the Christian life in general? Certain schools rose to lead the debate: the abstract school with its total conformity to divine will through annihilation of the self; Jesuit spirituality with its abandonment to the Holy Spirit; Saint-Jure's spirituality of uniting to Christ, annihilated in God; and Bérulle's spirituality of adherence to Christ's mysteries and states. Vigorous objections to spiritual authors and accusations and condemnations of heresy created a hostile environment and caused a number of works to undergo editing.[29]

Bérulle's work was no exception.

De Certeau wrote on the problem of mystical language and about the post-Tridentine attempt to remake a political and spiritual world of grace, taking the form with Bérulle of "a utopian ecclesiastical hierarchy that would articulate the secrets of mystical life." Functioning in secret groups, such as in the Saint-Sulpice seminaries, this interiorized world was based on the Calvinist model to reform society on the basis of scriptures.[30]

This reform, influenced by Calvinism, was not only introduced by Bérulle but reached a particular zenith first with the Oratory, well before the rise of the Sulpician seminary system.

Pseudo-Dionysius's was a "structural homology," as de Certeau described, between "mystical knowledge of the 'seer' and the ecclesial hierarchy." The sainted philosopher had "haunted five centuries of ecclesiastic reformism."[31] His "artificial 'language'"…"presented the model for a new science."[32]

Bérulle embraced this science fully in terms of his spiritual theology of priesthood.

De Certeau continued with an explanation of theology after the Renaissance. Scholastic, positive, and mystical theologies were characterized by their own language: the Scholastic by Aristotelian and nominalist language; the positive by scriptural and patristic language; and mystical theology by the Pseudo-

---

[29] Le Brun, "Le grand siècle de la spiritualité française et ses lendemains," 275–81, paraphrased.

[30] Michel de Certeau, *The Mystic Fable*, vol. 1, *The Sixteenth and Seventeenth Centuries*, trans. Michael B. Smith (Chicago and London: University of Chicago Press, 1992), 20–21. First published as *La fable mystique: XVIe – XVIIe siècle* (Paris: Gallimard, 1982), 35: "l'utopie d'une hiérarchie ecclésiastique articulant les secrets de la vie mystique…"

[31] Ibid., 90. In *La fable mystique*, 121: "…et jusqu'à Bérulle, Denys l'Aréopagite soit la référence dominante. Il pose une homologie de structure entre la connaissance mystique du 'voyant' (*oratikos*) et la 'hiérarchie ecclésiastique'…Denys a hanté cinq siècles de réformisme ecclésiastique auxquels il offrait une utopie speculative…"

[32] Ibid., 104. In *La fable mystique*, 143: "Par sa cohérence et son originalité lexicales…cette 'langue' artificielle présente le modèle d'une science nouvelle. Elle en est à la fois la condition et l'utopie."

Dionysian.[33] Mystical theology became independent at the turn of the seventeenth century.[34] De Certeau saw that the mystical journey had become a "self-imposed exile from the solidity of things," having been first determined by a reorganization of knowledge.[35]

Bérulle also reorganized ideals from tradition, utilizing concepts and language from these three branches of theology to construct his spiritual theology, resulting in an ahistorical sacerdotal spiritual theology unmoored from tradition, with recombined and redefined concepts.

Mystical writers, according to de Certeau, defended themselves by inventing an ancient mystical tradition or asserting that new words meant the same as ancient ones, by appealing to historical authority or to a secret tradition. This introduced the problem of a double reading and ambiguity in orthodox language.[36] De Certeau did not reference Bérulle directly as one of these *mystics* but it is clear that Bérulle, neither mystic, theologian, nor philosopher, entered into this class as he developed both a new grammar and a methodology based on a near-encyclopedic range of sources and ideals.

De Certeau wrote of the special practices and spaces formed by *mystics* which, arguably, could also characterize Bérulle and members of his Oratory, as this study will uncover. He wrote:

> they institute a "style" that articulates itself into *practices* defining a *modus loquendi* and/or a *modus agendi*…What is essential, therefore, is not a body of doctrines (which is the effect of these practices and above all the product of later theological interpretation), but the foundation of a field in which specific procedures will be developed: a *space* and an *apparatus*. The theoreticians of this mystical literature placed at the heart of the debates that at that time opposed them to "theologians" or "examiners" either the "mystic phrase" ("manners of expression," "turns of phrase,"

---

[33] Ibid., 107.

[34] Ibid., 107n126. The translator noted that the term "la mystique" was an elliptic form of "la théologie mystique." See also ix–x. The translator also noted he took the liberty to create an English term for which there is no equivalent in French. The term "la mystique" in French neither signifies mysticism, nor the mystical, nor the mystic but rather the field of the study of mysticism (as *physics* is a field). The translator coined the English term "*mystiques*" (always in italics) to denote this field. This translator's liberty adds no little confusion to de Certeau's already complex expressiveness.

[35] Ibid., 105. In *La fable mystique*, 145: "C'est l'entreprise mystique de partir chercher l'Un en s'exilant de la solidité des choses. Mais elle est d'abord déterminée par le mouvement qui réorganise le savoir. Je n'en retiens que deux éléments, également impliqués dans sa constitution en une science propre."

[36] Ibid., 110.

ways of "turning" words) or "maxims" (rules of thought or actions for "saints," that is, mystics). The reinterpretation of the tradition is characterized by an ensemble of processes that allow language to be treated differently—the entire contemporary language, not just the separate domain concerning theological knowledge or a patristical or scriptural corpus. Ways of acting organize the invention of a mystic body.[37]

Methods of the Era

De Certeau also described in detail the development and importance of methods in the centuries leading up to the seventeenth century. Methods applied to one field jumped boundaries and were combined and applied in others. In the Renaissance, the technical and social roles of methods became accentuated. According to de Certeau, the new science of mysticism involved a major development of methods, characterized by a mental and pedagogical technology (inherited from monastic tradition), the formation of a separate space, and a technique of rupture from what had gone before, with groups formed that constructed types of laboratories.[38]

Bérulle accomplished this development of method with the Oratory.

De Certeau also wrote, "Any theology eliminates the irreducibility of differences by the production of a 'tradition,' that is, by definition an 'essential' that clerical knowledge singles out, claims as its own, and regards as the common denominator of an oceanic plurality."[39]

---

[37] Ibid., 14–15. In *La fable mystique*, 26: "…elles instaurent un 'style' qui s'articule en *pratiques* définissant un *modus loquendi* et/ou un *modus agenda*…L'essentiel n'est donc pas un corps de doctrines (ce sera plutôt l'effet de ces pratiques et surtout le produit d'interprétations théologiques postérieures), mais la fondation d'un champ où se déploient des procédures spécifiques: un *espace* et des *dispositifs*. Les théoriciens de cette littérature placent au cœur des débats qui les opposent alors aux 'théologiens' ou 'examinateurs' soit les 'phrases mystiques' ('manières d'expression', 'tours' de langage, façons de 'tourner' les mots), soit des 'maximes' (règles de pensée ou d'action propre aux 'saints', c'est-à-dire aux mystiques). La réinterprétation de la tradition a pour caractéristique un ensemble de procès qui permettent de traiter autrement le langage—tout le langage contemporain, et non pas seulement la région qu'y découpe un savoir théologique ou un corpus patristique et scripturaire. Ce sont des manières de faire qui organisent l'invention d'un corps mystique."

[38] Ibid., 126–29.

[39] Ibid., 111. In *La fable mystique*, 155: "Elle élimine l'irréductibilité de différences par la production d'une 'tradition', c'est-à-dire par la définition d'un 'essentiel' qu'un savoir clérical découpe, s'approprie et tient pour le dénominateur commun d'une pluralité océanique."

Bérulle also created a new "theological" "tradition" of the priesthood, presented as canonical and essential, which was, at base, a spiritual theology.

Lastly, de Certeau noted that symbolism is a central problem in mystical language and that a theory of symbolism disintegrated at the end of the Middle Ages. "One axis of that theory…presumes that there must be a real analogy between the procedures (logical and rhetorical) that organize meaning and the succession or disposition of the facts. The link between the rhetorical and the 'ontic' has a strategic function here." In medieval times, a transfer from the linguistic to the theological became generalized, according to de Certeau.[40]

Bérulle's rhetoric was to reify key scriptural and patristic ideals into facts, transferring the metaphorical to ontological and historical categories, moved into place by his spiritual theology.

Textual Issues in the Study of the French School

Bremond noted that some theologians have disregarded the leaders of the French School, claiming their work was merely a mixture of dogmatic speculation and elevation.[41] Galy's research on the doctrine of sacrifice in the French School was an effort to examine this complex doctrine in light of the progress in scholarly conversation regarding which ideals might be considered pious and which precise theology.[42] However, serious methodological issues disallowing a close reading of texts faced Galy (and continue to face scholars of the French School today), including, as he described: how to know which works were original, many of which were undated and/or recorded oral transmissions; issues of definitions of key concepts which differed between authors; and the scope of French School writers' knowledge or ignorance of patristic texts, Aquinas, and the canons of the Council of Trent, as well as the plethora of diverse schools of thought present at the time of their writing.

---

[40]   Ibid., 90–91. In *La fable mystique*, 122: "Ne retenons qu'un axe de cette théorie. Elle suppose qu'il doit y avoir une analogie réelle entre les procédures (logiques ou rhétoriques) qui organisent le sens et la succession ou disposition des faits (dans 'une histoire du salut' et/ou dans un cosmos de la révélation). La jointure du rhétorique et de l'"ontique' y a une fonction stratégique."

[41]   Henri Bremond, *A Literary History of Religious Thought in France from the Wars of Religion Down to Our Own Times*, vol. 3, *The Triumph of Mysticism*, trans. K. L. Montgomery (London: Society for Promoting Christian Knowledge, 1928–36), hereafter *TM*, 573. The 1936 edition has been cited in this study. Originally published as *Histoire littéraire du sentiment religieux en France depuis la fin de guerres de religion jusqu'a nos jours,* vol. 3, *La conquête mystique: l'École française* (Paris: Bloud et Gay, 1921).

[42]   Galy, *Le sacrifice dans l'école française,* 10–16. This review follows Galy's analysis closely.

Galy also noted the difficulty in the comparison of these texts with any other system. Not being dogmatic treatises, they were neither directly speculative nor exhaustive, neither replying to objections nor shielding from ambiguity, as he described. The meaning of terms was not definite and was varied, with rigor in vocabulary lacking. The general purpose of these writings was to edify, not judge. He chose, therefore, to guard against deducing from any one text, but rather to note multiple evidences, differences and similarities of expressions, as well as the frequency of themes.[43]

In a similar vein, Dupuy commented that because Bérulle took from various sources, changing them to make them his own, it is difficult to attribute in his work what is owed to which influence. He did not direct his arguments to individuals but rather wrote long justifications in which key controversial points only appear as small details. He also avoided any Scholastic formulae.[44]

This present study depends, in part, on the experience and judgment of scholars of the French School in these matters. However, important previously unpublished texts made widely available in the twentieth century do contain references pointing to hidden ideals not heretofore explored in sufficient detail. In addition, where influences have not been noted by scholars, this study attempts to address additional possible influences on Bérulle's thought.

Bérulle's Rhetoric

Writing on philosophy in the sixteenth century, Kenny noted that humanists valued grammar, philology, and rhetoric over technical philosophical problems. The use of logic declined during this period. In Counter-Reformation philosophy, Catholic controversialists defended the notion that religious truths were within the scope of the human intellect, and that faith needed reason.[45]

Bérulle was formed in this environment and would use all these tools to accomplish his purposes in combating what he saw as the Huguenot threat.

Ferrari wrote about what she termed the "divine rhetoric" of Bérulle.[46] Ferrari's work was the first stylistic study of Bérulle's work, particularly of the

---

[43] Ibid., 13–16. See 16: as Galy put it, "Traiter chacune de leurs propositions comme une thèse, comprendre chaque terme en un sens strictement univoque serait une injustice grave et une erreur certaine qui mènerait vite à des impasses."

[44] Michel Dupuy, "Un guide de lecture pour Bérulle," *La Vie spirituelle* (April 1963): 462–75.

[45] Anthony Kenny, *The Rise of Modern Philosophy: A New History of Western Philosophy*, vol. 3 (Oxford: Clarendon Press, 2006), 2, 11–12, and 16.

[46] Anne Ferrari, *Figures de la contemplation: la "rhétorique divine" de Pierre de Bérulle* (Paris: Éditions du Cerf, 1997). In the following discussion, see especially 11–24, 28–42, 62–70, 297–318, 329, 341–56, and 373–90. Ferrari referenced the 1960 Montsoult ed. of Bérulle's

relationship between his spirituality and his style. Bérulle first studied philosophy with the Jesuits at Clermont College. The era in which Bérulle found himself was one of a renaissance in rhetoric, especially in the service of sacred discourse. The Council of Trent itself had attempted to promote a return to the fathers in order to reform this discourse. The Jesuits were at the center of the debate regarding rhetoric and attempted to create a program of studies, in which Bérulle was formed, which held to a Ciceronian rhetoric.[47]

After his time at Clermont, Bérulle began the study of law. His father, grandfather, and uncles were parliamentarians and wanted to make him a counselor of parliament as well. The rhetoric that these *gens de robe* were known for was rigorous and eloquent. Bérulle was to abandon his law studies after two years but, according to Dagens, he retained certain juridical arguments that can be traced in his work.[48] Thereafter, he returned to Clermont to study theology and then on to the Sorbonne. An ardent follower of St. Augustine and his *De doctrina Christiana*, Bérulle seized the idea that words should remain pure signs of the divine reality. Augustine's work was considered a model of the art of oratory. For Bérulle, rhetoric's purpose was not to please but to render God knowable by the heart through contemplation of the truth, which was to be frequently repeated and exalted. In time, Bérulle's style came to be seen as difficult and boring.

Bérulle followed the same principles that other writers on the subject of ecclesiastical rhetoric had recommended, including the practice of fashioning one's manner of speaking and preaching to each audience. As a controversialist involved in ongoing polemics with Calvinists, Bérulle's language was that of controversialist discourse, that is, concrete but filled with metaphors and striking images meant to shock. Bérulle made use of constructions favored during the Baroque period, including repetition, parallelism, opposition, antithesis, and oxymoron. He also had a tendency toward binary rhythm, parallelisms, and especially anaphora. His long, structured phrases sometimes included tertiary parallelisms that were almost synonymous. Ferrari noted that at times Bérulle approached pleonasm. He used the tripartite schema frequently, and replaced known categories by his own. For example, nature, grace, and glory became for Bérulle nature, sin, and grace.

Œuvres complètes, unless otherwise indicated. This review follows the author's exposition closely.

[47] Ibid., 24. See Jean Maldonat, "Discours inaugural de Maldonat," in J. M. Prat, *Maldonat et l'Université de Paris au XVIe siècle* (n.p., 1856), cited in Jean Dagens, "Notes bérulliennes: La source du bref discours de l'abnégation intérieure," *Revue d'histoire ecclésiastique* 27 (1931): 341.

[48] Ibid., 24–25. See Dagens, "Notes bérulliennes," 15n1 and 235.

Approaching the Baroque style, Bérulle also included paradoxical formulations and hyperbole, which played a major role in his rhetoric. His sayings "Dieu est l'homme, et l'homme est Dieu" and "Dieu se fait homme et l'homme devient Dieu" are two examples.[49] This kind of wordplay introduced ambiguities and gained Bérulle charges of heresy.

Ferrari ended her analysis with the observation that Bérulle's rhetoric was one of adherence to God. Bérulle intended that the text itself become a means of contemplation by elevation.[50] In this, he followed Pseudo-Dionysius, who wrote that the contemplative members of the hierarchy could acquire insight into the things of God by creating a ritual expression of contemplative insight, such as, for example, a theological treatise.[51]

Bérulle's Works: Comments on the Texts

While Bérulle published a number of works in his lifetime, it was Bourgoing who published a posthumous 1664 edition of his opus, known as the *Œuvres complètes*, co-edited by Gibieuf.[52] His preface to the edition served as a summary of Bérulle's thought. Besides the 1644 edition, the one often cited by scholars has been Migne's 1856 edition,[53] held, however, as inferior to the former in quality and with still-missing texts.[54]

Bérulle did not write on the priesthood per se but rather presented his ideals in terms of the Oratorian vocation in oral conferences, which, Dupuy noted, arguably, left a question as to his thinking on the priesthood itself. Known as *Collationes congregationis nostrae*, and consisting of notes taken by an auditor,

---

[49] Pierre de Bérulle, *Œuvres complètes*, Reproduction de l'Édition Princeps (Montsoult: Maison d'Institution de l'Oratoire, 1960), hereafter cited as *OC*, Montsoult ed., *Discours de l'état et des grandeurs de Jésus* (hereafter cited as *Grandeurs* in all editions), Discours 7, 276, and Discours 9, 318, quoted in Ferrari, *Figures de la contemplation*, 360.

[50] See Ferrari, *Figures de la contemplation*, 385–90.

[51] See James Miller on Pseudo-Dionysius in *Measures of Wisdom: The Cosmic Dance in Classical and Christian Antiquity* (Toronto: University of Toronto Press, 1986), 495.

[52] Pierre de Bérulle and François Bourgoing, *Les Œuvres de l'éminentissime et reverendissime Pierre cardinal de Bérulle,...augmentées de divers opuscules de controverse et de piété, avec plusieurs lettres: et enrichies de sommaires et de tables* (Paris: Antoine Estienne, 1644). Hereafter cited as *OC*, Bourgoing ed.

[53] *OC*, Migne ed.

[54] Bérulle and Thompson, *Bérulle and the French School*, 97. See also Jean Orcibal, "Les œuvres de piété du cardinal de Bérulle: essai de classement des inédits et conjectures chronologiques," *Revue d'histoire ecclésiastique* 57 (1962): 814, as cited in Guillén F. Preckler, *"État" chez le cardinal de Bérulle: théologie et spiritualité des états bérulliens* (Rome: Università Gregoriana, 1974), 3n16, hereafter cited as *État*.

these conferences spanned the first years of the founding of the Oratory between 1611 and 1615. The priesthood, in fact, became the life-long focus of Bérulle's activities.[55]

Bérulle's chef-d'œuvre and defense, titled *Discours de l'état et des grandeurs de Jésus par l'union ineffable de la divinité avec l'humanité, et de la dépendance et servitude qui lui est due et à sa très sainte Mère en suite de cet état admirable,* appeared in 1623.

Of particular note, Bourgoing and Gibieuf had attempted to hide the Platonic, Pseudo-Dionysian, and Rheno-Flemish themes in Bérulle's thought,[56] leaving certain texts out of the 1644 edition of his complete works. Bourgoing was concerned with possible continued accusations of Jansenism against the Oratory, as well as a perceived association with Neoplatonism. In an effort to defend Bérulle, Gibieuf appended a table of references to show Bérulle's fidelity to Aquinas.[57]

A renewed interest in Bérulle's opus in the 20th century sparked a return to the study of unpublished texts. Orcibal noted, in comparing published with unpublished materials, that the number of pieces kept by Bourgoing in his edition nearly doubles when unpublished works are taken into account. Orcibal also noted that the 1644 edition contained both interpolations and new compositions.[58]

Important for this study, in 1969, Dupuy published a doctrinal and historical study of certain previously unpublished pieces of Bérulle related to the priesthood.[59] Dupuy asked the question whether it would be efficacious to assemble the unpublished texts which were left aside by editors of the 1644 edition of his complete works, in order to uncover the doctrines that affected generations of priests. His answer was in the negative, citing the fact that much of Bérulle's sufficiently elaborated works on the topic of the priesthood had seen publication, and that what remained included pieces which posed critical questions. Bérulle himself complained that his conferences, for example, were

---

[55] See discussion by Michel Dupuy in Michel Dupuy and Pierre de Bérulle, *Bérulle et le sacerdoce: étude historique et doctrinale* (Paris: Lethielleux, 1969), 11–13, hereafter cited as *BLS*.

[56] *État*, 3. See Louis Cognet, *La spiritualité moderne (1500–1650)* (Paris: Aubier, 1966), 326–27, 377, and 471.

[57] Paul Cochois, "Bérulle, hiérarque dionysien," *Revue d'ascétique et de mystique* 37 (1961): 317–18. Cochois utilized the Migne edition.

[58] Orcibal, "Les œuvres de piété du cardinal de Bérulle," 814. See also 816–17, as cited in *État*.

[59] See *BLS*, 11–17, for this discussion.

often poorly copied.[60] Dupuy chose what he deemed only the most reliable among various copies of documents. Despite limitations, it is clear that certain central and repeated ideas are found in strong relief in these texts, which have found their way into French School tradition.

In 1995, a team of editors, managed by Michel Dupuy, began producing the first of a series of newly edited volumes of Bérulle's opus through Éditions du Cerf, also consulted and utilized for this study.[61]

Aspects of Priesthood to be Studied and Why

Guerra explored various kinds of priesthood, including Christian, ethnic, national, and hereditary priesthoods, as well as what he called the chthonic-mystery priesthood. The novelty of the Christian priesthood, he noted, is its participation in the priesthood of Christ, its emphasis on evangelization, and its particular sacrifice. The problems that pose themselves in the study of the Christian priesthood, according to Guerra, are the nature of its sacrifice, mediation, and representation.[62]

Bérulle faced these same issues in explicating his ideals. This study will demonstrate from evidence that, during an era of a resurgence of ancient ideals and texts, Bérulle adapted certain ideas from non-Christian priesthoods to meet what he considered the threats of Reformist and Renaissance thought.

In regard to issues attendant to representation, there are various aspects related to priesthood and configuration to Christ, according to Bifet: supernatural realities, doctrinal systematization, characteristic virtues, ascetical

---

[60]   Ibid., 15n5. See Pierre de Bérulle and Jean Dagens, *Correspondance du cardinal Pierre de Bérulle* (Paris and Louvain, 1937–39), 403, hereafter cited as *CB*.

[61]   The multi-volume, multi-year collaborative work is known as Pierre de Bérulle, *Œuvres complètes* (Paris: Édition du Cerf, 1995–2011), hereafter cited under each volume and year. Included in this multi-volume work are keys indicating the parallel numbering of works between the 1644, 1856, and 1995 editions. *Collationes congregationis nostrae* was published in French in *Œuvres complètes*, vol. 1, and known as *Conférences et fragments*, trans. Auguste Piedagnel, ed. Michel Dupuy (Paris: Oratoire de Jésus, 1995). It was also published in Latin in *Œuvres complètes*, vol. 2, *Collationes*, ed. Michel Dupuy (Paris: Oratoire de Jésus, 1995). Dupuy's references in *BLS* are to *Collationes congregationis nostrae*, manuscrit latin 18210 (Paris: Bibliothèque nationale). In this study, we refer to it as *Collationes* in all editions as specified, with individual pieces noted as "Coll.," followed by the number of each piece. These are paralleled in the 1995 edition of *Collationes*, as well as in the 1995 French translation *Conférences*.

[62]   Manuel Guerra, "Problemática del sacerdocio ministerial en las primeras comunidades cristianas," in José Capmany Casamitjana, *Teología del sacerdocio*, vol. 1, *Orientaciones metodológicas* (Burgos: Ediciones Aldecoa, S.A., 1969), 19–20 and 46–47.

means to achieve them, and communitarian organization.[63] Bérulle's spiritual theology of priesthood was constructed around these lines, including an attempt at an anti-Scholastic systematization, a challenge in attempting to analyze his work.

This study will delineate these and additional issues such as historical factors (political, sociological, juristic, and ethical) that might have had a bearing. Chief among these in Bérulle's project were configuration and conformity to Christ.

Configuration and Conformity in the Study of the Priesthood

In response to the Protestant threat and the call by Trent to reform the priesthood through seminary training, Bérulle constructed a spiritual theology of priesthood via a system of clerical formation to deal with unresolved issues related to configuration and conformity. These questions remain urgent ones today.

Costello wrote about what he called "priestly identity," examining the anthropology of sacerdotal formation in the light of the documents of the Eighth Synod of Bishops and Pope John Paul II's post-synodal apostolic exhortation on the formation of priests known as *Pastores Dabo Vobis*.

Costello accepted as a given the following encompassing definition of conformity to Christ and seminary formation's role in accomplishing it: "The purpose of seminary formation is to support the candidate in his desire to be transformed, psychologically and sacramentally, into a living image of Jesus Christ, head and shepherd of the Church, an idea put forth in the post-synodal document, *Pastores Dabo Vobis*."[64]

This stated goal had its formal beginning with Bérulle's construction of a new spiritual theology of priesthood through his system of formation for his Oratorians.

Costello's study related principally to the vast field of identity studies within psychology, with an anthropological focus that was both psychological and philosophical more than theological. The main problem he wished to address was "the difficulty encountered in forming a stable sacerdotal identity."[65]

---

[63] Juan Esquerda Bifet, "Estado actual de la reflexión teológica sobre el sacerdocio," in José Capmany Casamitjana, *Teología del sacerdocio*, vol. 1, *Orientaciones metodológicas* (Burgos: Ediciones Aldecoa, S.A., 1969), 206.

[64] Timothy Costello, *Forming a Priestly Identity: Anthropology of Priestly Formation in the Documents of the VIII Synod of Bishops and the Apostolic Exhortation Pastores Dabo Vobis* (Roma: Editrice Pontificia Università Gregoriana, 2002), 42.

[65] Ibid., 30.

This crucial need to stabilize sacerdotal identity formed the impetus for Bérulle's theorizing as well, in an attempt to meet Reformers' critiques regarding the widespread corruption of the clergy.

While the priesthood, according to Costello, "can easily become equated with a series of societal roles such as community leader, presider at liturgy, comforter of the bereaved..."[66] the Synod of Bishops was clear that "the priestly vocation finds its meaning and identity in values rather than roles. A role-orientation is inadequate because the priest is called to an ontological and theological self-transcendence that implies a willingness to transcend the role as well as the self."[67]

The issues surrounding the concept that the priest must rise above himself, as expressed in ontological and theological categories, as this study will highlight, also had a primary source in Bérulle's theorizing.

Costello pointed to O'Malley's analysis in his discussion of the various historical anthropological visions of seminary training during the centuries following Trent, considered "ethical-pessimistic," with a juridical approach with the goal of isolation for mission.[68]

This study will elucidate how during the era following Trent a comprehensive refashioning of the spiritual theology and identity of the priesthood took place, led by Bérulle, but in ways far outreaching this evaluation.

The Influence of the French School on the Second Vatican Council

In his 1971 article, Maritain explored the French School, and questioned how it was possible that a great number of churchmen remained under the influence of the French School despite having different doctrinal positions. Maritain answered that he believed that in their youth, they were more or less formed by that school in seminary, and were therefore unable to perceive the Platonic defects of a vague theology that had escaped rigorous intellectual systemization and therefore any kind of critical review. The result, he noted, was the production

---

[66] Ibid., 284.

[67] Ibid., 285. See also Luigi M. Rulla, Joyce Ridick, and Franco Imoda, *Anthropology of the Christian Vocation*, vol. 1, *Interdisciplinary Bases* (Rome: Gregorian University Press, 1986); L. M. Rulla, J. Ridick, and F. Imoda, *Entering and Leaving Vocation: Intrapsychic Dynamics* (Rome: Gregorian University Press, 1976), 234; G. Versaldi, "Priestly Celibacy from the Canonical and Psychological Points of View," in *Vatican II, Assessment and Perspectives: Twenty-five Years After (1962–1987)*, vol. 3, ed. R. Latourelle (Mahwah, NJ, 1989), 148–49.

[68] Ibid., 268–69. See J. O'Malley, "Diocesan and Religious Models of Religious Formation: Historical Perspectives," in Robert James Wister, *Priests: Identity and Ministry* (Wilmington, DE: M. Glazier, 1990), 54–70.

of an ideology rather than a theology, which had as its aim the inflaming of the heart. Maritain wrote that the school continued in his day to have an immense influence.[69]

This influence reached the Second Vatican Council, which Cancouët explored, including on the ideal of the relation of priests to Jesus. The first document the author treated was *Presbyterorum ordinis*, which clearly indicated that the priest's configuration to Christ included the notion of acting in the person of Christ the head.[70]

This conformity to Christ the head was found in the French School, and was one the author saw as based on a positive re-emergence of the Pauline ideal of the body of Christ.[71] In regard to the relation of priests to bishops, both Bérulle and Vatican II affirmed that the relation between them is of a mystical sacramental order and not only a practical order. The Council was concerned with the holiness of priests and took a decisive step, Cancouët noted, in the Church's understanding of a sanctity proper to priests as opposed to that of religious.[72]

The distinction between priests and religious became a key defense of Bérulle against Protestant criticism of the religious state as a state of holiness.

Dulles also treated the concept of the priesthood in Vatican II documents, which he saw as having been expanded from a cultic model to include clerical, pastoral, and kerygmatic aspects, as well as that of secular service. Dulles held that Vatican II overcame what he saw as the "excessive individualism of early modern theology of orders" found in seventeenth-century spirituality in which the priest was (arguably) "an isolated individual who has renounced the world for the sake of cultivating an otherworldly holiness."[73] He noted a problem in that the Second Vatican Council made preaching, teaching, and leadership co-equal

---

[69] Jacques Maritain, "À propos de l'école française," *Revue thomiste* (1971): 474–75, as cited in M. Cancouët, "Traces de la théologie et de la pratique de l'École française à Vatican II et au-delà," *Bulletin de Saint-Sulpice* 6 (1980): 214.

[70] "The office of priests, since it is connected with the episcopal order, also, in its own degree, shares the authority by which Christ builds up, sanctifies and rules his Body. Wherefore the priesthood, while indeed it presupposes the sacraments of Christian initiation, is conferred by that special sacrament; through it priests, by the anointing of the Holy Spirit, are signed with a special character and are conformed to Christ the Priest in such a way that they can act in the person of Christ the Head." Second Vatican Council, *Decree on the Ministry and Life of Priests, December 7, 1965 [Presbyterorum Ordinis]* (Washington, DC: National Catholic Welfare Conference, 1965), no. 2, quoted in Cancouët, "Traces de la théologie," 216–17.

[71] Cancouët, "Traces de la théologie," 217–18.

[72] Ibid., 220–27.

[73] Avery Dulles, "Models for Ministerial Priesthood," *Origins* 20 (1990): 287.

with the Christian priesthood, thus giving many functions to the priest which did not require ordination.

Jones summarized, however, that an enlarged view of the priesthood of Christ began with the French School, one that combined Trent's ideals with Protestant positions. Jones saw the French School in general as spanning the divide between a Protestant concern for preaching, non-cultic behavior, interior sacrifice, and love and Trent's focus on a sacramental and mystical priesthood with a new emphasis on both Christ's and the priest's interior dispositions to adore and sacrifice. The stress between cultic and non-cultic tensions would continue, he argued, to the present day.[74]

This study will explore the aspects which Dulles saw as being innovations of the Second Vatican Council and those Jones noted as influential, all having had expressions in the Reformist and Counter-Reformist currents of the sixteenth century, and having found their way into Bérulle's spiritual theology of priesthood in response to Reformers' critiques, thus expanding greatly the functions and certain powers of the priesthood, including a missionary impetus focused on preaching and direction.

Salient to this analysis, Dulles attempted to define what he saw as the current representational priesthood after Vatican II, including the notion that by indelible character, the priest becomes an ecclesial person, or public person. In representing Christ the head, the ministerial priesthood expresses itself in all the activities performed in the person of Christ the head. To be "transparent to Christ," and live the grace of priesthood, the priest must become "another Christ."[75]

This study will illustrate how this expansion of the role of the priest, and this transparency, located in the notions of public person and representative of Christ the head, found its zenith first in Bérulle's spiritual theology of priesthood.

French School Notions in Pastores Dabo Vobis

Terrien, former Superior General of the Society of Saint-Sulpice, the main contemporary inheritor of the French School tradition, wrote in detail about French School theological ideals related to the priesthood as found in recent magisterial documents.[76] Terrien's analysis is a critical benchmark for this study

---

[74] Michael Keenan Jones, "Toward a Christology of Christ the High Priest" (PhD diss., Rome: Editrice Pontificia Università Gregoriana, 2006), 351–52.

[75] Dulles, "Models for Ministerial Priesthood," 288.

[76] Lawrence Terrien, "Living Sacraments: Some Reflections on Priesthood in Light of the French School and Documents of the Magisterium," *Bulletin de Saint-Sulpice* 31 (2005): 243–59, hereafter cited as LS.

in highlighting key metaphysical concepts related to the spiritual theology of priesthood as they relate to present theological proposals.

While this study does not have a goal of directly addressing debates regarding these current trends specifically, it briefly delineates common themes to illustrate the pertinence of conducting this study in order to aid scholars in parsing both what could be "naïve appropriation[s] of tradition" (*naïve Traditionsaneignung*), as Gadamer described in his work, or antecedents found in the school that could be incorporated into present thinking through what he called a more nuanced "fusion of horizons" (*Horizontverschmelzung*).[77]

Terrien addressed the same text which Costello studied, *Pastores Dabo Vobis*, which, he noted, treated three key aspects of priestly identity: its Trinitarian foundations; its basis in the priest's special configuration to Christ the head of the Church; and the ideal of sacerdotal mission.[78]

All three aspects were influenced by Reform and Counter-Reform debates.

The Trinity, seen as the source of priestly identity in the document, according to Terrien, is so in terms of both *perichoresis* and mission, giving the priest a "relational" identity with a strong sense of mission.[79] Noting all ministry as an extension of the mission of the Son and the Spirit in the world, he noted that *PDV* developed "both Christological and Trinitarian dimensions…in treating configuration to Christ the head as well as the relationship between the ordained priesthood and the priesthood of all the faithful."[80]

This study will explore how the conceptualizations of mission, relation, configuration to Christ the head, and the linking of spiritualities between the ordained and laity were forged in the caldron of Reformist debates and represent in various ways reactions, inheritances, and aporias.

Terrien also treated the French School notion of Christ as *alter Christus* in *PDV*, which held the priest to be a sacramental representation of Christ as head and shepherd.[81] He cited *PDV* as basing this ideal in the larger identity of the

---

[77] Hans-Georg Gadamer, *Truth and Method*, 2nd printing (New York: Seabury Press, 1975), xxii. Originally published as *Wahrheit und Methode* (Tübingen: J. C. B. Mohr, 1972), xxii. Lowell Martin Glendon treated the subject of Gadamer's fusion of horizons in his dialogical analysis, "Jean-Jacques Olier's View of the Spiritual Potential of Human Nature: A Presentation and an Evaluation" (PhD diss., New York: Fordham University, 1983), 14–15. Glendon attempted to interpret what he called the negative spiritual anthropology of Olier (founder of the Society of Saint-Sulpice) to mine positive aspects for contemporary Sulpician priests.

[78] LS, 244, nos. 12–18.

[79] Ibid., 244. See *PDV*, no. 12.

[80] Ibid., 245.

[81] Ibid., 245.

Church itself as a "new priestly people…with a real ontological share in his one eternal priesthood, to which she must conform every aspect of her life."[82]

According to Terrien, in terms of the mission-oriented identity of the priest, the ideal of the priest as another Christ in *PDV* is to be grounded in service and sacrifice, not in an ideal that is above or apart from the Church. *PDV* described the priest's relationship with the Church as interiorly united to the relationality between Jesus Christ and the Church—the two relationships involving a kind of "mutual immanence" with the priest's "'sacramental representation' of Christ," the basis of his relationship with the Church.[83]

While *PDV* emphasized that "the ministerial priesthood does not of itself signify a greater degree of holiness with regard to the common priesthood of the faithful…"[84] Terrien noted that prior to the Second Vatican Council and in much of the Sulpician tradition, the ideal of the priest as an *alter Christus* lent to the idea that the priest was called to a special holiness. He nevertheless held that the first generation of French School figures considered the laity as *alteri Christi* as well, and their call to holiness the same call to configuration as other Christs.[85] Terrien noted Olier's ideal of the indwelling Christ in all Christians, as demonstrated by St. Paul's words, "It is no longer I who live, but Jesus Christ who lives in me."[86] Echoed in *PDV*,[87] this phrase was central in Bérulle's project as well, representing a key response to certain Reformist critiques which this study will highlight.

The document also points to the "spousal character" of the identity of the priest, rooted in Christ's identity as bridegroom.[88] Terrien quoted *PDV* regarding the purity and self-detachment that this spousal character involves.[89]

---

82   *PDV*, no. 13, quoted in LS, 245.

83   Ibid., no. 6, quoted in LS, 247.

84   Ibid., no. 17, quoted in LS, 247.

85   LS, 251.

86   J. J. Olier, quoting St. Paul (Gal. 2:20) in "Living Sacraments of Jesus Christ," in *Living for God in Christ Jesus* (an anthology of the writings of Olier published privately for the U.S. Province), 23, in turn quoted in LS, 251–52.

87   See *PDV*, no. 25: "While it is possible for God's grace to carry out the work of salvation through unworthy ministers, yet God ordinarily prefers to show his wonders through those men who are more submissive to the impulse and guidance of the Holy Spirit and who, because of their intimate union with Christ and their holiness of life, are able to say with St. Paul: 'It is no longer I who live, but Christ who lives in me' (Gal. 2:20)."

88   LS, 248–49.

89   *PDV*, no. 22, quoted in LS, 248: "the priest's life ought to radiate this spousal character which demands that he be a witness to Christ's spousal love, and thus be capable of loving people with a heart which is new, generous and pure, with genuine self-detachment, with full, constant and faithful dedication…"

Terrien also wrote about *PDV*'s enunciation of a central French School ideal and practice. He wrote, "Cultivating a constant awareness or consciousness of one's configuration to Christ will promote responsiveness to the call to holiness."[90] Terrien mentioned the term "states" (a key French School phrase) in relation to the states of life of laity, religious, and priests. He noted that in all three states, Christians are called in different ways to be "living sacraments," another key French School phrase.[91]

This call to frequent awareness was at the center of Bérulle's efforts to maintain conformity for his Oratorians.

The specific call to holiness for the priesthood, according to *PDV*, is that it must be Christological, that is, "the spiritual life of the priest is marked, molded, and characterized by the ways of thinking and acting proper to Jesus Christ, head and shepherd of the Church."[92] This spirituality is one that is ecclesial rather than private, meant to be a public witness, according to Terrien's reading of the document.[93]

Salient to this study, Terrien noted the current debate surrounding the notion of the priest as configured to Christ the head. In exploring the question as to whether this notion is definitive, Terrien responded in the negative, although he considered it the current official position. He did note that Pope John Paul II saw the limitations of this notion and tried to build correctives into the document, ones Terrien did not enumerate.[94]

The ideals of the priest as both public person and visible head of the Mystical Body in Bérulle's spiritual theology of priesthood were central to his rebuttal of Reformist critiques of the priesthood, and are the most outstanding and far-reaching of the aporias found in Bérulle's project, as this study will explore.

---

[90] LS, 249. Terrien follows this remark with a reference to *PDV*, no. 25, here expanded: "The bond with Jesus Christ assured by consecration and configuration to him in the sacrament of orders gives rise to and requires in the priest the further bond which comes from his 'intention,' that is, from a conscious and free choice to do in his ministerial activities what the Church intends to do. This bond tends by its very nature to become as extensive and profound as possible, affecting one's way of thinking, feeling and life itself: in other words, creating a series of moral and spiritual 'dispositions' which correspond to the ministerial actions performed by the priest." See also no. 57: "It is a question of a type of formation meant not only to ensure scientific, pastoral competence and practical skill, but also and especially a way of being in communion with the very sentiments and behavior of Christ the good shepherd…"

[91] Ibid., 252.

[92] *PDV*, no. 21, quoted in LS, 256.

[93] LS, 256.

[94] Ibid., 257–58.

Terrien addressed the fact that the French School has been criticized as having either a negative anthropology, or as being too positive (by Protestant theologians) in its conceptualization of the priest as living sacrament and *alter Christus*. He cited Bérulle's notion of the human as "néant capable de Dieu" as capturing this dichotomy.[95]

This particular kind of *néantisme*, as it is called, was arguably one of the central characteristics of Bérulle's spiritual theology, one fully explored by scholars.

Other ideas not mentioned by Terrien as found in *PDV* with links to Bérulle's project include abandonment to the Holy Spirit, the importance of the notion of "participation" as instrument, *imago Dei*, Christ's self-emptying (kenosis), and the relationship between self-emptying, purity, celibacy, and a new capacity to love.[96] Of particular interest is the notion of the priest as "a living and transparent image of Christ the priest."[97]

Of singular importance is the ideal of a special grace of priesthood that remedies the priest's human weakness by the holiness of Christ.[98] Also of note is the document's emphasis on the Eucharist as the culmination of the priest's pastoral charity, with an obligation to give his whole life a "sacrificial" dimension,[99] with a willingness to be "consumed" by others.[100] Other themes include the priest's vocation as part of the mystery of the Church,[101] the primacy

---

[95] Ibid., 255n16.

[96] *PDV*, nos. 1 and 13. See also no. 12: "The priest finds the full truth of his identity in being a derivation, a specific participation in and continuation of Christ himself, the one high priest of the new and eternal covenant." See also no. 20 in reference to the phrase "living instrument," and no. 21 in reference to Christ's self-emptying on the cross.

[97] Ibid., no. 12.

[98] Ibid., no. 20: "Therefore, since every priest in his own way represents the person of Christ himself, he is endowed with a special grace. By this grace the priest, through his service of the people committed to his care and all the People of God, is able the better to pursue the perfection of Christ, whose place he takes. The human weakness of his flesh is remedied by the holiness of him who became for us a high priest 'holy, innocent, undefiled, separated from sinners' (Heb 7:26)."

[99] Ibid., no. 23.

[100] Ibid., no. 28: "Finally, sacerdotal obedience has a particular 'pastoral' character. It is lived in an atmosphere of constant readiness to allow oneself to be taken up, as it were 'consumed,' by the needs and demands of the flock."

[101] Ibid., no. 35. Important to note is the strong link the document makes between the identity of the Church as mystery, communion, and mission and the identity of the priest. See also no. 59: "Since pastoral action is destined by its very nature to enliven the Church, which is essentially 'mystery,' 'communion' and 'mission,' pastoral formation should be aware of and should live these ecclesial aspects in the exercise of the ministry."

of grace and freewill in the call to priesthood, and its character as an oblation.[102] Also included in *PDV*, and reiterating the Council's *Optatam Totius*, is the French School (and Pseudo-Dionysian) idea of the priest entering the paschal mystery so as to become an initiator for others into the mystery.[103]

While Terrien located three main French School themes related to sacerdotal identity in *PDV* as Trinitarian foundations, mission, and configuration to Christ, undergirding and augmenting these themes are equally important ideas such as adherence, causality, potency, subsistence, the Mystical Body, theosis and indwelling, the will, the communication of idioms, mediatorship, and others. These will be taken up and studied in the works of Bérulle.

Conclusion

The nature of Bérulle's mainly orally-transmitted ideals related to the priesthood, coupled with his anti-Scholastic, Baroque style, does not dispose Bérulle's opus to scholarly inquiry. Each of a plethora of theological and philosophical ideals which Bérulle drew from tradition in support of his spiritual theology of priesthood was related to various others in a kind of chiaroscuro point and counterpoint, woven into a complex fabric of largely unstated polemical arguments and tied to often singularly defined or recombined notions related to positive theology and speculative mysticism. An adequate analysis first requires the separation of these concepts into his own categories, and a comparison of them with various ideals common to those found in tradition, which were taken up by polemicists during the Reformation and Counter-Reformation periods.

---

[102] Ibid., no. 35, as well as no. 36: "Freedom, therefore, is essential to vocation—a freedom which, when it gives a positive response, appears as a deep personal adherence, as a loving gift—or rather as a gift given back to the giver who is God who calls, an oblation…The free oblation, which constitutes the intimate and most precious core of a person's response to God who calls, finds its incomparable model, indeed its living root, in the most free oblation which Jesus Christ, the first of those called, made to the Father's will…"

[103] Pope Paul VI, *The Decree on Priestly Training: Optatam Totius* (Boston, MA: St. Paul Editions, 1965), quoted in *PDV*, no. 45: "Those who are to take on the likeness of Christ the Priest by sacred ordination should form the habit of drawing close to him as friends in every detail of their lives. They should live his Paschal Mystery in such a way that they will know how to initiate into it the people committed to their charge."

The Organization of This Study

Each chapter of this study will present an introductory background to each topic, relating it to tradition in general as well as proximate influences, including ideas current during the era surrounding Trent, the Reform, and Counter-Reform.

Chapter one serves as a presentation on methodology. Chapter two presents the historical context of the era under consideration, as well as a synopsis of Bérulle's life, times, influences, and project. The third chapter serves as a general overview of possible influences on Bérulle's project related to philosophy and speculative mysticism. Chapter four treats the rigorist influences of the era. The next three chapters address the highly complex Christological debates of the Reform and Counter-Reform, and their influences on Bérulle's thought. Chapters eight, nine, and ten treat Bérulle's spiritual theology related to the Trinity, the Mystical Body, and sacrifice. Chapters eleven and twelve present Bérulle's conception of the priest as mediator and public figure. Chapter thirteen explores Bérulle's notions surrounding sacerdotal character and grace. The next four chapters treat the topics of Bérulle's exemplarist spirituality, his ideas surrounding conformity and perfection, adoration and adherence, and the vows of servitude. Lastly, chapter eighteen presents Bérulle's notions surrounding the priest as image, followed by a concluding chapter and afterword.

Chapter 1
Methodological Considerations

Impetus for This Work

With an interest in the Roman Catholic crisis of clerical vocations, abuse, and cover-up, I focused my early doctoral research on possible psycho-social maladaptations in clerical identity. This focus evolved into the research question of whether clerical identity deficits might have a basis in clerical formation spirituality. Based on a recommendation of the late Dr. Jacques Gres-Gayer, noted scholar of 17th-century Jansenism at the Sorbonne, I first studied the formation manual for priests, widely utilized since the middle of the 17th-century until the Second Vatican Council, known as the *Traité des saints ordres*, long purported to be the teachings of Jean-Jacques Olier, yet heavily edited and largely penned by Louis Tronson.[1] Both were close followers of Pierre de Bérulle's ideals regarding the priesthood. This review, in turn, led to the realization, as noted, that there had been relatively little research on Bérulle's spiritual theology of priesthood, which I had come to see as mirrored in 20th-century official Church documents, as well as recent popular works on pastoral identity and spirituality.

General Challenges in the Study of the Priesthood

Perhaps the main challenges facing the study of the priesthood have been over-specialization, lack of coordination of research, and the august nature of the institution. Taking as a model the 19th-century geographer Sir Richard Burton, who refused to claim certainty as to the source of the Nile due to the lack of working instruments, I would argue that it is important to do the difficult work of forensic research based on evidence before claiming a particular theology of priesthood as canonical. Resisting the urge to suggest yet another of a myriad of current formulations in this, a polemical era similar to that of the 16th century, will require a holy restraint. Copious volumes on the spirituality and identity of the priesthood line shelves, attempts to fit together the many broad-brush strokes of disparate theological notions into one new hopeful icon or another. I hope this

---

[1] See Louis Tronson, Gilles Chaillot, Paul Cochois, and Irénée Noye, *Traité des saints ordres: 1676: comparé aux écrits authentiques de Jean-Jacques Olier (1657)* (Paris: Procure de la Compagnie de Saint-Sulpice, 1984). This work compares the work to Olier's authentic writings to discern which parts were penned by Tronson.

volume will serve as a foundational exploration for scholars to begin their own forensic analyses.

Challenges to Approaching Bérulle's Spiritual Theology of Priesthood

By way of apology, I would like to begin with a discussion of my own background and perspective. With the knowledge that the contemporary challenges of lowered vocations, moral failings, and high attrition affect contemporary Protestant as well as Roman Catholic pastoral identities, I took a wide-angle lens in exploring the underlying polemical themes of the Reformation and Counter-Reformation eras.

In terms of the current Roman Catholic priesthood, as noted, a return to tradition has been heralded as the answer to problems associated with the implementation of and the unforeseen effects of Vatican II, including principally what has been called the loss of the vertical dimension and the sense of the sacred, and one might argue, the perceived loss of the sense of the sacred priestly self.[2] However, I would argue, this current call to return to what some assert is *the* true theology of priesthood is to propose a return, in part, to Bérulle's particular spiritual theology of priesthood, systematically constructed in answer to the perceived threat of the Reformation.

Current debates might be characterized by dichotomies, such as high Christology vs. low, *alter Christus* vs. servant model, piety vs. social-justice orientation, and the ontological vs. the functional. This study will reveal hidden aspects underlying these themes which may aid scholars both in understanding the priesthood of Christ and in working through how the successors to the apostles participate in it.

As a Roman Catholic researcher, I am working with both welcome and sober constraints, fully assenting to the Church's tenets regarding the ministerial priesthood.

That said, I would argue that the theology of priesthood has, at times, been proposed as a closed matter, even though a systematized theology of priesthood has never been attempted other than that of the French School. Yet, as philosopher Jacques Maritain wrote now forty years ago, there is nothing more urgent than the renewal of the theology of priesthood: "Bénit soit le grand théologien qui, pour tirer le clergé de la crise où il se débat douloureusement,

---

2   See a more detailed discussion of the crisis of identity and my treatment of Gregory the Great's pastoral identity as found in *The Book of Pastoral Rule*: C. McGrath-Merkle, "Gregory the Great's Metaphor of the Physician of the Heart as a Model for Pastoral Identity," *Journal of Religion and Health* 50, no. 2 (2011): 374–88.

mettra un jour au point une juste théologie du sacerdoce, renouvelée de celle des vieux maitres! Ce sera là résponder à un des besoins plus urgents de notre temps."[3]

This study is an opening attempt to set the groundwork for scholars desiring to answer Maritain's call.

Specific Challenges

Several specific challenges faced me as I began my research, at first focused on Bérulle's spiritual theology of priesthood in relation to the *Traité*, including: the depth of the debates of the era under consideration, a seeming paucity of research on certain key ideas of this time period, the sheer complexity and volume of the canon of uniquely-defined ideas he put forth, and the difficulty in accessing pertinent texts in the U.S. This last challenge was remedied by a gracious grant on the part of The Crossland Foundation. Also, serendipitously, one of the libraries outside of France with the best collections of French School-related texts and with a solid general collection of texts is located only minutes from my home.

In terms of the limits of this study, while I am not a systematic theologian, my background provided me with a unique perspective and set of tools to conduct a descriptive survey and analysis of his system of spirituality, its underlying applied metaphysics, and its later reception. This background includes an undergraduate degree in French and Spanish literatures, a master's degree in theological studies with a certificate in Carmelite studies, a second master's degree in the history of philosophical ideas as set forth in the great texts of the Western tradition, as well as a full program of doctoral studies in spirituality and theology with a focus on the spiritual theology of priesthood.

Advanced professional studies and early experience as both an antiques appraiser and a commercial real estate appraiser provided a background in writing highly detailed descriptions and analyses separate from any interpretations or conclusions. Investigations in the commercial real estate field require laborious theoretical deconstructions, cataloguing, comparisons, and analyses of properties under study, as small changes in calculations in income potential, discount rates, and economic forecasting can result in large fluctuations in estimated value. I have applied similar caution in this study, in which I have come to see that seemingly minor nuances in meaning have yielded influential later interpolations.

The tracing of provenance is one of the most important tasks in determining the identity of an object of art. The hunt for authenticity, which I have always found compelling, drives appraisers, who are neither artists, architects, planners,

[3]   Maritain, "À propos de l'école française," 463–79.

developers, nor builders, and yet, their task is to see as these experts see in order to provide accurate, detailed, high-stakes valuations and advice to those making decisions wherein errors could cost millions of dollars.

Importantly, this study cannot be understood, nor its direct explication of Bérulle's thought and those of secondary sources, without these foundational caveats. The secondary works themselves could be characterized as treating minutia at length (necessitated by Bérulle's encyclopedic references), coupled with a hermeneutic of deference bordering on an obscurantism which, aside from being a stylistic weakness of the French School, could be seen, in some cases, as a veiled attempt to avoid scandal.

Readers of French School scholarship know that any explication of the singularly-defined vocabulary of the French School typically is lengthy. I chose to treat each main theme separately, citing and paraphrasing secondary authors' analyses as thoroughly as possible, utilizing the editions of Bérulle's works they themselves cited due to possible variations between editions.

Written so as to provide access to these ideas to the broadest number of scholars, this study fails to pursue conclusions or paths of inquiry obvious to specialists and, at the same time, errs on the side of caution by providing copious details needed for later specialized analyses.

In this effort I follow Schneiders, who noted that a formal method of research is required in the study of Christian spirituality, consisting of a "thick" description; a critical analysis of the phenomenon under scrutiny; and a constructive interpretation.[4]

My exposure, as well, to the American Psychological Association's publication methodology in writing two past articles was yet another impetus to review and cite pertinent scholars' work, attempting to present their research and conclusions accurately, something I had come to see as a practice missing in some philosophical and theological works.

The importance of including much seemingly extraneous material was based on my own reading into the various theologies of the priesthood as proposed by 20th-century authors. I saw them in a different light after studying Bérulle. The necessity of this approach may only be adequately defended in the future as I hope to address current debates. I have come to understand some contemporary documents as heirs to a chain of slippages linked to details treated in secondary works. Masters influencing the Second Vatican Council and theorizing particularly on the being and offices of Christ, I believe, will come under

---

[4]   Sandra Schneiders, "The Study of Christian Spirituality: Contours and Dynamics of a Discipline," in *Minding the Spirit: The Study of Christian Spirituality*, ed. Elizabeth A. Dreyer and Mark S. Burrows (Baltimore, MD: Johns Hopkins University Press, 1994), 5, 6.

reappraisal as French School theology, past and present, becomes better understood via this detailed cataloguing.

In addition, another motive for the artifice of seeming to hide behind others' work is past experience with the understandable dismissal of ideas thought to be either already addressed in the literature or a mere matter of opinion. It is hoped that the style I selected might foster a measured review of these ideas. For example, hazarding a critique of leading scholars' views on the Berullian priesthood would not have been possible without this kind of inclusion of secondary literature, which paints a pastiche, albeit obliquely, carrying readers to their own clear and sure appraisals of prevalent interpretations.

I also selected a newer but accepted style of providing a literature review which is not encapsulated in an opening chapter, but, rather, included in each chapter, due to the range of complex ideas requiring individual explication in light of both past tradition and current debates. This resulted in some repetition, as Bérulle himself used a catena-like style (also characteristic of formation literature), repetitively citing themes and sources which built upon each other.

The ongoing vocations and abuse crises facing the hierarchy, I believe, warrant the risks I have undertaken. This study provides a mirror, as reflected in the eyes of scholars of the French School, of the effects of both the Protestant Reformation and the Counter-Reformation on the spiritual theology of priesthood. It is a map of what I would call Bérulle's priestly identity creed, illuminated by a collection of finely sifted primary and secondary material.

Methodological Process

The specific combined methodology for this study shifted according to the exigencies of the material. First, I followed my primary investigative training in researching philosophical works according to the St. John's method (my *alma mater* in the graduate study of the history of philosophical ideas). This method includes a focus on primary texts and the basic pedagogical premise that the books themselves are the teachers rather than secondary experts.

In this vein, I first constructed a series of concept maps of all the highly organized ideals found in the *Traité*, and in so doing, located a list of themes that I could then use as a guide for locating themes in Bérulle's voluminous and unorganized talks and writings.

For this effort, I chose a method known as concept mapping, first developed by Dr. Joseph Novak at Cornell University in the 1970s, a system known to clarify and expand knowledge.[5] I had decided to pursue this method on the advice of a counter-terrorist expert who had conducted identity analyses of suspected terror cells in order to predict when particular individuals might act.

I wanted to analyze the identity of this particular priesthood by understanding the *actions* of the priest in *relation* to God and others.

When I first contacted Dr. Novak about my hopes to use this method, he counseled that it was best utilized for clarifying processes and might not be suitable for an identity analysis. He agreed, however, to review the maps I would create. After later doing so, he approved of their use. The publication of these maps and the analysis I conducted will follow this study at a later date.

After this preliminary close cataloguing of Berullian ideals found in the *Traité*, I then shifted my focus to study the notions Bérulle himself had developed, and this by way of prolegomenon only, to both an identity study of Bérulle and a study of the *Traité* itself, which I had come to see as requiring separate treatments.

Importantly, after my first analysis of the *Traité*, I came to see the importance of the Christological debates of the era under study. Thus followed a six-month review of these Christologies. In this, I pursued a trail of references provided by Dr. John F. Wippel, who graciously responded to my question on the possible essentialism found in the Christologies of the period.

Next, my task was to read and digitize various selections of Bérulle's work for word searching, outlining, and indexing of pertinent terms where indexing was not available.

The Study of a Priestly Spirituality

Schneiders noted that the field of spirituality is faced with the problem of how to organize scholarly research because of its interdisciplinary character. She provided the caution that doctoral research must be sufficiently broad and focused so as to neither make of the doctoral student "a shallow generalist" nor "an academic lone ranger."[6]

I chose to take a broad survey approach in certain chapters or the beginnings of chapters, making opening comparisons to influences on Bérulle's overall project. I attempted to find echoes in tradition on any number of points, as have other scholars, but without the depth or precision that a more focused work would mandate. I approached these particular sections from the perspective of standing in a literary future, pointing to more detailed discussions in later

---

[5]   See J. D. Novak, *Learning, Creating, and Using Knowledge: Concept Maps as Facilitative Tools for Schools and Corporations* (Mahwah, NJ: Lawrence Erlbaum & Associates, 1998).

[6]   Schneiders, "The Study of Christian Spirituality," 13.

chapters. Assertions made were by way of orienting readers who could then draw their own conclusions upon reading subsequent sections devoted to my detailed analysis of Bérulle's more recently edited direct quotes. This stylistic choice leaves an opening for the misinterpretation of these assertions as proof surrogates.

The study concludes with a foray into speculation, based on a larger view of Bérulle's project and meant to facilitate experts' work.

One of my key influences was the work of Edith Stein, whose use of the phenomenological method aided in her exploration of the spirituality of St. John of the Cross.[7] Whatever the limits of this particular school of thought, I was inspired by some basic tenets of phenomenological inquiry which seemed to me ideally suited for the research of historical spiritualities, including the use of a flexible narrative, empirical inquiry and reflection, a review of preunderstandings, the search for concealed meanings, the reconciling of larger ideas with particularities, and the ferreting out of ethical implications. Perhaps most importantly, this method encourages attempts to recover structures of meaning.[8]

The majority of direct quotations of Bérulle pertaining to the priesthood which were placed under close scrutiny were taken directly from primary-source pieces published for the first time in Dupuy's *Bérulle et le sacerdoce* in both French and Latin.

Also crucial to understanding French School scholars loyal to the Magisterium and their own religious orders are influences that these scholars appeared to have declined to explore in any depth: those of the Alexandrian School, the Florentine Academy, Duns Scot, De Vio, Suárez, Eckhart, Middle Platonism, and early and late Hermeticism. I elected to treat each of these possible influences only to the degree I thought necessary.

One central conceit of this study involves citing Thomas Aquinas' thought as a repeated benchmark. Since the first publication of Bérulle's works down to today, Aquinas has been pointed to as the inspiration of Bérulle's various proposals. It is not an exaggeration to say that Bérulle's priesthood has been hailed as "Thomistic."

Lastly, as to the possible contributions of this study, they include a demonstration of the importance of the study of both spiritual theology and philosophy in relation to theology, which, I would suggest, can be applied to a

---

[7]   Edith Stein, *The Science of the Cross* (Washington, DC: ICS Publications, 2002). Originally published as Edith Stein, *Kreuzzeswissenschaft: Studie über Joannes a Cruce*, vol. 1, *Edith Steins Werke* (Freiburg im Breisgau: Herder, 1954).

[8]   See Max Van Manen, *Phenomenology of Practice: Meaning-Giving Methods in Phenomenological Research and Writing* (London and New York: Routledge, Taylor & Francis Group, 2016).

variety of areas including ecclesiology, sacramental theory, Christology, and the Trinity. New insights gained can serve as the basis of my own and others' research on the identity of the priesthood itself, and pastoral identity in general across denominations and religions. Most specifically, this study illustrates the syncretism of the idea that the priest is "essentially" rather than ontologically different from the laity. Methodologically, this study can serve scholars in the field of spirituality in terms of highlighting the importance of the study of metaphysics underlying various spiritualities, and, for scholars in identity studies, of the suitability of the concept tracing of hidden ideals.

Chapter 2
Bérulle and Key Antecedents

Introduction

This chapter explores the life and times of Pierre de Bérulle, his founding of the Oratory, and the general characteristics of the French School of spirituality, as well as the rich intellectual milieu in which it took root. Next, an overview of Bérulle's project and an introduction to the spirituality of his Oratory is presented, followed by a review of key related developments in the history of the priesthood, including at the time of Trent and leading into the seventeenth century. An exploration of the importance of proximate figures concludes the chapter.

Background

Martelet wrote that the Counter-Reformation focused on four fronts in order to battle the threats of Protestantism: the real presence, the Eucharistic sacrifice, the sacrament of penance, and the priesthood. This counterattack was at the heart of defending a Catholic "identity." Its tone was Baroque, victorious, and triumphant. Martelet further described the Post-Tridentine world as being characterized by a missionary spirit, intense devotionalism, and a spirituality resting on repetition.[1] Martelet described this combination of ideas as confining priests to an "un ghetto ecclésiastique que les rigueurs du jansénisme vont encore asphyxier advantage."[2]

These traits were funneled into lay and sacerdotal spiritualities created by Bérulle for the purpose of renewing the priesthood in order to remake society.

Sedgwick wrote of the negative strain of Augustinian piety found in the thought and piety of Cardinal Bérulle: "The cardinal's devotional principles stressed the need for humility and self-abasement as an essential first stage in the process of redemption." Sedgwick detailed the influence of this piety found

---

[1]   Martelet, *Deux mille ans d'Église en question*, 150–51.
[2]   Ibid., 163–64 and 180. Quote taken from 181.

throughout Church history, characterized by an emphasis on the "helplessness of the human condition and the overwhelming power of divine grace."[3] Bérulle was an adherent of this spiritual anthropology, insisting that only through introspection can one realize one is nothing and in need of God's grace. As he wrote, "Nous naissons enfants d'ire de Dieu, esclaves du péché et du diable."[4]

This debased view of humanity included priests.

On the other hand, in the Tridentine world Martelet described, ecclesial identity was based on apostolicity, with a grandeur based on both Pseudo-Dionysian and Tridentine hierarchies.[5] Bérulle's system, based on divine hierarchy, was instituted in opposition to the Protestants' revolt against ecclesial hierarchy.[6] According to Martelet, Bérulle accented Trent's doctrine of indelible character by identifying the priest with Christ such that the priest became the mediator and source of all grace. The result, as Martelet termed it, was a cult of person and persona.[7]

Bérulle did not have an estimate of man as powerless in employing reason or will in achieving the good (as did later Jansenists). However, he did arrive at a concept of an annihilated will. For Bérulle, man's reason must also be annihilated and then, paradoxically, used in what he called the *science du salut*, not to obtain grace but to work continually to keep it.[8] Bérulle saw himself, in fact, as a defender of Augustinianism and specifically held to the limitations of reason and the greatness of divine will. In doing so, Williams argued, he contributed to a milieu that emphasized efficient grace.[9]

---

[3] Alexander Sedgwick, *Jansenism in Seventeenth-Century France: Voices from the Wilderness* (Charlottesville: University of Virginia, 1977), 5–6. In combating the errors of Pelagius, Augustine had argued that man's nature had been seriously damaged by sin, and so man could do no good without grace. Sedgwick wrote that Augustine's influence contributed to the Reformation and remained influential in the Post-Reformation Church.

[4] Ibid., 6, quoting Bérulle, *Œuvres de pieté*, 120, 979, hereafter cited as *OP* in all editions. Also quoted in J. Dagens, *Bérulle et les origines de la restauration catholique* (Bruges: Desclée de Brouwer, 1952), 290.

[5] Martelet, *Deux mille ans d'Église en question*, 180–81.

[6] Jean Orcibal, *Le cardinal de Bérulle: évolution d'une spiritualité* (Paris: Éditions du Cerf, 1965), 61.

[7] Martelet, *Deux mille ans d'Église en question*, 163–64 and 180.

[8] Williams, *The French Oratorians and Absolutism*, 197–99, quoting Bérulle, *Grandeurs, Discours* 2, no. 2, *OC*, Migne ed., 161. This review follows the author's exposition closely.

[9] Ibid., 443.

Mystic Vogue

According to Williams, during this period of French history, there was a turning inward to find authority lost in the Wars of Religion and an attempt thereby to flee feelings of doubt and sinfulness.[10] Included in this effort was an increase in pious practices and a greater emphasis on mystical experiences. Security was sought through interior adoration, personal sanctification, and a reliance on a personal experience of God.[11]

These characteristics also became part of Bérulle's sacerdotal spirituality as he proposed it to members of the Oratory.

The Life and Times of Pierre de Bérulle

Pierre de Bérulle was born in 1575 near Troyes, France, eleven years after the death of John Calvin, during the period of the Wars of Religion between French Roman Catholics and Calvinists, in which two to four million deaths resulted between 1562 and 1598.[12] Many in Bérulle's family, who belonged to the *nobles de robe* (lesser aristocrats holding judicial or administrative posts), were imprisoned or exiled during the wars. Countering Huguenot ideals came to be a lifelong passion for Bérulle.[13]

The subject of Bérulle's focus in countering what he perceived were attacks against the priesthood were ideals proposed by Calvin. A second-generation reformer and lawyer, Calvin had read theology and studied ancient languages.[14]

---

[10]   Ibid., 3.

[11]   Ibid., 8.

[12]   See Robert Knecht, *The French Religious Wars 1562–1598* (Oxford, UK: Osprey Publishing, 2002), 91.

[13]   This abbreviated biographical information was taken from the following works: Bérulle and Thompson, *Bérulle and the French School*; Louis Cognet, *Les origines de la spiritualité française au XVIIe siècle* (Paris: La Colombe, 1949); Jean Dagens, *Bérulle et les origines de la restauration catholique* (Bruges: Desclée de Brouwer, 1952); Ferrari, *Figures de la contemplation*; J. Huijben, "Aux sources de la spiritualité française du XVIIe siècle," *Supplément à la Vie spirituelle* 26 (January 1931): 17–46, hereafter AS; Yves Krumenacker, *L'école française de spiritualité: Des mystiques, des fondateurs, des courants et leurs interprètes* (Paris: Éditions du Cerf, 1998); Raymond Deville, *L'école française de spiritualité* (Paris: Desclée de Brouwer, 2008); and Williams, *The French Oratorians and Absolutism*.

[14]   Henry Beveridge, "Preface," in John Calvin, *Institutes of the Christian Religion*, trans. Henry Beveridge (Peabody, MA: Hendrickson Publishers, 2008), xi–xii. This edition was based on the 1845 English translation of Calvin's last Latin edition. Hereafter all editions will be cited as *Institutes*, with editions noted. Direct quotations taken from the *Institutes* will include the critical edition of the 1560 French text, Jean Calvin and J. D. Benoit,

He was eight years old when Luther presented his theses publicly. Schooled in both nominalist and terminist logic, he had also studied under conciliar theologian and historian John Major, a medieval Scholastic and follower of Duns Scot.[15] In 1534, Calvin separated from the Roman Catholic Church and his benefices after a conversion experience. Later that same year, Francis I was jailing and executing "anarchist" Protestants, with tens of thousands killed. Calvin fled to Switzerland and published the first version of his *Institutes of the Christian Religion* in 1536.[16] Warfield wrote that the *Institutes* "lies at the foundation of the whole development of Protestant theology…" and has "…unquestioned preeminence as the greatest and most influential of all dogmatic treatises."[17] Calvin attempted to place the work in a political framework, prefacing it with a letter to the King of France.[18] While Luther had wanted to reform the Church, Calvin wanted to "transform society."[19] So, too, Bérulle.

As a young man, Bérulle studied the classics under the rhetorician Jean Morel. After studying law, he entered the Jesuit College of Clermont in 1592, where he studied philosophy and theology until King Henry IV exiled the Jesuits in 1595. Maldonat, whose humanism emphasized the study of the fathers and the scriptures, had influenced the college. Later, he pursued studies for a time at the Sorbonne with noted theologians Gamaches and Duval. Duval, known for his commentaries on Aquinas, was considered a master of the spiritual life, and served with Bérulle as co-visitor of the Carmelite nuns whom Bérulle had introduced to France. Duval wanted to make the Sorbonne into a place that promoted the spiritual life, and he hoped to encourage the dissemination of mystical literature. Bérulle followed this reformist program at the Sorbonne, which sought the reunification of mystical and Scholastic theologies in response to the Reformers' ideals. Notably, he attracted his first Oratorians from the doctors of the Sorbonne who had studied with Duval: Bence, Gibieuf, Bertin, and Condren.

French Catholics had seen some two thousand religious houses and twenty thousand churches burned or sacked between 1559 and 1572 by Huguenots. Henry VI was to impose a Catholic restoration. Proponents of this movement included members of a group of "mystics" in Paris led by Barb Avrillot Acarie (later to become a Carmelite lay sister and a blessed), known as Madame Acarie's

---

Institution de la religion chrestienne (Paris: Vrin, 1957–60), and hereafter cited as *Institution*.

[15] Robert L. Reymond, *John Calvin: His Life and Influence* (Ross-shire, UK: Christian Focus Publications, 2004), 22–26.

[16] Beveridge, "Preface," xii–xiii.

[17] Reymond, *John Calvin*, 15.

[18] Ibid., 48.

[19] Beveridge, "Preface," xiii–xiv.

circle. The group, comprised of *petite bourgeoisie* and *nobles de robe*, held that the first duty of Christian was the interior life.

This would also become Bérulle's focus for priests.

In the circle were priests giving direction, including Duval and Gamaches. Benet Canfield, author of *La règle de perfection*, would have a great influence on the young Bérulle. Orcibal noted that Canfield's manual, *Exercice de la volonté de Dieu*, made him a popular spiritual director. His work was marked by a passive self-annihilation through an identification with Christ's self-annihilation. Orcibal referred to this as an *imitation ontologique* marked by a kind of spiritual conception or birth in the human will, so that by this joining with God's will, one can say: "je suis le volonté de Dieu." Orcibal noted that for Canfield, the light that gives unity to all works was not Christ but the divine essence. He cited the influence of Bernard, northern mystics, and anti-intellectuals in Canfield's proposal.[20]

Another profound influence was the Carthusian monk Richard Beaucousin, Bérulle's spiritual director, *l'oracle du monde dévot à Paris*, as Huijben called him, dying in the odor of sanctity in 1610.[21] After five years, his body remained incorrupt. Beaucousin was influenced by the spirituality of the Rheno-Flemish school of abstract mystics and such concepts as negation, self-abnegation, denial of the senses, and the negative ascent of a spiritual hierarchy by divine grace and illumination.

In the circle, clerical participation in the *vogue mystique* was proposed as part of this reform, with the requirement that spiritual practices conform to the ideal of an exalted clergy.

Protestant Controverses

Dubé wrote that at the age of seventeen, Bérulle began to participate in the Protestant *controverses*, or public disputes, and immersed himself for almost a decade in these efforts to convert public figures, becoming well-versed in the intricacies of the debates between Catholics and Huguenots. Not a first-rank *controversiste*, his work and considerable influence were as a spiritual director for

---

[20] Jean Orcibal, "Vers l'épanouissement du 17e siècle," in *Histoire spirituelle de la France*, 217–26, especially 223. See Benet Canfield, *Exercice de la volonté de Dieu*, in *La règle de perfection* (Paris, 1608), quote at 1, 2, fol. 5. See also 2, 4, fol. 6, 23 v°.

[21] J. Huijben, "Aux sources de la spiritualité française du XVIIe siècle," 26 (January 1931): 23. Huijben wrote a series of articles, hereafter referred to as AS: *Supplément à la Vie spirituelle* 25 (December 1930): 113–39; 26 (January 1931): 17–46; 26 (February 1931): 75–111; 27 (April 1931): 20–42; and 27 (May 1931): 94–122.

nobles and parliamentarians. Fundamental themes of Protestant theology, in which he became expert, later became the substance of Bérulle's own spirituality.[22]

Priesthood and the Founding of the Oratory

In 1599, Bérulle was ordained a priest. As described by his biographer Cérisy, in 1605, Bérulle experienced an interior illumination in which he was seized with a great desire to see the establishment of a congregation of priests.[23] In 1611, Bérulle founded the Congregation of the Oratory in support of ordinary priests who, unlike regular orders, were to serve local bishops, acknowledging their authority.[24]

Bérulle Begins His Project

While Trent had placed great importance on the founding of seminaries,[25] the Council decrees and canons were not received in France officially until 1619.[26] Bérulle, frustrated with this, focused his efforts on changing attitudes, for both the laity and priests.[27] In his spiritual conferences to his Oratorians, Bérulle exhorted his men to prayer and the ministry of the word, to intercession, and to honoring the mystery of the Incarnation. The interior life was considered part of the *perfection ecclésiastique*.[28] The first disposition demanded by Bérulle of the Oratorians was to live in the presence of God, the second being zeal for souls.[29]

The Oratorians were to model themselves after the primitive apostolic community, but in a new way, after the Ascension, as holy courtiers surrounding the prince. They were to have one object, Jesus Christ, and one activity: to attach

---

[22] Wilfrid Dubé, "Bérulle et les protestants, 1593–1610: contribution à l'étude de la controverse religieuse au début du 17e siècle" (PhD diss., University of Paris, 1966), 6–37. See Orcibal, *Le cardinal de Bérulle*, 21–48.

[23] See Habert de Cérisy, *La vie de cardinal de Bérulle* (Paris: Sebastian Hure, 1646), 320–21, cited in Stéphane-Marie Morgain, "La prêtrise selon Pierre de Bérulle: un état et une vie d'unité par intériorité et de société par son extériorité," *Société d'histoire religieuse de la France* 93, no. 1 (2007): 140.

[24] William Doyle, *Jansenism: Catholic Resistance to Authority from the Reformation to the French Revolution* (New York: St. Martin's Press, 2000), 15.

[25] Martelet, *Deux mille ans d'Église en question*, 158–59.

[26] Michel Dupuy, *Le Christ de Bérulle* (Paris: Desclée, 2001), 12.

[27] Anne H. Minton, "Pierre de Bérulle: The Search for Unity," in *The Roots of the Modern Christian Tradition* (Kalamazoo, MI: Cistercian Publications, Inc., 1984), 119.

[28] BLS, 94. See Coll. 292. This explication follows Dupuy closely.

[29] Ibid., 95. See Coll. 114, 117, 168, and 305.

themselves to him firmly and frequently. They were to belong to what Bérulle called the *chœur de Jésus* by participating in his life in a special way through a special actual grace, by becoming his *esclaves*, hiding themselves with Christ in God. This would be accomplished by being introduced into the mystery of his interior life and union with the Father.[30] Bérulle conceived of the link between priests and Jesus as greater than that of the apostles, since priests were to be united to him in his eternality. In this choir, they would unite themselves to His internal actions, to imitate him by participating in his internal dispositions, even to his union with the Father. Bérulle's special choir devoted to Christ's priesthood was an application of the Pseudo-Dionysian idea of choirs, used widely at the time. Of note, it was not ordination that conferred membership in the choir but a vow of servitude. Since Christ was priest by reason of the hypostatic union, Oratorians were to honor the hypostatic union specifically.[31] As visitator to the Carmelite nuns, Bérulle proposed they make vows of servitude to both Mary and Jesus. Inspired by Pseudo-Dionysius, he also imposed these same vows on his Oratorians, who were to form "un *chœur* ou un *ordre*, capable de diffuser sur les hiérarchies inférieures la lumière déifiante qu'ils recevront eux-mêmes par la Vierge et le Verbe incarné de la *déité fontale* du Père."[32] This choir pertained to the celestial hierarchy of love.[33]

He never spoke of the difference between the lay and ministerial priesthoods in this regard, urging Oratorians and Carmelite nuns alike to belong to this choir. According to Dupuy, this was consistent with his affective theology overall, which emphasized a vocation forged of an "exigence intérieure de progrès spirituel…"[34]

The Oratory was to especially honor two societies: the communication of the divine essence to the divine persons and the communication of the divine subsistence to the human nature of Christ.[35]

---

[30] Ibid., 100–101. See Coll. 164–65.
[31] Ibid., 100–102.
[32] Paul Cochois, *Bérulle et l'école française* (Paris: Seuil, 1963), 33.
[33] *BLS*, 102. See Coll. 205.
[34] Ibid., 103.
[35] See Bérulle, *OC*, vol. 7, *Discours de l'état et des grandeurs de Jésus*, ed. Michel Join-Lambert and Rémi Lescot (Paris: Oratoire de Jésus, 1996), Discours 8, 336–38. See 338n1.

The Vows of Servitude

Bérulle entered a grave controversy of his own related to his ideal of choirs and the vows he imposed on the Carmelite nuns, as we will detail.[36] The theological controversy that ensued over the orthodoxy of the vows led to the publication of *Discours de l'état et des grandeurs de Jésus*.

Key Collaborators

Bérulle, neither a theologian nor a metaphysician, was aided in his efforts by a doctor of the Sorbonne, Guillaume Gibieuf, who was first reader and corrector of Bérulle's *Grandeurs de Jésus*.[37] That said, theologians of the Sorbonne had called Bérulle's work "un verbiage mystique bon pour les femmes et qu'un étalage de platonisme à la mode."[38]

Another major influence on Bérulle's thought was Jean Duvergier de Hauranne, known as Saint-Cyran, so named after the monastery where he was abbot. An expert on patristic and Scholastic sources, for months during the year 1622 when Bérulle wrote his main defense, the two men spent six or seven hours together daily.[39] Saint-Cyran gave Bérulle references and texts he did not have time to research or study.[40] Their association had widespread ramifications in terms of Saint-Cyran's utilization of the Oratory as a method of spreading Jansenism, and, important to this study, perhaps Bérulle's absorption of patristic ideals, as this study will review.

Mature Years, Death, and Posthumous Publication of His Work

Considered a rival to Cardinal Richelieu, Bérulle had become regent to Louis XIII, and had favored the idea of the use of government coercion by the Church

---

[36] Bérulle and Thompson, *Bérulle and the French School*, 14. See Cochois, *Bérulle et l'école française*, 33–43.

[37] Ferrari, *Figures de la contemplation*, 9. See Philippe Sellier, "La rhétorique de Saint-Cyran, 1," in *Les deux abbés de Saint-Cyran: Chroniques de Port-Royal, 1977–1978* (Paris: Bibliothèque Mazarine), 43. See nos. 26–28.

[38] Étienne Gilson, *La liberté chez Descartes et la théologie* (Paris: Alcan, 1913), 180.

[39] TG, 53. See Jean Duvergier de Hauranne (Saint-Cyran), *Lettres chrétiennes et spirituelles de messire Jean du Verger de Hauranne, abbé de S. Cyran* (Lyon: J. Bapt. Bourlier & Laur. Aubin, 1674), 436, as cited in Cognet, *La spiritualité moderne*, 322.

[40] Michel Dupuy, "Le prêtre selon Duvergier de Hauranne (1581–1643)," in *L'image du prêtre dans la littérature classique, XVIIe–XVIIIe siècles: Actes du colloque organisé par le Centre "Michel Baude-Littérature et spiritualité" de l'Université de Metz, 20–21 novembre 1998*, ed. Danielle Pister (Peter Lang Verlag, 2001), 53.

in the abolition of Protestantism. Bérulle died in 1629 in the midst of a political conflict with Richelieu, after an undiagnosed illness lasting only several days.

Bérulle's complete works, published fifteen years after his death, were later considered outmoded and too luxurious, with followers attempting to simplify his ideals.[41]

French Spirituality of the Seventeenth Century

Spirituality during the seventeenth century, known as *le grand siècle de la spiritualité française*, was characterized by currents that drew on the Bible, Pseudo-Dionysius, and Rheno-Flemish and Carmelite spiritualities. Orcibal noted that the source of these was the Counter-Reformation, giving impetus for a new kind of *vie chrétienne* with a concentration on the sacraments, devotions, and *états de vie*. While many Catholics did not have access to a translated Bible for personal use, biblical themes abounded in various texts and artwork. Bérulle emphasized St. Paul and St. John, commenting on and paraphrasing the Christian scriptures. His emphasis on devotion to the Incarnate Word was both the cause and the consequence of familiarity with the Bible.[42]

Characteristics of Berullism, according to Cochois, included theocentrism, a mystical Christocentrism, devotion to the sovereign Mother of God, and an exaltation of the priesthood.[43]

Bremond gave a cogent summary of key aspects of the school, which placed a new emphasis on the virtue of religion, seen as crucial in meeting the neglect of the Mass and the rejection of the priesthood by Reformers.[44] The center of Bérulle's project revolved around his devotion to the Incarnate Word, not just the king and model of Jesuit spirituality, but also as perfect worshipper, even religion itself. As Bourgoing noted, Christ, for Bérulle, was "le grand sacrament de piété, et le sacrament primitif de la religion chrétienne."[45] Whereas Ignatius had emphasized the contemplation of the actions of Jesus, Bérulle focused on the idea of states or *états*, and called on Christians to adore by state not just by act, considered by Bérulle to be more profound. This adoration was not emanating from the faculties but rather a permanent imprint of one's being.[46] Bremond

---

[41] Louis Cognet, *Post-Reformation Spirituality* (New York: Hawthorn Books, 1959), 87.

[42] Jean Orcibal, "Vers L'épanouissement du 17e siècle," 227–31.

[43] Raymond Deville, *L'école française de spiritualité*, 19. See Cochois, *Bérulle et l'école française*, 146.

[44] *TM*, 27–28. See Denis Amelote, *La vie du père Charles de Condren, second supérieur général de la Congrégation de l'Oratoire de Jésus* (Paris, 1643), 78 and 85.

[45] Bourgoing, "Préface," *OC*, Migne ed., col. 98. Also cited in *TM*, 52.

[46] See Lettre 71, *OC*, Migne ed., cols. 1417–18. Also cited in *TM*, 31.

wrote, "Toute l'économie de notre sanctification personnelle se ramène à cette règle unique: se prêter, s'ouvrir, s'abondonner à la grâce, 'qui tire l'âme hors de soi-même par une sorte d'anéantissement et la transporte, l'établit, et l'ente en Jésus-Christ.'"[47]

The most important development in Berullism, according to Bremond, was the idea that the dispositions and mysteries of the life of Jesus are ever present and that we can gain fruit from them.[48] In contrast to Ignatius, who urged the practice of acts of humility, abnegation, and charity, with meditation followed by resolutions, Bérulle focused on adoring the being of Christ himself, while requesting a stable spirit like his—by doing so, one is drawn into an unchanging state of grace: "Nous tirons vie de ce mystère de vie; tirons donc aussi de l'état de grâce et de vie invariable en Dieu…"[49] For Bérulle, Christ adapts us to his states and mysteries, as his will is for us to appropriate them: "c'est à lui de nous approprier aux états et mystères qu'il voudra de sa divine personne, et a nous de nous y lier et d'en dépendre."[50] The fundamental idea of Berullism was that of Christ living in us.[51] This was accomplished through adherence, with other synonyms used to describe this, such as *appartenance, liaison, application,* and *servitude.*[52]

The Influence of Publications

Huijben wrote a series of articles on the sources of the French School that still serve today as a helpful window into a period of intense intellectual ferment following Trent.[53] Huijben noted that the Berullian School, as he called it, was the most important of various currents in the seventeenth century. Pertinent to any review of influences is a discussion of the spiritual currents of his era, fueled by a deluge of popular spiritual works.

From 1550 to 1610, there were 450 works on spirituality published in France, most translations of foreign works. French works were few due to the Wars of Religion. Some 110 works were new editions of the fathers. Only after King

---

47 Bremond, *TM*, 133. Bremond here quoted Bérulle, *OP* 112, *OC,* Migne ed., col. 1166.
48 *TM*, 56–59.
49 See *OP* 26, *OC,* Migne ed., col. 952. Also cited in *TM*, 61.
50 Ibid., cols. 940–41. See also *TM*, 62.
51 *TM*, 68. See Père Lloumeau, *La vie spirituelle à l'école du Bienheureux G. de Montfort,* 3rd ed. (Paris: Desclée, Lefebvre, 1913), 31–146.
52 Ibid., 107–8.
53 J. Huijben, "Aux sources de la spiritualité française du XVIIe siècle," *Supplément à la Vie spirituelle* 25 (December 1930): 113–39; 26 (January 1931): 17–46; 26 (February 1931): 75–111; 27 (April 1931): 20–42; and 27 (May 1931): 94–122.

Henry IV came to power in the late 1500s did the French ascetical and mystical movement spread, and it was not until 1600 that native writings on spirituality came to prominence.

Some 164 works originating from the Low Countries, including some German publications, were made available in France during that time, with considerable influence on Bérulle. Works relating to metaphysics and the spirituality of metaphysics were small in number, read by few, but also of major influence. The widely cited three great spiritual masters of influence, as Bremond called them, were Ruysbroec, Tauler, and Harphius. The terminology of the French School depended markedly on the mysticism of the Low Countries.[54]

Huijben noted that there are two forms of Christocentrism, in his opinion, although not exclusive, involving two kinds of union with Christ. The first involves adherence by faith and love to the loving reality of the Paschal mysteries centered in the Eucharist, with each person depending on the assistance of actual grace to accomplish supernatural acts. The second form involves a more permanent union, approaching a "state," which involves an increase in habitual grace such that Christ imprints and infuses in the soul his own dispositions. On the second, Huijben asserted, Berullism would focus.[55]

Bérulle found the basis for this mystical Christocentrism in St. Paul and St. John, in the fathers, and in Aquinas and the thirteenth-century dogma of the Mystical Christ, in which Christ as head and we as members form one mystical person.[56] Huijben noted that while Aquinas used the theology of justification in expounding on this ideal, the spirituality of this union with Christ was taken from elsewhere. In the fourteenth century, Ubertin de Casale wrote that our mystical identity with Christ flowed from the hypostatic union uniting the two natures in one person. He held that in the future, the contemplation of this mystery and the

---

[54] Ibid., 25: 113–39.

[55] Ibid., 27: 20–25.

[56] Ibid., 27: 25–26. See Thomas Aquinas, *ST*, 3.19.4, co., in *Summa theologiae ad codices manuscriptos vaticanos exacta cum commentariis Thomae de Vio Caietani ordinis Praedicatorum S. R. E. cardinalis*, vols. 4–12 of *Sancti Thomae Aquinatis doctoris angelici opera omnia iussu impensaque Leonis XIII P. M. edita* (Rome: Ex Typographia Polyglotta S. C. de Propaganda Fide, 1888–1906), 11: 246: "Respondeo dicendum quod, sicut supra dictum est, in Christo non solum fuit gratia sicut in quodam homine singulari, sed sicut in capite totius Ecclesiae, cui omnes uniuntur sicut capiti membra, ex quibus constituitur mystice una persona. Et exinde est quod meritum Christi se extendit ad alios, inquantum sunt membra eius: sicut etiam in uno homine actio capitis aliqualiter pertinet ad omnia membra eius, quia non solum sibi sentit, sed omnibus membris." See also *ST*, 3.48.2.1; *De veritate*, 29.7.11; *In ep. ad Col.*, 1, 24, lect. 6 (2).

development of all its possibilities would transform the world in what he called the golden age of the Holy Spirit, of the contemplative Church.[57]

In his attempt to restore in France the Mystical Body, torn asunder by disputes, Bérulle was to seek just such a transformation via his project of clerical renewal.

After the fourteenth century, the idea of the mystical Christ fell out of favor in the nominalist atmosphere of the times, according to Huijben. The idea of mystical union with Christ came to Bérulle through the writings of Saints Gertrude and Mechtilde, and Ludolphe le Chartreux. Bérulle's requirement to be in communion with the interior life of Christ was prefigured in St. Gertrude, according to Olier.[58] Both Gertrude and Mechtilde had an active Christocentrism—to do all by Christ and in union with him—a precursor, according to Huijben, of Bérulle's ideal of doing certain actions in honor of certain mysteries of Christ's life. Notably, in a revelation of Mechtilde between 1290 and 1298, she felt her heart so one with Christ that the two seemed one. This account was to have a major influence on a number of spiritual writers.[59]

One stream of Christocentrism influencing Bérulle was from the patristic and medieval eras, coming to him through Ludolphe le Chartreux's *La grande vie de Jésus-Christ*, which he could have known in translation.[60] The work detailed six ways of considering the passion of Christ: by imitation, by identification, through repose, compassion, admiration, and delight. Huijben quoted from the way of identification, in which one sees and feels in oneself nothing but Christ Crucified: "…considérons la Passion du Christ de façon à arriver à la parfaite transformation et identification au Christ Jésus…s'il veut que l'identification soit complète, il faudra que, sans plus se préoccuper d'autre chose, s'oubliant lui-même et tout le créé, il passe tout entier dans l'objet contemplé, au point de ne plus voir et sentir en lui-même que le Christ crucifié…"[61]

---

[57] Ibid., 27: 31. Ubertin de Casale, *Arbor vitae crucifixae Jesu Christi* (n.p., n.d.): "In hoc benedicto somno (Johannis apostoli supra pectus Domini) figuratur Ecclesia contemplativa, quae in fine temporum debet ad tam suavem gustum adduci contemplationis, ut vere requiescat in pectore Christi: quia sibi debet specialius revelari *arcanum unionis personalis in Christo, et istius unionis diffusio in corpus suum mysticum*, et transformatio mentium in delectum."

[58] Ibid., 27: 33. See J. J. Olier, "Lettre 156," in *Lettres spirituelles de M. Olier*, vol. 2 (Paris, 1862), 83–85.

[59] Ibid., 27: 31, 32–34. See St. Mechtilde of Hackeborn, *Liber specialis gratiae*, part 3, col. 27 (Paris, 1877), 230–231.

[60] Huijben did not cite this translation but would later translate from the original Latin, as we will detail.

[61] Ludolphe le Chartreux, *Vita Jesu Christi* (Paris, 1878), vol. 5, part 2, col. 58, n. 11, 10–11, quoted in AS, 27: 38. Huijben remarked that various schools of spirituality emphasized one

A central question Huijben addressed was whether Bérulle's ideal of the perpetuity of the mysteries of Christ's life had its origin in Ignatius of Loyola's *Exercises*, in the ideas of *composition du lieu* and what Pottier called *projections spirituelles*.[62] Huijben responded emphatically in the negative.[63]

Huijben ended the discussion by stating that the choice was between two distinct methods: one in which one proceeds as if one is present to a mystery, the other believing that the mystery is really, physically present. He referenced Aquinas in support of the idea that the mysteries are present everywhere by efficient causality, which he believed was the particular causality claimed by the school.[64] Bérulle's *Œuvres* included the following comment, "Nous suivons l'école de saint Thomas sur la question de l'Incarnation et en la matiere de la grâce, et en tout le reste, le plus que nous pouvons."[65] Pottier asserted, however, that his Thomist formation was *sorbonique* under Duval and de Gamache.[66]

or another of these ways of contemplating Christ, and that Ludolphe was inspired by Bonaventure in this schema, excepting identification.

[62] Aloÿs Pottier, *Le P. Louis Lallemant et les grands spirituels de son temps: essai de théologie mystique comparée* (Paris: P. Téqui, 1929), 98, quoted in AS, 27: 40.

[63] AS, 27: 40–41. See Marguerite d'Árbouze, *Traité de l'oraison* (Paris, 1625). At this juncture, and pertinent to the variety of opinions regarding the kinds of causality in relation to meditation and union with Christ, Huijben diverted to a heavy critique of the Ignatian method by Marguerite d'Árbouze. D'Árbouze also insisted, contrary to Bérulle, that these mysteries happened in the past, even while continuing in God in act. It is only their meritorious value that endures in act and worth.

[64] Ibid., 27: 42. See Aquinas, *ST*, 3.56.1, ad 3, in *Summa theologiae,* 11: 525: "Ad tertium dicendum quod resurrectio Christi non est, proprie loquendo, causa meritoria nostrae resurrectionis: sed est causa efficiens et exemplaris. Efficiens quidem, inquantum humanitas Christi, secundum quam resurrexit, est quodammodo instrumentum divinitatis ipsius, et operatur in virtute eius, ut supra dictum est. Et ideo, sicut alia quae Christus in sua humanitate fecit vel passus est, ex virtute divinitatis eius sunt nobis salutaria, ut supra dictum est; ita et resurrectio Christi est causa efficiens nostrae resurrectionis virtute divina, cuius proprium est mortuos vivificare. Quae quidem virtus praesentialiter attingit omnia loca et tempora. Et talis contactus virtualis sufficit ad rationem huius efficientiae. Et quia, ut dictum est, primordialis causa resurrectionis humanae est divina iustitia, ex qua Christus habet *potestatem iudicium facere inquantum Filius Hominis est*, virtus effectiva resurrectionis eius se extendit non solum ad bonos, sed etiam ad malos, qui sunt eius iudicio subiecti."

[65] Lettre 167, OC, Migne ed., col. 1501, quoted in AS, 26: 98–99. Huijben took some liberties with this quote, which reads: "…l'humanité du Verbe; que l'existence et non seulement la subsistence divine lui est attribuée en l'école de saint Thomas, laquelle nous suivons en cela et en la matière de la grâce et en tout le reste, le plus que nous pouvons."

[66] Pottier, *Le P. Louis Lallemant et les grands spirituels de son temps*, 86n2, quoted in AS, 26: 98n3.

This study will analyze the causality of the mysteries in light of Bérulle's innovations, a key characteristic of his spiritual theology.

La perle évangélique

The Carthusian monasteries of Cologne and Paris were centers of *propagande mystique* for proponents of the Catholic Renaissance. A vast press movement was established and published approximately sixty works on piety in the mid-1580s. *La perle évangélique* was one of these texts. A version was issued in 1602 and received approbations by two doctors of the Sorbonne. It was reportedly penned by an anonymous ecstatic, a female Dutch noble, who died at the age of 77 in 1540 and whose director was Ruysbroec. Huijben noted a stunning similarity between her work and that of Bérulle: notably, a total return to God through perpetual adherence via the benefits and passion of Christ in his humanity. Pertinent to the influence of her work on Bérulle's project, in her second work, *Temple de l'âme*, she presented her theory on the mystical liturgy that develops in the soul united to Christ, in relation to the various mysteries included in the liturgical cycle which she believed are always living and renewed in the soul. This was a doctrine Huijben noted was dear to Bérulle, although Huijben believed he did not know the work as there were no Latin or French translations.[67]

Huijben devoted an in-depth analysis to the influence of the work on Bérulle's thought.[68] Among key, shared themes he saw were the creature's absolute dependence on God, the importance of adoration, and that God is at the center of one's life. Huijben saw a new Christocentrism in *La perle*, with the soul residing continually in Christ, made "vn esprit, vne ame, et vn corps auec luy."[69] Under the influence of Beaucousin, Bérulle was to hold gradually that *La perle* had developed what St. John and St. Paul, the fathers, and Aquinas had taught. Bérulle's inheritance from *La perle* included the use of the verbs *imprimer* and *rayonner* to describe the communication of grace;[70] that creatures should not offer resistance as a *néant*;[71] that we are instruments of grace in the hands of Jesus

---

[67] AS, 26: 85.

[68] Ibid., 27: 94–122.

[69] Nicholas Van Essche, Philippe Despont, Ch. de Mallery, and Veuve de Guillaume de La Noüe, *La perle évangelique: tresor incomparable de la sapience divine, nouvellement traduict de latin en francois par les PP. Ch. lez Paris* (Paris, 1602), 1, 1, ch. 17, fol. 25, quoted in AS 27: 96.

[70] AS, 27: 96 and 105. See Van Essche, Despont, De Mallery, and De La Noüe, *La perle*, 1, 3, ch. 33, fol. 286.

[71] Ibid., 27: 105–6. See Lettre 239, *OC*, Migne ed., col. 1590, and Van Essche, Despont, De Mallery, and De La Noüe, *La perle*, 1, 2, ch. 5, fol. 135.

Christ, as his humanity is the instrument of the grace of the divinity;[72] the fundamental idea behind the vows of servitude to Jesus and Mary;[73] and the idea of honoring God not just by acts but by state.[74]

The Spirituality of the Oratory

Peirera and Fastiggi described the "French baroque oratory" of Bérulle as characterized by freestyle exaggeration, mannerisms, majesty, grandeur, and the pathos of the Baroque ideal classical order. Like other clerical orders of the era of secular priests not bound by vows, the Oratory followed their chief characteristics, which were the practices of continuous prayer and the love and honor of Jesus Christ in all phases of his life. The authors located five main themes in Bérulle's spirituality: a theocentrism emphasizing God's grandeur juxtaposed with creatures' nothingness; a Christocentrism based on Christ's example of debasement; the sacerdotal state; adherence to the mysteries of Christ's life; and servitude to Jesus and Mary.[75]

The authors also described Oratorian spirituality as having self-perfection as its primary goal with the perfection of others as its secondary goal. The first component of the spirituality was that of the clerical or sacerdotal ideal of giving God to humankind through the sacraments and giving man to God through service and teaching. A second component included the intimate love and honor of Jesus Christ the eternal priest.[76]

Returning to the Perfection of the Primitive Church

According to Bérulle, as Dupuy related, in the primitive Church there had been "trois beaux fleurons de la couronne sacerdotale:" authority, holiness, and the light of science. In the turbulent Post-Reformation era, Bérulle felt that authority had remained with prelates, holiness seemed too often reserved for religious, and the light of science had remained with academics. The dignity of the sacerdotal condition had been lost. His goal was to create a new congregation to reunite them.[77]

---

[72] Ibid., 27: 110. See *OC*, Migne ed., col. 1271, and Van Essche, Despont, De Mallery, and De La Noüe, *La perle*, 1, 3, ch. 32, fol. 284.
[73] Ibid., 27: 112. See Van Essche, Despont, De Mallery, and De La Noüe, *La perle*, 1, 3, ch. 41, fol. 78.
[74] Ibid., 27: 113. See Bérulle, préface, *OC*, Migne ed., col. 89.
[75] Pereira and Fastiggi, *The Mystical Theology of the Catholic Reformation*, 63, 70, and 206.
[76] Ibid., 193.
[77] *BLS*, 81, quoting Bérulle, *CB*, vol. 3, no. 891, quoted in *BLS*, 81.

The restoration of these flowers was the reclamation of the heritage of Jesus Christ. Bérulle:

C'est le vouloir et le conseil du Dieu sur nous; c'est à quoi il nous appelle, c'est pourquoi nous sommes assemblés: pour reprendre notre héritage, pour rentrer en nos droits, pour jouir de notre succession légitime, pour avoir le Fils de Dieu en partage, pour avoir part à son esprit, à sa lumière, à sa sainteté et à son autorité, communiquée aux prélats par Jésus-Christ, et par eux aux prêtres.[78]

Dupuy's Analysis

Returning to Dupuy's seminal study of the priesthood according to Bérulle, it is important to review his summary of the main characteristics of the cardinal's spiritual theology of priesthood. As he noted, for Bérulle, the Eucharist was an extension of the Incarnation.[79] As Bérulle wrote, "Cette plus grande merveille de l'Incarnation...(est) à proprement parler...l'original de ce mystère; et notre Eucharistie est comme la copie et l'extrait."[80]

Bérulle's defense of the sacrifice of the Mass and the priest's role in the Church took shape around this assertion.

Bérulle defined the priest, according to Dupuy, in the traditional manner: as the man of the Mass who offered the Body of Christ, with his functions being those of binding and loosing, governing, and edifying the body. In response to the Reformers' criticisms, Bérulle emphasized the ministerial aspect of priesthood.[81] The central idea of the priesthood for Bérulle was its call to perfection, again, not a new idea, but one of great emphasis in the Counter-Reform. Because he saw priests as mediators between God and humanity, holiness was crucial. Using the Pseudo-Dionysian ideal of spiritual radiation, Bérulle linked the holiness of priests to the sanctification of the faithful.[82]

Dupuy noted that while Bérulle characterized the priest as a man of sacrifice, the image of Christ, and a mediator, he never gave a clear picture of the role, powers, functions, and duties of the priesthood, other than his own sense of what sacerdotal function was. His insistence on the dignity of the priesthood, of

---

[78] Bérulle, *CB*, vol. 3, no. 891, quoted in Morgain, "La prêtrise selon Pierre de Bérulle," 152; see also Dagens, *Bérulle et les origines*, 375–76.

[79] *BLS*, 111. See *Discours de controverse*, 3, 9.

[80] *BLS*, quoting Bérulle, *OC*, 1, 5.

[81] Ibid., 71.

[82] Ibid., 75–76.

vocation as the desire for perfection, preceded, arguably, his shifting theological reflections and his turn toward his unique Christological synthesis, according to Dupuy, who saw the exemplarism in his project as a common thread that balanced his ideals, and his notion of choirs as reflecting an evangelical impulse to follow Christ. His vision did not distinguish between interior and exterior perfection, which Dupuy saw as a positive. Bérulle's depiction of the priest as transmitting the love of Christ by contagion, he deemed an imprecise vision.[83]

Dupuy touched on what he saw as less than felicitous aspects found in Bérulle's work, including those surrounding the priesthood. Bérulle's Christ is not only the perfect adorer, as this study will explore, but also the perfectly adored. A frequent theme for Bérulle was that priests have the office of praise to adore him, and this through being a choir of adorers. Dupuy asked rhetorically whether the adoration of the Father and the mystery of the Trinity were somewhat neglected in Bérulle's theology, even to the point of modalism. Christ becomes more the object of adoration than the means, pushing his role as mediator and his priesthood into the background. Dupuy held that so, too, the role of mediator for priests also remained blurred because they were simply more obligated than others to be such. Dupuy held this idea of Christ as adored was not a central part of his thought, and even declined after 1625. His later ideals situated adoration of Christ in a Trinitarian perspective and placed Christ's humanity in a more central place. The accent had moved from that of the Word Incarnate to Christ as he is, both God and man. Bérulle also later accented not just the adoration rendered by priests but their service to others.[84]

Historical Developments in Sacerdotal Spirituality

The Need for Pastoral Reform

This study will explore in detail the thought of both Luther and Calvin in terms of notions surrounding the priesthood. To provide the reader an overview of the Reformers' critiques, a review of the Church crisis as the Reformers encountered it is provided by McLaughlin, a professor of early modern Church history.

Approaching the era of the Reformation, both Scholastic theology and canon law, which were transmitted through late medieval manuals, lowered the sacrality of the priesthood, according to McLaughlin. According to these manuals, the

---

[83] Ibid., 243–49.
[84] Ibid., 180–82.

priest was to be a pastor, preacher, and counselor.[85] In addition, at this time, most priests were ignorant of Latin, and could not be recognized as priests due to their secular dress and social habits.[86]

Luther had responded to the crisis in clerical ranks by emphasizing the priesthood of all believers, denying indelible character and the conveyance of any potencies.[87] He rejected the Lord's Supper as a sacrifice offered by the priest to God. The true locus of ministry for Luther was preaching. Following Luther, local secular authorities became emergency bishops, and territorial state churches were formed with these local rulers becoming the heads of the church. Calvinists went much further than Luther, giving clergy a greater responsibility for disciplining moral and civic behaviors.[88]

Bérulle emphasized, in turn, a spirituality of sacrifice for both laity and priests, giving priests a central role in the spirituality of the laity as well, but with his principal ambition that of linking sacerdotal sacrality and mores.

While Luther and Calvin followed a line of Catholic Reformers, attempting to reform pastors' mores with a particular emphasis on spirituality, and returning to sources as guides in their efforts, the fathers at Trent, confronted with both theoretical and practical issues surrounding sacerdotal sacrality, focused, in part, on character on the one hand, while putting forward reforms in mores on the other.

Bérulle's project, also returning to sources, followed both lines as well.

The following is an overview of key historical trends in the theology of priesthood, which influenced Bérulle's thought.

Early Antecedents

The patristic ideals of the fourth and fifth centuries would be of major import for Bérulle's project, most notably, the Christological ideals of the fifth century pertaining to the relationship between the being of Christ and participation in his priesthood. During the fifth century, the priesthood was no longer seen as the prolongation of the work of the apostles, but rather a participation in the human-

---

[85] R. Emmet McLaughlin, "Clergy," in *Oxford Encyclopedia of the Reformation*, vol. 1 (New York and Oxford: Oxford University Press, 1996), 363.

[86] Marc Venard, "Le prêtre en France au début du XVIIe siècle," *Bulletin de Saint-Sulpice* 6 (1980): 197.

[87] See Luther, *WA* 6: 408.26–30: "Szo folget ausz dissem, das leye, priester, fursten, bischoff, und wie sie sagen, geistlich und weltlich, keynen andern unterscheyd ym grund warlich haben, den des ampts odder wercks halben, unnd nit des stands halbenn, dan sie seyn alle geystlichs stands…aber nit gleichs eynerley wercks."

[88] McLaughlin, "Clergy," 364–65.

divine being and function of Christ, as Garrigues, Le Guillou and Riou noted.[89] In the School of Alexandria, specifically, the basis of the ministerial priesthood included the mystery of the Incarnation in relation to the priesthood of Christ.[90]

This became so for Bérulle as well.

In the west, as of the third century, writers emphasized the duties of the priest, and concrete pastoral action. Augustine emphasized that the priest's acts of service are a prolongation of the service of Christ Priest, Mediator, and Good Shepherd. Gregory the Great, a key influence on clerical formation throughout the Middle Ages, emphasized the ministry of the Word, poverty, prayer, and contemplation. Isidoro de Sevilla, whose book *De ecclesiasticis officiis* also became one of the most influential in ecclesiastical formation in Gregory's era, treated liturgical ministry, preaching, and service to others with humility and charity. Notably, chastity was related to the celebration of the Eucharist.[91]

Bérulle's project of renewing the priesthood by means of a spiritual theology to meet the challenges of the Reformation took as its starting point these core Eastern and Western elements, and combined them with an emphasis, in part, on the main theological rebuttal by the fathers of Trent regarding the nature of sacerdotal character (which, nevertheless they did not clearly define, as this study will explore).

In the medieval era, Scholastics had occupied themselves with concerns regarding character, including Aquinas, Duns Scot, Albert the Great, and others.[92] Aquinas continued the originally Eastern tradition of considering the priest as the visible prolongation of Christ Priest. He defined character as a spiritual potential that configures a priest to Christ, who is priest by being mediator, so constituted by the hypostatic union.

At the same time, on a parallel track, schools or lines of sacerdotal spirituality emerged during the same period. Notably, the Anselmian line, which named holiness as union with Christ; that of Bernard, wherein the Word was spouse and friend; and the Franciscan School, emphasizing poverty and obedience to Christ.[93]

Lasting until the sixteenth century, the *devotio moderna* movement influenced a line of sacerdotal spirituality centered in the Low Countries,

---

[89] J.-M. Garrigues, M.-J. Le Guillou, and A. Riou, "Le caractère sacerdotal dans la tradition des Pères Grecs," *Nouvelle revue théologique* 93 (1971): 809–10.

[90] Juan Esquerda Bifet, *Teología del sacerdocio,* vol. 19, *Historia de la espiritualidad sacerdotal* (Burgos: Ediciones Aldecoa, S.A., 1985), 77.

[91] Ibid., 83–87.

[92] Ibid., 104. See footnote 6, especially Jean Galot, *La nature du caractère sacramentel: Étude de théologie médiévale,* 2nd ed. (Paris: Desclée de Brouwer, 1958).

[93] Ibid., 107.

emphasizing preaching and communitarian living. Key figures included Ruysbroec, Radewyns, Mombaer, Groote, and Kempis, with inspiration also from the thought of Eckhart, Tauler, and Suso.[94] The characteristics of the sacerdotal spirituality of the *devotio moderna*, according to Bifet, included an emphasis on the imitation of Christ, preaching, and methodization of prayer. There was a de-emphasis on both speculation and the concept of a descending ecclesiology. Devotion, affectivity, a "misticismo oscuro," and a withdrawal from the world were other traits. There was an exaltation of the dignity of the priesthood and an angelic holiness supposed, with the priest as mediator at Mass and in prayer.[95]

Bérulle absorbed much of this line of sacerdotal spirituality. He, however, did have an emphasis on speculation and a descending hierarchy.

Trent and Sacerdotal Spirituality in the Sixteenth Century

The Council of Trent focused on the indelibility of character, the reform of benefices, the authority required to ordain, the function of offering sacrifice, remitting sins, hierarchy of orders, residency of bishops, seminaries, and preaching. According to Hurtubise, there were four different visions of priesthood at the time: the man of the sacred, the good pastor, the holy priest, and the public figure who was characterized by good manners and commanded respect.[96]

Hurtubise explored the notion of what might be termed the Tridentine priest, and whether he was an ideal or a reality. He explored what effect Trent may actually have had and what changes occurred due to other influences or to subsequent interpretations of Trent. He noted certain challenges occurring subsequent to Trent, including the relegation of documents related to the council into archives, the influence of Post-Tridentine reformers such as Bérulle, and cultural and social influences (including Protestant pressures), as well as such influences as absolutism, the Pseudo-Dionysian hierarchicalism of the seventeenth century, and the emergence of a bourgeoisie intolerant of clerical ignorance. In fact, he asserted, the Tridentine Church and priest were as much a product of the interpretation and application of the council fathers' work as of

---

[94] Ibid., 123–25.

[95] Juan Esquerda Bifet, *Teología de la espiritualidad sacerdotal* (Madrid: La Editorial Católica, 1976), 292–93.

[96] Krumenacker, "Du prêtre tridentine au 'bon prêtre'," 123. See Pierre Hurtubise, "Le prêtre tridentin: idéal et réalité," in *Homo religiosus: autour de Jean Delumeau* (Paris: Fayard, 1997), 212.

the work itself, as they had been reticent to make any changes in the face of both Catholic and Protestant innovations.[97]

Venard held that there were actually two alternating visions of the priesthood discussed at Trent: that of the Pseudo-Dionysian mediator and that of the Gersonian shepherd.[98] However, according to Idigoras, insufficient theologies and a lack of moral rigor limited the model eventually proposed by Trent.[99]

At the time of Trent there were many books available on sacerdotal holiness, many of them remaining understudied today, according to Bifet.[100] Schools of sacerdotal spirituality developed, such as Benedictine, Carmelite, Augustinian, Ignatian, and Dominican schools. Of major influence leading up to Trent was the Spanish School.[101] In the Spanish School, seminaries had an emphasis on teaching, preaching, spiritual direction, and aggressive outreach.[102]

In terms of the secular clergy, the correction of mores and the restoration of discipline through the promotion of spirituality grew after Trent and became the basis for the sacerdotal spirituality of the seventeenth century. While before Trent, Catholic Reformers relied on spiritual humanism and a return to the scriptures and the fathers, various currents of reform separated into Calvinism and illuminism, as Catholic Reformers lost strength for lack of structure and doctrine, according to Certeau.[103]

Reasons for this weakening, we might suggest, could have been the dampening of theological debate and inquiry after the Council, along with the sealing of documents related to the Council.

The spirituality of the secular clergy in France in the late sixteenth century, difficult to explore because of societal upheaval, was still known for abuses.

---

[97] Hurtubise, "Le prêtre tridentin," 208–10. See Giuseppe Alberigo, "La 'réception' du concile de Trente par l'Église catholique romaine," *Irenikon* 58 (1985): 328.

[98] Marc Venard, *Histoire du christianisme*, vol. 8 (Paris: Desclée-Fayard, 1995), 860–72. Also cited in Hurtubise, "Le prêtre tridentin," 212.

[99] Ignacio Tellechea Idigoras, "El clero tridentino: entre ideal y realidad," *Ricerche per la storia religiosa di Roma* 337 (1988): 11–26. Also cited in Hurtubise, "Le prêtre tridentin," 212.

[100] Bifet, Teología del sacerdocio, 125. See A. Castellani, *Liber sacerdotalis*, Venetiis, 1523; CL. Le Jay, *Speculum sacerdotii*, Parisiis, 1559; R. Perautl, *De dignitate sacerdotali super omnes reges terrae*, n.p., n.d; J. Pfeffer, *Directorium sacerdotale*, n.p., 1482; J. Quintin, *Speculum sacerdotii*, Parisiis, 1559; P. Soto, *Lectiones de institutione sacerdotum*, Dillingen, 1558; J. Tritemio, *De vitae sacerdotalis institutione*, Maguntiae, 1494; San Juan de Capestrano, *Speculum Claricorum*, Venetiis, 1580.

[101] Ibid., 130–42.

[102] McLaughlin, "Clergy," 365.

[103] Michel de Certeau, "La réforme dans le catholicisme," in *Histoire spirituelle de la France*, 198–200.

Attempts were made to reform the clergy through the construction of seminaries and improved coursework, according to Certeau.[104] During the last twenty years of the century, the Baroque piety of Henry II had great influence, with grand processions with public flagellations. The French academy of the period was characterized by a "platonisme mystique et une cosmologie copernicienne tendant au panthéisme."[105]

Bérulle was firmly among the members of this academy at a time of deep social dislocation and doctrinal ambiguity, when the decrees of Trent had not yet been accepted in France.

Key Proximate Figures

Josse Clichtove and Juan of Ávila were important precursors of Bérulle's project and heavily influenced the reform of the clergy in the 16th century, although their works are relatively understudied. Bérulle borrowed certain key ideals, embellishing them, supporting them with his uniquely defined metaphysical notions, and forming them into his own amalgam. The following is an overview of the ideas of these important figures.

Josse Clichtove

Belgian Josse Clichtove, professional theologian and student of noted humanist and member of the Florentine Academy Jacques Lefèvre d'Étaples, was a major influence in the reform of the secular clergy leading up to Trent. His work on clerical reform (directed toward priests without pastoral duties) was one of the issues to which he most devoted himself, and yet it is the least studied. Many of his writings remain in manuscript form or in rare editions, placing a difficult filter on any comparison with Bérulle. Massaut has written the only in-depth treatment of Clichtove's ideas surrounding pastoral reform.[106] Clichtove's main work on the priesthood, *De vita et moribus sacerdotum*, was published in 1519, and reprinted four times between 1603 and 1609. He also proposed a program of clerical reform in a series of three sermons given at the Synod of Paris in 1515. In 1516, he wrote the *Elucidatorium ecclesiasticum* in order to explain the liturgy to

---

104 Ibid., 209–13.
105 Jean Orcibal, "Vers l'épanouissement du 17e siècle (1580–1600)," in *Histoire spirituelle de la France*, 220.
106 Jean-Pierre Massaut, *Josse Clichtove, l'humanisme et la réforme du clergé*, 2 vols. (Paris: Les Belles Lettres, 1968), 1: 9–22.

priests. Massaut held that his work was an important source of ideas influencing Trent as well as priestly spirituality in both the 16th and 17th centuries.[107]

Like other authors, he focused on the dignity of and the holiness demanded of the priesthood,[108] calling it an eminent *état*. Clichtove saw the priesthood's essence in sacrifice.[109]

Clichtove's Pseudo-Dionysian ideals surrounding the holiness of the priest were based on a frequent comparison of celestial and ecclesiastical hierarchies. Priests were to be in a radical separation from the laity and the world. Notably, Massaut asserted that this particular idea of radical separation was neither traditional nor ancient but rather characteristic of the modern priest, of whom Clichtove was a precursor.[110]

Prayer in the life of the priest was a controversial topic at the time: notably the link between mental and vocal prayer, and private and public prayer. Clichtove's program for the spiritual life of the priest included prayer that should occupy the majority of the priest's time, with an emphasis on asceticism as the main means of sanctification. For Clichtove, the priest's humility resembled an *exinanition*. In order to foster humility, the priest was to contemplate the grandeur of the divinity, considering the humanity of Christ and the mercy of God. In order to arouse the dispositions of humility and contrition, Clichtove proposed numerous ejaculatory prayers.[111]

The priesthood, for Clichtove, was to be considered a calling or vocation much like that of religious. Massaut held that Clichtove confused office, order, and state, conflating the state of perfection with interior perfection.[112]

---

[107] Ibid., 2: 105–24.

[108] Ibid., 2: 128n41, quoting Josse Clichtove, *De vita et moribus sacerdotum, singularem eorum dignitatem ostendens et quibus ornati esse debeant virtutibus explanans* (Paris: Simon de Colines, 1519), f° 147 r°: "Sicut templa et loca sacra sancto altaris sacrificio peculiariter sunt deputanda ac destinanda, quemadmodum supra ostensum est. Sicut etiam vestimenta et alia ornamenta ecclesiastica pervigili studio speciatim sunt adhibenda eidem ministerio, ut secundo hic dictum est loco, ita et ministri certo quodam delectu ac ordine constituendi sunt, qui ad altaris officium rite exquantur, ut non passim ac promiscue quivis se ingerant, ad tam arduum munus temere obeundum, sed ii soli qui a vulgo separati, ad id sanctificati sunt ac consecrati."

[109] Ibid., 2: 119, quoting Clichtove, *De vita et moribus sacerdotum*, f° 4 v°: "Et haec est temporum nostrorum conditio, status et qualitas, a quibus tamen ad finem usque seculi perdurabit sacerdotium istud evangelicum, sicut et sacrificium istud unicum et singulare, quod nonnisi per sacerdotes potest offerri."

[110] Ibid., 2: 125–26.

[111] Ibid., 2: 137–41.

[112] Ibid., 2: 353n47, quoting Clichtove, *De vita et moribus sacerdotum*, f° 2 r°–v°. Massaut quotes the following as an example of Clichtove's loose applications and combinations: "Ubi enim diligenter [sacerdotes] animadverterint quam insignis et ardua est ordinis

Massaut concluded that "Bérulle réalisa ce que Clichtove, un siècle plus tôt, avait réclamé."[113] Bérulle's Christocentrism and his and others' exaltation of the priesthood, according to Massaut, found a first expression in Clichtove's project, which he called *Pré-Contre-Réforme*, an attempt to answer Luther's attack against monastic vows and the separate character of the priesthood. Clichtove did so with an affective theology borrowing certain aspects from scholastic theology.[114]

A very different view of Clichtove's conceptualization of the priesthood is that of Lemaitre, who saw nothing new in his project but rather a repetition of themes from pastoral works of the past which Clichtove often cited.[115]

Arguably, much of the novelty of both Clichtove's and Bérulle's projects lay in how they recombined and emphasized certain historical ideals over others in their attempts to defend the priesthood.

Schillebeeckx, in his brief review of Clichtove's contribution, and aided by Massaut's analysis, clarified that Clichtove combined biblical, patristic, and medieval themes with those of what he called, without detail, "modern society."[116]

Juan de Ávila

Juan de Ávila, the main figure of the Spanish school of priestly spirituality, was an important precursor of many of Bérulle's ideals as well, and was held in high esteem by him.[117] A comparative study of Ávila's and Bérulle's spiritual theologies of priesthood, as well as a study of influences in Ávila's thought, are needed before conclusions can be drawn regarding the depth and breadth of Ávila's influence on Bérulle's thought. This introduction to Ávila's sacerdotal themes reveals similarities but also key differences. Ávila's ideals of humility and service, notably, were never assumed by Bérulle.

---

sacerdotalis professio, quam augustum est et sublime illius sortis ecclesiasticae officium, nemo eorum (ut reor) non studebit eam capessere vitae formam, quae deceat tam excelsam vocationem [...] quod suae dignitatis non habent rationem, neque quanta sit sui gradus ac ordinis celsitudo..."

113 Ibid.,, 2: 362.

114 Ibid., 2: 304, 352–64, 368–71, 392, and 405.

115 Nicole Lemaitre, "Le prêtre mis à part ou le triomphe d'une idéologie sacerdotale au XVIe siècle," *Revue d'histoire de l'Église de France* 85, no. 3 (1999): 289.

116 Edward Schillebeeckx, *The Church with a Human Face: A New and Expanded Theology of Ministry,* trans. John Bowden (New York: Crossroad, 1987), 195. Originally published as *Pleidooi voor Mensen in de Kerk: Christelijke Identiteit en Ambten in de Kerk* (Baarn, Holland: Uitgeverij H. Nelissen BV, 1985).

117 Bifet, *Teología de la espiritualidad sacerdotal,* 297. See also P. Pourrat, *Le sacerdoce: doctrine de l'école française* (Paris: Bloud and Gay, 1931); and Bourgoing, "Préface," *OC,* Migne ed., 109.

We would argue that key, sparse, and unelaborated ideals presented by Ávila in simple prose were later embellished, undergirded with metaphysical notions, and systematized by Bérulle.

Canonized in 1970, Ávila was named a Doctor of the Universal Church in 2012. Noting that Ávila had "an essential role in the historical development of the systematic doctrine of the priesthood," Pope Benedict XVI wrote: "Central to Master Ávila's teaching is the insight that, as priests, 'during the Mass we place ourselves on the altar in the person of Christ to carry out the office of the Redeemer himself' (*Letter 157*)." Notable for Benedict were Ávila's urging of the establishment of seminaries and his founding of the University of Baeza, the home of the Avilist sacerdotal school which perdured for centuries.[118]

Ávila wrote two systematic documents for friends participating in the Council of Trent: *Reformación del estado eclesiástico* (1551) and *Causas y remedios de las herejías* (1561). He also wrote *Tratado sobre el sacerdocio* (c. 1563), as well as various documents touching on sacerdotal themes, as found in a recent compilation of his works related to the priesthood.[119]

In general, and unlike Bérulle's, these works can be characterized by the treatment of practical problems, challenges, and reform ideals in relation to seminary training and pastoral practice. Lacking the exalted spirituality of the French School and its heavy metaphysical justifications, Ávila's approach was at the same time devotional and focused on a personal relationship between Christ and the priest as the basis for holiness.

García Mateo attempted to illustrate how Ávila developed a short reflection on the priesthood of Christ and of the hypostatic union as sacerdotal unction in response to attacks against the sacrament of orders,[120] a concept which Bérulle developed into a full metaphysic.

---

[118]   Benedict XVI, *Apostolic Letter: Proclaiming Saint John of Ávila, Diocesan Priest, a Doctor of the Universal Church* (Vatican City: Libreria Editrice Vaticana, 2012), no. 6, quoting John of Avila, *Letter 157*, Juan de Ávila, *Obras completas del Santo Maestro Juan de Ávila*, vol. 5 (Madrid, Spain: Biblioteca de autores cristianos, 1970–71), 571: "que en la misa nos ponemos en el altar en persona de Cristo a hacer el oficio del mismo Redentor, y hacemos intercesores entre Dios y los hombres para ofrecer sacrificio…"

[119]   See *Reformación del estado eclesiástico (Memorial Primero al Concilio de Trento)*, *Causas y remedios de las herejías (Memorial Segundo al Concilio de Trento)*, and *Tratado sobre el sacerdocio* in Juan de Ávila and Juan Esquerda Bifet, *Escritos sacerdotales* (Madrid, Spain: Biblioteca de autores cristianos, 2012), 67, 35, and 121 respectively.

[120]   Juan de Ávila, Sermón 3, 71, in Juan de Ávila, *Obras completas del Santo Maestro Juan de Ávila*, vol. 2: "*El Espíritu del Señor está sobre mí*, entended en cuanto hombre, que, en cuanto Dios, antes el Espíritu Santo procede de El y del Padre, y por tanto se ha de entender en cuanto hombre, y de esta manera le entendió San Joán en el c. 1, ca dice: *No le fue dado el Espíritu por medida*, porque le fue dada a la santísima ánima de Cristo grandísima copia

Ávila wrote of the eminent dignity of the priesthood, calling for prayer, study of the scriptures, praying the divine office, frequent confession, and daily Mass.[121] His emphases were on preaching and spiritual direction, with the priest working in the name and in the person of Christ. The priest was considered a mediator chiefly in liturgical prayer, and was to imitate the Poor Christ and be faithful to the action of the Holy Spirit and to Marian devotion. Ávila's Christological doctrine centered on Christ Priest, Mediator, and Redeemer, especially his interior sentiments and attitudes before the Father and in the Spirit. The theme of *miradas* is found in his work: the priest must gaze at the Father and Son without ceasing.[122]

Influenced by Erasmus, Ávila studied both the scriptures and the fathers, but whereas Erasmus had emphasized Christ as ethical model, Ávila stressed, as noted, a personal relationship with Christ, especially in his Passion. Juan of Ávila's work, *Audi, filia*, was written as a call to holiness and relationship with Christ. The French version of the text influenced Bérulle's notions of holiness pertaining to both laity and priests.[123] Other Erasmian influences included a strong humanist formation, and an emphasis on the Mystical Body.[124]

Bifet noted in his Introduction to a collection of Ávila's works treating the priesthood that the main characteristic of the Avilist sacerdotal school was that of an exemplary apostolic life: in addition to leading lives of prayer and penance, priests were to cultivate souls, teach children doctrine, and preach Christ crucified.[125] Unlike later figures who favored infrequent communion, Ávila was known for his promotion of frequent communion. Ávila wanted the Mass to be the center of evangelization and charity to be the central virtue of the life of the priest. In these aspects, he differed considerably from Bérulle, as this study will

---

de gracia, no como a los otros santos, *quia de plenitudine eius omnes accepimus*; fue ungido con el aceite y olio de gracia. David profeta: *Unxit te Deus, Deus tuus, oleo laetitiae prae consortibus tuis*. Más abundantemente le ungió que a ningún santo de antes." Also quoted in Rogelio García Mateo, "Cristología sacerdotal en Juan de Ávila," *Estudios eclesiásticos* 86, no. 336 (2011): 93.

121 Pourrat, *Le sacerdoce*, 14–17.

122 Bifet, *Teología del sacerdocio*, 133–42. See Juan de Ávila, *Tratado del amor de Dios* and *Audi Filia*, in Juan de Ávila, *Obras completas*, vol. 1.

123 John of Avila, *Audi, Filia*, trans. and intro. Joan Frances Gormley (New York: Paulist Press, 2006), ix–8.

124 See Florencio Sánchez Bella, *La reforma del clero en San Juan de Ávila*, 3rd ed. (Madrid: Ediciones Rialp, S.A., 1981), 56.

125 Juan de Ávila and Bifet, *Escritos sacerdotales*, introduction. See also Luis Muñoz and Martin Boswood, *Vida y virtudes del venerable varon el P. maestro Iuan de Ávila ...: con algunos elogios de las virtudes, y vidas de algunos de sus mas principales discipulos* (Madrid: Imprenta Real, 1635).

detail. Revered as a true reformer, Juan was noted for his own poverty and humility, as well as his devotion to the Humanity of Christ as Merciful Savior. Importantly, Bifet noted that Ávila's work was shortened by an early death, and was also truncated by a postconciliar problem which ran counter to the work of Trent, one he thought could repeat itself.[126]

The question this cryptic comment introduces is whether the rise of a Post-Reformation or proto-modern rigorism, mainly that of the French School of priestly spirituality, eclipsed Ávila's influence, a point this study would support, as we will explore.

In Juan of Ávila's work, as in Bérulle's, we see the theme of representation of Christ as tied to conformity and a spirituality of sacrifice. Writing on the doctrine of the priesthood according to Ávila, Palomero noted that Ávila's was a synthesis of moral, ascetical, and mystical theology. Participation in the priesthood of Christ meant a close friendship and a similarity of habits and of love.[127] Ávila held that this closeness was to actually transform the priest into Christ.[128] This union was to extend to being himself a sacrifice to God, ablaze in the fire of love.[129] This sacrifice of love reached even to the idea of the priest as victim with Christ, a theme basic to Bérulle's image of the priest.[130]

Palomero detailed what he saw as the influence of Ávila on the French School, including the themes of Christ Priest, the Incarnation, the heavenly sacrifice of Christ, *las tres miradas* of Christ (gazing at the Father, Himself, and humankind), and devotion to the Eucharistic and the Risen Christ, as well as pastoral zeal.[131]

A reading of Ávila's considerable opus related to the priesthood also reveals his mention of priests as public persons. Important to understanding Bérulle's and Protestant Reformers' adoption of this theme as detailed later in this study, Ávila's conceptualization applied only insofar as they were considered holders of

---

[126] Ibid., introduction, xxxix.

[127] Juan José Gallego Palomero, *Sacerdocio y oficio sacerdotal en San Juan de Ávila* (Córdoba: Caja de Ahorros y Monte de Piedad de Córdoba, 1998), 162 and 189.

[128] Ibid., 190, quoting Juan de Ávila, *Tratado sobre el sacerdocio*, in Juan de Ávila, *Obras completas*, vol. 3, 519: "Ha de ser la representación tan verdadera, que el sacerdote se transforme en Cristo y...siendo tan conforme, que no sean los dos, mas se cumple lo que San Pablo dice: *Que adaeret Deo, unus spiritus est*." Of note, the author leaves out the following (via an ellipsis): "y, como San Dionisio pone, *en semejanza de uno*."

[129] Ibid., 195, quoting Juan de Ávila, *Pláticas a sacerdotes 2*, in Juan de Ávila, *Obras completas*, vol. 3, 380: "Somos, padres mios, sacrificio de Dios, cuya parte se quemaba en honra de Dios y otra parte se comian los hombres; todos enteros hemos de ser encendido en el fuego del amor de Dios..."

[130] Ibid., 179. See *Tratado sobre el sacerdocio*, in Juan de Ávila, *Obras completas*, vol. 3, 504–506.

[131] Ibid, 259.

ecclesiastical office, and only to those activities they would conduct as public persons (such as offering the Mass and reciting the divine office) and, notably, as representatives of the universal Church.[132]

Philip Neri

Philip Neri's Congregation of the Oratory was founded in Italy in 1575, consisting of secular priests who lived in community but without vows. Devoted to saying daily Mass and preaching four sermons daily, Neri's men provided prayerful gathering places for the laity, characterized by popular devotions, discussions, and singing.[133] The spirituality of Neri included the desire for sanctity, which became in Bérulle's project a Christocentric mysticism with a focus on the priesthood, according to Peirera and Fastiggi.[134] Neri's spirituality developed five themes common also to the French Oratorian School. The first was a pure priesthood with an emphasis on "priesthood as a state that does not have to seek its perfection outside of itself," and also moderation, popular spirituality, joy, and method in prayer.[135]

Bérulle's spirituality shared several common characteristics with that of Neri, including a focus on prayer and interiority, sacramental piety, and an emphasis on the elevation of the heart toward God in love. Bérulle's project differed in his more structured approach, in a Pseudo-Dionysian mysticism borrowed from the Rheno-Flemish School, the abstract mysticism of Canfield, and Jesuit and Carmelite influences, according to the authors.[136]

---

[132] See Ávila's discussion, *Pláticas a sacerdotes 13,* in Juan de Ávila, *Obras completas*, vol. 3, 459. Ávila: "Para esto habéis de saber que las personas eclesiásticos todo lo que hacen tocante al oficio eclesiástico, lo hacen como personas públicas, como es el rezar sus horas canónicas y decir misas y lo demás. Y así, no mira Dios nuestro Señor a los merecimientos de aquel sacerdote en particular, sino mira a los merecimientos de toda la Iglesia universal, en cuyo lugar ofrece el sacerdote aquello; de manera que si el rey de Francis enviase unos legados y embajadores al rey de España sobre los negocios del mismo reino, a estos embajadores no los miraría el rey como personas particulares, ni les haría el tratamiento que sus personas en particular merecían, sino como a personas públicas que venían en lugar de todo el reino de Francia..."

[133] Henry Bowden Sebastian, "The Oratory of Saint Philip Neri," *Catholic Encyclopedia*, vol. 11 (New York: Robert Appleton Company, 1911), http://www.newadvent.org/cathen/11272a.htm.

[134] Pereira and Fastiggi, *The Mystical Theology of the Catholic Reformation*, 193–95, 197–98.

[135] Ibid., 200.

[136] Ibid., 204.

Notably, while Bérulle was considered a kind of disciple of Neri, his more rigorist and formalized spirituality differed considerably. Neri was known for his kindness, charisms, ecstasies and levitations.

Neri followed a traditional asceticism characterized by the moderation of his model, Cassian. His focus was on the practical and concrete.[137]

Bérulle's ambitions were greater than those of Philip Neri's Congregation of the Oratory, which did not occupy itself with spiritual direction of clergy or their formation. Bérulle wanted to make his Oratory a kind of *pépinière* for priests who were to lead a truly religious life and with a greater exigency than that of the rule of life of the Italian Oratory. Bérulle wrote that the new congregation held to the faith of the Italian Oratory, as well as the Oblates of St. Ambrose, founded by Charles Borromeo. The Oblates were characterized as being priests, simple clerics, or laypersons, living in service to a diocese, with a devotion to their archbishop. Bérulle wanted his Oratory to form priests to be at the service of the bishop, as the Jesuits were in service to the Pope.[138]

Instituted in 1578, the Oblates of St. Ambrose were characterized as being rigorist, hierarchical, communitarian, oriented to preaching and the sacraments, and meticulously organized. Borromeo's considerable contributions to the Council of Trent were the notion of residences for pastors, the fostering of diocesan synods, diocesan and parish regulations, and the foundation of seminaries, as well as parish missions.[139]

From the Company of Jesus, Bérulle took the ideal of combining the religious and apostolic life. Another source of inspiration for Bérulle was César de Bus, who founded the Congregation of Christian Doctrine in 1592. Bérulle closely followed his ideal of having his men catechize throughout the countryside. Insisting on austerity and contemplation, de Bus's main aim for his priests was to evangelize, particularly addressing the problems of the Reformers. Bérulle's objective surpassed that of de Bus (which did not include the idea of forming priests) with the goal of the reform of the clergy.[140]

---

[137] Antonio Cistellini, "Oratoire Philippin," in Marcel Viller, Charles Baumgartner, and André Rayez, *Dictionnaire de spiritualité: ascétique et mystique, doctrine et histoire*, hereafter cited as *DSAM*, vol. 11 (Paris: G. Beauchesne, 1982), cols. 853–875.

[138] *BLS*, 85–87.

[139] Roger Mols, "Saint Charles Borromée, pionnier de la pastorale moderne," *Nouvelle revue théologique* (1957): 715.

[140] *BLS*, 88–89.

The Theology of Priesthood in Bérulle's Era

When the Reformers denied that priests of the New Covenant were sacrificers, Catholic theologians answered with the defense that the priest is a minister of sacrifice and that the Mass is his proper function. To clarify how the priest was united with Christ, Catholics also responded that the priest himself participates in the offering that Christ makes to his Father.[141]

Bérulle's ideals also included the exaltation of the clerical state.

This theme was found among many writers, according to Le Brun, as a result of the sacerdotal literature (both ancient and modern) being published at the time, with John Chrysostom, Gregory the Great, Ambrose, and Gregory Nazianzen among the earlier works.[142]

The reform of the clergy remained an ongoing and serious concern following Trent. A central concern of numerous works in the era surrounding and after Trent was the spiritual problems of the clergy, with a goal of convincing priests of the need to rediscover the greatness of their task. These works were of two types: one addressed to parish priests, explaining their functions and guiding them in the exercise of their ministry, and the other addressed to all priests. Those destined for pastors, and following Aquinas and Gerson, included Pseudo-Dionysian themes including the threefold division of sacerdotal function: to purify, enlighten, and perfect, with the priest having as his mission the return of souls to their first source. One such work was La Rochefoucauld's *De l'état ecclésiastique* (1597).[143]

Additional themes found in the first category include the practical ideals associated with the mission of pastors to teach and to offer sacramental confession. Some works attempted to clarify pastoral responsibilities and the doctrines priests should transmit to the faithful. This category of works treated the dignity of the priesthood and the importance of the interior life.[144] Other works with which Bérulle would have been familiar and from which he borrowed ideas were a number of then-recent works on priesthood and perfection, including ones by de Molina, as well as de Besse, from whom he borrowed the importance of the royal priesthood. Perfection in sacerdotal identity, tied to the

---

[141] *BLS*, 45–50.
[142] Le Brun, "Le grand siècle de la spiritualité française et ses lendemains," 244–45.
[143] *BLS*, 56–57.
[144] Ibid., 56–58.

exalted role of mediator and provider of the Eucharist, and the need for prayer were themes treated in these works.[145]

Robert Bellarmine and the Theology of Order

Bellarmine was the initiator of the modern theological treatise on the sacrament of orders at the end of the sixteenth century, with his *De Sacramento Ordinis*.[146] It included topics such as a defense of orders as a true sacrament, its divine institution, and the promise of graces attached, as well as matters relating to ministry and ceremonies.[147] Bellarmine also wrote in his old age a brief exhortation on the perfection required of clerics. In it he treated such topics as ceremonial requirements, poverty, and reverence, citing Jerome and Bernard and their exhortations.[148] His main work, *Disputationes de Controversiis Christianae Fidei adversus hujus temporis Haereticos*, was published in three volumes in 1581, 1582, and 1593. A defense against Protestant critiques of the Mass, the sacraments in general, and the authority of the pope, it also treated ideas surrounding office, character, and the divinity and the humanity of Christ, including the *autotheotes* of the Son.

Having read the Reformers directly, Bellarmine responded to them, not with recourse to Trent but to the Christian scriptures and the fathers of the early Church.[149] One weakness in his approach, however, was the lack of any connection between the priesthood and the ministry of Jesus, according to Osborne.[150]

Bérulle's methodology resembled that of Bellarmine in returning to these sources. His work drew on Bellarmine's, as we will review.

---

[145]   Morgain, "La prêtrise selon Pierre de Bérulle," 142, nos. 13 and 14. See Pierre de Besse, *Royale prestrise, c'est-à-dire des excellences, des qualités requises et des choses défendues aux prêtres* (Paris, 1610); Clichtove, *De vita et moribus sacerdotum*, fol. 79. See also Antonio de Molina, *Instruccion de sacerdotes* (Burgos, 1608).

[146]   See Robert Bellarmine, *De Sacramento Ordinis Roberti Bellarmini*, in *Opera omnia*, vol. 5, ed. Justinus Fèvre (Paris: Ludovicum Vivès, 1870–74), 21–35.

[147]   See A. Michel, "Ordre: Théologie du XVIe siècle," in *DTC*, vol. 11 (1931): col. 1365. See also X. Le Bachelet, "Bellarmin, François-Robert-Romulus," in *DSAM*, vol. 2 (Paris: G. Beauchesne et ses fils, 1905), cols. 560–78.

[148]   Robert Bellarmine, "The Fourteenth Precept: On the Sacrament of Orders," in *The Art of Dying Well*, trans. John Dalton (London: Richardson and Son, 1847), 99–106.

[149]   Kenan B. Osborne, *Priesthood: A History of the Ordained Ministry in the Roman Catholic Church* (New York: Paulist Press, 1989), 282.

[150]   Ibid., 283 and 285.

Conclusion

Under the influences of an essentialist mystic vogue and an absolutist political climate—and deeply convinced of the promise of a renewed Catholic culture and an idealist academy rising from the rubble of the French Wars of Religion, Bérulle initiated a clerical formation movement to reform the Church. He did so via a spiritual theology that absorbed polemical ideals of Counter-Reformation France. Especially notable was his Christocentrism, shared in part with both Calvin and Luther, who, as Dolan noted, held that we receive everything from God, but only through Christ.[151]

Reclaiming what he saw as a lost heritage through a closer identification with Christ, Bérulle was, as this study will detail, to elevate the priesthood into a participation in the human-divine being and function of Christ himself, an Alexandrian inheritance.

In these efforts, Bérulle was far more than a mere mimic of early tradition or recent and important antecedents such as Clichtove or Ávila. The originality of his reform in the defense of the hierarchy, the Mass as sacrifice, the priesthood, and Catholic culture, lay in what was a broad, yet highly-detailed amalgam, aided by the charismatic communication of his ideals, and made possible by the weight and scope of his authority as both a political leader and prince of the Church.

Bérulle's special status gave him a place to stand and the leverage to shift the course of the spiritual theology of priesthood. His chief tools in this effort were the bright ideals found in the work of the Reformers themselves—Catholic and Protestant.

Next we turn to the landscape of philosophy upon which Bérulle charted his speculative mysticism and applied metaphysic.

---

[151] John Dolan, *History of the Reformation: A Conciliatory Assessment of Opposite Views* (New York: Desclee Company, 1965), 327.

Chapter 3
Philosophy and Speculative Mysticism

The Foci of This Analysis: Speculative Mysticism and Applied Metaphysics

Bérulle's is an important case study of a polemicized theological method utilizing ideas drawn from many and varied sources from the realm of speculative mysticism and metaphysics, the central foci of both his identity of priesthood and this analysis. It serves as a window into how a churchman of considerable political and ecclesial influence, with some theological and philosophical training, constructed and promulgated a spiritual theology of priesthood based on speculation, specifically grappling with problems Reformers brought to the fore.

There are several serious challenges in tracing direct and indirect philosophical influences, as noted, including Bérulle's tendency toward vague paraphrasing, his recombining and redefining of concepts, the difficulty in locating which sources came to him and how, and the sheer volume of notions that he applied in his project.

A key objective of this review is not to simply explicate influences in tradition but rather to highlight possible key benchmarks from which Bérulle came to deviate – a distinctly different task.

Added to these challenges is the reticence of scholars of the French School to delve into certain of Bérulle's possible sources of inspiration, as already noted, such as Middle Platonism, Hermeticism (early and late), Cabalism, the Rhineland mystics, Duns Scot and followers, De Vio, Suárez, and the Florentine Academy. One can speculate about the possible reasons for this: unfamiliarity with the intricacies of various historical versions of philosophical and theological ideas because of limits in training, the opaqueness of this period of intellectual history, denominational tensions and differences in historical scholarship, as well as a hesitancy to delve into controversial topics which could reveal Bérulle's sacerdotal spiritual theology as outside the thought of Aquinas and mainstream tradition.

The difficulty in correctly interpreting the application or misapplication of the myriad concepts treated in his work would involve a degree of tracing provenance for each individual aspect which is not possible in this study. We do, however, have the important detailed work of Yelle, Whannou, and Preckler on such foundational ideas as the holiness of Christ, subsistence, and the notion of *états* in his work, respectively, as well as the work of Dupuy on the priesthood according to Bérulle. These studies include substantial treatments from which conclusions are easily drawn or areas for additional study readily seen.

We also have the equally important contributions of other scholars, such as Bellemare, Cochois, Cognet, Dagens, Orcibal, and Carraud, who have treated many aspects of Bérulle's thought.

At times, this study will only locate kernels of possible philosophical influence, which Bérulle engineered into anomalous concepts. A trait of formation literature is to vaguely reference patristic sources at the margins, for example. To interpret various voices as directly influencing his thought would be to ascribe to him a rigor that was clearly lacking. To fail to attempt to locate certain strong, core ideals in tradition, however reinterpreted, would be to miss the opportunity to trace how he, in fact, did represent or misrepresent particular strains of philosophy and theology.

The following overview of certain salient influences serves as an introduction only. It is meant to find echoes in early and late streams of thought that Bérulle's rhetoric mimicked. Demonstrating these echoes with appropriate citations pertaining to each of Bérulle's myriad ideals is left for later chapters which treat each in proper detail and as brought into focus by specialized experts.

In this preamble, the objective is not to attribute influences as supported by the research of a broad range of specialized scholars, a task certainly required for further study, but merely to alert the reader to certain currents of thought as highlighted by some few but notable experts in the history of speculative mysticism, metaphysics, and spirituality.

Medieval Period

Bérulle's own speculative mysticism had its roots, in part, in the medieval period. To understand these roots, Copleston's thoughts about speculative mysticism and its relevance to the history of philosophy will be reviewed.[1]

Two prevalent themes found in this era were the relation of finite being to infinite being in general, and that of the human soul to God in particular. The mystical writers of this period were characterized by an affective piety and a desire to attract others to God. Their vernacular writings were a reaction against what they considered "Scholastic aridity and academic wranglings."[2]

---

[1] Frederick Copleston, *The History of Philosophy: Late Medieval and Renaissance Philosophy*, vol. 3, pt. 1 (New York: Image Books, 1963), 193–218.
[2] Ibid., 195.

Bérulle followed closely these trends, as this analysis will show, developing the relationship between the priest's finite being and that of God, and the priest's soul in relation to Christ, via an affective theology couched in a grandiloquence meant to convince and inspire.

The Revival of Religious Neoplatonism

Copleston wrote that towards the end of the Renaissance the cult of classical literature degenerated into Ciceronianism as a substitute for Aristotle.[3] Interest in classical literature led to a revival of interest in ancient philosophies, the most influential being that of Neoplatonism. The Platonists of this era were attracted to the religious side of Neoplatonism. They had a general dislike of the tendency toward naturalism, which they perceived in Aristotelianism. The Platonic tradition was seen as a source of renewal and reform for both church and state. They saw the humanistic Renaissance as in need of a doctrine that saw the human being as a microcosm and that held an ontological bond between the spiritual and the material.[4]

Bérulle, following later, was no exception.

The Fall of Aristotelian Logic: Philosophy at the Service of Positive Theology

Scholastic method and Aristotelian logic came under attack by a number of humanists who held logic to be subordinate to rhetoric. French humanist Pierre de Ramée, a Calvinist, insisted on the artificial character of Aristotelian/Scholastic logic. Men like Ramée were strongly influenced by the classics, especially Cicero. They stressed natural logic associated with speech. Luther himself, according to Copleston, was a "determined enemy of Scholastic Aristotelianism."[5]

The reform of the arts curriculum in Post-Tridentine Catholic schools included the purpose of attempting to explain all knowledge in the service of revealed theology, according to Lohr. This included Suárez's reinterpretation of Aristotle's metaphysics. Lohr also noted that a new Christian Aristotelianism "moved out of the mainstream of European intellectual history."[6] Professors

---

3   Ibid., 3 and 207–8.
4   Ibid., 210–11.
5   Ibid., 217 and 228.
6   Charles H. Lohr, "Metaphysics," in *Cambridge History of Renaissance Philosophy*, ed. C. B. Schmitt, Quentin Skinner, Eckhard Kessler, and Jill Kraye (Cambridge: Cambridge University Press, 1988), 617–18.

produced a new literary form, that of the *cursus philosophicus*. In these works authors reinterpreted parts of Aristotle's natural philosophy as metaphysics.[7]

This trend arguably influenced the spiritual theology of priesthood in Bérulle's efforts to link natural philosophy and metaphysics in his Christology, as this study will reveal.

There were a number of problems related to these works, including the fact that these authors had limited direct knowledge of Greek and Arabic sources and a limited acquaintance with medieval Latin authorities. These authors differed from their medieval counterparts who wrote as theologians attempting to show a fundamental harmony between Christian revelation and the Greeks. These writers, on the contrary, wrote as philosophers with an apologetic purpose. The summaries of Scholastic philosophers composed in the Counter-Reformation era included that of Eustache de Saint-Paul (who influenced Descartes), the author of the *Summa philosophiae quadripartita* in 1609. Notably, he was professor to Bérulle in developing his rhetorical skills in terms of expounding on metaphysical themes.[8]

Methodologies

Expanding on the discussion of methodologies, a review follows of the similarities between the methodologies of Calvin, Calvinists, and Bérulle.

Calvin and Calvinism

Calvin, a trained lawyer, was influenced by the French legal humanism of his age which gave him the tools to follow a methodology that included philology, approaching foundational texts directly while interpreting them within linguistic and historical parameters.[9]

Calvin's thought, according to McGrath, had direct links with the *schola Augustiniana moderna*, characterized by a strict epistemological nominalism or termism; a voluntarist understanding of the grounds of human merit and of the merit of Jesus Christ; extensive reference to Augustine and his doctrine of grace;

---

[7] Ibid., 618.

[8] Ibid., 620. See also Jean-Baptiste-Louis de Gonzague Fontaine (pseudonym Lascasas), *Le cardinal Pierre de Bérulle, devant la Champagne, son pays* (A. Berthelon, 1847), 52. Saint-Paul was a doctor at the Sorbonne and taught a seventeen-year-old Bérulle rhetoric, including asking him to write on metaphysical themes. Saint-Paul's 1609 work in Latin was considered a bestseller.

[9] Alister E. McGrath, *Reformation Thought: An Introduction* (Oxford, UK, and Cambridge, MA: Blackwell, 1993), 50–51.

a strongly pessimistic view of human nature; a radical doctrine of double predestination; and a rejection of the role of intermediaries such as habits of grace in justification.[10] This study will explore in greater depth Calvin's thought.

McGrath noted that there was a subtle but significant difference between Calvin and Calvinism on the issue of predestination, and Calvin's followers developed his ideas with an emphasis on systematization and a concern for methodology characteristic of that era. The doctrine of predestination was not central to Calvin's thought, but became central in later Reformed theology, with the theme of election dominating and taking on major political and social aspects. Whereas Calvin regarded Aristotelianism with suspicion, later Calvinist apologists utilized it. McGrath delineated four key characteristics of the Calvinist approach to theology: the role of human reason in exploring and defending theology; the presentation of theology based on a logically coherent and rationally defensible system; the use of Aristotelian philosophy (McGrath describes late Reformation writers as philosophical rather than biblical theologians); and a concern with the metaphysical and the speculative as they relate to the nature of God, the divine will, and especially predestination. Whereas Calvin's methodology was based on the historical phenomenon of Jesus Christ, Baeza, for example, began with general principles and then proceeded with a deductive and synthetic method in order to deduce their consequences for theology.[11]

Bérulle

Bérulle, too, took Christ in the scriptures and the fathers as his base, and was deeply influenced by the modern Augustinian school, especially in his pessimistic view of human nature and an extreme voluntarism, as this study will detail. His methodology also mirrored that of later Calvinists. His project clearly took on political and social aspects, and his approach was an attempt at a rationally defensible system that nevertheless was couched in a verbose, non-academic style. Focusing on Neoplatonic and Pseudo-Dionysian themes, Bérulle also addressed the nature of God, divine will, and his own version of assurance of sanctification for both priests and the perfect through frequent mental elevations, as this study will uncover.

---

[10]   Ibid., 84.
[11]   Ibid., 123–30.

Scholasticism and Humanism

Aspects of the two great intellectual currents of the medieval era, Scholasticism and humanism, were appropriated by the Reformers in quite diverse ways depending on geographical location. For example, the Reformation of Wittenberg directly worked with Scholasticism, whereas Erasmian humanism in early Reformed theology focused more on social and ecclesial ideals than theological notions.[12]

Devout humanism honored classical cultural ideals within works of spirituality, according to Le Brun. There was a trend to think of God as the principle and end of creatures, and man as his image and chief work with the role of referring creation back to God. There was, as well, an attraction to Stoicism.[13]

Bérulle reacted to these trends in various ways. Like Luther and Calvin, he was critical of Scholasticism, while reinterpreting Scholastic terminology in support of his own social and ecclesial ideals. In particular, even while condemning Stoicism, he came to absorb some notions which became central to his spiritual theology of priesthood, as future chapters will detail. Bérulle presented the priest as both the visible image of Christ and an image-maker himself, referring the laity back to God.

Scholasticism

The methodological and theological developments in late medieval Scholasticism had a major influence on a number of Reformers, notably Luther, according to McGrath's analysis. Humanist writers wanted to discredit the Middle Ages as an interval between antiquity and the Renaissance. The Reformers attacked theological method in general and Aristotle in particular.

Four issues were important for the Scholastics, according to McGrath.[14] Each, it can be argued, continued to have importance in Bérulle's response to Reformers. The first was the debate between realism (Thomists) and terminism (Scotists), which Bérulle attempted to reconcile.

The second debate was that between the logico-critical and historico-critical approaches to theology, the latter being a major influence as an origin of the Reformation. Bérulle's approach was, again, an attempt at a reconciliation of both, notably a referencing of the latter in support of the former.

---

[12] McGrath, *The Intellectual Origins of the European Reformation*, 184–85.

[13] Le Brun, "Le grand siècle de la spiritualité française et ses lendemains," 238–40.

[14] See Alister McGrath, "Scholasticism," in *Oxford Encyclopedia of the Reformation*, vol. 4 (New York and Oxford: Oxford University Press, 1996), 17–20, for the following discussion.

The third debate was between intellectualism and voluntarism. This study will illustrate how a certain voluntarism influenced Bérulle's priesthood as well.

The fourth major debate was on justification. The *via moderna* emphasized a positive human contribution, while the Reformers emphasized the absolute necessity of grace. Luther was to see the former as Pelagianism. Bérulle's approach mirrored more closely that of semi-Pelagianism, as this study will explore.

According to McGrath, Luther's critique of Scholasticism was that it was too rational, placed a wrong emphasis on human reason (having a misplaced priority for Aristotle, especially his ethics), and did not give precedence to the scriptures. He rejected the notion that one could attain goodness through repeated action as in the *Nicomachean Ethics*. The main complaint of the Reformers was that medieval Catholicism was a corrupt form of Christianity, joining pagan philosophy with the Gospel.

Bérulle, even while condemning Scholastic method, adopted and reinterpreted its nomenclature, as noted. Repeated prayer to maintain virtue and a mixing of pagan and Christian elements in his spirituality of priesthood were key characteristics, which this study will explore in detail.

The Via Moderna

Mahieu's was a severe critique of Ockham, who broke with Thomist Aristotelianism, beginning a trend known as the *via moderna*. Mahieu saw the movement as including the suppression of real or formal distinctions (there being only distinctions of reason) and the lack of distinction between essence and existence, substance and accident, the soul and its faculties, or the intellect agent and the passive intellect. Ockham failed to understand, according to the author, the theory of composite beings as presented by Aquinas and following Aristotle. For Ockham, intelligence cannot know a real universal that does not exist in things. With this, Mahieu asserted, the metaphysical became impossible, and the explanation of things could only be found in the will of God, psychology, and morality. The theological consequences included the lack of distinction between habitual grace and charity, as well as infused *habitus* and the soul itself. With the idea that by natural acts we prepare for grace Ockham also resurrected semi-Pelagianism.[15]

According to McGrath, a de-ontologizing of the relation of humanity to God was a feature of both the *via moderna* and the *schola Augustiniana moderna*.

---

[15]   Léon Mahieu, *Francisco Suárez: sa philosophie et les rapports qu'elle a avec sa théologie* (Paris: Desclée de Brouwer & Co., 1921), 7–8.

With both, there was a turn to the covenantal understanding of causality.[16] Trueman clarified that while Augustine held justification to be an ontological change, the Reformers, following the *via moderna*, held it was rather about relational change, a change in status, as a result of an emphasis on divine acceptance.[17]

The *via moderna*, a heterogeneous movement, could be generally characterized by voluntarism and the use of the logico-critical method, used in the fourteenth and fifteenth centuries to study both the role of supernatural habits in justification and the nature of the Incarnation. It included a general trend toward non-realist epistemology, which influenced the Reformers in their denial of any ontological aspect to justification, and was a continuation of a long-standing critique of *habitus* theology, which in high Scholasticism had included the idea that ontological changes happened in humanity requiring an ontological intermediate of the created habit of grace or charity. Notably, the council fathers did not mention *habitus* in their response to this controversy.[18] The late Augustinian tradition followed the *via moderna* in holding to the "priority of acts over habits," making the formal cause of both justification and merit extrinsic (the divine acceptance), rather than intrinsic (the created habits of grace).[19]

Bérulle addressed and absorbed the tendency of thinking of justification in personal or relational terms, as will be detailed, in his definitions related to the sanctification of priests, notably, the mechanisms of maintaining a special relation between the priest and the Word Incarnate.

McGrath saw the criticism of *habitus* theology as continued in the personalism of the Reformers.[20]

Indeed, a personalism could be attributed to Bérulle's spiritual theology of priesthood which required an annihilated will and frequent prayer to maintain union with Christ. These ideals will be explored in detail in the following chapters.

---

[16] McGrath, *The Intellectual Origins of the European Reformation*, 72–79, especially 77n46. See William J. Courtney, *Covenant and Causality in Medieval Thought: Studies in Philosophy, Theology and Economic Practice* (London: Variorum, 1984).

[17] Carl Trueman, "*Simul peccator et Justus*: Marin Luther and Justification," in *Justification in Perspective: Historical Developments and Contemporary Challenges*, ed. Bruce L. McCormack (Grand Rapids, MI: Baker Academic, 2006), 85–86.

[18] McGrath, *The Intellectual Origins of the European Reformation*, 72–79.

[19] Ibid., 85.

[20] Ibid., 77.

Mystical Experience and the Reformation

According to Baumgartner, controversies in the history of the study of mystical experience included those surrounding the nature of mystical contemplation, its differences with common prayer, and the relationship between contemplation and Christian perfection.[21] Both the Reformers and Bérulle deeply pondered these central questions, related as they were to justification and sanctification.

O'Brien asked the question, "What is 'mystical experience'?" He noted that twenty-three authors contributed their ideas on the history of this question in an article on contemplation in the *Dictionnaire de spiritualité*. The article treats such diverse forms of contemplation as that, for example, of the Hebrew prophets of the Servant, what has been called the Hellenic mysticism of John, and the double influence of Judaism and Hellenism in Paul's ideals on mystical experience. Stoic contemplation, for example, included the uniting of oneself to the work of the divine logos immanent in all things. For Plotinus, contemplation referred not just to the action of contemplating but also the being who contemplates, since beings exist only insofar as they participate in intelligence. Both Plato and Plotinus demanded perfection as a condition of contemplation. For Origen, one must move past the humanity of Christ before proceeding to prepare for the contemplation of the divinity. Gregory of Nyssa was to call it a great gift, and not simply the result of effort.[22]

Bérulle took great liberties in assembling ideals from various philosophical current in support of his spiritual theology of priesthood, which this study will detail.

Early Modern Platonism and Mysticism

Early modern continental Platonism has not been thoroughly explored by scholars, the main reason being that thinkers from that era combined ideas from a variety of sources. Attempting to trace back these ideas is extraordinarily difficult, according to Mercer.[23] The same is the case with the Platonic ideals of Bérulle, notably because he cited his sources so rarely and he combined ideals

---

[21]   Charles Baumgartner, "Contemplation: conclusion générale," in *DSAM*, vol. 2 (1953), col. 2171.

[22]   Elmer O'Brien, "Current Theology: Ascetical and Mystical Theology, 1952–1953," *Theological Studies* 15, no. 2 (June 1954): 290. See "Contemplation," in *DSAM*, vol. 2, pt. 2 (1950–52), cols. 1643–2193.

[23]   Christia Mercer, "Platonism and Philosophical Humanism on the Continent," in *A Companion to Early Modern Philosophy*, ed. Steven Nadler (Malden, MA: Blackwell Publishing, 2002), 36.

taken from various periods and thinkers so readily. His heavy reliance on the fathers, in particular, is notable.

Festugière, an authority on Hellenistic religions in relation to Christianity, wrote, "…when the fathers 'think' their mysticism, they platonize. There is nothing original in the artifice."[24] They were concerned with seeing God and understanding the divine mysteries, whereas Christianity's concern has been following Jesus, with the only mystery that of love. However, he added, certain Christian thinkers adopted a "philosophical spirituality," such as Chrysostom, Jerome, Cassian, Irenaeus, Basil, Benedict, and Ignatius, which Festugière attributed to the Alexandrian School, notably Clement and Origen. In the East, the teachers of contemplation were Evagrius, Gregory of Nyssa, and Pseudo-Dionysius, and in the West, St. Augustine and Gregory the Great. Mysticism took the form that "to be perfect is to contemplate, and that is to see God in an immediate vision." The mind (*nous*) is united to God in a contemplative life with no place for action.[25]

Louth responded that patristic mysticism differed from Platonic mysticism in certain aspects. God replaces the One, and the emphasis is on grace coming from the Incarnate Christ. The fathers' mysticism is about God's descent rather than the soul's withdrawal and ascent. In terms of the soul's relation to God, for Plato, the soul is already divine, and divinization is merely becoming what one is. Both Origen and Evagrius would follow this line, but later thinkers would reject this notion, holding to the ideal of *creatio ex nihilo*. Lastly, in terms of the role of moral virtues, for Platonists, the soul must control the body to be free of it, whereas for the fathers, while the moral virtues are purificatory, they are also both the means and the effect of the indwelling Christ.[26] Louth summarized by noting that Greek philosophy gave Christianity the idea of two lives: contemplative and active, the former being the ideal.[27]

This study will delineate how Bérulle attempted to combine the contemplative and the active as part of his Oratorians' spirituality, echoing certain aspects from both Platonic and patristic mystical traditions. While his basis for sacerdotal grace was the Incarnate Christ, his Oratorians' focus was to be on abstract "contemplation" of the unity of the divine essence, the humanity of Christ, and the hypostatic union. Essential aspects of Bérulle's asceticism would include withdrawal and ascent combined with a kind of personalist divine descent, and

---

[24] A. J. Festugière, *Contemplation et vie contemplative selon Platon*, 3rd ed. (Paris: J. Vrin, 1967), 5, quoted in Andrew Louth, *The Origins of the Christian Mystical Tradition: From Plato to Pseudo-Dionysius* (Oxford: Oxford University Press, 2007), 187.

[25] Festugière, *Contemplation*, 142, quoted in Louth, *The Origins of the Christian Mystical Tradition*, 188.

[26] Louth, *The Origins of the Christian Mystical Tradition*, 191–93.

[27] Ibid., 198. See C. Butler, *Western Mysticism* (London, 1922), 195–293.

this by a moral self-annihilationism that reached arguably to the ontological. The most complex aspect of Bérulle's project was his thought on the relationship between the practice of the virtues and infused grace in relation to the indwelling Christ. This relationship was at the center of both the Reformation and Counter-Reformation disputes on nature and grace, as well as Bérulle's spiritual theology of priesthood.

Renaissance Mysticism

Writing on Renaissance Mysticism, McGinn detailed ideals that were prevalent related to Platonism, *prisca theologia*, and Cabala. His review of Marsilio Ficino and Marsilio Giovanni Pico della Mirandola, two members of the Florentine Academy, serves to introduce these influences on Bérulle's thought. Known for their interest in *prisca theologia*, they sought out ancient wisdom about God and man found in the earliest revealed texts of all the Gentile religions (Zoroaster, the Hermetic corpus, the Orphic hymns, and Pythagoras).

Ficino thought of Hermes Trismegistus (an Egyptian sage and supposed author of the *Hermetica*) as the founder of theology, seeing his influence in Plato, Plotinus, and Proclus. Ficino held that this ancient wisdom reached its fulfillment in the Incarnation, in the Christian scriptures, and especially in Pseudo-Dionysius, Augustine, and Aquinas.[28] Ficino was a priest and leader of the Florentine Academy, a circle of thinkers who held to a Platonic mysticism that consisted in the immortality of the soul as realized through contemplation. In fact, divinization was central to the Florentines' effort to unite Christianity with Platonism. He wrote, "our rational soul is able to become God" ("*potest animus noster aliquando fieri deus*"). The soul becomes "clothed with divine substance as with a new form; and through this form it almost becomes God, and through this form it then performs all its operations as some god rather than as a soul." ("*substantiam divinam induitur quasi formam, per quam paene fit deus, per quam omnes deinde operationes agit ut deus aliquis potius quam ut anima*").[29]

---

[28] Bernard McGinn, *The Varieties of Vernacular Mysticism 1350–1550* (New York: Crossroad Publishing Company, 2012), 250–52. This review follows the author's exposition closely. See Marsilio Ficino, *Platonic Theology*, English translation by Michael J. B. Allen with John Warden, Latin text by James Hankins with William Bowen, 6 vols. (Cambridge: Harvard University Press, 2001–6), 14.1 [4: 224–25], quoted in McGinn, *The Varieties of Vernacular Mysticism*, 267.

[29] Marsilio Ficino, *Marsilio Ficino: Platonic Theology*, 14.1 [4: 224–25]. See 225n2 where the editor notes the use of "God" and "a god." Also quoted in McGinn, *The Varieties of Vernacular Mysticism*, 267.

Ficino's idea of the unity of the soul with God was in rapture, in which the soul attains God by also reconciling its own bodily elements with those of the world's body. Ficino claimed this was the unity to which Zoroaster and Plato also referred: "Zoroaster calls 'the flower of the mind' the center itself of the soul which Plato calls 'the mind's head.'" (*"Zoroaster ipsum animae centrum, quod Plato nominat mentis caput"*).[30] As with Plato, he held the soul to be a mirror of the divine countenance. Ficino was known for the idea of "Platonic love," which harnessed the power of erotic love to ascend to the beauty of God. Ideal love was the intense love between two people (ideally men, for both Plato and Ficino) who refrain from physical expression in order to harness this power. McGinn noted that this construct was a powerful one at the time in Renaissance society.[31]

Pico echoed this schema, with the ascent of the soul beginning with the sight of the male body. The goal of finding heavenly beauty could only be reached with a separation from the body through ecstasy.[32]

This study will explore in detail some of Bérulle's ideas which suggest echoes of the Academy, including emphasis on union with Christ through a frequent effort at mental elevations, as well as his interpretation of Christ as divine substance and the Holy Spirit as quasi-formal cause. In particular, Ficino's possible influence on Bérulle's Christology will be detailed.

The Influence of Augustine's Spirituality

While Bérulle is considered to have been impacted by Augustinian philosophy, as this study will examine in detail, it is beyond the scope of this study to compile an in-depth catalogue of this influence. Important for this analysis is the less well-defined phenomenon of Augustinian piety in vogue at the time that had a notable impact on the era and on Bérulle's thought. His return to the fathers, including Augustine, was marked by a tacit acceptance of ideals, many times without

---

[30] Ficino, *Platonic Theology*, 13.5 [4: 212], quoted in McGinn, *The Varieties of Vernacular Mysticism*, 266. See Zoroaster on *"noou anthei"* from *Chaldean Oracles*, n. 28b, and Plato, *Phaedrus*, 248a.

[31] McGinn, *The Varieties of Vernacular Mysticism*, 255–62. See Ficino, *De Amore*, 7.15, in Marsilio Ficino and Sears Reynolds, *Marsilio Ficino: Commentary on Plato's Symposium on Love*, 2nd ed. (Dallas, TX: Spring Publications, 1985).

See also Ficino, *Platonic Theology*, 14.4 [222], quoting his own statement from *On Love*: "Ubi constat animum divino uri fulgore, qui in formoso homine micat quasi speculo atque ab eo clam raptum quasi hamo trahi sursum ut deus evadat."

[32] Ibid., 280. See Giovanni Pico della Mirandola, *Commento sopra una canzone di Benivieni*, 3.2, in Giovanni Pico della Mirandola and Sears Reynolds Jayne, *Commentary on a Canzone of Benivieni* (New York: P. Lang, 1984), 125.

attribution and paraphrased, making it difficult to pinpoint. Following is an opening survey of Augustine's influence by various commentators.

In the waning of the Renaissance, faith for both Catholics and Protestants reflected an Augustinianism characterized not by doctrines to which one adheres but by a gift by which one believes—an inward disposition rather than an external commitment.[33] This focus on disposition over external commitment was central to Bérulle's vision of a reformed priesthood.

Dagens detailed Augustine's influence on Bérulle's thought. Augustine was considered a master of the interior life, and was a major inspiration of the Acarie group and Bérulle. The Augustinianism of the era preceding Bérulle at first was an attempt at an Augustinian humanism, trying to bring together Plato, Neoplatonism, Hermeticism, antiquity, and Christianity. Dagens called Bérulle's Augustinianism both Christocentric and a kind of Christian Socratism in that Bérulle both lauded and condemned ancient culture. Berullian doctrine was founded on a profound meditation (a Pauline ideal already found in Augustine) on the Incarnation, considered as a mystery of abasement and humiliation. Self-knowledge was important in order to know God, but true wisdom consisted in piety and the *science des saints*.[34] Several key challenges in the history of the study of Augustine, however, were that his ideas were occasional, typically studied in isolated quotations or "sentences," were used as proof texts without recourse to the study of complete sources, or were misattributed.[35]

The Reformation was as much a debate about Augustine as about the primacy of the scriptures, according to McGrath. An edition of his works was completed in 1506 and contributed not only to a renewal of his thought, but to a more exacting study, which corrected previous errors of attribution and understanding.[36]

Knowledge of the self, again, an aspect of Christian Socratism, was part of the spiritual life in the seventeenth century as it was in the Middle Ages, according to Le Brun. Authors insisted on knowledge of self as leading to knowledge of God. Psychological moralism took different forms at this time, as affected by Jansenism or influencing spiritual direction, for example. Influential works included those on the topic of Christian character.[37]

---

[33] William James Bouwsma, *The Waning of the Renaissance: 1550–1640* (New Haven: Yale University Press, 2000), 101.

[34] Jean Dagens, "Le XVIIe siècle, siècle de Saint Augustin," *Cahiers de l'association internationale des études françaises*, nos. 3–5 (1953): 31–38.

[35] McGrath, *The Intellectual Origins of the European Reformation*, 169.

[36] Ibid., 169–72.

[37] Le Brun, "Le grand siècle de la spiritualité française et ses lendemains," 260–61.

One feature of the Post-Tridentine era was a patristic positivism, with a particular interest in Augustine, whose interpreters on free will and the necessity of grace came under scrutiny. The return to patristics in general was complex and was not necessarily characterized by orthodoxy. McGrath, arguably, thought the fathers had probably little influence on the Reformed Church.[38]

Nominalism and Mysticism

In Dress's analysis, explicated by Ozment, and referring to the intersection between mysticism and nominalism in late medieval literature, it was nominalism's theologically "stringent epistemology," resulting in "the denial of demonstrative knowledge of God, which became the peculiar jumping off place for mysticism." For Dress, "Dionysian negation and nominalist economy work together to prepare the way for a distinctive 'affective transcendentalism'."[39]

Ozment wrote that the most salient ideal of late medieval mystical traditions was that of a shared divine/human nature. The idea "that 'likeness' *(similitude)* is the *sine qua non* for saving knowledge and relationship" was held by many "mystical thinkers." As he continued, "these common medieval doctrines, to be sure in exaggerated form, become the very pillars of mystical theology."[40] Conversely, the nominalism of the period insisted that God's and man's relation was covenantal, not ontological, as noted, challenging the idea that only like can know like.[41]

As we will detail, Bérulle's spiritual theology of priesthood held God as transcendent and distant and yet at the same time in continual close relation to the priest through an affective transcendentalism of frequent elevations. His ideals would emphasize likeness as key to salvation, but this only through a covenant-like vow of servitude in order to maintain union.

Ozment questioned whether a young Luther might not have represented a synthesis between nominalism and mysticism. He was a devotee of medieval

---

[38] Alister E. McGrath, *Iustitia Dei: A History of the Doctrine of Justification*, 2 vols., 2nd ed. (Cambridge: Cambridge University Press, 1998), 90 and 173–76.

[39] Stephen Ozment, "Mysticism, Nominalism and Dissent," in *The Pursuit of Holiness in Late Medieval and Renaissance Religion*, ed. Charles Trinkaus with Heiko A. Oberman (Leiden: E. J. Brill, 1974), 68–69. See Walter Dress, *Die Theologie Gersons: eine Untersuchung zur Verbindung von Nominalismus und Mystik im Spätmittelalter* (Gütersloh: C. Bertelsmann, 1931), 51, 54, 69ff.

[40] Ozment, "Mysticism, Nominalism and Dissent," 77. See also footnote 2.

[41] Ibid., 78. See M. H. Carré, *Realists and Nominalists* (London: Oxford University Press, 1946), 110; Guilelmus de Ockham and Philotheus Boehner, *Philosophical Writings: A Selection* (London: Nelson, 1962), xxvii.

mysticism, was a trained Ockhamist, and had annotated Tauler and Biel, as well as edited *Theologia Deutsch*. Ozment opined that while Luther rejected basic axioms from both traditions, including similitude, he held to the union of the soul with Christ.[42]

Cranz agreed with and responded to Ozment, writing that the progress from late medieval nominalism and mysticism to Luther's thought was yet another effort to deal with Platonist ideals related to union, knowledge, and symbolism.[43] Cranz saw Luther as influenced by Augustine and Pseudo-Dionysius, yet ultimately rejecting, arguably, a formula of mysticism with his personal union of faith. Cranz wrote:

> Luther will go beyond the conformity of the will and the mind which could be found in nominalism, but he will not go back to the universality of Augustine or to the impersonality of Proclus and of Pseudo-Dionysius. Thus he explains in a Sermon: "The Lord does not say that your thoughts will be in me or that my thoughts will be in you but rather that you, you are in me, and I, I am in you….The Lord does not speak of a mere thought….but rather that I am in him with body, life, soul, piety, and justice, with sins, foolishness, and wisdom, and that he, Christ, is in me with his holiness, justice, wisdom, and blessedness"…[44]
>
> "But faith makes of you and Christ as it were one person (quasi unam personam) so that you are not separated from Christ, but cleave to him, as if you were to say: 'I am Christ' and as if he in turn were to say 'I am that

---

[42] Ibid., 91–92.

[43] F. Edward Cranz, "Cusanus, Luther, and Mystical Tradition," in *The Pursuit of Holiness in Late Medieval and Renaissance Religion*, ed. Charles Trinkaus with Heiko A. Oberman (Leiden: E. J. Brill, 1974), 93. See also 101, where the author notes Luther's early pointing to the identification of the knower with the known, referencing Aristotle, *De anima*, 3, 4 429a22 in Sermon of 1515, *Luthers Werke: Kritische Gesammtausgabe* (Weimar: Hermann Böhlau, 1883–), hereafter cited as *WA*, 1: 29.18–20: "Sic enim Aristoteles ait: Intellectus impossibilis [*sic pro*: possibilis] est nisi [*sic pro*: nihil] eorum, quae intelligit, sed potentia est ipsa omnia, et ipse est quodammodo omnia."

[44] Luther, "Sermons of John," 6–8, in Luther, *WA* 33: 225.18b–27b: "Aber der Herr saget nicht: deine gedancken von mir sind in mir oder meine gedancken sind in dir, sondern du, du bist in mir und ich, ich bin in dir, er nennet nicht einen schlechten gedancken, sondern das ich in jme mit leib, leben, Seele, frömkeit, Gerechtigkeit, mit sünden, torheit und weisheit sey, und er, Christus, widerumb in mir auch sey mit seiner heiligkeit, gerechtigkeit, weisheit und seligkeit." Quoted in English in Cranz, "Cusanus, Luther, and Mystical Tradition," 101; author's English translation. See also Martin Luther, *Luther's Works*, (hereafter *LW*) American ed., ed. Jaroslav Pelikan, Helmut T. Lehmann, and Christopher Boyd Brown, 75 vols. (Philadelphia and St. Louis: Fortress Press, 1955), 23: 144.

sinner'."[45] And if faith is now what defines the true self or the 'I' of the saved Christian, Luther is explicit that there is nothing substantial or thing-like about it: "I am accustomed to speculate in this way (sic imaginari), as if there were no *quality* in my heart which is called faith or righteousness, but in their place I put Jesus Christ."[46]

In a seeming echo of Luther's personalist unicity, Bérulle presented a certain kind of unicity with Christ in which the priest became closely identified with Christ.

The Influence of Eckhart

A comprehensive exploration of the possible direct or indirect influence of Eckhart's thought on Bérulle's is warranted before any conclusions can be drawn. That said, a similarity between their rhetorical styles, which deliberately introduce ambiguities meant to startle and a common divergence from efficient causality, characterize their work. Like Bérulle, for example, Eckhart's rhetoric involved paradox, oxymoron, and neologisms, and creating novel definitions.[47]

Schürmann noted, for example, that Eckhart's analogy differed from that of Aquinas, in that, as Schürmann wrote, for Eckhart, "The structure of the act of being of beings is not measured by, but identified with the one being that is God."[48] Schürmann held that proportionality based on predicamental analogy between substance and accident was rejected by Eckhart and was of Neoplatonic origin.

---

[45] Luther, *Commentary on Galatians*, WA 40.1: 285.5–7: "Sed fides facit ex te et Christo quasi unam personam, ut non segregeris a Christo, imo inherescas, quasi dicas te Christum, et econtra: ego sum ille peccator." Quoted in English in Cranz, "Cusanus, Luther, and Mystical Tradition," 101; author's English translation. See also *LW* 26: 168.

[46] Luther, in Luther's addendum to a letter of Melanchthon to Brenz, May, 1531, in Martin Luther, *Martin Luthers Werke: Kritische Gesammtausgabe, Abteilung Briefe*, vol. 6 (Weimar: Hermann Böhlaus Nachfolger, 1930–85), 100.49–101.1: "Et ego soleo, mi Brenti, ut hanc rem melius capiam, sic imaginari, quasi nulla sit in corde meo qualitas, quae fides vel charitas vocetur, sed in loco ipsorum pono Iesum Christum." Quoted in English in Cranz, "Cusanus, Luther, and Mystical Tradition," 101–102.

[47] See Bernard McGinn, *The Harvest of Mysticism in Medieval Germany*, vol. 4, *The Presence of God: A History of Western Christian Mysticism* (New York: Crossroad Publishing Company, 2005), 116.

[48] Reiner Schürmann and Meister Eckhart, *Meister Eckhart, Mystic and Philosopher: Translations with Commentary* (Bloomington: Indiana University Press, 1978), 176–77. Originally published as *Maître Eckhart ou la joie errante: Sermons allemands traduits et commentés* (Paris: Éditions Planète, 1972).

Gilson, in turn, noted that perfection, according to Eckhart, was merely imputed to the created. Gilson wrote, "Being is, so to speak, imputed to beings by God, without ever becoming their own being, about in the same way as in Luther's theology justice will be imputed to the just without it ever becoming their own justice."[49]

According to Eckhart, wrote Schürmann, "Being and all perfections are allotted to the created things *ze borge*, on loan."[50] While Aquinas and Aristotle understood being according to various degrees of perfection and modes of being, Eckhart did not conceive analogy in terms of proportionality.[51] The author felt that Eckhart's ontology was characterized by a "fleetingness of borrowed being" as opposed to that of Aquinas, which consisted of and reflected the autonomy of analogical beings.[52]

Importantly, Eckhart was criticized for his stress on formal rather than efficient causality.[53] At trial, Eckhart defended the idea that we and the Second Person of the Trinity are in a sense the same by appealing to the *inquantum* principle, that is, that we are identical to the Son insofar as we are sons, in a univocal sense.[54]

Eckhart and Origen on the Word

Schürmann's analysis is also helpful in situating how Bérulle envisioned the Incarnate Word in relation to the priest. Writing more on Eckhart's notions surrounding analogy, he noted that "the Scholastic theory of analogy is derived

---

[49] E. Gilson, *History of Christian Philosophy in the Middle Ages* (New York: Random House, 1955), 441, quoted in Schürmann and Eckhart, *Meister Eckhart*, 177. See also 253n59.

[50] See Meister Eckhart, *Book of Divine Consolation*, in Meister Eckhart, *Die deutschen und lateinischen Werke*, ed. Josef Quint, Deutsche Forschungsgemeinschaft (Stuttgart: Kohlhammer 1936–), DW V, 37, 5, quoted in Schürmann and Eckhart, *Meister Eckhart*, 177.

[51] Schürmann and Eckhart, *Meister Eckhart*, 177–78.

[52] Ibid., 179.

[53] Bernard McGinn, *The Mystical Thought of Meister Eckhart: The Man from Whom God Hid Nothing*, (New York, NY: Crossroad Publishing Company, 2001), 180.

[54] Ibid., 118. See Gabriel Théry, "Edition critique des pièces relatives au procès d'Eckhart contenues dans le manuscrit 33b de la bibliothèque de Soest," *Archives d'histoire doctrinale et littéraire du moyen âge* 1 (1926–27): 129–268. See also McGinn, *The Mystical Thought of Meister Eckhart*, 245n19, quoting Eckhart, *Expositio sancti Evangelii secundum Iohannem* for example, in Meister Eckhart, *Meister Eckhart: Die deutschen und lateinischen Werke herausgegeben im Auftrag der deutschen Forschungsgemeinschaft*, 3 (Stuttgart/Berlin: Kohlhammer, 1936–): 103.12–14, n.118: "Ait ergo: *verbum caro factum est* in Christo, *et habitavit in nobis*, quando in quolibet nostrum filius dei fit homo et filius hominis fit filius dei."

from Aristotelian ousiology and Neoplatonic cosmology; but Eckhart's understanding of being… transcends both."[55] The author held that the theory of analogy is insufficient in attempting to understand Eckhart's ontology. Eckhart, along with other Neoplatonists, saw being as continuously bestowed on beings. Like Plotinus, Eckhart held asceticism to be necessary to climb the steps of the emanations. The path that Eckhart envisioned was most often *abegescheidenheit*, or detachment or renunciation. Detachment progressively turned into the core of his ideals, as well as the idea of a kind of letting go, a serenity or releasement (*gelâzenheit*).[56]

Pertinent to Bérulle's project, Schürmann noted that while for Aquinas, the intellect has the power to confer intelligibility on objects, which is accomplished by the production of the word in the mind in relation to knowledge of the world, for Eckhart the detached man conceives and engenders the Word itself. Eckhart broadened this as well to include deification, where the "act of knowledge becomes the operative identity in the reciprocity of begetting."[57]

For Eckhart, it was through obedience that man becomes one with God as their wills become one, an idea owed to Eastern patristics, where the birth of the Son/Word occurs in the heart of the believer. Eckhart's idea of the detached man actually begetting the Son himself was an idea taken from Origen. Schürmann wrote, "For Origen, the union of the Word and the soul is accomplished by knowledge: to acquire knowledge is to become one with the Word."[58]

The basis for Eckhart's voluntarist mysticism was his ideal that God is pure intellect and not being. Being is always caused and so intellect must be the cause of being.[59]

---

[55]   Schürmann and Eckhart, *Meister Eckhart*, 180.

[56]   Ibid., 16 84–5 and 185–86.

[57]   Ibid., 24. Schürmann cited Aquinas, *Commentary on Aristotle's De anima* 3, ch. 4, lecture 9, no. 724, in Aristotle, Kenelm Foster, Silvester Humphries, and Ivo Thomas, *Aristotle's De Anima: In the Version of William of Moerbeke and the Commentary of St. Thomas Aquinas* (London: [s.n.], 1951), 423.

[58]   Ibid., 25. See also 23–24. See Origen, *Commentary on the Song of Songs*, 1, in Deutsche Akademie der Wissenschaften zu Berlin, *Die griechischen christlichen Schriftsteller der ersten Jahrhunderte*, vol. 8 (Berlin: Akademie-Verlag, 1925), 91, 1, 5. The author wrote that this tradition influencing Eckhart probably began with Clement of Alexandria, and was developed philosophically by Hippolytus and Origen, becoming "a systematized theology of union with God in Methodius, Gregory of Nazianzus, and Maximus." See 231n36, where the author noted this hypothesis was proposed by Hugo Rahner in "Die Gottesgeburt: Die Lehre der Kirchenväter von der Geburt Christi aus dem Herzen der Kirche und der Gläubigen," in *Symbole der Kirche* (Salzburg: Müller, 1964), 11–18 and 40ff.

[59]   Burkhard Mojsisch, "Meister Eckhart," *Stanford Encyclopedia of Philosophy*, published January 4, 2006, revised April 25, 2011, http://plato.stanford.edu/entries/meister-eckhart/#Bib.

In this study, possible echoes of these lines of thought will be explored in Bérulle's essentialist union with the Word Incarnate, as well as in how Bérulle envisioned his Oratorians' union with the Word Incarnate through meditation, and their giving Christ to their charges.

Christianized Stoicism

Verbeke, in his study of Stoicism in the ten centuries encompassing the medieval era, noted that the issue touches many authors who were often unaware of their Stoic leanings. Not hard to recognize if preserved in their original form, Stoic ideals changed with those who attempted to incorporate them.[60] Stoicism played a large role in the evolution of philosophical and theological thought during that era, although there was not a major influx of thought through the availability of translations.[61] By the medieval era, certain of its aspects were mainly accepted, being principally in "the background, never having been condemned by the Church."[62] Stoic writings were still not available in Latin, with the early Stoics not even available in the original Greek. The sources of Stoic thought were in secondary sources such as Simplicius, Arab-speaking philosophers, and Seneca.[63]

Following the chaos of the Wars of Religion, the Catholic Reformation sought to "discipline every aspect of life," a desire which Stoicism supported.[64] The movement called Neostoicism arose in response. The severe philosophy of Stoicism seemed a good counter to the moral chaos and anarchy of the era. Church fathers were cited as a way to promote the idea that Stoicism was compatible with Christianity. Guillaume Du Vair wrote on Stoicism in the vernacular for a wide popular audience in a preface to his translation of Epictetus, *Philosophie morale des Stoïques*, appearing in 1594.[65]

---

[60]   Gerard Verbeke, *The Presence of Stoicism in Medieval Thought* (Washington, DC: Catholic University of America Press, 1983), vii–viii.

[61]   Ibid., 1.

[62]   Ibid., 5–6.

[63]   Ibid., 6–7, 8n24. See Paul Faider and Paulus pseud.? Pompilius, *Études sur Sénèque* (Gand: van Rysselberghe & Rombaut, 1921), 137.

[64]   William J. Bouwsma, *A Usable Past: Essays in European Cultural History* (Berkeley and Los Angeles, CA: University of California Press, 1990), 63. See John Bossy, "The Counter-Reformation and the People of Catholic Europe," *Past and Present* 47 (May 1970): 51–70. See also Justus Lipsius, *De constantia libri duo, qui alloquium praecipuè continent in publicis malis* (n.p., n.d.), 9, on the topic of *apatheia*.

[65]   Jill Adrian Kraye, "Moral Philosophy," in *Cambridge History of Renaissance Philosophy*, ed. C. B. Schmitt, Quentin Skinner, Eckhard Kessler, and Jill Kraye (Cambridge: Cambridge University Press, 1988), 370–72. See Günter Abel, *Stoizismus und frühe Neuzeit: Zur Entstehungsgeschichte modernen Denkens im Felde von Ethik u. Politik* (Berlin

A Stoic Influence: Christ as the Temple of God

Epictetus held that Zeus was immanent and could be identified with the natural order. His *Encheiridion* was translated into Latin in 1497 and became very popular in France in Bérulle's period, including with theologians who found it compatible with Christianity.[66] Epictetus wrote: "But if our souls are so bound up with God and joined together with Him, as being parts and portions of His being, does not God perceive their every motion as being a motion of that which is His own and of one body with Himself?"[67]

This ideal, according to Dupuy, had become a kind of substitute for the Stoic doctrine of the Logos: an immanent force and principle of cohesion. For the Rheno-Flemish, for example, the air that one breathes or the drop of water in the ocean were meant to evoke the intimacy of union with God rather than a static spatial representation. This was vulgarized, according to Dupuy, into a static schema such that all of nature becomes the temple of God, thus calling into question the place of Christ.[68] Bérulle assumed this ideal in writing of "'l'étendue' de l'Être incréé qui 'contient' toutes choses," Dupuy wrote, an ideal recalling Pseudo-Dionysius.[69]

It would, perhaps, be through the influence of Maximus that Bérulle absorbed key Stoic notions.

---

and New York: De Gruyter, 1978); Guillaume Du Vair and G. Michaut, *De la sainte philosophie: philosophie morale des stoïques* (Paris: J. Vrin, 1945); Gerhard Oestreich, Brigitta Oestreich, and H. G. Koenigsberger, *Neostoicism and the Early Modern State*, trans. David McLintock (Cambridge: Cambridge University Press, 1982); Léontine Zanta, *La renaissance du stoïcisme au XVIe siècle* (Paris: H. Champion, 1914).

[66] Margaret Graver, "Epictetus," *Stanford Encyclopedia of Philosophy*, Spring 2013 ed., Edward N. Zalta, http://plato.stanford.edu/archives/spr2013/entries/epictetus.

[67] Epictetus, *Discourses* 1, in Epictetus and William Abbott Oldfather, *The Discourses as Reported by Arrian, The Manual, and Fragments*, vol. 1, Loeb Classical Library (Cambridge: Harvard University Press, 1946), 14, 6, 103: "ἀλλ᾽ αἱ ψυχαὶ μὲν οὕτως εἰσὶν ἐνδεδεμέναι καὶ συναφεῖς τῷ θεῷ ἅτε αὐτοῦ μόρια οὖσαι καὶ ἀποσπάσματα, οὐ παντὸς δ᾽ αὐτῶν κινήματος ἅτε οἰκείου καὶ συμφυοῦς ὁ θεὸς αἰσθάνεται;"

[68] Michel Dupuy, *Bérulle: une spiritualité de l'adoration* (Tournai, Belgium: Desclée & Co., 1964). Hereafter noted as *BSA*. Dupuy cited the Migne edition even if correcting it with the Bourgoing edition. See 229–30.

[69] Ibid., 230, quoting Bérulle, *Grandeurs*, 6, no. 6, col. 250. See also Pseudo-Dionysius, in Pseudo-Dionysius, Colm Luibhéid, and Paul Rorem, *Pseudo-Dionysius: The Complete Works* (New York: Paulist Press, 1987), chapter 7.

The Influence of Maximus

Moore, writing on Stoic influences apparent in Maximus the Confessor's work, wrote that in his advanced Christological and eschatological works, Maximus held to a Neoplatonic Monothelitism.[70] Moore posited that the Eastern mystical tradition of ascesis and self-denial held to the "complete negation of one's personal, egocentric will, and the absolute reception of the will of Christ, as the prerequisite for *theôsis*, or divinization." A major difference existed between the "the doctrine of the transference of natures (i.e., the Athanasian/Apollinarian formula that 'God became man so that man may become God')," and the thought of Maximus in which "the individual human being, the person, had to relinquish his or her own autonomy, and yield place to an over-powering Will of God."[71] As Thunberg wrote, with Maximus "the soul received God as a substitute for [its] own ego."[72]

This "transference of natures" doctrine moved from "the soteriological sphere of the early Christian *kerygma*" to become "transplanted in, or grafted upon, the pagan Hellenic tradition, resulting in Monophysitism," moving the Incarnation from the cosmological to the personal in terms of its effect on human nature.[73]

The question arises as to whether in Bérulle's kenotic spirituality for both laity and priests, God is given the role of a substitute for the ego. This analysis will explore this question.

The Spirituality of Duns Scot

As already noted, that Gibieuf felt obligated to catalogue the Thomistic influences in Bérulle's *Discours de l'état et des grandeurs de Jésus* hints at the pressure to downplay any association between his sacerdotal spirituality and that of the Subtle Doctor and Scotist Reformers.

According to Balic, the Scotist and Franciscan schools have become synonymous over time, and he noted that one can speak of a spirituality according to Duns Scot. Certain characteristics of his thought have had influence

---

[70]   Edward Moore, "Monophysitism and the Evolution of Theological Discourse in Christian Neoplatonism," in *Metaphysical Patterns in Platonism: Ancient, Medieval, Renaissance, and Modern Times*, ed. John F. Finamore and Robert M. Berchman, International Society for Neoplatonic Studies (New Orleans: University Press of the South, Inc., 2007), 142.

[71]   Ibid., 143.

[72]   Lars Thunberg, *Man and the Cosmos: The Vision of St. Maximus the Confessor* (Crestwood, NY: St. Vladimir's Seminary Press, 1985), 89, quoted in Moore, "Monophysitism and the Evolution of Theological Discourse," 143–44.

[73]   Moore, "Monophysitism and the Evolution of Theological Discourse," 144.

in the realm of spirituality, including the idea that only infinite being has being, his emphasis on love, meditation on Christ to unite with God, and that all grace is received in and by Christ.[74]

Of particular note is an article Hayen wrote, treating the difference between Duns Scot's emphasis on essence and that of Aquinas on existence. Particularly pertinent to this study is the question he raised regarding any difference the teachings of Duns Scot or Aquinas might make in the formation of priests, with such ideals as the justice of God, charity, the evangelical counsels, and the gifts of the Holy Spirit.[75]

An example Hayen gave was that of Duns Scot's answer to the question of whether it was legitimate for a prince to baptize a child against the wishes of the parents. He answered in the affirmative, based on a univocal order of power and authority.[76] This analysis will explore the various ideals related to univocity which Bérulle put forward as an attempt to defend the power and authority of priests.

That said, to parse the applied or misapplied metaphysics of a "Scotist" spirituality would be a complex scholarly project, one much needed to fully understand the era under consideration and Bérulle's influence on the current theology of priesthood, in particular

Despite this critical lacuna, it will not be difficult for the reader to see in Bérulle's spirituality the echoes of these and other applied notions labeled as "Scotist." The question arises as to how to read them in the light of French School scholars' works which, in the main, only offer a trail of inference and vague references to these "Scotist" influences, again reflecting a reticence bespeaking unresolved issues.

At best, this study can highlight where scholars have noted these strains, and attempt to frame them in terms of how Bérulle himself hinted at Scotist ideals in the rhetoric of his spiritual theology of priesthood.

The Influence of Pseudo-Dionysius

Perhaps the greatest influence on Bérulle's spiritual theology of priesthood was that of Pseudo-Dionysius, an influence that will be explored in detail through this study, particularly in light of French School scholars' commentary and analysis. Rorem provides an introductory window into the scope of the influence of this

---

[74] Charles Balic, "Duns Scot," in *DSAM*, vol. 3 (1957), cols. 1801–7 and 1815.

[75] André Hayen, "Deux théologiens: Jean Duns Scot et Thomas d'Aquin," *Revue philosophique de Louvain*, 3rd series, 51, no. 30 (1953), especially 289.

[76] Ibid., 269. See John Duns Scot, *Opera omnia*, vol. 8, ed. Luke Wadding (Lyon: Sumptibus Laurentii Durand, 1639), 275–76, 1.4.4.9, nos. 1 & 2: "In parvulo Deus habet maius ius dominii quam parentes: universaliter enim in potestatibus ordinatis, potestas inferior non obligat in his, quae sunt contra superiorem."

late 5th or early 6th-century Christian philosopher-become-saint, thought for centuries to have been the direct disciple of St. Paul. In the Middle Ages, his local hierarchy of clergy and laity expanded into an authoritarian universal plan, according to Rorem. Neoplatonism's *exitus reditus* became both chronological and eschatological as it evolved into salvation history, and as the three ways became moral purification, intellectual illumination, and unitive perfection. One aspect of this particular interpretation of Neoplatonism was the unitive perfection of priests as crucial in mediating salvation through the building of the kingdom of God, co-equivalent with the Roman Catholic Church, according to Rorem. Pseudo-Dionysius's authority was considered apostolic, although certain humanists and Reformers did have misgivings.[77]

Conclusion

Whereas Luther and Calvin held that reason had been influenced by the Fall, and so philosophy had been compromised,[78] Bérulle, rather, used a plethora of combined philosophical notions in support of his positive spiritual theology of priesthood, drawing deeply from the same traditions which shaped the Reformers.

Bérulle, rejecting Scholastic method, nevertheless used and reinterpreted its nomenclature. Following an era when, as Mahieu held, the metaphysical was replaced with the will of God, psychology, and morality, Bérulle's was an attempt at a reconstructed metaphysic characterized by just these aspects.

We will explore how Bérulle addressed two key questions in constructing a spiritual theology to meet the Reformers' critiques of the priesthood: in what precisely did the relationship between the finite being of the priest and the infinite being of God consist; and the question of the nature of the relationship of the soul of the priest to Christ. In this, he wished to emphasize the ontological bond between the spiritual and the physical, and in so doing, we would suggest, reinterpreted natural philosophy as metaphysics in support of the ideal of the priest's close union with Christ.

Arguably, following a possible Maximian transposition of the Stoic logos, the soul of the priest would come to receive God as a substitute for his own ego, as this study will support. Adding to this transmogrification, however, was a

---

[77] Paul Rorem, *Pseudo-Dionysius: A Commentary on the Texts and an Introduction to Their Influence* (New York: Oxford University Press, 1993), 238–39.

[78] Peter Harrison, "Philosophy and the Crisis of Religion," in *Cambridge Companion to Renaissance Philosophy* (Cambridge: Cambridge University Press, 2007), 239.

covenantal de-ontologization wherein the priest was urged to work at all times to maintain his unicity with Christ, as this analysis will also highlight.

We will review how Bérulle, like Eckhart, rejected proportionality and constructed a spiritual theology of priesthood of imputed being dependent at all times on the will of God.

First, the next chapter explores the rigorism of Bérulle's era and its influences on Bérulle's project in order to understand how a unique moralism entered his spiritual theology and prepared the way for the centuries-long influence of the French School in both Christian and sacerdotal spiritualities.

Chapter 4
Bérulle's Rigorist Spirituality

Introduction

A central question that now presents itself is whether Bérulle's sacerdotal spirituality represents a chain in the link of historical monastic and clerical spiritualities, or whether it was a new development. In order to address this question, this chapter will serve as an opening account of key monastic themes found in Bérulle's spirituality, which will be explored and expanded in proper depth in later chapters.

First, we review currents in monastic and clerical culture, as well as key precedents leading up to Bérulle's era, followed by a focused review of the spirituality of the Oratory in light of monastic ideals.

Lastly, a brief review of the possible shared characteristics of Berullian and Jansenist spiritualities follows, which will give an introductory perspective for understanding Bérulle's spiritual theology of priesthood.

Background

There had been a long history of what has been called episcopal or urban monachism, in which bishops would insert their clerics into community living and celibacy, such as with Victrice de Rouen.[1] St. Augustine also had within his own episcopal residence a monastery of clerics. This form of living was the precursor to both later forms of religious life and the life of canons regular.[2]

Bérulle's houses for priests located in dioceses at the service of bishops followed in some fashion this tradition.

Gregory the Great, whom Bérulle both mentioned and emulated also, sought to reform the priesthood of his day by a return to monastic discipline. He wrote

---

[1] O. Rousseau, "Sacerdoce et monachisme," in *Études sur le sacrement de l'ordre* (Éditions du Cerf, 1957), 215–21.
[2] Ibid., 219–20. See Augustine, *Serm.* 355.

a pastoral manual, *The Book of Pastoral Rule*, required reading for bishops throughout the Middle Ages.[3]

Gregory, notably, fostered a sacerdotal identity and spiritual direction similar to that of the desert ascetic, considered a holy man, whom Brown considered a "locus of power who also exerted social power" in the East of late antiquity as ascetic, outsider, and mediator. Bacchi saw this identity as not merely an Eastern phenomenon, but shared, for example, with Augustine. Gregory adopted this ideal.[4]

These characteristics are also reminiscent of Bérulle's emphasis on spiritual direction for priests, and his fundamental vision of priest mediators requiring a high degree of holiness.

Monastic Reform and Rigor

There have been various attempts at monastic reform over the centuries.

Writing on reform and spirituality in the sixteenth century, de Certeau noted that, already in the early years of the sixteenth century, reform focused on clergy and religious with the idea of defining roles and promoting a greater fidelity and conformity to disciplines. Monastic Reformers emphasized mysticism, economic reform, and rigid moralism variously.[5]

Massaut wrote on the connection between the humanism of the era and its interplay with spirituality, notably monastic spirituality. French humanism at the beginning of the sixteenth century was influenced by Petrarch, Gerson, St. Augustine, and St. Bernard, with the majority of humanists being monks and supportive of monastic and clerical reforms. As Massaut noted, reform and humanism were inseparable ideals in France, with humanists working to restore a pure and primitive institution of monasticism.[6] Renaudet noted that at the

---

3   For a synthesis of the literature on the influences on Gregory's thought, see McGrath-Merkle, "Gregory the Great's Metaphor." See Gregory the Great and George Demacopoulos, *The Book of Pastoral Rule* (Crestwood, NY: St. Vladimir's Seminary Press, 2007).

4   Peter Brown, "The Rise and the Function of the Holy Man," in *Society and the Holy in Late Antiquity* (Berkeley and Los Angeles: University of California Press, 1982), 122–26, quoted in L. F. Bacchi, *The Theology of Ordained Ministry in the Letters of Augustine of Hippo* (San Francisco: International Scholars Publications, 1998), 187. See also 188–95.

5   De Certeau, "La réforme dans le catholicisme," 195–97.

6   Massaut, "Le XVIe siècle," 186–93.

beginning of the sixteenth century, theologians abandoned the study of the mystics, the Bible, and the fathers to humanists.[7]

Important to this study, the semi-Pelagian debate between divine grace and human agency was taken up again at the time of the Reformation. Weaver, studying the roots of the controversy, noted the Semi-Pelagian heritage as having been derived from the Origenist tradition of the desert fathers, with the controversy erupting in the monastic community at Hadrumetum (now Sousse, Tunisia) about the year 426 C.E. in response to Augustine's insistence on salvation as a gift. Their ideal of the monastic life rested, on the contrary, on the idea that by one's own agency (with grace) one can and should shape one's life through monastic discipline specifically to attain God.[8]

The question arises as to whether the Oratorian program of priestly formation represented an effort to attain God through human agency, in line with the monastic culture of the 16th century and unanchored by systematic theological reflection?

Introduction to Bérulle's Project

As noted, Bérulle desired to form a special society of priests who lived in community under the authority of their local bishop. Following the Catholic Reformers Clichtove, Neri, and Ignatius of Loyola, he wished to take key aspects of monastic spirituality and apply them to Oratorian society and formation.

This absorption by Bérulle of monastic ideals is a major and understudied aspect of his spiritual theology of priesthood.

The Oratory and Monastic Ideals

Taveau, in his work written for men in formation, detailed the aspects of asceticism that comprised the Oratorians' program, calling Bérulle's an *haute ascèse*, focused on a renouncement of self to the point of slavery.[9]

Dupuy noted that in answer to Calvin's critique that religious orders were like the Corinthians who were divided as to which religious leaders they followed,

---

[7] Ibid., 193. See A. Renaudet, *Préréforme et humanisme, à Paris pendant les premières guerres d'Italie, 1494–1517* (Paris: E. Champion, 1916), 596–97, referenced in Massaut, "Le XVIe siècle," 193.

[8] Rebecca Harden Weaver, *Divine Grace and Human Agency: A Study of the Semi-Pelagian Controversy*, North American Patristic Society, Patristic Monograph Series 15 (Macon, GA: Mercer University Press, 1996), ix and 1.

[9] Claude Taveau, *Le cardinal de Bérulle: maître de la vie spirituelle* (Paris: Desclée de Brouwer, 1933), 235–312. Taveau cited the Migne edition, corrected by the Bourgoing edition.

Bérulle responded with the claim that the priesthood was the work of Christ. For Bérulle, the priest was consecrated to honor the being of Christ, whereas religious orders honored only some aspect of his virtues or mysteries. Bérulle:

> Je vous requiers, (ô Jésus) qu'en cette piété, devotion et servitude spéciale au mystère de votre Incarnation soit...notre esprit et notre différence particulière d'entre les autres sociétés saintes et honorables qui sont en votre Eglise; lesquelles semblent avoir voulu saintement partager la robe que vous avez laissée montant en croix, en partageant entre elles la variété de vos vertus et perfections par lesquelles elles vous servent en la terre, les unes ayant choisi la pénitence, les autres la solitude, d'autres l'obéissance, pour marque, pour objet et pour exercice de leur institution.[10]

Bérulle wished to establish a congregation that was neither secular nor religious but rather a kind of intermediary.[11] He insisted on elements of the religious life such as poverty, chastity, and community life, along with the praying of the office and a rigorous daily schedule of private devotions, but he rejected a rule, constitutions, or solemn vows.[12] He worried any formalization would make the congregation into simply an ecclesiastical state. He insisted the congregation had Jesus Christ as founder: "En cette petite congrégation, nous désirons n'avoir et reconnaître que Jésus pour fondateur; car il est l'auteur de la prêtrise et le chef des prêtres."[13]

Theirs was to be a society made by the divine persons with no other tie than that of charity, or the Holy Spirit: "Il est à propos qu'en l'honneur de la première société du monde, source de toute autre société, c'est-à-dire en l'honneur de la Très Sainte Trinité, reconnue seule et adorée en la seule Eglise chrétienne, il y ait une société qui n'ait autre lien que celui de la charité, c'est-à-dire du Saint-Esprit, qui est le lien même et l'unité de la Très Sainte Trinité..."[14]

Dedicating their lives to the will of their bishops, Oratorians were called to take on a large variety of tasks even while living communally in their own houses. While their stated purpose was to reform the clergy, not replace them, they found themselves called to serve in parishes and missions and to oversee colleges, even

---

[10]   *Grandeurs,* 1623 ed., 8, 13, quoted in *BLS*, 182–83.

[11]   Ibid., 236n28, quoting Bérulle, *CB 90*: "intérmediaire (media) entre les séculiers et les religieux." Also quoted in *BLS*, 236n28.

[12]   Ibid., 236–39.

[13]   Bérulle, Lettre 165, *OC*, Bourgoing ed., quoted in *BLS*, 238.

[14]   Bérulle, BLS, *OR* 15, no. 1, 289. The abbreviation "*OR*" references texts related to the Oratory as first published in *BLS*. The first number following refers to the number assigned to the piece, the second refers to the numbered paragraph.

two seminaries. Their daily lives were not well known, but it is known that communal and private prayers were frequent, the office taking first place, being that their principle function was praise and intercession.[15]

Bérulle believed that leading a life in community was almost essential to the pursuit of perfection. They were to lead a life of contemplation, followed by action, as victims consecrated to God through work ("être des victimes consacrées à Dieu par le travail").[16]

They must be separated from the world, having no contact with the laity except in ministry, so that the laity might never see them as anything but priests.[17] Bérulle urged them to love without measure, holding all that the world embraces in horror, working for God in all things: "Qu'ils prennent bien garde que, du fait qu'ils sont séparés du monde et liés à cette congrégation, ils sont engagés totalement et non partiellement; qu'ils aient en horreur tout ce que le monde aime et embrasse…"[18]

Their lives were to reflect modesty and simplicity. They were to practice detachment, abnegation, and self-perfection, guarding their senses.[19]

Bérulle's Conferences

Bérulle treated these concepts in detail in his oral conferences which provide a window into the monastic ideals he held, and which are worthy of further analysis.

Bérulle presented the main object of his Oratorians as that of knowing Christ through a constant occupation, and of attaching themselves to him. Their two duties toward Christ were homage and imitation, with their prayer consisting of meditation on the divine attributes of Christ, characterized by a simple, affectionate interior discourse with him. Their meditation on the mysteries of Christ's life was to include examining his interior actions such that their souls should become tightly united to his. Notably, imitation of Christ was to include imitation of Christ in his vision of God, never allowing their occupations to interrupt their regard of him interiorly. They were to always remain in the presence of God and remember his Passion, although the practice of recollection might vary according to whether one was a beginner or more advanced.[20]

[15]   *BLS*, 203–11.
[16]   Ibid., 216, quoting Relation du Perrin, Archives nationales, M 233.
[17]   Ibid., 217.
[18]   Ibid., Bérulle, *OR* 32, no. 1, 345.
[19]   See *BLS*, *OR* 31, 341–43.
[20]   Bérulle, *OC*, vol. 1, *Conférences et fragments* (1995), Conferences from 1611 and 1612. See especially pp. 2–19 and 76–77. References to this text are to the French-language version.

Bérulle outlined how his Oratorians might obtain a recollection without interruption, which was through faith and frequent acts of love. Dupuy referenced the idea that for Bérulle, recollection could pass beyond both nature and the supernatural to arrive at a third category, that of *la vie éminente*, as this study will explore. As Bérulle held: "…il n'y a aucun de nos devoirs qui puisse nous séparer de cette vie intérieure avec Jésus-Christ…Pour que le présence de Dieu se maintienne fermement, non pas à la façon d'un état mais à la manière d'une disposition…"[21]

He urged that Oratorians remain at all times regarding Christ, as Christ himself remained in his own vision of God at all times. For example, each time they entered or left a room they were to attempt to maintain a meditative focus. Bérulle:

> …chacun s'appliquera à ne jamais entrer dans sa chambre ou dans celle d'un autre ou bien à sortir sans avoir salué l'image de Jésus-Christ, de la bienheureuse Vierge Marie ou d'un autre Saint et, en imitant ainsi Jésus-Christ qui était à la foi sur le chemin et en possession de la vision de Dieu, à mener ses occupations extérieures de telle sorte qu'aucune ne nous empêche de le regarder, lui, intérieurement.[22]

Bérulle seemed to be attempting to bring the Oratorians into a new way of being. He noted three ways of possessing the Holy Spirit: that of possessing but not acting; producing acts of charity but not under the impulse of the Holy Spirit; and acting at all times under the inspiration of the Holy Spirit.

He urged his Oratorians to act in this third manner, as instruments of Jesus Christ as the one who acts. In this, God not only possesses one's soul, according to Bérulle, but also one's faculty to act. By uniting themselves thus to God and all his operations, they would achieve the ultimate disposition, a Scholastic ideal referencing the gift of form. Bérulle:

> …ceux qui suivent l'impulsion de l'Esprit saint ont donné à Dieu a la fois leur volonté et leur liberté pour agir exactement quand il faut, à un tel degré qu'ils ne sont que comme l'instrument de Dieu agissant en eux et par eux. Et ce n'est pas un instrument inerte, comme le serait un mort,

---

This edition prefers to present a non-numeric order, under section title headings. This is a primary text with commentaries.

[21] Ibid., 67–70, Bérulle, *Recueillement, Actes d'amour*, and *Présence de Dieu*. See also introduction, xxi. Quotes taken from 67 and 70.

[22] Ibid., 12–13, Bérulle, *Règles*, January 1612.

mais un instrument vivant…Soyons donc attentifs à ne rechercher que Dieu et ses operations saintes et à nous unir à lui, car l'union est la disposition ultime. [23]

Of note, Dupuy pointed to Bérulle's ideal that God honors dispositions of the soul more than actions, and noted whether a theologian would ask if this were not a Pelagian notion in that, for Bérulle, dispositions were in the realm of human acts. Bérulle held: "Car Dieu estime plus et récompense plus les dispositions de l'âme que les actions extérieures, et ce qui apporte le plus d'honneur à Dieu, ce sont les dispositions de l'âme, et non les actions."[24]

The Oratorians were to acquire this interior life by always elevating themselves to God during exterior actions and by walking always with Christ. Dupuy noted that Bérulle justified this voluntarism in saying that on earth we should do more acts of will than intelligence. Bérulle:

Un point est à noter: c'est que nous devons accomplir un nombre beaucoup plus grand d'actes de la volonté que de l'intelligence. Dans l'état de gloire, les actes de l'intelligence et ceux de la volonté seront jusqu'à un certain point à égalité, car l'opération de l'intelligence sera aussi importante que celle de la volonté. Au contraire, en ce monde, puisque les réalités divines nous sont proposées "d'une manière un peu obscure et dans un miroir," c'est la preuve que c'est moins à l'intelligence de s'en occuper qu'à la volonté, à qui elles sont proposées pour qu'elle les aime de tout son cœur et de toutes ses forces.[25]

If Oratorians followed their program of always turning to God, he would give not only graces, but also his own *essence*. Bérulle told them: "c'est que Dieu, lui, ne donne pas seulement sa grâce et toutes sortes de biens extérieurs à lui, mais lui-même, sa proper essence."[26]

Dupuy clarified, arguably, that Bérulle's voluntarism was one of attachment to the will of God rather than his essence, as Bérulle insisted was the purview of the saints in heaven: "Aux saints du ciel il est donné de s'attacher à l'essence

---

[23] Ibid., 90–92, Bérulle, *L'Avent du Seigneur*, December 2, 1612. Quotes taken from 91 and 92. See 92n3 where Dupuy noted that the expression "disposition ultime" was a Scholastic expression denoting the gift of form.

[24] Ibid., 107n1. See Bérulle, *L'attention au chœur*, January 1613. Quote taken from 107.

[25] Ibid., 130–31, Bérulle, *Présence de Dieu*, July–August 1613. See 131n1 for Dupuy's comment.

[26] Ibid., 132, Bérulle, *Union de l'âme avec Dieu*, July–August 1613.

divine; au contraire, sur la terre c'est à la seule volonté de Dieu qu'il nous est permis de nous attacher."[27]

To pray for this glory, Bérulle urged, notably, a frequent meditation on the Resurrection, especially the power given to priests by Christ after the Resurrection.

> La meilleure disposition pour honorer la Résurrection est de penser que par elle il nous à acquis telle ou telle grâce particulière sans que nous ayons contribué pour notre part à la gloire de sa Résurrection, tandis que nous avons contribué beaucoup à l'ignominie de sa Passion…
>
> Le pouvoir accordé par Jésus-Christ après sa Résurrection nous conduit au zèle à l'égard des âmes, puisqu'il n'a pas voulu exercer par lui-même son pouvoir sur les âmes, mais par nous ses indignes ministres…[28]

The following key passage reveals a decided rigorism in Bérulle's formation, seemingly to point to a kind of theandrism. Oratorians were not to act according to their natural emotions but by the influence of grace. As all of Christ's actions proceeded from his divinity, so all their actions should emanate from the grace and Spirit of Jesus Christ. Bérulle:

> C'est pourquoi nous ne devons nous servir de nos yeux, par example, ou des autres parties de notre corps, que de la manière dont Jésus-Christ lui-même s'en servirait. Le second moyen est de ne pas nous déterminer selon une émotion de la nature, mais selon l'impulsion de la grâce. Comme en Jésus-Christ toutes les actions provenaient de sa divinité—ce qui leur permettait d'être divinement humaines et humainement divines—, de même, en nous, toutes nos actions doivent émaner de la grâce de l'Esprit de Jésus-Christ, moyennant quoi elles lui seront agréable.[29]

It is important to note that "the Spirit of Jesus" was a common phrase in Bérulle's era, referring to the third person of the Trinity operating in and by the humanity of the Word, as André Rayez wrote.[30] Bérulle's work included the use of the word "Spirit" and "spirit" without distinction. In fact, the liberal use of capital letters

---

[27] Ibid., 229, Bérulle, *Pour Dieu quitter des biens terrestres et quitter des biens spirituels*, July 1614. See 229n1.

[28] Ibid., 204, Bérulle, *Honorer spécialement un mystère*, March 1614.

[29] Ibid., 86, *La modestie*, November 1612.

[30] André Rayez, "Dons du Saint-Esprit: III. Période Moderne: Les Spirituels," in *DSAM*, vol. 3 (1957), cols. 1604–10.

in the 17th century makes it difficult to discern the difference between the spirit of Jesus and the Spirit of Jesus considered as the Holy Spirit in Bérulle's work. Dupuy was careful to explain that Bérulle did not separate the Spirit from He who sends, the Christ.[31] That said, an underlying question presents itself as to whether Bérulle held that Oratorians possessed the Holy Spirit in person, as we will further explore.

Continuing with our analysis, while Bérulle insisted that he focused on the will rather than the intellect, he did claim that we can know the divine perfections, albeit obscurely. Each day, he urged his Oratorians to take a moment of reverence for one of the perfections, such as the holiness or goodness of God. Because God exists in his perfections, which can be communicated, Oratorians could participate in them "d'une certaine façon."[32]

For those just entering the congregation, Bérulle urged that they disdain all creatures, love nothing outside of God, and desire nothing else but to become holy.[33] As Dupuy remarked, however, in order to avoid a Pelagian interpretation, Bérulle insisted that one cannot procure holiness but only dispose oneself through self-emptying.[34]

That said, it would be the prominence of the necessity to constantly dispose oneself which was at the heart of Bérulle's rigorism.

To the question of whether Bérulle's spirituality represented merely a high monastic ascesis in vogue in the sixteenth century or rather the more exaggerated spirituality of the Jansenist movement about to spread throughout France and beyond, a review of the similarities between Oratorian and Jansenist spiritualities gives light.

Similarities between Oratorian and Later Jansenist Spiritualities

According to Williams, the key characteristics of the Oratory were an abstract spirituality, soul searching, a valuation of mystical phenomena, and longing for union and perfection, as well as a concern for moral reform coupled with a Baroque near-masochistic severity.[35]

Jansen and Saint-Cyran, already mentioned as key collaborators of Bérulle, worked together to promote an Augustinian penitential theology (c. 1625),

---

[31]   *BLS*, 120. See also discussion on 173–74, especially footnote 59.
[32]   Bérulle, *OC*, vol. 1, *Conférences et fragments* (1995), 281, *Perfections divins…*, November 1614.
[33]   Ibid., 31, *À celui qui entre dans le Congrégation*, May 1612.
[34]   Ibid., 99–100, *Humilité d'esprit*, January 1613. See 100n2.
[35]   Williams, *The French Oratorians and Absolutism*, 91.

according to Sedgwick, some fourteen years after the founding of the Oratory, and they hoped that Bérulle's Oratory would be the means by which the theology would displace the laxism of the Jesuits.[36]

Krumenacker wrote of the shared characteristics between Jansenists and Oratorians, including a very strict moral rigorism; an Augustinian theology of grace; a pessimistic anthropology highlighting the misery of the human creature; and a high value assigned to contrition.[37] He cited some of the factors that played a role in the nearness of the two groups, including personal rapport and links of fidelity; the will to defend Augustine; opposition to Jesuits; a penchant for an austere religion; interiorized piety; an independent spirit in regards to authority; and an ecclesiology that elevated bishops and priests but also insisted on the participation of the laity.[38]

The consequences of the closeness between the Jansenists and Oratorians transformed the Oratory, according to Krumenacker, after the time of Bérulle. The Oratory lost many seminarians because of the suspicion of Jansenism, and had to close seminaries and houses of study.[39]

Conclusion

Of particular note in this review are the monastic currents of the era leading up to Bérulle's, which included an increased rigor and a scholarly separation from systematic theological reflection, as well as a series of Catholic reformist efforts at creating priestly societies with tenets borrowed from monastic spirituality. Bérulle's efforts seem to be in line with his times.

Also noteworthy, however, are the similarities between Berullian and later Jansenist spirituality and the use by Jansen and Saint-Cyran of the Oratorian movement to spread their ideals.

Thayer is a defender of the positive aspects of the spirituality of the French School, disagreeing that its neantism was pessimistic.[40] He asserted that critics confuse the psychological with the ontological in the Neoplatonic concepts found in its spirituality. Thayer rightly emphasized, as have many authors in the

---

[36] Sedgwick, *Jansenism in Seventeenth-Century France*, 49.
[37] Krumenacker, *L'école française de spiritualité*, 472.
[38] Ibid., 480.
[39] Ibid., 481.
[40] David D. Thayer, "All or Nothing," unpublished manuscript. Prof. Thayer has served as editor of the *Bulletin de Saint-Sulpice* and is a Sulpician formator.

Sulpician tradition, the positive aspects of its spirituality, including its missionary impulse arising from its foundations in mysticism, its emphasis on sacrificial love, service, and humility, and its emphasis on the Eucharist as the center of sacerdotal spirituality.[41]

While the later practices of sacerdotal spirituality may have differed due to an evolution in the ideals and their applications within the sacerdotal spirituality of the French School, as, for example, under the leadership of Jean Jacques Olier, who was considered the leading enemy of Jansenism,[42] the scope of this study does not permit a judgment in that regard, except insofar as scholars have noted surviving Berullian themes.

While not discounting the positive aspects of the very complex spirituality of the French School or of its founder, this review has highlighted key rigorist elements in Bérulle's project which we will explore in this analysis.

At first inspection, it appears that Bérulle borrowed concepts present in ancient monasticism, as we will also explore, and applied them to the spirituality of the Oratory. Further analysis will reveal whether and how this spirituality represented a new negative ethicist strain in sacerdotal spirituality, also influencing the spiritual theology of priesthood.

With this as background, here follows an examination of the Christological controversies of the era under consideration.

---

[41] See David D. Thayer, "Living the Life of a Prophet," unpublished manuscript.
[42] See Bérulle and Thompson, *Bérulle and the French School*, 79. See Bremond, *TM*, 277–87.

Chapter 5
Christological Controversies and Divine Union

Introduction

To understand the Christology of Christ as sole priest according to the Reformers, is to begin to understand the basis of their arguments regarding the relationship between grace and nature, justification and sanctification, Calvary and the Eucharist, the individual believer and Christ and the Church. The central questions under consideration in these debates were how Christ saves as high priest, and how we are united to him.

As importantly, to understand the underlying spiritualities and spiritual theologies of the Reformers is to begin to understand the applied and underappreciated metaphysics they proposed, as well as the deepest convictions fueling their reformist zeal and theological constructs.

We would argue that a lacuna in broad awareness across confessions of the ideas lying beneath the surface of the theological debates of the era has resulted in an under-interpretation of the complex Christological arguments which lay at the heart of the Reform and which, as this study will indicate, reshaped the spiritual theology of the Roman Catholic priesthood.

This chapter presents opening accounts of Reformist Christologies and spiritualities circulating at the time of the Reformation, which Luther and Calvin represented in some fashion through their prominent positions. Provided by scholars, some working without attribution, these accounts include Protestant or convert perspectives, not necessarily flowing in the mainstream of philosophical or theological opinion. These voices are needed to paint a picture of key Christological themes in light of Reformist spiritualities, a decidedly controversial perspective, as we will detail.

Also treated are related ideals during the time of Trent, as well as Bérulle's era, that also form the backdrop for the development of Bérulle's Christology. Introductory critiques of Bérulle's Christocentrism are included to frame the discussion before the conclusion of the chapter, in which we stand in a literary future, pointing to possible Reformist echoes in Bérulle's rhetoric and project, which will be either substantiated or rejected in future chapters.

Background

The Christ of Luther, Calvin, and Trent

Christological arguments were the foundation of Luther's attack against indulgences, the hierarchy, the priesthood, and the Mass. These arguments, in turn, rested on Luther's well-developed Christology of Christ as High Priest.

Zur Mühlen wrote that Luther had condemned the sale of indulgences by proclaiming that sins are not forgiven by the power of indulgences but, rather, by Christ, in his Person and through his office as sole head of the Church. He alone suffered for our salvation. Luther also emphasized the two natures as distinct yet with one person: through the hypostatic union Christ partakes in the attributes of the divine nature as servant. This, as Zur Mühlen noted, was the issue of the relationship of the unity of Christ's divinity and humanity come to the fore once again in the Reformation.

Luther's was an Incarnation-oriented Christology, following a nominalist-Ockhamist tradition in rejecting mystical devotion in favor of the incarnate Christ. By the communication of attributes, derived from the hypostatic union, one could know God hidden in the humanity of Christ through the word of God.[1] As noted, Luther asserted the priesthood of all believers, rejecting sacramental character.

According to Jones, the Council of Trent responded, addressing Christ's priesthood in terms of redemption, justification, ordination and hierarchy, liturgy, and sacrifice, and so the priesthood was seen mainly in terms of jurisdiction and hierarchy. The council fathers neglected to address key aspects related to the complaints of Reformers regarding needed reforms, such as preaching, the scriptures, and the priesthood of all believers.[2]

As Jones summarized, Calvin held to the limitation of the sacrifice of propitiation to Jesus alone, with only the sacrifice of praise and honor available to all.[3] Calvin invited all believers into the *société de Christ*.[4]

---

[1] Karl-Heinz Zur Mühlen, "Christology," in *Oxford Encyclopedia of the Reformation*, vol. 1 (New York and Oxford: Oxford University Press, 1996), 314–22.

[2] Jones, "Toward a Christology of Christ the High Priest," 219.

[3] Ibid., 196–207. See *Institution*: 2.15.6: "Car combien que nous soyons pollus en nous, estans faits Sacrificateurs en luy (Apocal. I, 6), nous avons liberté de nous offrir à Dieu avec tout ce qu'il nous a donné…"

[4] Ibid., 198. See *Institution*, 4.1.3.

Luther's and Calvin's Spiritualities in Light of the Christological Debates

Both Luther and Calvin rejected the idea of mystical union. Luther held to the idea of union as established by baptism, and Calvin to union by faith.[5] Calvin, particularly, focused on piety, as the title of his chief work indicated: *The Institutes of the Christian Religion, Containing Almost the Whole Sum of Piety and Whatever It Is Necessary to Know in the Doctrine of Salvation: A Work Well Worth Reading by All Persons Zealous for Piety, and Lately Published: A Preface to the Most Christian King in Which This Books is Presented to Him as a Confession of Faith.*[6]

First, we review Luther's notions surrounding union with Christ.

Luther and Theosis

While Luther rejected Pseudo-Dionysian mysticism with its ideal that the Christian could meet God in the apex of the soul,[7] and the word *theosis* did not appear in his works, the words *deificatio* and *Vergottlichung* did occur frequently. Also, while scholars of Luther recognize the idea of Christ dwelling in us, they have not framed the discussion in terms of participation, ignoring, downplaying, or even denying deification, according to Lehninger.[8]

That said, the speculative mysticism of Meister Eckhart was an important inspiration for Luther. The *Theologia Deutsch*, a work that highly influenced Luther, incorporated Eckhart's thought.[9] Luther edited the work, writing in its

---

[5]   Bernard McGinn, "Mysticism," in *Oxford Encyclopedia of the Reformation*, vol. 3 (New York and Oxford: Oxford University Press, 1996), 122.

[6]   See Jones, "Toward a Christology of Christ the High Priest," 190. See also the first edition of John Calvin's work, *Christianae religionis institutio, totam fere pietatis summam, & quicquid est in doctrina salutis cognitu necessarium: complectens: omnibus pietatis studiosis lectu dignissimum opus, ac recens editum: Praefatio ad Christianissimum regem Franciae, qua hic ei liber pro confessione fidei offertur* (Basel: Thomam Platterum & Balthasarem Lasium, 1536).

[7]   D. H. Tripp, "The Modern World: The Protestant Reformation," in *The Study of Spirituality,* ed. Cheslyn Jones, Geoffrey Wainwright, and Edward Yarnold (New York: Oxford University Press, 1986), 344.

[8]   Paul Lehninger, "Luther and Theosis: Deification in the Theology of Martin Luther" (PhD diss., Milwaukee, WI: Marquette University, 1999), 1.

[9]   Ibid., 86. See Kenneth Scott Latourette, *A History of Christianity,* vol. 1 (New York: Harper & Row, 1975), 540–42.

preface: "…no book except the Bible and St. Augustine has come to my attention from which I have learned more about God, Christ, man, and all things."[10]

For Eckhart, the believer is the eternal son of God:[11]

God begets his Son or the Word in the soul and, receiving it, the soul passes it on, in many forms, through its agents, now as desire, now in good intentions…These are all his and not yours at all…The deed is his; the word is his; his birth is his; and all you are his, for you have surrendered self to him, with all your soul's agents and their functions and *even your personal nature*.[12]

According to Lehninger, Eckhart's were not figures of speech but rather a definition of participation in which "we lose our identity, and God becomes multi-hypostatic."[13]

However, Luther was careful to say that union with God is not substantial. He wrote that since the Lord is spirit, we are one in spirit with him, "not substantially."[14] He disagreed with the idea that grace and sin are accidental

---

[10]   Luther, *WA* 1: 378.21–23: "Und das ich nach meynem alten narren rüme, ist myr nehst der Biblien und S. Augustino nit vorkummen eyn buch, dar auß ich mehr erlernet hab und will, was got, Christus, mensch und alle ding seyn." *LW* 31.74 [sic] 75, quoted in Lehninger, "Luther and Theosis," 95.

[11]   Lehninger, "Luther and Theosis," 87–89. See Andrew Weeks, *German Mysticism* (Albany, NY: State University of New York, 1993), 81.

[12]   Meister Eckhart, "Sermon on the Eternal Birth," in *Late Medieval Mysticism*, Library of Christian Classics, vol. 13, ed. Ray C. Petry (Philadelphia: Westminster, 1957), 182–83, quoted in Lehninger, "Luther and Theosis," 89. Lehninger italicized the final phrase. German edition: Meister Eckhart and Franz Pfeiffer, *Meister Eckhart* (Göttingen: Vandenhoeck & Ruprecht, 1906), Sermon 3, 21.40–22.13: "Got der gebirt in der sêle sîne geburt unde sîn wort unde diu sêle enpfâhet ez unde biutet ez fürbaz bî den kreften in maniger wîse, nû in einer begerunge, nû in guoter meinunge…ez ist allez sîn und niht dîn bî niute…Diz werc ist sîn, diz wort ist sîn, disiu geburt ist sîn und allez daz daz dû bist alzemâle. Wan dû hâst dich gelâzen unde bist ûz gegangen dînen kreften und iren werken unde dîns wesennes eigenschaft." Translated by R. B. Blakney, *Meister Eckhart: A Modern Translation* (New York and London, 1941), 109–17.

[13]   Lehninger, "Luther and Theosis," 91.

[14]   Ibid., 118, quoting Luther, *WA* 1: 28.39–29.2: "Ita nec nos qui sumus caro sic efficimur verbum, quod in verbum substantialiter mutemur, sed quod assumimus et per fidem ipsum nobis unimus, qua unione non tantum habere verbum sed etiam esse dicimur. Sic enim Apostolus ait: Dominus Spiritus est, et qui adhaeret domino unus spiritus est. Et Ioh. 3. Sic est omnis qui ex spiritu natus est, item: quod ex spiritu natum est., spiritus est."

forms adhering to the soul. Rather, he held that God strips the *esse* of our intellect of all form and prepares it to receive a new form, which is the Word.[15]

Luther's Union with the Word

Luther rejected the legalism of the Church of his day, which inspired fear of hell and scrupulosity, as well as a bondage to indulgences and penances. He systematically constructed a spirituality and applied metaphysic based on a theology of union with the Word outside of institutional constraints.

Bouyer's highly detailed treatment of the spiritualities of the Protestant Reformers and their sources is an important window into Luther's spiritual landscape.

Bouyer wrote that his attempt at this exploration was a difficult task because Barthian, Bultmannian, and neo-Lutheran schools "…united in their insistence that where true Protestantism is concerned, mysticism is the most unacceptable reality of all…the element in Catholicism that justified Protestant opposition more than any other."[16]

The central problem Luther confronted regarding the manner in which we are saved was both personal and spiritual, according to Bouyer. Luther rejected a legalistic concept of holiness as something achieved through ascetical practice. Two foundational intuitions became the bases of his reform: the word of God as God's personal intervention in one's life; and faith in that word as the most important act. Exteriorly, this signaled a reform of Church life to re-center on the word, but interiorly, it meant faith became a deeply personal experience between God and the believer.[17]

Bouyer attempted the task of locating the negative element in Luther's great spiritual movement. Nominalist philosophy (associated with late Augustinian theology) played a role, as already noted, as well as tendencies in the intellectual and spiritual environments of the Middle Ages that had spread, including the loss of the idea of divine transcendence as defined by the fathers over and against ancient ideals.

---

[15]   Ibid., 131, quoting Luther, *WA* 56: 218.20–219.2: "Non impletur nisi quod vacuum est, Non construitur nisi quod inconstructum est. Et Vt philosophi dicunt: Non inducitur forma, nisi ubi est priuatio forme precedentisque expulsio, Et: intellectus possibilis non recipit formam, nisi in principio sui esse sit nudatus ab omni forma et sicut tabula rasa."

[16]   Louis Bouyer, *Orthodox Spirituality and Protestant and Anglican Spirituality*, trans. Barbara Wall (London: Burns & Oates, 1969), 57. This explication follows Bouyer's thought closely.

[17]   Ibid., 63–64.

Bouyer theorized that in these movements either God became our highest experience of ourselves, as in the spirituality of the Low Countries, or God became totally transcendent, with the need to self-annihilate to enter into relationship with him. With the collapse of what he termed theistic metaphysics, the "two corruptions—monism and the most radical dualism" became the "two poles of a world where the infinite has once more become that *apeiron* or simple negation of the human order that existed in pre-Christian Greek thought."[18]

This collapse was both the cause and the effect of nominalism, according to Bouyer, which he credited with the reduction of being to act and the loss of the notion of distinct and stable substances. Both were the products of the mind being absorbed in itself and of human sensibility taking itself as the chief end. In the realm of spirituality, he felt this produced both Pelagianism and Luther's rejection of it.[19]

For Bouyer, at the heart of the misunderstanding between the concept of nature as true creation bound to God versus nature as foreign and opaque to God was the notion of sanctifying grace inhering in the soul. Luther rejected sanctifying grace because for him it excluded or downplayed actual grace. Bouyer noted that Aquinas had the insight that sanctifying grace had no meaning or purpose without actual grace to which we became disposed and dependent under its effect, and that later successors to Aquinas lost this same insight.[20]

Notwithstanding Protestant theologians' objections to the contrary, Bouyer held that Luther relied heavily on the mysticism of essence as found in the Pseudo-Dionysian tradition as expressed in the mysticism of the Low Countries, particularly Tauler and the *Theologia Deutsch*. He also depended on the mystical marriage doctrine of St. Bernard's commentary on the *Song of Songs*. Luther valued the hidden God of Pseudo-Dionysian mysticism and combined it with the Christic mysticism of Bernard, characterized by its emphasis on the cross, while, however, rejecting Bernard's ideal of a glory also possible on earth through an ecstatic union with God.[21]

Bouyer noted that the spirituality that Luther sought to inculcate in the faithful was promoted by the two catechisms that he wrote, which promoted

---

[18] Ibid., 64–65.

[19] Ibid., 65–66.

[20] Ibid., 68.

[21] Ibid., 69. Bouyer credits the discussion on medieval mystics and Luther to the following sources: H. Jaeger (without attribution); Rufus Jones, *Some Exponents of Mystical Religion* (London, 1930), 114ff.; O. Scheel, "Taulers Mystik und Luthers reformatorische Entdeckung," in *Festgabe D. J. Kaftan* (Tübingen, 1920), 298–318; H. Strohl, *Luther jusqu'en 1520*, new ed. (Paris: Presses universitaires de France, 1962), 193ff *et seq.*; and W. von Lowenich, *Luthers Theologia Crucis*, 2nd ed. (Munich, 1954).

study of the Bible, key to Protestant spirituality. Notably, Bouyer wrote that Luther's "reduction of the Canon of the Mass to the words of consecration, the Preface and Sanctus" merely brought to the fore another tendency in medieval piety "where the Presence overshadows the sacrifice, and the Communion itself is seen only from the angle of the individual reception of the presence."[22]

For Luther, the distinction between faith and works became that between the source and effects of the Christian life, or, in other words, the interior life of the Christian's soul in contact with Christ, and the external life of the Christian. As Bouyer wrote, for Luther, "the inner man is king and priest through his direct bond with Christ" and his life of love and service flows from that. The life of every Christian is priestly. This distinction between the inner and outer man Bouyer credited to a negative medieval Augustinianism influenced by Neoplatonism. Bouyer saw two dangers in this scenario: the devaluation of the ministerial priesthood and the conflation of the Church with society and civil authority, the latter being a trend since the fourteenth century.[23]

Calvin and Calvinist Spiritualities

Turning to Calvin and Calvinism, Bouyer noted that Calvin's notion of a return to the ideal of the primitive and purified Church was his innovation. Still bound by an "inadequate notion of divine transcendence, inherited from nominalism," Calvin's most important contribution to Lutheranism and to Reformed piety, according to Bouyer, was his doctrine of sanctification and the way in which he connected it to justification.[24]

With Calvin's doctrine of double predestination (with both condemnation and salvation willed by God), salvation through external means became possible, as with a Christian society. This particular rejection of substantial sanctification, according to Bouyer, led to detailed external rules and a system of punishment. A paradox resulted—the separation of grace and works but the need, all the same, to sanctify the actions of the justified.[25]

Calvin's most important contribution to Christian spirituality, according to Bouyer, was the idea that God's glorification was the end of Christianity. Calvin restored the theocentrism lost by Luther's emphasis on saving grace in personal justification based on an anthropomorphic medieval piety. For Calvin, humanity is saved to give God glory through obedience to the divine will and by

---

[22] Ibid., 73.
[23] Ibid., 75–76.
[24] Ibid., 84–85.
[25] Ibid., 88–89.

conforming all one's thoughts to God's will alone. Bouyer noted here, again, a problem with this spirituality—that God's transcendence depends on man's nothingness.[26]

Sheldrake wrote that the adoration of God's glory and union with Christ are at the heart of Calvinist spirituality. Calvin addressed mystical union as "'that joining together of Head and members, that indwelling of Christ in our hearts—in short, that mystical union' by which 'we put on Christ and are engrafted into his body.'"[27] Sanctification took first place with Calvin, compared to justification with Luther. Both fear and piety were equally found in Calvin, according to Sheldrake, leading to a need for assurance of salvation. Both the scriptures and the Eucharist were central for Calvin in incorporating us into Christ's body, the process being a gradual one. In terms of the Eucharist, Calvin did write of a "true and substantial partaking of the body and blood of the Lord."[28] Instead of a stress on private devotion or individual spiritual perfection, however, Calvinist piety placed a focus on Christ and neighbor, calling on laity and clergy to place every part of their lives in service, including the reform of society.[29]

Importantly, as Canlis described, Calvin reworked the ideal of the ascent of the soul, central to mystical theology, to become the core of the Reformers' ideals pertaining to both theology and piety.[30] For Calvin, the author noted, ascending was neither "a matter of the soul's latent powers nor of conscientious Christian endeavor but of communion: it is participation in Christ's own response to the Father…"[31]

Next we turn to Calvin's spirituality of union with Christ as explored by various authors.

---

[26]   Ibid., 93.

[27]   *Institutes*, (1960), 3.12 [sic], 11.10, quoted in Philip Sheldrake, *New Westminster Dictionary of Christian Spirituality*, 1ˢᵗ American edition (Louisville, KY: Westminster Knox Press, 2005), 162. *Institution*: "Parquoy l'eslève en degré souverain la conionction que nous avons avec nostre chef, la demeure qu'il fait en noz cœurs par foy, l'union sacrée par laquelle nous iouissons de luy, à ce qu'estant ainsi nostre il nous départisse les biens ausquels il abonde en perfection."

[28]   *Institutes*, 4.17.19, quoted in Sheldrake, *New Westminster Dictionary of Christian Spirituality*, 162–63. *Institution*: "…ie reçoy volontiers tout ce qui pourra server à bien exprimer la vraye communication que Iesus Christ nous donne par la Cène en son corps et en son sang…"

[29]   Sheldrake, *New Westminster Dictionary of Christian Spirituality*, 162.

[30]   Julie Canlis, *Calvin's Ladder: A Spiritual Theology of Ascent and Ascension* (Grand Rapids, MI: W. B. Eerdmans Pub. Co., 2010), 1–2.

[31]   Ibid., 3. See *Institution*: "Or ils ne cognoissent point la façon de descendre dont nous avons parlé, qui est pour nous eslever au ciel."

Calvin's Unio Mystica

Seng-Kong Tan wrote a revealing analysis of Calvin's doctrine on union with Christ, noting that scholars have argued that Calvin's notion of *unio mystica* is important for understanding both the *Institutes* and his spirituality overall. Tan noted the need to first examine the Chalcedonian *distinctio sed non separatio*, a central underlying principle for Calvin.[32] Its importance lies not only in Calvin's soteriology and pneumatology, but also in his doctrine of justification and sanctification, and in his Trinitarian ideals. Tan also noted that Calvin recognized a real distinction between the divine persons, represented by mutual relationships, although he rejected such categories as essence, processions, and relations.[33]

Edmonson's treatment of the metaphysics of Calvin's Christology clarified this development in light of Servetus' rejection of the hypostatic union and of the distinctiveness of the two natures. Servetus had accused Calvin of Nestorianism.[34] Edmonson noted Dominice's critique that the human nature of Christ had value for Calvin only in union with the divine nature.[35]

For Calvin, according to Tan, union with Christ was founded on the "pretemporal electing will of God the Father" and the "covenantal union God made with Himself." Christ, in exercising his kingly office, is mediator of God's rule. Through the hypostatic union, according to Calvin, we share in Christ's sonship and life in heaven. Although Christ's atonement is in the past, his mediation continues such that our union "is a participation of act and being, since Christ's identity is inseparable from his mission," continued Tan. Calvin wrote of our engrafting into Christ's body and participation not only in his benefits but in Himself.[36] Here Tan opined that union with God, for Calvin, may

---

[32] Seng-Kong Tan, "Calvin's Doctrine of Our Union with Christ," *Quodlibet Online Journal of Christian Theology and Philosophy* 5, no. 4 (Oct. 2003): 1, http://www.quodlibet.net /articles/tan-union.shtml#_edn3. See Alister E. McGrath, *A Life of John Calvin: A Study in the Shaping of Western Culture* (Oxford, UK: Basil Blackwell, 1990), 149.

[33] Ibid., 1n7.

[34] Stephen Edmonson, *Calvin's Christology* (New York: Cambridge University Press, 2004), 204.

[35] Ibid., 210. See Max Dominicé, *L'humanité de Jésus, d'après Calvin* (Cahors: A. Coueslant, 1933), 48.

[36] *Institutes* (1960), 3.2.24, quoted in Tan, "Calvin's Doctrine of Our Union with Christ," 2n26; *Institution*: "Car ce que nous espérons salut de luy, n'est pas pource qu'il nous apparoisse de loin, mais pource que, nous ayant unis à son corps, il nous fait participans non seulement de tous ses biens mais aussi de soy-mesme."

be applied both to the Trinity without distinction and to Christ himself, as the "bond" of our adoption.[37]

Tan pointed to Calvin's reciprocity in participation, Christ in us, and our engrafting into him, with an emphasis always on the communal rather than the personal. This participation involves the double but inseparable grace of justification and regeneration.[38]

In so framing righteousness and holiness in the *unio mystica*, even with a term such as "put on Christ," Calvin addressed the Roman Catholic critique of legality, according to Tan. The restoration of the *imago Dei* for Calvin was both mortification of the flesh and regeneration of the spirit. His ideal of similitude, according to Tan, was a union in which Christ "transfers His virtue to us."[39]

Notably, Calvin rejected Manichean emanationism and Neoplatonic mysticism even while admitting we are to be deified eventually.[40] Tan noted that while Calvin did not write of an essential participation, it was "ontic," noting that Calvin had disagreed with Osiander's notion of essential righteousness, asserting that he had confused our union with that among the persons.

Calvin and Union with Christ

Tamburello, writing on Calvin's notions surrounding union with Christ, noted that Reformation scholars have begun in recent years to pay attention to the influence of medieval movements on the Reformers, as well as the presence of mystical themes in Luther's work. While Calvin criticized the *Theologia Deutsch* and Pseudo-Dionysius, for example, there were mystical influences in both Calvin's training and the themes found in his work.[41]

---

[37] *Institutes*, 3.6.3, cited in Tan, "Calvin's Doctrine of Our Union with Christ," 2n29; *Institution*: "Car si Dieu nous adopte pour ses enfans à ceste condition que l'image de Christ apparoisse en nostre vie, si nous ne nous addonnons à iustice et saincteté, non seulement nous abandonnons nostre Créateur par une desloyauté trop lasche, mais aussi nous le renonçons pour Sauveur." This 1560 French critical edition does not include the Latin phrase: "nostrae adoptionis vinculum."

[38] Tan, "Calvin's Doctrine of Our Union with Christ," 3.

[39] John Calvin, "The Commentaries on the Epistles of Paul the Apostle to the Hebrews," 4:10, in John Calvin, *The Comprehensive John Calvin Collection*, CD-ROM (Albany, OR: AGES Software, 1998), quoted in Tan, "Calvin's Doctrine of Our Union with Christ," 5–6; *Institution*: "...nous avons qu'il a esté conceu du Sainct Esprit: à fin que en toute plénitude son humanité feust sanctifiée, pour espandre le fruict de sa sanctification sur nous."

[40] Tan, "Calvin's Doctrine of Our Union with Christ," 6.

[41] Dennis E. Tamburello, *Union with Christ: John Calvin and the Mysticism of St. Bernard* (Louisville, KY: Westminster John Knox Press, 1994), 1–2, hereafter cited as *UC*.

One neglected topic, according to Tamburello, had been Calvin's notion of union with Christ. While Calvin used the term "unio mystica," generally it has not been viewed as referencing the idea of mysticism. Criticisms of mysticism include that of Ritschl, who held it is individualistic and isolating, quietistic, opposed to the ethics of the Reformation, elitist, and restricted to religious, a form of works righteousness, and opposed to evangelical doctrine in that it posits a kind of equality with God.[42] Kolfhaus, as well, put forth the criticisms that mystical experience includes the "annihilation" of the person and absorption into God's essence; that it refers to an unmediated union (with no need of the Church or sacraments); and that it posits an "enjoyment of the fullness of salvation."[43]

Tamburello asserted that much of medieval mysticism was built on Neoplatonic themes, and it is important to try to understand any connection between Neoplatonism and Calvin. While Calvin made no mention of Neoplatonism, he did make numerous references to Plato in the 1559 edition of the *Institutes*, and Platonic themes are found, including the body as prison, the immortality of the soul, the existence of two worlds, contemplation, and the longing for a return to a state of purity.[44] Calvin, however, did not share the Platonic notion of degrees of purification—one is either saved or damned.[45]

Various authors have weighed in on mystical themes and the *devotio moderna* movement in relation to Calvin's thought. Calvin had contact with the Brethren of the Common Life in several ways, including his time at the College of Montaigu. The spirituality of Calvin showed a resemblance in vocabulary and in some of his ideas to the *De imitatione Christi*, as well as the writings of Groote.[46] These shared themes and characteristics include the transcendence of God, and the concepts of election, holiness, and the glory of God.[47] The Brethren had

[42] Ibid., 4–5. See Albrecht Ritchl, *A Critical History of the Christian Doctrine of Justification and Reconciliation*, vol. 1, trans. John S. Black (Edinburgh: Edmonston and Douglas, 1872), 3: 112 and 163.

[43] Ibid., 5. See Wilhelm Kolfhaus, *Christusgemeinschaft bei Johannes Calvin,* Beiträge zur Geschichte und Lehre der Reformierten Kirche, vol. 3 (Neukirchen: Buchhandlung d. Erziehungsvereins, 1938), 126–27.

[44] Ibid., 15. See Jean Boisset, *Sagesse et sainteté dans la pensée de Jean Calvin: essai sur l'humanisme du Réformateur français* (Paris: Presses Universitaires de France, 1959), 255–84.

[45] Ibid., 15. See *Institution,* 3.24.12: "Comme le Seigneur par la vertu de sa vocation conduit ses esleus au salut, auquel il les avoit préordonnez en son conseil éternel, aussi, d'autrepart, il a ses iugemens sur les réprouvez, par lesquels il exécute ce qu'il a déterminé d'en faire." See also Boisset, *Sagesse,* 261–62.

[46] Ibid., 16. See Lucien Joseph Richard, *The Spirituality of John Calvin* (Atlanta: John Knox Press, 1974), 122–27.

[47] Ibid., 16–17. See Richard, *The Spirituality of John Calvin,* 180–83.

transferred monastic exercises to the laity, also reflecting an antimonastic thought characteristic of the new devotion and influencing the Reformers.[48]

Tamburello summarized Calvin's ideals regarding the basis of unity with Christ in the following statement: "The Holy Spirit brings the elect, through the hearing of the gospel, to faith; in doing so, the Spirit engrafts them into Christ."[49]

Calvin wrote about a twofold communion with Christ corresponding to the double grace of justification and sanctification. In Calvin's commentary on Galatians 2:20 ("It is no longer I that live, but Christ lives in me"), Calvin noted that Christ lives in us in two ways: "The one consists in His governing us by his Spirit and directing all our actions. The other is what He grants us by participation in His righteousness…"[50] In the first communion, Christ lives in us through the power of the Spirit (referencing justification), and in the second communion he gradually makes us rich with spiritual gifts (sanctification).[51]

Calvin did at times write about our having a share in Christ's "substance." Calvin wrote (in reference to Eph. 5:30 and Genesis, "flesh of my flesh"): "…we grow into one Body by the communication of His substance."[52]

The author noted that Calvin rejected Osiander's notion of "essential righteousness" as a kind of pantheism. Calvin denied that Christ's essence is mixed with ours.[53] Calvin clarified that this is not a transfusion of his substance into us.[54]

---

[48] Ross Fuller, *The Brotherhood of the Common Life and Its Influence* (State University of New York Press, 1995), xiii and 5.

[49] *UC*, 86.

[50] Ibid., 86. John Calvin, *John Calvin's New Testament Commentaries,* vol. 11, *The Epistles of Paul to the Galatians, Ephesians, Philippians, and Colossians,* trans. T. H. L. Parker (Grand Rapids: Wm. B. Eerdmans Publishing Co., 1965), 43; *Corpus Reformatorum* (Brunswick: C. A. Schwetschke, 1863–1900), 50: 199, hereafter cited as *CO*: "Porro vivit Christus in nobis dupliciter. Una vita est, quum nos spiritu suo gubernat atque actiones nostras omnes dirigit. Altera quod participatione suae iustitiae nos donat…"

[51] Ibid., 87. See John Calvin, Letter 2266, Peter Martyr Vermigli, 8 August 1555, *CO*, 15: 723: "…nisi quod divina spiritus virtute vitam e coelis in terram transfundi agnosco: quia nec per se vivifica esset caro Christi, nec vis eius ad nos usque nisi immensa spiritus operatione perveniret. Ergo spiritus est qui facit, ut in nobis habitet Christus, nos sustineat atque vegetet, omniaque capitis officia impleat." The second communion is the effect of the first: "Illius prioris…fructus est ac affectus."

[52] Calvin, *John Calvin's New Testament Commentaries*, 208–9, *CO*, 51: 225, quoted in *UC*, 87: "…ita nos, ut simus vera Christi membra, substantiae eius communicare, et hac communicatione nos coalescere in unum corpus."

[53] *UC*, 87–88. See *Institution*, 3.11.5: "cependant ie luy nie que l'essence de Christ soit meslée avec la nostre."

[54] Ibid., 88. See Calvin, *The Gospel according to St. John 11–21 in the First Epistle of John,* trans. T. H. L. Parker, in John Calvin, David W. Torrance, and Thomas F. Torrance,

Notably, Calvin wrote that we do not come into communion with Christ by virtue of our own holiness. He wrote, "Rather, we ought first to cleave unto him so that, infused with his holiness, we may follow whither he calls."[55]

Bérulle's Responses

Bérulle's response to Luther's notions on the hypostatic union and his rejection of devotion, as well as to Calvin's notions on election, would rest on the centrality of the will of the Father, and the priesthood of Christ from the moment of the Incarnation, confirmed by oath:

> Le Christ inaugure son sacrifice dès sa naissance, bien plus, dès sa conception. En entrant dans le monde, il dit: "Tu m'as formé un corps." C'est la victime. "Alors, j'ai dit: voici viens."
>
> La parole du serment, qui vient après la Loi, institue le Fils, parfait pour toujours. C'est la parole du serment par lequel le sacerdoce du Christ est institué…
>
> Ce sacerdoce plut tant au Père qu'il le voulut éternel. Il déplaît tant aux hérétiques qu'ils voudraient qu'il n'existât pas. Dieu le Père le voulut si bien éternel, qu'il le confirma par un serment.[56]

The idea that, by the Incarnation, human nature is elevated by union with the divine nature is a basic article of the faith developed by the fathers, according to Magnard.[57] "The fathers, especially the Greek fathers, began from the so-called *physico-mystical* conception of the redemption," as Carmody described, with the Incarnation seen as a physical union between the Word and a single human nature, containing all of humanity. By this union, the presence and action of the Word saves humanity. Cyril's, in particular, was a Word-flesh Christology at its

---

Commentaries, vol. 5 (Grand Rapids: Eerdmans, 1959), 148. See *CO*, 47: 387: "Unde etiam colligimus, nos unum cum Christo esse, non quia suum in nos substantiam transfundat, sed quia spiritus sui virtute nobiscum vitam suam et quidquid accepit a patre bonorum communicet."

[55] *Institutes of the Christian Religion*, ed. John T. McNeill, trans. Ford Lewis Battles (Philadelphia: Westminster Press, 1960), 3.6.2, quoted in *UC*, 100; *Institution*: "veu qu'il nous faut premièrement que d'estre saincts adhérer à luy *(a)*, afin qu'il espande de *(b)* sa saincteté sur nous | pour nous faire suyvre là où il nous appelle…quum potius adhaerere primo illi oporteat ut eius sanctitate perfusi sequamur quo vocat."

[56] *BLS*, *OR* 15, no. 5, 292.

[57] Pierre Magnard, "L'Incarnation selon le cardinal de Bérulle," in *Port-Royal et l'école française de spiritualité: colloque de Port-Royal des Champs, 15–16 septembre, 2006, Chroniques de Port-Royal*, 110–11.

peak. The intimate union of the Word and flesh for him was the means of the flesh becoming a life-giving instrument (*organon*) of the Word in our divinization, notably in the Eucharist.[58] Echoing this physico-mystical conceptualization, Bérulle called the priest an *organe*, with the Word Incarnate and the priest intimately united, as this analysis will detail.[59]

Bérulle held that the Incarnation was the fourth order of the universe, after nature, grace, and glory.[60] He developed a notion of a sacerdotal state as closely tied to the state of the hypostatic union of Christ the Priest. Bérulle told his Oratorians: "La dignité du sacerdoce du Christ vient de l'union hypostatique. Celle de notre sacerdoce, de l'union spéciale que nous avons avec le Christ par l'état sacerdotal."[61]

Cochois noted that the substance of the mystery of the Incarnation (hypostatic union) was itself the principle of divinization for Bérulle, independent of any kenotic economy, because, as he wrote, for Bérulle, the economy was an epiphany of its substance.[62] We will explore how the Incarnation became, for Bérulle, the principle of divinization for priests as well.

Importantly, as Orcibal wrote, Bérulle had attempted to meet the Calvinists' claim that theirs was a "profoundly lived Christocentric spirituality." Seeing this as an attack on ecclesiastical hierarchy, he looked to the sacerdotal prayer of Christ to support the idea that mission among men must have the same rank as the processions among the persons of the Trinity.[63] He promoted this conflation with his interpretation of the Incarnation, as we will explore.

In this focus on the Incarnation, Bérulle followed Ficino. Bérulle was called a follower of the fifteenth-century Florentine Academy, according to Morgain,[64] and followed Ficino in attempting a philosophical basis for his defense of the

---

[58] James M. Carmody and Thomas E. Clarke, *Word and Redeemer: Christology in the Fathers* (Glen Rock, NJ: Paulist Press, 1966), quote taken from 7. See also 91.

[59] See *BLS, OR* 22, no. 5, 317.

[60] Julien-Eymard d'Angers, "L'exemplarisme bérullien: les rapports du naturel et du surnaturel dans l'œuvre du cardinal de Bérulle," *Revue des sciences religieuses* 31 (1957): 123. See Bérulle, in Pierre de Bérulle and Olivier Piquand, *Discours de l'estat et des grandeurs de Jésus par l'union ineffable de la divinité avec l'humanité* (Paris: Siffre Fils et Cie, 1865), 17–18, 161; Migne ed., cols. 157, 220. See also 301–2, col. 280, where Bérulle combined the orders of grace and glory into one.

[61] *BLS, OR* 8, 279.

[62] Cochois, "Bérulle, hiérarque dionysien," 37: 334.

[63] Orcibal, *Le cardinal de Bérulle*, 59–61.

[64] See Stéphane-Marie Morgain, *La théologie politique de Pierre de Bérulle, 1598–1629* (Paris: Publisud, 2001), 388.

faith. Ficino had claimed that priests could find in the Platonic Academy tools to bring unbelievers back to the Church on philosophical grounds.[65]

Lauster noted that Ficino had placed the Incarnation as the foundation of his Christology as well, viewing it as the descent of the pre-existent Logos. Particularly applicable to this study, and to be detailed, Ficino combined the Platonic theory of cognition with the Christian doctrine of grace, which Lauster called the "divine formation of the intellectual power." He wrote that for Ficino, "the thinking of divine ideas necessarily transforms the soul because God works as the moving and the forming power."[66]

Collins clarified that the primary purpose of Ficino's Platonic theology was to oppose secular Aristotelianism by proving that philosophy cannot be separated from religion and is related to the worship of its object. He integrated the Platonic doctrine of unity and power with the Thomistic doctrine of being and act. For Ficino, causation involved influence, a flowing of originating power into the effect. The more dependent the effect on its cause, the more pervasive its efficacious power.[67]

Important, and applicable to this study, is Hankins' opinion that Ficino's project was not an effort to establish an esoteric philosophical religion but rather a reformed one, in which contemplation and a universally-appealing Christ superseded legalism.[68]

Bérulle forged a complex Word Christology. Called the "Apôtre du Verbe incarné" by Pope Urban VIII,[69] Bérulle proposed ideals surrounding both Christian and sacerdotal spiritualities which had as their starting point the importance of the Incarnation in relation to the priesthood of Christ.

Vieillard-Baron explored Bérulle's image of man in relation to the Incarnation, writing that Bérulle's borrowed from a Renaissance cosmology in which humankind was between the angels and demons, part-animal and part-angel. Writing on the idea of possession, Bérulle would present two extremes:

---

[65]   Peter Serracino-Inglott, "Ficino the Priest," in *Marsilio Ficino: His Theology, His Philosophy, His Legacy*, ed. Michael J. B. Allen, V. Rees, and Martin Davis (Leiden: Brill, 2001), 11.

[66]   Jörg Lauster, "Marsilio Ficino as a Christian Thinker: Theological Aspects of His Platonism," in *Marsilio Ficino: His Theology, His Philosophy, His Legacy*, ed. Michael J. B. Allen, V. Rees, and Martin Davis (Leiden: Brill, 2001), 56–60.

[67]   Ardis Collins, *The Secular Is the Sacred: Platonism and Thomism in Marsilio Ficino* (The Hague: Martinus Mijhoff, 1974), 7, 22, and 106.

[68]   James Hankins, "Marsilio Ficino and the Religion of the Philosophers," *Rinascimento* 48 (2009): 101–21.

[69]   Dagens, *Bérulle et les origines*, 291. Dagens noted that the exact source of this title is not known, but he had no doubt of its veracity.

deified man (Jesus) and satanized man. Seen in these terms, the Incarnation was an invasion by God of human nature, according to the author.[70]

The question arises whether Bérulle's priest himself became a deified Renaissance man following the exemplar of Christ. Part-animal, part-angel, the Oratorian struggled through frequent prayer to maintain union with Christ. The next question presents itself of whether Christ had to, in a sense, take over the priest for him to be a true priest and mediator? We will explore these questions in this study.

Bérulle's Political Theology

By way of preamble, we present the thoughts below of several writers focusing on the intersection of the political views and religious beliefs of Bérulle, cardinal and statesman, as he came to apply his theological constructs to the defense of both the Mystical Body and society against what he saw as the Huguenot threat.

According to Minton, Christology had become a tool in Counter-Reformation France and Spain to permit the exaltation of authority, and to provide a model of virtues such as obedience, submission, humility, and suffering. Minton saw Bérulle's focus on Christ as a polemical stance against Calvinists who were suspicious of devotion to Christ. Minton noted that Bérulle's ideas were a blend of accepted doctrine and unorthodox ideas, reflecting a radical corruption of human nature, the powerlessness of humans to effect salvation, a shift in emphasis to a personal encounter with God's grace in Jesus, a stress on the emptying of Christ, and the overpowering force of Christ's divine nature in the person of Jesus.[71]

Committed to the eradication of heresy, Bérulle incorporated ideas taken from the Huguenots, particularly the transcendence of God, according to Minton, who questioned whether his religious synthesis was for political goals or vice versa. In her opinion, the issue of power was the underlying theme in his discussion of Christ's attitude. Being a political enemy of Richelieu and a key figure in the *dévot* party that opposed him, Bérulle promoted a spirituality of

---

[70] Jean-Louis Vieillard-Baron, "L'image de l'homme chez Descartes et chez le cardinal de Bérulle," *Revue philosophique de la France et de l'étranger* 182, no. 4 (Oct.–Dec. 1992): 407–8. See Bérulle, *Traité des Énergumènes, OC*, Migne ed., 835–836: "Le créateur, situant l'homme, qui est son image, au milieu du monde, c'est-à-dire entre le ciel et l'enfer, quant à la résidence; entre le temps et l'éternité, quant à la durée; entre lui et le diable quant à la liberté; et entre les anges et les animaux quant à la nature, il en fit comme un point et un centre auquel toutes les parties du monde se rapportent…"

[71] Anne H. Minton, "The Figure of Christ in the Writings of Pierre de Bérulle (1575–1629)" (PhD diss., New York University, UMI Dissertation Service, 1979), 8–10.

submission and withdrawal from the world.[72] Minton noted Bérulle's fascination with the call to priesthood and the priest's participation in the role of Christ Priest as stemming from his focus on the polemics of the Huguenot debates.[73]

Another analysis of the political and theological overlaps of Bérulle's thought is that of Milbank, who wrote that the Incarnation for Bérulle involved "the kenotic and deificatory exchange and fusion of worshipping and worshipped." The Incarnation became the basis for the argument in favor of kingly rule. This new order was "paracosmic" for Bérulle, and was "the participation of the creation in God through the newly realized cosmic body of Christ."[74]

Cognet noted that Bérulle presented a marked historicism in his treatment of the Incarnation as the center of history and as a new order in the universe.[75]

In writing on Bérulle's extended meditation on the life of Jesus and the mysteries of his life, Beaude noted a historicity without continuity, which was characterized by a temporality of the instant moment as Bérulle attempted by his rhetoric itself to elevate readers to adhere to eternal mysteries.[76]

Milet's socio-psychological study traced the shift from theocentricity to Christocentricity in the seventeenth century and forward, attributable to the influence of the French School. Rejecting Scholasticism, the school isolated itself from theocentricity, favoring the historical person of Christ, in favoring a humanism, arguably, that held Christ as the most human man. The school's approach also rejected the traditional approach of union with God via the example and intercession of Christ. Now, only in Christ was God known and loved.[77]

Of note for this review of Bérulle's interpretation of sacerdotal mediation, Milet wrote that under this "autonomous christocentricity" the status of the priest changed profoundly from one who brought prayers to God to he who brings grace to humanity. This, he thought, influenced the Christocentric turn in the twentieth century as well, notably elements predominating in the texts of the Second Vatican Council, including frequent references to Christ Priest, the concern for sacerdotal formation to restore Christocentricity, and the theme of

---

[72] Ibid., 12–28.

[73] Ibid., 61.

[74] John Milbank, "Liberality versus Liberalism," in *Religion and Political Thought*, ed. Michael Hoelzl and Graham Ward (London and New York: Continuum International Publishing Group, 2006), 232.

[75] Cognet, *Les origines de la spiritualité française*, 64.

[76] Joseph Beaude, "Historicité et vie mystique: La vie de Jésus du cardinal de Bérulle," *Archives de Philosophie* 29 (1986): 571–82.

[77] Jean Milet, *God or Christ: The Excesses of Christocentricity* (New York: Crossroad Publishing Company, 1981), 111–16.

Christ as perfect man in *Gaudium et Spes*. Milet wrote that the *Decree on the Ministry and Life of Priests*[78] was added *in extremis* and was a return to Christocentricity. The Priest was no longer a man of God but a representative of Christ.[79]

Conclusion

Bérulle looked to a myriad of traditional and Reformist Christological formulations in responding to the lived spiritualities of Luther and Calvin. An understanding of the debates and underlying Reformist spiritualities and applied metaphysics is crucial to parsing Bérulle's complex spirituality of priesthood.

Numerous ideals related to the history of mysticism include divine union, contemplation, the vision of God, deification, the birth of the Word in the soul, ecstasy, and radical obedience to the divine will.[80] Bérulle ranged freely through these and other categories related to mystical experience in his Christological constructions in support of the exalted nature of the priesthood and the holiness required of priests. His was an effort to catalogue and assign new significance to traditional ideals, referencing them, many times without attribution.

Outlined below are key Reformist and Counter-Reformist themes reviewed in this chapter which had echoes in Bérulleé rhetoric and which will be explored in greater depth in later chapters.

Like the Florentine Academy, Bérulle brought together various popular ideals with those of Christianity in the effort to restore the unity of the Church. Bérulle's Christology, focusing on the Incarnation and the hypostatic union, willed and emanating from the Father, as the wellspring of grace, and available through his own unique syncretistic system of mystical devotion, was similar in some regards to Ficino's thought.

As this study will elucidate, Bérulle mixed his particular interpretations of Dionysian mysticism, Rheno-Flemish themes, Scotism, and Thomism in his project to reform the clergy, in loose concepts surrounding principal and formal causes, actuated by a grace-causing meditation on divine ideas.

---

[78] Second Vatican Council, *Decree on the Ministry and Life of Priests, December 7, 1965* [*Presbyterorum Ordinis*].

[79] Jean Milet, *God or Christ*, 182–89.

[80] Bernard McGinn, *The Foundations of Mysticism*, vol. 1, *The Presence of God: A History of Western Christian Mysticism* (New York: Crossroad Publishing Company, 1991), xv–xvii.

Like the Reformers, Bérulle also placed piety at the center of his project for both laity and priests. As Preckler remarked, for Bérulle, the light of piety led to perfection rather than the light of faith leading to salvation.[81] Importantly, for Bérulle, the piety of priests led to redemption, as this analysis will explore.

Following Bellarmine, who had responded to Luther's invisible Church by insisting on the visible aspects of the Church,[82] Bérulle focused on Christ the invisible head of the Church, with the priest being the visible head. In this, he developed an ideal asserted by Trent against the Reformers of a new, visible priesthood into which the older priesthood had given way.[83]

Luther's spiritual theology, focused on a personal relationship with the Incarnate Christ, was based on a conception of theosis, influenced by Eckhart, as receiving the form of the Word by faith, and his rejection of both *habitus* and substantial grace. We will argue this spirituality found an echo in Bérulle's rhetoric, depicting Christ as divine substance, as well as in his proposal of a unique relationship between the priest and the Word Incarnate.

Luther's ideal of union by Baptism and Calvin's of union by faith were also both echoed in Bérulle's essentialist mystical union of the priest with Christ, held in place by a personalist faith experience, as later chapters will detail.

Luther's personalism found a parallel, as well, in Bérulle's sacerdotal spirituality, in that a personal affective union with Christ was requisite for the highest use of sacerdotal powers.

Also, the opposing effects of nominalism, which Bouyer categorized as either God becoming the highest experience of ourselves or so transcendent that one must annihilate oneself to enter into relationship, are found in Bérulle's spiritual theology of priesthood as the priest became both the visible image of Christ and head of the Mystical Body, as well as a kenotic vessel and immolated victim.

---

[81] *État*, 126. See *Narré des persécutions soulevées par les vœux*, 27, 404. Preckler utilized the Montsoult edition of the *Œuvres complètes*, as well as the Migne edition of the *Œuvres de piété*, which he deemed more complete, albeit correcting the text, if necessary, using the former. He also used Dupuy's 1964 edition of Bérulle's unpublished texts on the priesthood, as well as Dagens' edition of Bérulle's correspondence, and various sources for unpublished texts as noted and as explicated in the index of Bérulle's works cited.

[82] Franco Buzzi, "La 'scolastica barocca' come risposta alla Riforma e ai tempi nuovi," in *Per il Cinquecento religioso italiano: clero, cultura, società: atti del Convegno internazionale di studi, Siena, 27–30 giugno 2001*, ed. Maurizio Sangalli (Roma: Edizioni dell'Ateneo, 2003), 87.

[83] Council of Trent – 1545–1563: Session 23, ch. 1, in Heinrich Denzinger, Peter Hünermann, and Helmut Hoping, *Enchiridion symbolorum definitionum et declarationum de rebus fidei et morum = Kompendium der Glaubensbekenntnisse und kirchlichen Lehrentscheidungen* (Freiburg, Basel, Wien: Herder, 2014), 1563: "in ea novum esse visibile et externum sacerdotium, in quod vetus translatum est."

That said, Bérulle was to respond not with what Bouyer held was a nominalist reduction of being to act and the loss of the notion of substance, but, arguably, with a reduction of being to action, and the Stoic notion of Christ as the substance of the priest, as we will detail.

Luther's ideal of the Presence overshadowing the sacrifice, and the Reformist ideal of adoration as the only sacrifice, would have a parallel of sorts in Bérulle's emphasis on the internal attitude of Christ as perfect adorer in the Mass.

Bérulle himself focused on the mediation of the Church, the sacraments, and the priest, incorporating the electing will of God in his particular treatment of the Incarnation, which made us sons of the Son. Bérulle's rhetoric echoed the notion of engrafting and union with Christ in his concept of the priest participating in mediation, as we will explore.

Bérulle's emphasis on the Incarnation as sacerdotal act and as an act of redemption combined the substance and economy of the Incarnation. This, it could be argued, was an attempt to form a basis for viewing the priest as a victim of the redemption and conjoined instrument of Christ, not just in dispensing the sacraments but at all times.

Making the Incarnation into the fourth order of the universe, Bérulle created a sacerdotal state closely tied to the hypostatic union. This sacerdotal state he considered one of the mysteries of the life of Christ by means of which the priest, elevated to participate through frequent effort, became head of the celestial city on earth.

All this was accomplished through adherence to Christ through these frequent mental elevations, mirroring Calvin's cleaving and notions on servitude. Calvin's notion of election and the need to assure it was reflected in this system where priests, in a certain sense, had to maintain their election as priests.

Countering Calvin's insistence on the limitation of the sacrifice of propitiation to Jesus alone, with only the sacrifice of praise and honor available to all, Bérulle proposed a system of honor and adoration by *anéantissement* for both laity and priests.

As adoration of God's glory was at the heart of Calvin's spirituality, it became so for Bérulle's sacerdotal spirituality. In his response to Calvin's emphasis on Christ's priesthood begun in glory, Bérulle placed priests in relation to Christ via adoration, with an emphasis on the imitation of the glorified Christ's psychological states of stability, perfection, and impassability.

We can see Calvin's anti-hierarchical invitation to believers to enter into the "society of Christ" as another theme in Bérulle's exemplarist defense of both the Church and the society of priests as based on the exemplar of the society of the Trinity.

In light of the Reformist turn to an incarnational Christ as sole mediator, it would be Bérulle's interpretation of the holiness of Christ, a key Christological construct, which formed the basis of his defense of the priesthood. We review it now.

Chapter 6
The Holiness of Christ

Introduction

The issue of the need for holiness on the part of priests was predominant in the period of the Reform and Counter-Reform. Bérulle sought to defend the objective holiness of the priesthood by utilizing key Christological ideals current in the Reform and Counter-Reform. For this reason, an in-depth review is warranted of Yelle's 1938 treatise on the theme of the holiness of Christ in Bérulle's thought.

Background

Yelle presented the complex foundations of Bérulle's spirituality as based on the contemplation of the Incarnate Word and the doctrine of the Mystical Body.[1] Bérulle's motive, according to Yelle, was to address what he saw as heretics denying the divinity of Christ, who admitted only a union between Christ and God by means of habitual grace. To do so, Bérulle focused on uniting more closely the members of the Mystical Body with their head, by showing the Mystical Body as a prolongation of the Incarnation, and by insisting on the personal union of the humanity of Christ with the divinity. There followed what Yelle called the most difficult aspect of Bérulle's Christology and his theology overall: his notion of the relationship between the substantial holiness and the accidental holiness of Christ.[2]

The Mystical Body and Substantial Holiness

Yelle began his discussion of Bérulle referring only briefly to the great controversy over the vows of servitude Bérulle imposed upon the Carmelites and his Oratorians, and Bérulle's later defense, *Grandeurs de Jésus*, which we will

---

[1]   *Le mystère.* This review follows the author's exposition closely.
[2]   Ibid., 121–22, see footnote 2.

explore.[3] With these vows, Bérulle hoped to initiate especially priests into a participation in the holiness of Christ.

Yelle addressed how Bérulle understood the manner in which the divine life which is within the soul of Jesus is passed from the head to the members of the Mystical Body, as well as his understanding of the problem of the Mystical Body in terms of the "substantial" sanctification of the humanity by the divine subsistence of the Word.

Yelle addressed the idea of the substantial holiness of Christ, its relation to accidental holiness, and the notion of subsistence, which the author thought important to understand in relation to Bérulle's Christology and Christocentrism.[4]

Beginning with the Trinity, Bérulle treated such aspects as unity of essence, persons, generation, and relation. Bérulle saw the generation in time of the Word within the unity of and as the prolongation of the eternal generation of the Word, taking from Saints Cyril and Hilary the idea that the eternal communication of essence is the exemplar of the communication in time of subsistence.[5]

The Notion of Relation

Bérulle placed considerable importance on the concept of relation in terms of the relationship between the accidental holiness and the substantial holiness of Christ. He considered Trinitarian relations as constitutive of the divine persons and as their origins, insisting that there is no subsistence in the divinity without relations: "Mais en Dieu les relations sont constitutives des personnes divines…, sont origines des personnes divines…, et il n'y a subsistence en la Divinité que par relations…"[6]

Yelle commented that it is by virtue of the communication of idioms that we can attribute to Christ his essential holiness, but, in the case of Bérulle, there was not only a communication of idioms but a communication of holiness such that, as Bérulle wrote, "l'Incarnation …sanctifie l'humanité de la divinité."[7]

The communication of holiness included the communication of the divine subsistence or the divine sonship for Bérulle. In order to understand the manner

---

[3]   Ibid., 20. Yelle referenced the Migne edition of Bérulle's collected works for his study, as well as the first volume of Bérulle's correspondence edited by J. Dagens.

[4]   Ibid., 26–27.

[5]   Ibid., 30.

[6]   *OP* 119, 2, quoted in *Subsistence*, 32.

[7]   *Grandeurs*, 7, no. 9, col. 282, quoted in *Le mystère*, 35. Yelle consulted the Migne edition for all works cited.

in which this holiness is communicated one must understand the Christological terminology Bérulle used.[8]

Subsistence

Bérulle held that the perfections of the divine persons come from the unity of the essence common to the divine persons, with the perfections of Jesus coming from this subsistence. It is the unity of the subsistence that established the Incarnation. He also held that as in the Trinity the unity of essence is the source of all the grandeurs of the persons, so the unity of person is the source of grandeurs and communications made to the humanity of Christ: "Car Dieu y communique sa subsistence, et par sa subsistence son essence, et en son essence les perfections de son essence comme subsistantes personnellement en cette humanité."[9] Yelle asked exactly what Bérulle meant by the word *subsistence*, and what he saw as the structure of the union that the sanctifying subsistence of the Word establishes between the human nature and the divine nature. In order to answer those questions, he noted that one must understand Bérulle's distinction between substance and economy in the Incarnation.[10]

At issue were his ideals regarding the "states" of the Incarnate Word and their relation to the subsistence of the Word. Bérulle held that the Incarnation of the Word is the basis not only of the sanctification but the divinization of all the states and mysteries of Christ: "Car l'Incarnation du Verbe est la base et le fondement de la dignité suprême, c-est-à-dire, non seulement de la sanctification, mais aussi de la déification de tous états et mystères..."[11] This emphasis on the subsistence of Jesus, which forms the center of the substance of the mystery of the Incarnation, is reminiscent of both Saints John and Paul, in Yelle's opinion.[12]

Yelle noted that since the latter part of the fourteenth century, Christological controversies had arisen surrounding the ideas of person and nature. Theological thought regarding the Incarnation was dominated by the ideas of subsistence, essence, and existence—terms also linked to the idea of substantial holiness. One issue was the question: in what does the formal constituent of the subsistence consist? All three words occur many times together within *Grandeurs de Jésus*, and are applicable to Bérulle's idea of substantial holiness. Referring obliquely to De Vio, Yelle explained, "Essence et subsistence se distinguent comme chose

---

[8]   *Le mystère*, 35.
[9]   *Grandeurs*, 3, no. 9, col. 204, quoted in *Le mystère*, 37.
[10]   *Le mystère*, 37.
[11]   *OP* 17, no. 2, col. 940, quoted in *Le mystère*, 39.
[12]   *Le mystère*, 40.

terminée et terme. La nature humaine du Christ, privée de subsistence humaine, est terminée par la subsistence du Verbe."[13] Bérulle wrote:

> Le dénûment de la subsistence humaine dans la nature humaine, est une privation d'une chose bien plus liée et plus inséparable, bien plus propre et plus INTRINSÈQUE à la nature, qui n'est pas la franchise et la liberté au regard de la personne qui entre en servitude…Car la nature ne peut être séparée de son être personnel que par l'auteur même de la nature…L'être personnel entre dans le ressort de la nature, en est LE TERME comme L'ACCOMPLISSEMENT et faisant en une CERTAINE MANIÈRE PARTIE DE LA PROPRE SUBSTANCE des choses, au lieu que la franchise n'est qu'un simple accident et qualité qui se passe et se perd sans l'intérêt du sujet, et n'entre que dans les conditions de l'état et non de la personne.[14]

Yelle noted that this passage included terms used by De Vio to define personality.[15]

The humanity of Christ, for Bérulle, did not have a human existence. He also noted that some texts suffered from a lack of logical order and reflected the influence of a Suarezian modalism. Yelle wrote, "…Suárez ajoute la subsistence, ce mode substantiel à l'essence dèjá actuée par l'existence."[16] For Bérulle, the

---

[13] Ibid., 46. Yelle pointed to footnote 4, which is missing.

[14] *Grandeurs*, 2, no. 10, col. 177, quoted in *Le mystère*, 45–46. Yelle took some liberties with the Migne edition. For example, Migne capitalized some words, and omitted the wording "and slavery" after the word "servitude."

[15] *Le mystère*, 46n2. See Tommaso de Vio Cajetan, *Commentaria*, 3.4.2, 12 in Aquinas, *Summa theologiae*, 11: 74–81: "Ex hoc quod realitas personalitatis est terminus ultimus natuae patet primo difficultas de identitate et diversitate ejus a natura singulari. Est enim quodammodo idem, et quodammodo non idem; sicut terminus est termniato et non est illud…" See also 11, "Quod assumitur, trahitur ad aliquid completius, ipsum incompletum existens: et hoc est contra rationem personae, quae maximam completionem habet." The author noted that Bérulle never quoted De Vio but must have known his work through other authors.

[16] Ibid., 47. See Suárez, *Disputationes metaphysicae*, in *Opera omnia*, 26 (Paris: Vivès, 1856), 34.4.9: "Tamen in eo quod supponit, et in quo cum præcedenti convenit, scilicet, quod existentia substantialis, intrinsece, formaliter et essentialiter sit ipsamet subsistentia, impugnatur hæc opinio a Cajetano, 3 part., quæst. 4, art. 2, et aliis, qui eum sequuntur, cujus rationes statim latius videbimus tractando ejus sententiam. Summa omnium est, quia juxta prædictam sententiam cogitatur natura tanquam immediatum subjectum susceptivum existentiæ, et existentia ponitur ut actus immediatus naturæ; suppositum autem ponitur ut quid immediate resultans ex esse, et essentia substantiali. Item juxta illam opinionem confunditur in substantiis completis compositio ex natura et supposito cum

subsistence is the substantial *terme* that establishes being. Because only substances subsist, Bérulle placed subsistence in the category of substance: "Cette humanité…est dénuée d'une chose si grande et si intime à son essence comme est la subsistence, et, selon le Docteur angélique, de son existence…"[17]

Yelle then referenced Mersch's critique that the French School masters held a pessimistic view of human nature, which did not allow for a full understanding of the Incarnation, with the hypostatic union absorbing the humanity of Christ into a divine glory and function, and with the subsistence of the Word replacing Christ's human personality.[18]

Yelle remarked that Bérulle maintained a duality of natures against Monophysitism, and the unity of the hypostasis against the Nestorians. Bérulle insisted on the independence of the Word in regard to both the Father and the Holy Spirit, and therefore the unique dependence of the humanity on the Word. He also insisted that the Word is the sanctifying unction of the human nature. This statement, Yelle noted, addressed the apprehension of those critics who saw an Apollinarian tendency in what Yelle called the "cajétano-thomiste" notion of subsistence.[19]

The next question Yelle addressed was in what this union between the divinity and humanity consists, as it had been the source of criticism. Yelle noted that Bérulle based his ideal of this unity on Saint Cyril's "union selon l'hypostase (secundum subsistentiam unitum)."[20] He noted that the key to understanding this conceptualization of the formal constituent of the hypostatic union is to be found, not in the fathers, but in Aquinas, explained by De Vio. In explicating the Incarnation as a union, Aquinas referred to the idea of union as distinct from assumption: the union being the end of the action, and the assumption the action itself, by which the person of the Eternal Word takes on the human nature within

---

compositione ex esse et et essentia. Hæc autem falsa videntur, quia natura non est proximum susceptivum existentiæ, sed suppositum, juxta sententiam D. Thomæ, 3 part. quæst. 17, art. 2, in corpore, et ad. 4. Et ideo (juxta ejusdem doctrinam) solum suppositum est principium operationis, terminus generationis vel nativitatis, subjectum filiationis, et similia; ergo existentia non est actus immediatus naturæ, nec natura est proximum susceptivum existentiæ, sed inter eas mediat subsistentia, quæ cum natura constituit proximum susceptivum existentiæ." See also Suárez, *De Incarnatione*, in *Opera omnia*, 17 (Paris: Vivès, 1860), 3.1.11.3.

[17] Ibid., 47–48. See *Grandeurs*, 2, no. 10, col. 177.
[18] Ibid., 48n1. See Émile Mersch, *Le corps mystique du Christ*, vol. 2, 2nd ed. (Paris and Bruxelles, 1936), 331 and 337.
[19] Ibid., 51–54.
[20] Ibid., 59–61n2. See St. Cyril, *Anathématisme*, 2.

the unity of his subsistence.[21] Bérulle, however, joined the ideas of union and appropriation in an example of Baroque hyperbole: "En cette communication, il y a une application très puissante, une union très intime, une appropriation très parfaite du Verbe à cette humanité, et de cette humanité au Verbe."[22]

Yelle noted that Bérulle emphasized the idea of the humanity in Christ's being and his acts as a "conjoined instrument" of the divinity in order to realize the work of redemption. However, Bérulle preferred the specific expression of this union as a personal union, or a union of subsistence.[23]

Bérulle contemplated *l'Homme-Dieu*: "Ces deux natures si différentes sont en lui, et en sa personne, sans confusion, sans séparation: il nous les faut considérer sans séparation aussi…"[24] Within Bérulle's purpose of emphasizing the union of natures in the unity of person was his other purpose of illustrating that the operations of Jesus Christ as Savior are neither purely human nor purely divine but are, as he called them, operations that are "humainement divines, et divinement humaines."[25]

---

[21] Ibid., 62n3. See Aquinas, *ST*, 3.2.8, co., in *Summa theologiae*, 11: 42–43: "Respondeo dicendum quod, sicut dictum est, unio importat relationem divinae naturae et humanae secundum quod conveniunt in una persona. Omnis autem relatio quae incipit esse ex tempore, ex aliqua mutatione causatur. Mutatio autem consistit in actione et passione. Sic igitur dicendum est quod prima et principalis differentia inter unionem et assumptionem est quod unio importat ipsam relationem: assumptio autem actionem secundum quam dicitur aliquis assumens, vel passionem secundum quam dicitur aliquid assumptum.

"Ex hac autem differentia accipitur secundo alia differentia. Nam assumptio dicitur sicut in fieri: unio autem sicut in facto esse. Et ideo uniens dicitur esse unitum: assumens autem non dicitur esse assumptum. Natura enim humana significatur ut in termino assumptionis ad hypostasim divinam per hoc quod dicitur *homo*: unde vere dicimus quod Filius Dei, qui est uniens sibi humanam naturam, est homo. Sed humana natura in se considerata, idest in abstracto, significatur ut assumpta: non autem dicimus quod Filius Dei sit humana natura.

"Ex eodem etiam sequitur tertia differentia: quod relatio, praecipue aequiparantiae, non magis se habet ad unum extremum quam ad aliud; actio autem et passio diversimode se habent ad agens et patiens, et ad diversos terminos. Et ideo assumptio determinat terminum et a quo et ad quem, dicitur enim assumptio quasi *ab alio ad se sumptio*: unio autem nihil horum determinat. Unde indifferenter dicitur quod humana natura est unita divinae, et e converso. Non autem dicitur divina natura assumpta ab humana, sed e converso: quia humana natura adiuncta est ad personalitatem divinam, ut scilicet persona divina in humana natura subsistat."

[22] *Grandeurs*, 6, no. 5, col. 249, quoted in *Le mystère*, 63n2. One sees in this quote an instance of chiasmus.

[23] *Le mystère*, 63.

[24] *Vie de Jésus*, 25, 481, quoted in *Le mystère*, 74n1.

[25] *Vœu à Dieu*, 627, quoted in *Le mystère*, 76. This is another chiastic phrase.

The next question that Yelle addressed was the exact nature of the substantial holiness of Christ. There were a number of applications in Bérulle's schema, reflecting the unity of the subsistence of Christ in the hypostatic union, including the union of Mary with Jesus, as well as Christ in relation to the Eucharist, and lastly, the saints in relation to Christ.[26]

Anointing and Substantial Holiness

First, Yelle attempted to understand Bérulle's notions of anointing and of substantial holiness under the terms of consecration and formal holiness, and in their relationship to accidental holiness.[27]

Bérulle defined the anointing of Christ as the substantial sanctification of the humanity by the divinity, and took as his base the scriptural passage from Psalm 45:8 ("…therefore God, your God, has anointed you…"). Bérulle interpreted this text in the same fashion as did St. Augustine, as the anointing of Christ as part of the hypostatic union rather than as a consequence of the glorification of Christ merited by his death.[28] Bérulle saw the humanity penetrated by the divinity in the Incarnation, which was destined for our salvation: "Dieu est en ce petit corps, et la plénitude de la divinité y habite corporellement, et c'est le corps de Dieu même…"[29]

It is this psalm, according to Yelle, upon which all the arguments of authority were brought to bear (especially since the seventeenth century) in favor of the idea of substantial holiness, whether it be consecratory or formally sanctifying.

Yelle clarified that there are two kinds of consecration of the humanity of Christ for Bérulle: the first is by the Father for the Son, and the other is by the Son, which he gives himself: "qu'il a consacré à soi-même par soi-même, c'est-à-dire par l'onction et application de sa divine essence."[30] At this point, Yelle entered into a discussion of Bérulle's vision, as he moved easily from generation to mission and from mission to anointing, seeing the temporal generation of the Son as an extension of the eternal generation. According to Bérulle, "C'est une expression des grandeurs de Jésus en deux choses, en sa génération éternelle et en sa mission temporelle: *Tu es Christus Messias*…ce ne peut être que par l'ineffable communication de la subsistence de ce Fils à la nature humaine."[31]

---

[26] *Le mystère*, 79.
[27] Ibid., 79.
[28] Ibid. See 81n1.
[29] *Vie de Jésus*, 25, 483, quoted in *Le mystère*, 81.
[30] *Le mystère*, 81–82.
[31] *OP* 35, no. 3, col. 971, quoted in *Le mystère*, 84.

For Bérulle, the anointing of the humanity of Christ by the divinity is a temporal extension of the eternal generation of the Word. It is accomplished by God the Father upon the humanity of the second person of the Holy Trinity. This is the consecration of Christ, as we will review in detail.[32] In Bérulle's words, it is an anointing of substantial grace rather than just accidental grace.[33] Yelle made the point that Bérulle considered this a royal anointing.[34]

In this, we perhaps see echoes of the eternal generation controversy regarding the aseity of Christ, in which Reformers denied emanationism and asserted the saving power of Christ over the authority of a "necessary" institutional hierarchy, which we will explore in detail in the next chapter.

Yelle asked whether Bérulle's was an attempt to highlight the royalty of Christ. He noted that in the dedication to the King of France, which prefaces *Grandeurs de Jésus*, this idea is delineated: Jesus the Man-God is also King. This royalty is spiritual and the reason why heads of state must recognize Christ.[35]

The ideas of priesthood, redemption, and mediation are connected for Bérulle. As Yelle wrote: "L'onction sacerdotale établit le Christ dans son état de Médiateur de Rédemption."[36]

Yelle wrote that for Bérulle, the *termination* of Christ's humanity satisfied divine justice, resulted in a juridical appurtenance, and was the basis of Christianity. In the following passage, the degree of this appropriation by means of this anointing and sacerdotal consecration, expressed in legalistic terms, is evidenced:

Le Verbe éternel, comme personne substituée au droit de la nature humaine, et personne divine et incréée, s'approprie cette humanité, l'unit à soi, la rend sienne, repose et habite en elle comme en sa propre nature, la tire hors des limites d'un usage commun et naturel, l'OINT ET LA CONSACRE DE L'ONCTION DE SA DIVINITÉ, et prend droit et autorité sur elle et sur ses actions…Car tout ce qui est en Jésus-Christ est fondé en l'hypostase de sa divinité. Et le Verbe éternel, comme suppôt et suppôt divin de cette nature humaine, est le propriétaire de toutes ses actions et souffrances, les soutient, les relève et les déifie en sa propre personne.[37]

---

[32] *Le mystère*, 87.
[33] Ibid., 88n1. See *Grandeurs*, 7, no. 7, col. 277.
[34] Ibid., 92.
[35] Ibid., 92–93. *Dédicace*, in *Grandeurs*, 115–130.
[36] Ibid., 95n5. See *OP* 12, no. 2, col. 925.
[37] *Grandeurs*, 2, no. 10, col. 176, quoted in *Le mystère*, 96.

For Bérulle, it is the grace of substantial union with the Word that renders Christ holy and a mediator capable of offering sacrifice, which results in the substantial holiness of the humanity. This anointing supposes a sacerdotal vocation.[38]

For Bérulle, the substantial anointing, the divine consecration of Christ, as both priest and victim, is the basis of our redemption through an adequate satisfaction. Yelle wrote that just as with Aquinas and Augustine, there was a synthesis in Bérulle's thought between two great currents of thought on the priesthood of Christ: that of the Eastern church, which emphasized the divine aspect, and that of the West, which emphasized the human. The humanity of Christ, which is assumed, is something that is separated from the human race at the moment of the Incarnation, consecrated, and sanctified as a victim, according to Bérulle: "C'ést en ce mystère que cette hostie...de la même instant qu'elle es produite, est consacré par l'onction de la Divinité et par l'union ineffable et hypostatique..."[39]

Yelle finally noted that there was an exaggeration in Bérulle's ideal of royalty in regard to the Mystical Body as a result of Christ not being made king by means of capital grace. Rather, an aspect of capital grace flows from the exercise of his royalty.[40] The substantial anointing consecrated Christ as king and head of creation and as mediator of both redemption and religion. In addition, the appurtenance of the humanity to the subsistence of the Word was founded not only on the title of creation but also on the title of generation, according to Bérulle:

> Car au lieu que la nature divine appartient au Verbe par génération et non autrement, et que les choses créées ne lui appartiennent que par création (à laquelle se réduisent, et en laquelle sont fondées toutes les autres voies d'appartenances qu'elles ont au Créateur), cette humanité appartient au Verbe éternel par création comme toutes les choses créées: et elle lui appartient encore par génération, qui est le même titre par lequel lui appartient la divinité.[41]

Substantial Holiness: The Formal Sanctification of the Holiness of Christ

Yelle wrote that in the twentieth century many theologians explained the substantial holiness of Christ in terms of consecration. However, in the

---

[38] *Le mystère.* See 97.
[39] Ibid., 98–99. See *Grandeurs*, 11, no. 4, col. 361.
[40] *Le mystère*, 105.
[41] Ibid., 100–101. See *Grandeurs*, 6, no. 2, col. 259.

seventeenth century, there was an insistence on the formal substantial holiness of Christ. The primary sources for Bérulle's ideas on this point were Suárez and Gamaches. While there were other authors weighing in on this, Bérulle was not familiar with them. Suárez himself held that Christ's humanity was made holy through the grace of union.[42] In contradistinction, Aquinas' treatment of the holiness of Christ supported the reasons why the humanity was made holy by means of habitual grace alone.[43]

Various theologians, including Medina, J. Vincent, Nazario, and Vázquez, also held to this idea. held that habitual grace was not absolutely necessary for Christ to be formally made holy, in line with the thought of the early fathers (that

---

[42] Ibid. See 106n1 and 2. See Francisco Suárez, *De Incarnatione*, disp. 18, sect. 1 (Lyon, 1608), 359: "Je dis que l'humanité du Christ, ou le Christ comme homme, formellement de par la grâce d'union, a été absolument saint et agréable à Dieu." See Francisco Suárez, *Commentaria ac Disputationes in Tertiam Partem D. Thomae*, 7.1. disp. 18, sec. 1, no. 5, in *Opera omnia*, 17 (Paris: Ludovicum Vivès, 1860), 576: "Dico ergo primo, humanitatem Christi, seu Christum ut hominem, formaliter ex vi ipsius gratiæ unionis fuisse absolute et simpliciter sanctum, et Deo gratum." See also no. 3: "Secunda principalis sententia est, non indiguisse Christum gratia aliqua creata, ut esset sanctus, et gratus Deo, etiam secundum humanitatem. Hanc sententiam pauci ex scholasticis Theologis attingunt; videtur autem sumi ex communi sententia Sanctorum, assertentium, per gratiam unionis sanctificari animam et corpus Christi, quos statim referam; ex hoc enim fundamento concludi videtur, propter sanctificationem non fuisse Christo habitualem gratiam necessariam. Et hæc sententia est sine dubio vera." See also Philippe de Gamaches, *Summa theologica* (Paris, 1627), 3.7.

[43] Ibid., 108. See Aquinas, *ST*, 3.7.1, ad 1, 2, and 3, in *Summa theologiae*, 11: 106–7: "Ad primum ergo dicendum quod Christus est verus Deus secundum personam et naturam divinam. Sed quia cum unitate personae remanet distinctio naturarum, ut ex supra dictis patet, anima Christi non est per suam essentiam divina. Unde oportet quod fiat divina per participationem, quae est secundum gratiam.

"Ad secundum dicendum quod Christo, secundum quod est naturalis Filius Dei, debetur hereditas aeterna, quae est ipsa beatitudo increata, per increatum actum cognitionis et amoris Dei, eundem scilicet quo Pater cognoscit et amat seipsum. Cuius actus anima capax non erat, propter differentiam naturae. Unde oportebat quod attingeret ad Deum per actum fruitionis creatum. Qui quidem esse non potest nisi per gratiam.

"Similiter etiam, inquantum est Verbum Dei, habuit facultatem omnia bene operandi operatione divina. Sed quia, praeter operationem divinam, oportet ponere operationem humanam, ut infra patebit; oportuit in eo esse habitualem gratiam, per quam huiusmodi operatio in eo esset perfecta.

"Ad tertium dicendum quod humanitas Christi est instrumentum divinitatis, non quidem sicut instrumentum inanimatum, quod nullo modo agit sed solum agitur: sed tanquam instrumentum animatum anima rationali, quod ita agit quod etiam agitur. Et ideo, ad convenientiam actionis, oportuit eum habere gratiam habitualem."

the grace of union sanctified the body and soul of Christ). Yelle pressed the idea that this concept did not recognize the communication of idioms.[44]

Bérulle's idea of consecration was of a perfection superior to that of the accidental holiness of habitual grace. Bérulle wrote:

> O humanité sacrée,...vous êtes sainte d'une sainteté ...émanée de l'essence et personne divine comme de son acte et de sa forme propre, et je vous considère et adore comme sainte, et non par aucune forme de sainteté adjointe et accidentelle, mais par la divinité même qui vous rend sainte d'une sainteté substantielle, d'une sainteté incréée, d'une sainteté primitive et radicale, d'une sainteté constituant l'ordre et l'état admirable de l'union hypostatique...[45]

Bérulle held the source of the sanctification of the humanity to be both the person of the Word and the divine nature of the Word. He wrote, "...la sainteté de Jésus est la personne du Verbe..."[46] and "C'est la nature et substance de Dieu même, qui est la grâce communiquée personnellement à cette humanité et qui la sanctifie et déifie en lui."[47]

The Accidental Personal Holiness of Christ

Yelle questioned whether Bérulle neglected the notion of accidental holiness, although he acknowledged that Bérulle admitted that the soul of Jesus did have accidental grace, pertinent to his role as head of the Mystical Body and how grace flows from him to the members.[48] Echoing the above quote, Bérulle noted that the humanity of Christ "...est sainte par la divinité même, et non par aucune forme ou sainteté adjointe et accidentelle, et en tant qu'elle est élevée dans le trône même de la divinité par l'union personnelle..."[49]

As already discussed, a key component of the French School of spirituality was its interpretation of the efficacy of the mysteries of Christ and the participation by the faithful in his states, in light of the writings of Aquinas.[50] Yelle, however, was careful to note that the humanity of Jesus as it is united to the

---

[44] Ibid., 108.
[45] *Élévation troisième*, no. 16, cols. 520–21, quoted in *Le mystère*, 109–10.
[46] *OP* 110, col. 1127, quoted in *Le mystère*, 115. See footnote 3.
[47] *Grandeurs*, 7, no. 8, col. 280, quoted in *Le mystère*, 118.
[48] *Le mystère*, 127.
[49] Ibid., 121–22, quoting Bérulle, *Vœu à Dieu*, 629.
[50] Ibid. See 131n1.

divinity is an efficient cause of the life of grace, but only as an instrumental cause dependent on the divinity.[51]

In order to explain the influence of Christ on the Mystical Body, Bérulle compared Christ to the notion of substance: "Comme les accidents et propriétés fluent de la substance et ont leur être et leur dépendence en elle, ainsi les effets de la grâce ont leur racine en vous et leur subsistence en vous, ô humanité déifié!"[52] Yelle wrote that in order to understand the consequences of Bérulle's notion that Christ is our "mystical" subsistence, one must understand its origin and three periods of the development of this ideal. First, for Aquinas the notion of mystical efficacy of the sufferings of the redemption was based on the idea that the head and members form one mystical person. The second period was that of Thomists in the late sixteenth and early seventeenth centuries, including De Vio, Hosius, Victoria, Medina, and Nazario, (all, notably, without attribution) who viewed Christ as a kind of hypostasis with his Mystical Body. The third period saw the authors of spirituality, such as Francis de Sales, Canfield, Bérulle, and others, use this ideal to motivate Christians to obtain union with Christ.[53]

For Bérulle, the humanity of Christ, stripped of its own subsistence, was consecrated and sanctified substantially by the subsistence of the Word, and accidentally by created grace, to become the head of the Mystical Body and the conjoined instrument of the divinity. His adopted sons are called to partake in the accidental sanctity by losing, mystically speaking, their subsistence, so that Christ can become their "mystical" subsistence.[54] Yelle insisted that Bérulle employed mystical hyperbole in this regard, remarking that a univocal interpretation of Bérulle's thought would lead to heresy while an analogical interpretation would not. He held that Bérulle exploited this metaphysical image of abnegation and union with God by arguing the Pauline ideal, as noted, that "yet I live, no longer I, but Christ lives in me" (Galatians 2:20).[55]

Bérulle demanded that we lose our own human self, speaking of an annihilation rather than a loss of subsistence: "Mais notre subsistence…n'est anéantie que quant à l'usage et à la moralité, et en son autorité et non en son

---

[51] Ibid., 131–32.

[52] Ibid., 133. See *Grandeurs*, 2, no. 4.

[53] Ibid., 135. See Mersch, *Le corps mystique du Christ*, vol. 2 part 3, ch. 6 and 9.

[54] Ibid., 136. See footnote 1, referencing the discussion on the difference in terminology between mystics and theologians in Jacques Maritain, *Distinguer pour unir; ou, Les degrés du savoir*, 3rd ed. (Paris: Desclée, de Brouwer et cie, 1932), 658–68; and R. Garrigou-Lagrange, "Le langage des spirituels comparé à celui des théologiens," *Supplément à la Vie spirituelle* 49 (Dec. 1, 1936): 257–76.

[55] Ibid., 136–37.

existence."[56] Yelle saw this not as an ontological annihilation but a spiritual one, a kind of abnegation. He was careful to make the point that Bérulle was not writing about an ontological notion of subsistence but, again, about an analogy in which the notion of the mystical subsistence is realized in the order of an accidental union and operation.[57]

McKay, expanding on Yelle's analysis, reiterated that the Word had, for Bérulle, "property" over the actions of the human nature.[58] McKay pointed to the fact that Bérulle seemed to occasionally "assimilate substance to subsistence" in writing about what he called the "substantial" and "essential" sanctity of Christ. As Bérulle held: "Comme aussi il y une substance, s'il était loisible de parler ainsi, c'est-à-dire il y a une subsistence commune, qui étant en la nature divine, est aussi en la nature humaine et unit ces deux natures en unité de personne."[59]

Bérulle's calling the humanity of Christ substantially holy, was, as McKay noted, central to his theology of grace. McKay also noted that one of the critiques of Bérulle was that the humanity of Christ was presented as being united to the divine essence. He countered with the defense that the subsistence of the divine Word is "si intime à la Divinité, qu'il a identité et est une même chose avec l'essence divine…"[60]

McKay claimed that for Bérulle, the distinction between subsistence and essence or nature disappeared when speaking of God, due to divine simplicity. She held that he was demonstrating that the Word unites the human nature to the essential sanctity of God. Bérulle, speaking to Christ: "Béni soyez-vous à jamais et en votre divnité, et en votre humanité, et en votre subsistence, qui lie pour jamais cette humanité à votre divine essence, et qui rend cette humanité sainte de la plus grande sainteté qui puisse être communiquée à aucune autre créature, c'ést-à-dire la rend sainte par la même sainteté que le Père donne à son Fils, que le Fils et le Père donnent au Saint-Esprit, qui est la sainteté de la divine essence!"[61]

---

[56] *OP* 132, no. 3, col. 1166, quoted in *Le mystère*, 138.
[57] *Le mystère*, 139.
[58] TG, 178. See *Grandeurs*, 2, no. 10, col. 175: "propriété." McKay utilized the Migne edition of the collected works, as well as Dagens' edition of Bérulle's correspondence. McKay noted that Dupuy had provided her with his translation of *Collationes* prior to its publication. She also referenced various unedited pieces published by Dupuy in 1972, as noted in the Works Cited section of this study.
[59] *Grandeurs*, 9, no. 4, col. 328. Also quoted in TG, 197.
[60] *Grandeurs*, *OC*, 9, no. 4, col. 329. Also quoted in TG, 197–98.
[61] *Grandeurs*, 2, no. 14, col. 186. Also quoted in TG, 198–99.

McKay argued that Bérulle understood that the substantial sanctification of Christ is different from the essential holiness of God: "le rend Saint des saints, bien qu'en une autre manière."[62]

Sacerdotal Anointing

McKay also described Bérulle's concept of the anointing of Christ as both a royal and a sacerdotal unction, as discussed. In this, Christ has the role of both mediator of redemption and mediator of religion: "Dieu est en ce petit corps...Dieu a mis la vie, la religion et la rédemption de l'univers."[63]

According to McKay, Bérulle's synthesis of this ideal with Neoplatonic hierarchicalism and exemplarism was original: through Christ as head, God communicates with all beings not only as exemplar, but also as efficient cause.[64] McKay described Christ's continual influence (his term, *influer*, with the root being *influere* in Latin) over the Mystical Body, according to both Bérulle and Scholastics, as a kind of immensity.[65]

Bérulle's Priest: Formal and Substantial Holiness and Character

Arguably, Bérulle's was an attempt to meet Luther's objections both to substantial union with Christ and to the notion of accidental grace. However, it was not simply how life passes from Christ to the Mystical Body that was of concern to Bérulle, but how Christ operates in the priest. The substantial sanctification of Christ, we will argue, was to become the basis for the sanctification of the priest as well, first, by virtue of character, and then by virtue of sacerdotal grace, as this study will detail.

According to Yelle, and important to this study, Bérulle moved from the idea of Jesus as the living image of the Eternal Father to the notion of character and what he called a Greek etymology enforcing a substantial reality, that of an impressed and terminated application of the penetration of the subsistence. Bérulle wrote of the Son, "Il est le caractère de la substance du Père, qui lui donne et communique impressivement sa propre substance. Et il veut être le sceau et le caractère imprimant sa propre essence et subsistence en la nature humaine."[66]

---

[62] TG, 200. See *Grandeurs*, 2, no. 4, col. 163.

[63] Bérulle, *Vie*, 25, col. 483. Also quotes in TG, 202.

[64] TG, 203.

[65] Ibid., 208–11. See *OP* 18, col. 941.

[66] *Grandeurs*, 5, no. 9, col. 238, quoted in *Le mystère*, 89.

To activate this character, in a manner of speaking, Bérulle's priest was to work to maintain a moral union with Christ wherein Christ's mystical subsistence would somehow replace that of the priest.

Conclusion

Yelle's critique that Bérulle did not understand the communication of idioms is supported by Ocáriz, Seco, and Riestra, who pointed out that the hypostatic union changed nothing in Christ's human nature, as Chalcedon insisted that the properties of each nature remained unimpaired. If his human nature had been made holy by the grace of union, then it would have necessarily changed. Christ, in fact, needed habitual grace for his human nature "to be raised to the supernatural order."[67]

It would be an error to interpret all of Bérulle's notions as applied to the spiritual theology of priesthood to the status of categorical systematic statements, as scholars have remarked. That said, in this crucial aspect, Yelle has demonstrated that, in fact, his spiritual theology was not simply an effort at analogous interpretation but was itself based on an erroneous systematic theology.

As the *termination* of the humanity satisfied justice and resulted in a juridical appurtenance, so too, Bérulle's Oratorian's subsistence, as mystically stripped, assumed the subsistence of Christ, leading to the sacerdotal claim to an authority the Reformers rejected, as this study will explore.

Just as the grace of union made Christ holy and a mediator of religion, not just redemption, capable of sacrifice, so, too, the priest, through the grace of union with Christ, was made mediator of redemption and capable of sacrifice, separated from the rest of men, as we will explore. In this, the priest became a mediator in the order of being, rather than in solely the moral order through intercession, the remission of sin, and the conferral of grace.[68]

The next chapter will treat perhaps the greatest and least studied controversy of Calvinism in relation to the priesthood, that of the doctrine of eternal generation. In his response, Bérulle would attempt to anchor his sacerdotal

---

[67] F. Ocáriz, L. F. Mateo Seco, and J. A. Riestra, *The Mystery of Jesus Christ*, corrected reprint (Gateshead, England: Athenaeum Press Ltd., 2008), 178–79.

[68] John A. Hardon, *The Catholic Catechism* (Garden City, NY: Doubleday, 1975), 165–67. See discussion on the mediation of Christ as compared to others. Mediation in the order of being is incommunicable and reserved to Christ.

Christosyncretism described in this chapter to a Trinitarian exemplarism based on emanationism, clearly extant in tradition and rejected by Reformers.

Chapter 7
Eternal Generation and Emanationism

Introduction

The question of how we are saved, so central to the Reformation, was in direct response to the Church's claim to the necessity of priests and the hierarchy as agents in the divine plan of salvation, which included a centuries-old strain in tradition emphasizing a mediation based on natural causation and emanationism. As a prelude to exploring aspects of Bérulle's doctrine related to this theme, this chapter will explore Calvin's and his followers' rejection of eternal generation and a necessary emanationism used to legitimate the power, authority, and saving agency of the hierarchy and priesthood.

Background

Call to Ministry, Authority, Trinitarian Processions

The divine call to ministry was at the center of the Reformation debates.[1] Protestants objected to the ideal of a presbyteral priesthood, claiming that it was of pagan origin and an affront to the priesthood of Christ.[2] Bérulle responded with a defense of the hierarchy and the role of the priest based on the idea of mission, with the assertion that authority is based on the Trinitarian processions.[3]

A particularly close identification between the priest and the Trinitarian processions was Bérulle's concerted defense against the Calvinist rejection of apostolic succession and hierarchical authority as based on an emanationism that denied the power of the God-Man as savior in time.

---

[1]   Dupuy, *Le Christ de Bérulle*, 167.
[2]   P. Idiart, "Prêtre païen et prêtre chrétien," in *Études sur le sacrement de l'ordre* (Paris: Éditions du Cerf, 1957), 325.
[3]   *BLS*, 66–68.

The Eternal Generation Controversy

Questioning of the Nicene formulation of eternal generation occurred at the time of the Reformation.[4] The following review will focus on Calvin's and Calvinist notions surrounding eternal generation as reflected in their spiritualities, anthropologies, and ecclesiologies.

The *Dictionnaire de théologie catholique*'s treatment of the Trinity and the Protestant crisis, in the section entitled "The Protestant Crisis and Its Repercussions in Catholic Theology," notes that the first Reformers did not attack the dogma of the Trinity. In an extensive discussion of Calvin's Trinitarian doctrine, no mention was made of his treatment of eternal generation.[5] Neither was it mentioned in Margarie's exposition of eternal generation in *The Christian Trinity in History*.[6] Farrelly also wrote, "Calvin was so faithful to the Christian trinitarian belief that he approved of the execution of Servetus (1553) as a heretic because he denied the Trinity."[7]

Warfield noted that Calvin and other Reformers have sometimes been represented as merely following tradition on the Trinity, which was not a matter of dispute with Rome.[8] Warfield, rather, insisted on the importance of Calvin's innovations, citing Bauer as seeing Calvin at the beginning of "a radical transformation of the doctrine of the Trinity."[9]

Calvin's Writings

A short review follows with key quotes taken from Calvin's Chapter Thirteen of the *Institutes*, which treats the Trinity. Fundamental and antecedent to considerations of the Trinity was the foundational idea for Calvin of Christ's role in the economy of salvation (which he specifically addressed in this chapter):

---

[4]   Robert L. Reymond, *'What Is God'? An Investigation of the Perfections of God's Nature* (Ross-shire, UK: Christian Focus Publications Ltd., 2007), 307–9.

[5]   A. Michel, "Trinité: La crise protestante," in *DTC*, vol. 15, pt. 2 (1950), cols. 1766–68.

[6]   Bertrand de Margerie, *The Christian Trinity in History*, Studies in Historical Theology, vol. 1, trans. Edmund J. Fortman (Still River, MA: St. Bede's Publications, 1982).

[7]   M. John Farrelly, *The Trinity: Rediscovering the Central Christian Mystery* (Rowman & Littlefield Publishers. Inc., 2005), 110.

[8]   Benjamin Breckenridge Warfield, *Calvin and Calvinism* (Grand Rapids, MI: Baker Book House, 1931; reprint, 1981), 192.

[9]   Ibid., 194. See Ferdinand Christian Bauer, *Die christliche Lehre von der Dreieinigkeit und Menschwerdung Gottes in ihrer geschichtlichen Entwicklung*, vol. 3 (Tübingen: C. F. Oslander, 1843), 42–43. Warfield quoted Bauer, who opined that when Calvin writes on the Trinity, he "inclines to a mode of apprehending it in which the ecclesiastical *homoousia* is transmuted into a rational relation of subordination."

"Out of the eternal God there is no salvation, no righteousness, no life. All these are in Christ. Christ, consequently, is eternal God."[10] As Haroutunian noted, "The main point of Calvin's insistence on the deity of Christ was that he was the agent of our salvation...."[11]

Key to Calvin's position on eternal generation was his defense of the Trinity of persons developed, in part, in his arguments against Servetus, an anti-Trinitarian. Calvin wrote the following (which Beveridge footnoted as being a heresy held by Gilbert, bishop of Poitiers):

> Whosoever says that the Son was essentiated by the Father, denies his self-existence. Against this, however, the Holy Spirit protests, when he calls him Jehovah. On this supposition, then, that the whole essence is in the Father only, the essence becomes divisible, or is denied to the Son, who, being thus robbed of his essence, will be only a titular God. If we are to believe these triflers, divine essence belongs to the Father only, on the ground that he is sole God, and essentiator of the Son. In this way, the divinity of the Son will be something abstracted from the essence of God, or the derivation of a part from the whole. On the same principle it must also be conceded, that the Spirit belongs to the Father only. For if the derivation is from the primary essence which is proper to none but the Father, the Spirit cannot justly be deemed the Spirit of the Son. This view, however, is refuted by the testimony of Paul, when he makes the Spirit common both to Christ and the Father. Moreover, if the person of the Father is expunged from the Trinity, in what will he differ from the Son and Spirit, except in being the only God? They confess that Christ is God, and that he differs from the Father. If he differs, there must be some mark of distinction between them. Those who place it in the essence, manifestly reduce the true divinity of Christ to nothing, since divinity cannot exist without essence, and indeed without entire essence.[12]

---

[10] "The Unity of the Divine Essence in Three Persons Taught, in the Scriptures, from the Foundation of the World," in *Institutes*, 1.13.13. *Institution*: "Outreplus, si hors de Dieu il n'y a nul salut, nulle iustice, nulle vie, certes en contenant toutes ces choses en soy il est démonstré estre Dieu."

[11] J. Haroutunian, "Introduction," in John Calvin, Joseph Haroutunian, and Louis Pettibone Smith, *Commentaries* (Philadelphia, PA: Westminster Press, 1958), 46, quoted in Jones, "Toward a Christology of Christ the High Priest," 214.

[12] *Institutes*, 83, 1.13.23. See footnote 3, referencing Bernard, *In Cantica Canticorum, serm.* 80, on the heresy of Gilbert of Poitiers. *Institution*: "Car quiconque dit que le Fils soit essencié du Père (puisque tells abuseurs forgent des noms contre nature), il nié qu'il ait estre propre de soy. Esprit contredit à tels blasphemes, le nommant Iehova, qui vaut autant

Lastly, Calvin rebutted Lombard regarding eternal generation: "For instance, what avails it to discuss, as Lombard does at length (lib. 1 dist. 9), whether or not the Father always generates? This idea of continual generation becomes an absurd fiction from the moment it is seen, that from eternity there were three persons in one God."[13]

Bray wrote that Calvin refused to give primacy to the divine essence, as he noted had been done in the Middle Ages by attempts to define God in philosophical terms. Calvin believed that rejecting Trinitarian relations as mere results of natural causation, and focusing on the persons and their voluntary relationships, would restore devotionalism.[14]

Bérulle, himself, would define God in philosophical terms, emphasizing the divine essence, also focusing on an exemplarism based on the ideas of person, Trinitarian relation, and causation. These would form the basis of his spiritual theology of priesthood, including his formulations of sacerdotal character, grace, and piety, as we will explore.

à dire comme celuy qui est de soy et de sa proper vertu. Or si nous accordons que toute essence soit au seul Père, ou elle sera divisible, ou elle sera du tout ostée au Fils: et par ce moyen estant despouillé de son essence, il sera seulement un Dieu titulaire. Si on veut croire ces bavars, l'essence de Dieu ne conviendra qu'au Père seul, d'autant que luy seul a estre, et qu'il est essentiateur de son Fils; par aussi l'essence du Fils ne seroit qu'un extrait ie ne say quell, tire comme par un alembic de l'essence de Dieu, ou bien une partie découlante du total. Davantage, ils sont constraints par leur principe de confesser que l'Esprit est du Père; car si c'est un risseau découlant de la première essence, laquelle selon eux n'est propre qu'au Père, il ne pourra estre tenu ne réputé Esprit du Fils, ce qui est toutefois rembarré par le tesmoignage de sainct Paul, quand il le fait commun tant au Fils qu'au Père. Outreplus, si on efface de la Trinité la personne du Père, en quoi sera-il discerné du Fils et de l'Esprit, sinon entant qu'il sera seul Dieu? Ces phantastiques confessant que Christ est Dieu, et néantmoins qu'il diffère d'avec le Père. Or icy il faut avoir quelque marque de discretion, en sorte que le Père ne soit point le Fils. Ceux-cy la mettant en l'essence anéantissent notoirement la vraye déité de Iesus Christ, laquelle ne peut estre sans l'essence, voire toute entière."

13 Ibid., 88, 13.29. *Institution*: "Car de quoy servira-il de disputer si le Père engendre tousiours, veu que quand ce poinct est conclud qu'il y a eu de toute éternité trois personnes résidentes en Dieu, cest acte continuel d'engendrer n'est qu'une fantasie superflue et frivole."

14 Roger Beckwith, "The Calvinist Doctrine of the Trinity," *Churchman* 115, no. 4 (2001): 309. See G. L. Bray, *The Doctrine of God* (Leicester: Inter Varsity Press, 1993), 197–294.

Christ as Autotheos

Reymond wrote that Calvin had to choose between Nicene's "very God of very God" and *autotheos* [God in and of himself].[15] One aspect of the Nicene-Constantinopolitan fathers' doctrine of the Trinity which sixteenth- and seventeenth-century Reformers questioned was the term "begotten out of the Father." Reymond wrote about some of the fathers, without attribution:

> They show no apparent awareness that such teaching by implication *denies to the Son and the Spirit the attribute of self-existence* that is necessarily theirs as divine Persons of both the tri-personal Yahweh of the Old Testament and the triune God of the New Testament, and without which they could not be *theotic* at all inasmuch as self-existence is an absolutely essential attribute of the three persons.[16]

Reymond wrote that these fathers' language suggested subordination both in modes of operation and in essence in that the Son is not God *a se* but only out of [*eke*] the Father by a continuous generation. He cited Macleod as deeming this tritheism.[17] Calvin saw the Father as the beginning of deity but only in respect to order.[18] As Reymond wrote about Calvin, "he endorsed the doctrine of the Father's eternal generation of the Son, not with respect to his essence as deity, but

---

[15] Reymond, *'What Is God?'*, 86.

[16] Ibid., 308.

[17] Ibid., 309. See Donald Macleod, *Behold Your God* (Ross-shire, UK: Christian Focus Publications, 1991), 201.

[18] Calvin, *Institution*, 1.13.24: "Ce qu'ils prennent pour une maxime est faux, assavoir que toutes fois et quants que le nom de Dieu se trouve sans queue (comme l'on dit), il se rapporte au Père seul. Mesmes aux passages qu'ils amènent ils descouvrent trop lourdement leur ignorance, pource que là le nom du Fils est mis à l'opposite; dont il appert qu'il y a comparaison de l'un à l'autre, et que pour ceste cause le nom de Dieu est particulièrement donné au Père. Ils répliquent: Si le Père n'estoit seul vray Dieu, il seroit son Père à ce conte. Ie respon qu'il n'y a nul inconvénient, à cause du degré et ordre que nous avons dit, que le Père soit nommé Dieu spécialement, pource que non seulement il a engendré de soy sa sagesse, mai aussi est Dieu de Iesus Christ, selon qu'il est médiateur; de quoy il sera ailleurs traité plus au long." Also quoted in Reymond, *'What Is God?'*, 310.

See also 1.13.26: "Quant à ce qu'ils obiectent, que si Christ est vrayement Dieu il seroit mal nommé Fils de Dieu, désia i'ay respondu, puisque lors il se fait comparaison d'une personne à l'autre, que le nom de Dieu n'est point pris absolument, mais qu'il est spécifié du Père entant qu'il est le commencement de déité, non pas en donnant essence a son Fils et à son Esprit, comme ces phantastiques babillent, mais au regard de l'ordre que nous avons déclairé."

with respect to his Sonship that he derives from the eternally 'generated' relationship in which he stands to the Father."[19]

Many of Calvin's successors argued that the three persons were united (as in the Cappadocian *perichoresis*) only at the level of person, not of essence.[20] Reymond quoted Warfield: "The principle of [Calvin's] doctrine of the Trinity was…the force of his conviction of the absolute equality of the Persons."[21]

Butin wrote about Calvin's "tendency toward a 'perichoretic' model of hypostatic relations," noting that Calvin's "emphatic and consistent articulation of the constant interpenetration of the trinitarian *hypostaseis* in the external, economic work of God, however, was of far more significance for the history of the doctrine of the Trinity."[22] Butin asserted that this was Calvin's attempt to recover patristic insights into the economic Trinity and its "enablement of human response…"[23] According to Butin, Calvin reflected an Augustinian emphasis on the strict equality of the *hypostaseis*.[24]

As Warfield wrote, these ideas of Calvin created a party that was to become the Reformed churches, which held the aseity of Christ; a stress on the equality of the persons; and a rejection of subordinationism in regard to the relations of the persons.[25]

Murray noted that students of historical theology are aware of "the furore which Calvin's insistence upon the self-existence of the Son as to his deity aroused at the time of the Reformation."[26] Meier, writing on the controversy, noted that Bellarmine acknowledged that Calvin did not depart from doctrine in his conception of the *autotheotes* of the Son."[27] Bellarmine, rather, faulted Calvin

---

[19]   Reymond, '*What Is God?*', 310. See *Institution*, 1.13.25: "Et voilà pourquoy nous confessons que le Fils, entant qu'il est Dieu, sans avoir esgard à la personne a son estre de soy-mesme; entant qu'il est Fils, nous disons qu'il est du Père; par ce moyen son essence est sans commencement, et le commencement de sa personne est Dieu."

[20]   Ibid., 311. See also Bray, *The Doctrine of God*, 202.

[21]   Warfield, *Calvin and Calvinism*, 257–58, quoted in Reymond, '*What Is God?*', 314.

[22]   Philip Walker Butin, *Revelation, Redemption and Response: Calvin's Trinitarian Understanding of the Divine-Human Relationship* (New York and Oxford: Oxford University Press, 1995), 130–31.

[23]   Ibid., 125.

[24]   Ibid., 44.

[25]   Warfield, *Calvin and Calvinism*, 251.

[26]   John Murray, "Systematic Theology," in *Collected Writings of John Murray* (Edinburgh: Banner of Truth, 1982), 4: 8, cited in Reymond, '*What Is God?*', 320.

[27]   Georg August Meier, *Die Lehre von der Trinität in ihrer historischen Entwickelung* (Hamburg: F. und A. Perthes, 1844), ii, 58–59, cited in Warfield, *Calvin and Calvinism*, 230–31. See Robert Bellarmine, *Opera omnia*, vol. 2 (Paris: Ludovicum Vives, 1870), 334: "Calvinum existimo quoad modum loquendi sine dubio errasse, et dedisse occasionem, ut de illo scriberentur, quae scripta sunt a nostris….Sed quamquam haec ita se habeant:

for the reasons he called the Son *autotheos*. Bellarmine argued that Calvin relied on Augustine, who wrote that Our Lord "is called Son, with reference to the Father (*ad patrem*) and God with reference to Himself (*ad seipsum*)." Bellarmine continued, "But, it is not the same thing to say that the Son is God *ad se*, and that he is God *a se*."[28] Pétau agreed. Warfield, however, maintained Calvin made no such error in confusing terms but that it was doubtful whether Calvin believed that begetting involved any communication of essence, since it is the person of the Father who begets and it is the person of the Son who is begotten, not the essence common to the Trinity.[29] Warfield maintained there remained much unclear as to Calvin's exact beliefs, as his assertions were inconsistent.[30]

Warfield wrote that Pétau, however, took Calvin to mean that the Son "has his essence not from the Father but from Himself…"[31] Pétau insisted that Calvin rejected the doctrine and that his ideas were heretical. Pétau wrote that everyone "has his essence from him by whom he is begotten; since generation is just the communication of the nature,—whether, as in created things, in kind, or, as in the divine production of the Word, in number. It is indeed impossible to form any conception of generation without the nature, and some communication of the essence, occurring to the mind."[32]

---

tamen dum rem ipsam excutio, et Calvini sententias diligenter considero, non facile audeo pronunciare, illum in hoc errore fuisse. Siquidem docet, Filium esse a se respectu essentiae, non respectu personae, et videtur dicere velle, personam esse genitam Patre, essentiam non esse genitam, sed esse a se ipsa, ita ut si a persona Filii removeas relationem ad Patrem, sola restet essentia, quae est a se ipsa."

[28] Warfield, *Calvin and Calvinism*, 280. See Aurelius Augustinus and Johann Kreuzer, *De Trinitate (Bücher VIII–XI, XIV–XV, Anhang Buch V)* (Hamburg: Felix Meiner Verlag, 2001), 372, 5.6.7: "Si autem huic sic putant resistendum esse sermoni qua pater quidem ad filium dicitur et filius ad patrem, ingenitus tamen et genitus ad se ipsos dicuntur non ad alterutrum; non enim hoc est dicere ingenitum quod est patrem dicere quia et si filium non genuisset nihil prohiberet dicere eum ingenitum, et si gignat quisque filium non ex eo ipse est ingenitus quia geniti homines ex aliis hominibus gignunt et ipsi alios – inquiunt ergo."

[29] Ibid., 257–58 and 281–82.

[30] Ibid., 260.

[31] Ibid., 256.

[32] Denis Pétau, "De Trinitate," 11, 5, quoted in Warfield, *Calvin and Calvinism*, 256. In Latin, *Dogmata theologica Dionysii Petavii e Societate Jesu*, 3 (Paris: Ludovicum Vivès, 1865), 252a: "Siquidem ab eo habet essentiam, a quo est genitus; quoniam generatio ejusdem est naturae communicatio, vel specie, ut in creatis rebus fit, vel numero, ut in divina Verbi productione. Neque enim vel cogitando concipi potest generatio, quin natura, et essentiae communicatio quaedam occurrat animo."

Warfield noted that a number of "Romanists" were opposed to Calvin's notions, believing they seemed like Sabellianism or tritheism.[33]

Calvin's Eternal Generation

Both aspects of the doctrine of eternal generation, eternality and generation, were issues of importance at the time of the Reformation.[34] For example, according to Reymond, Calvin's core issue with the eternal aspect of generation was that of an erroneous conception of eternity as timelessness. He asserted that Calvin held God's eternality to be everlastingness. If Christ is a timeless deity in regard to humanity and his plan for us, then we are still in our sins, because if God has only knowledge, as opposed to foreknowledge, then, perhaps, for God, Christ somehow has not yet come.[35] Reymond declared the Calvinist view of predestination means that God's decree governs all destinies and makes the Son "the Christian's sovereign king."[36]

Warfield clarified that Calvin's rejection of this aspect of eternal generation referred to the notion of "ceaseless" generation, referencing Sheldon who wrote: "Like Origen, the Nicene fathers seem to have conceived of the generation, not as something accomplished once for all, but as something parallel with the eternal life of the Son, ever complete and ever continued."[37]

Calvin's attempt to develop this doctrine has been the subject of debate. For example, Warfield noted that Bauer held that "…the new construction of the Trinity already foreshadowed in Calvin was to revolve around Christ; but around Christ as God-Man conceived as the mediating principle between God and man…"[38] Disagreeing with this, Warfield rather believed that the doctrine of the Trinity for Calvin was "a postulate of his profoundest religious emotions; was given, indeed, in his experience of salvation itself."[39]

---

[33] Warfield, *Calvin and Calvinism*, 260–61. See also 253n93 referencing Gisbert Voet, *Selectae disputationes theologiae*, 1 (n.p., 1648), 453–54.

[34] Jung Suck Rhee, "A History of the Doctrine of Eternal Generation of the Son and Its Significance in the Trinitarianism" (master's thesis, Calvin Theological Seminary, 1989), 2.

[35] Reymond, *'What Is God?'*, 87.

[36] Ibid., 165.

[37] Henry C. Sheldon, *History of Christian Doctrine*, 2nd ed. (New York: Harper & Bros., 1886), i, 202, quoted in Warfield, *Calvin and Calvinism*, 247n85.

[38] Warfield, *Calvin and Calvinism*, 194–95. See Bauer, *Die christliche Lehre*, 44–45.

[39] Ibid., 195.

While the Scholastic emphasis was on Christ's humanity in this role of mediator as God and man,[40] for Calvin, the divinity of Christ was important to an understanding of how Christ saves. Christ is mediator according to both natures: "We know that he is God, manifested in the flesh, but his heavenly power is also to be thought upon in his Person as a minister, in his human nature."[41]

Christ's Mediatorship as Priest, Prophet, and King

Importantly, the mission and mediatorship of Christ as *autotheos*, for Calvin, found expression in his offices as priest, prophet, and king.

Although not original to Calvin, his ideas regarding the threefold office were taken up by the convert Cardinal John Henry Newman, who was to greatly influence *Lumen Gentium*.[42]

Conclusion

Calvin's concerns centered on the importance of Christ as the divine agent of salvation, mediating through both natures, as God-Man and savior, in personal relation with each believer.

Calvin, well familiar with the tradition emphasizing emanationism, sought an egalitarian Trinity and an *autotheotic* Christ to support his architectonic of a depraved humanity redeemed via predestination and the salvific mission and office of the divine man. Key to this project were the rejection of an eternally-generative God outside time, as well as a rejection of a necessary and continual Neoplatonic subordinationism. This Neoplatonism was fueled in the Tridentine

---

40 See Aquinas, *ST*, 3.26.2, s.c., in *Summa theologiae*, 11: 286: "Sed contra est quod Augustinus dicit, in lib. IX, *de Civ. Dei*: *Non ob hoc est mediator Christus, quia est Verbum. Maxime quippe immortale et maxime beatum Verbum longe a mortalibus miseris. Sed mediator est secundum quod homo.*"

41 Calvin on Matt. 3:16, in John Calvin, *Commentary on a Harmony of the Evangelists, Matthew, Mark, and Luke* (n.p., n.d.), quoted in Butin, *Revelation, Redemption and Response*, 65–66. In Latin, John Calvin, *Harmonia ex Euangelistis tribus composita, Matthaeo, Marco, & Luca* (Geneva: Apud Eustathium Vignon, 1582), 56: "Scimus quidem ipsum esse Deum manifestatum in carne, sed in persona quoque ministri et humana eius natura coelestis virtus consideranda est."

42 Jones, "Toward a Christology of Christ the High Priest," 17. See Calvin, *Institution*, 2.15.1: "Parquoy, afin que la foy trouve en Iesus Christ ferme matière de salut pour se reposer seurement, il nous convient arrester à ce principe: c'est que l'office et charge qui luy a esté donnée du Père quand il est venu au monde consiste en trois parties. Car il a esté donné pour Prophète, Roy et Sacrificateur."

world by the popularity of Pseudo-Dionysian ideals regarding the identity of God as monad and the hierarchy of the spiritual ascent of the soul, as well as the necessary role of clerics in that ascension, whose rule on the basis of a natural and necessary causation the Reformers sought to abolish. Calvinist divine generativity, if extended in the mission and offices of Christ, resided also at the level of the person of Christ. This generativity is effectively a byproduct of divine will and personal faith, both outside the control of "Romanist" philosophers and the Church hierarchy.

In turn, a voluntarism is seen in Calvin and the Reformed churches that followed, as salvation is restricted to only the few willed by God to be saved.

The following analysis will detail what could be seen as Bérulle's response, which paralleled a number of Calvinist ideals come to be reflected in his spiritual theology of priesthood itself.

Chapter 8
Bérulle's Trinitarian Mechanics

Introduction

This chapter will treat the Trinitarian aspects of Bérulle's Christocentrism, including exemplarism, emanationism, mission, and the role of the divine persons in the life of the priest. Perhaps of greatest consequence for Bérulle's sacerdotal spiritual theology was his interpretation of the doctrine of eternal generation as the basis of the mission and authority of the priesthood. This analysis will explore key influences, his movement from emanation to mission to sacerdotal anointing, and his view of how the persons of the Trinity operate, somehow, in relation to the priest.

Emanationism

While Luther had called Christ the "mathematical point" of the scriptures,[1] Bérulle called Christ "the sun:" "Jésus est le vrai centre du monde et le monde doit être en un mouvement continuel vers lui. Jésus est le soleil de nos âmes duquel elles reçoivent toutes les grâces, les lumières et les influences."[2]

This rhetoric would have an echo in how Bérulle saw the persons of the Trinity operating in relation to the priest and, particularly, in how the priest participated in Christ's priesthood.

Trinity and Mission

Rétif explored the themes of Trinity and mission in Bérulle's thought. Ten years after his ordination, a text containing many of the details of Bérulle's thoughts on the priesthood appeared in 1609. It came to be known as the *Discours de controverse*.

---

[1] Klaas Zwanepol, "A Human God: Some Remarks on Luther's Christology," *Concordia Journal* 30, nos. 1–2 (Jan.–Apr. 2004): 49. See Martin Luther, *Tischreden: (1531–1546)*, vol. 2 (Weimar: Hermann Böhlau, 1912), 439.25–26: "Christus est punctus mathematicus sacrae scripturae."

[2] *Grandeurs*, in *OC*, vol. 7 (1996), Discours 2, 85.

Bérulle, having been involved for almost a decade with the Protestant controversies, wrote three discourses: one on the mission of pastors, the others on the sacrifice of the Mass and the real presence of Jesus Christ in the Eucharist. The first discourse was entitled "De la mission des pasteurs en l'Église." In it, Bérulle treated the link between the divine processions and the temporal missions of the Son and Spirit, and that between the temporal missions and the mission of the Church.[3]

Bérulle elaborated on the theology of mission based on the Trinity. His argument was as follows: only God (the Father) can send without being sent. On what basis do the Reformers claim to send without having themselves been sent? Bérulle cited Augustine (erroneously) as holding that mission and procession were synonymous. Bérulle explained his thoughts on the link between procession and mission:

(Dieu) veut que la mission tienne entre les hommes le même rang que la procession aux personnes divines, esquelles, selon saint Augustin, ces deux termes de mission et de procession disent une même chose. Tellement que comme après le Père de lumière, duquel descend et procède toute lumière créée et incréée, selon l'apôtre, il n'y a aucune personne subsistante en la très sainte Trinité, que par la voie de la procession; aussi n'y a-t-il aucune fonction divine et subsistante en l'Église de Dieu pour le salut des hommes, que par la mission...[4]

The Priest in Society with the Trinity

Cochois wrote that for Bérulle, God is the model and end for all creatures, in a kind of "Trinitarian exemplarism."[5]

Returning to Cognet's critique, he further explained that Bérulle's exemplarism was based on a concept of Trinitarian relation which served as an ontological schema repeating itself analogically.[6]

As described in the following passage, Bérulle considered the priesthood as the greatest state and power in the Church, an exemplar of Trinitarian interior unity and external society. Tied to both God and the world, the priests lives his life in society with the Trinity. Bérulle described the priest's association with the

---

[3]   André Rétif, "Trinité et Mission d'après Bérulle," *Neue Zeitschrift für Missionswissenschaft* 13 (1957): 1–2.

[4]   *Discours de controverse*, OC, Migne ed., 673, quoted in Rétif, "Trinité et Mission d'après Bérulle," 3.

[5]   Cochois, *Bérulle et l'école française*, 85.

[6]   Cognet, *La spiritualité moderne*, 333.

persons of the Trinity, offering the Son to the Father. The virtue of the Spirit is communicated to him to do this such that he enters into the person of Christ, doing the great work of the Eucharist, which brings him into a new relation with the Father, Son, and Spirit, as well as with the sacred humanity. Bérulle:

> La vie ecclésiastique par ses propres conditions intérieures et par ses fonctions extérieures nous lie à Dieu et au monde. C'est une vie de société avec le Père éternel, avec son Fils unique, avec leur Saint Esprit, et avec l'Église que le Fils de Dieu a fondée, que le Saint-Esprit régit en la terre, que le Père éternel possède au ciel: "Quand il lui aura tout soumis" (1 Cor. XV, 28), c'est-à-dire au Père. "Soyons en communion (société) avec le Père et son Fils Jésus-Christ" (I Jean, I, 3).
>
> Que de dispositions sont requises en la vie ecclésiastique au regard de tous ces sujets-là! Que de vertus doivent être acquises et pratiquées!
>
> L'association aux Personnes divines est admirable. Nous offrons le Fils au Père par la vertu du Saint-Esprit. Nous entrons en la Personne de Jésus-Christ, et, in Persona Christi, nous faisons ce grand œuvre de l'Eucharistie…nous offrons cette grande, unique, éternelle hostie de louange, et nous l'offrons pour tout le monde. La vertu du Saint Esprit nous est communiquée pour faire cette opération et oblation. Nous recevons ce que nous avons offert; et en cette eucharistie nous avons une liaison nouvelle au Père, au Fils, au Saint Esprit et à l'humanité sacrée de Jésus; et nous avons liaison comme opérant vers eux et par eux un si grand œuvre. Quelle abstraction, quelle élévation, quelle appropriation à Dieu requiert une si grande opération et un si saint ministère![7]

The Ideal of the Archetype

Dupuy summarized that in the mission of the priest, Bérulle looked to the notion of archetype in light of the mystery of the Trinity and the divine processions. In defending the hierarchy and the role of the priest, he concentrated on the scriptural ideal that as the Father sent Christ, so Christ sends priests. The prolongation of the mission of Christ in the priest's mission, for Bérulle, was the restoration of the link between man and God known as "religion." The priest was the necessary instrument of the return of all things to God. True faith, in this schema, which was current at the time, lay in believing not by reason of evidence (a Scotist, and in some cases, Reformist position) but by reason of the legitimate authority found in the priest, who himself was under obedience, as was Christ.[8]

[7]   *BLS, OR* 13, nos. 4 to 5, 284–85. See also no. 3.
[8]   Ibid., 66–68, paraphrased.

Emanationist Spirituality

Cochois clarified how Bérulle's spirituality of the mysteries was emanationist in that Bérulle transposed, according to Cochois, the notion of God's "rayon théarchique" emanating the divine perfections to that of Christ's deified humanity continually deifying a new creation, imprinting perfections according to the various mysteries of his life.[9] The hypostatic union became the origin of all emanations of grace, according to Bérulle: "(état de l'union hypostatique), qui est la source et l'origine de toutes les opérations saintes, de toutes les émanations de grâces…"[10] Howells wrote that this was not a Neoplatonic emanation as by stages, but an emanation from the unity of the humanity and the divinity.[11] So, Christ engenders Christians, contains them, and is their world. Bérulle:

> En ces deux émanations nous recevons un être et un être différent; nous sommes établis en deux mondes et deux mondes aussi différents. En l'un nous recevons l'être de la nature, en l'autre, nous recevons l'être de la grâce. En l'un nous entrons en ce monde que nous voyons; en l'autre nous entrons en un monde que nous adorons. Là ce Jésus qui est notre père et principe nous engendre et produit, nous forme et établit en lui-même. Tellement que, comme il est notre principe, il est notre univers encore; il est notre monde et nous vivons en lui. Nous sommes créés et établis en lui, ce dit l'Apôtre: "Créés en Jésus-Christ." II est notre univers et notre monde, et le monde des grâces et faveurs de la Divinité, comme le premier monde est le lieu qui enclot et contient les créatures de la Divinité. Jésus donc est un monde, et est notre monde.[12]

Oratorian Mission and Emanation

The Oratorians and the Carmelites had as their purpose the prolongation of the mission that Jesus received from the Father, which was the glory of God in the

---

9   Paul Cochois, "Bérulle et le pseudo-Denys," *Revue de l'histoire des religions* 159, no. 2 (1961): 191–92.

10   TG, 175. See *Grandeurs*, in *OC*, Migne ed., 2, no. 3, col. 163.

11   Edward Howells, "Relationality and Difference in the Mysticism of Pierre de Bérulle," *Harvard Theological Review* (April 1, 2009): 241. See *État*, 63.

12   Pierre Bérulle, *Œuvres de piété (166–385)*, ed. Michael Dupuy, *OC*, vol. 4 (Paris, 1996), OP 209, 101. See also Jean-Michel Le Lannou, "Le 'sacrifice du moi' selon Bérulle," *Revue des sciences religieuses* 78, no. 2 (2004): 223, hereafter SM.

salvation of souls.[13] Cadoux wrote, "Pour Bérulle la mission des prêtres est à l'image de la mission temporelle du Fils qui puise elle-même son modèle dans la génération éternelle du Verbe."[14] Bérulle linked generation and the office of priesthood in his emanationist ideals in a conference to Oratorians: "Il [Christ] est la première émanation du Père et l'unique en qualité de géneration. Le sacerdoce adjoint à la filiation et émané d'icelle, et peut-être le premier de ses offices…"[15]

Preckler pointed to a passage revealing Bérulle's thought on the theme of continual creation and reminiscent of Eckhart and the Rheno-Flemish theme of participation in the eternal generation of the Word. Bérulle:

> Chercher toutes les voies de se lier à Dieu, croître tous les jours en liaison et union avec lui: faire journellement une prière particulière à N. Seigneur, qu'il se daigne glorifier en nous par notre même être et qu'il daigne honorer en nous sa génération éternelle par la génération de notre être qui n'est autre chose qu'une continuelle production, ce que nous devons d'autant plus désirer que cette production continue de notre être est pour rendre hommage par état à cette émanation qui est source de toute autre émanation en Dieu et hors de Dieu.[16]

According to Rétif, Bérulle's doctrine of temporal mission and eternal procession had one principle or movement with a double effect: the rapport between the two was not simply one of origin but of similitude and exemplarity. There were three moments in the history of salvation for Bérulle: the generation of the Word, the Incarnation of the Son, and the mission of the Church. He considered the mission of the Word Incarnate as the origin of the sanctification of all other missions. Bérulle's priest was to achieve the full circle of love begun in the eternal processions, continued in the mission of Christ and the Church and, at last, returning humanity to the Father. The missionary priest was to be a link in the chain and must be intimately united to God, detached and pure, placing himself in the *courant trinitaire*, as Rétif called it. Bérulle: "Il nous faut donc présentement adorer Dieu envoyant son fils au monde, car cette mission est

---

[13] Virgile Blanchard, "La spiritualité christocentrique de Pierre de Bérulle dans les écrits des premières années de l'Oratoire de France, 1611–1615," (PhD diss., Université d'Ottawa, 1978), 244.

[14] Richard Cadoux, "Le Sacrement de l'Incarnation: l'exemplarisme dans *Les grandeurs de Jésus* du cardinal Pierre de Bérulle" (master's thesis, Université Catholique de Lyons, 1993), 12.

[15] *BLS, OR* 7, 278.

[16] Bérulle, Archives nationales, carton M. 233, quoted in *État*, 143n173.

origine de sanctification pour toutes les autres missions, et sans le grand mystère de l'Incarnation par lequel le Père envoie son fils, il n'y a rien qui puisse être agréable à Dieu, tout ètant de nous ou du diable: c'est de cette grande mission qu'il nous faut occuper, et non point de l'áutre."[17]

From Mission to Sacerdotal Anointing

Reviewing more closely Yelle's analysis, Bérulle passed from generation to mission and then from mission to anointing because he saw the temporal generation of the Son as an extension of the eternal generation of the Word. Bérulle:

> C'est une expression des grandeurs de Jésus en deux choses, en sa génération éternelle et en sa mission temporelle: *Tu es Christus Messias.* C'est la pierre angulaire, c'est l'expression de la filiation divine communiquée à l'homme ENVOYÉ et OINT sur son peuple: car si le Messie est le Fils de Dieu vivant, ce ne peut être que par l'ineffable communication de la subsistence de ce Fils à la nature humaine.[18]

Bérulle also wrote:

> …et le Père ne l'envoie pour s'incarner que par le même pouvoir par lequel il l'engendre soi-même: tellement que le principe de sa génération éternelle est le principe de sa mission…, aussi cette mission…comprend et emporte avec soi la génération ineffable de ce même Verbe éternel, à laquelle cette humble naissance se trouve heureusement liée et conjointe par le moyen de cette mission, comme par un lien commun qui tient à l'émanation éternelle, comme à son origine, et à l'émancipation temporelle comme à son effet…et conjoint en un même Fils de Dieu incarné, sa naissance divine et éternelle, et sa naissance humaine et temporelle.[19]

---

[17]   Rétif, "Trinité et Mission d'après Bérulle," 5, quoting Bérulle, *CB,* vol. 3, 40.

[18]   *OP* 35, no. 3, col. 971, quoted in *Le mystère*, 84.

[19]   *Grandeurs*, 11, no. 2 (354), quoted in *Le mystère*, 86. It is important to note that Aquinas addressed the idea of whether mission is eternal or only temporal. He asserted that generation is exclusively eternal whereas mission is temporal. Thomas did write that it could be said that mission includes the eternal procession, with the addition of the temporal effect. Procession then can be both eternal and temporal, but not in the sense of a double relation to the principle. See Aquinas, *ST*, 1.43.2, ad 3, in *Summa theologiae*: "Ad tertium dicendum quod missio non solum importat processionem a principio, sed

The Roles of the Trinitarian Persons in Relation to the Priesthood

Bérulle restored within his spiritual theology of priesthood the notion of relation as the result of causation, which Calvin had rejected. In doing so, however, and in direct echo of Calvin, he focused on the economic persons operating, somehow, in relation to the priest himself. Just as Calvin had emphasized the constant interpenetration of the economic Trinity, so too Bérulle placed this constant interpenetration inside the priest, as we will now explore.

Morgain wrote that Bérulle associated the priesthood (as a similitude between imitations and archetypes) not just with the mystery of the Incarnation but also with redemption, the Church, and the Trinity.[20] For Bérulle, there existed a special link between the priest and each of the divine persons: "Notre fonction…'nous lie au Père éternel produisant son Fils,…nous lie au même Fils comme produit et formé par nous dans les âmes; fonction qui nous élève et ainsi nous conjoint aux choses (les) plus grandes qui soient dans le temps et dans l'éternité.'"[21]

Cochois clarified Bérulle's thought on the relationship between the priest and the persons of the Trinity. Because the Father produced the spirit of priesthood of Jésus-Christ, Bérulle's priest had to adhere to the Spirit to receive the Father's influences. The bond of priests with the thearchic source only became perfect through mystical servitude, as will be detailed later in this analysis."[22]

Cochois noted that for Pseudo-Dionysius, the ministerial priesthood was only a particular kind of mediation within the spiritual hierarchy, including an angelic or mystical priesthood.[23] In his humanity, Christ must pass through the angelic hierarchy in his relations with the Father. This mystical priesthood was the result

---

determinat processionis terminum temporalem. Unde missio solum est temporalis. – Vel, missio includit processionem aeternam, et aliquid addit, silicet termporalem effectum: habitudo enim divinae Personae ad suum principium non est nisi ab aeterno. Unde gemina dicitur processio, aeterna scilicet et temporalis, non propter hoc quod habitudo ad principium geminetur: sed geminatio est ex parte termini temporalis et aeterni."

[20] As previously quoted; see *OP* 288, *OC*, Migne ed., quoted in Morgain, "La prêtrise selon Pierre de Bérulle," 146.

[21] *Mémorial de quelques points servans à la direction des Supérieurs en la Congrégation de l'Oratoire de Iesus* (Paris, 1632), hereafter *Mémorial*, 8, quoted in *BLS*, 167. The author noted in footnote 23 that the priest also links the soul to the Holy Spirit as well. See also 173.

[22] See *OC*, Montsoult ed., 2, 24, 7–8, quoted in Cochois, "Bérulle, hiérarque dionysien," 37: 338.

[23] Cochois, "Bérulle, hiérarque dionysien," 37: 335–36.

not of the hypostatic union but of union with the *déité fontale* of the Father.[24] Following in this tradition, in order to receive the spirit of priesthood, Bérulle insisted, Oratorians were to adore the fecundity of the Father as the source of eternal emanations and adhere to the Holy Spirit:

> …adhérons à cet Esprit éternel…pour concevoir son Saint-Esprit; et pour produire au monde son dessein et son œuvre au nom de Père, du Fils et du Saint-Esprit, et en l'honneur de leurs processions éternelles…origine de tout ce qui doit à jamais émaner de Dieu en son Église. Car le Père éternel engendrant son Fils a engendré cet œuvre (*l'Oratoire*) s'il est sien, et produisant le Saint-Esprit il a produit cet esprit au monde (*l'esprit de prêtrise que l'Oratoire se propose de renouveler*)…[25]

A question for further research is whether Bérulle's answer to Calvin's insistence on Christ as *autotheos* was his emphasis on the Son as an emanation of the Father.[26] As Bérulle held:

> Le Fils de Dieu est la première émanation du Père et en cette qualité il est la source et l'exemplaire de toutes les autres émanations de Dieu et en soi et hors de soi et de nature et de grâce et de gloire et de l'union hypostatique. En effet il s'est uni lui-même à une nature humaine et est cause et forme ou quasi-forme de cette nature qu'il a prise comme en l'informant par sa propre subsistence. En quelque genre que ce soit, le premier est la règle des autres. De même en Dieu, le Fils de par son émanation est principe de l'Esprit saint. Et comme le Père en se

---

[24] Ibid., 336, referencing Bérulle's frequent use of the term. See *Grandeurs*, 5, col. 230; 5, col. 237; 6, col. 246; 7, 3, col. 267.

[25] Bérulle, Archives nationales, M 215, 3, 1, quoted in Cochois, "Bérulle, hiérarque dionysien," 37: 338.

[26] Perl noted Origen's notion of participation, designating the relation between the Father and the Son. All, including the Son, are deified by participation in the Father's divinity. See Eric Perl, "Methexis: Creation, Incarnation, Deification in Saint Maximus Confessor" (PhD diss., New Haven, CT: Yale University, 1991), 93, citing Origen, *Commentarii in evangelium Joannis*, in *Origenes Werke*, vol. 2, ed. E. Preuschen, *Die griechischen christlichen Schriftsteller der ersten drei Jahrhunderte* (Leipzig: Hinrichs, 1903), 54; *PG* 14, 108B–109. Perl wrote, quoting Origen: "For instance, he clearly explains that the Father alone is αὐτόθεος and ὁ θεός (with the article), while the Son is only θεός. 'Everything, then, besides the God himself (τό αὐτό θεος),' including the Son, 'is deified by participation in his divinity.'"

contemplant lui-même produit le Fils comme son image vivante, ainsi en contemplant et aimant le Fils, il produit l'Esprit saint.[27]

Bérulle's Notion of the Son as Autotheos

As Whannou explained, Bérulle (following Gamaches) held that Jesus emanated always from the Father, he is sovereign, and his humanity depends only on himself since he completes and terminates it. The second person is independent, but his human nature is dependent on the Trinity as a creature and on the Word as that which confers his perfection.[28] This schema was perhaps in direct response to Calvin's *autotheos* argument.

Bérulle emphasized incommunicability as a property of person, an idea put forth by a number of theologians in the Middle Ages: "En ce mystère auguste, il n'y a qu'une personne subsistante en deux natures différentes par-dessus les lois de l'auteur du monde, qui donne à chaque nature sa subsistence propre, intrinsèque et incommunicable à tout autre sujet."[29] Calvin, too, held to this incommunicability.[30]

Egan wrote, "In fact, Bérulle speaks of a second Trinity: Jesus' body, soul, and divinity. Because of the Incarnation, the adored Trinity becomes the adoring Trinity:"[31] "nous avons deux trinités saintes, divines et adorables en nos mystères: trinité de subsistence en unité d'essence au premier, au plus haut, et au plus auguste mystère de la foi, en la personne du Père, du Fils et du Saint-Esprit; et trinité d'essence en unité de subsistence, au sacré mystère de l'Incarnation, en l'essence de l'âme, en celle du corps, et en la divinité de Jésus."[32]

---

[27] Pierre Bérulle, *Œuvres de piété (1–165)*, ed. Michael Dupuy, *OC*, vol. 3 (Paris, 1995), *OP* 126, 344.

[28] See Charles A. Whannou, *Subsistence chez Bérulle: essai historique et doctrinale sur la place et l'importance de la notion de "subsistence" dans la spiritualité bérullienne de la divinisation* (Porto-Novo, République du Bénin: Imprimerie Notre-Dame, 1993), 77. Hereafter cited as *Subsistence*. See *Grandeurs*, 6, no. 7, 252. See Philippe de Gamaches, *Summa Theologica* (Paris, 1627), In primam, 1.26.2: "terminatio naturae humanae per hypostasim Verbi." Whannou utilized the following editions of Bérulle's work: *OC*, Monsoult ed. and Migne ed. As the Migne edition has many small errors, the author used, in the case of Bérulle's *Œuvres de piété*, both Migne and Monsoult paginations, in that order.

[29] Ibid., 78–79. See *Grandeurs*, 4, no. 4, 215.

[30] See *Institution*, 70, 1.13.6: "En premier lieu i'appelle Personne une résidence [subsistentiam] en l'essence de Dieu, laquelle estant rapportée aux autres est distincte d'avec icelles d'une propriété incommunicable."

[31] Harvey D. Egan, *An Anthology of Christian Mysticism*, 2nd ed. (Collegeville, MN: Liturgical Press, 1996), 484.

[32] Bérulle, *Grandeurs*, 3, 8, 156 (1996).

Aumann noted that this happens through the means of the Holy Spirit, who, according to Bérulle, is sterile in the immanent Trinity but becomes fecund outside the Godhead: "le Saint-Esprit a cela de propre d'être stérile et fécond tout ensemble: stérile en soi et fécond hors de soi-même."[33]

In this rhetoric, it could be argued, we see Christ elevated as a second Trinity himself, perhaps in response to Calvin's insistence on Christ's aseity.

Bérulle's Sacerdotal Pneumatology: The Oratorians' Life in the Spirit

Dupuy wrote that Bérulle proposed that the Oratorians live a life in the Spirit. This life is something of degrees, with the Spirit living in all the faithful but often somehow dormant. The principle of Oratorians' actions was to no longer be that of nature but the Holy Spirit within, as they renounced themselves and lived continually in God's presence.

Bérulle also noted that priests were not only sanctified by created grace but by the Holy Spirit "en Personne." Priests were instruments of God in the administration of the sacraments. If they allowed themselves to be led by the Spirit, they would become perfectly docile instruments just as the humanity of Christ was the instrument of the divinity: "Sa sainte humanité était l'instrument par lequel sa divinité se faisait connaitre. De même en nous les actions doivent être comme le moyen par lequel la grâce de Dieu et l'Esprit-Saint qui habite en nous se manifestent."[34]

According to Taveau, Bérulle did not treat overtly the gifts of the Holy Spirit, but the relation of the priest to the Holy Spirit was the most important aspect of his "art d'adhérer."[35]

The Role of the Spirit of Jesus

The Spirit of Jesus was depicted by Bérulle, by way of analogy, as if a quasi-formal cause, directing and animating the Oratorians' spirits: "Nous ne devons agir que par l'Esprit de Jésus dirigeant, animant, appliquant *(et)* remplissant notre esprit comme la forme remplit la matière, comme la cause première applique les causes

---

[33] Jordan Aumann, *Christian Spirituality in the Catholic Tradition* (San Francisco, CA: Ignatius Press, 1985), 224. Quote taken from Bérulle, *Grandeurs*, 9, 208 (Migne edition).

[34] *BLS*, 106–7, paraphrased. See Coll. 102.

[35] Taveau, *Le cardinal de Bérulle*, 224–25, quoted in Rayez, "Dons du Saint-Esprit."

secondes et la principale applique les instrumentales, comme l'âme anime et vivifie le corps et comme l'Esprit de Dieu doit régir tous les esprits créés."[36]

Bérulle frequently detailed what Cochois referred to as a Trinitarian mystique in referring to an adherence to Jesus which allows us to emanate from him and receive his Spirit: "nous faut *(-il)* adhérer à lui, comme adhérant au Père; il nous faut émaner de lui, comme émanant de son Père; il nous faut recevoir son Esprit, comme étant celui qui le produit avec le Père."[37]

As Bérulle related, "le fondement de la vie spirituelle soit en nous une réalité substantielle et non pas accidentelle, comme la grâce."[38] What is this substantial reality for Bérulle?

Holtzen wrote on the union with the Holy Spirit according to Pétau, as we will explore.[39] For Pétau, the divine indwelling of the Christian was proper to the Holy Spirit alone and a substantial indwelling, not an accidental form as he believed Aquinas held.[40] In contradistinction, the Scholastic tradition held that since the divine persons are inseparable in nature, whatever they do *ad extra* is an action of this nature, and of all three persons.[41]

Conclusion

Any lack of awareness on the part of scholars regarding the importance of the eternal generation debate in relation to the development of the theology of the priesthood may have been due to a failure to understand the doctrine in relation to the debate and its significance. This, again, may be due to the centuries-long sequestering of texts and discouragement of debate after Trent, or, perhaps, like the Reformers themselves, scholars had turned their focus on Christ *a se* rather

---

[36] Bérulle, Arch. De l'Oratoire, 1 bis, pièce 12, 9, quoted in Cochois, "Bérulle, hiérarque dionysien," 37: 331.

[37] *OP* 5, col. 914, quoted in Cochois, "Bérulle, hiérarque dionysien," 37: 340. See *Grandeurs*, 3, no. 5, col. 196; *OP* 11, col. 925; *Grandeurs*, 7, no. 4, col. 269; 7, 7, col. 276; 11, 5, cols. 362–63; *OP* 87, 2, cols. 1071–72. See also L. Cognet, "Bérulle et la théologie de l'Incarnation," *XVIIe siècle* 29 (Oct. 1955): 330.

[38] *OC, Conférences et fragments* (1995), *Vie intérieure et extérieure*, March 1612, 20.

[39] Thomas L. Holtzen, "Union with God and the Holy Spirit: A New Paradigm of Justification" (PhD diss., Milwaukee, WI: Marquette University, 2002).

[40] Ibid., 31–32, quoting Denis Pétau, "De Trinitate," 8, 5, in *Dogmata theologica Dionysii Petavii e Societate Jesu*, 3 (Paris: Ludovicum Vivès, 1865), 466b: "...evidens est ex eorum decretis, justitiae, ac santitatis statum, non creata re ulla, vel qualitate, sed ipsa Spiritus sancti substantia, tanquam principali forma in nobis perfici."

[41] Gerard S. Sloyan, *The Three Persons in One God* (Englewood Cliffs, NJ: Prentice-Hall, Inc., 1964), 101–2.

than Christ as the second person of the Trinity, having themselves been influenced by the Christocentrism of the *via moderna*. Perhaps, also, Scotist influences, as already discussed, prepared the way for a lack of the key distinction between *ad intra* and *ad extra* operations. This brief review suggests that there is a case to be made that Bérulle had become aware of the significance of Calvin's ideals in relation to the priesthood.

This review confirms Rhee's idea, as well, that the processions are an important and long-neglected notion. It is arguable that a major but unconscious shift occurred in Trinitarian Christology in the Reformation and Counter-Reformation periods, which similarly affected a shift in the spiritual theology of priesthood.

Bérulle's project resembled Calvin's in having been influenced by a negative Augustinian piety that required a God-Man as mediator for a debased humanity. Again, unlike in Augustine's view, priests were to become themselves sources of grace, participating in the incommunicable mediation of the being itself of Christ.

Both Calvinist and Berullian negative anthropologies required an economic Trinity of persons united at the level of person, a Trinity who *willed* salvation for a few rather than being a Trinity in essence generative and infinitely *willing* to share the intimacy of divine life with all.

Calvinism required, on the one hand, an extrinsicism in the divine human relationship to support his notions on predestination and election, whereas Bérulle required the heroic effort of the priest to maintain election for himself and the faithful via a mystic kenotic spirituality based on a Pseudo-Dionysian return of the debased soul to God via both the will and the sacraments, as we will detail.

In Calvinism, the immanent Trinity was replaced by an economic Trinity of co-equal persons operating in time, guaranteeing ecclesial and political freedom via an *autotheotic* Son, a spiritual king. In Berullism, a romanticized immanent Trinity, which also became a Neoplatonic economic Trinity operating through a kind of *autotheotic* priesthood, guaranteed a Gallican ecclesial and political freedom in the person of the priest as the de facto fourth member of the Trinity and as sole dispenser of grace. Christ was to rule France, a kingdom subordinate to the heavenly kingdom. As head of the Mystical Body, Christ was represented by the visible head of the Mystical Body, the priest, in whose person the authority of the entire hierarchy rested.

This Christocentrism was also based on a Word Christology with a key fault. As Ocáriz, Seco, and Riestra noted, when there is a de-emphasis on the idea that Christ became man to share our nature so as to redeem us, soteriology is deformed.[42] While it is true that Christ is mediator because he is God, he mediates through his humanity.[43]

So, too, Bérulle's spiritual theology of priesthood was likewise deformed by associating the Trinitarian persons, notably the Word and the Spirit, in too close relation to the person of the priest. This schema of the priest as a necessary link based on a Trinitarian emanationist exemplarism brings us to the question of whether, in Bérulle's spiritual theology of priesthood, all the priest's actions became theandric.

While the work of the Incarnation is one action, common to all three persons, Bérulle's sacerdotal identity denied this causality for the sake of an exemplar causality needed to defend the role of the priest in the sacrifice of the Mass and of the role of the hierarchy in general. In defense of the priesthood, Bérulle not only returned to an emanationism Calvin had rejected, but he securely anchored it, arguably, in a kind of multi-hypostatic and autotheotic spiritual theology of priesthood.

Considering divine persons apart from being, and de-ontologizing the generativity of the Trinity, leaving it a matter of person and will, led to a kind of Calvinist voluntarism in Bérulle's spiritual theology of priesthood.

The following chapter details how Bérulle utilized the doctrine of the Mystical Body to reconstruct a new church/state with the priest as visible head.

---

[42] Ocáriz et al., *The Mystery of Jesus Christ*, 60.
[43] Ibid., 141.

Chapter 9
Christ and His Mystical Body

Introduction

A central question at the time of the Counter-Reform in France was how to restore society and the Church devastated by war. This chapter will explore Bérulle's answer as he proposed it in a spirituality based on the doctrine of the Mystical Body. Included in this analysis will be a multitude of notions Bérulle brought to bear in his polemics surrounding this theme, and taken up at this time, including rebellion, religion and the virtue of religion, ecstasy of being, sacerdotal subsistence, relation, and more. Lastly, a review of challenges associated with Bérulle's spiritual theology of the Mystical Body will follow. First, however, we will explore the idea of Christ as subsistent religion, an idea fundamental to Bérulle's project.

Rebellion and the Virtue of Religion

A central Calvinist assertion was that Christ is the one true worshipper as *leitourgos* (Hebrews 8:2).[1] Calvin called genuine religion both confidence in and fear of God, along with reverence and worship without "ostentatious" ceremonies,[2] in opposition to what he called the papists' rejection of pure doctrine regarding worship through the sanction of worshipping angels and saints.[3]

Bérulle came to respond to Reformist criticisms with an emphasis on the virtue of religion, as well as servitude and the Eucharist as our duties toward God, as Orcibal detailed. Bérulle's depiction of the Eucharistic Christ as perfect adorer and our union with him were stressed and described in a sentence left out of his published work: "Adorons-le…en son Eucharistie adorant son Père

---

[1] Ross Mackenzie and Christopher Kiesling, "Reformed and Roman Catholic Understandings of the Eucharist," *Journal of Ecumenical Studies* 13 (1976): 70.
[2] See *Institution*, 1.2.2: "Voilà que c'est de la vraye et pure religion, assavoir la foy coniointe avec une vive crainte de Dieu…veu que tous monstrent belle apparence, mais bien peu s'y adonnent de cœur."
[3] Ibid., 1.12.1. Calvin referred to this as the superstitious worship of "a tribe of minor deities." *Institution*: "une multitude de petits dieux."

éternel...unissons nos actions à ses actions, notre adoration à la sienne..."[4] Dupuy wrote that, for Bérulle, Christ has three duties: to pray, appease and obtain, as only God can fittingly praise God. In this light, the Eucharist is a cult rendered to the Father in union with the perfect adorer.[5]

Bremond noted that Bérulle's emphasis on the virtue of religion was crucial in meeting the rejection of the Mass and the priesthood by Reformers.[6]

Minton wrote on Bérulle's search for unity in answer to what the cardinal saw as the rebellion of the Calvinists, who he believed denied Christ in denying the Eucharist. His goal became to unify Christianity through a relationship with God. Minton prefaced her analysis by writing about the fruitless attempt to understand religious ideas outside of their historical contexts and how critical it is to see Bérulle's project in context: "Often throughout history...we Christians have divorced religious ideas and symbol systems from their own historical setting. Then we propose them as an ahistorical model..."[7]

In attempting to heal the division between the human person and God, Minton wrote that Bérulle placed key importance on union with God as both the source of holiness and the means to escape a world of death. In this project, his focus was on conformity to the will of God, with the goal of the Christian to be transformed by grace. This served not just as an answer to the Huguenots but also as a corrective to the Renaissance emphasis on reason. The figure of Christ and his submission (which restored unity and order to the cosmos) became central to Bérulle.[8] As discussed, Bérulle came to incorporate into his system of thought the religious ideals of the Huguenots, in particular, notably that of the transcendence of God.[9]

Bérulle constructed his own symbol system in defense of the unity of the Roman Catholic faith, using ideas from many diverse sources taken outside their original historical contexts. The virtue of religion became central in reaching this transcendent God.

---

[4] Orcibal, *Le cardinal de Bérulle*, 62, quoting *OC,* Migne ed., *Discours de controverse*, 2, 2 and 7, 2, cols. 683 and 769.

[5] Dupuy, *Le Christ de Bérulle*, 162.

[6] *TM*, 78 and 85.

[7] Minton, "Pierre de Bérulle," 105. See also 106–7.

[8] Anne H. Minton, "The Spirituality of Bérulle: A New Look," *Spirituality Today* 36, no. 3 (Fall 1984): 210–19.

[9] Minton, "The Figure of Christ," 13.

Background

Aquinas wrote that the whole rite of the Christian religion was derived from Christ's priesthood.[10] Following Cicero, he also held religion to be a moral virtue annexed to justice, as it concerns the rendering of what is due. Religion regards our relation to God, but it is not a theological virtue and does not have God as its direct object but rather the acts that honor him.[11]

On the contrary, De Vio called religion a theological virtue. Following Pseudo-Dionysius in asserting that an inferior nature touches at its height the base of a superior nature, he saw religion as the greatest of the moral virtues, "participating" in the nature of a theological virtue. For De Vio, religion had God as an object, by offering him one's *mens*, actions, and exterior things.[12]

Heck discerned this evolution and the renewal of the sense of the word "religion" as a removal from the realm of ethics.[13] Staubinger, in turn, would add that religion became no longer an assemblage of acts, but also "the total gift of man to God, with all his personality."[14]

Bérulle and Religio

Dupuy wrote that Bérulle distinguished between the natural and supernatural life, and between the meditations of philosophers and the prayers of Christians. To tend to one's natural end of beatitude and perfection via natural morality was

---

[10] See Aquinas, *ST*, 3.63.3, co., in *Summa theologiae,* 12.1: 35: "Secundo autem deputatur quisque fidelis ad recipiendum vel tradendum aliis ea quae pertinent ad cultum Dei. Et ad hoc proprie deputatur character sacramentalis. Totus autem ritus Christianae religionis derivatur a sacerdotio Christi. Et ideo manifestum est quod character sacramentalis specialiter est character Christi, cuius sacerdotio configurantur fideles secundum sacramentales characteres, qui nihil aliud sunt quam quaedam participationes sacerdotii Christi, ab ipso Christo derivatae."

[11] Raymond Saint-Jean, "Religion, Vertu de: I. Théologie Scolastique," in *DSAM*, vol. 13 (Paris: Beauchesne, 1988), cols. 308–20. See Aquinas, *ST*, 2-2.81–82.

[12] Ibid., col. 311. De Vio in *Commentaria, Summa theologiae*, 9: 185: "sanctitas autem directe respicit mentem, et mediante mente respicit et alia virtutum opera, et etiam religionis opera…"

[13] Erich Heck, *Der Begriff religio bei Thomas von Aquin; seine Bedeutung für unser heutiges Verständnis von Religion* (München: F. Schöningh, 1971), 216–19, cited in Saint-Jean, "Religion," col. 315.

[14] Heinrich Straubinger, *Religionsphilosophie mit Theodizee*, 2nd ed. (Freiburg: Verlag Herder, 1949), 145: "le don total de l'homme à Dieu, avec toute sa personnalité," cited in Saint-Jean, "Religion," col. 315.

not enough for Bérulle, who wrote of the Christian: "C'est par une relation à Dieu, comme à sa fin, qu'il se réfère lui-même à Dieu, ainsi que toutes ses actions…Et c'est cela que consiste l'oraison, qui est élévation de l'esprit (*mens*) à Dieu."[15]

Bérulle, wanting to demonstrate that faith was rooted firmly in Christ himself, held that whereas before the Incarnation and the institution of the Eucharist, religion consisted in human acts, now after the Incarnation, it was the God-Man himself, *substance divine*, which became the expression of religion itself.[16] Bérulle:

> Le Fils de Dieu se communique á l'homme par la voie de la religion; il est l'objet de sa créance; il est l'hostie de son sacrifice; il est la grâce de son sacrement; il est la vie, la nourriture et le soutien de nos âmes.
>
> Le Fils de Dieu se donne à l'homme pour l'homme, pour faire vivre Dieu en l'homme et l'homme en Dieu. Il se donne à l'homme par voie de religion, établissant en soi-même le corps et l'état d'une religion nouvelle. Et au lieu qu'auparavant la religion subsistait dans les actions de l'homme vers Dieu, et le commerce entre Dieu et l'homme par la voie de la religion se faisait par le moyen de quelques accidents émanés de Dieu vers l'homme et de l'homme vers Dieu, maintenant ce commerce consiste en un fonds et en une substance divine. Car c'est Dieu même que l'homme reçoit en ses mystères et c'est Dieu même que l'homme offre en ses sacrifices. Et ainsi cette religion est toute substantielle et divine, et nous avons Dieu réellement présent au milieu de nous en la terre, comme nous l'aurons présent au ciel.[17]

For Bérulle and the French School, the virtue of religion was influenced by both the *mystique de l'essence* of the Pseudo-Dionysian-inspired Rheno-Flemish school and the devotion to the humanity of Jesus of the Carmelites, according to Noye.[18] Humankind participates in the movement of return of all divine works to God. The three movements that draw us to God are divine consecration (by nature); as a new creation (by grace); and by our own will. Bérulle noted that because the human will of Christ is totally turned to God in the hypostatic union, therefore, humankind cannot realize our religion except by entering (by the grace

---

[15] *Collationes*, 145, manuscrit latin 18210, Bibliothèque nationale, quoted in Dupuy, *Bérulle: une spiritualité de l'adoration*, 61. Dupuy noted that he utilized the Migne edition in his work, with corrections provided by the more complete Bourgoing edition.

[16] Dupuy, in *OC* (1995), *OP* 9, 47–48. Quote taken from Lettre 144 of 1617, *CB*.

[17] Ibid., 49.

[18] Irénée Noye, "Religion, Vertu de: II. École Bérullienne," in *DSAM*, vol. 13 (1988), col. 316.

of adoring the humanity of Jesus) into the religious movement of the Son. Servitude and sacrifice are two elements of the religion of the Incarnate Word, according to Bérulle. The Christian must enter into these dispositions as Jesus Christ did—with a total *appartenance* or belonging to God through abnegation and renunciation, as we will treat in detail.[19]

This religion restores the tie that sin had broken, as Dupuy noted.[20] Religion is centered on Christ's submission to the Father by which he restored unity and order to creation, and which Bérulle believed Protestants had rejected.[21]

In this schema, Bérulle introduced a voluntarism and ethicism that would be a key aspect of his system of thought.

The Priesthood in the Service of Unity and Society

Orcibal wrote that a chief characteristic of Bérulle's spirituality was the idea of unity, which opposed the Reformers who rejected veneration of Mary and the saints, ecclesiastical authority, and the monarchy, as well as priests who rejected the authority of bishops. Notably, as already cited, Bérulle linked sacerdotal character to mystical passivity for which the hypostatic union was the model. Bérulle wished to develop priests into conjoint instruments by placing them in the choirs of Jesus and Mary, and of the sacred humanity under the title of head.[22]

In this Bérulle attempted to make the priest one with Christ and a link in the chain of redemption. Bérulle emphasized the priesthood as both a unity and a society to his Oratorians. Bérulle noted, "Ainsi la prêtrise, qui en sa généralité est l'état et le pouvoir le plus éminent de l'Église, est un état et une vie d'unité par intériorité et de société par son extériorité."[23]

The depth and breadth of the role of the priest, and the society of Oratorians, particularly, in maintaining unity will be detailed in this analysis.

Religio *and* Analogia Entis

Von Balthazar gave a cogent analysis of the metaphysics of the Oratory, noting that all its theological notions were rooted in the fundamental relation of *analogia entis*, expressed as *religio* for the creature:

---

[19] Ibid., cols. 316–18. See *OP* 123, *OC*, Migne ed., cols. 1150–51.

[20] *BLS, OR* 18, no. 4, 300ni.

[21] Minton, "Pierre de Bérulle," 116.

[22] Orcibal, *Le cardinal de Bérulle*, 140. See Jean Orcibal, *Origines du jansénisme*, vol. 2 (Paris: Vrin, 1947), 336–40; Paul Cochois, "Bérulle, initiateur mystique: les vœux de servitude" (PhD diss., Institut catholique de Paris, 1960), 44 and 278–82.

[23] *OR* 13, no. 3, in *BLS*, 284.

Both in His being and in His consciousness Jesus Christ is the point where glory is transformed into worship; indeed, since He is personally God in human nature, the transformation is total and perfect: 'You alone serve God as he deserves to be served, that is, with an infinite service, and you alone adore Him with an infinite adoration…From all eternity there was an infinitely adorable God, but there was still not an infinite adorer…O grandeur of Jesus, precisely in His state of abandonment and servitude…since from now on we have a God served and adored without any kind of defect and a God adoring without a [selfish] interest in His divinity.' This precision is not just ontological, because it is expressed by Christ's own act of adoration; and yet it is not just functional either, for the particular act totally corresponds to the ontological situation of the God-Man. To express the unity of the two aspects Bérulle invents the idea of 'state' (*état*). This denotes the psychological and existential dimension of Jesus' ontological reality; constantly and precisely, His actions reveal His being.[24]

For Bérulle, in his quest for unity and in defense of the Mass and the priest's participation in the Eucharistic sacrifice, the virtue of religion for the Christian moved from the moral order with God as its end to a unique ontological schema with God as its immediate object, in relation to the Christian, however, via moral striving.

The act of worship became dependent on being inside the praise of the perfect adorer. For the priest, the act of worship, whether personal or public, also became dependent on being inside the sacrifice of Christ the perfect adorer at all times, and this through a moralistic striving, dependent on frequent mental elevations, as we will explore.

The Mystical Body

To fully understand Bérulle's take on Christ as Subsistent Religion Himself, it is important to see its full flowering in his doctrine of the Mystical Body.

---

[24] Hans Urs von Balthasar, in Hans Urs von Balthasar, John Kenneth Riches, and Brian McNeil, *The Glory of the Lord: A Theological Aesthetics*, vol. 5, *The Realm of Metaphysics in the Modern Age* (Edinburgh: T. & T. Clark, 1991), 119–22, also quoting Bérulle, *OC*, Montsoult ed. 183–84. Originally published as *Herrlichkeit: Eine theologische Ästhetik* (Einsiedeln: Joannes, 1961–69), 121.

Background

Of the numerous debates of the Reformation and Counter-Reformation influencing Bérulle's construction of his spiritual theology of priesthood, that pertaining to the doctrine of the Mystical Body was one of the most crucial, although he does not mention the phrase "le corps mystique" often. In defense of the unity of the Church and its authority over the state, Bérulle placed the priesthood in a central role in maintaining this unity, a unity he built with the Neoplatonic idea of oneness. According to Houdard, Bérulle meant for his Oratorians as priests to be the means to "recompose" the Mystical Body.[25]

In order to emphasize the unity of Christ the head with his members, Bérulle emphasized the Eucharist as a prolongation of the Incarnation, which itself became the center of his spirituality, asserting the personal union of the divinity and humanity of Christ in the Incarnation.[26] In order to accomplish this, Bérulle followed Bellarmine, who utilized what Buzzi called a Baroque Scholastic polemic of calling Christ the hypostasis of the Church.[27]

According to McGrath, whereas Augustine had argued for the unity of the Church in the Donatist controversy of the early fifth century, the Reformers argued that grace was far more important than unity. Opponents of the Reformation, in turn, argued that the Church itself was the guarantor of the faith.[28]

For Bérulle, according to Morgain, to disobey was to leave both the state and the Mystical Body. The Reformers' desire to separate politics from the church was met with Bérulle's ideal that the state be subject to the rule of the Mystical Body: "l'État de Jésus est une royaume auquel les royaumes et les États doivent servir."[29]

---

[25] Sophie Houdard, "Sacerdoce et direction spirituelle: Le prêtre et la représentation du corps mystique," in *L'image du prêtre dans la littérature classique (XVIIe–XVIIIe siècles): Actes du colloque organisé par le Centre "Michel Baude—Littérature et spiritualité" de l'Université de Metz, 20–21 novembre 1998*, ed. Danielle Pister (Peter Lang Verlag, 2001), 113.

[26] Orcibal, *Le cardinal de Bérulle*, 68. See also discussion in *Le mystère*, 122n2.

[27] Buzzi, "La 'scolastica barocca' come risposta," 88. See R. Bellarmine, *Disputationes de Controversiis Christianae Fidei adversus hujus temporis Haereticos*, 1 (n.p., n.d.), contr. 3. bk. 1, ch. 9, col. 536, E: "Cum dicitur Ecclesia corpus Christi, vox illa Christi potest commode referri, non tam ad Christum ut caput, quam ad eundem Christum ut hypostasimeius corporis."

[28] McGrath, *Reformation Thought*, 132.

[29] Morgain, *La théologie politique de Pierre de Bérulle*, 230.

The Doctrine of the Mystical Body as Spirituality

The doctrine of the Mystical Body, according to Mersch, occupied a major role in the writings of the masters of the French School, specifically Bérulle, Condren and Olier, their ideals on the topic being very much the same to him.[30] According to Mersch, the influences on Bérulle's thoughts on the topic are not easily distinguishable. Bérulle spoke of attachment to Christ as a kind of slavery and incorporation, and used an idea of the Greek fathers that the Incarnation stored up in Christ the life of all humankind.

To paraphrase Mersch, both the scriptures and the fathers had already held our incorporation in Christ to be the principle that should govern all conduct. That said, and important to this study, the French School's doctrine of the Mystical Body became a system of spirituality. Christ, our head, became the norm of our activity, our relations with Christ in God being similar to those that unite Christ's humanity with his divinity. When Christians act, they act as a prolongation of Christ's activity and so are united with his same mission, which emanates from the Father. For Bérulle, our actions "have God, not only as their first beginning, but also as their first exemplar and ultimate norm."[31] Mersch explained: "To know what the conduct of a Christian should be, we must in the first place consider, not the Christian himself—he is merely a participation—nor the relation between the two natures in Christ—this is simply a mediation indicating a higher principle—instead, we must first study the relations that unite the three divine Persons in the inner life of the Trinity."[32]

The Mystical Body and the Notion of Subsistence

Whannou conducted a study of Bérulle's notion of the word *subsistence*, in which the lines of Bérulle's construction of the Mystical Body in defense of the Eucharist and the priesthood can be found, as based on various theological stances of the period. For this reason, this analysis will review it in some depth here.[33] It serves as a clarification of Yelle's analysis.

Whannou summarized that Bérulle's Christology was a spiritual theology of divinization and divine filiation. The center around which Bérulle organized his

---

[30] Émile Mersch, *The Whole Christ: The Historical Development of the Doctrine of the Mystical Body in the Scriptures and Tradition*, 2nd ed., trans. John R. Kelly (Milwaukee: Bruce Publishing Company, 1938), 531–55. Originally published as *Le Corps Mystique Du Christ* (Paris: Desclée de Brouwer, 1936).

[31] Ibid., 540.

[32] Ibid., 540.

[33] *Subsistence.* This review follows the author's exposition closely.

doctrine was the unity of the subsistence of Christ, an idea influenced by Augustine, Leo the Great, and Cyril.[34]

It is important to note that the influence of these sources did not include faithfulness to their original meaning necessarily. Whannou's was an attempt to highlight veins of possible influence rather than direct correlations.

Whannou explained that Bérulle defended the mediation of the Church by asserting the idea that the Mystical Body is centered on the Church's mission and on its position as mediator of divinizing grace. The Church, for Bérulle, is an exemplar of the transcendental relation in which she participates. Central to Bérulle's theology, according to Whannou, is the contemplation of the Mystical Body in relation not only to the hypostatic union, but also to the eternal generation of the Word as source and prototype of all renewal in the Church, a link which is not simply one of exemplarity but also of participation. Participating in the humanity of Christ by participation in the Church is also to participate in the source of the grace of the Mystical Body, which is the hypostatic union by which humankind is divinized. Therefore, the Mystical Body's unity is not only based on the unity of the Trinity but also on the two natures of the person of the Word. This union between Christ and Christians imitates the hypostatic union.[35]

Christ as Both Christian and Sacerdotal Subsistence

Lethel wrote in his preface to Whannou's work that the notion of subsistence in Bérulle's thought was one of the most difficult, especially his idea of the privation of subsistence in the humanity of Christ.[36] While the notion of subsistence spans the fields of history, anthropology, metaphysics, and exegetical hermeneutics, as Whannou noted, he chose to focus on the history of the usage of the term in Bérulle's work in relation to his spiritual doctrine, first detailing several senses of the word *subsistence*. The common sense of the word *subsist* is to "continue in being." The theological sense of the word comes from the Latin *subsistentia* or *hypostasis*, meaning "person." However, Whannou held that there appeared to be a problem at times in Bérulle's work with a copyist substituting *substance* for *subsistence*.[37]

---

34 Ibid., 221. See footnote 23 referencing Augustine, *In Ioannis Evangelium*, tract. 111; Leo the Great, *Letter to Flavian*, ch. 3; Cyril of Alexandria, *Quod unus sit Christus*.

35 Ibid., 244–45.

36 Ibid., préface, François-Marie Léthel, 16.

37 Ibid., 25–30.

Bérulle, as Whannou explained, was influenced by his professor at the Sorbonne, Gamaches, who used the term in reference to the existence of God, the hypostatic union, and the Trinity. Specifically, he used it in terms of the subsistence of God: "nam cum essentia divina realiter formaliter sibi identificet tres personas, non minus perfecte in his existit, nec maiorem cum illi facit compositionem, quam si quarta & communis subsistentia poneretur."[38] Gamaches asserted that the person or subsistence of Christ completes the human nature of the Word: "terminatio naturae humanae per hypostasim Verbi."[39]

Whannou took pains to note that the juridical sense of the word meant to remain in force in a firm and stable manner, and that Bérulle's vision was influenced by his juridical background.[40] The notion of *état* is important in relation to the notion of subsistence for Bérulle. Whannou wrote:

> "État" désigne la condition dans laquelle le Verbe incarné et les créatures "subsistent." Dans le langage bérullien, "état signifie" (sens spirituel) la **disposition perpétuelle et permanente d'un sujet**, la **stabilité** de sa situation, de sa manière de vivre, sa connaturalité avec une perfection donnée, ainsi que son attitude de passivité. Autrement dit, "il s'agit d'une disposition de l'âme, d'une **certaine durée** qui donne à la vie intérieure une teinte particulière aussi longtemps qu'elle persiste."[41]

Bérulle also used the phrase "subsister par Lui" to indicate that God is the subsistence of all being as origin and end. God contains everything such that all of creation depends on God essentially.[42] God alone is the *Ens subsistens*, with all others participating in him.[43] This relation Bérulle described as follows: "…relation non accidentelle, mais **substantielle**, non particulière, mais universelle et absolue en tous les degrés et en tous les états de son être; **relation essentielle** perpétuelle et nécessaire vers son Dieu…"[44]

Bérulle held that the creature must necessarily and at all times be conjoined to God as to its first cause ("l'être créé qui a toujours nécessairement besoin d'être

---

[38] Ibid., 30, quoting Gamaches, *Summa Theologica*, In primam, 1.4.2.
[39] Ibid., quoting Gamaches, *Summa Theologica*, In primam, 1.26.2.
[40] Ibid., 31. See *Dictionnaire de l'Académie Française*, vol. 2 (Paris: J.B. Coignard, 1694), 508.
[41] Ibid., 31, quoting also F. Jetté, "État," in *DSAM*, vol. 4, pt. 2 (Paris: Beauchesne, 1961), col. 1378. See also Guillén F. Preckler, *Bérulle aujourd'hui: 1575–1975: pour une spiritualité de l'humanité du Christ* (Paris: Beauchesne, 1978), 37.
[42] *OP* 196, art. 1, 1289, quoted in *Subsistence*, 32.
[43] *Subsistence*, 35.
[44] *Grandeurs*, 6, no. 6, 252, quoted in *Subsistence*, 46.

conjointe à Dieu, comme à sa cause première").[45] Additionally, without adoration and sacrifice the creature cannot *subsister*.[46]

The Privation of Subsistence

Whannou noted that Bérulle was the first to mention the idea of the privation of the human subsistence of Christ in relation to the kenosis of Christ and the ideal of abnegation. Bérulle held that the Word is *anéanti* in assuming human nature *destituée* of its own personality, referring to Christ's self-naughting in Philippians 2:6–11.[47] There are two forms of exinanition of the Word: the privation of subsistence of the human nature and the *anéantissement* of love or the kenosis of the Word in uniting itself to our nothingness, in other words, the subsistence of the person of the Word in the humanity. Bérulle wrote: "cette humanité est privée de sa subsistence et personnalité propre et est douée de celle du Verbe éternel..."[48] This phrase caused the orthodoxy of Bérulle to be placed in doubt. According to the author, a similar phrase ("Que l'humanité de Jésus s'est dépouillée de sa propre subsistence") was taken from a defective version of the vow and was subsequently censured by Lessius, as we will review.[49] The author noted that Bérulle, however, used similar expressions to refer to Jesus having been dispossessed of his subsistence, such as *dépouillement, dépossession, dénuement,* and *privation*.[50]

Bérulle made the point of insisting that the humanity conserves "l'intégrité de son être et de son existence."[51] Whannou noted the same insistence in other authors. Juan de Rada wrote, for example, that being deprived of human personality did not diminish the perfection of the human nature of Christ. As a Scotist, he defined personality by incommunicability rather than individuality. Important to this study, in this schema, the personality adds only a negation, as subsistence belongs to the order of relation.[52]

---

45   *Grandeurs*, 6, no. 6, 251, quoted in *Subsistence*, 47.
46   *Subsistence*, 47. See *OP* 162 (1221) 1056.
47   Ibid., 58. See *Collationes*, 287.
48   *Grandeurs*, 2, no. 11, 187, quoted in *Subsistence*, 59–60.
49   *Grandeurs*, 2, 244–45, quoted in *Subsistence*, 60.
50   *Subsistence*, 60. See Archives Nationales de Paris, M. 233, 15–16; *OP* 72 A; 89 C; G 2, 11, 187.
51   *Subsistence*, 61. See *OP* 206 D; *Grandeurs*, 2, no. 4, *OC*, 173–74.
52   Ibid., 61. See footnote 17. See also Juan de Rada, *Controversiae theologicae inter S. Thomam et Scotum super Tertium Sent.*, 3, controv. 1, a. 1 (Rome, 1615). We cite the Venice, 1618 edition: "Pars negatiua probatur. Quia si persona diceret huiusmodi entitatem positiuam, esset in natura humana aliqua entitas inassumptibilis a Verbo, sed consequens est falsum: ergo & Antecedens. Probatur sequela maioris. Quia illi vltimae entitati, quam addit

The Notion of Subsistence and Ecstasy of Being

Dupuy defended Bérulle as following De Vio, writing that he was not writing of an absence of subsistence in the absolute sense, since the human nature received an infinite actuation in the Word.[53] Whannou's analysis attempts to understand what Dupuy might have meant by this statement and raises historical arguments and questions beyond the scope of this study, but worthy of inspection in order to find any possible links to Bérulle's notions surrounding the priesthood.

Whannou asked what, for Bérulle, was the formal constituent of the Man-God.[54] He noted that Bérulle relied on various Scholastics, particularly on De Vio, who proposed the personality as the terminus of the human nature, and the formal constituent of its existence. Bérulle called it "terme propre et accomplissement substantiel de cette nature."[55]

Bérulle also depended on Capreolus, according to Whannou, who posited *l'extase de l'être* as explaining the hypostatic union. Capreolus placed the formal constituent of the person in existence.[56] This would have major ramifications for Bérulle's spiritual theology of priesthood, which this analysis will detail.

Galot noted several difficulties with the theory that the constitutive principle is found in existence (attributing this idea to Capreolus and later, Billot). In this theory, the human nature of Christ has no human existence, but only a divine one, thus affirming an "ecstasy of being." However, Christ's deprivation of a human "to be" is problematic in light of the Council of Chalcedon, Galot insisted. He noted that the theory brings into question the idea of the hypostatic union in that the union is accomplished within the divine nature and not just the divine person, thus making it a substantial union rather than a hypostatic union. In this

---

persona supra naturam, repugnaret assumi, & communicari vt quo: quia persona est incommunicabilis existentia. Probatur minor argumenti. Quia secundum Damascenum, libro tertio Orthodoxae fidei, quod est inassumptibile, est incurabile. At asserere aliquid esse incurabile in natura humana, est inconueniens; Ergo."

[53] Ibid., 61. See footnote 17 referencing *BSA*, 216, and De Vio's idea of the of the absence of *l'esse humain* in *Commentaria*, Aquinas, *ST*, 3.17.2. in *Summa theologiae*, 11: 223–229.

[54] *Subsistence*, 68–75.

[55] Bérulle, *Grandeurs* 12, no. 2, 374, quoted in *Subsistence*, 75–76.

[56] *Subsistence*, 75. See Jean Galot, *La personne du Christ: recherche ontologique* (Bruxelles: Duculot-Lethielleux, 1969), 18–19. See Johannes Capreolus, *Defensiones theologicae divi Thomae Aquinatis.*, vol. 5 (Tours, 1879), In *IV Sent.*, 2, 3, d. 5, q. 3, a. 3. See also 24–25, where Galot also pointed to De Vio as holding to the notion of ecstacy of being, as well: "Selon la théorie de Cajetan, la personne est constituée par un mode de la substance avant que ne vienne l'actuation par l'existence; l'application de cette notion au Christ implique l'extase de l'être."

way, the *esse ad* and *esse in* of Christ are identical.[57] Galot referred to Garrigou-Lagrange's opinion on the subject, namely, that the humanity in this scenario "n'a pas seulement l'extase de la connaissance et de l'amour par la vision béatifique, mais l'extase par l'être lui-même, en tant qu'elle existe par l'être éternel lui-même du Verbe."[58]

Whannou summarized that the hypostatic union has a logical, not ontological consequence: that of the communication of idioms.[59]

The Unity of Subsistence and Relation

Whannou related that for Bérulle, "La subsistence qui donne existence à la nature prise par le Verbe, en est aussi le constitutif formel ou la forme constitutive qui pose le Verbe Incarné comme Relation dans la Trinité et, à un niveau analogue, entre Dieu et les hommes."[60] Important to this study, this idea of person as relation, according to Galot, carried with it certain difficulties, as it should have differing distinctions in speaking of the Trinity, Christ, or human beings.[61] In Bérulle's exemplarism, these distinctions were not clear, notably in regard to the priest's relation to Christ and the Trinity, as this analysis will explore.

Whannou defended Bérulle's expression of the unity of subsistence as the same unity of the Incarnate Word of the apostolic faith and held especially by the Greek fathers. In this, he particularly followed Cyril, as noted. Whannou explained and quoted Bérulle's thought: "...le Verbe Incarné est Fils de Dieu en ses deux natures 'non par grâce, mais par nature.' Il est toujours Celui qu'Il était 'dès le commencement'; Il est déifié 'non par opération mais par communication de la Divinité, non par inhabitation, mais par subsistence et non en union mais en unité de subsistence.'"[62]

The author explained that Bérulle's use of the word *subsistence* in its Christological sense was founded not on the idea of relation in regard to the Trinity, but on the notion of the unicity of subsistence, which presupposed that the human nature of Jesus does not exist except in his union with the Word: his nature has no other formal constituent than the person of the Word. It is the

---

[57] Jean Galot, *Who Is Christ: A Theology of the Incarnation* (Chicago: Franciscan Herald Press, 1980), 291–92.

[58] Réginald Garrigou-Lagrange, *De Christo Salvatore* (Turin: R. Berruti, 1946), 314, quoted in Galot, *Who is Christ*, 18.

[59] *Subsistence*, 73.

[60] Ibid., 76–77.

[61] Galot, *La personne du Christ*, 31–52. See his discussion of the problems associated with defining person as relation in each of these contexts.

[62] *Subsistence*, 83–84. Whannou also quoted *Grandeurs*, 11, no. 7, 350.

hypostatic union that is the source and foundation of the Mystical Body as exemplary and efficient cause of the grace of the Mystical Body.[63] In this hierarchical schema, the Son is the source and exemplar of all other emanations of nature, grace, and glory.[64]

Bérulle repeatedly taught that the eternal generation is the source of all revival in the Church and that it is through the operation of the Holy Spirit that humanity and God are made one person. Bérulle turned to the idea of substantial grace in this assertion: "La divine essence est une grâce substantielle et vous ô humanité sainte, comme unie au Verbe, vous êtes une autre sorte de grâce substantielle et subsistante personellement en la sainteté divine et incréée."[65]

Christ's humanity was made (as Whannou expressed it) *consubstantielle* with the Word and so the foundation of all grace.[66] Importantly, Bérulle asserted that Jesus had "[une] grâce infinie," "une grâce incréée qui est la subsistence divine," and so, therefore, "[une] capacité infinie." This is in contradistinction to Aquinas, who held that the grace of the humanity of Christ is finite.[67]

Bérulle held that Christ's soul subsists in the divinity, and that all things subsist, then, in him. The following explanation by Whannou clearly delineated Bérulle's logic, quoting him: "Dieu en effet assume, en Lui, tous les états humbles et 'abjects' des hommes, en sorte qu'ils sont 'existants et établis dedans l'être divin'; ils sont dès lors 'appuyés par la subsistence du Verbe et sont unis personellement à une grandeur et majesté infinie...'"[68] Whannou further explained, "Ces états sont des instruments de grâce pour ceux qui auront à y participer; mais, déjà, en Jésus, toute l'humanité participe à la grâce, en attendant que chaque homme adhère à cette volonté de Dieu. Nous retrouvons ainsi, en cette terminologie, comment la 'subsistence', la 'source' et le 'fondement' de toutes choses sont dans le Christ..."[69]

---

[63]   Ibid., 85–86.

[64]   Ibid., 87. See footnote 6. See also *OP* 95 D.

[65]   *Grandeurs*, 2, no. 5, 175, quoted in *Subsistence*, 88. The author noted in footnote 9, regarding the substantial character of sanctifying grace, that Bérulle followed the Greek fathers, the Rheno-Flemish, and Peter Lombard more than Aquinas. See Cochois, "Bérulle, initiateur mystique," PhD diss., 187ff.

[66]   *Subsistence*, 88. See *Grandeurs*, 8, no. 6, 290.

[67]   *OP* 34 A, quoted in *Subsistence*, 88. See Aquinas, *ST*, 3.7.11.

[68]   *Vie de Jésus*, 23, 497, quoted in *Subsistence*, 89.

[69]   *Subsistence*, 89. See *Collationes*, 125 / 19 Mars 1613.

Substance and Property

For Bérulle, Christ is the "all" of the Mystical Body, a concept which supposed the idea of the lack of subsistence of the Mystical Body as proposed by Nazario.[70] Whannou went on to write, quoting Bérulle, that Christians participate in the grace of the Incarnation as they are "renfermées en sa substance." For Bérulle, the grace of union equals the habitual grace of Christ. For Bérulle, Christ is not only the head of the Mystical Body but also our principal.[71] This analysis will explore this distinction in Bérulle's particular interpretation of causality in relation to the priest.

According to Whannou, Bérulle relied heavily on Nacchianti regarding the relationship between the head and members of the Mystical Body.[72] One must be *enté* (grafted) onto Jesus.[73] Jesus is the *substance* of both the Mystical Body and the order of grace.[74]

For Bérulle, Christ alone is "subsistent" at the level of grace, while we are but a relation to him. Grace, for Bérulle, is not a gift of divinization and sanctification but a relation with Christ: "Il faut vivre et subsister dans le Fils de Dieu et ne faut avoir vie ni subsistence qu'en Lui; vois le rayon du soleil, il n'a point de subsistence en soi, il est tout subsistant au soleil…"[75]

This subsistence in Christ begins with baptism; however, this union is not only an exemplar of that between the Word and the humanity, which is assumed, but also of that between the Father and the Son.[76] The only property that the creature possesses is his *indigence*.[77] This indigence, according to Whannou, involves not only understanding one's own impoverished existence but also actually renouncing one's own self-subsistence. As Bérulle held, the grace of subsisting in the Mystical Body is "'la grâce de mort,' 'd'anéantissement,' 'et non

---

[70]   *Subsistence*, 90. See *Grandeurs*, 2, no. 7, 178; and J. P. Nazario, *Commentarium in III partem*, vol. 3 (n.p., 1620), 18, f° 152 r°, 449.

[71]   Ibid., 90, quoting *OP* 16.

[72]   Ibid., 91. See J. Nacchianti, *Opera*, vol. 2, *Enarrationes in divi Pauli epistolos ad Ephesios et Romanos…* (Venice, 1564), f° 177 v°–178 v°, especially f° 34 v°–35 r°.

[73]   Ibid., 92. See *Mémorial*, 4, 619.

[74]   Ibid., 92. See *Grandeurs*, 2, no. 5, 175. In footnote 31, Whannou wrote that the word '*substance*' is used in this instance in the sense of 'hypostasis.'

[75]   *OP* 84 A, quoted in *Subsistence*, 94–95.

[76]   *Subsistence*, 95–96. See *OP* 142, C; CI (1116) 948; 27, 2 (957) 790. See also 99, footnote 68: The author noted that it is an important distinction that Bérulle preferred the idea of subsisting in Christ rather than in God, as nothing subsists directly in God.

[77]   Ibid., 96. See *OP* 136 B.

de subsistence.'"[78] This denuding of subsistence is not a depersonalization, argued Whannou, but becoming pure potential.[79]

Subsistence and Priesthood

The author explained Bérulle's logic: as we Christians are incorporated into God's Son, becoming one in the Mystical Body, we can then offer praise as we are united to the state of the grace of the mysteries of his life which he left us so that they can subsist in us.[80] Also, in receiving communion, we become *sépulcres vivants* of Jesus, who takes possession of our members.[81]

Whannou explicated the link between Bérulle's notions of subsistence and the Mystical Body as applied to his defense of the power of the priest, subsisting in Christ the head. Whannou wrote, also quoting Bérulle:

> La consécration, qui transforme le pain et le vin, se réalise "in Persona Christi," par une sorte de "subsistence" dans le Christ-Tête, propre aux prêtres. Par leur participation à l'onction de Jésus Christ, en effet, ils entrent dans une intimité profonde avec les Personnes divines, et, demeurant "in Persona Christi," ils font l'Eucharistie. Dans leur fonction sacrée, "leur personne est assumée par celle du Christ," ils revêtent la "Personne du Christ et son sacerdoce." Ils participent ainsi du privilège d'opération qui relève de sa personne.[82]

Considering that the priest remains *in persona Christi*, he participates not only in the mystery of the Incarnation, but also in that of the Resurrection, according to Bérulle: "En la consécration, il faut être en Jésus Christ produisant son Corps en la subsistence du Verbe, en la vertu de Saint-Esprit, par même puissance par laquelle Dieu l'a ressuscité."[83]

The author traced the originality of the links Bérulle made between subsistence, person, and the Church. Whannou wrote:

> Le terme "subsistence" est utilisé et défini à propos du mystère de Jésus en Lui-même—originalité bérullienne—comme un équivalent de

---

[78] Ibid., 97. See *OP* 140 (1177) 1010.

[79] Ibid., 98. See Bérulle, Archives nationales, M 233, n. 2, 15–16; *OP* 73, A.

[80] Ibid., 100. See footnote 74. See Nacchianti, *Opera*, 1: 113.

[81] Ibid., 102. See *Grandeurs*, 4, 218; *Œuvres de controverses* 1, 6, 689.

[82] *Subsistence*, 102, quoting *OR* 13. See also *Ms de Nantes O*, f° 22 r°–23 r°; *Mémorial*, 33, 834; *OR* 15.

[83] Bérulle, *Ms de Nantes O*, folio 26 r°–27 r°; also f 22 r°, ff, quoted in *Subsistence*, 102.

"Personne." Il est question de l'unique "subsistence" du Verbe Incarné, de la relation de cette "subsistence" au Père et à l'humanité déifiée, et enfin, de l'entrée des hommes, par ce mystère, dans la filiation adoptive; c'est donc le sens christologique qui émerge ici avec des implications ecclésiologiques.[84]

Subsistence and the Oratorians' Vows

Whannou wrote that the Oratorians were invited to honor Jesus as he is in his person or subsistence, which Bérulle defined as relation both to the Father and to his own assumed humanity. For Bérulle, human beings received in the hypostatic union a new grace of entering into the relation of the subsistence of the Word to the Father because they were now related to the deified humanity. Purified humankind becomes a member of the Mystical Body by union with the humanity of the Word, who allows them to enter within the unity of his divine person such that they return to their Father and their God. Bérulle:

> ...de nous référer au Fils de Dieu qui est relation en sa personne, et relation en la personne du Père, auquel il réfère tout ce qu'il est en ses deux essences éternelle et nouvelle, et généralement tout ce qui lui appartient; et se réfère, non simplement par affection....mais par la condition et l'état de sa personne divine, qui n'est pas seulement relative, mais la relation même; relation éternelle et nécessaire, relation immutable et invariable, relation subsistante et personnelle."[85]

To enter into the subsistence of Christ is a gift to those predestined for this grace. As Whannou wrote, through baptism, Christ comes to dwell in all Christians, but it is not enough. One must consent to subsist in Christ and refer oneself to him who is *relation* to the Father. Importantly, this dynamic became the ideal of the vows.[86] It was also not enough that the priest be ordained but that he also must enter into a more profound relation through the vows of servitude, as this analysis will detail. Bérulle's intention was to emphasize to both Oratorians and Carmelites that abandonment and a mystical passivity, meaning a radical conformity of the will, were necessary for our divinization. This conformity found its exemplar in the privation of the human subsistence of the humanity of Jesus.[87]

---

[84] *Subsistence,* 125.
[85] Bérulle, *OP* 87, 2 (1071) 905, quoted in *Subsistence,* 126.
[86] Ibid., 126.
[87] Ibid., 132.

Luther's and Calvin's Graft

Whannou noted that, for Bérulle, the state of the humanity of the Word and its dependence was both a graft and an ontological transplantation. The union of the humanity with the subsistence of the Word is an ontological transplantation which is the exemplar of the state of servitude for the Christian, involving a mystical graft in Christ. The author asked whether Bérulle may have been influenced by Calvin, who referenced John 15.[88]

Calling Bérulle's ideal analogical, the author wrote that Bérulle noted that the humanity of the Word *cede* to the subsistence of the Word "le droit qu'elle a de subsister en soi-même, pour ne subsister qu'en la personne divine."[89]

For Bérulle, and only after having received grace, one must ratify this dependence by an oblation of servitude to subsist in Christ analogically as the humanity subsists in the Word.[90]

In the following quote referenced by McKay, the interplay between substance and relation is made clear. Bérulle:

> Or comme en Dieu il n'y a que substance et relation, ainsi Dieu, formant son œuvre principal à son image et semblance, a voulu qu'il fût compris dans ces deux catégories de substance et de relation. Jésus-Christ son Fils incarné en est la substance comme étant la grâce incréée: et notre grâce consiste en relation vers lui comme étant en quelque façon les accidents de cette substance qui ne sont que par lui, que pour lui et qu'en lui, et ne sont considérables que comme quelque chose de lui.[91]

Capacity, Stripping, and Passivity

Bérulle, writing on the idea of *capacité de Dieu*, distinguished between a natural capacity linked with creation and a supernatural capacity related to grace. In the case of the former, man is "indigent de Dieu, capable de Dieu, rempli de Dieu,

---

[88]   Ibid., 133–34. Whannou referenced John 15 in Calvin's first edition, *Institution de la religion chrestienne: en laquelle est comprinse une somme de piété, et quasi tout ce qui est nécessaire à congnoistre en la doctrine de salut: Composée en latin par Iean Calvin, et translatée en françois, par luymesme: Avec la préface addressée au treschrestien roy de France, Francoys premier de ce nom: par laquelle ce présent livre luy est offert pour confession de foy* (1541), 217: "Je suis, dit-il, la Vigne, vous êtes le cep…"

[89]   *Grandeurs*, 2, no. 10, 185, quoted in *Subsistence*, 135.

[90]   *Subsistence*, 138.

[91]   *OP* 119, col. 1145, quoted in TG, 207.

s'il le veut."[92] In the second ideal, he considered the saints as having taken on a total passivity and self-annihilation, creating a void that God can fill: the greater the capacity, the greater the holiness. In this way, a person who is disposed by abnegation can receive the resemblance of God in and by Jesus: "plus nous nous déperdons nous-même, plus nous évacuons nous-mêmes (s'il faut parler ainsi), plus nous sommes remplis de Dieu."[93]

The goal of the vow of servitude is mystical passivity, with the state of capacity being a radical stripping, both active and passive, which accompanies sanctifying grace.[94] Whannou also noted that for Bérulle, it was not enough to live with Christ who lives in us by faith and love, but rather one must live inside Christ by what he called a kind of "extase dionysienne et bérullienne." Bérulle illustrated this in his call to the Carmelites of Toulouse: "Mais passez plus outre en cette voie de vie, de grâce et d'amour avec Lui. **Vivez en Lui**, car Il est en vous ou plutôt soyez toutes transformées en Lui-même, en sorte que ce soit Lui et non pas vous qui soit **subsistant**, qui soit vivant, qui soit régissant, qui soit opérant et agissant en vous…"[95]

This mystical ecstasy is what makes for a spiritual transformation in God, according to Whannou. The author pointed to the similar ideals of Bonaventure's sixth degree of contemplation, as well as the annihilated and divinized will of Canfield, and the deiformity of Gagliardi as sources.[96] Whannou noted that for Bérulle, however, this transformation passes from a psychological level to an ontological level—one that is not simply a subjective experience, but a transformation of the will, which is possessed by Christ's will and intelligence.[97] The soul is transformed into God, according to Bérulle: "Dieu s'unit tellement l'âme qu'il opère le tout en elle, de sorte que ce n'est plus l'âme qui opère toutes ces actions saintes….Dieu la transforme en soi-même de telle sorte…que Dieu et le Saint ne font qu'un."[98]

---

[92] *OP* 115, quoted in Subsistence, 173. See also *OP*, 150 regarding "capacité de Dieu."
[93] *OP* 136 B, quoted in *Subsistence*, 174. See discussion 173–76.
[94] Ibid., 178.
[95] *CB*, vol. 2, 342–43, Jan. 1623, quoted in *Subsistence*, 194. See footnote 13 for additional references. Bolding is Whannou's.
[96] *Subsistence*, 194. See nos. 16 and 17, citing Bonaventure, *Itinerarium*, 7, 4, 102; Benet Canfield, *Le règle de perfection* (Paris: Presses universitaires de France, 1982), II, 7, f° 26 r°, 76; Achilles Galliardi and Isabella Cristina Berinzaga, *Breve compendio di perfezione cristiana, e "vita di Isabella Berinzaga" per la prima volta pubblicata, con introduzione e note di Mario Bendisciolo* (Firenze: Libreria editrice fiorentina, 1952), 141–44.
[97] Ibid., 195.
[98] *OP* 107 C, quoted in *Subsistence*, 195.

Whannou argued that this spirituality of subsistence in Christ is a divinization that is essentially Trinitarian because it is Jesus that transforms us in God, realized by the Spirit, and for the glory of the Father.[99] That said, the spirituality of Bérulle, according to Whannou, is essentially a participation in the divine filiation of Christ.[100]

Bérulle's Christology as Spirituality

Cyril's influence, already noted, included Christological formulations that would be judged Monophysite. For example, the *mélange* of two natures such that we are transformed into sons of God by grace is Cyril's, as well as the idea that Jesus imprints in us his form and character as Son.[101] Certain problems arose regarding Bérulle's ideas about the union of the two natures of the Word Incarnate. Bérulle had accepted the perichoresis or interpenetration of the two natures as held by Cyril, and while certain copyist errors did exist, as well as those introduced by his adversaries, there were certain propositions of Bérulle that reflected a Cyrillian perichoresis.[102]

Privation of subsistence was the exemplar for Christian abnegation for Bérulle, which was founded on his interpretation of Cyril. A formula of the vows of servitude, which was defective, as we have explored, reflected the idea of privation of subsistence as a deficiency or defect, in which case it should have been censored. It is not a defect in Christ that we must imitate, but rather abnegation.[103]

Three expressions are associated with Bérulle's doctrine of divinization: the humanized divinity, the divinized humanity, and the divinely human and humanly divine actions. The first two expressions were judged Monophysite because it is not the divinity that is incarnated but the Word. Bérulle attempted to say that Aquinas explained how this could be understood in a non-heretical manner.[104] Bérulle continued to insist that the entirety of the holiness of Christ comes from the grace of union as a formal holiness.

---

99   *Subsistence*, 197.
100   Ibid., 212.
101   Ibid., 219–220. See 220n119. See also Cyril of Alexandria, *Thesaurus*, 24 et seq.
102   Ibid., 223–24.
103   Ibid., 228–32.
104   Ibid., 233. See Aquinas, *ST,* 3.16.4, ad 2, in *Summa theologiae,* 11: 204: "Ad secundum dicendum quod, si ea quae ad defectum pertinent Deo attribuantur secundum divinam naturam, esset blasphemia, quasi pertinens ad diminutionem honoris ipsius: non autem pertinet ad Dei iniuriam si attribuantur ei secundum naturam assumptam."

Subsistence and Its Pertinence to Bérulle's Spiritual Theology of Priesthood

What, if any, influence does a view of subsistence as particularly related to Christ's ecstasy of being have on Bérulle's spiritual theology of priesthood? Detailed study would be required to explore these influences and Bérulle's appropriation of them.

That said, Hastings' review, dependent on that of Diepen, of the consequences of the doctrine of ecstasy of being leads to points to consider for this analysis.

Hastings asserted that if one considers De Vio's view that an essence could be actuated by the divine existence, then there is no reason why it should be limited to the hypostatic union.[105] This doctrine of Christ's ecstasy of being leads necessarily to one of three errors. The first is Pantheism, which reflects a union of potency of human nature and the act of divine existence. The second is essentialism, which, in order to escape Pantheism, as he noted, must deny the real distinction between essence and existence, and so reduce beings to essences. The last, Monophysitism, in order to avoid the latter two errors, must deny any existential reality to Christ's human nature.[106]

Considering French School scholars' warnings not to understand Bérulle's thought in anything but in an analogical way, one must ask whether Bérulle's version of the doctrine of ecstasy of being was reflected somehow in his spirituality and psychology of priesthood, and whether it resulted in placing within the spiritual theology of priesthood itself some aspects of the three possible errors that Hastings noted: Pantheism, essentialism, or Monophysitism. Each possibility will be considered in the following sections.

Pantheism

Thompson insisted that Bérulle's Neoplatonic emanationism had been cleansed of any Pantheism.[107] This study, however, will detail how Bérulle's elevations may have, in fact, been influenced in part by Eckhart's Pantheism, characterized by the need to habitually attempt oneness with the Infinite, as McClintock and

---

[105] Adrian Hastings, "Christ's Act of Existence," *Downside Review* 73 (1955): 156. See also H.-M. Diepen, "Le critique du baslisme selon Saint Thomas d'Aquin," *Revue thomiste* 50 (1950): 82–118, 290–329; and H.-M. Diepen, "L'unique Seigneur Jésus-Christ," *Revue thomiste* 53 (1953): 28–81.

[106] Ibid., 153. Hastings's response to the doctrine was to deny divine actuation of Christ's human nature by formal causality and to affirm Aquinas's notion that the nature has its own existence which both is substantial and has a *secundum quid* character similar to an accident.

[107] Bérulle and Thompson, *Bérulle and the French School*, 85.

Strong described it. Further study might trace the influence of the hard-to-distinguish varieties of early Scholastic Pantheism on Bérulle's thought, especially the idea that God alone has true being as substance of all of things. The authors also suggested that the mystics of the fourteenth century, who had such influence on the Reformers, had borrowed a Scholastic materialism and placed it in a "spiritualized" form.[108] Is this the case with Bérulle? Whannou's study, as already outlined, suggested this.

Monophysitism

For Bérulle, Christ is the subsistence of both the Christian and the priest, thus reflecting an affective theology of the indistinct union of love and will. For the priest, in particular, Christ acts as if by way of principal cause in all actions, not simply during the consecration, suggesting an annihilation of the will at all times. Might this lead to the accusation of an applied idealized spiritual Monophysitism, or perhaps Monothelitism? Further study is required.

Essentialism

Bérulle's priest has the Holy Spirit in person, not just by accidental grace (as opposed to the laity), as this analysis will explore. The sacerdotal anointing of Christ flows to the priest such that his state is that of perfection itself, held in permanent relation to Christ, actuated by frequent acts of the will by way of elevations.

In what ways might this view of the closeness of the priest to Christ and the Spirit be essentialist?

The possible roots of the essentialism found in the Christology of the sixteenth century and its place in the polemics of the Reformation is beyond the scope of this analysis, but a brief summary of critiques of two figures already noted as influences on Bérulle's thought is warranted. Ocáriz, Seco, and Riestra, citing Bilot, noted that De Vio's placing of the formal constituent of the hypostatic union in the substantial mode has had as a chief objection that this substantial mode, "which is nothing more than a termination, seems to be

---

[108] John McClintock and James Strong, "Pantheism," in *Cyclopaedia of Biblical, Theological, and Ecclesiastical Literature*, vol. 7 (New York: Harper & Brothers, 1894), 620–21: "In the 14th century the practical extravagance of the schoolmen's pantheism was repeated by the Mystics, not, however, in a materialistic, but in an idealistic form. They held creatures to be in and of themselves a pure nullity and God alone to be the true being, the real substance of all things."

superfluous."[109] They posited that De Vio did not have a grasp of being as act.[110] The question is whether this essentialism found its way into Bérulle's spiritual theology of priesthood, again through an idealized spirituality emphasizing that the priest has no subsistence of his own.

The same authors also critiqued Suárez, "because for him *existence* is the ultimate actualization of substance, something which is added to the complete substance already constituted in being, can only do so as an accident, as something added on. But the hypostatic union cannot be conceived as something accidental…" They continued, "what lies at the root of these complications is inadequate metaphysical understanding of the act of being, and, in the case of Suárez, that essentialism which comes from denying the real distinction between being and essence."[111]

Bérulle's adoption of a kenotic Christology was based on a Scotist substance-accident model as applied to the hypostatic union.

Van Driel wrote about the difference between what he called classical Christology and kenotic Christology.[112] He wrote of two strategies developed to answer questions related to person and nature: that of Aquinas and his followers and that of Duns Scot and others. Aquinas thought of the relation between the

---

[109] Ocáriz et al., *The Mystery of Jesus Christ*, 118n93. See De Vio, *Commentaria*, 3.4.2.12, in Aquinas, *Summa theologiae*, 11: 77: "Ex hoc namque quod realitas personalitatis est terminus ultimus naturae, patet primo difficultas de identitate et diversitate eius a natura singulari. Est enim quodammodo idem, et quodammodo non idem: sicut terminus est terminato quasi idem: et quasi non idem. Est enim aliquid eius, scilicet terminus, et non est illud…" See also 3.4.2.11, in Aquinas, *Summa theologiae*, 11: 76–77: "Auctoritas est divi Thomae, in III *Sent.*, dist. V, qu. III, art. 3, dicentis: 10: *Quod assumitur, trahitur ad aliquid completius, ipsum incompletum existens: et hoc est contra rationem personae, quae maximam completionem importat.*" Also quoted in *Le mystère*, 46n2.

See also Tommaso de Vio Cajetan, *De ente et essentia*, ch. 5, n. 84, (n.p., n.d.). See also L. Billot, *De Verbo Incarnato*, 7th ed. (Rome: Gregorianum, 1927), 88.

[110] Ibid., 118n93.

[111] Ibid., 119n94. Note that the English translation of this text is awkward. See Francisco Suárez, *Disputationes metaphysicae*, in *Opera omnia*, vol. 26 (Paris: Vivès, 1856), 31.13.18: "Unde cum existentia nihil aliud sit quam essentia in actu constituta, sicut essentia actualis per seipsam, vel per sua intrinseca principia est formaliter limitata, ita etiam existentia creata limitationem habet ex ipsa essentia, non ut est potentia in qua recipitur, sed quia in re nihil aliud est quam ipsamet actualis essentia."

See also A. Michel, "Hypostase," in *DTC*, vol. 7 (1970), 418–21; J. I. Alcorta, *La teoría de los modos en Suárez* (Madrid: Consejo Superior de Investigaciones Científicas, Instituto "Luis Vives" de Filosofía, 1949); and J. Solano, "De Verbo Incarnato," in *Sacrae Theologiae Summa*, vol. 3, 3rd ed. (Madrid: Editorial Católica, 1953), 42–53.

[112] Edwin Chr. van Driel, "The Logic of Assumption," in *Exploring Kenotic Christology: The Self-Emptying of God*, ed. C. Stephen Evans (New York: Oxford University Press, 2006), 265–90.

two as analogous to that of the whole to its parts, with parts sharing in the original *esse* (which Driel called existence) whereas accidents do not. This part-whole model was applied to the hypostatic union, where the Word's *esse* becomes the *esse* of the human nature.[113] Duns Scot preferred the substance-accident model. In this model, Driel wrote, "The relationship between the person of the divine Word and its human nature is analogous to the relation between a subject and an accident."[114] He wrote that Duns Scot's most important argument was that the divine Word can only assume individual substance-natures that are not yet personified.[115]

So, in its relationship with the Word Incarnate, did not just the priesthood but the human nature of the priest become, in Bérulle's kenotic Christosyncretist spirituality, a mere accident of the divine substance? Did he become somehow one with Christ as a depersonalized *néant*, either or both metaphysically and psychologically speaking?

In his effort to defend the priesthood, Bérulle drew from a wide range of sources, combining various ideals into a sum larger than their parts. Did Bérulle introduce these three errors via an affective theology and essentialist spirituality that made the priest one with Christ?

Bérulle's innovative interpretations were in response to the immediacy and personal relationship with Christ that the Reformers urged, and had serious repercussions in the spiritual theology of priesthood, with core Thomistic ideals vitiated by central faults suggested in this chapter, and warranting further study by experts.

Mersch's Critique

We end this chapter with Mersch's thoughts on Bérulle's ideals:

---

[113] Ibid., 271–72. See Aquinas, *ST*, 3.2.6, ad 2, in *Summa theologiae*, 11: 37: "Verbum autem Dei ab aeterno esse comletum habuit secudum hypostasim sive personam: ex tempore autem advenit ei natura humana, non quasi assumpta ad unum esse prout est naturae, sicut corpus assumitur ad esse animae; sed ad unum esse prout est hypostasis vel peronae. Et ideo humana natura non unitur accidentaliter Filio Dei."

[114] Ibid., 273.

[115] Ibid., 274. See John Duns Scot, q. 19, sec. 19.61–19.62, in *Opera Omnia*, 26 (Paris: Ludovicum Vivès, 1891), 287. See esp. 19.61: "Et quod hoc sit possibile de quacumque, probatur ratione, quia quaecumque natura est simpliciter in potentia obedientiali ad dependendum ad personam divinam ; si ergo esset aliqua entitas positiva, quia natura esset in se personata, illa entitas esset assumpta a Verbo, et tunc natura in Christo esset personata simul duplici personalitate, quod est impossibile, quia si creata, igitur per illam est formaliter incommunicabilis alteri personae, et per consequens personae Verbi non communicatur, et ita in ipso non personatur."

His constant refrain is "adherence, dependence, a manner of acting derived from Jesus," a complete stripping off of self in order to be a capacity, a pure capacity for Jesus, distrust of self in order to experience to the full the influence of Jesus. The supernatural life comes to us, not from a living God, but from a dying God—what the author means is clear; it is therefore a grace of self-annihilation, a spirit of death, an operation wherein God "confiscates" our whole being.[116]

Paraphrasing Mersch, one effect of the school pertaining to the rigorisms of the seventeenth century and the problems associated with Jansenism included the fact that those theologians remaining within the Church did not agree with the Protestants that sin vitiates the substance of our nature, but they did maintain that holiness cannot be a result of our own actions except as acts of abstention. Mersch held that the abasement of the Incarnation, the cross, and even the glory of heaven and the tabernacle were all regarded in the French School as part of a sacred annihilation which prevents us from appreciating the humanity and goodness of the Word who should be accessible to humankind. The hypostatic union, according to the way they conceived it, he wrote, absorbs the humanity into a glory and a function that are divine. These ideas placed the very idea of the Mystical Body in jeopardy, Mersch argued. While the humanity of Christ is raised to the grace of headship precisely because of his closeness to us, rather, in this schema, our humanity is minimized and restricted.[117]

Conclusion

Bérulle's treatment of the spiritual theology of the Mystical Body and its relationship with priesthood focused on a unique participation of the priest with the persons of the Trinity, especially Christ, who becomes the priest's "spiritual"

---

[116] Mersch, *The Whole Christ*, 531–55. See 542, quoting Bérulle in English, *OP* 190, in *Les Œuvres de l'eminentissime et reverendissime Pierre Cardinal de Bérulle, instituteur, et premier Superieur General de la Congregation de l'Oratoire de Iesus-Christ nostre Seigneur: Augmentées de divers opuscules de controverse & de pieté, auec plusieurs lettres: et enrichies de sommaires & de tables* (Paris: Chez Sebastien Huré, au Cœur-bon, et Frederic Leonard, à l'Escu de Venise, 1657), 722. In French; "Adherence, Dependance & Conduite deriuée de Iesus, comme de celuy qui est le Souuerain Pasteur des ames..."

[117] Ibid.

substance and subsistence, with the priest's person being assumed by Christ, as we will explore.

With the priest participating in Christ's own ecstasy of being, it could be argued, Bérulle's spiritual theology of priesthood took on pantheist, Monophysite, and essentialist overtones via an essentialist and kenotic spirituality that attempted to move psychological states into ontological categories.

At the heart of the polemics of his era was a question pertinent to this analysis which Welch asked: "Who does the priest represent in his distinctive actions?" He wrote:

> There are two inadequate theories of the relationship between the head and body: one "Pelagianism," and the other "Monophysite"; each has implications for understanding the representative role of the priest. The former theory supposes that Christ, as head, functions as another member of the body. It supposes that the distinctive actions of both head and members exist side-by-side, like two people who pull one rope in order to reach a certain goal. But certainly the head is not just another member of the body. The distinctive actions of both head and members ought not to be understood as exercised in tandem, side-by-side. For it is Pelagian to think that the Church has some sort of independent or autonomous power to sanctify. This hides the Church's radical dependence upon Christ. If the ordained priest is understood to represent this kind of principal agency, then the true headship of Christ is not sacramentalized. Another theory supposes that Christ the head, as principal agent, acts alone. According to this theory, the agency of the members is simply absorbed into Christ; there is no agency, save his. This theory collapses the Church into Christ in a kind of ecclesiological Monophysitism. It cannot express the free character of unity between Christ and the Church. If the ordained priest is understood to represent this kind of principal agency, the role of the assembly is eliminated, or completely taken over by the priest, as representing the head.[118]

In some sense, as we will explore, Bérulle's priest operated under both theories: as an *organe* of Christ in an essentialist relation with Christ in the order of holiness, and so imbued with spiritual power. This power, however, was dependent on a semi-Pelagian effort at prayer for its full exercise.

---

[118] Lawrence J. Welch, "Priestly Identity Reconsidered: A Reply to Susan Wood," *Worship* 70, no. 4 (July 1996): 315.

Bérulle, perhaps, lost a fuller understanding of Christ as the head of the human race, united with every person, which is the presupposition of redemption. He is head of the Mystical Body only by virtue of the humanity of His own soul.[119] Instead, Bérulle held to the idea of the virtue of religion as an ontological schema with God as its immediate object, and only available via moral striving.

Bérulle's polemicized spirituality of the Mystical Body was crucial in his defense of the priesthood. The priest is he who makes sacrifice, and so the key to understanding Bérulle's use of the Mystical Body as a bulwark against what he saw as rebellion and disunity is the notion that sacrifice is necessary for humankind to subsist in God. This doctrine of sacrifice is the subject of the next chapter.

---

[119] Ocáriz et al., *The Mystery of Jesus Christ*, 283–84. See footnote 112 for the discussion on the distinctions between types of headship.

Chapter 10
Bérulle's Sacrificial Spirituality

Introduction

The essence of priesthood being sacrifice, both Reformers and Counter-Reformation polemicists struggled with the idea of the Mass as sacrifice, and the identity of the presider at Eucharist. This chapter will explore Bérulle's own response and his ideals as cohered in his sacrificial sacerdotal spirituality, as various scholars have outlined them. Notions related to kenosis, annihilation, and Bérulle's system of *néant*, as it has been called, will be explored.

Background

Daly wrote that the Council of Trent rose to the defense of the Mass against the Reformers' claim that a true sacrifice requires immolation absent in the Mass. The council fathers, however, did not specify the exact nature of the Mass as sacrifice. This was left to subsequent debate, which was considerable. The center of these debates was whether there was a destruction or real change in Christ as victim.[1]

---

[1] Robert J. Daly, "Robert Bellarmine and Post-Tridentine Eucharistic Theology," *Theological Studies* 61 (2000): 248. See Robert Bellarmine, *De missa*, in *Disputationes de Controversiis Christianae Fidei adversus hujus temporis Haereticos* (Ingolstadt, 1581–93), vol. 3 (Paris: Tri-Adelphorum, 1613), 10.5.5, 720: "Explicatis vocibus Missæ, & sacrificii, sequitur ut ipsa quæstio explicetur; Utrum Missa sit sacrificium. Porrò quæstio principalis cum hæreticis huius temporis, non est de sacrificio spirituali, aut improprio. Fatentur enim Philippus in Apologia Confessionis Augustanæ, & Martinus Kemnítius in Examine Tridentini Concilii & Brentius in Confessione Vvirtembergensi, & alii, Missam, sive sacram cœnam multis modis sacrificium dici posse: sed de sacrificio externo visibili, verè, ac propriè dicto; ac potissimum de ipso genere sacrificii propriè dicti, id est, de oblatione visibili Deo facta ministerio sacerdotum." See also Maurius Lepin, *L'idée du sacrifice de la messe d'après les théologiens depuis l'origine jusqu'à nos jours*, 2nd ed. (Paris: Beauchesne, 1926), 383–84; Edward J. Kilmartin, *The Eucharist in the West: History and Theology*, ed. Robert J. Daly (Collegeville: Liturgical Press, 1998).

Attacks against the Mass were attacks on the identity of what it meant to be Catholic, according to Strenski.[2] The history of discourse about sacrifice in France extended to a "cosmic drama involving self-annihilation and expiation" that had begun in Tridentine theology and was fostered by a Rococo sacrificial spirituality, including that of the French School.[3]

These attacks were also on the identity of the priesthood itself. If all laity could participate in Christ's sacrifice of praise, as emphasized by the Reformers, of what importance is the priest? How should he participate in the priesthood if the "essence" of priesthood is sacrifice?

Bérulle's defense of the Mass and the priesthood focused on Christ's interior state of immolation at the sacrifice of the Mass, and upholding particularly the priest's identity in terms of this sacrifice. St. Augustine and St. Aquinas' conception of the Eucharistic sacrifice as a sign of an interior sacrifice[4] was the basis of Bérulle's rebuttal of Reformist rejections of external sacrifice. In this effort, he strove to first develop a kenotic and sacrificial spirituality for both the laity and priests.

The Priest and Sacrifice

Dupuy remarked that at the heart of Bérulle's Christocentrism was the desire of humanity to praise God, and the duty to do so by sacrifice. In this task, the priest had a central role. For Bérulle, sacrifice was *anéantissement* and oblation more than immolation. Christ's oblation continues in heaven, and Christ remains in

---

The notion of the priest's self-communication as the completion of the sacrifice did, in fact, continue in dogmatic theology into the twentieth century. See Johann Auer and Hugh M. Riley, *A General Doctrine of the Sacraments and the Mystery of the Eucharist*, trans. Erasmo Leiva-Merikakis (Washington, DC: Catholic University of America Press, 1995), 102. Originally published as Joann Auer and Joseph Ratzinger, *Allgemeine Sakramentenlehre und das Mysterium der Eucharistie* (Regensburg: Friedrich Pustet Verlag, 1971).

[2] Ivan Strenski, *Contesting Sacrifice: Religion, Nationalism, and Social Thought in France* (Chicago: University of Chicago Press, 2002). See 1–11.

[3] Ibid., 4 and 12–13.

[4] See Aquinas, *ST*, 3.22.2, co., in *Summa theologiae*, 11: 257: "Respondeo dicendum quod, sicut dicit Augustinus, in X *de Civ. Dei, omne sacrificium visibile invisibilis sacrificii est sacramentum, idest sacrum signum*. Est autem invisibile sacrificium quo homo spiritum suum offert Deo: secundum illud Psalmi: *Sacrificium Deo spiritus contribulatus*. Et ideo omne illud quod Deo exhibetur ad hoc quod spiritus hominis feratur in Deum, potest dici sacrificium."

an *état d'hostie* in heaven.[5] Priests were to sacrifice themselves as they sacrificed Christ:

> Jésus-Christ est victime; que le prêtre soit une victime; il ne doit être autre chose en sa vie, en son geste et actions, qu'une hostie immolée à la gloire de Jésus...Le prêtre sacrifie Jésus. Qu'il sacrifie donc soi-même aussi! Et comme Jésus en cet autel par le ministère du prêtre n'est que pour la gloire et adoration de son Père et pour l'application de la grâce et amour de son Père aux pécheurs, qu'aussi le prêtre ne soit en terre et en l'Église que pour ces deux intentions.[6]

This sacrificial spirituality was not limited to priests. Bérulle emphasized that Christian life itself is a continual death, and that the spirit of the school of Jesus is the spirit of abnegation, as we have explored. Priests, however, were to be the first in this school.[7]

Blanchard noted that, as of 1614, Bérulle proposed annihilation such that the Holy Spirit would become the principle of the Oratorians' being. Not only is Jesus Christ an example of annihilation, but all beings are nothing in God's presence. Bérulle asked that his Oratorians render perpetual honor to the state of abandonment and annihilation, because the annihilation of the divinity in the humanity of Christ was likewise permanent. The soul must self-annihilate to subsist in the Son's deified humanity.[8] Bérulle:

> En Jésus-Christ, l'humanité n'avait pas de subsistence qui lui était propre. Elle était privée de toute personnalité et toute sustentée par la personne du Verbe. Ainsi nous devons demeurer en Jésus-Christ afin que par lui nous accomplissions toutes choses, nous vivions en lui, ce qui certainement arrivera si, en toutes choses, nous cherchons sa gloire, complètement morts à nous-même et au monde en l'honneur de cette grande captivité qu'il avait dans son enfance, de sa divinité, dis-je, de sa sagesse, de son intelligence, de sa raison et sa vie animale.[9]

---

5   Bérulle, *OP* 80, no. 1, quoted in *BLS*, 126. See 124–26n17.
6   Bérulle, *OR* 6, no. 4, 277; also quoted in *BLS*, 132.
7   *BLS*, 132. See *OP* 134.
8   Blanchard, "La spiritualité christocentrique," 112–31.
9   Ibid, 124, quoting Coll. 62, January 1615. See also footnote 74, where the author noted that in the *Collationes*, the terms *persona* and *personalitas* were employed as synonyms.

Daeschler summarized Bérulle's version of abnegation, writing that it was not just a voluntary act of religion, but rather a necessity of supernatural life—that our nature must be stripped and vitiated.[10]

A review of the ideals of Christian sacrifice, self-emptying, and nothingness in relation to union with Christ in his sacrifice is required in order to place Bérulle's thought in this ascetical tradition.

Influences in the History of Mysticism

Bérulle borrowed ideals from a long tradition in forging his sacrificial spirituality. Louth wrote that Philo, for example, held the soul as only a created image of the Logos, and so, in order to know oneself, one must become aware of the "absolute nothingness of created being (*en pasi tou genetou…oudeneian*)."[11] McGinn called this "self-naughting."[12]

Again, St. Paul's repeated phrase "in Christ" had an impact as well in this spirituality, as McGinn noted, exemplified in Gal. 2:19–20: "I have been crucified with Christ, and I live now not with my own life but with the life of Christ who lives in me."[13]

Bérulle saw this passage as referring to a kind of destruction of the self, replaced by the Spirit of Christ: "Par cette source permanente nous entendons l'Esprit qui habite en nous. C'est de lui que parlait saint Paul: 'Je vis, non ce n'est pas moi qui vis, main c'est le Christ qui vit en moi.' Ce "moi" détruit en lui, c'est l'Esprit du Christ qui le remplaçait. Cela s'emplique par le principe suivant: la génération de l'une suit la corruption de l'autre."[14]

Bérulle's Kenosis

Calling Bérulle's doctrine on the union with Christ revolutionary, Hankey noted that Bérulle provided a sacrificial way of living for all believers who were taught

---

[10] R. Daeschler, "Abnégation: II. Tradition patristique, médiévale, moderne," in *DSAM*, vol. 1 (Paris: Beauchesne, 1937), cols. 73–101.

[11] Philo, *De Somniis*, 1.60, Loeb Classical Library, vol. 5 (Cambridge: Harvard University Press, 1934), quoted in McGinn, *The Foundations of Mysticism*, 39. See Louth, *The Origins of the Christian Mystical Tradition*, 25–26.

[12] McGinn, *The Foundations of Mysticism*, 39.

[13] Ibid., 73.

[14] Bérulle, *Collationes*, 292 / March 1612, quoted in Blanchard, "La spiritualité christocentrique," 134–35.

how to do so by priests educated in his system. Hankey held that in this way lay life was transformed.[15]

In Bérulle's Neoplatonic exemplarist schema of the return to God, priests give the laity the power to sacrifice, according to Dupuy. As the Father communicated his essence to the Son, and the Son to our humanity through Mary, so priests communicate Christ's body and life to us so that we might offer an acceptable sacrifice.[16]

Importantly, at the center of Bérulle's project in opposition to the Reformers' emphasis on the priesthood of all believers were priests who were not merely dispensers of the sacraments but *hosties immolées*. Bérulle:

> Ensuite de cette pensée et vérité, nous porterons tous, par le devoir et l'esprit de cette institution, un honneur et amour spécial à Jésus-Christ, nous tenant désormais comme hosties immolées à son service, ainsi qu'il a daigné être hostie immolée pour nous à Dieu son Père, et nous mettant du tout entre ses mains, comme organes de son Esprit et instruments de sa grâce, ainsi qu'il est en son humanité l'instrument joint personnellement à la Divinité.[17]

According to Cochois, in being immolated victims, as Bérulle called them to be, they would unite the sacrifice of redemption to the sacrifice of praise, just as the hypostatic union became in his schema the principle of both redemption and divinization.[18]

The Doctrine of Sacrifice

Following is a more detailed exploration of the notion of the requirement of *anéantissement* on the part of Christians as based on Christ's self-abasement.

---

[15] Wayne J. Hankey, "From St. Augustine and St. Pseudo-Dionysius to Olier and Bérulle's Spiritual Revolution: Patristic and Seventeenth-Century Foundations of the Relations between Church and State in Québec," *Laval théologique et philosophique* 63, no. 3 (Oct. 2007): 542. See Aquinas, *ST*, 3.4.2 and 3.2.6.

[16] Dupuy, *Le Christ de Bérulle*, 124.

[17] *OP* 192, 1270–71, quoted in Blanchard, "La spiritualité christocentrique," 224–25.

[18] Cochois, "Bérulle, hiérarque dionysien," 37: 333–34. Notably, at the end of his life, Bérulle constantly offered himself to God as a *victime de la rédemption*, wishing to belong to the Son's *état* as victim of God, "portant les péchés des hommes en hommage et adoration de ce que Jésus-Christ en a porté par son état de victime…" See Bérulle, Testimony of Marie de Saint-Jérome, Archives nationales, M 233, no. 8, 2, quoted in Cochois, "Bérulle, hiérarque dionysien," 37: 334.

Galy wrote that most works on the French School have treated spirituality rather than theology, passing over the doctrine of sacrifice which is at the core of its spirituality. Galy's work was the first thorough treatment of the doctrine of sacrifice in the French School, with various preceding scholars either praising the doctrine or critiquing it as arbitrary and not essential. His research was an effort to examine this complex doctrine in light of the progress in scholarly conversation regarding which ideals might be considered pious and which precise theology.[19] Despite the serious methodological issues Galy pointed to, as already noted, his remains a salient study.

As this analysis has explored, Bérulle held that Christ began his Passion from the moment of the Incarnation in a double *anéantissement*, which consisted of his nature being reduced to a *néant* in a created nature (yet still existing), as well as in his human nature being deprived of its own subsistence.[20] As noted, this giving up of human subsistence was Bérulle's model for the Christian life. Bérulle wrote, "Comme au mystère de l'incarnation, il y a une sorte d'anéantissement de la nature humaine qui est dépouillée de sa proper subsistence pour être établie en la personne du Verbe, aussi en la grâce, il y a une sorte d'anéantissement de nous-mêmes et d'établissement en Jésus."[21]

De Lubac argued, however, that those who see in Bérulle the assertion that spiritual beings lack their own nature or essence are incorrect. He quoted Bérulle in his discussion regarding past thinkers on the ideal of living in Christ:

> Nous avons encore une autre émanation de Dieu, et bien plus obligeante à nous sanctifier, c'est celle de Jésus; Jésus en est le principe, et nous naissons de lui…nous entrons en Jésus. Saint Paul nous appelle les créés en Jésus-Christ…comme nous avons deux émanations de Dieu, et deux êtres différents, nous avons aussi deux entrées en mondes bien divers, et à des fins bien diverses. Car en la cration première, nous entrons en ce monde que nous voyons, et en la creation seconde nous entrons en un monde que nous adorons; c'est-à-dire nous entrons, nous vivons, nous opérons en Jésus: *Creati in Christo Jesu.* Et comme il est notre principe, il est notre univers aussi, il est notre monde et nous vivns en lui.[22]

---

[19] Galy, *Le sacrifice*, 10–12.

[20] Ibid., 28–30.

[21] *OC,* Migne ed., 701–2; Gaston Rotureau, *Le cardinal de Bérulle: opuscules de piété* (Paris: Aubier, 1943), Opuscule 151, 451, quoted in Galy, *Le sacrifice*, 31n15.

[22] Bérulle, Opuscule 125, 2, in Rotureau, *Le cardinal de Bérulle*, 381 and 415–416, quoted in Henri de Lubac, *Le mystère du surnaturel* (Paris: F. Aubier, Éditions Montaigne, 1965).

Christ's Sacrifice according to Galy

Bérulle held that the sacrifice of Christ was that of his humanity, consecrated to the cult, offered to God, with its appropriation by the divine essence in which it became the *hostie* of the Father.[23] Central to Bérulle's economy of *anéantissement* was his idea of Christ's perpetual interior oblation, even in heaven: "Jésus-Christ a trouvé l'invention d'établir une partie de sa passion dans l'état de sa gloire, y réservant ses cicatrices."[24] Bérulle defined Jesus' entire life in terms of oblation and servitude, as a victim from the moment of conception whose function in the state of *hostie* was adoration and expiation: "et il est naissant comme hostie, et hostie de louanges, et comme hostie qui reçoit son accomplissement en ce mystère et y fait sa fonction et son office, rendant louanges et adoration au Père éternel."[25]

This state included the Mass: Bérulle wrote of an immolation and an effusion of invisible but real blood operating at the words of consecration.[26] It was, as Galy, termed it, a virtual sacrifice. Bérulle wrote: "une immolation sans occision…et en somme un sacrifice vrai et parfait sans être pourtant un sanglant sacrifice."[27]

Important to this study, Galy noted that Christ's action as priest at the Mass is an interior action within the human priest who is his member, as we will explore.[28]

Ferrari's Analysis

Ferrari clarified associations in Bérulle's defense of the Mass as sacrifice. For Bérulle, according to Ferrari, the emphasis was not on the sacrifice of the Mass but rather on the interior mysteries of the life of Christ. Ferrari pointed to Bérulle's notion of the three sacrifices of Jesus: the perpetual sacrifice of his glory, the second in the Eucharist, and the third on the cross. The last two are inseparable for Bérulle: the cross as immolation and the Eucharist as the interior oblation which transforms the cross into a sacrifice: "Vous avez une viande, mais non une hostie présente en l'Eucharistie sans le sacrifice de la crox […]; vous avez un meurtre et non un sacrifice en la coix sans l'oblation et intérieure et

---

23   Galy, *Le sacrifice*, 33–34, quoting *Grandeurs*, Migne ed., 360–361.
24   Bérulle, *OP*, (54) 201–202, quoted in Galy, *Le sacrifice*, 65.
25   Bérulle, *Grandeurs*, 360, quoted in Galy, *Le sacrifice*, 46.
26   Bérulle, in Rotureau, *Le cardinal de Bérulle*, Opuscule 88, 309, quoted in Galy, *Le sacrifice*, 93.
27   *OC*, Migne ed., 703, quoted in Galy, *Le sacrifice*, 94.
28   Galy, *Le sacrifice*, 101–3.

sacrificielle que le Fils de Dieu a faite de soi-même en l'Eucharistie en Sion. L'un sacrifice de rédemption, l'autre sacrifice de religion."[29]

In this, again, Bérulle attempted to meet the Reformers' insistence that the sacrifice is only that of praise.

Carraud on Sacrifice as a Lutheran Aporia

Carraud held that Bérulle's concept of the *néant* was the most operational in his work, joining the ontological with the Christological, and that Bérulle's rejection of philosophy gave him a dependence on an underlying obsolete metaphysic.[30] In a later study, Carraud also explored the link between the spirituality and metaphysics of sacrifice, as well as that of Bérulle's and Condren's ideal of the *néant* in relation to Condren's notion of sacrifice.[31] Carraud's aim was to explore the link between this spirituality of sacrifice and the metaphysical, in order to illustrate the further link between what he called the Berullian-Condrenian theory of the *néant* and Condren's doctrine of sacrifice.[32]

Notably, he quoted Balthasar on the general nature of both sacrifice and the nature of Eucharistic sacrifice: that "…il faut avoir constamment à l'esprit que le mot n'est utilisé que par analogie."[33]

Carraud observed that the analogical use of a concept often results in an aporia that demarcates rather than clarifies extreme terms.[34] This idea is pertinent to the concept of Eucharistic sacrifice and important to this study. He referenced Aquinas, asserting that for him, destruction is not the essence of sacrifice, a problematic point at the time of the Reformation in relation to the Mass, as this analysis has noted. The Lutheran and Zwinglian rejection of the sacrificial nature of the Mass had at its core the insistence on the nature of sacrifice as immolation and so involving the destruction of a victim. Carraud held that this insistence on immolation became a Catholic aporia, essentially a Lutheran inheritance.[35] In the

---

[29] Bérulle, *OP*, 87, 261, in Anne Ferrari, "La notion de sacrifice dans l'école française de spiritualité et à Port-Royal," in *Port-Royal et l'école française de spiritualité: Colloque organisé par la Société des Amis de Port-Royal (15–16 septembre 2006)*, ed. Helene Michon and Laurence Devillairs, *Chroniques de Port-Royal,* vol. 57 (Paris: Bibliothèque Mazarine, 2007), 74.

[30] Carraud, "De l'état," 245–47.

[31] Vincent Carraud, "De la destruction: Métaphysique et idée du sacrifice selon Condren," *Archivo di filosofia* 76 (2008): 335.

[32] Ibid., 335.

[33] Hans Urs von Balthasar, "Don du Christ et sacrifice eucharistique," *Communio* 10, no. 3 (1985): 5–6, quoted in Carraud, "De la destruction," 332n3.

[34] Carraud, "De la destruction," 332.

[35] Ibid, 334.

half-century following the Council of Trent, various theories were proposed by theologians regarding the nature of the sacrifice present in the Mass, but they all agreed that immutation, viewed as immolation, was essentially a sacrifice.[36]

The French School of spirituality was to have no qualms about addressing these issues and was to develop a doctrine of sacrifice, making it the essential duty of religion, and, according to Galy, establishing the rapport between sacrifice and priesthood.[37]

Le Néantisme *of Bérulle*

Continuing with Carraud's analysis, he termed Bérulle's project a *système du néant*.[38] Bérulle treated categories of *néant*: a *néant* by nature (*néant métaphysique*), a *néant* of sin (*néant moral*), and a *néant* of grace (*état anéanti* of grace), as this analysis will detail. He did so, according to Carraud, in an openly anti-philosophical spirit, which rejected both the love of self and the love of nature in favor of the abnegation of the Christian self. This spirit was at heart an anti-Scholastic reaction, which did, in fact, use the Neoplatonism of the abstract school. Bérulle's was an attempt to address the crisis in both the philosophy and theology of that time.[39]

Carraud attempted to explicate Bérulle's doctrine of the *néant* in order to contribute to the understanding of the *néant* in the early seventeenth century. Carraud did so, relating it to Christology, while relying on Orcibal and Cognet's analyses. Carraud pointed out that the theme of unity of spirit in the early seventeenth century (see 1 Cor. 6:17), upon which depended the sense of the word *adherence*, had three models: that of the medieval contemplative tradition of spirituality; that of the Mystical Body; and that of Neoplatonism, especially Pseudo-Dionysian, with the mystical being understood as fusion, requiring a separation not only from everything besides God, including all creatures, but also from oneself. Bérulle:

> La théologie mystique tend à nous tirer, à nous unir, à nous abîmer en Dieu. Elle fait le premier par la grandeur de Dieu, le second par son unité, le troisième par sa plénitude. Car la grandeur de Dieu nous sépare de nous-mêmes et des choses créées, et nous tire en Dieu. Son unité nous

---

[36] Ibid., see discussion, 332–33, esp. 332n5. See Aquinas ST, 2-2.85.3, ad 3 in *Summa theologiae*, 9: 218: "Sacrficia proprie dicuntur quando circa res Deo oblatas aliquid fit…"

[37] Ibid, 335. See *BLS*, 123–35, and Galy, *Le sacrifice*, 109.

[38] Carraud, "De l'état," 211–47.

[39] Ibid., 212–16.

reçoit et nous unit en lui. Et sa plénitude nous perd, nous anéantit et nous abîme dans l'océan immense de ses perfections, comme nous voyons que la mer perd et abîme une goutte d'eau.[40]

Gilson named Bérulle *l'apôtre de l'unité divine*.[41] As Carraud explained, quoting Bérulle, "La foi propose, pour Bérulle, trois unités: 'l'unité d'essence en la divinité que nous adorons; l'unité d'amour en La Trinité que nous admirons; l'unité de subsistence en l'Incarnation que nous professons'."[42]

Carraud asserted that the Rheno-Flemish current of mysticism influencing Bérulle was "profondément volontariste, qui tient que l'essence de l'homme réside dans la volonté: l'union à Dieu s'acomplit par l'absorption—volontaire—de la volonté humaine dans la volonté divine."[43] In the Rheno-Flemish school, following Eckhart, Carraud noted that all was to be transcended and denied, with no intermediary between the soul and God, not even the humanity of Christ.[44]

Huijben noted that Bérulle would follow *La perle* in the idea that the creature should offer no resistance to God as *néant*.[45] As authors have noted, Bérulle's Christocentrism and the importance of the Incarnation came after an early period of his interest in abstract mysticism. Carraud wrote, however, that Bérulle faced the problem of how to reconcile the neantist mysticism of union without intermediary of the abstract school with a devotion to the Incarnation. According to Carraud, all of Bérulle's Christology and its concomitant anthropology would be an attempt to address this problem. Bérulle's concepts of *néant*, *anéantissement, adherence*, and *servitude* would be crucial in this effort.[46] Carraud here referred to Cognet's definition of adherence: "L'adhérence est en quelque façon, une participation à l'union hypostatique et, du même mouvement, elle nous fait entrer en Dieu."[47]

The definition of annihilation for Bérulle included three senses: *l'abnégation* (the exclusion of obstacles);[48] *exinanition* (the double kenosis of the Word);[49] and

---

[40] Bérulle, *OC* (1995), *OP* 12, 57, quoted in Carraud, "De l'état," 222.

[41] Gilson, *La liberté chez Descartes et la théologie*, 170, quoted in Carraud, "De l'état," 222n46.

[42] Carraud, "De l'état," 222–23n46, quoting Bérulle, *Grandeurs*, 3, Migne ed., col. 200.

[43] Ibid., 223–24.

[44] Ibid., 225.

[45] AS, 27: 105–6. See Van Essche, Despont, De Mallery, and De La Nouë, *La perle*, 1.2, ch. 5, fol. 135. See also *OC*, col. 1590.

[46] Carraud, "De l'état," 227.

[47] Cognet, *La spiritualité moderne*, 353–54, quoted in Carraud, "De l'état," 227n65.

[48] Carraud, "De l'état," 230, quoting Bérulle, *OC, Conférences et fragments* (1995), 237 / *Collationes* (1995), 212: "Nostrum est remouere dumtaxat impedimenta."

[49] Ibid., 231, quoting Bérulle, *OC, Conférences et fragments* (1995), 235 / *Collationes* (1995), 211: "[…] dans le Christ Seigneur il y a deux sortes d'anéantissement, à savoir, d'une part

in the state of glory "une autre anéantissement, sans aucune doute, de l'essence même de l'âme,"[50] in which "il est certain qu'il n'y a plus en elle que Dieu et que c'est Dieu seul qui opère."[51]

Bérulle's Theory of Relation, Le Néant, and Sacrifice

Dupuy believed that Bérulle arrived to the point of holding the human being to be a pure relation,[52] although he conceded this was figurative language.[53] Bérulle wrote: "Que je me réfère à vous, comme vous m'y référez par la puissance et éminence de votre Être et par la condition propre de mon être qui n'est qu'une ombre inséperable de votre Être et une simple relation à vous!"[54]

Carraud related that the Neoplatonism of continuous creation was adapted by Bérulle to include integration of one's being with Christ. He illustrated the importance of the Berullian thesis of relation in the following quotation: "Ô mon Seigneur Jésus, faites que je vive et subsiste en vous, comme vous vivez et subsistez en une personne divine! Soyez mon tout, et que je fasse partie de vous en votre corps mystique, comme votre humanité est partie d'un divin composé subsistant en deux natures si différentes."[55]

Carraud insisted that all of Bérulle's thought revolved around the theme of relation in which he opposed the "science" of Aristotle with that of Christ. Bérulle went so far as to say that our being itself is a relation: "Notre être est un rapport

---

celui de la personne humaine, puisque la nature humaine en lui ne subsiste pas avec sa personalité propre, et d'autre part l'anéantissement de sa divinité puisqu'il n'apparaît pas dans la majesté mais dans 'la forme d'un esclave'." In Latin: "[…] in Christo Domino duplicem fuisse exinanitionem, unam videlicet personae humanae cum per personalitatem propriam non subsistat in ipso natura humana, et aliam Divnitatis suae exinanitionem cum non appareat in maiestate sed 'in formam servi'."

50   *OC, Conférences et fragments* (1995), 237 / *Collationes* (1995), 212, quoted in Carraud, "De l'état," 235. In Latin: "[…] agnoscamus aliam possibilem […] annihilationem ipsiusmet videlicet essentiae animae."

51   Ibid., *Conférences et fragments* (1995), 236 / *Collationes* (1995), 211, quoted in Carraud, "De l'état," 233. In Latin: "Ita etiam, cum se communicat animae post supra dictam abnegationem, est quidem annihilate: quo autem modo nescimus, sed certum est Deum solum in ea esse, illum solum operari."

52   Ibid., xxxiv, citing *OP* 192, in *Œuvres de piété (166–385)*, ed. Michael Dupuy, *OC*, vol. 4 (Paris, 1995).

53   Ibid., xxxiv, citing *OP* 228, 3.

54   Bérulle, *OP* 192, 66.

55   *Grandeurs*, 2, no. 6, Migne ed., col. 168, quoted in Carraud, "De l'état," 236n104. Bérulle insisted that this kind of subsisting in God is by way of analogy only. See also *OC, Collationes* (1995), 65–66.

à Dieu."[56] As a *néant*, we do not place any obstacle between us and God, becoming "capable de Dieu."

Returning to the theme of capacity in Bérulle's work, Carraud opined that it is a key part of Bérulle's anthropology. As we worship and imitate through spiritual abnegation the *état anéanti* of Jesus Christ (the ontic model of annihilation, Carraud noted), we return to our original state, the pre-creational *néant*, becoming capable of God.[57]

Turning now to Carraud's second study, in which the Berullian-Condrenian theory of the *néant* and Condren's doctrine of sacrifice are explored,[58] Carraud related and commented on Gibieuf's description of Bérulle's three ways of being a *néant*: that of the nothing before creation out of which God draws us, that of the nothing of sin, and that which we must enter along with the Son by abasing ourselves.[59] As noted, Carraud called the idea of the three *néants* (*ontologique, moral, et spirituel*) "une système du néant."[60]

Important to this analysis, Carraud commented that this system of *néant* not only rejects the univocity of its era (such as that of Suárez), but also does not have a basis in the analogy of being, because not only is there no rapport between infinite and finite being (existence), but also, in fact, there is no analogous concept.[61]

The Condrenian concept of sacrifice, based on the same exemplarism as Bérulle's, was, according to Carraud, characterized by a radical rejection of the analogy of being. In fact, it necessitated the destruction of being.[62] Carraud asserted that Condren misused a traditional (Thomistic) metaphysical determination that created being has its being from a cause of which it is an effect, by affirming the nothingness of created being and the need for self-destruction. Thus, he charged Condren with transposing a metaphysical doctrine into a spiritual doctrine. He quoted Condren: "Le sacrifice étant institué pour reconnaître Dieu, comme Auteur de tout l'être, et pour honorer son souverain

---

[56] *OC* (1996), *OP* 180, 39, quoted in Carraud, "De l'état," 239.
[57] Carraud, "De l'état," 241.
[58] Carraud, "De la destruction," 335.
[59] Ibid., 342, quoting Gibieuf, Bourgoing ed., 135; Migne ed., no. 136, col. 1170: "Il y a trois sortes de néant: le néant duquel Dieu nous tire par la création, le néant où Adam nous met par le péché, et le néant où nous devons entrer avec le Fils de Dieu s'anéantissant soi-même pour nous réparer."
[60] Ibid., 342.
[61] Ibid., 342n4, paraphrased.
[62] Ibid., 342–43.

domaine sur l'être créé, il demanderait la consomption et la destruction entière de cet être."[63]

Carraud ends his discussion with the observation that the combination of these two systems of *néant* and sacrifice-destruction linked metaphysics, morals, Christology, and liturgy, but with radical deficits in each.[64]

Cochois noted that the mystical annihilation of Bérulle and Condren may have used different terminologies but were much the same.[65] The following analysis will suggest that Condren's notions of a radical sacrificial spirituality were already in full flower in Bérulle's thought.

The Destruction of Nature by the Supernatural

According to Hankey, Bérulle's was a "radically new Christocentric Catholicism…based in a reinterpretation of the formula of Chalcedon" in which Christ sacrificed "his humanity to his divinity from all eternity."[66]

We will now explore the sacrifice of the self.

Le Sacrifice du Moi

Le Lannou conducted an investigation into Bérulle's ideas on being and its sacrifice, which was centered on piety, a piety that demanded the suppression of all obstacles to the love of God, and which he characterized as radically antihumanist. Bérulle called it the "demission de son être."[67] What was this abdication of being? As Bérulle insisted, "l'être n'est pas essentiel et nécessaire à la créature."[68]

For Bérulle, to be is to be referred to God. Le Lannou asked what must one do to be in this exclusive relation to God? The love of God demanded for Bérulle that we renounce self-love and die to self.[69] In a second instance of the notion of

---

[63] Charles de Condren, *L'idée du sacerdoce et du sacrifice de Jésus-Christ* (Paris, 1697), 41, quoted in Carraud, "De la destruction," 344.

[64] See Carraud, "De la destruction," 346–48.

[65] Cochois, "Bérulle, hiérarque dionysien," 37: 332.

[66] Wayne J. Hankey, "Philosophy as Way of Life for Christians? Iamblichan and Porphyrian Reflections on Religion, Virtue, and Philosophy in Thomas Aquinas," *Laval théologique et philosophique* 59, no. 2 (2003): 210–11.

[67] *OC*, vol. 6, *Courts traités: Bref discours de l'abnégation intérieure, Traité des énergumènes, Trois discours de controverse, Autres œuvres de controverse*, ed. Michel Dupuy (Paris, 1997), 22, quoted in SM, 205–6.

[68] *OC* (1996), 39 and 116, quoted in SM, 214.

[69] SM, 207–8. See *OC* (1996), 346.

simple relation, Bérulle, addressing God, insisted: "vous êtes ma substance et je ne suis qu'une simple relation à vous."[70]

Le Lannou pointed out that Bérulle rejected Aristotle's thesis regarding the substantiality of nature as anterior to relation.[71] Le Lannou remarked that nature, for Bérulle is merely "une vaine pretension à l'auto-position," which, according to Le Lannou, Bérulle thought imposed, "ontologiquement," a love of self.[72] Bérulle noted that "cette catégorie de relation est une des plus petites, *tenuissimae entitatis*; et c'est la catégorie la plus puissante et la plus importante dans le monde de la grâce qui ne subsiste et ne consiste que'en relation en Dieu."[73]

Le Lannou summarized that Bérulle's fundamental ontological thesis was that God is sole substance, and anything outside of him is insubstantial.[74]

Bérulle's piety demanded not only a free consent to this relation, but an adherence to the movement toward God.[75] Bérulle held that "la créature a une imperfection quasi comme essentielle, en qualité de chose créée, se joignant et attachant facilement à ce qui est créé" which is changed into almost "une inclination comme essentielle…de désunion…avec Dieu."[76]

Further clarifying the demands of Bérulle's piety, Le Lannou called it a piety that demanded a kind of destruction of one's personality, resulting in a depersonalization.[77]

Bérulle clarified that the first creation was in God, and the second in Christ. Grace separates us from ourselves and establishes us in Christ, forming us into a living image ("l'image de son Fils incarné").[78] Le Lannou wrote, quoting Bérulle: "'par la soustraction de l'existence et subsistance humane,' nous conduira au 'monde intelligible et archétype,' puisque 'Jésus est une monde.'"[79] This was essential liberty for Bérulle, according to Le Lannou.

---

[70] Ibid., 66, quoted in SM, 215.
[71] Ibid., 208. See *OC* (1996), 108, for a discussion of Bérulle's opinion of the inadequacies of ancient philosophy.
[72] Ibid., 209.
[73] *OC* (1996), 164–65, quoted in SM, 210–11.
[74] Ibid., 214.
[75] Ibid., 217. See *OC* (1996), 21.
[76] *OC, OP* (1996), 55, quoted in SM, 219.
[77] SM, 220.
[78] Ibid., 226. See *OC, OP* 227, (1996), 141.
[79] Ibid., 226. See *OC*, Montsoult ed., 1083; *OP* (1996), 58; and *Courts traités* (1997), 224.

Spirituality of Contingency or Indigence?

Bérulle saw relation as both indigence and the capacity for God, according to Dupuy.[80] For Bérulle, relation was neither like a property of being nor like a predicament, but rather a constituent of being, without which one is nothing, an idea taken from Duns Scot, according to Bellemare.[81] For Duns Scot, the creature tended to non-being: "Creatura ita tendit in non-esse…quia est ex nihilo."[82]

Bérulle took this further, writing, "la créature est indigente," and the humanity of Christ is "très indigente."[83]

Néantisme *and Pious Theologizing*

Balthasar, pointing to Bérulle, criticized a kind of "pious theologization of metaphysics" which "is forgetful of every worldly encounter of actual Being and springs over this, if all spirits communicate *only* in God as their common sun." Rather, "ultimately it is Jesus, God's Word and Son, who comes to meet us *immediately* in all sensible and intellectual knowledge." He continued,

> Thus this philosophy of spirit also lacks the decisive experience of reality: the shock of a head-on encounter with *another* ego, a dialogue between an I and a Thou which is radically open to its own vulnerable depths of being. This shock was missing in Bérulle, Condren and Fénelon, which is why their elevated spirituality retains something spectrally unreal, journeying in a world of ideas without a basis in Nature, crudely stated: something elitist for spiritual aristocrats for which, not without reason, the merciless guillotine of the real 'comrades' stands waiting.[84]

In this thoughtful critique, Balthasar brings to mind the confrontation of the French Revolution with the French hierarchy of the late eighteenth century, the inheritor of Bérulle's ideals. This analysis begs the question whether the elevated and essentialist spirituality of Bérulle's priesthood, based on pure relation and without a basis in nature, allowed the priest to be in a true personal relationship with Christ. Also, how could this priest relate to others and their vulnerability if his own ego was closed to the vulnerability of his own being?

---

[80] *BSA*, 52n44. See *OP*, 8, 122, 147. This review follows the author's exposition closely.

[81] Ibid., 52. See Robert Bellemare, *Le sens de la créature dans la doctrine de Bérulle* (Paris: Desclée de Brouwer, 1959), 122ff.

[82] John Duns Scot, *In 2 Sent.*, d. 1, q. 3, arg. 4; cf. q. 2, arg. 3, in *Opera omnia*, Wadding ed., quoted in *BSA*, 281.

[83] *BSA*, 281, quoting Bérulle, Marseille, 22 (66 D), fol. 75.

[84] Balthasar, Riches, and McNeil, *The Glory of the Lord*, 481.

Conclusion

To answer Reformers' emphasis on sacrifice as praise, Bérulle constructed a spiritual theology of priesthood that upheld priests' necessary place as mediators and sacrificers by constructing a sacrificial spirituality which envisioned the priest as *victim immolée* himself, who also must sacrifice himself as he sacrifices Christ.

Carraud observed that Bérulle had to reconcile his first emphasis on the mysticism of union without intermediary as well as the neantism of the abstract school with his later devotion to the Incarnation. Bérulle took the devotional Christ that he found in his interactions with the Carmelites and transformed him into the Cosmic Christ and exemplar ego, in union by way of a pseudo-annihilation with both laity and priests.

Important to this study, Carraud's crucial observation that Bérulle's was a radical rejection of both univocity and analogy of being points to clear ramifications for Bérulle's spiritual theology of priesthood. Christ can only operate through the priest to the degree that he somehow sacrifices himself to cede place to Christ.

The next chapter will explore how this schema was utilized by Bérulle in his doctrine of the priest as the mediator of redemption himself.

Chapter 11
The Priest as Mediator of Redemption

Introduction

A central question that came to the fore again at the time of the Reformation was that of how the priest participates in the mediation of Christ. The following chapter outlines Bérulle's thoughts on the mediation of priests who participate in the state of Christ's priesthood and the mysteries of his priestly life, a mediation that extends to spiritual direction and their comprehensive authority as Pseudo-Dionysian hierarchs.

Background

The Counter-Reformers criticized Protestant pastors for not having a "vocation" as defined by Catholic theologians: the calling to a function by hierarchical authority, often synonymous, according to Dupuy, with mission. Calvin and others held that there was an exterior vocation given by the hierarchy and an interior one given by God.[1]

Dupuy held that Bérulle would follow the Catholic understanding of vocation, but in countering Calvin, he emphasized a personal calling or *voie*, equating it with mission as based on an exemplarist notion of mission. Dupuy lamented this, writing that he considered it a loss of ecclesial value.[2]

This use of exemplarism was Bérulle's chief method of combating what he saw as rebellion against authority. The chief question became, "How does the hierarchy mediate salvation?" D'Angers wrote that the Church, the Mystical Body, became the image of the divine nature for Bérulle, and the mission of the apostles a reflection of the processions. The Eucharist was an imitation of the

---

[1] BLS, 97–98. See John Calvin, "Commentarius in Genesin," in *Joannis Calvini opera quae supersunt omnia*, CO, 23: 238: "…promissio non generaliter accipitur pro externo verbo, quo Deus suam gratiam tam reprobis quam electis conferebat, sed ad efficacem vocationem quam intus obsignat per spiritum suum restringi debet."

[2] Ibid., 99–100. See Coll. 275.

Incarnation, as well as the image of eternal generation and divine fecundity. The Church reproduced the characteristics of the Incarnation in the mission of its apostles, sacraments, prayer, and in souls who must receive the image of the divine model and reproduce it by their own supernatural efforts.[3]

This was particularly the case for Bérulle's Oratorians, for whom the participated priesthood meant being holy mediators of holiness.

Christ as Mediator

McGinn noted that debates over mysticism preceded this era, including the questions whether mystical experiences replace the mediation of Christ and whether they encourage antinomianism and the denial of the mediation of the sacramental Church. The Reformers attempted to address questions regarding mysticism, and their responses varied considerably. While Luther insisted on a mystical union established in baptism, with God becoming one with man in temptation and suffering, he rejected speculative mysticism. One of Calvin's specific responses was to proclaim Christ as sole mediator.[4]

According to Jones, mediation is the key to understanding Calvin's Christology in which there is no need for priests.[5] As discussed and cited, Calvin emphasized the doctrine of the three offices or functions of Christ (as priest, prophet, and king), which became a central theme of the Reformation.[6]

As if in response to Calvin's priest, prophet, and king theme, Bérulle called the anointing of the priest greater than that of prophets, kings, or religious.[7]

The Priest as Holy Mediator of Holiness

The issue of the holiness and mediatorial character of the priest was not a new one. Donatists had insisted the priest was the source of holiness rather than a mere mediator, a position Augustine would counter.[8] Returning to an important passage, already cited, Bérulle understood Augustine (erroneously) as holding

---

[3] D'Angers, "L'exemplarisme bérullien," 133–39.

[4] McGinn, "Mysticism," 119–24. See *Institution*, 3.20.21: Calvin insists that Christ has the "titre de seul médiateur."

[5] Jones, "Toward a Christology of Christ the High Priest," 215–16.

[6] Jones, "Toward a Christology of Christ the High Priest," 17. See also Jean-Yves Lacoste, *Encyclopedia of Christian Theology*, vol. 1, 2nd ed. (New York: Routledge, 2005), 290–91, and *Lumen Gentium*, 25–27.

[7] *BLS, OR* 23–25, no. 1, 318.

[8] Gerald O'Collins and Michael Keenan Jones, *Jesus Our Priest: A Christian Approach to the Priesthood of Christ* (Oxford: Oxford University Press, 2010), 88.

that mission and procession were synonymous, in an exemplarist attempt to defend the priest's mission as founded in the society of the Trinity.[9] Morgain explained this parallelism as found in Bérulle's defense:

> Dans le souci de combattre le théocentrisme exclusif de Jean Calvin, Bérulle emprunte à Denys l'Aréopagite, l'idée de la "chaîne dorée" qui, issue de l'Un ne reconduit à l'Un qu'au terme d'un parcours à travers tous les intermédiaires hiérarchiques. Et ailleurs, dans certains passages platoniciens, il montre que l'Église est la parfaite image de son archétype, c'est-à-dire la Trinité dont elle possède la "fécondité divine," la "pluralité des ministères" et, cependent, l'unité… Dans *l'Opuscules de piété* 288, Bérulle dit en effet: "L'Église est un œuvre d'unité et de société. Ainsi la prêtrise."[10]

Bérulle believed that the Reformers' rebellion blocked the mediatorship of Christ, tearing apart the Mystical Body: "Nous adhérons à son corps réel par la communion à l'Eucharistie, et à son corps mystique par la communion de l'Église."[11] Bérulle confused hierarchical proximity with physical proximity to Christ, according to Morgain, believing that the closer one is in intimacy, the more efficacious the mediation.[12]

In the context of a Pseudo-Dionysian efficiency and exemplarism, Bérulle's notion of vocation was not simply a state of life, but a very particular form of communion with the life and grace of Jesus Christ, noted Blanchard. Bérulle was interested in the *intérieur* of the mysteries of the Incarnation, insisting that there were certain vocations that honored certain mysteries. In the case of the vocation of the perfect, one must honor the mystery of the interior life of the Man-God. The object for Oratorians was participation in the life of the Man-God through honoring the mystery of Christ's interior life: "De même qu'au ciel, Dieu est pour les saints toutes choses et en toutes choses, de même en la terre, le Fils de Dieu doit être toutes choses pour nous et nous devons le considérer en toutes choses."[13]

In Bérulle's explication of this notion of vocation in one of his conferences, he noted that Carmelites and Oratorians, being advanced in the spiritual life,

---

9   *Discours de controverse*, OC, Migne ed., 673, quoted in Rétif, "Trinité et Mission d'après Bérulle," 3 (see ch. 8, n. 4).

10 Morgain, "La prêtrise selon Pierre de Bérulle," 144, quoting Bérulle, OC (1996), OP 288, 315.

11 Bérulle, *Dédicace au roi*, OC, *Grandeurs* (1996), 21, quoted in Morgain, *La théologie politique de Pierre de Bérulle*, 392.

12 Ibid., 371–72.

13 Coll. 230, quoted in Blanchard, "La spiritualité christocentrique," 69.

must aspire to communication and a special participation: "d'aspirer à cette communication et à cette participation spéciales dont nous venons de parler, s'il daigne en faisant appel à sa seule miséricorde nous y appeller." Dupuy noted that in an old translation of this particular conference, this phrase regarding the aspiration to this special communication was omitted, as it had been open to the charge of *mystiquerie*.[14]

Cognet clarified that the mediation that the priest was able to effectuate in Bérulle's project was not merely a necessary effect but by way of entering into a special state of adherence.[15] They were to be attached to the Incarnation itself, which Bérulle described as "…l'Incarnation, auqel nous appertenons et en vertu duquel nous opérons et nous traitons avec le monde."[16]

Cochois' Analysis

For Bérulle, the state of priesthood required two things: great perfection and a special bond with Jesus Christ, conjoining with him in a special manner, according to Cochois. With these two notions, Bérulle developed a double theology of priesthood: the first aspect being that of the priest as hierarch/mediator of deifying grace (associating Neoplatonic themes with a theology of mission, which was central in his notions regarding spiritual direction); and the second aspect associating sacramental participation in the priesthood of Christ (which was an aspect of the traditional theology of order). Bérulle:

L'état de prêtrise requiert de soi-même deux points:

premièrement une très grande perfection et même sainteté, car c'est un état saint et sacré en son institution, c'est un office divin en son usage et ministère et c'est même l'origine de toute la sainteté qui doit être en l'Eglise de Dieu;

secondement il requiert une liaison particulière à Jésus-Christ Notre Seigneur, auquel nous sommes conjoints par ce ministère en une manière spéciale et par un pouvoir si élevé qu'il ne convient pas même aux anges en l'état de la gloire.[17]

---

[14] Bérulle, *OC, Conférences et fragments* (1995), piece dated January 1615. See Dupuy's comment at 303n2, 303. See also Blanchard, "La spiritualité christocentrique," 64–68, and Dupuy's discussion of vocation, *BLS*, 97–100.

[15] Cognet, *La spiritualité moderne*, 358.

[16] *BLS, OR* 14, 287.

[17] Bérulle, *OP* 192, no. 2, col. 1270, quoted in Cochois, "Bérulle, hiérarque dionysien," 37: 323.

Bérulle also held there were two types of priesthood: the royal priesthood of the baptized and that of the sacramental participation of priests, according to Laurentin. The former corresponded to an interior attitude of Christ the High Priest and a mystical participation of the Church in this interior attitude (which corresponded to the order of the personal life of grace). The latter corresponded to sacramental participation in the power of Christ the High Priest. Both types of priesthood were not separable for Bérulle, according to Cochois, as the substantial holiness of the deified humanity of Christ is not separable from the hypostatic union.[18]

Jesus was priest by state, and so priests must become so by state by subsisting in him in a kind of psychological and ontological ecstasy, according to Cochois' reading of Bérulle. In order to extend the priesthood to all their activities, they must extend this mystical union/ontological ecstasy realized by their ordination to all their activities. Cochois insisted this was more than a disappropriation, made possible only through Jesus himself taking possession of them. To be sure, Bérulle asked Carmelite nuns to do the same, but in the case of priests, it was in terms of sacramental participation in Christ's power, argued Cochois.[19]

Bérulle as Hierarch

In the second part of this article, published a year later, Cochois explored how Bérulle saw himself as a hierarch, especially in terms of the direction of souls, thanks to a dossier of unpublished pieces assembled by Gibieuf, including written testimonies by Carmelites.

At his early retreat at Verdun, in 1602, Bérulle had a mystical experience in which an interior voice reassured him: "...ne crains point, fie-toi en moi, ton cœur est en ma main, il ne parlera que par moi."[20] In 1607, a similar illumination assured him that he would not work in the court of Henry IV but in that of Jesus: "annuntiate inter gentes studia eius."[21] A Carmelite testified that Bérulle, shortly before his death, thought this one of the most important events of his life, a time when he spent many days as if he were no longer on earth.[22]

---

[18] Ibid., 324. See R. Laurentin, *Marie, l'Église et le sacerdoce: étude théologique* (Paris: Nouvelle editions latines, 1953) 2.

[19] Ibid., 330–32. See Bérulle, Arch. De l'Oratoire, 1 bis, pièce 12, 9 (see ch. 8, n. 36).

[20] Bérulle, *Retraite du cardinal de Bérulle*, 12, Archives nationales, M 233, col. 1304, quoted in Cochois, "Bérulle, hiérarque dionysien," 38: 355.

[21] Bérulle, Archives nationales, M 233 and Psalm 9:12, quoted in Cochois, "Bérulle, hiérarque dionysien," 38: 355–56.

[22] Cochois, "Bérulle, hiérarque dionysien," 38: 356. See Marie de Saint-Jérôme, Archives nationales, M 233, no. 8, folio 6.

As Cochois detailed, as superior of the Oratory and spiritual master, Bérulle never constructed a rule for his Congregation, but his talks to his Oratorians formed a program of initiation through the vows of servitude. The idea of the hierarch as initiator and mediator (for Bérulle, in this case, as a superior) was, again, a Pseudo-Dionysian influence. He addressed the following to the superiors of the Oratory—urging them to participate in angelic functions and purity:

> …il y a deux sortes de personnes: les uns qui reçoivent et les autres qui communiquent l'esprit, la lumière et la grâce de Jésus. Les premiers sont tous les fidèles, et les seconds sont les prêtres et les Supérieurs, qui départent leurs influences aux inférieurs et doivent imiter les anges supérieurs et les ordres éminents entre les anges qui purgent, qui illuminent, qui enflamment ceux qui leur sont soumis et subordonnés. Puisque Dieu nous appelle aux fonctions angéliques, disposons-nous aussi à une vie angélique et à un exercice et ministère si élevé, si saint et si efficace.[23]

Mediation, the Direction of Souls, and the Authority of Priests

In answering the Protestant and illuminist claim to an immediate dependence on God without intermediary, Bérulle spoke of divine authority as resting on those who direct souls—a key defense of the authority of the priesthood and hierarchy.

Dupuy wrote on the direction of souls, of keen interest to Bérulle, who considered it a sacerdotal mission and not the purview of religious, as was then current practice.[24]

Bérulle's ideas on spiritual direction were also based on the Pseudo-Dionysian notion of mediation. He held that the ecclesiastical state was not only sacred but "même l'origine de toute sainteté qui est en l'Église de Dieu."[25] According to Bérulle, there was a parallel between the angelic and ecclesiastical hierarchies. While the celestial spirits form a hierarchy of love, the visible hierarchy, which is based on authority, must also become a hierarchy of love. Following the Pseudo-Dionysian ideals of purifying, illuminating and perfecting, Bérulle treated illumination as the most excellent of sacerdotal functions: "Car ils [les supérieurs] sont obligés de donner cet esprit [de cette congrégation] à leurs inférieurs et de les disposer à cette grâce et lumière par leur conduite, ce qu'ils ne peuvent faire

---

[23] *OP*, Migne ed., OP 191, no. 3, col. 1268, quoted in Cochois, "Bérulle, hiérarque dionysien," 38: 359.

[24] *BLS*, 140–42. This review follows the author's exposition closely.

[25] *OR* 1, no. 2, quoted in *BLS*, 146.

sans cette éminence. Car les philosophes nous enseignent qu'il faut avoir l'acte pour le donner à ceux qui ne l'ont qu'en puissance…"[26]

For Bérulle, the ministry of the Oratorians in the direction of souls was linked to the Father producing the Son: "il tend à faire naître et former ce Jésus dans les cœurs; il tend à donner son corps et son esprit au monde; il tende à donner une nouvelle naissance à celui qui est né de toute éternité dans le sein du Père…"[27] In imitation, the priest was to "produire le Fils et son Esprit dans les âmes."[28]

Bérulle did not distinguish between psychological and ontological levels in terms of defining the priest's role as mediator, as Dupuy explained.[29] He was a visible image of an invisible reality. This Pseudo-Dionysian idea of imitation is echoed in other Berullian themes, as the Incarnation imitates the divine unity, as the Virgin Mary is the image of the divine paternity, and as priests in community reflect the union of the three persons.[30]

Bérulle noted that God wished to "conjoindre" the priest to his action over souls.[31] According to Bérulle, this kind of instrumentality requires a docility on the part of priests to divine inspiration, as they were instructed directly by God. In terms of directing souls, Bérulle believed that the grace of God led souls as infallibly as a sacramental grace obtained *ex opere operato*. Dupuy preferred to think of this not as an example of illuminism but rather one of Pseudo-Dionysian mediatorship.[32]

Priests were to respect and honor souls whom they direct because they are part of the Mystical Body.[33] All persons could give adoration to God as *hosties* themselves, whom priests could then offer back to God.[34]

In granting priests this special power over souls, Bérulle followed not only Pseudo-Dionysius, but also the notion in tradition that the apostolic office could lay claim to all charismata.[35]

---

[26] *OC*, vol. 8, *Discours de l'état et des grandeurs de Jésus, Narré, Approbations, Élévations, Vie de Jésus, Mémorial de direction, Élévation vers sainte Marie-Madeleine*, ed. Joseph Beaude, Blandine Delahaye, Michel Join-Lambert, and Rémi Lescot (Paris, 1996), *Mémorial*, 13, 385. See *BLS*, 146n5, referencing this passage. The author noted that this is a theme more Aristotelian than Pseudo-Dionysian. For Bèrulle, the priest could not give a sanctity which he did not first have, and this under the rubric of causality, as we will detail.

[27] Bérulle, *Mémorial*, 9, col. 816, quoted in *BLS*, 173.

[28] Ibid., 15, quoted in *BLS*, 174.

[29] *BLS*, 149 and 151. See *Mémorial*, 22.

[30] Ibid., 151. See *OR* 18, no. 1.

[31] Bérulle, *Mémorial*, 8, quoted in *BLS*, 152.

[32] *BLS*, 154.

[33] Ibid., 165. See *Mémorial*, 4.

[34] Bérulle, *Mémorial*, 8, quoted in *BLS*, 167.

[35] See J. Wilhelm, "Charismata," in *Catholic Encyclopedia* 3, http://www.newadvent.org/cathen/0588e.htm.

Conclusion

Bérulle's return to a Pseudo-Dionysian interpretation of sacerdotal mediation, wherein the priest must be holy to mediate, was an attempt to address the critiques leveled against a corrupt clergy. It was not enough for Bérulle to insist, with Trent, that the sacraments produced grace *ex opere operato* regardless of the state of the soul of the priest. Decades after Trent, corruption remained in a France torn by the Wars of Religion.

Bérulle looked to the fathers and more recent theorizing to expand priestly identity from a participation in the priesthood of Christ to a participation in the holiness of Christ. This holiness permitted priests to be the visible image of Christ the head, and heads themselves of the Mystical Body.

The following chapter explores the complex notions Bérulle borrowed to accomplish this effort through his particular fashioning of the priest into a public person.

Chapter 12
The Priest as Public Person

Introduction

In an effort to recompose the Mystical Body in the face of Protestant critiques of the Church, Bérulle's priests were no longer private persons, according to Houdard, but produced the *respublica christiana* wherein every priest is called to become a divine person. The priesthood became a public service for the common good. Bérulle:

> La fin de cet esprit sacerdotal est de servir Dieu par la prière et le sacrifice et le prochain par les sacrements. Et cela, au nom de Dieu et au nom du peuple: server Dieu au nom de peuple, dispenser au peuple les dons de Dieu.
>
> Aussi cet esprit fait-il jouer un role, non plus privé, mais public, ou plûtot rend notre personne, non plus profane ou quelconque, mais sacrée, non plus commune mais divine.[1]

Perhaps applicable to Bérulle's particular interpretation of the priest as public person is Harnack's criticism that the Roman Catholic priesthood in many of its aspects followed that of pagan Rome.[2] In this chapter, the evolution of the notion of public person will be explored, followed by a review of the Reformation debates surrounding private vs. public persons, as well as Luther's, Calvin's, and Calvinist notions in relation to Christ as public person. Next, Bérulle's ideas regarding the priest as public person in relation to the divine persons will be outlined.

---

[1]   Houdard, "Sacerdoce et direction spirituelle," 113–14, quoting Bérulle, *Finis huius novi instituti*, in *BLS*, 315.

[2]   J. Pohle, "Priesthood," in *The Catholic Encyclopedia*, 12. See Adolf von Harnack, *Das Wesen des Christentums* (Leipzig, J. C. Hinrichs, 1902), 157.

Background

Mauss wrote that there had been a devolution in ancient Roman law regarding the Latin concept of *persona* as mask: it had become more than a right to assume a certain role. While all Roman citizens had a civil *persona*, some became religious *personae*, with certain masks and rituals become the purview of some privileged families of religious *collegia*. Stoicism's voluntarist and personal ethics further enriched the Roman notion of person, making it into a moral person. In turn, Christianity made this moral person a metaphysical entity.[3]

The Roman notion of public person was eventually incorporated into canon law, according to Gy. Citing Mülejans, Gy remarked that only a public person had the power to act in the name of the people.[4] Aquinas, for example, called the bishop a public person, who alone could be called a prelate and to whom alone full power in the dispensation of the sacraments belonged.[5]

The concepts of public person and ecclesial office became central at the time of the Reformation. Bérulle's defense against what he saw as the Protestant rebellion against authority and the rejection of apostolic succession focused on various religious, moral, and metaphysical ideals surrounding "person," notably Christ's person and his public life, as well as the person of the Holy Spirit given to the apostles by Christ—both in relation to his defense of the priest as public person.

---

[3] Marcel Mauss, "A Category of the Human Mind: The Notion of the Person, the Notion of the Self," trans. H. D. Halls, in *The Category of the Person: Anthropology, Philosophy, History*, ed. Michael Carrithers, Steven Collins, and Steven Lukes (Cambridge: Cambridge University Press, 1985), 13–19.

[4] Pierre-Marie Gy, *The Reception of Vatican II Liturgical Reforms in the Life of The Church* (Milwaukee, WI: Marquette University, 2003), 21–22. See Hans Mülejans, "Publicus und privatus im römischen Recht und im älteren kanonischen Recht unter besonderer Berücksichtigung der Unterscheidung Ius publicum und Ius privatum" (PhD diss., Munich: Max Hueber, 1961), 14.

[5] Aquinas, *ST*, 3.supp.26.1, co., in *Summa theologiae*, 12.2: 50: "Sed, cum Ecclesia sit *congregatio fidelium*; congregatio autem hominum sit duplex, scilicet oeconomica, ut illi qui sunt de una familia, et politica, sicut illi qui sunt de uno populo: Ecclesia assimilatur congregationi politicae, quia ipse populus Ecclesia dicitur; sed conventus diversi vel parochia in una dioecesi, assimilantur congregationi in diversis familiis vel in diversis officiis. Et ideo solus episcopus proprie praelatus Ecclesiae dicitur: et ideo ipse solus, quasi sponsus, anulum Ecclesiae recipit. Et ideo ipse solus habet potestatem plenam in dispensatione sacramentorum, et iurisdictionem in foro causarum, quasi persona publica: alii autem secundum quod ab eis committitur."

Public vs. Private in Reformist Controversies

Public vs. Private Persons

Koerner noted that Luther held that individuals could represent various groups, including in the past or present, in the domestic, political, and apostolic realms. However, for Luther, only Christ could represent the Church in terms of acting on behalf of, or standing in proxy for.[6] As Koerner wrote:

> Against Rome, which based its authority precisely on its power to represent Christ personally through its officers—the bishops and priests— Luther discerns church only in the personal, hidden, and inner encounter of the believer with Christ. Accorded the status of priests, but representing only themselves, individuals confront god individually, in their "own person," and in a concealment that neither persons nor institutions can dispel. This had been the message of the first words of Luther's Invocavit sermons delivered to a rebellious Wittenberg in 1522: "The summons of death comes to us all, and no one can die for another…I will not be with you then, nor you with me."[7]

Trepanier explored the Protestant Revolution as he saw it develop in theology, law, and community, including the notion of public person. He cited Berman's analysis that Luther had challenged the idea of the church as a law-making body. Luther rejected the two-swords theory for the two-kingdoms theory—with the church governed by the Gospel and overseeing issues of grace and faith only. Social, political, and legal authority were the domain of earthly rulers exclusively.[8]

---

6   Joseph Leo Koerner, *The Reformation of the Image* (Chicago, IL: University of Chicago Press, 2004), 378. See Peter Brunner, *Nikolaus von Amsdorf als Bischof von Naumburg: eine Untersuchung zur Gestalt des evangelischen Bischofamtes in der Reformationszeit* (Gütersloh: G. Mohn, 1961); and Hans-Ulrich Delius, "Das Naumburger Bischofsexperiment und Martin Luther," in *Martin Luther und das Bischofsamt* (Stuttgart: Calwer Verlag, 1990), 131–40.

7   Luther, *WA* 10.3: 1.15–2.16: "Wir sind alle zum tode gefoddert und wird keiner fur den andern sterben…ich werde denn nicht bey dir sein noch du bey mir." *LW* 51: 70, quoted in Koerner, *The Reformation of the Image*, 378.

8   Lee Trepanier, "The Protestant Revolution in Theology, Law, and Community," *First Principles,* ISI Web Journal, 208, available at http://www.firstprinciplesjournal.com /articles.aspx?article=1503. See Harold Berman, *Law and Revolution*, vol. 2, *The Impact of*

Salient to this analysis, Luther emphasized the difference between public and private persons in his theology, with civil authorities alone having jurisdiction as public persons.[9] The priesthood of all believers meant no other mediator than Christ was needed for salvation, and all had the vocation to minister to others, rather than what was believed to be the Roman Catholic ideal of vocation as that pertaining to the "spiritually perfect."[10] Luther did away with priestly office, seeing the Church as founded on Peter's faith, not Peter himself.[11]

With these assertions, the Reformer struck at the root of ecclesial authority: the sacrality of the priest as representative of Christ.

The idea of public person was also an important one to the Reformers in relation to both Christ and Adam. Christopher Hill detailed the concept of "public person" in the Reformation era. "Representative," "public," or "common person" were terms used interchangeably. Both Adam and Christ were considered public persons, both representatives of humankind: the former's sin meriting all punishment, the latter paying the penalty for that sin.[12] Luther's concern that Christ be seen as a public person, not a private one, was based on his emphasis on what Christ did for us—the *pro me* of Luther's Christology, according to Zwanepol.[13] Luther saw Christ's kenosis not as his becoming man but as laying aside his divine attributes. For Luther, the Atonement cost God.[14]

Nacchianti attempted to demonstrate, against the extrinsicism of Calvin, that our satisfaction did injure Christ. Christ, being one with us in the Mystical Body, continues to suffer in his members, who are natural, not adopted sons.[15]

---

the Protestant Reformations on the Western Legal Tradition (Cambridge: Harvard University Press, 2003), 40–41.

[9]   Ibid., 209–10. See Berman, *Law and Revolution*, 25–26 and 68.

[10]   Ibid. See Berman, *Law and Revolution*, 41–44.

[11]   Auer and Riley, *A General Doctrine of the Sacraments*, 103.

[12]   Christopher Hill, *The Collected Essays of Christopher Hill*, vol. 3, *People and Ideas in Seventeenth Century England* (Amherst: University of Massachusetts Press, 1986), 300. See Martin Luther, *Commentary on Galatians*, English translation (1807), 1, 304.

[13]   Zwanepol, "A Human God," 42. See Luther, *WA* 40.1: 448.2–7: "Hoc est vitium omnium Sophistarum et patrum, ut faciant Christum privatam personam, verum; sed non ibi consistendum; nondum habes Christum, per hoc non vocatur; sed quando datur tibi ista innocentissima persona, quod fit Rex et sacerdos meus, servit mihi, exuit sanctitatem et vult esse peccator: volo te portare; da ghet Christus an."

[14]   Ibid., 45. See Hans Joachim Iwand, *Nachgelassene Werke*, vol. 5, *Luthers Theologie* (München: Chr. Kaiser, 1974), 129. See also *WA* 17.2: 438.36–439.1: "War ists, das der blosse glaub selig mach und uns nichs koste, aber dannocht hat es got etwas gekostet, und also vil, das seyn ayniger Son hatt mussen mensch werden und uns erlösen."

[15]   Orcibal, *Le cardinal de Bérulle*, 95–96. See Nacchianti, *Opera*. See also A. Piolanti, "De 'una persona mystica' quadam Jac. Nacchianti," *Euntes docete* 10 (1957): 236–43; Bellemare, *Le sens de la créature*, 165ff.

Bérulle's own project, as detailed, included the idea that Christ's kenosis began at the moment of the Incarnation, with an emphasis on a similarly kenotic sacrificial spirituality for Christians. Bérulle's focal point was a kenotic representational sacerdotalism that found its rationale in both.

Luther and the Ideal of Public Office

Wengert explored in-depth the idea of public ministry during the Reformation. Luther argued against the idea of two estates, writing that all Christians belong to one *Stand* or walk of life.[16] Luther explained ordination and the public office of ministry thus: "Therefore the priesthood should be nothing other in Christianity than an officeholder: as long as he is in [such an] office, he carries out [its duties]; where he is deposed, then he is a peasant or citizen like any others." The Reformer had rejected the idea of sacerdotal office.[17]

The word "public" was strongly contested in the Augsburg Confession. Luther held that the eschatological purpose of church government was to shout from the rooftops (Matt. 10:27). Whereas Luther was criticized for usurping authority, according to Wengert, he, in fact, was against the notion of a private call or self-appointed preachers. Reformers tied the public call with the offices of Christ: pastor, preacher, and teacher. Far from a bottom-up ecclesiology, according to Wengert, it is Christ vesting the office, not the laity.[18]

Wengert concluded that authority for the Reformers rested in the Word, not in the person. Wengert wrote, "Thus, the person is transparent. One does not see the minister at the front, but rather sees Christ; one does not hear the preacher's words from the pulpit, but rather hears Christ's word; one is not received at the

---

[16] Timothy J. Wengert, *Priesthood, Pastors, Bishops: Public Ministry for the Reformation and Today* (Minneapolis, MN: Fortress Press, 2008), 6–7. See *WA* 6: 407.10–19: "Man hats erfunden, das Bapst, Bischoff, Priester, Kloster volck wirt der geystlich stand genent, Fursten, Hern, handtwercks und ackerleut der weltlich stand, wilchs gar ein feyn Comment und gleyssen ist, doch sol niemant darub schuchter werden, unnd das aufz dem grund: Dan alle Christen sein warhafftig geystlichs stands, unnd ist unter yhn kein unterscheyd, denn des ampts halben allein, wie Paulus i. Corint. Xij. Sagt, das wir alle sampt eyn Corper seinn, doch ein yglich glid sein eygen werck hat, damit es den andern dienet, das macht allis, das wir eine tauff, ein Evangelium, eynen glauben haben, unnd sein gleyche Christen, den die tauff, Evangelium und glauben, die machen allein geistlich und Christen volck." *LW* 44: 127. The author is translator.

[17] *WA* 6: 408.18–21: "Drumb solt ein priester stand nit anders sein in der Christenheit, dan als ein amptman: weil er am ampt ist, geht er vorh, wo ehr abgesetzt, ist ehr ein bawr odder burger wie die andern." *LW* 44: 129, quoted in Wengert, *Priesthood*, 11.

[18] Wengert, *Priesthood*, 42–43.

Table by the host pastor, for Christ is the host; and one certainly does not receive the pastor's body and blood, but receives Christ's."[19]

The Issue of Private Masses and Priests as Public Figures

Luther also wrote repeatedly about and questioned the validity of what he saw as a grave evil: private Mass.[20] He wrote that in private Masses the "sacrament-priest" had become the "sacrifice-priest," who performed a blasphemous act of crucifying the Lord again, and charging money.[21] Luther questioned whether the priest in a private Mass was still acting as a public figure. Catholics responded that the priest was a private person in this instance.[22] For Luther, the private Mass was a denial of the word of God, as it should be derived from the word.[23] The kind of priests who had evolved for the purpose of saying Masses for a fee neither preached, baptized, nor performed charitable works, according to Luther.[24] He drew on Scholastic metaphysics to support his claims, writing, "In the private Mass, there is no efficient, formal or final cause of the sacrament. Therefore, there

[19]   Ibid., 105. See Gordon Lathrop, *The Pastor: A Spirituality* (Minneapolis: Fortress Press, 2006).

[20]   Robert C. Croken, *Luther's First Front: The Eucharist as Sacrifice* (Ottawa: University of Ottawa Press, 1990) 57. See especially Martin Luther, *Von der Winkelmesse und Pfaffenweihe* (1533) and *Die Disputation contra missam privatam* (1536), in Luther, *WA* 38: 171–256, and *WA* 39.1: 134–73.

[21]   Ibid., 58–59 and 80. See Luther, *LW* 38: 152; *WA* 38: 199.23–33: "Ist Christus meinung, (wie gesagt) das man das Sacrament solle aus teilen der gemeine Christi, jren glauben zu stercken und Christum zu loben offentlich, Du aber hast ein eigen werck draus gemacht, das dein sey und du volnbracht hast on zuthun der andern, Und solchs werck andern mit geteilet und umb geld verkaufft, Was kanstu hie leugnen? ...Und bist schlecht widder Christum geweyhet, zu thun alles, was widder jn ist."

[22]   Ibid., 59–60. See Luther *LW* 38: 165; *WA* 38: 211.14–22: "Es gilt auch nicht, ob man hie wolt fürwenden, Ein Winckelpriester sey eine offentliche person, offentlich geweyhet etc, der man gleuben solle, wie man einem Notario odder offentlichen schreiber gleubt, Denn, wie gesagt, diese sache ist Geistlich und nicht Weltlich, Zu dem, so gleubt man auch Weltlich keinem Notario allein, wo er nicht zeugen da zu hat, So sind auch seine sachen offenbar, die man sihet und hört, Hie aber sind keine zeugen Sondern eine eintzele person, welche im tunckeln munckelt und unter dem hütlin spielet, und spricht darnach, sie habe es so und so gemacht, dem solle man gleuben und unser seligkeit drauff setzen, Nein, das gilt nicht ..."

[23]   Ibid., 59. See Luther, *LW* 38: 155–56; *WA* 38: 202–3.

[24]   Ibid., 60. See Luther *LW* 38: 179; *WA* 38: 222.26–31: "Sie Predigen nicht, Sie Teuffen nicht, Sie reichen das Sacrament nicht, Sie Absolvirn nicht, Sie beten nicht (on das sie die wort des Psalters lören und wispeln), Sie sind jnn keinem ampt der seelsorgen nach bey den sterbenden etwas thun, Sondern es ist das unnutz, faul, mussig gesinde, die allein das Sacrament (wie sie meinen) handeln und für ein opffer und werck verkeuffen."

is no sacrament."[25] He held that the efficient cause of the Mass (for the benefit of all) was Christ; the formal cause was the institution itself for the remission of the sins of the living (not the dead); the final cause was the announcing of Christ's death until he returns in glory. In the private Mass, there was no annunciation, nor any feeding of the faithful.[26]

The Council of Trent responded to Luther's critique by defending private Masses, calling them "truly common."[27] Bérulle's rhetoric, in seeming response, included a strong identification of the priest as public person at all moments, at one with Christ, who acts as if by way of principal cause even beyond sacramental acts, as we will explore.

Calvinism and the Public Person

According to Hill, the idea of public person was held by the exponents of theology as well, including Calvin.[28] Covenant theory was influenced by the increased importance of contracts and debtor-creditor relations. Whereas in medieval sacramental theory the symbolism of the sealing of transactions could be found, for example, in the marriage ring or the laying on of hands, Protestants emphasized faith over works, and denied sacramental grace. Promises and covenants were now the key: intentions must be true, and therefore, the state of mind of the Christian was important.[29]

Calvin, a trained lawyer, saw justification in legal terms: the covenant with God did away with the need for saints' intervention. God entered into obligation with his elect, thus replacing the covenant of works with that of grace. Christ's covenant with the elect was as a representative person.[30]

Bérulle's own project emphasized the idea of the priest as public person and visible head of the Church, in society with the Trinity. Bérulle's system of mystical initiation through the vows of servitude for his Oratorians seemingly mirrored

---

[25] Luther, *WA* 39.1: 142.9–11: "In missa privata non est causa efficiens nec formalis nec finalis sacramenti. Ergo non est ibi sacramentum." Quoted in Croken, *Luther's First Front*, 65.

[26] Croken, *Luther's First Front*, 65. See *WA* 39.1: 142.11–143.12: "Causa efficiens est, quod Christus instituit sacramentum, ideo non ut unus solus eo fruatur, sed tota ecclesia aut multi…Formalis causa est ipsa institutio Christi, ut vescamur sacramentum altaris in remissionem peccatorum…Finalis causa est annuntiatio mortis domini, donec veniat."

[27] Ibid., 121. See *Canons and Decrees of the Council of Trent*, trans. H. J. Schroeder (St. Louis, MO, and London: B. Herder Book Co., 1960), 147.

[28] Hill, *The Collected Essays*, 300. See Leonard J. Trinterud, "The Origins of Puritanism," *Church History* 20 (March 1951): 48.

[29] Ibid., 301–2.

[30] Ibid., 303–4.

the idea of a covenantal obligation. This system served Bérulle's spiritual theology of priesthood, as he constructed a spiritual theology of the priest as public person and visible head of the Church by assuring, through frequent mental elevations, that his intentions and inner states of mind were consistent with his high calling.

The Imputation of Christ's Righteousness

Venema analyzed Calvin's doctrine of the imputation of Christ's righteousness in relation to justification, which had been the topic of debate among Calvinists.[31] We, here, summarize Venema's and Shepherd's treatments of this topic.

At issue was the notion of Christ's "active" obedience to the requirements of the law and his "passive" obedience in enduring penal sanction under the law.[32]

Perhaps applicable to this analysis is Shepherd's thesis that Calvin had restricted imputation of righteousness to the passive obedience of Christ, and had defined justification as forgiveness of sins. Shepherd had noted that the terminology of passive and active obedience arose among later Calvinist Scholastics, and even as early as 1563. Shepherd also noted that this doctrine, which he held was a consensus opinion of Reformed orthodoxy, introduced the idea of meritorious works on the part of Christ, transforming the notion of justification by grace into justification by works, accomplished by Christ as mediator over the course of his entire life, in active obedience to the Father.[33]

Venema responded to Shepherd's analysis by defending Calvin as having supported a comprehensive view of justification. Calvin saw Adam as a "public" person, an expression of later Calvinism. Adam was ordained to act not just for himself, but also for his descendants.[34] So, too, Christ, as mediator and the new Adam, fulfilled all righteousness under the law during his entire life, from the moment of his Incarnation. Christ's righteousness was comprehensive, with his

---

[31] Cornelis Venema, "Calvin's Doctrine of the Imputation of Christ's Righteousness: Another Example of 'Calvin against the Calvinists'?" *Mid-Atlantic Journal of Theology* 20 (2009): 15–47. This review follows the authors' expositions closely.

[32] Ibid., 17.

[33] Ibid., 19–24. See Norman Shepherd, "The Imputation of Active Obedience," in *A Faith That is Never Alone: A Response to Westminster Seminary California*, ed. P. Andrew Sandlin (La Grange, CA: Kerygma Press, 2007), 249–78; and Norman Shepherd, "Justification by Works in Reformed Theology," in *Backbone of the Bible: Covenant in Contemporary Perspective*, ed. P. Andrew Sandlin (Nacogdoches, TX: Covenant Media Press, 2004), 114–18.

[34] Ibid., 38; *Institution*, 2.1.7: "Qui est-ce qui se souciera de l'origine de l'âme, après avoir entendu qu'Adam avoit reçeu les ornemens qu'il a perdus, non pas moins pour nous que pour soy, entant que Dieu ne les luy avoit point baillez comme à un seul homme un particulier, mais afin que toute sa lignée en iouist avec lui communément?"

obedience imputed to all believers, not just in terms of the forgiveness of sins but also their righteousness and holiness, a holiness imputed by Christ's holiness.[35]

Did the Calvinist passive and active obedience controversy have a parallel in Bérulle's reference to active obediential potency and holiness?

Further study of this later Calvinist controversy is needed, as well as an examination of the interplay between Calvinist and Roman Catholic polemicists. However, this cursory review of another Christological controversy further points to the fact that Bérulle's project may have been influenced by yet another of many complex debates requiring research in order to fully understand the shaping of sacerdotal spiritual theology in the Counter- and Post-Reformation eras.

The Calvinist idea of Christ's meritorious works via obedience may have had an echo in Bérulle's view of the divinizing mysteries of the life of Christ as meritorious causes of grace, including sacerdotal grace and mission.

In what might be seen as an instance of justification by works made possible through an annihilated will and the passivity of the vows of servitude, Oratorians, as public persons, were urged to become immolated victims, to take on the sins of the laity.

The Holiness, Authority, and Doctrine of the Priest as Public Person

As noted previously, Bérulle wanted the three *fleurons* of the sacerdotal crown—holiness, authority, and doctrine—to be brought together again in a reformed priesthood.[36] Bérulle attempted to argue against Protestants claiming priests did not exist in the Christian scriptures by referring both to the Levitical priesthood and to the foundation of the priesthood in natural law.[37] Priests are called to the same Levitical heritage of renouncing earthly wealth and being set apart for public ministry. The priest's possession is to have a participation in Jesus Christ in these three gifts, which are the gifts of the three persons.[38] Bérulle:

> Ce sont les prélats et les prêtres qui y sont appelés; ce sont eux que Jésus-Christ en l'Évangile nomme le sel de la terre; c'est à eux qu'appartiennent ces trois qualités. Il donne aux particuliers la foi, l'espérance et la charité; et il donne aux personnes publiques ces trois autres dons: sainteté, autorité et doctrine. Et c'est le fonds de l'héritage de la tribu de Lévi, c'est-à-dire,

---

[35] Ibid., 46–47.
[36] *BLS*, 81. See *CB* 891.
[37] Ibid., 65–66. See *Discours de controverse*, 2, 10. This review follows the author's exposition closely.
[38] Ibid., 81.

du clergé, appelé de ce nom, qui signifie en grec héritage, pour montrer qu'ils n'ont point de possession en la terre, et que tout le bien que Jésus-Christ leur a laissé, est cette possession du ciel et cette participation à lui-même; c'est-à-dire à sa sainteté, à sa lumière et à son autorité, comme adorant et recevant l'autorité du Père, la lumière du Fils, la sainteté de Saint-Esprit.[39]

Bérulle affirmed that in the sacrament of orders, the priest is sanctified not as a private person (as with other sacraments) but as a public person and as a main figure of the Christian City, whose duty it is to promote the coming reign of Christ and without whom this state would not exist. In this, one sees perhaps a transposition of Luther's insistence on public authority back to that of the priest's authority, perhaps a mirror of the Roman pagan priest as public person:

Dans les autres sacrements l'homme est sanctifié selon lui-même, seulement en tant qu'il est personne privée; mais par celui-ci, il l'est en tant que personne publique et partie principale de la cité chrétienne. Quand ils entendent: "Que ton règne vienne," que les prêtres se souviennent qu'ils en sont partie principale et que leur devoir est de le promouvoir. Nous faisons partie de cet état, et parties nobles et principales, sans lesquelles cet état ne peut subsister.[40]

The Public Person and Sacerdotal Character and Grace

Dupuy detailed how Bérulle depicted sacerdotal grace as something more than personal, but rather part of the priest's mission in the Church, calling the priest a public person, whether in terms of saying a Mass publicly or privately. Bérulle wrote, "Dans la célébration de la messe, nous remplissons une fonction publique pour l'Église qui a le droit d'exiger de nous ce service. Aussi, sauf pour un motif particulier et une juste raison, nous devons célébrer la messe chaque jour."[41]

Dupuy noted that in the twentieth century, sacerdotal character had taken on the notion of a "transformation of being" such that the all the priest's actions have a "new value."[42] Dupuy held the opinion that Bérulle's notion of character is far from this idea but is rather functional, with the grace of order sanctifying the priest only insofar as he is a public person.[43]

---

[39] *CB*, vol. 3, no. 891, referenced in *BLS*, 81. Here quoted directly.
[40] *BLS*, *OR* 22, no. 5, 317, quoted in Houdard, "Sacerdoce et direction spirituelle," 114.
[41] Coll. 208, quoted in *BLS*, 105.
[42] *BLS*, 189–90.
[43] Ibid., 190.

A closer look at a key conference will be helpful in seeing how Bérulle's ideas took shape. In this conference, Bérulle delineated what the Oratorians owed to God as priests, here treated in more depth. As priests, they must consider themselves instruments, saying that instruments are for action, and so too priests. Bérulle:

> Et comme prêtres nous avons à considérer que nous sommes instruments du Fils de Dieu pour travailler à sa gloire dans les âmes, coopérant à leur salut. L'instrument n'est que pour l'action; aussi nous ne sommes que pour l'action….L'instrument est pour l'action même de la cause principale. Nous sommes pour la même action du Fils de Dieu, c'est-à-dire pour travailler au salut des âmes à son honneur et gloire. L'instrument est en la main de celui qui est le principal agent et nous sommes comme en la main de Jésus-Christ qui se sert de nous aux fonctions et ministères qu'il désire.[44]

Laboring for the Son of God, priests are "pour travailler, pour opérer."[45] This appears, as Dupuy suggested, to be a reference to their function as public persons and as instruments of authority. Bérulle urged his Oratorians to works of charity, by which they would represent the person of Christ: "nous représentons la Personne de Jésus-Christ qui en la terre autrefois a été en ces labeurs et qui y serait toujours s'il était en la terre…"[46]

The priest, according to Bérulle, is to pray the daily divine office as a public person as well, and in so doing, his thoughts would be divinized: "la pensée est divinisée."[47] This shows the strong link between the actions of the priest as leader of prayer for the sake of the Church, a public service even if done privately, and the notion of divinization through prayer. Bérulle saw the holiness of the priest achieved through the exercise of public prayer, a prayer for the sake of the people. Bérulle called on his Oratorians to make satisfaction for the sins of the people and for the salvation of others: "Car il convient spécialement au prêtre qui doit remettre les péchés des peuples…"[48] In a seeming reference to Luther's emphasis on the *pro me* of Christ's public personhood, Bérulle defended priests as "personnes publiques" in relation to a share in Christ's humiliation and death, taking part in his Passion through the application of its graces:

---

[44] Ibid., *OR* 75, no. 6, 408–9.
[45] Ibid.
[46] Ibid., 410, *OR* 75, no. 8.
[47] Ibid., 385, *OR* 59, no. 3.
[48] Ibid., 342, *OR* 31, no 4.

S'humilier *en son nom* particulier et au nom de la *nature humaine* comme *personnes publiques* de la part qu'elle a eue seule entre toutes créatures à ce grand méfait *de la mort* de son Dieu....Prendre grande part à cette passion par l'application des grâces qui nous y sont acquises par icelle.[49]

The Person of Christ and the Priest in Relation to the Public Person Debate

As already noted, Aquinas called the priest an instrument.[50] However, Bérulle found this appellation insufficient, according to Dupuy, calling the priest an *organe* of Christ.[51] Dupuy noted that, as Aquinas had called the humanity of Christ a conjoint instrument,[52] Bérulle invited one curate to be the "instrument conjoint au Fils de Dieu."[53]

A redacted text, held to represent his thoughts, reflects the ideals of a profound union between the priest and Christ:

Il a daigné nous choisir pour un si grand œuvre et a voulu que nous en fussions les instruments et coadjuteurs. Et il y a plus: car non seulement nous sommes ses instruments et coadjuteurs, mais nous agissons et parlons en sa personne et comme si c'était lui-même. Et plût à Dieu que comme nous paraissons en sa personne et qu'il met ses paroles en notre bouche, que son Esprit fût en nos cœurs et que notre vie ne fût qu'une consommation de la sienne! C'est une conjoncture admirable que celle de Jésus-Christ avec nous en ce sacrement. Et elle va imitant la part que Dieu a bien voulu donner à la Vierge au mystère de l'Incarnation. Car comme Dieu s'est uni à la Vierge pour accomplir le grand œuvre de l'Incarnation

---

[49]   *OC* (1995), *OP* 79, nos. 1 and 2, 245. The italics are Bérulle's.

[50]   Aquinas, *ST*, 3.63.2, co., in *Summa theologiae*, 12.1: 32: "minister autem habet se per modum instrumenti…"

[51]   *BLS*, 116, quoting Bérulle in the following texts: *CB*, vol. 3, no. 893; *OR* 22, no. 5; *OP* 87, no. 2; *OR* 15, no. 3.

[52]   Aquinas, *ST*, 3.62.5, co., in *Summa theologiae*, 12.1: 27: "Respondeo dicendum quod, sicut dictum est, sacramentum operatur ad gratiam causandam per modum instrumenti. Est autem duplex instrumentum: unum quidem separatum, ut baculus; aliud autem coniunctum, ut manus. Per instrumentum autem coniunctum movetur instrumentum separatum: sicut baculus per manum. Principalis autem causa efficiens gratiae est ipse Deus, ad quem comparatur humanitas Christi sicut instrumentum coniunctum, sacramentum autem sicut instrumentum separatum. Et ideo oportet quod virtus salutifera derivetur a divinitate Christi per eius humanitatem in ipsa sacramenta."

[53]   *BLS*, 117. See *CB*, no. 138; *Mémorial*, 4.

de son Fils, ainsi pouvons-nous dire que ce Fils incarné Jésus-Christ notre Seigneur s'unit avec nous pour accomplir son Eucharistie.[54]

For Bérulle, the priest is above all he who renders present the body of Christ through transubstantiation by virtue of the Holy Spirit.[55]

Dupuy argued that Bérulle's use of the term *personne* needed a clarification only metaphysics could give, referring to it as a principle of operation. The priest has a part in the action of Christ when consecrating. In this sense he is linked to the person of Christ, argued Dupuy. Referring to John 17:6, Bérulle explained that it is to the deified humanity, to the divine person, that the priest is united in the offering of the Mass, which makes priests his members.[56]

In the following quote, Bérulle appears to differentiate, however, the functional instrumentality of the priest as public person and as compared to the intimate union of the priest as a member of Christ in private life: "être attaché au Christ, comme un membre à la tête, comme un instrument à la cause principale; comme membre pour la vie intérieure, privée; comme instrument pour les fonctions extérieures, sacerdotales."[57]

In Persona Christi

Bérulle explained how the priest is anointed. Bérulle echoed the scriptural phrase "putting on Christ," a Pauline phrase cherished by Reformers, also combining it with the notion of being inside the person of Christ.

By the priesthood of Christ, the priest "puts on the Person of Christ," operating, as Dupuy translated it, "en la Personne du Christ" ("in Persona Christi operamur"). Added to these assertions was the notion that the person of Christ assumes the priest's person to do the works of Christ:

Le Christ est prêtre, et prêtre par l'onction de sa Divinité même. Nous, nous sommes prêtres par l'opération du Christ oint lui-même: il nous oint de son Esprit et nous consacre à lui comme prêtres. Il faut considérer, bien peser, adorer le sacerdoce du Christ.

---

[54] Ibid., *OP* 82, 117, here presented as an expanded quote from *OC* (1996), *OP* 280, 299–300 (revised numeration). Dupuy introduced this opuscule with the comment that this text is known through the Bourgoing edition with a note in the margin: "Cet écrit contient des pensées excellentes de l'auteur, mais il n'est pas achevé et même il semble que ses pensées ont été recueillies par un autre."

[55] Ibid., 119. See *OR* 11, 5.

[56] Ibid., 117–18.

[57] *BLS, OR* 37, no. 1, 356.

De même que nous sommes membres du Christ par l'Incarnation: "c'est l'os de mes os," de même, par le sacerdoce du Christ, nous revêtons la Personne du Christ. Nous opérons en la Personne du Christ. Et il se produit une sorte d'assomption merveilleuse de notre personne par la Personne du Christ pour opérer les "merveilles du Christ," en sorte que nous fassions les œuvres du Christ. "Œuvrez pour la nourriture qui ne passe pas, mais demeure pour la vie éternelle." Ceci vaut spécialement pour nous, prêtres, qui consacrons le Christ.[58]

In Bérulle's thought, argued Dupuy, the priest is united to the deified humanity, not the Word. That said, it is the Word that gives the priesthood its theological dimension, according to Dupuy. By the Incarnation, priests are united to Christ's person. Priests must cede their own persons and enter into the person of Jesus, as Dupuy put it, not just at Mass, but also at all times. This is a spiritual notion rather than a metaphysical one, Dupuy argued:

C'est la personne qui agit. Mais elle agit selon sa nature et, dans le cas du Christ, ou bien selon sa nature humaine, ou bien selon sa divinité. Or l'offrande qu'il fait de lui-même est acte du Christ selon sa nature humaine: c'est en tant qu'homme qu'il est le Souverain Prêtre. Cependant, comme il apparaît dans la transsubstantiation, cette offrande est rendue possible du fait que sa nature humaine est revêtue de la puissance divine que lui confère sa subsistence dans le Verbe. C'est précisément à cette humanité déifiée que le prêtre est uni dans l'offrande de la messe. Il est de "Ceux que le Père a choisis et fait siens avant tous les siècles et qu'il a donnés à son Fils incarné dans la plénitude des temps, selon cette parole: Tui erant et mihi eos dedisti [John 17:6], et que le Fils tire tous les jours dans l'unité de sa divine Personne, les liant à son humanité déifiée et les faisant ses membres."[59] L'expression "Instrument conjoint du Fils de Dieu en la terre"[60] dit tout cela avec concision et précision: instrument conjoint, non pas du Verbe bien sûr, mais du Fils de Dieu en la terre.

Que cette distinction ne fasse pas perdre de vue ce que la relation du prêtre au Verbe a d'étonnant: c'est elle qui donne au sacerdoce sa dimension théologale; c'est elle qui insère la réflexion sur le sacerdoce dans la théologie entendue au sens précis de discours sur Dieu. Le Christ est prêtre en raison de son union hypostatique. Les "siens" sont prêtres en raison de leur relation au "Fils de Dieu en la terre." Bérulle insiste sur ce

---

[58]   Ibid., *OR* 15, no. 3, 291.
[59]   *OP* 87, no. 2, quoted in *BLS*, 118.
[60]   *CB*, no. 138, quoted in *BLS*, 118.

point en reprenant l'opposition classique nature-personne. Par l'Incarnation, le Christ a revêtu la nature humaine qu'il a partagée avec l'humanité. A la Cène il unit les prêtres, non plus seulement à sa nature, mais même à sa Personne.[61]

Telle est l'affirmation centrale qui fonde tout l'effort spirituel du prêtre, sous l'aspect de dépouillement comme sous celui de renouvellement. L'union à la Personne du Fils de Dieu est pour le prêtre exigence de renoncement. Il faut que sa propre personne cède pour ainsi dire à celle du Fils de Dieu, comme ce fut le cas pour l'humanité de Jésus....Il lui faut entrer dans la Personne de Jésus, non seulement pour célébrer la messe, mais durant toute sa vie. Nous dirions aujourd'hui qu'il doit renoncer à sa personnalité pour s'identifier à son sacerdoce.[62]

Mysteries of the Life of Christ as Public Person

Molien wrote on the relationship between the states of Christ in relation to the priesthood.[63] Priests were called to adhere particularly to the interior states of Jesus during his public life and ministry.[64] Bérulle:

nous avons aussi une grande obligation en ce temps [Feast of the Baptism] à renouveler notre adhérence au Fils de Dieu. Car c'est à présent que sa vie publique nous est proposée. Auparavant il a mené une vie secrète, privée, particulière, inconnue et ordinaire, se montrant seulement comme homme, quoiqu'il fût Dieu et homme tout ensemble. Mais maintenant il commence une vie publique en laquelle il se découvre le Messie, l'oint du Seigneur et paraît Fils de Dieu au monde. Aussi cette vie commence par une déclaration et manifestation de sa filiation divine de la part du Père éternel en son baptême. Or comme le Fils de Dieu commence cette nouvelle manière de vie, il nous faut honorer cette vie publique de trois ans, ses prédications, ses miracles, ses conversations avec les âmes et l'état intérieur de son âme en chacun de ces points, renouvelant notre adhérence, liaison et piété vers lui en ce nouvel état. Mais prenons garde que parlant si souvent entre nous de nous renouveler en l'esprit de piété et en l'adhérence au Fils de Dieu et pour l'amour de lui à sa très sainte

---

61   *BLS, OR* 15, no. 3, 291, quoted in *BLS*, 119.
62   Ibid., 118–19.
63   A. Molien, *Le cardinal de Bérulle: histoire—doctrine—les meilleurs textes*, vol. 1 (Paris: Beauchesne, 1947), 291–94.
64   Ibid., 292. See *OP* 59, Migne ed., cols. 1033–34.

Mère, nos œuvres correspondent fidèlement aux lumières et aux avis qu'il plaît à Dieu de nous en donner, et que cette piété envers Jésus et Marie et tout ce qui concerne leur service et nos devoirs envers eux soit de jour en jour plus particulière, plus parfaite, plus éminente; et d'autant plus encore que c'est cette piété qui nous distingue des autres sociétés de l'Église de Dieu.[65]

Public Person and Holy Spirit

Melanchthon emphasized in the fifth article of the Augsburg Confession that, through offices, God "gives the Holy Spirit who produces faith, where and when he wills, in those who hear the gospel." He condemned the notion of Anabaptists and others that held that one can obtain the Holy Spirit without the external word, through one's own devices.[66]

Calvin was said to have "the incarnation of the Holy Spirit as his basic principle of ecclesiology," according to Sloyan.[67] In terms of the priesthood, Calvin objected to the idea that priests "have" the Holy Spirit, no matter what the state of their souls.[68]

In his defense of the Mass as sacrifice and the priesthood, Bérulle focused on the role of the Holy Spirit in the life of the priest as public person. The following passages are taken in order from Bérulle's talk, "Finis Huius Novi Instituti," with Dupuy's analysis interspersed.[69] The following sentence, in particular, highlights the relationship between the priest as public person and the Holy Spirit for Bérulle. The Spirit plays a public, not private role, rendering the priest's person no longer profane but sacred and divine (here provided in Dupuy's French translation and in the original Latin):

---

[65] *OP*, vol. 3 (1995), *OP* 66, 220–21, quoted in part in Molien, *Le cardinal de Bérulle*, 292, referencing the Migne edition.

[66] Wengert, *Priesthood, Pastors, Bishops*, 34, quoting Philipp Melanchthon, "The Apology of the Augsburg Confession," 5.1–4, in *The Book of Concord: The Confessions of the Evangelical Church*, ed. Robert Kolb and Timothy J. Wengert (Minneapolis: Fortress Press, 2000), 38 and 40.

[67] Sloyan, *The Three Persons*, 98–99. Note that this is in contrast to Bouyer's opinion, as cited, that Calvin refused the work of the Holy Spirit in humankind other than in the gift of understanding the scriptures.

[68] See *Institution*, 3.4.20: "Ils se vantent d'avoir le sainct Esprit, mais par leurs faits ils le nient."

[69] *BLS, OR* 22, 315–17.

Aussi cet Esprit fait-il jouer un rôle, non plus privé, mais public, ou plutôt rend votre personne, non plus profane ou quelconque, mais sacrée, non plus commune, mais divine.[70]

Ille itaque spiritus publicam, non privatam, eamque sacram, non profanam vel communem, divinam, non vulgarem, personam induit seu confert.[71]

Referring to the above passage, Dupuy noted the difficulty in the precise meaning of "induere personam," which he translated as "se masquer," or "tenir un role," and which he believed showed a permanence to the sense of the word *persona*, despite, as he put it, the metaphysics attributed by theology. He also noted that the Latin word "conferre" implied a juridical sense of a functional investiture.[72] For this reader, the question remains whether Bérulle indicated, rather, a change in the priest himself, which made a public role possible.

Below, Bérulle insisted that priests received neither the grace of Christ nor that of the Holy Spirit but rather the Holy Spirit in person, so that priests can give grace to others. Dupuy noted that this statement was reminiscent of Pétau's ideal, as reviewed, which Dupuy believed Bérulle borrowed from the Greek fathers.[73] Bérulle:

Noter qu'il a été dit aux apôtres et qu'on répète aux prêtres: "Recevez l'Esprit-Saint," et non pas seulement la grâce de l'Esprit-Saint. La raison pourrait en être ceci: alors que dans les autres sacrements, excepté l'Eucharistie, on reçoit une grâce du Christ ou de l'Esprit-Saint, plutôt que l'Esprit-Saint lui-même, ici l'Esprit-Saint est d'abord donné en personne, pour qu'en nous et par nous il donne sa grâce et ses autres dons. Aussi l'esprit sacerdotal ne consiste-t-il pas seulement en l'infusion d'une disposition spirituelle, comme la charité ou les vertus de pauvreté et de solitude mais en l'infusion de l'Esprit-Saint lui-même. Et cet esprit est l'Esprit-Saint. Il ne s'agit donc pas d'une simple motion spirituelle, mais de l'Esprit-Saint lui-même.[74]

---

[70] Ibid., *OR* 22, no. 2, 315.
[71] Ibid., *OR* 22, no. 2, 313, Latin version.
[72] Ibid., *OR* 22, no. 2, 313 and 315. See footnote 1.
[73] Ibid., 120n51.
[74] Ibid., *OR* 22, no. 2, 315–16.

The Holiness of the Priest and Possession of the Holy Spirit

Returning to the topic of the holiness of the priest as both objective and subjective, a closer look at Dupuy's analysis of Bérulle's thought reveals, in fact, the conflation of the two.

The priesthood was a state or order of holiness according to Bérulle, with the supernatural capacity of conferring grace. Pointing to Soto's opinion, Bérulle held that priests themselves were permeated (*imbuantur*)[75] with grace. Therefore, a distinct holiness was required of them: "Puisque les sacrements sont instruments de la Passion du Christ et tiennent de lui leur capacité surnaturelle de conférer la grâce, la raison demande que les ministres en soient promus à un ordre de sainteté, secondement, pour une dispensation digne de ces sacrements, qu'ils soient revêtus de la grâce, dit Soto (IV, dist. 24. Q. 1. Art. 1)."[76]

Bérulle noted that just as Christ was holy by the hypostasis of the Word, so priests are holy by the Holy Spirit, which is received not simply by an infusion of grace. In the sacrament of orders, Bérulle insisted, the Holy Spirit acts by his form, or at least by the power of his form:

> Dieu est saint de par sa propre essence. Le Christ l'est, en tant qu'homme, de par l'essence divine qui lui est communiquée hypostatiquement. Les prêtres le sont, de par l'Esprit-Saint qui leur est infusé: "Recevez le Saint Esprit," non pas seulement par l'infusion d'une grâce. Si l'Esprit-Saint n'était pas donné dans tous les sacrements du fait de l'infusion de la grâce, il le serait quand même dans le sacrement de l'ordre, où il agit par sa propre forme ou du moins par le pouvoir de sa forme: "Recevez l'Esprit-Saint." C'est de lui-même qu'ont besoin ceux qui doivent dispenser aux autres sa grâce.[77]

Bérulle proposed that just as the Word's union with the humanity made it disposed to purchase or liberate humankind, so too, in the priest, a human nature is united to the Holy Spirit making the priest disposed to sanctify humankind:

---

[75] Ibid., 313, no. 3, Latin version.

[76] Ibid., *OR* 22, nos. 2 and 3, 316. Dupuy chose to translate the Latin *imbuantur* with the French word *revetû* (which could be translated "clothed," as in "clothed with virtue"). This translation perhaps gives a more extrinsic connotation. See Académie française, *Dictionnaire de l'Académie Française*, 4th ed. (Paris: chez la veuve de B. Brunet, 1762), for the sixteenth-century definition. See http://artflsrv01.uchicago.edu/cgi-bin/dicos /pubdico1look.pl?strippedhw=revetu.

[77] Ibid., *OR* 22, no. 3, 316.

C'est pourquoi, de même que le Christ est dit venir de l'Esprit-Saint: "Ce qui est né d'elle vient de l'Esprit-Saint" et que l'Incarnation du Christ est appropriée à l'Esprit-Saint, de même l'ordination sacerdotale est opérée spécialement par l'Esprit-Saint lui-même: "Recevez le Saint-Esprit." Dans le Christ la nature humaine fut unie au Verbe divin et par là fut apte à racheter le genre humain. Dans le prêtre une personne humaine est unie à l'Esprit-Saint et par là rendue apte à sanctifier le genre humain.[78]

The Priest as Public Person Who Has Received the Holy Spirit Himself

Bérulle once again reiterated in the following passage that the priest as public person, as representative of Christ, is filled with the Spirit. Bérulle insisted that just as God is in Christ to reconcile the world, so he is in the priest to sanctify it. As detailed, the priest is an *organe* of God, meant to sanctify the world as Christ reconciled it. He is filled with God, and receives the Holy Spirit, as Christ gave the Holy Spirit to his apostles:

Un prêtre, rempli du Saint-Esprit, est dans l'Église de Dieu comme une personne publique, un représentant de Dieu, celui qui tient sa place. C'est ainsi qu'il convient que Dieu "opère tout en tous." En l'Église militante, comme en la triomphante, il sera "tout en tous." C'est pourquoi, de même que Dieu était dans le Christ pour se réconcilier le monde, Dieu est dans le prêtre pour sanctifier le monde. Et le prêtre est l'organe de Dieu. Etc. Jésus-Christ édifiant l'Église, Homme-Dieu. Le prêtre, servant à Dieu en cette Église, est homme de Dieu, plein de Dieu: "Recevez le Saint-Esprit," qui est Dieu.[79]

The Priest Doing the Works of Christ

As just discussed, Bérulle held that Christ was anointed by the Holy Spirit, which Dupuy remarked was reminiscent of Pétau.[80] Bérulle also emphasized that the priest was called to do the same works as those of Christ, again in a different manner. In both cases, Bérulle appears to make cautious qualifications to avoid criticism. Referring back to the analysis of the Reformers' view of the role of Christ as public person whose works during his life and Passion were considered, it is clear that Bérulle is here rebutting the position that Christ is the sole mediator of grace by making the priest a public person:

---

[78] Ibid., *OR* 22, no. 4, 316–17. Dupuy called this imprudent. See *BLS*, 120.
[79] Ibid., *OR* 22, no. 5, 317.
[80] Ibid., *BLS*, 317m.

Le Christ est dit oint du Saint-Esprit: "Comment Dieu l'a oint d'Esprit-Saint." C'est-à-dire: en tant que la grâce du Saint-Esprit fit qu'il fut oint de la divinité elle-même, comme dit Vasquez. Ainsi le prêtre, comme le Christ bien que d'une autre manière, est oint de l'Esprit-Saint: "Recevez le Saint-Esprit." De même que le prêtre est appelé à des œuvres semblables à celles auxquelles le Christ fut appelé, mais de manière différente, de même il est oint aussi du même Saint-Esprit, mais de manière différente. [81]

Conclusion

Putting on the person of Christ, entering into the person of Christ, being assumed by the person of Christ—with a seemingly Baroque repetition, this vocabulary was used to construct a spiritual theology of priesthood that comprehensively asserted an essentialist relationship between the priest and Christ, also dependent on the notion of the possession of the person of the Spirit by the priest as public person.

This study illustrates that the roots of this emphasis on the priest as public person were to be found in a devolved classical notion of the priest as public representative, as well as in Reformist ideals that attempted to de-emphasize the minister as image of Christ and his role in the work of redemption via a greater transparency. This same transparency was adopted into Bérulle's spiritual theology of priesthood, serving to cement the unicity between the person of the priest and that of Christ, making the priest, rather than merely an image, a transparent image of Christ, the topic of a future chapter.

First, we turn to Bérulle's conflation of sacerdotal character and sacerdotal grace, a schema resulting in further conflations of ideals surrounding the notion of image in its legal and official sense, and as related to grace, faith, and charity.

---

[81]   Ibid., *OR* 22, no. 6, 317.

Chapter 13
Sacerdotal Character and Sacerdotal Grace

Introduction

In this chapter, the Reformist objections to the idea of sacerdotal character, Trent's truncated response, and Bérulle's oblique treatment are explored. Next, the question of character as a category of being, as well as various historical proposals from which Bérulle may have borrowed ideals, is treated. Sacerdotal character in relation to sacerdotal grace, sanctifying grace, and special graces, as well as the politics of the grace debates in the period before and during his lifetime, are then explored. Bérulle's notions surrounding the priest's production of the Word in souls are also discussed. Lastly, we explore the "ontological vs. functional" debate regarding the nature of character in Bérulle's project.

Background

For Bérulle, concepts related to sacerdotal grace, sacerdotal character, sanctifying grace, and, specifically, special graces formed an important part of his response to the Reformers' objections to both a corrupt clergy and the ministerial priesthood in general. This came at a time of prolonged, multiple disputes regarding the nature of grace both within and outside the Roman Catholic Church.

The interplay between sacerdotal character, sacerdotal grace, and various other conceptualizations of grace, as understood and debated at the time, formed the ontological glue, so to speak, of Bérulle's reform of the priesthood, a priesthood dependent on a sacerdotal spirituality of servitude and adherence. As with other themes, Bérulle did not treat the topic systematically for a variety of possible reasons. Bérulle had rejected the rigors of Scholasticism, wished to argue points on the same grounds as Reformers, and perhaps wanted to avoid criticism. Other possible reasons might have been that the Council canons and decrees were not accepted until 1619 in France, or that any debate regarding character was discouraged after the Council.

Finding patterns in this crucial area of Bérulle's thought is difficult but made possible by situating it within the Reformist controversies of the era. Bérulle was concerned with justifying the necessity of priests as mediators. Their mediation depended, on the one hand, on the notion of a unique objective holiness attributable to priests, and on the other, on a program of sacerdotal spirituality to guarantee a corresponding subjective holiness. Bérulle attributed the former to character, and the latter to grace. That said, character and grace were not mutually exclusive in his thought, being conflated in an emanationist exemplarism, as we will explore.

Luther's Critique and Trent's Response

During the Reformation, accusations against immoral priests brought the issue of the validity of the sacrament of orders to the fore. The fathers of Trent were forced to confront Luther's rejection of the sacramental character of ordination.[1]

According to Pintard, challenges confronting Trent on the subject of orders were considerable, including those to the theology of apostolic function, the manner in which apostolic function is transmitted, and its various expressions. Luther's objection to the permanency and authority of the priesthood and the hierarchy lay in his belief that neither could be supported by either scriptural or patristic authority.[2]

The problem of priests returning to the lay state had created a crisis of conscience regarding indelible character,[3] and widely divergent opinions on the nature of indelible character had existed on the part of theologians prior to Trent.[4] The council fathers avoided any definition of the nature of character because of the still-extant debates.[5] They also avoided determining the connection between character and the non-repeatability of a sacrament by maintaining the language of the Council of Florence. They wanted to avoid a

---

[1] Martin Luther, *De captivitate Babylonica ecclesiae, praeludium Martini Lutheri*, October 1520, WA 6: 560: "Hoc sacramentum Ecclesia Christi ignorat, inventumque est ab Ecclesia Papae: non enim solum nullam habet promissionem gratiae ullibi positam, sed ne verbo quidem eius meminit totum novum testamentum. Ridiculum autem est asserere pro sacramento dei, quod a deo institutum nusquam potest monstrari. Non quod damnandum censeam eum ritum per tanta saecula celebratum, sed quod in rebus sacris nolim humana commenta fingi, nec liceat astruere aliquod divinitus ordinatum quod divinitus ordinatum non est, ne ridiculi simus adversario."

[2] J. Pintard, "Caractère sacerdotal et fidélité," *Esprit et vie* 84 (1974): 164–65.

[3] Ibid., 162. See C. Vogel, "Le retour du presbytre au rang des laïcs," *Revue des sciences religieuses* (Jan. 1973): 56–122.

[4] Pintard, "Caractère sacerdotal et fidélité," 163. See Galot, *La nature du caractère sacramentel*.

[5] Hervé-Marie Legrand, "The 'Indelible' Character and the Theology of Ministry," *Concilium* 74 (1972): 58.

"consequential link between the impression of the character and the impossibility of the priest becoming a layman once again."[6] As Pintard summarized, on the level of faith there was no doubt at Trent about the existence of indelible character. However, the fathers conceded a limited understanding of its nature.[7]

A number of the strongest objections of the Reformers remained in full force and largely unaddressed when Bérulle rose to meet them, over fifty years after Trent. The need to address certain objections can be traced, perhaps, to the failure of the council fathers to define the nature of character, a lacuna that remains today.

Bérulle and Character

Dupuy noted that Bérulle preferred the idea of vocation over character, rarely mentioned character, and took some liberties with its etymological sense. Bérulle represented the character of both baptism and priesthood as a *lien*, a new relation to Christ granting a permanent power: "…nous sommes liés à Jésus-Christ…" In this, according to Dupuy, he followed the Scotist idea of character as relation, an idea hard to sustain, according to Dupuy, after Trent had defined it.[8]

Dupuy thought Bérulle's was a juridical notion similar to others in that era, including that of Bellarmine, who had attempted to define character as a moral, not physical power, a result of the divine assistance wherein a pact with God gave assurance. This conceptualization, it could be argued, mirrored the voluntarism of the Reformers' emphasis on God's free election.[9]

Dupuy argued that this tie for Bérulle was more of a gift, and had more of a biblical sense than that of a contract. The basis of character, and the priesthood's permanence, for Bérulle, was Christ's own unchangeability and the conservation

---

6   Ibid., 58.
7   Pintard, "Caractère sacerdotal et fidélité," 161–163.
8   *BLS*, 188, esp. footnote 3. See *OR* 15, no. 2, 290–91; *OR* 18, no. 2, 297 and 192–93.
9   Ibid., 188n3. See Robert Bellarmine, "De Effectu Sacramentorum," ch. 19, *De sacramentis in genere*, in *De Controversiis Christianae Fidei*, 3 (Naples, 1856–58), controv. 1, bk. 2: "Est tamen hic notandum, istam potentiam non videri physicam, sed moralem. Non enim character attingit effectum, sed tantum operari dicitur, quia ubicumque est talis character Deus ex pacto adest, et concurrit ad effectum supernaturalem producendum, quod non facit ubi non est talis character."

of his power,[10] which is the permanence of the hypostatic union: Christ is human even in heaven, a priest forever.[11]

A closer examination of Bérulle's ideas surrounding character follows.

Character and Category of Being

The main question facing any discussion of character, according to Persich, is into what category of being it falls—a question that remains a matter of dispute.[12] Pourrat articulated that this question, arising in the thirteenth century, was as follows: "To what category of being should it be ascribed and what are the exact relations it establishes between Christ and the faithful?"[13] In the case of the priesthood, this question also applies.

Bérulle, in his conceptualization of character, drew on a rich and complex history of metaphysical concepts. A larger study is needed to ascertain the scope of various ideals influencing Bérulle's thought; however, a few thinkers figure prominently, representing various lines of thought and possible influence.

Pourrat detailed that Alexander of Hales, for example, held that character inheres in the soul and is not a mere relation, but is, rather, a *habitus*, a quality that perfects the soul intrinsically, making it fit to receive grace. For Alexander, character entails assimilation to Christ. In terms of sacerdotal character, this involves an assimilation to Jesus as sovereign priest.[14]

---

[10] Dupuy, 188. See *OR* 11. Dupuy also referenced Aquinas, *ST*, 3.63.5, ad 2, in *Summa theologiae*, 12.1: 38: "Et ideo, quantumcumque voluntas moveatur in contrarium, character non removetur, propter immobilitatem principalis moventis."

[11] Ibid., 189. See *Coll.* 38 and 110. See also Hebrews 5:6 (cited in *OP* 80, no. 1) and Hebrews 7:25.

[12] Nicholas C. Persich, "The Priesthood of the Mystical Body" (PhD diss., Rome: Pontificio Instituto Angelico; St. Louis: Society of the Congregation of the Missions, 1951), 55.

[13] P. Pourrat, *Theology of the Sacraments* (St. Louis, MO, and Freiburg: B. Herder, 1910), 246. Originally published as *La théologie sacramentaire: étude de théologie positive* (Paris: Lecoffre, 1907).

[14] Ibid., 246–47. See Alexander Hales, *Summa Universae Theologiae* (n.p., n.d.), 4.8.membr.8.1: "Character est aliquis habitus relucens, in anima impressus perpetuo, quo discernatur fuisse sanctificatio baptismi, Nec est habitus ad agendum simpliciter, sed est ad disponendum ad gratiam quantum est in se dum homo est viator, et ad discernendum, ovem dominicam a lupis."

Aquinas placed character in the category of an instrumental potency,[15] and held that character is a participation in the priesthood of Christ.[16] Aquinas was also the first to depart from the notion that character belonged to the category of *habitus*, one requiring grace for perfection. Aquinas' rejection was based on the fact that if it were a *habitus*, then a priest saying Mass in mortal sin would invalidate the sacrament.[17] In terms of character as the second species of quality, *potentia*, Aquinas wrote: "…character conveys a spiritual potency ordained to whatever pertains to divine worship."[18] God is the principal agent of character, which is both a physical and instrumental power, superior to the natural

---

[15] Galot, *La nature du caractère sacramentel*, 174. See Thomas Aquinas, *Sent.* 4.4.1.1, in *Scriptum super Sententiis magistri Petri Lombardi*, ed. Maria Fabianus Moos, vols. 3–4 (Paris: P. Lethielleux, 1933–47), 4: 150–51: "*Sicut* enim cujuslibet existentis in aliqua natura, sunt aliquae operationes propriae, *ita* etiam in spirituali vita regenerati, ut Dionysius dicit in 2 c. *Eccles. Hier.* Ubicumque autem sunt operationes propriae, oportet quod sint principia propria illarum operationum. Unde *sicut* in aliis rebus sunt potentiae naturales ad proprias operationes, *ita* etiam renati ad vitam spiritualem habent quasdam potentias, secundum quas possunt illa opera: quae potentiae sunt similes illis virtutibus quibus sacramenta efficaciam habent sibi inditam; quia *sicut* sacramenta causant gratiam instrumentaliter…*ita* recipientes characterem operantur divina per ministerium. Minister autem est sicut instrumentum ejus cui ministrat…Et ideo tam virtus sacramenti quam minister qui est character est instrumentalis."

[16] George Edward Dolan, *The Distinction between the Episcopate and the Presbyterate according to the Thomistic Opinion* (Washington, DC: Catholic University of America Press, 1950), 29. This review follows the author's exposition closely. See L. Audet, *Notre participation au sacerdoce du Christ* (Quebec: Université Laval, 1938), 26. See Aquinas, *ST*, 3.63.3, s.c., in *Summa theologiae*, 12.1: 34: "Sed character aeternus est ipse Christus: secudum illud *Heb.* I: *Qui cum sit splendor gloriae et figura*, vel character, *substantiae eius*. Ergo videtur quod character proprie sit attribuendus Christo."

[17] Ibid., 29. See Aquinas, *ST*, 3.63.2, s.c., in *Summa theologiae*, 12.1: 31: "Sed contra, Philosophus dicit, in II *Ethic.*: *Tria sunt in anima: potentia, habitus et passio.* Sed character non est passio: quia passio cito transit, character autem indelebilis est, ut infra dicetur. Similiter etiam non est habitus. Quia nullus habitus est qui se possit ad bene et male habere. Character autem ad utrumque se habet: utuntur enim eo quidam bene, alii vero male. Quod in habitibus non contingit: nam habitu virtutis *nullus utitur male*, habitu malitiae nullus bene. Ergo relinquitur quod character sit potentia."

[18] Ibid., 33. See Aquinas, *ST*, 3.63.2, co., in *Summa theologiae*, 12.1: 31–32: "sacramenta novae legis characterem imprimunt inquantum per ea deputamur ad cultum Dei secundum ritum Christianae religionis…Divinus autem cultus consistit vel in recipiendo aliqua divina, vel in tradendo aliis. Ad utrumque autem horum requiritur quaedam potentia: nam ad tradendum aliquid aliis, requiritur potentia activa; ad recipiendum autem requiritur potentia passiva. Et ideo character importat quandam potentiam spiritualem ordinatam ad ea quae sunt divini cultus."

potencies of the soul.[19] Aquinas did not place character in the essence of the soul but in a power or faculty of the soul.[20]

According to Cross, Aquinas held that character is a quality which inheres in the intellect, configuring the threefold structure of the mind to its Trinitarian

---

[19]   Ibid., 33–34. See Aquinas, *ST*, 3.63.4, ad 2, in *Summa theologiae*, 12.1: 36: "…essentia animae est subiectum potentiae naturalis, quae ex principiis essentiae procedit. Talis autem potentia non est character: sed est quaedam spiritualis potentia ab extrinseco adveniens." See also 3.64.1, co., in *Summa theologiae*, 12.1: 41: "operari aliquem effectum contingit dupliciter: uno modo, per modum principalis agentis; alio modo, per modum instrumenti. Primo igitur modo solus Deus operatur interiorem effectum sacramenti. Tum quia solus Deus illabitur animae, in qua sacramenti effectus consistit. Non autem potest aliquid immediate operari ubi non est.—Tum quia gratia, quae est interior sacramenti effectus, est a solo Deo, ut in Secunda Parte habitum est. Character etiam, qui est interior quorundam sacramentorum effectus, est virtus instrumentalis, quae manat a principali agente, quod est Deus.

  "Secundo autem modo homo potest operari ad interiorem effectum sacramenti, inquantum operatur per modum ministri. Nam eadem ratio est ministri et instrumenti: utriusque enim actio exterius adhibetur, sed sortitur effectum interiorem ex virtute principalis agentis, quod est Deus." See also 3.62.1 and 4.

[20]   Galot, *La nature du caractère sacramentel*, 190. See Aquinas, *Sent.* 4.4.1.3, in *Scriptum super Sententiis*, ed. Moos, 4: 158: "Unde *sicut* gratia quae est spiritualis vitae principium est in essentia animae sicut in subjecto, *ita* et character qui est spiritualis potentia est sicut in subjecto in naturali potentia animae, et non in essentia animae, ut Quidam dicunt, nisi mediante potentia animae."

model, and that it is instrumental in the process of receiving grace.[21] Duns Scot held, however, that character is a relation.[22]

In the following review, various aspects of these influences can be discerned, however mixed and vague their flavors, in Bérulle's rhetoric.

By far the greatest influence on Bérulle's notions regarding character was Pseudo-Dionysius. Garrigues, Le Guillou, and Riou's review of his thought on Christ as mediator in both angelic and ecclesial hierarchies bears repeating in terms of sacramental character.[23] For Pseudo-Dionysius, Christ as head of the ecclesiastical hierarchy retains his place beneath the angels in the celestial hierarchy, as noted,[24] with all acts of priesthood associated with thearchic

[21] See Aquinas, *Sent.* 4.4.1.1, in *Scriptum super Sententiis*, ed. Moos, 4: 149: "Differunt autem in hoc, quia Quidam ponunt istis relationibus non subesse aliquod accidens absolutum, sed immediate in anima fundari istas relationes.

"Hoc autem esse non potest, quia signum per formam quam sensibus vel intellectui imprimit, facit aliquid in cognitionem venire. *Similiter etiam* nihil distinguitur ab alio nisi per aliquam formam. Similitudo etiam est relatio super unitate qualitatis fundata, ut dicitur in V *Meta*. Unde patet quod quaelibet illarum relationum quam importat character, requirit aliquam formam substratam; et cum non sit forma substantialis, quia forma substantialis in sacramentis non datur, relinquitur quod forma substrata sit qualitas quaedam, cujus unitas consignificationis similitudinem facit."

See also Aquinas, *Sent.* 4.4.1.3, in *Scriptum super Sententiis*, ed. Moos, 4: 159: "Ad secundum dicendum quod assimilatio in bonitate praecipue est ad Deum per voluntatem, sed assimilatio in esse et posse magis est ex parte intellectus; quia ex hoc ipso quod aliquid esse immateriale habet, intellectivum est et potentiam habet quodammodo infinitam, secundum quod intellectus universalium est, quae quodammodo infinita sunt virtute. Et ideo cum conformitas characteris respiciat spiritualem potestatem, magis competit intellectivae parti quam affectivae." Also cited in Richard Cross, *Duns Scot* (New York and Oxford: Oxford University Press, 1999), 139.

[22] Cross, *Duns Scot*, 139. See Duns Scot, *Opera omnia*, vol. 11.2, 578, 4.3.1.Scholum 1: "Sacramentum enim est signum formaliter, et relatio rationis, et refertur ad invisibilem gratiam, ut correlativum et signatum."

[23] See Pseudo-Dionysius, *EH*, 372A, cited in J.-M. Garrigues et al., "Le caractère sacerdotal dans la tradition des Pères grecs," 815. Greek citations taken from Pseudo-Dionysius, Beate Regina Suchla, Günter Heil, and Adolf Martin Ritter, *Corpus Dionysiacum* (Berlin: de Gruyter, 1990), hereafter cited as *CD*. See *CD*, 63.11–64.4: "Οὕτω γάρ, ὡς ἡ θεολογία τοῖς θιασώταις ἡμῖν παραδέδωκε, καὶ αὐτὸς Ἰησοῦς, ὁ θεαρχικώτατος νοῦς καὶ ὑπερούσιος, ἡ πάσης ἱεραρχίας ἁγιαστείας τε καὶ θεουργίας ἀρχὴ καὶ οὐσία καὶ θεαρχικωτάτη δύναμις, ταῖς τε μακαρίαις καὶ ἡμῶν κρπείττοσιν οὐσίαις ἐμφανέστερον ἅμα καὶ νοερώτερον ἐλλάμπει καὶ πρὸς τὸ οἰκεῖον αὐτὰς ἀφομοιοῖ κατὰ δύναμιν φῶς." This review follows the authors' exposition closely.

[24] Garrigues et al., "Le caractère sacerdotal dans la tradition des Pères grecs," 815. See Pseudo-Dionysius, *CH*, 181C. *CD*, 23.10–14: "Ὁρῶ γὰρ ὅτι καὶ αὐτὸς Ἰησοῦς ἡ τῶν ὑπερουρανίων οὐσιῶν ὑπερούσιος αἰτία πρὸς τὸ καθ᾽ ἡμᾶς ἀμεταβόλως ἐληλυθὼς οὐκ ἀποπηδᾷ τῆς ὑπ᾽ αὐτοῦ ταχθείσης τε καὶ αἱρεθείσης ἀνθρωποπρεποῦς εὐταξίας, ἀλλ᾽ εὐπειθῶς ὑποτάττεται ταῖς τοῦ πατρὸς καὶ θεοῦ δι᾽ ἀγγέλων διατυπώσεσιν."

power.[25] Conflating the orders of grace and ordination,[26] sacerdotal character became a mark of perfection.[27]

Sacerdotal Character in Relation to Grace

An important consideration in any study of character, according to Galot, is the question of the relationship between grace and the power associated with character. For Aquinas, as noted, the power of character concerned sacramental actions, distinct from the order of grace, although he did posit a *habitus* of grace.[28] For him, character as a sacrament is a sign of invisible grace, but of itself it is specifically configuration to Christ.[29] Another possible influence was Vázquez and his notions surrounding special graces, as this analysis will detail.

---

[25] Ibid., 815–16. See Pseudo-Dionysius, *EH*, 513A, *CD*, 113.1–5: "Δοκεῖ γάρ μοι τὰ λόγια κλῆρον ὀνομάσαι θεαρχικόν τι δῶρον ὑποδηλοῦν ἐκείνῳ τῷ ἱεραρχικῷ χορῷ τὸν ὑπὸ τῆς θείας ἐκλογῆς ἀναδεδειγμένον, πλήν γε ὅτι τὸν θεῖον ἱεράρχην οὐκ αὐτοκινήτως χρὴ τὰς ἱερατικὰς ποιεῖσθαι τελεσιουργίας, ἀλλ᾽ ὑπὸ θεῷ κινοῦντι ταύτας ἱεραρχικῶς καὶ οὐρανίως τελεσιουργεῖν."

[26] Ibid., 816.

[27] Pseudo-Dionysius, *EH*, 512A–B, quoted in Garrigues et al., "Le caractère sacerdotal dans la tradition des Pères grecs," 816: "Le caractère (σφραγίς), cruciforme (de la signation liturgique à l'Ordination) manifeste la cessation des désirs charnels et une vie à l'imitation de Dieu constamment *tournée vers la très divine vie humaine de Jésus* qui est allé jusqu'à la croix et la mort avec l'*impeccabilité théarchique*, et qui signe ceux qui vivent ainsi comme semblables par la forme à la forme de la croix, *icône de sa propre impeccabilité.*" *CD*, 111.21–26: "Ἡ σταυροειδὴς δὲ σφραγὶς τὴν ἁπασῶν ὁμοῦ τῶν σαρκικῶν ὀρέξεων ἀνενεργησίαν καὶ τὴν θεομίμητον ζωὴν ἀφορῶσαν ἀκλινῶς εἰς τὴν ἀνδρικὴν Ἰησοῦ θειοτάτην ζωὴν ἄχρι σταυροῦ καὶ θανάτου μετὰ θεαρχικῆς ἀναμαρτησίας ἐληλυθότος καὶ τοὺς οὕτω ζῶντας ὡς ὁμοειδεῖς ἐνσημαίνοντος τῇ σταυροειδεῖ τῆς οἰκείας ἀναμαρτησίας εἰκόνι."

[28] Galot, *La nature du caractère sacramentel*, 183. See Aquinas, *Sent.* 4.4.1.1, in *Scriptum super Sententiis*, ed. Moos, 4: 151: "Et ad hoc quod has operationes bene exerceat indiget habitu gratiae, sicut et aliae potentiae habitibus indigent."

[29] Ibid., 184. See Aquinas, *ST*, 3.63.3, ad 2, in *Summa theologiae*, 12.1: 35: "Ad secundum dicendum quod character sacramentalis est res respectu sacramenti exterioris: et est sacramentum respectu ultimi effectus. Et ideo dupliciter potest aliquid characteri attribui. Uno modo, secundum rationem sacramenti. Et hoc modo est signum invisibilis gratiae, quae in sacramento confertur.—Alio modo, secundum characteris rationem. Et hoc modo signum est configurativum alicui principali, apud quem residet auctoritas eius ad quod aliquis deputatur: sicut milites, qui deputantur ad pugnam, insigniuntur signo ducis, quo quodammodo ei configurantur. Et hoc modo illi qui deputantur ad cultum Christianum, cuius auctor est Christus, characterem accipiunt quo Christo configurantur. Unde proprie est character Christi."

The Politics of Grace

To understand Bérulle's thoughts on both sacerdotal character and sacerdotal grace, it is helpful to look at the polemics of grace in the era. Minton wrote that issues of power and authority in France had been in the forefront from the time of Bérulle's youth, and were posed theologically in the grace disputes of the period. Minton noted that Bérulle, perhaps, had these as the basis of his religious system, including his discussion of Christ's attitudes, his emphasis on church over state, and his spirituality of obedience, submission, and withdrawal.[30]

These, too, became closely related to his ideas regarding sacerdotal character and grace. The conversion, submission, and unity of the priest with Christ was at the center of Bérulle's project to legitimize authority and reform the priesthood, with the priest being the first to be transformed by grace through submission to the will of God.

The difficulty with Bérulle's interpretation, as Mersch described and this analysis has detailed, is that the Christian's humanity became minimized and restricted along with Christ's.[31] To explore this question further, a review is necessary of Bérulle's various ideas regarding the priest's graced transformation and union with Christ.

Sacerdotal Grace

According to Aquinas, a grace is given to the priest along with character.[32] Bérulle asked his Oratorians to recall this, the grace of their vocation.[33] As already discussed, however, for Bérulle, priests are not sanctified by created grace, but by the Holy Spirit.[34] Filled with the Holy Spirit, or God, the priest becomes an *organe* of God, and has the authority then to sanctify others. Notably, priests are also rendered holy by the exercise of their office: "Cette servitude nous rend saints par notre office."[35]

---

[30] Minton, "The Figure of Christ," 26–27.

[31] Mersch, *The Whole Christ*, 553.

[32] Bifet, *Teología del sacerdocio*, 105–7. See Aquinas, in *Summa theologiae, ST*, 3.63.5.1: "Ad primum ergo dicendum quod aliter est in anima gratia, et aliter character. Nam gratia est in anima sicut quaedam forma habens esse completum in ea: character autem est in anima sicut quaedam virtus instrumentalis, ut supra dictum est."

[33] *BLS*, 97. See Coll. 113.

[34] Ibid., 107. See Coll. 292, 307, and *OR* 22, no. 2, 312.

[35] Ibid., 201. See *OR* 82, no. 11, 424.

Sanctifying Grace

Specifically, Aquinas held that the sacrament of holy orders confers an increase of sanctifying grace which disposes a priest to exercise power.[36] The power of orders for Aquinas was charismatic, with this sanctifying grace aimed at the sanctification of the priest in order to excel in holiness.[37]

Reviewing Whannou's analysis, for Bérulle, Christ alone is "subsistent" at the level of grace while Christians are but a "relation" to him. Sanctifying grace, for Bérulle, was not a gift of divinization and sanctification but a relation with Christ.[38]

Christ's humanity is made, as Whannou termed it (although Bérulle did not write this), "consubstantial" with the Word and so participates in being the origin and foundation of all grace.[39] As noted, Bérulle made a distinction in that the grace of the humanity of Christ is infinite in contradistinction to Aquinas who held it to be finite.[40]

As Dupuy wrote, while the priest was a conjoint instrument of Christ, for Bérulle, he was also a member of Christ, just like the laity. "…le Fils tire tous les jours dans l'unité de sa divine Personne, les liant à son humanité déifiée et les faisant ses membres."[41] While the priest was to subsist in a certain manner in

---

36 Persich, "The Priesthood of the Mystical Body," 96–97. See Aquinas, *ST*, 3.supp.35.1, co., in *Summa theologiae*, 12.2: 64: "Respondeo dicendum quod *Dei perfecta sunt opera,* ut dicitur *Deut.* XXXII. Et ideo cuicumque datur potentia aliqua divinitus, dantur ea per quae executio illius potentiae potest congrue fieri. Et hoc etiam in naturalibus patet: quia animalibus dantur membra quibus potentiae animae possunt exire in actus suos, nisi sit defectus ex parte materiae. Sicut autem gratia gratum faciens est necessaria ad hoc quod homo digne sacramenta recipiat, ita etiam ad hoc quod homo digne sacramenta dispenset. Et ideo, sicut in baptismo, per quem fit homo susceptivus aliorum sacramentorum, datur gratia gratum faciens; ita in sacramento ordinis, per quod homo ordinatur ad aliorum sacramentorum dispensationem."

37 Ibid., 97. See Aquinas, *ST*, 3.supp.35.1, ad 3, in *Summa theologiae*, 12.2: 64: "Ad tertium dicendum quod ad idoneam executionem ordinum non sufficit bonitas qualiscumque, sed requiritur bonitas excellens: ut sicut illi qui ordinem suscipiunt super plebem constituuntur gradu ordinis, ita et superiores sint merito sanctitatis. Et ideo praeexigitur gratia quae sufficiebat ad hoc quod digne connumerentur in plebe Christi: sed confertur in ipsa susceptione ordinis amplius gratiae munus, per quod ad maiora reddantur idonei."

38 *Subsistence*, 88. See *Grandeurs*, 8, no. 6, 290.

39 Ibid., 88. See *Grandeurs*, 8, no. 6, 290.

40 Ibid., 88–89. See *OP* 34 A. See also Aquinas, *ST*, 3.2.11, co., in *Summa theologiae*, 11: 50: "Et ideo omnis operatio illius hominis subsecuta est unionem. Unde nulla eius operatio potuit esse meritum unionis."

41 *OP* 87, no. 2, quoted in *BLS*, 195n1.

Christ in order to act *in persona Christi*,[42] the laity too were urged to subsist in Christ. As with Aquinas, sacerdotal character demanded, however, a particular call to be holy.

Dupuy continued his analysis, noting that Bérulle held that in comparison to sacerdotal grace, sanctifying grace is "la plus éminente et importante."[43] While the greatest spiritual goods were common to all,[44] priests, as already noted, must be the first in *l'école de Jésus* in terms of abnegation.[45] The greatest purpose of the priesthood, which demanded holiness, was in dispensing sanctifying grace.[46]

Grace as Ex Officio *Obligation*

Bérulle asserted that while participation in the divine nature is communicated by habitual grace, in terms of priests and the exercise of their office, participation is also by the help of a special grace to which they are obliged *ex officio* and which they must work to obtain: "Tous ceux qui reçoivent la grâce de Dieu deviennent, il est vrai, 'participants de la nature divine.' Pourtant cette participation à la vie divine n'est pas communiquée à tous par la grâce habituelle commune; elle n'est communiquée que par un secours spécial. Et Dieu a obligé les prêtres en vertu de leur office à chercher à l'obtenir."[47]

Bérulle called the grace of vocation habitual, and both interior and exterior: "Mais il y en a une que d'une certaine façon on appellee habituelle, et c'est celle qu'on nomme la grâce de la vocation, aussi bien extérieure qu'intérieure." In this, Dupuy saw Bérulle responding to the Reformers' idea of an interior vocation apart from an exterior one dependent on a bishop's call. The exterior vocation referred to the abandonment of the world, while the interior related to the grace to live according to the Spirit. In this interior grace of vocation, there was a constant need for the perpetual actions of grace, and special divine assistance.[48]

Special Possession by the Spirit of Jesus

Bérulle spoke of the notion of a special grace by which Jesus takes possession of certain souls. Bérulle was to say also that the Spirit of Jesus carries a direct and

---

42 *BLS*, 196. See *Grandeurs*, 8, no. 13, and *OR* 39, no. 4.
43 Bérulle, *OP* 180, no. 3, quoted in *BLS*, 197.
44 *BLS*, 197. See *OR* 19, no. 7.
45 Ibid., 198. See *OP* 134.
46 Ibid., 199–200n18. See *OR* 22, no. 5. This idea was found in Molina, *Instruccion de sacerdotes,* tr. 1, ch. 16.
47 Coll. 69, *OC, Conférences et fragments* (1995), 313–14.
48 See Bérulle, *Quand on reçoit une grâce; défauts à éviter*, October 1613. *OC, Conférences et fragments* (1995), 155, See 155n1.

immediate possession of them as something more than by the common infusion of grace. All the members (of Christ) are vivified, but there are more noble parts (such as priests and the perfect) where grace operates more surely and efficaciously:

> Ces deux derniers dépendent de notre usage et volonté. L'Esprit de Jésus emporte une possession et direction immédiate de Jésus sur nous comme chose plus sienne que par l'infusion commune de la grâce. Tous les membres sont vivifié par l'âme; mais il y a des parties plus nobles et vitales où elle opère plus sûrement et efficacement, outre la vie commune qu'elle communique à toutes les parties du corps également; car elles ne sont pas toutes capables également de ses effets.[49]

Therefore, Bérulle's Oratorian, as priest, was filled with God himself through sacerdotal grace, but also was called to a special infusion of sanctifying grace as well.

"State" of Priesthood as State of Grace?

In his talks with the Oratorians, Bérulle attempted to link a canonical sense of the phrase *état de prêtrise* and a theological *état de grâce*, but without precision, as Preckler wrote.[50]

Bérulle specifically attempted to link the state of the priesthood and the state of grace by priests' association in the Oratory, Dupuy explained. Bérulle treated at some length how the Oratory was a society that mirrored the societies of the Trinity and the Incarnation. Tied to God by the spirit of charity and the state of their spirit of servitude, Bérulle asserted that Oratorians had a new tie with the Spirit of Jesus both by state and by character, through a new grace that God wanted to give the Church. It appears, then, that the tie is not simply that of character, but one that creates a special state of grace through the vow of servitude: "Comme assemblés pour recueillir cette nouvelle grâce que Dieu veut faire en son Église, nous sommes lies à lui par l'Esprit de Jésus et par l'état de notre servitude envers lui."[51]

Bérulle told his Oratorians that belonging to the choir of Jesus demanded an additional grace, one that permitted them to honor, respect, and desire

---

[49] *BLS, OR* 18, no. 4, 300.
[50] *État*, 51. See *BLS, OR* 80, 416–19.
[51] *BLS, OR* 18, no. 2, 297. This review follows the author's exposition closely.

participation—that is, to be hidden with Christ in God: "Cette appartenance demande, outre la grâce ordinaire, une grâce actuelle spéciale."[52]

States and Grace

Revisiting Bérulle's ideas surrounding the mysteries in relation to grace, Bérulle's conceptualization of how the Christian and the priest participate in the mysteries of Christ's life was based on the idea that the humanity of Christ acts as an efficient, instrumental cause of grace in souls.[53] Adhering to the states of the Incarnation causes grace in the soul because Christ and the members of the Mystical Body form "une seule personne mystique."[54] This idea represents, noted Walsh, not only an efficient causality but an "intrinsic modality, an inner form, to the grace caused by each mystery."[55] But what exactly is this intrinsic modality?

McKay explored Bérulle's theology of grace, notably in relation to Bérulle's notion of states as means of grace. She clarified that Christ, sharing his states, thereby imprints on souls his own dispositions, accomplishing this in three ways, according to Bérulle. He evokes similitude, brings about divinization, and aids in the reunion of the spiritual world with the divine exemplar.[56]

How the soul reunites with the divine exemplar is central to how Bérulle envisioned that the priest unites with Christ, and will be treated in the next chapter.

Eminent Grace, the Way of Eminence, and Spiritual Immensity

Central to how Bérulle envisioned sanctifying grace adding to sacerdotal grace are his notions regarding the way of eminence and the notion of a spiritual immensity apart from that of immensity proper. Marion wrote that Bérulle had popularized Canfield's nihilistic mysticism and a particular rediscovery of the

---

[52] Ibid., 101. See Coll. 165. See 101n43 where Dupuy also referenced *OR* 80, no. 1, in which Bérulle noted that priests are called to sanctifying grace, that is, to holiness.

[53] Eugene Aloysius Walsh, "The Priesthood in the Writings of the French School: Bérulle, de Condren, Olier" (PhD diss., Washington, DC: Catholic University of America, 1949), 75. See *Le mystère*, 129.

[54] Ibid., 76–77, quoting AS, 26: 99–100.

[55] Ibid., 77.

[56] TG, 220–21.

way of eminence in which an infinite God can only be reached by love.[57] This combination held major implications for the priesthood.

Bérulle wrote of a kind of spiritual immensity in Christ: "Comme il y a en Dieu une immensité d'être qui remplit toutes choses, aussi en ce nouvel être, état et vie de Jésus, il y a une sorte d'immensité spirituelle, une dignité, une grandeur qui doit remplir tout esprit crée et occuper toute vie capable de cette vie."[58] This applied to both laity and priests.

Bérulle called on Oratorians to be prepared to preach by disposing themselves to an eminent grace, not only *in potentia*, but also *in actu*.[59] Bérulle used the term *éminente* frequently and synonymously with the idea of greatness, but his use of the word seems to point to a suggestion of the way of eminence in the Pseudo-Dionysian tradition, that is, of a theory of participation wherein all things are radiating from God who is all that is.[60] In terms of the priesthood, Bérulle's urging his Oratorians to contemplate and accept and renew all the liaisons they have with Jesus was seemingly to activate this grace: "'Religion' vient de 'relier.' Or le Christ est tout dans la religion et le lien qui par elle nous unit au Père; et il a institué sur lui-même la voie et la religion les plus éminentes, lui qui est la voie vers le Père."[61]

Grace as Emanation

As discussed, Bérulle, following the author of *La perle évangélique*, used the verbs *imprimer* and *rayonner* to describe the communication of grace.[62] He also described that we have two beings, two emanations from God, established in two worlds: one of nature and the other the *être de la grâce*.[63]

What is this emanation, transfusion, and union? Taveau noted that Bérulle's concept of grace did not fit a typical double model of grace based on infused virtues and gifts of the Spirit. Rather, Taveau saw a seamless garment between habitual grace and the infused virtues with the greatest mystical union.[64] Bérulle

---

[57] Jean-Luc Marion, "The Idea of God," in *Cambridge History of Seventeenth-Century Philosophy*, vol. 1, ed. D. Garber and M. Ayers (Cambridge: Cambridge University Press, 1998), 271–73.

[58] *OC* (1995), *OP* 35, 120.

[59] *BLS, OR* 85, 428.

[60] See A. Gaudel, "Eminence: Méthode d'," in *DTC*, vol. 4, pt. 2 (1911), col. 2428.

[61] *BLS, OR* 18, no. 4, 300.

[62] *AS*, 27: 105. See Van Essche, Despont, De Mallery, and De La Nouë, *La perle*, 2, ch. 1, fol. 130, and 1.3, ch. 33, fol. 286.

[63] *OP*, 1131, quoted in Taveau, *Le cardinal de Bérulle*, 140–41.

[64] Ibid., 166–68.

did not speak of the gifts of the Holy Spirit. Rather, the divine motions can grow, if no obstacles are present, to become what Taveau called a *conduite habituelle* in the soul.[65]

The De Auxiliis *Controversy and the Syncretist System of Grace*

McKay wrote that Bérulle must have known about the *De Auxiliis* controversy, but that no direct reference to it was found in his works.[66] Dupuy described Bérulle as a young priest who would have been well aware of the *De Auxiliis* controversy. He indicated in his conferences to his Oratorians that man's role was to remove obstacles and dispose himself to grace through abnegation, imitation of Christ, and prayer; it is God, however, who establishes and conserves us in grace.[67]

Vázquez' thought, which Bérulle referenced, featured in this particular controversy as he held to the necessity of special helps of grace, insisting that we should ask repeatedly for grace for individual good works.[68] In Bérulle's urging his Oratorians to frequent prayers to maintain their tie with Christ, there appears to be an echo of a view similar to Vázquez's syncretist position in the debate.

Producing Grace in Souls through Contemplation

Bérulle insisted that all grace comes through priests: "Mais toute la grâce de l'Église est donnée à la prêtrise. Elle n'est communiquée que par le prêtre."[69]

Taveau also studied Bérulle's program of mystical initiation, with special reference to grace and how Bérulle envisioned that it was conveyed by priests. Bérulle called on Oratorian superiors to practice contemplation in order to produce the Son of God and his spirit in souls:

---

[65]   Ibid, 222 and 226.

[66]   See TG, 88–91.

[67]   Michel Dupuy, "Bérulle et la grâce," *XVIIe siècle* 43, no. 1 (1991): 40–41. See *OC*, Migne ed., col. 1149, *OP* 177. Bérulle: "L'être de la créature a besoin de sa puissance pour être conservé; le péché des enfants d'Adam a besoin de sa miséricorde pour être effacé, et la grâce du juste de sa sainteté pour être consommée."

[68]   Ulrich G. Leinsle, *Introduction to Scholastic Theology*, trans. Michael J. Miller (Washington, DC: Catholic University of America Press, 2010), 327–30. See Gabriel Vázquez, *Commentariorum ac Disputationum in Primum Secundae Sancti Thomae Tomus secundus* (Lyon, 1631), 321b–356b.

[69]   *OC* (1996), *OP* 290, no. 2, 322.

Car le Père contemplant soi-même produit son Fils, et aimant son Fils en soi-même produit le Saint-Esprit. C'est aussi en la contemplation et en l'amour des choses célestes et divines, que nous devons produire le Fils de Dieu et son esprit dans les âmes. Et les supérieurs doivent se rendre éminents en la contemplation et piété, pour être dignes d'imiter en l'Église ces deux productions de la Divinité, que nous savons être par contemplation et par amour.[70]

Superiors were to elevate themselves to enter into Christ's *lumiéres*.[71]

Taveau wrote that Bérulle was familiar with St. Teresa and St. John's ideal regarding infused prayer, a passive state wherein God acts and the soul receives. The author followed with two passages wherein Bérulle described how he envisioned infused contemplation in relation to divinization and ministry. Oratorians were to be in an elevated contemplative state, ravished, and so, open to God's operations:

Ici vous êtes tirées à Dieu, élevées à lui, unies à lui, heureusement perdues et absorbées dans l'abime de ses grandeurs et perfections divines…Même vous entrez en conversation, en privauté et en familiarité avec Dieu…Vous portez ses opérations saintes; et se vérifie cette grande parole de Jésus: *Pater meus usque modo operatur, et ego operor* (Joan. V: 17). En cet heureux commerce et communication avec Dieu, vous êtes entre ses mains, ouvertes à sa puissance, exposées à son opération, mises en l'état que le grand Denis appelle, *pati divina*, et il vous tire, il vous élève, il vous ravit, il s'applique à vous et vous transforme en lui.[72]

Toutes les grâces que Dieu nous donne sont pour opérer, et c'est pour cela qu'il les donne. Quelques-uns distinguent la théologie en mystique et pratique; mais c'est une distinction que je ne voudrais point apporter à la grâce. Toutes les grâces que Dieu distribue en la terre sont données pour mieux opérer.[73]

Transformed in God, given graces in order to *opérer* as men and as priests, Bérulle insisted on not distinguishing between what he called mystical and practical theology, insisting that all graces are given in order to act, work, and operate.[74]

---

[70] *Mémorial*, 821, quoted in Taveau, *Le cardinal de Bérulle*, 80.
[71] *Grandeurs*, 159–60, quoted in Taveau, *Le cardinal de Bérulle*, 81.
[72] *Lettres*, 1334, quoted in Taveau, *Le cardinal de Bérulle*, 84–85.
[73] *OP*, 1143, quoted in Taveau, *Le cardinal de Bérulle*, 85.
[74] Taveau, *Le cardinal de Bérulle*, 85.

As already detailed, Ficino had combined the Platonic theory of cognition with the Christian doctrine of grace into a theory of the intellectual power in which "the thinking of divine ideas necessarily transforms the soul because God works as the moving and forming power."[75] This analysis suggests that Bérulle may have been influenced by this ideal.

Perl had concluded that Maximus' doctrine consisted of a thoroughly essentialist doctrine of grace in which both perfection and existence follow essence—to be is to be good, to fail is to fall into non-being.[76] Bérulle's particular interpretation maintained an echo of this doctrine.

Importantly, Taveau remarked that Bérulle, "…séduit par le réalisme de la sainte humanité du Christ cause instrumentale de toutes grâces, il considère de préférence l'action du Saint-Esprit au travers de l'âme de Notre-Seigneur."[77]

Taveau clarified that this grace of the Son was, as Whannou also noted, a grace of death, not of life. According to Bérulle, "La grâce que le Fils de Dieu est venu établir au monde, est une grâce de mort, et non de vie: une grâce d'anéantissement, et non de subsistence; une grâce d'appauvrissement, et non de suffisance et abondance…"[78] This death required a separation from oneself to enter into Him, his grace and glory: "Nous devons nous séparer de nous-mêmes et nous incorporer en lui…c'est la voie qu'il tient pour nous mettre en sa grâce et en sa gloire."[79]

Character in Relation to the Debate Regarding Ontological vs. Functional Priesthoods

A central question regarding character has been whether it effects an "ontological" change in the priest. Dupuy ventured into this debate.

For Bérulle, the sacerdotal anointing is "émanée de celle de Jésus."[80] In treating this topic, Dupuy entered into a discussion regarding the accusation that Bérulle had a notion of *un sacerdoce ontologique*. He noted, in answer, that perhaps there had been confusion between the idea of *état sacerdotal* and *adoration par état*, that is, confusing the mystical theme of adoration by state and the exemplarist notion of a state that adores. Dupuy defended the Platonic exemplarist ideal of the state of the priesthood honoring the priesthood of Christ

---

[75] Lauster, "Marsilio Ficino as a Christian Thinker," 59–60 (see ch. 5, n. 66).
[76] Perl, "Methexis," 260.
[77] Taveau, *Le cardinal de Bérulle*, 227.
[78] *OP*, 1177, quoted in Taveau, *Le cardinal de Bérulle*, 251.
[79] *OP*, 1164, quoted in Taveau, *Le cardinal de Bérulle*, 251.
[80] BLS, 189. See *OR* 11.

as opposed to an incorrect notion of the subjective state of the priest.[81] We will explore the idea of adoration by state in detail.

For Dupuy, Bérulle's was a "functional" priesthood in that priests were instruments, and were described by Bérulle in terms of their duties toward the laity more than in terms of what they were in and of themselves.[82] For Bérulle, he argued, they were to be "instruments du Fils de Dieu."[83]

Dupuy's defense of Bérulle's priesthood as functional rather than ontological points to similar discussions on the priesthood today, which is beyond the scope of this analysis. That said, this discussion points to the fact that the central question in this debate is not whether there is an ontological change but what kind of ontological change occurs.

Dupuy argued that those who think Bérulle's priesthood is "ontological" rather than functional confuse an exemplarist state of priesthood which honors Christ and a subjective state of the priest. Bérulle, we would argue, confused the two in his ideal of a conjoined instrumentality and his particular exemplarist spirituality. Considerations regarding being, essence, and act figure into this conceptualization.

Conclusion

The transformation of the priest through grace, for Bérulle, depended on a view of grace in diametrical opposition to that of the Reformers who held that justification was based on absolute certainty, uniformity among all the justified, and unforfeitableness. Following the teachings of the Church, Bérulle's spiritual theology of priesthood reinforced the ideal of sanctifying grace with its three characteristics, which, Pohle noted, are uncertainty, inequality, and admissibility,[84] and to a fault, as he resorted to a semi-Pelagian voluntarism to maintain grace. His spiritual program of initiation and sanctification for priests was also an attempt, however, to reconcile the Reformers' concerns by focusing on the idea of priesthood as a stable state, sharing a basic metaphysic with the lay spirituality of the perfect, and given an additional permanence via a kind of vow. In this can be seen the influence of the grace debates on Bérulle's spiritual theology of priesthood.

---

[81]   Ibid., 190n13.

[82]   Ibid., 198.

[83]   Ibid., 19, quoting *OR* 75, no. 6.

[84]   See J. Pohle, "Sanctifying Grace," in *Catholic Encyclopedia,* vol. 6, http://www.newadvent.org/cathen/06701a.htm, for these distinctions.

Bérulle's was an attempt to rebut Luther's rebellion against the hierarchy, and in doing so, he presented the priest as a "slave" to Christ through a spirituality of servitude. This move resulted in a shifting of the weight of the basis of ecclesial authority from the hierarchy to that of the person of each individual priest.

While Bérulle insisted on the objective state of holiness of the priest against Reformist objections, his Oratorians had to resort to frequent prayer to maintain a state of union with Christ, a union which was greater than what habitual grace could convey. Vocation, then, for Bérulle, mirrored in some way a kind of covenantal ideal. Sacerdotal character was relational and only somehow activated through a sacerdotal grace, a grace dependent on a submission of the will through the vow of servitude and a use of the intellect at the service of the will in frequent mental elevations.

Numerous points have been alluded to in this review, albeit preliminarily, due to Bérulle's lack of precision and avoidance of clearly defined categories. Both the nature of grace and that of character were hotly debated in the past and are still unresolved today. Might this have led to a lack of awareness on the part of contemporary scholars of the complexity of the issues in Bérulle's day and their implications for the theology of priesthood?

Bérulle's conflation of character and grace are understandable in the light of the Pseudo-Dionysian vogue of his day wherein, as scholars have noted, there was a parallel conflation of celestial and ecclesial hierarchies.

Various conjectures present themselves for exploration. Borrowing from Mersch's critique that the Christian's humanity is restricted when the humanity of Christ is restricted, could it be said that by Bérulle's definition of the grace of headship, the priest's humanity is restricted as well? In a sense, the Word becomes an overpowering presence in the life of the priest. However, in another way, the priest's humanity could also be said to be elevated as visible head of the Church.

In the service of this elevation, Bérulle drew on the concepts of the way of eminence and *pati divina* [to undergo the divine things], as well as on a Christic immensity to pull the priest into an elevated order of grace. Important here is Preckler's observation regarding the imprecision in Bérulle's differentiation between the state of priesthood and the state of grace, which we will explore in more detail. Ideas such as infusion, possession by the Spirit of Jesus, and possession of the Holy Spirit are terms Bérulle explored in terms of these states.

Just as Perl noted that Maximus held to an essentialist doctrine of grace, so too, did Bérulle: the priest must be good in order to be fully a priest. His participation in the priesthood of Christ depended on his ceding his subsistence to that of Christ. Again, referencing Carraud's analysis, thus was created a spiritual theology of priesthood through a notion of character based on a radical denial of both univocity and analogy.

As already cited, Taveau's insightful comment is salient: "seduced by the realism of the sacred humanity of Christ, instrumental cause of all grace," Bérulle preferred the "action of the Holy Spirit by means of the soul of our Lord."[85] This perhaps was the result of a misconstrued exemplar causality, making the priest trapped, as it were, inside the humanity of Christ upon which he must frequently meditate, yet at the same time acting as Christ at all times and with his authority.

Bérulle's emphasis on exemplar causality is the subject of the next chapter.

---

[85]   Taveau, *Le cardinal de Bérulle*, 227.

Chapter 14
Bérulle's Exemplarist Spirituality

Introduction

Mancha wrote about the possibility of a causal overdetermination and double effect in his discussion of instrumental causality in relation to the theory of premotion, a topic of considerable debate in Bérulle's era.[1] The question that is presented for consideration at the outset of this chapter is whether Bérulle may have attempted to combine the ideas of exemplar causality and essential relation, active obediential potency, and the necessity of special helps such that a kind of causal overdetermination and double effect resulted as well—with Christ operating at all times, somehow, as principal agent in relation to the priest.

In this chapter, the interpretation of causality held by Calvin and Reformed theologians is reviewed, an interpretation which Bérulle met with an emphasis on exemplar causality. Next, a pivotal historical change in the theory of participation is explored, which lent support to Bérulle's voluntarist vision of the union between the priest and Christ. Following, Bérulle's thinking on causality in relation to the priesthood is treated in terms of such concepts as the humanity of Christ, grace, obediential potency, instrumentality, and the mysteries of the life of Christ. Lastly, several scholars' analyses of the thought of Aquinas regarding exemplar causality, indwelling, and the divine ideas are reviewed. This review will be helpful in determining which of Bérulle's ideas related to the priesthood might be considered unorthodox.

---

[1]   Louis A. Mancha, Jr., "Aquinas, Suárez and Malebranche on Instrumental Causation and Premotion," *International Philosophical Quarterly* 52, no. 3 (Sept. 2012): 335–53. See Thomas Aquinas, *De potentia Dei*, in *Quaestiones disputatae de potentia Dei*, trans. English Dominican Fathers (Westminster, MD: Newman Press, 1952), 3.7.obj. 6: "Sed dices, quod virtutes naturales non possent durare, sicut nec alia entia, nisi virtute divina continerentur.—Sed contra, non est idem operari ad rem et operari in re. Sed operatio Dei qua virtutem naturalem vel facit vel in esse conservat, est operatio ad illam virtutem constituendam vel conservandam. Non ergo propter hoc potest dici, quod Deus in virtute naturali operante operetur."

Background

Calvin: Faith as Formal Cause

While Trent had pronounced on the nature and causes of justification,[2] the main question regarding the causality of the sacraments that faced the fathers and continued after the Council of Trent was whether the sacraments have a physical efficiency. Calvin had attacked the Roman Catholic position on the causality of the sacraments both before and after the Council, holding to faith alone as the instrument with which we receive the promises of God.[3]

Varied applications of Aristotelian metaphysics were prominent in sixteenth- and seventeenth-century Reformed theology, according to Fesko. Calvin had used metaphysics and Aristotelian fourfold causality in explaining his views on the relationship between holiness and good works. Calvin named the mercy of the Father as the efficient cause of obtaining eternal life; Christ and his obedience as the material cause; faith as formal or instrumental cause; and both the demonstration of divine justice and the praise of God's goodness as final cause.[4]

Bérulle responded with an emphasis on an exemplar causality, foundational in his vision of priesthood.

---

[2] Council of Trent – 1545–1563: Session 6 (January 1547), "Decree on Justification," ch. 7, in J. Neuner and J. Dupuis, eds., *The Christian Faith* (Bangalore and New York, 2001), 810. See also Heinrich Denzinger, Peter Hünermann, and Helmut Hoping, *Enchiridion symbolorum definitionum et declarationum de rebus fidei et morum = Kompendium der Glaubensbekenntnisse und kirchlichen Lehrentscheidungen* (Freiburg, Basel, Wien: Herder, 2014), 1547: "Huius iustificationis causae sunt: finalis quidem gloria Dei et Christi ac vita aeterna; efficiens vero misericors Deus, qui gratuito abluit et sanctificat [*cf. 1 Cor 6,11*] signans et ungens [*cf. 2 Cor 1,21s*] 'Spiritu promissionis Sancto, qui est pignus hereditatis nostrae' [*Eph 1,13s*]; meritoria autem dilectissimus Unigenitus suus, Dominus noster Iesus Christus, qui 'cum essemus inimici' [*Rm 5,10*], 'propter nimiam caritatem, qua dilexit nos' [*Eph 2,4*], sua sanctissima passione in ligno crucis nobis iustificationem meruit [*can. 10*], et pro nobis Deo Patri satisfecit; instrumentalis item sacramentum baptismi, quod est 'sacramentum fidei,' sine qua nulli umquam contigit iustificatio. Demum unica formalis causa est iustitia Dei…"

[3] Daniel Iturrioz, *La definición del Concilio de Trento sobre la causalidad de los sacramentos* (Madrid: Ediciones FAX, 1951), 331, 347–48.

[4] See John V. Fesko, "Metaphysics and Justification in Sixteenth- and Seventeenth-Century Reformed Theology," *Calvin Theological Journal* 46 (2011): 29–47. See also *Institution*, 3.14.17: "la cause effeciente de nostre salut est la miséricorde de nostre Père céleste, et la dilection gratuite qu'il a eu envers nous. Pour la cause matérielle…Christ avec son obéissance…De la cause qu'on appelle instrumentale…la foy…Quant à la cause finale…pour démonstrer la iustice de Dieu, et glorifier son bonté…"

A Spirituality of Causality

Evolution from the Logical to the Ontological

Bérulle's ideals surrounding how the priest participates in Christ had an important precursor in the thought of Maximus. Maximus's Platonic doctrine of participation became the Neoplatonic doctrine of emanation in which the One produces being as an effect, and form causes being. Perl wrote:

> A vital step in the movement from Platonism to Neoplatonism is the transformation of the theory of participation into a theory of causation of being. Both Plato and the Neoplatonists adhere to the Parmenidean insight that to be is to be intelligible... From this principle, Neoplatonism concludes that the cause of intelligibility is the cause of being....Plato argues that the forms cause things to be what they are; for instance, Beauty causes beautiful things to be beautiful. But Neoplatonism goes a step further. If to be is to be intelligible, then that which makes a thing to be what it is, its formal cause, is what causes it to exist. It comes to be by receiving this form, and if it ceases to have this identity, if it is deprived of its form, it ceases to be itself, and so ceases to be. The chief hallmark of Neoplatonism is this doctrine of formal cause as cause of being.[5]

Perl noted that in Maximus's doctrine an explanatory principle became a dynamic causal principle, wherein a logical relation became an ontological one. Perl further elucidated that the Neoplatonic union of logic and ontology created a participation that became "metaphysical motion" (exitus/reditus).[6]

For Pseudo-Dionysius, in turn, the metaphysics of creation was determined by the understanding of participation in which the act of creation is the self-multiplication and the self-impartation of God.[7]

Following these influences, we would argue, Bérulle moved the priest's participation in Christ's mediatorship into the order of being via a particular unorthodox interpretation of exemplar causality, which we will now review.

---

[5] Perl, "Methexis," 23–24.
[6] Ibid.
[7] Ibid., 64–66.

Grace and Causality

The Scholastic tradition held that, since the divine persons are inseparable in nature, whatever they do *ad extra* is an action of this nature and all three persons. In the West, grace was a work of efficient causality of the entire Trinity, through the divine nature and via the Incarnation, according to Sloyan.[8]

Bérulle's ideals, however, as already noted, were similar to that of Pétau, who was an innovator in holding sanctification to be the work of the Holy Spirit, by a substantial union, not merely a substantial presence: the Holy Spirit is the formal cause of the soul's justice.[9]

Causality and Obediential Potency

Bérulle himself noted that according to Suárez and others, we take part in natural acts as principal causes, but we take part in supernatural acts only as instruments of God as principal cause. This is based, as already explored, on the theology of obediential potency that requires a submission to God on the part of Christians in general, as well as priests, as we will review in detail.[10] In holding to the main thrust of this concept, Bérulle followed tradition. However, it would be his and Suárez's particular interpretation of obediential potency that would make a significant mark on Bérulle's spiritual theology of priesthood.

Instrumental Causality and the Person of Christ in the Life of the Priest

As already cited, Bérulle described the causality of the Spirit of Jesus by using the analogies of how form fills matter: "Nous ne devons agir que par l'Esprit de Jésus dirigeant, animant, appliquant, remplissant notre esprit, comme la forme remplit la matière, comme la cause première applique les causes secondes et la principale applique les instrumentales…"[11]

Bérulle's notion of sacerdotal instrumentality, according to Dupuy, was based on the exemplar of the humanity of Christ as instrument. According to Bérulle, "Sa sainte humanité était l'instrument par lequel sa divinité se faisait connaître. De même en nous les actions doivent être comme le moyen par lequel la grâce de Dieu et l'Esprit-Saint qui habite en nous se manifestent."[12]

---

[8]   Sloyan, *The Three Persons*, 101–3.
[9]   Holtzen, "Union with God and the Holy Spirit," 29–35.
[10] See *BLS, OR* 43, no. 4. 367.
[11] Ibid., *OR* 14, 287.
[12] Coll. 102, quoted in *BLS*, 107.

This causality extended, for Bérulle, to all facets of his Oratorians' ministry, requiring assent and obedience to be in "union with their cause," in any ministerial function, including in the confessional: "L'on doit grandement peser qu'entrant au confessionnal, c'est pour être instrument de Dieu. Pour tant, avoir grande union, grand rapport et grande relation à notre cause qui est Dieu."[13]

Dupuy held the opinion that, in fact, in regard to the sacraments, Bérulle considered priests to be inside the person of Christ, more than instruments, since even instruments have an "efficacité propre."[14]

Active Obediential Potency

The manner in which the soul of the priest is to reunite with the divine exemplar was central to Bérulle's defense of his idea that the priest maintain oneness with Christ. Bérulle used the idea of an active obediential potency in his program of sacerdotal spirituality. Specifically, Bérulle leaned on Suárez' notion of an active obediential potency in his interpretation of causation.[15] This idea figured prominently in the debates on grace and has recently been critiqued by Leinsle.[16]

Theologians recognized that the ability to obey the will of God in supernatural operations (that is, beyond natural operations) is a passive ability to obey. Suárez' thesis, published in 1590 in his commentary on Part III of the *Summa*, was based on two related questions: What proper power or potency enables Christ's

---

[13] *BLS, OR* 84, 427.

[14] Ibid., 152.

[15] See Francisco Suárez, *De Sacramentis in Genere, de Baptismo, de Confirmatione, de Eucharistia usque ad Quæstionem LXXIV*, in *Commentaria ac Disputationes in Tertiam Partem D. Thomae*, disp. 9, sec. 1, no. 21, in *Opera omnia*, 20 (Paris: Ludovicum Vivès, 1860), 147: "...quaenam sit illa virtus, per quam possunt instrumenta Dei concurrere, quando elevantur. Diximus enim, non esse rem aliquam supperadditam, sed esse ipsammet entitatem rei, quæ hoc ipso, quod creata est, et subordinata primo agenti, est in potentia obedientiali active, ut efficiat quidquid non implicat contradictionem respectu illius. Haec enim ratio obedientialis potentiæ communis est sacramentis, quorum elevatio divina solum in hoc consistit, quod Deus altiori modo concurrit dando auxilium sufficiens, ut res operetur secundum hanc potentiam. Necque ad hoc refert, quod sacramenta sint imperfecta in sua entitate. Quia hic concursus non fundatur in naturali eorum perfectione, sed in prædicta virtute obedientiali et in infinita Dei virtute, cui omnia subordinantur. Et ideo nihil refert, quod sacramenta consistant in motu, vel sono, dummodo aliquid entitatis habeant. Quanquam fortasse non efficiant solum per ipsum motum, qui est ens imperfectum, seu modus entis, et significatur nomine ablutionis vel unctionis, sed per ipsasmet res quæ moventur, vel applicantur, dum sacramenta fiunt, vel accipiuntur, ut per oleum, aquam, species panis, etc.; sic enim dixit Augustinus aquam esse, quae corpus tangit et cor abluit."

[16] Leinsle, *Introduction to Scholastic Theology*.

humanity to operate miraculously as an instrument of the divine Logos? Second, is there an active obediential power (rather than passive) that elevates created things to the status of God's instruments?[17]

In the following text, Bérulle treated the necessity of obedience in order for priests to perform supernatural acts as instruments of God. He utilized Suárez's notions as applied to creatures in support of the necessity of the vows of servitude and the requirement that his Oratorians be instruments in the hands of God as He is the only principal cause. His emphasis was on the need for humility and obedience:

> Noter la justification remarquable fournie par la théologie de la puissance obédientielle et s'en servir pour renforcer l'inclination à l'obéissance. Car, d'après les meilleurs théologiens et Suárez, l'âme ne concourt aux actes surnaturels ici-bas et au ciel que comme instrument de Dieu, par une puissance non pas naturelle, mais obédientielle. Sur la voie de Dieu, embrassons donc la voie de l'obéissance, nous qui ne pouvons tendre à Dieu par des actes surnaturels que selon une puissance obédientielle, tant ici-bas qu'au ciel; nous, dis-je, qui pour tendre à Dieu n'avons de puissance qu'obédientielle, n'avons d'autre voie que l'obéissance.
>
> Selon cette opinion, nous agissons aux choses naturelles comme causes principales, mais aux surnaturelles de la grâce et de la gloire interne et externe, nous n'agissons que comme instruments aux mains de Dieu qui est l'unique cause principale. Ne soyons donc que comme instruments, et en la dépendance de Dieu et en la soumission à Dieu, ou par la voie de sagesse, si Dieu nous y a mis, ou par la voie d'obéissance, en laquelle c'est à nous de nous mettre.
>
> Noter que cette opinion de théologie de la puissance obédientielle fonde l'humilité et l'obéissance en l'esprit; et pour cela, il le faut noter et s'en servir.[18]

Leinsle detailed objections to Suárez' notion of an active obediential potency, including a subtle Pelagianism, a confusion of the natural and supernatural orders, and the appearance of denying the necessity of grace. Importantly, Leinsle noted that Suárez' notion of *status* appears to be an elevation that is something higher than that of a creaturely endowment through a union with an external

---

[17] Ibid., 324–27. See Francisco Suárez, *De Incarnatione*, disp. 31, s. 5, in *Opera omnia*, 18 (Paris: Ludovicum Vivès, 1877).

[18] *BLS, OR* 43, no. 4, 367.

cause (although presuming an active, intrinsic power which is perfected through the union).[19]

Arguably, Bérulle may have applied the Suarezian ideal of active obediential potency to priests insofar as he saw the need for them to make frequent acts of obedience (and so, the will) to be instruments of God. His use of the ideal of an active obediential potency disposed Bérulle's spiritual theology of priesthood to the problems pointed to by Leinsle: a subtle Pelagianism, a confusion of natural and supernatural orders, the denial of the need for grace (in their need for frequent elevations to maintain union, although Bérulle conceded God's grace was needed to make them); and an elevation beyond a creaturely endowment, thus imputing an active, intrinsic power (which Bérulle seemed to attempt to compensate for by the notion of obedience and humility).

Causality and the Mysteries of the Life of Christ

For Bérulle, the concept of likeness featured prominently in relation to exemplar causality. According to McKay, a question that arises about Bérulle's thought is whether the likeness between the Christian's mystical subsistence in Christ and the sacred humanity's subsistence in the Word is not just an extrinsic likeness but also an effective one. This appears so, McKay concluded, because the Incarnate Word is both the exemplar and efficient cause of the life of grace, as noted.[20]

Bérulle's most original contribution to the theology of grace, according to McKay, was that of how capital grace is communicated via states. In Christ, human states become both divinized and perpetual: "Or, tous ces états et mystères sont déifiés, et partant ont une dignité divine, une puissance suprême, une opération sainte, et sont accomplis pour la gloire de Dieu et pour notre utilité particulière…"[21] Christ did this so as to free human states from sin and make them capable of honoring God: "…Dieu voulant que sa grâce surabonde sur le péché, et que tous les états de la nature humaine infecté par icelui, soient honoré de sa grâce et de sa grâce suprême, qui est la grâce et l'union hypostatique…"[22] These graces perdure in heaven in Christ's glorified soul. For Bérulle, the states are meritorious because they participate in the abnegation of the Word from the moment of the Incarnation, which was meritorious. McKay referred specifically to the exemplarity of the states as the original contribution, with Christ

---

[19] Leinsle, *Introduction to Scholastic Theology*, 325.
[20] TG, 252. This review follows the author's exposition closely.
[21] *OP* 17, no. 2, col. 940, quoted in TG, 215.
[22] *OP* 17, nos. 1 and 2, col. 940, quoted in TG, 215.

imprinting on souls his dispositions effecting similitude, divinizing us, and reuniting the spiritual world with the divine exemplar.[23]

The Challenges of a Misconstrued Exemplarism

The next question that presents itself is how Bérulle understood the relationship between efficient and exemplar causality. As Ocáriz, Seco, and Riestra explained, in line with Aquinas, all things that Christ accomplished in his life were saving acts but only through the power of the divinity, extending through all time and space. The principal efficient cause of the grace of salvation can only be God, through the humanity of Christ.[24]

The authors clarified, "All the mysteries...even though they happened successively in times past, constitute a single, unique cause of our salvation: all of them, together and at the one time, work our salvation, when in the Church (particularly in the sacraments) the fruit of the redemption is applied to each person. This does not prevent particular mysteries of Christ's life from having a special connection (by way of exemplary cause) to particular aspects of salvation. For example, the Resurrection of our Lord is, above all, the model (exemplary cause) of our future resurrection at the end of time..."[25]

What exactly is this special connection for Bérulle? The answer lies, in part, in the realm of the divine ideas.

Doolan explored the exemplarism of the divine ideas according to Aquinas. A review of his discussion will clarify key aspects of Berullian exemplarism as well as its ramifications in regard to his spiritual theology of priesthood.

First, according Aquinas, the divine ideas are not generative principles, but rather creative ones. Even though the divine exemplars are the cause of form in physical substances, their causality does not compromise the operations of nature, since the proximate causes of generation are natural agents, not the divine ideas.[26]

---

[23] Ibid., 220–21.

[24] Ocáriz et al., *The Mystery of Jesus Christ*, 291–92. See Aquinas, *ST*, 3.56.1, ad 3, in *Summa theologiae*, 11: 525 (see ch. 2, n. 64). See also *ST*, 3.52.8 and 3.48.6.2.

[25] Ibid., 292.

[26] See Thomas Aquinas, *De veritate*, 3.1, ad 5, in *Quaestiones disputatae de veritate*, vol. 22 of *Sancti Thomae de Aquino opera omnia iussu Leonis XIII P. M. edita*, vol. 1, fasc. 2, *QQ. 1– 7* (Rome: Ad Sanctae Sabinae, 1970), 101: "ideae existentes in mente divina non sunt generatae nec sunt generantes si fiat vis in verbo, sed sunt creativae et productivae rerum." Quoted in Gregory T. Doolan, *Aquinas on the Divine Ideas as Exemplar Causes* (Washington, DC: Catholic University of America Press, 2008), 170. See also 248. This review follows the author's exposition closely.

According to Doolan's analysis of the thought of Aquinas, "although the essences of finite beings do not participate in their exemplar ideas, they do participate in the exemplar that is God's nature" through which created essences receive and are limited in *esse*. This limitation is dependent on the formation of divine ideas, which determine the limited modes of being (*esse*) received. While a created essence's "mode of being is determined by its divine idea…its actuality is determined by the finite being's participation in the likeness of the divine nature."[27]

For Bérulle, Christ acts as proximate cause, thus compromising the operations of nature, serving as a generative rather than a creative principle: instead of priests participating solely in their own essences, they participate in the idea of the Son.

Next, Bérulle's conceptualization of divine exemplarity will be reviewed, which includes the idea that priests participate in the idea of the Son, the Word, as resemblance himself.

Klima's analysis of the medieval problem of universals is helpful in viewing the particular application of emanationism found in Bérulle's spiritual theology of priesthood as related notably to illumination. For Aquinas, the divine ideas are in the divine mind as things understood: the multiplicity of ideas does not include the multiplicity of the divine essence.[28] Augustine considered divine illumination as an irradiation of the intelligible light of divine ideas, accessible only to the few.

---

[27] Doolan, *Aquinas on the Divine Ideas as Exemplar Causes*, 249–50. See Aquinas, *ST*, 1.44.3, co., *Summa theologiae*, 4: 460: "Respondeo dicendum quod Deus est prima causa exemplaris omnium rerum. Ad cuius evidentiam, considerandum est quod ad productionem alicuius rei ideo necessarium est exemplar, ut effectus determinatam formam consequatur: artifex enim producit determinatam formam in materia, propter exemplar ad quod inspicit, sive illud sit exemplar ad quod extra intuetur, sive sit exemplar interius mente conceptum. Manifestum est autem quod ea quae naturaliter fiunt, determinatas formas consequuntur. Haec autem formarum determinatio oportet quod reducatur, sicut in primum principium, in divinam sapientiam, quae ordinem universi excogitavit, qui in rerum distinctione consistit. Et ideo oportet dicere quod in divina sapientia sunt rationes omnium rerum: quas supra diximus *ideas,* id est formas exemplares in mente divina existentes. Quae quidem licet multiplicentur secundum respectum ad res, tamen non sunt realiter aliud a divina essentia, prout eius similitudo a diversis participari potest diversimode. Sic igitur ipse Deus est primum exemplar omnium."

[28] Gyula Klima, "The Medieval Problem of Universals," *Stanford Encyclopedia of Philosophy*, pub. Sept. 10, 2000, rev. July 8, 2013, 14–15, http://plato.stanford.edu/entries/universals-medieval/. Pagination was assigned to a printed copy of the online edition. See footnote 17 referencing Aquinas 1 *SN*, d. 36, q. 2, aa. 1–3.

This implies, according to Klima, that human nature is "naturally defective in its noblest part, precisely in which it was created after the image of God."[29]

This error was reflected in Bérulle's neantist sacerdotal spiritual theology. It appears that for Bérulle, finite beings (including priests), participate in the idea of the Word or the Son as resemblance. It also appears that there may be no distinction for Bérulle between the exemplarism of the divine idea of the Word and that of the divine nature. Therefore, it seems, Bérulle may have confused intellectual exemplarism (which involves a perfect likeness between a divine idea and a finite being) with the exemplarism of the divine nature (which involves degrees of imitation).[30] Although he allowed for degrees of participation, his conceptualization of union with God suggests that *esse* is not limited in his spiritual theology of priesthood.

Several questions present themselves. Was there an exaggeration both of the nothingness of humanity and of God as principal cause in Bérulle's spiritual theology of priesthood? Are priests expected to possess God through love and the will here on earth to an inordinate degree and as a basis of their participated priesthood? Is Bérulle's vision of deification similar to an intellectual salvation inside a Cosmic Christ, following in some fashion Nicholas of Cusa?[31] Does Bérulle's spiritual theology of priesthood support the idea of a quasi-substantial union with the Word as resemblance himself and a quasi-hypostatic union with the person of the Spirit? The following analyses may assist us in coming to some conclusions.

---

[29] Ibid., 17–18. See P. V. Spade, *A Survey of Medieval Philosophy*, Version 2.0, 1985. Available online at http://www.pvspade.cpm/Logic/docs/Survey%202%20Interim.

Spade quotes Augustine, "On Eighty-Three Different Questions," in Augustine and Almut Mutzenbecher, *Sancti Aurelii Augustini, De octo Dulcitii quaestionibus*, Corpus Christianorum, Series Latina, vol. 44a (Turnholt: Brepols, 1975), 46.2: "Sed anima rationalis inter eas res, quae sunt a deo conditae, omnia superat et deo proxima est, quando pura est; eique in quantum caritate cohaeserit, in tantum ab eo lumine illo intelligibili perfusa quodammodo et inlustrata cernit non per corporeos oculos, sed per ipsius sui principale quo excellit, id est per intelligentiam suam, istas rationes, quarum uisione fit beatissima. Quas rationes, ut dictum est, siue ideas siue formas siue species siue rationes licet uocare, et multis conceditur appellare quod libet, sed paucissimis uidere quod uerum est."

[30] See Doolan, *Aquinas on the Divine Ideas as Exemplar Causes*, 247.

[31] See Nancy J. Hudson, *Becoming God: The Doctrine of Theosis in Nicholas of Cusa* (Washington, DC: Catholic University of America Press, 2007), 200.

Greenstock's Analysis

Greenstock addressed the challenges inherent in this exemplarism when he wrote on what he called a "profound theological problem:" that of the gap between the Latin and Greek fathers' ideas regarding the supernatural relations between God and man. While the Latins focused on the unity of the divine essence, applying it, by appropriation, to all *ad extra* operations to explain the soul in a state of grace, the Greeks held to a personal relationship between the soul and the Divine persons based on more than "mere" appropriation.[32]

Greenstock provided a brief history of the development since ancient times of this latter line of thought, applicable to this analysis. He began with Pétau, proceeding to a revival of his thought in modern existential philosophies emphasizing contact with God through immanent experience (wherein God is revealed as transcendent being, in whom all things exist).

Greenstock noted that theologians responded to these existential philosophies by questioning whether it is possible for a more personal relationship between the soul in grace and the divine persons. *Mystici Corporis* then intervened, asserting efficient causality to be held in common by the Trinity, that any relation between the soul and a divine person would be in conflict with Trent, and that a material causality would be absurd.[33]

Greenstock then asked the question: How are we to understand the doctrine of exemplar causality in terms of the spiritual life of the soul?[34]

By extension, how might we understand the doctrine in the spiritual life of the priest?

Greenstock explained that the basis for exemplar causality in the thought of Aquinas was that it was something internal to the mental process: it cannot exist outside the intelligent cause and so it is clearly distinguished from the internal form that enters into the constitution of the effect.[35] Aquinas excluded the idea of God playing the part of a formal intrinsic cause as a kind of Pantheism. At this point, the notion of image features prominently, as it did for Bérulle.

---

[32] David L. Greenstock, "Exemplar Causality and the Supernatural Order," *Thomist* 16, no. 1 (January 1953): 1–2.

[33] Ibid., 3. See Catholic Church, *Encyclical Letter (Mystici Corporis Christi) of His Holiness Pius XII on the Mystical Body of Jesus Christ and Our Union with Christ Therein* (London: Catholic Truth Society, n.d.), 48, no. 78. Greenstock did not specify the nature of the conflicts he saw with Trent.

[34] Ibid. For the following discussion, see 3–4 and 7–18.

[35] Ibid., 4, quoting Aquinas, *De veritate*, 3.1, co. In *Quaestiones disputatae de veritate*, 22.1.2: 100: "forma quam aliquid imitatur ex intentione agentis qui praedeterminat sibi finem."

Aquinas held that there are two types of image: ontological and intentional. The intentional or intellectual image belongs to the order of knowledge and implies a relation between the intellect and its object. The second is the ontological image that "has its foundation in the real order, as something that reproduces or copies the thing of which it is an image in its very being."[36] Grace is an image in the second sense. It is a formal participation in the divine nature, reproducing imperfectly the divine nature. The divine essence is the exemplar of grace and is common to the three persons. Grace is not just an effect of efficient causality but also produces effects of adopted sonship and the indwelling of the Trinity.[37]

Greenstock then asked the question: Is there a more personal relationship between the soul and the individual divine persons from the point of view of exemplar causality?

Aquinas held that adopted sonship is attributed to the Holy Spirit (as sanctifier of souls). Relations are brought about not just because Christ won redemption, but also because, as Greenstock wrote, "his eternal sonship is the exemplar on which our adoption is based."[38]

There is a difference between the role of grace in adoption and the role of the three divine persons in adoption. Greenstock noted, "Adoption is the effect of grace insofar as grace is a formal participation in the divine nature."[39] We are sons of the whole Trinity. While adopted sonship is a created imitation of the eternal sonship of the second person, which is the exemplar of our own, the efficient causality of our sonship must be common to all three persons. It is appropriated to the Father, with the Son being the exemplar, and the Holy Spirit the sanctifier. The formal cause is grace as a participation in the divine nature. Greenstock explained, "Its exemplar cause is to be found in all Three Persons, as identified with the divine nature, but in a special way with the Second Person, whose eternal sonship is the divine model of our adoption."[40]

---

[36] Ibid., 15.

[37] Ibid., 17.

[38] Ibid., 18n23, quoting Aquinas, *Sent.* 3.10.2.1, sol. 3. In *Scriptum super Sententiis*, ed. Moos, 3: 344: "Potest etiam notare formalem causam, et hoc *dupliciter: vel* inhaerentem *vel* exemplarem.

"*Si inhaerentem,* sic adoptati sumus per Spiritum sanctum cui appropriatur caritas...

"*Si vero designat causam exemplarem formalem,* sic sumus adoptati per Filium. Unde dicitur *Rom.,* VIII, 29: '*Quos praescivit conformes fieri imaginis Filii sui, ut sit ipse primogenitus in multis fratribus*'."

[39] Ibid., 19.

[40] Ibid., 19. See Aquinas, *ST,* 3.23.2, ad 3, in *Summa theologiae,* 11: 265–66: "Ad tertium dicendum quod, sicut dictum est, filiatio adoptiva est quaedam similitudo filiationis aeternae: sicut omnia quae in tempore facta sunt, similitudines quaedam sunt eorum quae

As just cited, in terms of the Incarnation, Christ's Resurrection, for example, is the exemplar of ours. The mysteries of Christ's life have a direct bearing on ours as exemplars to which we as members of his Mystical Body are expected to conform.[41] All causality is an essential and not a personal attribute, as Greenstock noted. However, as the author continued, there is a close relationship between formal and exemplar causes because the formal cause plays the major part in conforming the effect produced to the exemplar idea of it in the mind of the agent. There can be a similarity between a quality of a created effect and a proper attribute belonging to a divine person. Thus, the doctrine of appropriation.[42]

Aquinas' teaching on the divine missions and divine indwelling is relevant here. For Aquinas, the indwelling is the "real and substantial" presence of the Trinity in the soul which is "distinct from the general presence of God in all His creatures through His divine immensity."[43] This presence presupposes the existence of the soul and the creation in it of grace. Grace is the formal cause of the indwelling, but only insofar as it gives rise to the theological virtues that have as their object God.[44]

The presence of immensity, required as a prerequisite for the indwelling, was overlooked by Suárez, and according to Greenstock, has been a source of much confusion. There are many relationships between the soul in the state of grace and the Trinity, but "only one relationship that effects this real and substantial presence of the Trinity which we call the presence of the indwelling:" this is the fundamental relationship.[45]

Herein lies the central challenge in Bérulle's spiritual theology of priesthood. The priest may have a number of kinds of relationships with the persons of the Trinity, but there is only one kind of indwelling and it must be of the Trinity, not only of one person.

Any personal activity is excluded for two reasons, according to Greenstock: the complete identity of the nature in all Three and the identity between God's power and his operation in the *ad extra* operations. The persons act through one common nature, and there can be no multiplication of essential attributes of God.

---

ab aeterno fuerunt. Assimilatur autem homo splendori aeterni Filii per gratiae claritatem, quae attribuitur Spiritui Sancto. Et ideo adoptatio, licet sit communis toti Trinitati, appropriatur tamen Patri ut auctori, Filio ut exemplari, Spiritui Sancto ut imprimenti in nobis huius similitudinem exemplaris."

[41] Ibid., 19–20. See Aquinas, *ST*, 3.56.1, ad 3 (see ch. 2, n. 64).
[42] Ibid., 20–21.
[43] Ibid., 21.
[44] Ibid., 22–23.
[45] Ibid., 24–25.

Exemplar Causality and Mission

Greenstock then asked the question: "How is it, then, that certain theologians have found a place for exemplar causality within the framework of the Divine Missions?"[46]

One might add, have they also found a place for exemplar causality in the framework of the priesthood in relation to the divine missions?

Greenstock answered that, if so, it is probably because theologians have not distinguished between the notions of mission, indwelling, and assimilation. These are connected to grace but different.

The perfections that flow from grace produce a sealing, or an assimilation to the three persons, as the perfections (of the intellectual order) impress the soul with a likeness to the Word, while others (pertaining to love and power) give likeness to the Holy Spirit and the Father respectively. Importantly, assimilation is an effect of indwelling, not the formal cause of it, and it is attributable to the exemplar causality of individual persons by appropriation. As Greenstock wrote, "The eternal processions of the Persons are not the direct causes of the created effects, but only insofar as they include essential attributes of intellect and will." For example, wisdom is appropriated to the Son as the image of the Father.[47]

Important to this analysis, if considering character as an assimilation to Christ, it must be remembered that any assimilation to Christ is assimilation to God, a distinction lost, perhaps, in Bérulle's particular interpretation of exemplar causality.[48]

According to Greenstock, theologians who hold to "a more personal relationship between the soul and the individual Persons of the Trinity through the medium of exemplar causality have not understood the connection between the divine exemplar and the doctrine of assimilation which is based on appropriation." Again, it "is the divine essence which is the exemplar, either as it is in itself, or as it is communicated to the Persons." For example, the Spirit is "the personification of divine goodness and holiness, and these are essential attributes."[49]

---

46 Ibid., 26.

47 Ibid., 26–28. See 27 for quote.

48 See Michael James Ryan, "Character (in Catholic Theology)," in *Catholic Encyclopedia,* vol. 3 (New York: Robert Appleton Company, 1908), 2, http://www.newadvent.org /cathen/03586a.htm.

49 Greenstock, "Exemplar Causality and the Supernatural Order," 30–31. See Aquinas, *ST,* 1.39.7 and 8, esp. 7, ad 2, in *Summa theologiae,* 4: 407: "Ad secundum dicendum quod, si sic appropriarentur essentialia attributa Personis, quod essent eis propria, sequeretur quod

Greenstock ends his analysis with the assertion that, for Aquinas, "grace, as an invisible Mission of the Trinity, brings the Persons into contact with the soul in a new way, as the objects of its knowledge and love. This real and substantial presence far exceeds anything which could be attained or imagined along the lines of exemplar causality…"[50]

Indwelling as Applied to Bérulle's Spiritual Theology of Priesthood

In this analysis of Bérulle's spiritual theology of priesthood, one question perdures: What, then, is the special relation of the priest with Christ and with the Spirit according to Bérulle, and is it a heterodox interpretation?

Chirico's exploration of various speculations regarding the divine indwelling and distinct relations to the indwelling persons can assist us in parsing this issue.[51]

There are three central questions regarding the divine indwelling, according to Chirico. Each applies to this study: in what way is God said to be present in a special way in the souls of the just; is there a relationship between the soul and each of the three persons or only one; and how does this relationship arise?[52]

Echoing Greenstock, Chirico noted that there are certain norms regarding any indwelling theory, norms taken from the encyclical *Mystici Corporis*: no explanation is permissible according to which the just soul passes beyond the sphere of creatures; nothing in the line of efficient causality can be attributed to one person alone (as detailed); the divine persons inhabit the soul inasmuch as they are present to it in a way that they are known and loved in a way that is unique and transcends all nature; and the union of the indwelling differs from the beatific vision only by reason of the earthly state.[53] Chirico referenced Michel, who clarified Pétau's position during the era when the matter came to the attention of theologians. For Pétau, the union of the soul terminates in the person of the Holy Spirit. This is not a hypostatic union but a union whose term is his person just as the person of the Word is the proper term of the hypostatic union.[54]

---

una persona se haberet ad aliam in habitudine formae. Quod excludit Augustinus, in VII *de Trin.….*"
[50] Ibid., 31.
[51] Petro F. Chirico, "The Divine Indwelling and Distinct Relations to the Indwelling Persons in Modern Theological Discussion" (PhD diss., Rome: Pontificiae Universitatis Gregorianae, 1960). This review follows the author's exposition closely.
[52] Ibid., 1.
[53] Ibid., 3–4.
[54] Ibid., 11. See Michel, "Trinité," col. 1851.

Chirico wrote that the criticisms of Pétau's thought and that of his successors are generally three. The first objection is that the proponents of personal relations have misinterpreted the Greeks. The other two objections deny the possibility of personal relations. The second holds some kind of influence of the persons in the soul, implying an efficient causality on the part of persons, while the third objection denies the possibility of ontological relations to the divine persons that are not hypostatic. The only thing proper to the divine persons in the Trinity is the hypostatic function. Therefore, any union with a divine person if it is to be proper must be the hypostatic function, but that is impossible, for we know there is but one such union—the Incarnation.[55]

Sons of the Son Theory

Important to this analysis, Chirico treated the "Sons of the Son" theory, an outgrowth of Pétau's thought, and arguably similar to Bérulle's. According to Mersch's treatment, sonship of the Trinity is denied and instead, our adoptive sonship of the Father is justified on the basis of the Incarnation, by which we are made real participants in the filiation of the Son. This theory is marked by two ideas: the supernatural as a communication of the Trinity and an emphasis on our incorporation in Christ. This Trinitarian concept of the supernatural has three elements: communication of the Trinity as Trinity; the unique personal self-donation of God; and a unique effect that transcends the categories of Aristotle, adapting the finite to the infinite.[56]

These three elements were applied to Christ the head, a key theme in Bérulle's spiritual theology of priesthood.

The first, the supernatural as a communication of the Trinity as Trinity, refers to the fact that in the Incarnation, Christ's human nature is so united to the Word that Christ is truly the Son of God. Because the Son does not exist except in relation to the Father and the Holy Spirit, in him the Trinity is communicated to creatures as Trinity. Also, the human nature of Christ is so deified, filialized, and perfected that it can infuse the whole human race with Trinitarian deification, as already seen.

God's personal self-donation is next considered in this theory. The Incarnation is a common operation of the Trinity in their one nature. The person of the Son is given to the created humanity, making Christ God. Chirico wrote,

---

[55] Ibid., 13–14. See P. Galtier, *L'habitation en nous des trois personnes*, 2nd ed. (Rome: Pont. Università Gregoriana, 1950), 3–143.

[56] Ibid., 71–72. See Émile Mersch, "Filii in Filio," *Nouvelle revue théologique* 65 (1938): 551–82, 681–702, and 809–30.

"And this giving of the Second Person to Christ's human nature is communicated by Him to His members so that all become sons of the Father as He is, though in a more restricted sense."[57]

According to this theory, there is a new effect that adapts the finite to the infinite. In the Incarnation, this effect adapts the humanity to be the humanity of God and the humanity of the Son. In order for the humanity to belong to the Word, there must be a change, a perfecting. This change in the human nature of Christ is grace. This grace is in fact threefold: the grace of union, the grace that is called ordinary created grace, and *gratia capitis*.

The grace of union is the substantial sanctification and filiation that the humanity of Christ has from its being the humanity of the Word. This grace of union produces the second grace, ordinary sanctifying grace, which makes for the individual and internal holiness of the humanity of Christ. The third grace is that of the habitual grace in Christ which then flows into the members of Christ. The grace that is in Christ is essentially filial. If we possess this kind of grace through our union with Christ, then we are also sons.[58]

This theory centers on the role of Christ as head of the Mystical Body. Christ as head is the source of the immediate union with the other persons. We become attached to the Holy Spirit of the Son and so are deified. Also, as Christ spirates the Holy Spirit and since men have the Holy Spirit as brother, then the spiration now takes place in humankind. We spirate the Holy Spirit along with Christ.[59]

The theory depends on two factors, according to Chirico: that grace is essentially filial and relates us in a special way to the Son; and that since we are related to the Son, we share his relationships with the other divine persons. The author did not believe that Mersch proved that the relation arising from the Incarnation and redemption is of such a nature that it carries with it a further relationship to the Father and the Son. Chirico argued:

> If there is a special relation to the other Persons of the Trinity because of the Incarnation, this must be for one or more of three reasons: the fact that the Son has assumed a human nature like our own; the fact that grace is produced through the instrumentality of this human nature; or the fact (if it is a fact) that grace as it is in Christ takes on a modality that it would not have had without the incarnation of the Son, and that through this

---

[57] Ibid., 73. See Mersch, 681–83 and 812–14.
[58] Ibid., 74–75.
[59] Ibid., 75. See E. Mersch, *La théologie du corps mystique*, vol. 2, 4th ed. (Bruges: Desclée de Brouwer, 1954), 139–45.

modality which is present in grace as imparted to us we are related to the Father and the Spirit through the Son.[60]

The author eliminated as the root of special relations to the three divine persons the idea that we share the same kind of humanity as the Son. Our physical connection to Christ is generic, not causal: being of the same nature does not provide the basis of a real relationship. If we assert that we are related to the Son and through him to the other persons by physical sharing of the same nature, we must assert that all humanity has the same relationship. No relationship can be traced back to the Father and the Holy Spirit from the mere instrumentality of Christ's human nature in the production of grace. Nor does the author see any grounds for a relationship to all three persons in some filial modification of grace derived from the Incarnation. Filial obedience was Christ's basic virtue. We do share in this filial characteristic if we are related to all three persons by grace. This must be because of the very nature of grace irrespective of any modification introduced into it by its being the special grace of Christ.[61]

Mersch's idea that grace through Christ causes a Trinitarian relationship is false, according to the author, because it is ultimately based on the false principle that a real relationship to a person implies a real relationship to the relations of that person. Our relationship to Christ does not entail a sharing of the divine processions. It is based only on the sharing of something created.[62]

Chirico noted additional objections to proper ontological relations, including the idea that if there is such a relation it ought to have been revealed at the time of the apostles.[63]

Another objection presents itself as applicable to Bérulle's particular emphasis on Christ as head of the Mystical Body. Ocáriz, Seco, and Riestra clarified that Christ is head of the Mystical Body as the result of his being the head of humanity, united to every human being. He is head of the Mystical Body for those who have accepted the fruit, as they wrote, of an already given redemption.[64] As the Council of Quiercy (833) stated, "there is not, never was nor ever will be any person for whom Christ our Lord had not suffered."[65]

In this light, Bérulle's notion of the priest as visible head of the Mystical Body and agent of redemption appears to be a conflation of redemption and sanctification.

---

[60]   Ibid., 76–77.
[61]   Ibid, 77–79.
[62]   Ibid., 79. See V. de Broglie, *De gratia* (unpublished manuscript, copied in Paris).
[63]   Ibid., 88–89.
[64]   Ocáriz et al., *The Mystery of Jesus Christ*, 283n112–284.
[65]   Ibid.; see 300 regarding Jansenism in light of the Council of Quiercy (*DS* 624).

Conclusion

The causality of the sacraments and the nature of both sacramental character and grace remain open questions today. The challenge of the conflation of configuration and conformity also remains.

Cunningham summarized that any theories of indwelling that explain the Trinitarian presence from the point of view of God as cause, principle, or 'operating' are irreconcilable with Aquinas. Direct union to one individual divine person by means of exemplarity and assimilation is not possible. The presence of the Trinity conforms and assimilates a human being to God by making him a true image of the three persons because he is conjoined by real union, not appropriation.[66]

Further research is needed to determine the similarity of Bérulle's thought to that of Pétau. That said, this analysis supports the argument that in terms of both sacerdotal character and grace, a spiritual theology of priesthood based on exemplar causality cannot rely on a divine person as formal cause or on an essential relation or union with one divine person.

Returning to the question of the possibility of causal overdetermination and double effect in terms of Christ's operating as principal agent in relation to the priest at all times, a full answer is beyond the scope of this study. Suffice it to say that Bérulle's particular exemplar causality, his ideals of a quasi-substantial union with Christ and essentialist relation with the Holy Spirit as quasi-formal cause, along with his notions surrounding an active obediential potency and the requirement of special helps, suggest the need for a deeper exploration of the influence of the debates on grace on the theology of priesthood.

---

[66] Francis L. B. Cunningham, *The Indwelling of the Trinity: A Historico-Doctrinal Study of the Theory of St. Aquinas* (Dubuque: Priory Press, 1955), 337–40.

Chapter 15
Priesthood, Conformity and Similitude

Introduction

Bérulle's treatment of conformity and similitude took a prominent place in his rebuttal of Reformers' notions regarding free will in relation to union with Christ and in his construction of the metaphysics of the Oratory. This area of Bérulle's thought is perhaps the most complex, linking to ideas such as the intellect, nature, participation, perfection, holiness, the divine ideas, and most especially the priesthood considered as state.

The chapter ends with important critiques posed by both Maritain and Balthasar.

Free Will

One of the biggest philosophical issues dividing Catholic and Protestants in the sixteenth century was free will, a central issue for Luther in the context of salvation, according to Kenny. The Thomistic emphasis in the debate was on the intellect, including the idea that the knowledge of one's final goal determines the direction of one's free will. Scotists, however, as well as the Scholastic theologians of the late medieval *via moderna*, insisted on the volitional and affective aspects, advocating a double voluntarism: the sovereign will of God and the submission of the will to that of God through a cooperation with grace. Trent's response sided with neither Thomism nor Scotism, but simply held that certitude of faith was anathema.[1]

Bérulle attempted to fill this vacuum against a Reformist piety, which he saw as continuing to destroy the unity of the Church. Bérulle created a spiritual theology of priesthood which reflected volitional and affective characteristics as well, with the full exercise of sacerdotal power dependent on a radical obedience to and intense union with God.

---

[1] Kenny, *The Rise of Modern Philosophy*, xiii–19. See especially 5. See Luther, *WA* 7: 146.5–7: "sed simpliciter debui dicere 'liberum arbitrium est figmentum in rebus seu titulus sine re.' Quia nulli est in manu sua quippiam cogitare mali aut boni," quoted in Kenny.

Nominalism, denying the possibility of knowing God, asserted that only his will could be known.[2] The Company of Jesus took form in this climate, according to Dupuy. Bérulle, a student of these ideas, focused, as did the Jesuits, on the independence of God: God freely willed the Incarnation in which He manifested himself.[3]

Conformity in Relation to Union and Indwelling

As McGinn detailed, conformity of the will with that of God was a fundamental issue particularly in the debates regarding mysticism during the Reformation, and the question of in what union with God consists.[4]

It was a central preoccupation for Bérulle.

Bremond detailed two schools of ascesis with which Bérulle was familiar: the one seeking virtue by means of pagan philosophy, and the one seeking virtue only in relation to and conformity with Christ. Traditional ascesis, he asserted, is anthropocentric, one of affirmation. Its aim is to develop and discipline the will through intense activity. In this school, Christ is the model, and Christian virtue consists in imitation. Berullian ascesis, on the other hand, was theocentric, consisting in the suppression of the ego and emphasizing the unitive life. The aim was the submission and annihilation of the will, self-surrender. Christ in this model becomes our life, as we become a living image of him.[5]

Importantly, Cunningham noted that the doctrine of the indwelling had not been formulated in the Middle Ages but, rather, only arose with Protestantism. The most difficult double-edged question that indwelling posed, as already reviewed, was the following: How is God present in the soul, and how is this presence brought about? While Trent asserted that the Holy Spirit dwells within, Cunningham noted that as a result of the stresses of the controversies in the Post-Reformation era, the Church had forgotten this dogma.[6]

So, too, Bérulle.

Union of Conformity, Union of Mystical Subsistence

According to Blanchard, Bérulle defined the life of union for the ecclesiastic as both a union by conformity to Jesus Christ and one defined by the mystical

---

[2] Dupuy, *Le Christ de Bérulle*, 22.
[3] Ibid. See 21–27 for discussion.
[4] See McGinn, "Mysticism," 119–24.
[5] *TM*, 117.
[6] Cunningham, *The Indwelling of the Trinity*, 2–6.

subsistence of the soul within the humanity of the Savior through the grace of the Holy Spirit. The Spirit of Jesus Christ had the role of the principle of life and operation in the soul. Jesus was both the cause and the exemplar of the life of grace.[7] Blanchard noted that Bérulle called his Oratorians to give honor to God, an honor which consisted in the exercise of the presence of God through prayer and meditation as well as imitation. These exercises would bring them into conformity with Jesus Christ through a participation in the life of Christ in his various states and mysteries.[8] Only then would they be able to take on hierarchical mediation.[9]

Importantly, as Whannou clarified, one could conform completely to the image of the Son of God passively through grace and actively through ascesis, by conforming to this state of Jesus, in order to enter by him into Trinitarian communion.[10]

Conformity: From Disposition, to Capacity, to Mystical Subsistence

McKay elucidated Bérulle's thinking on these matters by detailing key influences and describing the historical evolution of thinking on the nature of conformity from that of the divine will in Augustine's thought, to capacity in Pseudo-Dionysius' thought, to divine likeness in the fulfillment of one's own nature in the thought of Aquinas:

> Augustine suggested that the degrees of closeness to God were actually degrees of "disposition": One approached God not by going from place to place but by conforming one's will to the divine will.[11] Pseudo-Dionysius employed a similar notion of conformity, specifying it as "capacity": "Each rank around God conforms more to him than the one further away…Do not imagine that the proximity here is physical. Rather what I mean by

---

[7]   Ibid., 132. Blanchard, "La spiritualité christocentrique," 132.

[8]   Blanchard, "La spiritualité christocentrique," 33–35. Blanchard consulted the 1644 and 1856 editions of Bérulle's works, J. Dagens' edited volumes of Bérulle's correspondence, and unpublished materials available in the National Archives, in the National Library, and at Avignon.

[9]   Ibid., 34–35. See Cochois, "Bérulle, initiateur mystique," PhD diss., 30.

[10]   *Subsistence*, 239. See 292, where Whannou noted that he utilized Bérulle's *OC*, Montsoult ed. and Migne ed. As the Migne edition has many small errors, the author used, in the case of Bérulle's *Œuvres de piété*, both Migne and Montsoult paginations, cited in that order.

[11]   TG, 113. See Jean Pépin, "Univers dionysien et augustinien," in *Aspects de la dialectique* (Paris: Desclée de Brouwer, 1956), 187.

nearness is the greatest possible capacity to receive God."[12] Centuries later, Thomas Aquinas cautioned that beings can only be "measured" within the universal order if "distance" is transferred out of the category of quantity or actual space and into the category of quality. Since God is omnipresent, a thing cannot be distant from God in a physical way, but can be near or far in terms of its "likeness" to God and its "truth," i.e. the fulfillment of its own nature.[13]

This last distinction, conformity in relation to the fulfillment of one's own nature, as this study has explored, was missing in Bérulle's *néantisme*, notably in relation to the spiritual theology of the priesthood.

A Special Participation

Important to this analysis, Bérulle distinguished between imitation and participation in terms of the average lay person as opposed to priests and the perfect. While imitation was for all Christians, participation was reserved for special souls, in which Jesus Christ communicated participation in his own life. This came about through a special grace different from common grace, as noted.[14]

Whannou noted that, for Bérulle, God was substance and *formaliter* (not just *efficienter*) in being, not just action.[15] However, Bérulle later nuanced his ideals when he wrote about sanctity and participation. He wrote that while the saint is entirely consumed in God, he is all that God is but only through similitude: "Le saint est si entièrement consommé en Dieu qu'il est tout ce que Dieu même est non pas toutefois par égalité, mais par similitude seulement..."[16]

---

[12] TG, 113, also quoting Pseudo-Dionysius, Letter 8, in Pseudo-Dionysius, Luibhéid, and Rorem, *Pseudo-Dionysius: The Complete Works*, 274 (1092B). This is an English-language translation of J. P. Migne, *Patrologiae Cursus Completus, Series Graeca III* (Paris, 1857), with some changes according to the then-forthcoming 1990 edition of *Corpus Dionysiacum*. See *CD*, 180.12–16: "καὶ γὰρ ἑκάστη τῶν περὶ θεὸν διακόσμησις θεοειδεστέρα τῆς μᾶλλον ἀφεστηκυίας ἐστί...Καὶ μὴ τοπικῶς ἐκλάβοις, ἀλλὰ κατὰ τὴν θεοδόχον ἐπιτηδειότητα τὸν πλησιασμόν."

[13] TG, 113. See Edward P. Mahoney, "Metaphysical Foundations of the Hierarchy of Being according to Some Late Medieval and Renaissance Philosophers," in *Philosophies of Existence: Ancient and Medieval*, ed. Parviz Morewedge (New York: Fordham University Press, 1982), 169–72.

[14] Blanchard, "La spiritualité christocentrique," 107. See Coll. 166 and 167.

[15] *Subsistence*, 171. See *OP* 157, 2 (1215), 1049.

[16] *Subsistence*, 171–72. See *Ms de Nantes O*, fol. 115 v°–116 r°.

Blanchard summarized that, for Bérulle, the Spirit is subsistent, living in the soul personally of he who first destroys the self.[17]

Again, this is in contradistinction to Aquinas' notion of participation as fulfillment of one's nature. As Cochois wrote, mystic servitude was the perfection of the relation that makes men priests.[18] This servitude was considered a state of perfection, a term known in tradition, and reviewed in detail here.

States of Perfection

According to Dupuy, even before the Reformation, the expression *état de perfection* had been criticized, given the notion that religious were called to acquire the state of perfection whereas prelates were called to a state of the exercise of perfection for the sake of others. The Reformers, affirming justification by faith, criticized the notion that only certain Christians were called to this state, and that religious leaders with obvious faults believed themselves perfect and above the laity.[19]

By the end of the sixteenth and beginning of the seventeenth centuries, the ideal of perfection became extreme, and much was written about it. Bérulle was of this school, and insisted, for example, that priests should "frapper de terreur ceux qui n'aspirent pas à la perfection."[20]

One main question at the beginning of the seventeenth century was that of the relationship between various approaches to mysticism and perfection, another facet of the union through conformity debate, as Dupuy detailed. Contemplation and perfection are not necessarily related. To avoid this assumption, two types of contemplation were proposed: natural (or Platonic), which was viewed as useless to the pursuit of perfection, and supernatural, which was infused and considered a way of perfection. Dupuy argued that Bérulle was in the latter camp.[21]

Bérulle's program of initiation and contemplation for his Oratorians was an attempt to obtain both union and perfection through frequent mental elevations. The question is whether Bérulle's ideal surrounding states reflected a response to Reformist reactions against the notion of states of perfection. The complexities of his reinterpretation of traditional notions warrant a detailed discussion.

---

[17] Blanchard, "La spiritualité christocentrique," 132–35.
[18] Ibid., 169, referencing Cochois, "Bérulle, hiérarque dionysien," 37: 342.
[19] Michel Dupuy, "Perfection, VI: 16e–17e siècles," in *DSAM*, vol. 12, pt. 1 (1984), col. 1132. See *Institutes*, 4.13.11, and Luther, *De votis monasticis*, in *WA* 8: 609; *LW* 44: 251–400.
[20] *BLS, OR* 12, 283, quoted in Dupuy, "Perfection," cols. 1138–39.
[21] Dupuy, "Perfection," col. 1145. See *Collationes*, 145.

Essentialist Introversion: The Influence of La perle évangélique

The necessity for a high degree of sanctity enumerated in *La perle évangélique* was a major influence on Bérulle, according to Huijben, and included the notion of stability achieved through meditation. The author of *La perle* wrote, "Pour ce nostre esprit est icy esleué et auec l'esprit de Iesus-Christ est introduit en la montagne de la diuinité... et en la presence diuine est *stabilié* par vne simple pensee, pur regard et amour indepeint, pour contempler continuellement Dieu..."[22]

Huijben referenced Bourgoing's opinion of Bérulle's notion of states in relation to disposition: "Par cette disposition, explique Bourgoing, l'on ne donne pas seulement les fruits, mais le fonds: non seulement les accidents, mais la substance: non seulement les actions, les paroles et les souffrances, mais aussi l'être, l'essence et l'intime de l'âme."[23]

Huijben explained that the notion of states in Bérulle's thought linked his notions of *être* and *essence*. *La perle* also would use terms such as *être*, *essence*, and *essentiel*: "En ce que tu te conuertis ainsi à moy et demeures en moy, voila i'imprimeray en ton esprit vne certaine *essentielle*, vnique, eternelle, diuine, delectable, paisible et ioyeuse *essence*."[24]

As already noted, the idea of an essential activity of the soul is from the medieval mysticism of the Low Countries and the Rhineland, dependent on a Scholasticism that did not always distinguish between the nature of the soul and its faculties, or the nature of *mens*.[25]

Huijben concluded that Bérulle's idea of adherence by state was an adaptation of *La perle*'s *introversion essentielle*.[26] There is also a link with the *vie suressentielle* or the *vie suréminente*, common terms in his era referring to the third stage of spiritual development of those living habitually at the *fine pointe* of the soul. Essential activity at this stages becomes predominant, according to Huijben. The writer of *La perle* wrote: "A la vie superessentielle paruiennent ceux qui resignans leur volonté..." This notion of a stable life of the perfect linked to surrender of the will resembles that of the state of servitude of Bérulle.[27]

---

[22] Van Essche, Despont, De Mallery, and De La Noüe, *La perle*, 1, 2, ch. 17, fol. 154–55, quoted in AS, 27: 100.
[23] Bourgoing, "Préface," in *OC*, Migne ed., col. 89, quoted in AS, 27: 113.
[24] Van Essche, Despont, De Mallery, and De La Noüe, *La perle*, 1, 2, ch. 1, fol. 130, quoted in AS, 27: 113–14.
[25] AS, 27: 115n2.
[26] Ibid., 27: 116–17.
[27] Van Essche, Despont, De Mallery, and De La Noüe, *La perle*, 1, 2, ch. 29, fol. 167, quoted in AS, 27: 117–18.

This essential servitude, obtained through adoration and adherence, was the model of sacerdotal spirituality for Bérulle's Oratorians, as instituted by the vow.

Incarnation, Priesthood, and *État*

Bérulle applied the notion of state to the Incarnation and the priesthood in support of his ideals regarding perfection in relation to priesthood. We now return to Preckler, who conducted an important study of the many meanings of the word "état" in Bérulle's work and in Bérulle's time, in the spheres of law, politics, and the "state" of the Church itself. A detailed review of his study is warranted for this analysis of the priesthood, itself a state, according to Bérulle.

Preckler began with a summary of the thought of Aquinas, who devoted several questions to the notion of states in the Church: the *état des évêques*, and the *état des religieuses*.[28] The word had been used by theologians and spiritual writers in various ways, the most frequent since the time of the patristic era being a state of prayer or a state of the spiritual life described in psychological terms. Aquinas also noted a three-part division in the spiritual life in terms of states, belonging to beginners, proficients and the perfect. Within this background of the language of institutions with juridical nuances, that of theology with metaphysical nuances, and that of spirituality with psychological nuances, Preckler argued, Bérulle's uses of the word should be analyzed.[29]

Of key interest to this analysis of Bérulle's spiritual theology of priesthood, Preckler quoted Suárez's definition of the word (which includes the two elements of perfection and stability) as that which Bérulle would follow in whatever way he used the term: "…cum (…) personae attribuitur, duo semper indicat, scilicet, *perfectionem* in aliqua conditione, vel modo existendi eius *quietem seu immobilitatem* in illa."[30]

Suárez, known to be an influence on Bérulle's thought, held that there were five conditions required for this state of perfection: it must be an external act of profession demonstrating the embrace of a mode of life which is visible; it is an obligation of permanence; the obligation must be entered into with solemnity; the purpose must be for the exercise of works of perfection; and the actions of the state must be external.[31]

Although they were not religious vows, Bérulle's vows of servitude seemed to have followed these five principles, as this study details, an attempt to inaugurate

---

[28] *État*, 8. See Aquinas, *ST*, 2–2.83–86.
[29] Ibid., 7–11.
[30] Francisco Suárez, "De statu perfectionis et religionis," in *Opera omnia*, vol. 15 (Paris: Vivès, 1859), 1, no. 1, quoted in *État*, 11.
[31] Ibid., "De statu perfectionis et religionis," 5, nos. 6 and 7, 28–30.

his Oratorians into a program of spiritual practice intended to create and maintain a stable state of perfection along the lines of religious life.

The Holiness of Christ and the State of the Priesthood

That said, for Bérulle, the state of the priesthood (as opposed to religious life) was not only the most holy state in the Church but (as Preckler wrote, "in the spirit of Dionysian mediations"), it was holy and sacred in its institution and the origin of all the holiness in the Church.[32] For Bérulle, the underlying reason for all states (canonical or spiritual) within the Church was Christ, who was called to the "…état de l'Incarnation, état d'Homme-Dieu, état de filiation divine dans la nature humaine."[33]

The basis of the superior holiness of the state of priesthood was the priest's tie to Christ by indelible character. Bérulle considered them tied both by state and by character: "Les prêtres sont liés à Jésus-Christ par leur état et par leur caractère perpetual et ineffaçable, indissoluble même par les forces de l'enfer, qui est une sorte de lien plus grand et plus fort que celui du vœu solennel."[34]

For Bérulle, the firmness and stability of the sacerdotal state had their origin in Christ, not in a religious vow or through any action of the priest. The priesthood of the Oratorians was dependent on the priesthood of Christ and on his action, his consecration:

> Cette société exige la pratique, plutôt que le vœu; elle est appelée par un état qui résulte, non d'un vœu, mais d'une consécration par le Christ: le sacerdoce lui-même est en effet un état, à ce point insigne, qu'il a pour forme et pour exemplaire du sacerdoce du Christ. Et c'est un état au service du sacerdoce du Christ; c'est un état qui puise sa stabilité dans la consécration du Christ qui s'est consacré des prêtres; c'est un état solide et stable, au point qu'il dure pour l'éternité: "prêtre pour toujours, au point qu'il continue même en enfer; c'est un état qui imite et adore par son éternité et sa solidité la solidité et l'éternité du sacerdoce du Christ; c'est un état qui doit sa solidité et sa stabilité, non pas à nous, mais au Christ, non à un vœu ou à l'Église, mais au serment du Père éternel qui établit le

---

32 *CB*, vol. 1, no. 89, 166, quoted in *État*, 42n38. Bérulle: "état de prêtrise…est le premier et le plus saint état de l'Église de Dieu." See also n. 39, quoting *OR* 1, 260: "l'état ecclésiastique…est saint et sacré en son institution et même l'origine de toute sainteté qui est en l'Église de Dieu."

33 *OP* 141, cols. 1177–78, quoted in *État*, 42.

34 *BLS*, *OR* 18, 297, quoted in *État*, 43. See also 41–42.

sacerdoce du Christ (notre sacerdoce est en effet dépendance du sacerdoce du Christ), non à un vœu, comme l'état religieux, c'est-à-dire à notre action (le vœu que nous faisons est action), mais à l'action du Christ; c'est-à-dire qu'il doit à la consécration du Christ sa stabilité et son être.[35]

Stability and Perfection

Preckler wrote that Bérulle made the hypostatic union of the Word with our human nature a state, and one that was "l'origine (*hauriens*), le prototype (*exemplar*), et la finalité (*inserviens*)" of the priesthood.[36]

Bérulle used the terms state and order interchangeably. Notably, he wrote about the orders of nature, grace, and glory, defining them respectively: the order of nature wherein all creatures have a natural participation in the being of God; the order of grace (including the glory of humans and angels) in which intelligent beings participate accidentally in the holiness and felicity of God; and the order of glory, which is that of the hypostatic union in which the humanity of Christ receives the subsistence of the Word. All three orders were, according to Bérulle, "trois sortes d'émanations et operations de Dieu hors de son essence…"[37]

Preckler noted a Pseudo-Dionysian influence in this equating of emanations and operations.[38] Bérulle combined the orders of grace and glory into one in the second category, and Preckler asked whether Bérulle's third order centering on the *état de l'Incarnation* surpassed the order of glory, a schema similar to that of Harphius.[39]

Preckler also analyzed Bérulle's use of the word *état* in terms of the Trinity, the Incarnation, the hypostatic union and the humanity of Christ.[40] Bérulle

---

[35] BLS, *OR* 15, no. 2, 289, quoted in *État*, 43, using the Latin version. The French version as translated by Dupuy is provided here. See 290–91.

[36] *État*, 43–44; see BLS, *OR* 10, 282; *OR* 20, 304.

[37] *Discours*, 3, no. 9, 105–6, quoted in *État*, 55–56.

[38] *État*, 57.

[39] L. Cognet, *Introduction aux mystiques rhéno-flamands* (Paris: Desclée, 1968), 296. See also Cognet's discussion, 299–300, also cited in *État*, 61. See Hendrik Herp (Harphius), *Theologia Mystica*, 1 (Cologne: Melchior Novesanius, 1538), 1.7. fol. 6r: "…L'Incarnation a rapport à la perfection de l'homme lui-même, et par conséquent à la perfection de l'univers, en cela qui'l (le Christ) donne au genre humain son accomplissement en ce qui regarde la nature aussi bien que la grâce et même la gloire….Et c'est pourquoi, quand bien même l'homme n'eût pas péché, Dieu néanmoins se fût incarné, ca il convenait que l'homme atteignît à la perfection selon la nature, la grâce et la gloire, de telle sorte que la nature humaine pervînt à sa plus haute diginité," quoted in Cognet, *Introduction aux mystiques rhéno-flamands*, 296, also quoted in *État*, 61.

[40] *État*, 64.

manifested a clear case of exemplarism in calling the *état du mystère de l'Incarnation* the image of the divine world—the Trinity.[41] Preckler included the following "striking" passage, with characteristic flexibility in terminology. Bérulle:

> C'est la naissance de l'ordre et de l'état de l'union hypostatique, lequel porte hors de Dieu la sainteté la plus haute et la plus éminente qui soit possible, et la plus proche de la sainteté superessentielle de Dieu même, que cet ordre et état suprême enclôt et comprend en soi-même, comme sa forme et son principe. Or cette sainteté nouvelle en la terre et au ciel, et cette grâce admirable de l'union hypostatique, a sa naissance en la naissance de Jésus, et prend son origine en ce mystère, et d'icelui se dérive et s'étend en tous les autres mystères de Jésus, en tous ses états, et en toutes ses œuvres. Car, à proprement parler, les autres mystères du Fils de Dieu, sont mystères ou d'actions ou de souffrances saintes; mais ce mystère est un mystère de substance, et mystère produisant au monde la substance même de la sainteté, de laquelle procèdent, et en laquelle reposent ses actions et ses souffrances saintes, et en laquelle subsistent tous les autres états divers et divins qu'il a, soit en la terre, soit au ciel. Reconnaissons donc ce mystère comme mystère de Vie, comme mystère de Lumière, comme mystère de Sainteté, comme mystère de substance et non seulement d'action ou d'accident; comme mystère de sainteté substantielle, de sainteté primitive, de sainteté originale et fondamentale, de tous les mystères, de toutes les œuvres, et de tous les états de Jésus. Et recueillons de ce mystère une grâce, une sainteté, une lumière, une vie, une vie de lumière, une lumière de vie en Jésus, comme effets propres et procédant de l'état et de la condition de ce mystère auquel le Fils de Dieu se va donnant et manifestant au monde. Dont nous voyons qu'en icelui, plus qu'en aucun autre temps, en aucun autre état, en aucun autre mystère de sa vie, il donne vie et connaissance de lui-même…[42]

In explicating Bérulle's analogical application, as Preckler termed it, he noted that Bérulle held the hypostatic union to be stable and perfect, and "la source et

---

[41] Ibid., 80–81.

[42] *Grandeurs*, 11, no. 4, 345–46, quoted in *État*, 83–84. Preckler noted Rheno-Flemish and Dionysian influences in the word "superessentielle." See Cognet, *Introduction aux mystiques rhéno-flamands*, 273ff.

l'origine de toutes les operations saintes, de toutes les émanations de grâce…,"
including the special state of the Virgin Mary, the Eucharist, and the priesthood.[43]

Dupuy noted a particular passage in which Bérulle considered that just as the
holy humanity was elevated and made subsistent in the person of the Word, so
too, the Word Incarnate wished to associate Mary with the divine order, not in
her nature but by the office of maternity. Just so, he wished to also elevate his
apostles "en quelque manière."[44]

According to Preckler, essential to Bérulle's doctrine of state is that Christ is
the cause of divinization thanks to the supreme power of his state as the Man-
God in the Incarnation: this state of the Word is "principe, fin, et prototype" of
all grace. Preckler summed up this spirituality as a Trinitarian *néantisme* based
on a Christological exemplarism.[45] Bérulle:

> Or en ce mystère il y a perte et plénitude d'être tout ensemble, et aussi y a-
> t-il voie d'honorer Dieu dans le fonds de l'être, cette manière portant perte
> de soi-même, et étant nécessaire que la créature soit retirée de soi-même
> et se perde, pour être établie en Dieu et l'honorer en cette manière si intime
> et si sainte. C'est pourquoi l'abnégation est le fondement de la discipline
> chrétienne.[46]

Clarifying the notion of adoration by state, Preckler continued that Bérulle did
not define the soul, but he did attempt to define adoration by state: it is free, by
the power of both God and Christ; it is passive, in that the soul can only offer
thoughts and action; it is permanent in the *fond* of the soul; and it is modeled
after the Incarnation as a profound abnegation and divinization. The *infinies
voies* of the Man-God are the divine states of souls imprinted by Christ in
imitation of his own deified states.[47]

Preckler pointed to Huijben's analysis of Scholastic concepts in relation to
Bérulle's thought. The Scholastics failed to distinguish *habitus* from activity or
the nature of the soul from its faculties, or to explain the nature of the *mens*, as
already referenced. Here presented is Huijben's thought in some depth.

> Malheureusement les mystiques du moyen-âge ne distinguent pas
> toujours très nettement entre l'*essence* ou *nature* proprement dite de
> l'âme, qui n'opère pas, et ce que les scolastiques appellent la *voluntas ut*

---

43 *Grandeurs*, 2, no. 3, 173, quoted in *État*, 84–85.
44 *Discours de controverse*, 3, 9, quoted in Dupuy, *Le Christ de Bérulle*, 116.
45 *État*, 141–42, quoting *OP* 148, no. 6, col. 1192.
46 Ibid.
47 *État*, 142–44.

natura, simplex intelligentia, habitus primorum principiorum, synderesis, etc. Il est vrai que les scolastiques eux-mêmes n'étaient pas d'accord sur la distinction à établir entre la nature de l'âme et ses facultés, ni sur l'explication à donner du *mens*. Même chez Bérulle il n'est pas toujours facile de discerner si par *état* il entend un habitus ou bien une activité proprement dite, quoique réduite à sa simple expression.[48]

Holiness and Perfection

Bérulle was very interested in the idea of holiness, the first divine perfection. Dupuy held that he was unique in presenting his conception of holiness as a belonging to a sacred world. There are two generally held meanings of the word holiness: moral purity and consecration for separation. For Bérulle, sanctity was union with God, separation from the world and a consecration to God, as well as an infinite distance from sin and separation from all that is created: "La sainteté consiste en l'union et en la communication que Dieu fait de soi-même à l'âme."[49]

Dupuy asked whether one might consider Bérulle's concept of holiness as owing as much to the Reformers as to his familiarity with the Bible.[50] This holiness applied to both Christians in general and priests in particular.

In contrast, Aquinas emphasized that religious merely made professions regarding poverty, chastity, and obedience. He rejected the notion that the practice of austerities signaled greater holiness.[51]

As Sheldrake noted, Calvinist piety stressed the corporate, covenant relationship, which included the Church. His focus was on Christ and neighbor rather than private devotion or spiritual perfection.[52] This is in contradistinction to the opinion of Tamburello and Richard, as discussed, that his spirituality was individualistic. More study is needed to understand in what ways it might have been both, perhaps based on a rejection of individualistic mysticism but still supporting the individual's direct access to God via a personalist piety.

In defense of the notion of private piety and the pursuit of perfection, Bérulle responded with a notion of perfection which included the need for covenant-like vows. In terms of his Oratorians, this piety included living in community as public persons in the service of the Church.

---

[48] AS, 27: 115n2, quoted in *État*, 144. Huijben indicated page 155 in error.

[49] Bérulle, manuscrit 467, *Marseille*, 19 (107 C), Bibliothèque municipale de Marseille, quoted in Dupuy, *BSA*, 299. See discussion, 297–99.

[50] *BSA*, 306.

[51] Jones, Wainwright, and Yarnold, *The Study of Spirituality*, 298–99. See Aquinas, *ST*, 2.2.184ff.

[52] Sheldrake, *New Westminster Dictionary of Christian Spirituality*, 162–63.

Huijben defended Bérulle's vision of the pursuit of holiness by asserting that for Bérulle, perfection was the work of God's grace in the French School, with man cooperating by abandoning himself to God, with the performance of mortification and virtue only thereafter following.[53] This study supports the idea that his ideals surrounding perfection and holiness were more complex.

Dupuy noted that Bérulle held that the priest's role in the Eucharist and his role as mediator require great holiness.[54] The state of the priesthood for Bérulle was both a state and an order of holiness. As God is holy by his essence, and Christ by the hypostatic union, so priests are holy by the Holy Spirit who not only infuses them with grace, but also dwells in them himself. Urging a separation from the world greater than that of monastics, priests must imitate God in his own infinite separation from the world before returning to serve others without any other commerce than as a priest. Bérulle: "…Dieu donne à sa créature et ne reçoit rien de sa créature, ainsi nous ne devons avoir aucun commerce intéressant avec la créature, mais lui départir ce que nous avons reçu de Dieu pour son utilité particulière, sans intérêt et sans retour."[55]

Bérulle described the state of the priesthood as a state and order of holiness, not just virtue, as with religious:

> On peut en déduire que l'état de prêtrise est état et ordre de sainteté, et non seulement de vertu, comme il suffit à l'état religieux. Distinguons donc l'état sacerdotal de l'état religieux. Et à ce dernier, accordons l'état de vertu; mais à l'état sacerdotal, l'état de sainteté institué par le Christ, l'auteur même de la sainteté.[56]

Bérulle credited Pseudo-Dionysius's ideals, in particular, regarding the perfection required of priests as being greater than that of religious. Bérulle:

> Tout ce qui est de la perfection intérieure et de la communication avec Dieu en sa plus haute éminence est inférieur à la dignité de cet état et opération. Tout ce que la vie monastique suppose en cette abstraction et éminence nous est propre, plus qu'aux ermites et religieux, selon Saint Denys…
>
> Bien plus, la perfection des anges eux-mêmes nous est inférieure: nous sommes appelés plus haut.

---

[53] Huijben, AS, 26: 100, cited in Walsh, "The Priesthood in the Writings of the French School," 87.

[54] Morgain, "La prêtrise selon Pierre de Bérulle," 142. See *OC* (1996), *OP* 297, 349–55.

[55] *BLS, OR* 13, no. 7, 285.

[56] Ibid., *OR* 22, no. 3, 316.

Mais cette abstraction et élévation doit en nous être différente de celle des ermites et religieux. Et elle doit plus imiter Dieu en sa séparation et abstraction de l'être créé. Car, comme Dieu est infiniment séparé de tout être par l'éminence, élévation et sainteté de son être, il est ce nonobstant conjoint à sa créature et intime à icelle par son opération, direction et application…[57]

Bérulle also delineated what Oratorians owed to God as men, Christians, and priests. As men, they owed fidelity in the battle against the flesh; as Christians, to recognize the gift of the Son and their belonging to him by giving themselves completely to him. As Christians they were to "regarder, imiter et nous transformer en cet objet nôtre qui est Jésus-Christ." As Christians they were to offer themselves as victims, citing Romans 12:1.[58]

However, Oratorians were required do more than imitate Christ and live austere lives, even transforming themselves into Christ as living victims (as should the laity); they must live their entire lives as if they were instruments of a principal cause. They should live only for him. Bérulle:

Et ces deux points, savoir est cette grande liaison d'honneur et de dépendance de notre Seigneur Jésus-Christ et ce grand désir de la perfection chrétienne doivent être tenus comme essentiels à l'institution de la prêtrise. Et sur iceux sont fondés tous les devoirs et obligations des prêtres: le grand zèle qu'ils doivent avoir de l'honneur de Jésus; la vraie imitation de sa vie et de ses mœurs; la grande coopération à ses desseins; le grand respect et service à son Église; la grande propagation de son État et de son Royaume en la terre; la plénitude de lui, la pauvreté et vacuité de tout le reste, qui est de nous regarder comme des instruments de ses mains, morts en nous-mêmes et animés par lui et pour lui, sans mouvement ni application que celle qui vient de lui et pour lui, comme l'instrument n'opère que par la cause principale qui le meut et l'applique; comme hosties immolées a Jésus, instruments de sa grâce, ses coopérateurs et aides: "Christi adiutores," parties nobles de son État et de son Royaume, ne vivant que pour lui.[59]

---

[57] Ibid., *OR* 13, nos. 6–7, 285.
[58] Ibid., *OR* 75, nos. 1–6, 407–8.
[59] Ibid., *OR* 23–25, no. 2, 319.

Cognet's Critique

Cognet summarized that in making the main object of the adoration of the Incarnate Word the divine essence in the unity of its perfections, Bérulle depicted Christ as adoring the divine essence in himself, which Cognet considered "une grandiose immanence."[60] Cognet wrote that Bérulle had constructed an ontology of priesthood that infinitely transcended its social and temporal realization.[61] One must ask whether Bérulle's spiritual theology of priesthood did not also take on the same immanentist grandiosity.

The portrait of Bérulle's priest and his required perfection depicted the need to reach for a state of perfection higher than the angels. Bérulle expressed the following in reference to the Oratorians' association with the society of the Trinity: "Or, comme en ce regard notre vie est une vie de société extérieure, comme au regard de Dieu c'est une vie d'élévation et société intérieure, tout ce qui sert à la perfection d'une société entre dans la condition de la vie ecclésiastique."[62]

The question arises whether these passages reflect an absorption of an Eckhartian-influenced imputed Lutheran perfection. This Lutheran heritage of justification, filtered again through Calvin's ideals regarding union with Christ, resulted in a priest who must frequently work toward perfection through union with Christ of whom he is the visible image.

Canfield's notion of perfection, as discussed by McKay, can also be detected, wherein perfection is reduced to a single point of unity with the divine will. Through obedience and internal union of intellect and affectivity with the divine movements, there is an absorption of the self into the will of God.[63]

Sacerdotal Perfection and Pseudo-Dionysius

Pseudo-Dionysius held that the goal of the hierarchy is to be "our greatest likeness and union with God."[64] In the following quote can be seen the specifically sacerdotal pursuit of perfection as based in the concept of theurgy or "work of

---

[60] Cognet, *Les origines de la spiritualité française,* 65.

[61] Ibid., 73.

[62] *BLS, OR* 13, no. 8, 285–86.

[63] TG, 40. See Canfield, *La règle de perfection.*

[64] Pseudo-Dionysius, in Pseudo-Dionysius, Luibhéid, and Rorem, *Pseudo-Dionysius: The Complete Works,* 200, *EH,* 392A. *CD,* 68.16–17: "Εἴρηται τοίνυν ἡμῖν ἱερῶς, ὡς οὗτός ἐστι τῆς καθ᾽ ἡμᾶς ἱεραρχίας σκοπός· ἡ πρὸς θεὸν ἡμῶν ὡς ἐφικτὸν ἀφομοίωσίς τε καὶ ἕνωσις."

God."[65] In this, the Berullian sacerdotal themes of assimilation, emanation, elevation, dispositions, stability, mystic initiation, and stability may have had their greatest source:

> Jesus enlightens our blessed superiors, Jesus who is transcendent mind, utterly divine mind, who is the source and the being underlying all hierarchy, all sanctification, all the workings of God, who is the ultimate in divine power. He assimilates them, as much as they are able, to his own light. As for us, with that yearning for beauty which raises us upward (and which is raised up) to him, he pulls together all our many differences. He makes our life, dispositions, and activity something one and divine, and he bestows on us the power appropriate to a sacred priesthood.
>
> Approaching therefore the holy activity of the sacred office we come closer to those beings who are superior to us. We imitate as much as we can their abiding, unwavering, and sacred constancy, and we thereby come to look up to the blessed and ultimately divine ray of Jesus himself. Then, having sacredly beheld whatever can be seen, enlightened by the knowledge of what we have seen, we shall then be able to be consecrated and consecrators of this mysterious understanding. Formed of light, initiates in God's work, we shall be perfected and bring about perfection.[66]

For Pseudo-Dionysius, hierarchs must imitate God by "endlessly reminding ourselves of God's sacred works and doing so by sacred hymns and acts." Hierarchs praise the works by Jesus, and behold with the mind's eyes for a

---

[65] Ibid., 52. The editors wrote that Pseudo-Dionysius used the term "theurgy" to mean "work of God" not in the sense of a Iamblichan objective genitive indicating a work directed to God but of a subjective genitive meaning God's work.

[66] Ibid., 195–96, *EH*, 372A–372B. *CD*, 63.11–64.14 (see ch. 13, n. 23): "Οὕτω γάρ, ὡς ἡ θεολογία τοῖς θιασώταις ἡμῖν παραδέδωκε, καὶ αὐτὸς Ἰησοῦς, ὁ θεαρχικώτατος νοῦς καὶ ὑπερούσιος, ἡ πάσης ἱεραρχίας ἁγιαστείας τε καὶ θεουργίας ἀρχὴ καὶ οὐσία καὶ θεαρχικωτάτη δύναμις, ταῖς τε μακαρίαις καὶ ἡμῶν κρείττοσιν οὐσίαις ἐμφανέστερον ἅμα καὶ νοερώτερον ἐλλάμπει καὶ πρὸς τὸ οἰκεῖον αὐτὰς ἀφομοιοῖ κατὰ δύναμιν φῶς ἡμῶν τε τῷ πρὸς αὐτὸν ἀνατεινομένῳ καὶ ἡμᾶς ἀνατείνοντι τῶν καλῶν ἔρωτι συμπτύσσει τὰς πολλὰς ἑτερότητας καὶ εἰς ἑνοειδῆ καὶ θείαν ἀποτελειώσας ζωὴν ἕξιν τε καὶ ἐνέργειαν ἱεροπρεπῆ δωρεῖται τῆς θείας ἱερωσύνης τὴν δύναμιν, ἐξ ἧς ἐπὶ τὴν ἁγίαν ἐρχόμενοι τῆς ἱερατείας ἐνέργειαν ἐγγύτεροι μὲν αὐτοὶ γινόμεθα τῶν ὑπὲρ ἡμᾶς οὐσιῶν τῇ κατὰ δύναμιν ἀφομοιώσει τοῦ μονίμου τε καὶ ἀνεξαλλάκτου τῆς αὐτῶν ἱερᾶς ἱδρύσεως καὶ ταύτῃ πρὸς τὴν μακαρίαν Ἰησοῦ καὶ θεαρχικὴν αὐγὴν ἀναβλέψαντες ὅσα τε ἰδεῖν ἐφικτὸν ἐποπτεύσαντες ἱερῶς καὶ τῆς τῶν θεαμάτων γνώσεως ἐλλαμφθέντες τὴν μυστικὴν ἐπιστήμην ἀφιερώμενοι καὶ ἀφιερωταὶ φωτοειδεῖς καὶ θεουργικοὶ τετελεσμένοι καὶ τελεσιουργοὶ γενέσθαι δυνησόμεθα."

conceptual contemplation, and then proceed to sacred acts (consecration). They pray that, like Christ, they might perform the divine things. They must cling to him by conformity through sinlessness.[67] In this can be seen the themes of contemplation of the mysteries of the life of Christ, adherence, and conformity, echoed also in Bérulle's project.

This effort at contemplation and stability in pursuit of divinization must be constant, according to Pseudo-Dionysius, through a self-naughting which grants capacity, as we have reviewed:

Now I think it is quite evident to those with an understanding of hierarchies that in all sustained effort to reach the One, by the complete death and dissolution of being of what is opposite, intelligent beings are granted the immutable capacity to mold themselves completely on the form of the divine...One must fearlessly confront any disastrous backsliding. There must never be any decline in the sacred love of truth. Indeed one must ceaselessly and prayerfully be raised up as much as one

---

67 Ibid., 221–22, *EH*, 441C–444B. *CD*, 92.2–93.10: "Τὸ θεομίμητον δὲ πῶς ἂν ἡμῖν ἑτέρως ἐγγένοιτο μὴ τῆς τῶν ἱερωτάτων θεουργιῶν μνήμης ἀνανεουμένης ἀεὶ ταῖς ἱεραρχικαῖς ἱερολογίαις τε καὶ ἱερουργίαις; Τοῦτο ποιοῦμεν ὡς τὰ λόγιά φησιν εἰς τὴν αὐτῆς ἀνάμνησιν. Ἔνθεν ὁ θεῖος ἱεράρχης ἐπὶ τοῦ θείου θυσιαστηρίου καταστὰς ὑμνεῖ τὰς εἰρημένας ἱερὰς θεουργίας Ἰησοῦ τῆς θειοτάτης ἡμῶν προνοίας, ἃς ἐπὶ σωτηρίᾳ τοῦ γένους ἡμῶν εὐδοκίᾳ τοῦ παναγεστάτου πατρὸς ἐν πνεύματι ἁγίῳ κατὰ τὸ λόγιον ἐτελείωσεν. Ὑμνήσας δὲ καὶ τὴν σεβασμίαν αὐτῶν καὶ νοητὴν θεωρίαν ἐν νοεροῖς ὀφθαλμοῖς ἐποπτεύσας ἐπὶ τὴν συμβολικὴν αὐτῶν ἱερουργίαν ἔρχεται καὶ τοῦτο θεοπαραδότως· ὅθεν εὐλαβῶς τε ἅμα καὶ ἱεραρχικῶς μετὰ τοὺς ἱεροὺς τῶν θεουργιῶν ὕμνους ὑπὲρ τῆς ὑπὲρ αὐτὸν ἱερουργίας ἀπολογεῖται πρότερον ἱερῶς πρὸς αὐτὸν ἀναβοῶν· Σὺ εἶπας «Τοῦτο ποιεῖτε εἰς τὴν ἐμὴν ἀνάμνησιν». Εἶτα τῆς θεομιμήτου ταύτης ἱερουγίας ἄξιος αἰτήσας γενέσθαι καὶ τῇ πρὸς α ὑτὸν Χριστὸν ἀφομοιώσει τὰ θεῖα τελέσαι καὶ διαδοῦναι πανάγνως καὶ τοὺς τῶν ἱερῶν μεθέξοντας ἱεροπρεπῶς μετασχεῖν ἱερουργεῖ τὰ θειότατα καὶ ὑπ' ὄψιν ἄγει τὰ ὑμνημένα διὰ τῶν ἱερῶς προκειμένων συμβόλων. Τὸν γὰρ ἐγκεκαλυμμένον καὶ ἀδιαίρετον ἄρτον ἀνακαλύψας καὶ εἰς πολλὰ διελὼν καὶ τὸ ἑνιαῖον τοῦ ποτηρίου πᾶσι καταμερίσας συμβολικῶς τὴν ἑνότητα πληθύνει καὶ διανέμει παναγεστάτην ἐν τούτοις ἱερουργίαν τελῶν. Τὸ γὰρ ἓν καὶ ἁπλοῦν καὶ κρύφιον Ἰησοῦ τοῦ θεαρχικωτάτου λόγου τῇ καθ' ἡμᾶς ἐνανθρωπήσει πρὸς τὸ σύνθετόν τε καὶ ὁρατὸν ἀναλλοιώτως ἀγαθότητι καὶ φιλανθρωπίᾳ προελήλυθε καὶ τὴν πρὸς αὐτὸν ἡμῶν ἑνοποιὸν κοινωνίαν ἀγαθουργῶς διεπραγματεύσατο τὰ καθ' ἡμᾶς ταπεινὰ τοῖς θειοτάτοις αὐτοῦ κατ' ἄκρον ἑνώσας, εἴπερ καὶ ἡμεῖς ὡς μέλη σώματι συναρμολογηθῶμεν αὐτῷ κατὰ τὸ ταὐτὸν τῆς ἀλωβήτου καὶ θείας ζωῆς καὶ μὴ τοῖς φθοροποιοῖς πάθεσι κατανεκρωθέντες ἀνάρμοστοι καὶ ἀκόλλητοι καὶ ἀσύζωοι γενώμεθα πρὸς τὰ θεῖα μέλη καὶ ὑγιέστατα. Χρὴ γὰρ ἡμᾶς, εἰ τῆς πρὸς αὐτὸν ἐφιέμεθα κοινωνίας, εἰς τὴν θειοτάτην αὐτοῦ κατὰ σάρκα ζωὴν ἀποσκοπεῦσαι καὶ τῇ πρὸς αὐτὴν ἀφομοιώσει τῆς ἱερᾶς ἀναμαρτησίας εἰς τὴν θεοειδῆ καὶ ἀλώβητον ἕξιν ἀναδραμεῖν. Οὕτω γὰρ ἐναρμονίως ἡμῖν τὴν πρὸς τὸ ὅμοιον κοινωνίαν δωρήσεται."

can toward it and strive always to be uplifted in a sacred fashion toward the ultimate perfection of the Deity.[68]

Mysteries of the Life of Christ and the Deification of States

Spirituality of the Mysteries

Referencing Lécuyer's 1952 analysis, O'Brien noted that the idea of the "presence of Christ by the perpetuity of his mysteries was a beautiful commonplace of the fathers."[69] Lécuyer wrote that if the mysteries of Christ are ours and by them he assimilates us more to himself, then it is Jesus himself who lives these mysteries in us. Therefore, Christians must be the prolongation of the redemptive Incarnation.[70]

Théron called this Christocentrism *théandrisme*.[71]

In the following section, the exact nature of the causality of the mysteries of the life of Christ is explored.

States, the Divine Exemplar, and Participation Through Prayer

McKay wrote on Bérulle's theology of states in relation to grace, expanding on Preckler's analysis. The grace of Incarnation is a new state of human existence for Bérulle, and gives the new possibility of abiding in and communicating with the divine exemplar. McKay wrote of Bérulle:

> The permanence of this mystery in turn qualifies the homage which the state of the Incarnation renders to the Trinity. Because it perfectly expresses and imitates the divine paternity, filiation, and union of love, the

---

[68]   Ibid., 207, *EH*, 401B–C. *CD*, 76.22–77.8: "Ἀλλ' ἔστι που δῆλον ὡς οἶμαι τοῖς τῶν ἱεραρχικῶν ἐπιστήμοσιν, ὅτι ταῖς διηνεκέσιν ἐν συντονίᾳ πρὸς τὸ ἓν ἀνατάσεσι καὶ ταῖς τῶν ἐναντίων ὁλικαῖς νεκρώσεσι καὶ ἀνυπαρξίαις τὸ ἀναλλοίωτον ἴσχει τὰ νοερὰ τῆς θεοειδοῦς ἕξεως. ...καὶ ἀφόβητον ἀεὶ πρὸς τὴν ἐπ' αὐτὴν ὀλέθριον ὕφεσιν οὐδὲ τοῦ ἱεροῦ τῆς ἀληθείας ἔρωτος ἐν καταλήξει ποτὲ γενέσθαι, προσεχῶς δὲ καὶ αἰωνίως ἐπ' αὐτὴν ὅσῃ δύναμις ἀνατείνεσθαι τὴν ἐπὶ τὰ τελεώτερα τῆς θεαρχίας ἀναγωγὴν ἱερῶς ἀεὶ διαπραγματευόμενον."

[69]   O'Brien, "Current Theology," 276. See J. Lecuyer, "La pérennité des mystères du Christ," *La Vie spirituelle* 87 (1952): 451–63.

[70]   Lecuyer, "La pérennité des mystères du Christ," 462.

[71]   H. Théron, "Le théandrisme spirituel de Bérulle," *L'année théologique augustinienne* 12 (1952): 187–90, quoted in O'Brien, "Current Theology," 276.

Incarnation permanently offers honor to God. Underlying this Berullian insight is the Neoplatonic idea that insofar as an emanated reality regards and images its prior, it is honoring that prior.[72]

Preckler held, arguably, that Bérulle's unique theory on the presence and virtues of the mysteries of Christ's life was similar to Thomistic doctrine, and noted that the liturgical movement has also posed the problem of the presence of the mysteries.[73]

Bérulle held that Christ's acceptance and oblation of mortality at the moment of the Incarnation was an act of servitude and adoration—setting aside the glory of the Word at that moment. This divine oblation deified all the states of his life: "Le nouveau vivant que Dieu fait sur la terre...vie de grâce et de gloire connaissant et adorant celui qui l'a fait et lui a donné ce nouvel état, qui n'était point encore dans les états de Dieu, et qui doit régir et sanctifier les autres."[74]

For Bérulle, the interior states of the mysteries of Christ produce the "states" in the *fond* of chosen souls.[75] In virtue of Bérulle's doctrine of the subsistence of the assumed humanity, Bérulle applied the concept of deification to all the states and mysteries which also become the instruments of divinization for souls. Bérulle considered the mysteries of the life of Jesus as the meritorious causes of grace, the exemplar causes of resemblance, and the efficient causes of both the general and special applications of grace, according to McKay.[76] The second causality, exemplar causality, is unique to Bérulle, in that participation in Christ is emphasized in regard to a personal incorporation into Jesus. According to Bérulle, "Jésus...en ses états et mystères est lui-même notre partage, et nous donnant une part universelle en lui, il veut que nous ayons une part singulière en ses divers états, selon la diversité de son élection sur nous et de notre piété vers lui."[77]

This participation, through prayer, included Bérulle's formula, according to Preckler: "Soyez donc en moi, ô Jésus, vivez en moi, opérez en moi, former et figurez en moi vos états et vos mystères."[78]

---

[72] TG, 174–75.
[73] *État*, 151, referencing the theories of Dom O. Casel in Th. Filthaut, *Die Kontroverse über die Mysterienlehre* (Warendorf, 1947). See also L. Bouyer, *La vie de la liturgie: une critique constructive du mouvement liturgique* (Paris: Éditions du Cerf, 1956), 115ff.
[74] Bérulle, *OP*, 129, cols. 1161–1162, quoted in *État*, 173. See also 173–78.
[75] *État*, 151–53.
[76] Ibid., 162.
[77] *OP* 17, 2, cols. 940–41, quoted in *État*, 165.
[78] *Elévation à Jésus* (1625), no. 12, 530, quoted in *État*, 162.

Preckler thought that Bérulle's emphasis on abnegation prevented any dangers in this form of spirituality.[79]

Maritain's Critique of Bérulle's Ideals Surrounding Character and State

Maritain, two years after the publication of Dupuy's work on Bérulle and priesthood, wrote on what he called "the notion of the priesthood that has been imposed for a long time now by the French School." He detailed what he considered Bérulle's key philosophical errors that contributed to then-current problems facing the priesthood.[80] It is included in this study as it serves as an overarching critique against which any conclusion might be measured.

The first error he pointed to involved Bérulle's notion of *state*, which Maritain noted could mean various things, such as a functional state in society (military, medical, etc.), or an existential state (married or eremitical, for example). Maritain located a third meaning, that of the "existential state of the human creature *in the Church and before God,*" whether applied to the Christian in terms of the human condition or to those who adopt it to help in progress toward divine union.

At this point the distinction between functional and existential states is of major importance for Maritain, who held that the sacerdotal state is a functional one insofar as it relates to the holy function of the priest who transmits the grace of sacraments, in contradistinction to the state of consecrated life, which he considered an existential state.

The slippage between these two definitions, Maritain asserted, was a problem for Bérulle, whom he referred to as a "confused mystical Platonist" and whom he saw being influenced by Pseudo-Dionysius, as well as by the need to bolster the self-consciousness of the sanctity of the clergy by virtue of their office or mission.[81] Maritain defended his interpretation: "their spirituality must consist above all in losing their own subsistence in order to live solely in the Person of Christ, who never ceases to draw them into the unity of the divine Person." He pointed to Bérulle's phrase already cited, "Le Fils les tire…dans l'unité de sa divine Personne, les faisant ses membres."[82]

---

[79]   *État*, 166.

[80]   Jacques Maritain, "Apropos of the French School," in *Untrammeled Approaches*, trans. Bernard Doering, with a preface by Ernst R. Korn (a pseudonym for Heinz R. Schmitz) (Notre Dame, IN: University of Notre Dame Press, 1997), 424. Originally published as "À propos de l'école française," *Revue thomiste* (1971): 463–79. This review follows the author's exposition closely.

[81]   Ibid., 424–25.

[82]   Ibid., 427, quoting Bérulle, *OP* 87, no. 2. See footnote 8. See also *BLS*, 195n1.

While Maritain agreed with Bérulle's insistence on the holiness toward which a priest must aim, he insisted that Bérulle was seriously mistaken in making what he saw as an imperceptible step from affirming the perfection to which a priest is called in order to exercise his function, to affirming a perfection of the state of life conferred at the same time as his sacramental powers. This state, as we have outlined, according to Bérulle, was superior to the religious state and made the priest the source of all sanctity in the Church, and a member of Christ's own sacerdotal order.[83]

Maritain continued his appraisal of Bérulle's notions surrounding the priest, quoting Dupuy: "He [the priest] cannot be defined as a superchristian. *For he is not just that.* But it is urgent that he be at least that."[84] Dupuy continued, "The priest is united to Christ more than as an instrument, he is conjoined to Him, he is not only in His hand, he is in a sense His hand itself; he is a member of Christ."[85]

The basis of the superiority of Bérulle's sacerdotal state was, as Maritain continued, that "the sacerdotal anointing emanates from that of Jesus,[86] who (and this is the thesis dearest to Bérulle) is a priest because of and as a direct consequence of the hypostatic union…"[87]

Maritain also commented on Dupuy's interpretation that Bérulle held that it is sacerdotal character by which the priest is consecrated to God rather than by vows, as is the case with religious.[88] Maritain objected to the idea of a kind of concomitant sacerdotal "state of sanctity" with the rebuttal that the nature of the indelible character holds even in hell, making a link between sanctity and priesthood all the more dubious.[89] Maritain suggested that Bérulle confused sacerdotal character with sacerdotal grace.[90] Bérulle himself noted the same permanence in hell, insisting that this fact supported the idea of the stability of the sacerdotal state: "Et c'est un état au service du sacerdoce du Christ; c'est un état qui puise sa stabilité dans la consécration du Christ qui s'est consacré des

---

[83]   Ibid., 427n5 and 7. See Cochois, *Bérulle et l'école française*, 26 (who, in turn, cited *CB*, vol. 1, 118).

[84]   *BLS*, 190 [*sic*] [200], quoted in English only, "Apropos of the French School," 427. Italics are Maritain's.

[85]   *BLS*, 195n1. See *OP* 87, no. 2, quoted in Maritain, "Apropos of the French School," 428n10. Maritain clarified that they are not members in the sense that Christians are members of the Mystical Body, but "*members* of His divine Person itself."

[86]   Maritain, "Apropos of the French School," 428. See *BLS*, 189.

[87]   Ibid., 428.

[88]   Maritain, "Apropos of the French School," 428. See *BLS*, 191.

[89]   *BLS*, 192. See *OR* 22, no. 3.

[90]   Ibid., 429.

prêtres; c'est un état solide et stable, au point qu'il dure pour l'éternité: 'pretre pour toujours', au point qu'il continue même en enfer…"[91]

Maritain listed the ideas that suggested this confusion: the sacerdotal consecration as the same as that of the consecration of Christ radiating on the priest; the idea of conjoined instruments; the fact that the priest must "enter into the person of Jesus, not only to celebrate Mass, but during the whole of his life."[92] Maritain asserted that the grace of priesthood that Bérulle conceived was that which emanated "from the priesthood of Christ into the soul of the priest like a ray of the hypostatic union," something which can be lost.[93]

Maritain then cited the Thomistic theologians De Vio and John of St. Thomas as holding (with Aquinas) that it is by reason of his capital grace as head of the Church, not the grace of union (as Bérulle held), that Christ possesses priesthood.[94] He critiqued Garrigou-Lagrange for his opinion that it is the hypostatic union which constitutes the basis for Christ as both priest and Mediator.[95] Maritain's argument is complex and deserves repetition:

> I think this theological thesis must be flatly rejected. It forgets that Christ IS first Mediator *in His very being* as the Incarnate Word, or as Man-God, before ACTING as such; for "to be a priest" is to have the power to exercise a meditating action and, above all else, to offer sacrifice. Hence it is *radically* by reason of the substantial grace of the hypostatic union, by reason of that fact that through this grace He is man, but it is *proximately* and formally by reason of His capital grace—of the grace of the virtues and the gifts (understood in as much as He is head of the Church) which is present in His soul in limitless fullness—that Christ is the priest of the new and eternal alliance, just as it is proximately by virtue of this grace of the virtues and the gifts that He does all that He does.
>
> Christ is mediator in *His very being* by reason of the substantial grace of the hypostatic union. And He is mediator *in His action* by reason of the infinite sanctifying grace that reigns in His soul; it is in virtue of this

---

[91] *BLS, OR* 15, no. 2, 290–91.

[92] *BLS*, 119, quoted in Maritain, "Apropos of the French School," 429–30.

[93] Maritain, "Apropos of the French School," 430.

[94] Ibid., 430.

[95] Ibid., 431. See Réginald Garrigou-Lagrange, *Le Sauveur et son amour pour nous* (Paris: Éditions du Cerf, 1933), 190–93. Maritain emphasized that Garrigou-Lagrange wrote with some hesitation, in the form of an opinion only.

personal grace—which is also His capital grace—that He carried out that work…[96]

Maritain also attempted to clarify the difference between the mediation of Christ and that of the co-redemption of all Christians who participate in Christ's priesthood and who are called to apply his merits. Citing Aquinas, only Christ's mediation is perfective (bringing about as its proper term union with God), while others are dispositive (in the case of the laity) or ministerial and functional (in the case of priests).[97]

He then detailed how the priesthood of priests is related to the priesthood of Christ, which is derived formally and directly from his capital grace. The anointing that the priest receives conveys both the grace of priesthood (as a modality of habitual grace, and calling for actual graces) and the character and accompanying powers. He is a non-conjoint instrument. But, Maritain continued, if one holds to the priesthood of Christ as coming formally and directly from the substantial grace of the hypostatic union, one with the Word, then the priest is a conjoined instrument, his hand the same as the Divine hand. Maritain asks, "How can any clear and precise theology of priesthood be constructed on such a basis? The priest's person must be replaced by the person of Christ such that the priest must lose his own subsistence. This results in being transpersonalized, and this is the reason that the sacrament puts him in a state of sanctity. He is an incomplete priest only until he reaches immanent sanctity…"[98]

Maritain, however, insisted that he did not attribute this theology to Bérulle because not only did his ideas lack the precision of a systematic theology, but he even attempted to avoid it. Maritain said that Bérulle and his followers perhaps found repugnant the idea of submitting lofty spiritual ideals regarding the priesthood to theological reasoning out of some kind of humility. Unfortunately, concluded Maritain, they misplaced the true grandeur of the priesthood by introducing a number of false ideas, including the idea that the priest's is a loftier state than that of the laity and that he is an *alter Christus* not just on the altar but

---

[96] Ibid., 431. See footnote 30, in which Maritain remarked that there is only a distinction of reason between the personal and capital graces of Jesus.

[97] Ibid., 432n35 and 434. See Aquinas, *ST*, 3.26.1: "Ad primum ergo dicendum quod prophetae et sacerdotes veteris legis dicti sunt mediatores inter Deum et homines dispositive et ministerialiter: inquantum scilicet praenuntiabant et praefigurabant verum et perfectum Dei et hominum mediatorem. – Sacerdotes vero novae legis possunt dici mediatores Dei et hominum inquantum sunt ministri veri mediatoris, vice ipsius salutaria sacramenta hominibus exhibentes." See also Marie-Joseph Nicolas, *Théotokos, le mystère de Marie* (Paris, 1965), 189–90.

[98] Ibid., 434–435.

in all he does. Finally, Maritain suggested that the vagueness and voluntarism of these ideals assisted in allowing them to remain in vogue for three centuries.[99]

Maritain argued, as well, on behalf of the notion of a holy function and functional mediation, noting that Bérulle, on the contrary, held it to be an existential state.[100] It is not clear whether Maritain was aware of Aquinas' notions surrounding objective holiness, but his point is well taken and expressive of the idea that Bérulle held to a kind of essentialist change in the priest himself.

Maritain's support of this claim was based on Bérulle placing the priest inside the person of Christ at all times from a sacerdotal anointing emanating as a consequence of the hypostatic union.

Balthasar's Major Critique of the Metaphysics of the Oratory

In addition to pointing to Bérulle's pious theologizing, Balthasar devoted a section of his essay on Bérulle to the metaphysics of the Oratory, in which he described (as already noted) its theology as rooted in the fundamental relation of the *analogia entis*, expressed in creatures by *religio*. The immensity of God's grandeur is juxtaposed to the essential nothingness of creatures. The God-Man Jesus Christ is the bridge between God's absolute glory and our humanity. He wrote: "Ontologically and psychologically, he is the full reality of analogy." Calling Bérulle prudent and circumspect, he also wrote that Bérulle answered the question of how what is temporal in Jesus becomes eternal. By inventing the idea of "state," Bérulle expressed both the act of Christ's adoration and the ontological aspect as God-Man. "State" denoted for Bérulle the "psychological and existential dimension of Jesus' ontological reality; constantly and precisely, his actions reveal his being."[101]

Balthasar pointed to Odo Casel's version of the "theology of the mysteries" as integrating the states of human life into the state of the God-Man. Balthasar compared Bérulle to Eckhart, who emphasized that the love of God is always "now" and grounded in the eternal processions. Bérulle thought of the life of faith as a participation in the ontological and psychological state of the "perfect adorer." In this belief, Bérulle gave a metaphysical foundation to the Pauline concept of the indwelling Christ by faith. Balthasar asserted that Bérulle removed what he called the poison of the Platonism of Eckhart and Rusbroec, which held that the creature lives more in its divine idea.

---

[99] Ibid., 424–27.

[100] Ibid., 424–25 and 439.

[101] Balthasar, *The Glory of the Lord*, 119–21. This review follows the author's exposition closely.

Balthasar admitted, however, that his metaphysics neglected the ethics of the love of neighbor.[102]

For Bérulle, Balthasar continued, the creature was to become a "pure relation" to God. He must "relate to Christ in a way analogous to the relation of his anhypostatic human nature to His divine person." Balthasar noted that Condren, Bérulle's disciple, went even further by comparing sacrificed man to the accidents of bread and wine, with Christ becoming our substance, a notion this analysis has highlighted as already present in Bérulle's spiritual theology of priesthood. Balthasar asserted that Bérulle held this "identification of God with being" as an inheritance of the German mystics where the "essential work," the birth of God, was the beginning of all external works of evangelization. However, in the French School, Balthasar saw a preoccupation with personal encounter, resulting in Catholic openness to the world actually decreasing.[103]

Balthasar's position that Bérulle's thought was rid of the poison of a certain Platonism does not hold in the light of this analysis. Of note, however, is the fact that Balthasar wrote his opinions before the publication of Dupuy's analysis of Bérulle's unpublished texts and that of Preckler's study of Bérulle's notion of states.

Conclusion

The state of the hypostatic union, which Bérulle considered beyond the orders of nature, grace, and glory, formed the basis for Bérulle's emphasis on the stability and perfection of the clerical state. Christ's humanity was deified, and through the absence of its own subsistence and in a state of servitude, realized the highest mystical state. In an *état de vie voyagère*, nevertheless, Christ was in the state of glory from the first moment of the Incarnation, thus allowing all the states of his life a permanent irradiation of the virtues of each mystery to each soul. Christians and priests were to imitate Christ and could, therefore, be in a state of sonship.[104]

Union by conformity became, with Bérulle, indwelling by mystical subsistence. Not only did the thinking of divine ideas transform the soul by the working of God as the moving and forming power, following Ficino, it became the divine idea of Christ himself living again through the believer, and especially the priest.

---

[102]   Ibid., 121–24.
[103]   *État*, 255–257.
[104]   Ibid., 255–57.

In the next chapter, we will explore how the priest was to accomplish and maintain this nihilistic union in Christ through adoration and adherence, both themes echoing Reformist themes.

Chapter 16
Sursum Corda

Introduction

This chapter will explore how Bérulle reacted to the debates surrounding sanctification with the notions of adoration and adherence. Constructing an adoration by annihilation, Bérulle took notions from various thinkers to form Christian and sacerdotal spiritual theologies based on an essentialist relation maintained through prayer. In terms of the Oratorian, adoration and adherence were necessary for a full participation in Christ's priesthood as holy mediators of redemption and holiness.

Adoration

Background

According to Orcibal, Bérulle's spirituality emphasized adoration as a defense of the Eucharist. Bérulle insisted that, as a result of the Incarnation, Christ had incorporated himself into humanity in order to found a religion based on the adoration of this mystery.[1]

Dupuy noted that, for Bérulle, the Incarnation was the adoration that Christ gave to the Father, a state honoring both the union and the relations between them. This adoration is extended in the Eucharist by priests who are the instruments of this adoration. While Trent had emphasized the Mass as a sacrifice, in reaction to the Reformers, Bérulle wanted to include the idea of supplication described in the Letter to the Hebrews, and so he gave adoration and praise first place. Dupuy raised the question of whether Bérulle had been influenced by the Reformers' position that sacrifice is only praise in the heart of the believer. He answered in the negative, noting that Bérulle's conception was focused on praise as the work of Christ, present in the Eucharist.[2]

Bérulle's conceptualization of adoration in this polemical effort, linking it to the notions of adherence and participation, was unique and had as its main aim

---

[1]   See Orcibal, *Le cardinal de Bérulle*, 59–61.
[2]   *BLS*, 128–29.

the defense of the need for a ministerial priesthood, both in terms of the sacraments and in governance, and took its main foundation the Reformist accent on sacrifice as personal praise.

Balthasar described what he called the first obligation of the creature to honor God, according to Bérulle:

> This primordial act does not originate in the creature's free deliberation and self-reflection, but is the response of homage to God's will for glorification…He "makes our soul adore the divine majesty, not only by its own thoughts and affections but also by the operation of His divine Spirit, who acts in our spirit, and makes it bear and feel the power and sovereignty of His being over all created beings…"[3]

For Bérulle, the adoration of both the Christian and the priest is only possible inside the adoration of Christ. To understand Bérulle's ideals surrounding adoration and adherence, a review of Reformers' notions surrounding participation, justification, and sanctification is warranted.

Luther's Objection, Trent's Response, and Bérulle's System

Luther had dismissed the Augustinian notion that justification is based on an internal righteousness, infused by God, insisting rather that the Passion of Christ alone justified sinners, according to Koerner. In terms of adherence, Luther considered that the Reformers were restoring apostolic purity by adherence to God's word.[4]

Trent followed tradition in seeing justification as both an event and a process.[5]

However, these questions remained at the time of Bérulle as he attempted, with his new system of spirituality for both laity and priests, to demonstrate, against the French Huguenots, how sanctification occurred through union with the perfect adorer, Christ, both in the sacrifice of the Mass and as a result of personal and frequent prayer.

Bérulle met Reformist critiques with the creation of a spiritual theology of priesthood based on sacrifice and adoration both in the Mass and in the life of

---

[3]   Balthasar, *The Glory of the Lord*, 119–20, also quoting Bérulle, Migne ed., cols. 1417–18: "Or une des opérations de Dieu, est de faire que notre âme adore la majesté divine, non seulement par ses propres pensées et affections; mais aussi par l'opération de son esprit divin, qui agit dans notre esprit, et lui fait porter et sentir la puissance et souveraineté de son être sur tout être créé…"

[4]   Koerner, *The Reformation of the Image*, 385.

[5]   McGrath, *Reformation Thought*, 113–16.

the priest. Key notions surrounding Calvin and Calvinist polemics regarding the Eucharist would be his points of departure.

Calvin and Reformed Theology

A central question for the Reformers was whether the Eucharist provides what faith alone cannot. In other words, whether the sacraments are insignificant.[6] Key to the Reformers' questioning was the rejection of the notion that we receive the benefits of Christ's death through the actions of a priest.[7]

Sursum Corda

Using the idea of raising hearts and minds to Christ on high in glory as an argument against transubstantiation, Calvin saw himself firmly in the tradition of St. Augustine, as well as the Council of Nicaea in its call to avoid fixing attention on symbols.[8]

Central to the Reformed Church's rejection of transubstantiation was not what happens to the elements, but rather what happens to us.[9]

As detailed, Bérulle met what he perceived as an attack against the real presence and the Mystical Body with the notion of Christ as subsistent religion, with the believer inside the adoration of Christ himself. This grafting onto Christ encompassed the notion of sanctification through participation in the mysteries of the life of Christ, not just at the Mass, but also through adoration in everyday life. This became central, as well, in Bérulle's spiritual theology of priesthood.

Faith as Firm and Sure Knowledge

Calvin defined faith as firm and sure knowledge.[10] Calvin also insisted that Christ cleaves to *us* rather than we to him. Calvin: "[not] only does he cleave to us by an

---

6   Gordon E. Pruett, "A Protestant Doctrine of the Eucharistic Presence," *Calvin Theological Journal* 10 (November 1975): 142–43.

7   Ibid., 153.

8   Jack Kinneer, "Calvin's Use of the Sursum Corda," *Roots of Reformed Worship* (November 1998): n.pp.

9   Mackenzie, in Mackenzie and Kiesling, "Reformed and Roman Catholic Understandings of the Eucharist," 74. Mackenzie wrote that what was central was "…the transformation of our humanity in the life, death, and Resurrection of Jesus Christ. In the Spirit on the Lord's day we participate in that conversion."

10 Calvin, *Institution*, 3.22.7: "Maintenant nous avons une entière définition de la foy, si nous déterminons que c'est une ferme et certaine cognoissance de la bonne volonté de Dieu

indivisible bond of fellowship, but with a wonderful communion, day by day, he grows more and more into one body with us, until he becomes completely one with us."[11]

In contrast, for Bérulle, the duty of religion was to adore God through Christ through adherence, slavery, and incorporation.[12]

We would argue that Calvin's concept of a firm and sure knowledge, fundamental to Calvin's conceptualization of predestination, found echoes in Bérulle's method of frequent prayer that could guarantee and maintain a firm and sure union with Christ. Notably, the echo was of a kind of grafting referred to by Reformers.

Bérulle and Adoration by Annihilation

Bérulle was familiar with Harphius, who had defined adoration as "Adorare est ad Deum, qui solus est adorandus, tota mentis intentione tendere."[13] According to Dupuy, this *mentis intentio* was realized in Bérulle's vow of servitude.[14] Dupuy asked how Bérulle conceived of the union with God that results from adoration. Bérulle used an oft-cited passage from St. Paul: "Qui adhaeret Domino, unus spiritus est" (I Cor 6:17). This *adherence* in Bérulle's time, in *La perle*, as well as according to Canfield, was that of the union of wills, as detailed. For Bérulle, this took the form of the movement of the will that results from adoration: "Par la connaissance, l'âme en la terre possède Dieu, non pas tel qu'il est en lui-même, mais tel qu'il est en elle…par l'amour, l'âme possède Dieu dès la terre, tel qu'il est en lui même…l'amour nous transporte de nous en lui en nous déifiant, en nous transformant en Dieu."[15]

Continuing with Dupuy's analysis, for Bérulle, the soul must use all its powers to annihilate itself in God, giving it the capacity for God, as we have explored.[16] The key text in parsing how Bérulle saw *anéantissement* as an effort at adoration

---

envers nous; laquelle, estant fondée sur la promesse gratuite donnée en Iesus Christ est révélée à nostre entendement, et séellée en nostre cœur par le sainct Esprit."

[11] Calvin, *Institutes* (1960), 3.2.24, quoted in Tan, "Calvin's Doctrine of Our Union with Christ," 7. *Institution*: "Et non seulement adhère à nous par un lien indissoluble, mais par une conionction admirable et surmontant nostre entendement il s'unist iournellement de plus en plus à nous en une mesme substance."

[12] See Mersch, *The Whole Christ*, 533.

[13] Hendrik Herp, *Theologiae mysticae libri tres*, 1 (Cologne, 1611), 2.85, quoted in *BSA*, 61.

[14] *BSA*, 61.

[15] Ibid., 63. See 64. Bérulle, *Grandeurs* 9, no. 1, col. 318.

[16] *OP* 158, quoted in *BSA*, 74.

is the following: "Il faut mourir par homage à l'Être immuable…adorant son Être par notre *néant*."[17]

In the case of the Rheno-Flemish, the will was considered one of the powers proceeding from the *fond*. Likewise in *La perle*, the *fond* or depth of the soul became "essence" or "spirit," with God as its center, with three powers in the *fond* underneath which God resides and where man could be united to him. To enter this *fond*, one must annihilate the three powers of memory, intelligence, and will. Bérulle was not interested in this schema.[18] Important to this study, for Bérulle, God is not at the center of the soul, but rather sin is. For Bérulle, the human person is corrupted by original sin in his *fond*, or as he expressed it, *quasiment* in his essence. He wrote: "La creature a une imperfection quasi-comme essentielle en qualité de chose créée, se joignant si facilement à ce qui est créé."[19]

Dupuy defended the vows of servitude as the expression of a completely engaged will. He framed Bérulle's adoration in terms of the notion of continual creation. In every instance, the creature adores a God who is always loving.[20]

Returning once again to Bérulle notion of adoration by state, Dupy described it as a kind of mystical state to which the vows disposed. However, this state was more of a juridical one (a state of religion) and became the idea that to adore by state is more or less to adore by being. In his *Grandeurs de Jésus*, for example, the two expressions are hardly distinguishable.[21]

Bérulle wrote, attempting to describe a kind of adoration deeper than the action of the will:

> Les anges adoraient bien au ciel par les actions de leur entendement et volonté, mais non pas de cette sorte d'adoration, dont nous parlons, qui est bien différente…qui n'est pas simplement émanante des facultés de l'esprit et dépendante de ses pensées; mais qui est solide, permanente et indépendante de ses puissances et des actions et qui est vivement imprimée dans le fond de l'être créé et dans la condition de son état.[22]

Bérulle wrote of this essential relation of the creature's movement toward God: "Dieu, créant et formant tout choses, les réfère et les rapporte toutes à soi-même, (ce) qui est un movement inséparable de la création même, et inséparable aussi

---

17   Bérulle, Archives nationales, M 233, 170 A, quoted in *BSA*, 76.

18   *BSA*, 79.

19   *OP* 150, quoted in *BSA*, 77n4. Dupuy noted that Bérulle was not willing to commit to an essential imperfection, which would be unorthodox.

20   *BSA*, 113–15.

21   Ibid., 129–30.

22   Bérulle, *Grandeurs*, 11, no. 6, quoted in *BSA*, 139.

de la créature, et un mouvement si vivement imprimé dans l'être de la créature par la puissance du Créateur, qui lui est plus intime que son être propre."[23]

Neoplatonism, then, according to Dupuy, allowed Bérulle to think of adoration as an act of the spirit rather than an act of the faculties of the spirit: an act of adoration in the center of one's soul. For Bérulle, only by the conversion of spirit was there true adoration, which is permanent, and which involves a "permanent movement."[24]

Bérulle frequently referred to the hierarchy of the states of life, whether mineral, vegetable, animal, or spiritual. The adoration and service of God by state, for Bérulle, consisted in a new kind of life. Following Plotinus, where reason is found even outside the activity of the intelligence, and where all being contemplates, Bérulle conceived of adoration by state as an intelligible relation to God and as a movement of the soul towards God.[25] This life was also an act of being, according to Dupuy. Bérulle held to the formula "Comme l'âme est la vie du corps, ainsi l'esprit de Dieu est la vie de l'âme…et est non seulement infus de Dieu, mais Dieu-même."[26] Bérulle cited as an example Mary, who was given a perpetual inclination towards Jesus and an elevated state as well as an elevated nature. She possessed a love which was imprinted in her essence and in her nature.[27]

Dupuy pointed to Bérulle's following influences he traced to Duns Scot: the conception of the *ens commune* as either that of God or of creatures and the mode of existing as not important, whether limited or unlimited, substantial or accidental, given that Bérulle concentrated on the idea of essence more than that of existence.[28]

---

[23] Bérulle, *OP* 123, quoted in *BSA*, 140.

[24] *BSA*, 140–41. See Bibliothèque nationale 25066 (165 A), 17.

[25] Ibid., 142. See Plotinus, A. H. Armstrong, and Porphyrius Neoplatonicus, "On Nature and Contemplation and the One," in *Plotinus*, vol. 3 (London: William Heinemann, 1967), 8.8, 384: "Ταῦτα μὲν οὕτω. Τῆς δὲ θεωρίας ἀναβαινούσης ἐκ τῆς φύσεως ἐπὶ ψυχὴν καὶ ἀπὸ ταύτης εἰς νοῦν καὶ ἀεὶ οἰκειοτέρων τῶν θεωριῶν γιγνομένων καὶ ἑνουμένων τοῖς θεωροῦσι καὶ ἐπὶ τῆς σπουδαίας ψυχῆς πρὸς τὸ αὐτὸ τῷ ὑποκειμένῳ ἰόντων τῶν ἐγνωσμένων ἅτε εἰς νοῦν σπευδόντων, ἐπὶ τούτου δηλονότι ἤδη ἓν ἄμφω οὐκ οἰκειώσει, ὥσπερ ἐπὶ τῆς ψυχῆς τῆς ἀρίστης, ἀλλ᾽ οὐσίᾳ καὶ τῷ ταὐτὸν τὸ εἶναι καὶ τὸ νοεῖν εἶναι."

[26] *OP* 153, quoted in *BSA*, 143. Dupuy noted in footnote 51 that these were not the terms of Aquinas (*ST*, 1–1.110.1 and 2), but rather those of Augustine (*City of God*, 19, 26). Dupuy also noted that Pétau would expound on the subject and in a less than happy manner.

[27] *BSA*, 144–45.

[28] Ibid., 175. See footnote 13. See Étienne Gilson, *Jean Duns Scot, Introduction à ses positions fondamentales* (Paris: Vrin, 1952), 105n1.

Bellemare's Critique

In Bellemare's treatment of ontology in Berullism, the central question was that of the nature of the divine essence, which Bérulle emphasized. Bellemare asked whether Bérulle's was an ontology or a henology.[29] Bellemare referenced, in turn, Gilson's analysis of Plotinus' thought in which the One and the Good is identified with the being of the Christian God, thus transposing the emanation of the many from the One into the Christian emanation of beings from the one Being. Bellemare argued that Bérulle's was rather the God of the Bible. Dupuy, in turn, argued that Bérulle's thought could not be strictly characterized in regard to either.

Dupuy also wrote that immutability was one of the most important divine attributes for Bérulle, who held it as a requirement for adoration: the states of Jesus, therefore, must be constant and unchanging.[30]

So, too, for his Oratorians.

Adoration and Priesthood

By way of background, we first review some key Christological concepts from which Bérulle drew in linking the adoration of the humanity of Christ and the priesthood.

As Dupuy described, Bérulle, as a Scotist, did not separate creation and Incarnation, holding that humanity was created in order to conform to the image of Christ: "Il le rend souverain entre ses oeuvres, et, lui étant le seul Dieu éternel, invisible et universel, il le met comme un Dieu temporel, visible et particulier au milieu de ses oeuvres."[31] Bérulle would emphasize adoration as the means to achieve this conformity.

Important to this study, as already referenced in our treatment of McKay, Bérulle was criticized for holding that the humanity of Jesus was united to the divine essence instead of to the person of the Word.[32] We would argue that in this, Bérulle hoped to create a closer link between both the Christian and the priest with Christ.

---

[29]   Ibid., 178–79. See Bellemare, *Le sens de la créature*, 93–94, referencing Étienne Gilson, *L'être et l'essence* (Paris: Vrin, 1948), 41–42.

[30]   Ibid., 199–200.

[31]   *BSA*, 195–96. See *Grandeurs*, 11, 367. See also 195n18 on this Scotist conception, widespread in theological education in the early seventeenth century.

[32]   Ibid., 198n25. Dupuy argued Bérulle was merely thinking abstractly.

Referencing the immutability of God, both as divine attribute and in terms of temporal presence, Bérulle looked to the states of Jesus, which were considered to last forever and to have the immutability that adoration requires, according to Dupuy. For Bérulle, these states remain always present in their efficaciousness (for example, the passion and the wounds of the risen Christ).[33] Bérulle:

> Jésus donc porte ainsi en soi-même un état regardant et adorant son état éternel…Car nous parlons d'une adoration qui est par état, et non par action; d'une adoration qui n'est pas simplement émanante des facultés de l'esprit, et dépendante de ses pensées; mais qui est solide, permanente et indépendante des puissances et des actions, et qui est vivement impimée dans le fond de l'être créé et dans la condition de son état.[34]

One issue for Bérulle was the obstacle of multiplicity. Annihilation by abnegation was to negate multiplicity by a return to interior unity.[35] As already noted, Bérulle turned to the metaphysical idea of subsistence to justify this abnegation: taking the *dénouement* of the human subsistence of Christ and applying it to the spiritual life. The consequence, according to Dupuy, was an invitation to renounce one's will, as did Christ, moving a metaphysical category to a psychological category.[36] This renunciation also required an extreme separation from the world and oneself, as noted.[37]

As Dupuy noted, only in union with the humanity of Christ is one led to annihilation.[38] He conveyed, "Comme l'humanité de Jésus n'a être, vie et subsistence qu'en la divinité, aussi nous ne devons avoir vie et subsistence qu'en son humanité et en sa divinité."[39]

Bérulle proposed the adoration of the humanity of Jesus as it subsisted in the Word, such that the human actions of Jesus were the actions of God: the Eternal Word "entre en possession de l'état, des actions et des souffrances de la nature humaine, pour en disposer selon son divin vouloir.."[40] Bérulle then related this to human actions: "Illius sacra humanitas erat instrumentum quo eius divinitas se manifestabat, ita in nobis actiones naturales debent velut medium esse, a quo

---

[33] Ibid., 200–201. See *Collationes*, Bibliothèque nationale, manuscript latin 18210, 285.
[34] Bérulle, Grandeurs, 11, 6, col. 364 (Migne ed.), cited in *BSA*, 201.
[35] *BSA*, 210.
[36] Ibid., 216–17.
[37] Ibid., 218. See Bérulle, Archives nationales, M 233, 75 B.
[38] Ibid., 218.
[39] *OP* 130, 4, quoted in *BSA*, 221.
[40] *BSA*, 225. See *Grandeurs*, 2, no. 11, col. 180.

gratia Dei et Spiritus Jesu Christi habitans in nobis se prodat."[41] Dupuy noted that in this belief Bérulle was incorrect, in that while our actions should manifest the divine indwelling, they are natural. Bérulle's was an attempt at adoration as an effort to reach the principle of the actions of Jesus.[42]

These ideals can be found in the way Bérulle expected his Oratorians to live the grace of priesthood by obtaining the same dispositions as Christ.[43]

How exactly were Oratorians to live out this grace of priesthood? The answer was an emphasis on adoration, focusing on relation. Dupuy explained this relationship. Bérulle held to the notion that Christ was not simply united to God, but was God, a notion based on the principle of his actions, rather than the actions themselves. Dupuy noted that this was a psychological approach that caused confusion. Morainvillier accused Bérulle of Monothelitism for having written of the humanity of Jesus "que sa vie, son état, ses mouvements et ses actions ne sont plus d'elle, ni à elle proprement."[44] Dupuy argued that, for Bérulle, the actions of Christ were not important but rather his being, and coming to know him and adore him as he is in himself.[45]

Dupuy wrote that in Scholastic terms, there was only a relation of reason between God and the humanity of Jesus. Bérulle concentrated on the relation between the Father and the Son, of which the humanity had a part. Adoration focused on this permanent relation.[46]

The question again presents itself whether there is an implied theandrism in Bérulle's notion of relation, and whether it made its way into Bérulle's spiritual theology of priesthood such that all the priest's actions became theandric.

---

41   *Collationes*, 102, quoted in *BSA*, 225.
42   *BSA*, 225n40.
43   Ibid., 225. Dupuy: "En fait, on retrouve objectivé et transposé au Christ un problème spirituel qui hante Bérulle depuis toujours, depuis en particulier que le *Bref Discours de l'Abnégation* s'essayait à isoler l'"apex mentis': Bérulle, comme tant d'autres, cherche à atteindre le niveau de l'âme où s'opère l'union à Dieu. Dans les *Collationes*, il insiste sur ce que les oratoriens ont activement à transformer en eux: le niveau le plus profond qu'il se propose d'atteindre est celui des 'dispositions'; car elles ont plus de valeur que les actes qui les manifestent…"
44   Louis de Morainvillier, *Réponse à un libelle diffamatoire sous le nom de l'ami de la verité* (Paris: Estienne, 1622), deuxième grief, quoted in *BSA*, 225n41 and 226.
45   *BSA*, 226.
46   Ibid., 227.

Adherence

Influence of La perle

Huijben had pointed to *La perle évangélique* as the source of Bérulle's notion of adherence, in particular the idea of adherence to the interior and exterior life of the Son, the leitmotiv of *La perle*. Molien summarized that the word *adherence* was frequently used in *La perle*,[47] and defined adherence as offering oneself to the action of the Word Incarnate, a heroic effort such that nothing of ourselves is left. Only then can Jesus thus imprint his states and effects in our souls, his mysteries, sufferings, and glory.[48] Following are two passages illustrating the similarities between Bérulle's thought and that of the author of *La perle*. Bérulle:

> Le premier de tous les mystères est celui de l'Incarnation, auquel chacune de vos âmes doit être particulièrement dédiée…Dans la vie (voyagère du Fils de Dieu), il y a la *vie intérieure* et la vie *extérieure*. L'*extérieure* c'est toutes les actions du Fils de Dieu, c'est toutes le actions du Fils de Dieu, ses souffrances, sa pauvreté et toutes les autres choses semblables, que vous honorez par vos exercices extérieurs. L'autre partie de la vie de Jésus est la *vie intérieure* qu'il avait sur la terre *vers Dieu son Père*…c'est de cette vie que vous devez vivre, ce doit être l'object continuel de vos âmes, qui doivent participer et adhérer à cette vie de Jésus-Christ, et recevoir de lui *participation aux pensées de sa bienheureuse âme* sur la terre…Il ne demande autre chose qu'à *reposer son esprit en vous*, car il l'y a mis, non afin que le vôtre vive, mais le sien seulement, et que vous soyez remplies et occupées de lui seul…Il faut que vous preniez en lui une vie nouvelle, imitant sa vie voyagère, afin qu'il vous rende dignes d'y participier, c'est à dire que vous fassiez les actions des vertus avec participation de l'esprit dans lequel Notre-Seigneur opérait les siennes…Soyez donc adhérantes et participantes à cette vie du Fils de Dieu.[49]

La perle:

> Quand nous iettons nostre volonté dans la volonté de Dieu…et nostre desir en son desir…at nostre intention dans l'intention de Dieu…ainsi veritablement nous sommes vestus de Iesus-Christ, et faisons et operons

---

[47] A. Molien, "Bérulle," in *DSAM*, vol. 1 (1937), cols. 1546–47. See also AS, 27: 122.
[48] Ibid., cols. 1564–65. See *OP* 78, col. 1054.
[49] Bérulle, *OC*, Migne ed., cols. 1309–11, quoted in AS, 27: 97–98.

toutes choses par luy…(mais) nous deuons non seulement nous occuper en l'humanité de Iesus-Christ, ains par les merites de l'humanité entrer dans la belle diuinité, à ce que puissons en nous sentir ce qui est en Iesus-Christ, en *esprit*, cést à sçauoir, en *ame* et en *corps*.[50]

Dupuy proposed that this was a voluntarist spirituality that found its theological basis in a certain Scholastic thesis regarding the nature of affective union, a thesis in which on earth the path of love, rather than knowledge, transformed the soul into God. According to Bérulle, "Par la connaissance, l'âme en la terre possède Dieu, non pas tel qu'il est en lui-même, mais tel qu'il est en elle…par l'amour, l'âme possède Dieu dès la terre, tel qu'il est en lui-même…l'amour nous transporte de nous en lui en nous déifiant, en nous transformant en Dieu."[51]

A Voluntarist Beatitude

Dupuy defended Bérulle's thesis as having first been formulated by Aquinas, who held that the love of God ranked before knowledge, with charity being more excellent than faith.[52] However, according to both Aquinas and John of St. Thomas, beatitude is constituted by an active intelligence, whereas Duns Scot held it to be an act of the will.[53] Bérulle's logic consisted in the fact that if union

---

[50]   Van Essche, Despont, De Mallery, and De La Nouë, *La perle*, 1, 1, ch. 43, fol. 84–85, quoted in AS, 27: 99.

[51]   *Grandeurs*, 9, no. 1, col. 318, quoted in *BSA*, 64.

[52]   *BSA*, 64n23. See Aquinas, *ST*, 2–2.23.6, co., in *Summa theologiae*, 8: 170: "Respondeo dicendum quod, cum bonum in humanis actibus attendatur secundum quod regulantur debita regula, necesse est quod virtus humana, quae est principium bonorum actuum, consistat in attingendo humanorum actuum regulam. Est autem duplex regula humanorum actuum, ut supra dictum est, scilicet ratio humana et Deus: sed Deus est prima regula, a qua etiam humana ratio regulanda est. Et ideo virtutes theologicae, quae consistunt in attingendo illam regulam primam, eo quod earum obiectum est Deus, excellentiores sunt virtutibus moralibus vel intellectualibus, quae consistunt in attingendo rationem humanam. Propter quod oportet quod etiam inter ipsas virtutes theologicas illa sit potior quae magis Deum attingit. Semper autem id quod est per se magis est eo quod est per aliud. Fides autem et spes attingunt quidem Deum secundum quod ex ipso provenit nobis vel cognitio veri vel adeptio boni, sed caritas attingit ipsum Deum ut in ipso sistat, non ut ex eo aliquid nobis proveniat. Et ideo caritas est excellentior fide et spe; et per consequens omnibus aliis virtutibus. Sicut etiam prudentia, quae attingit rationem secundum se, est excellentior quam aliae virtutes morales, quae attingunt rationem secundum quod ex ea medium constituitur in operationibus vel passionibus humanis."

[53]   Ibid., 64–65, citing Duns Scot, *In IV Sent.*, dist. 49, q. 4, in *Opera omnia*, Wadding ed. See especially q. 2, n. 20: "Dico igitur ad quaestionem, quod beatitudo simpliciter est

in heaven is a deification based on the will, this same deification can take place on earth. Dupuy expanded on Canfield's thought, explaining that he held to the ideal of God's essential will, identifying the will of God with God himself, as discussed. Dupuy saw this Scotism as giving a philosophical basis to a mystical theology that allowed for a union with the essential will of God, thus allowing deification.[54] As discussed, Dupuy also noted, arguably, that Bérulle was not claiming an essential adherence to the divine essence here on earth but rather an adherence to and a union with the divine will.[55] Dupuy argued that Bérulle did not fully embrace the idea of deification, but rather the transmutation of the will.[56]

Transfusion Rather than Imitation

As this study has explored, the fundamental idea of Berullism was that of Christ living in us, which was to be accomplished through adherence.[57] Adherence, for Bérulle, was tied closely with the notion of imitation.

According to de Certeau, the theme of imitation predominated in terms of devotion to Christ in the works of sixteenth-century humanists.[58] Bérulle's version of imitation required Christians to make a constant effort to conform their interior life to the interior life of Jesus, according to Cognet. This effort was to result not simply in an imitation of Christ but rather in a transfusion into his being. By doing so, the soul participates "in a way" in the hypostatic union.[59]

Adherence and the Priesthood

As Cognet explained, for the priest, it meant the obligation to enter into a special state of adherence to Christ who communicated to him his priesthood, making him a mediator.[60]

Bérulle invited Oratorians to adhere to and to honor Jesus Christ in his public acts as preacher and miracle worker, and in his conversations. As noted, they were to adhere to the interior states of his public life through the dispositions of

---

essentialiter et formaliter in actu voluntatis, quo simpliciter et solum attingitur bonum optimum, quo perfruatur."
[54] Ibid., 65. See Benet Canfield, *La règle de perfection* (Paris, 1608).
[55] Ibid., 67. See *Collationes*, manuscrit latin 229, June 1614, Bibliothèque nationale.
[56] Ibid., 65–67.
[57] *TM*, 68 and 107–8.
[58] De Certeau, "La réforme dans le catholicisme," 203–4.
[59] Louis Cognet, *Post-Reformation Spirituality*, 70–73.
[60] Cognet, *La spiritualité moderne*, 358.

their souls, in a stable manner. In this, Bérulle compared the stability of union with Christ to the beatific vision of the saints.[61] This adherence was to be accomplished by means of the liturgical cycle, through the various feasts honoring the events of Christ's life.[62] Bérulle: "et puisque nous [Oratorians] faisons profession spéciale d'adhérer à Jésus, comme prêtres de Jésus, avons soin de rechercher cette science de Jésus, de recevoir de cet esprit de Jésus, de nous conformer aux desseins et voies de Jésus."[63]

While all Christians have as objects of faith and piety the three unities (of the Trinity in God, the humanity and the divinity of Christ, and the virginity with the maternity of the Virgin), Oratorian superiors were to adhere not simply to Jesus Christ but to the unity of the essence of the Trinity and the fecundity of the divine persons in order for them to conceive the knowledge and love of God in souls, in honor and imitation of the divine processions:

> Adhérons à l'unité de son essence et à la fécondité de ses personnes pour concevoir l'esprit d'unité, de sapience, de charité et de fécondité sainte et spirituelle dans son Église…En la vertu et puissance de cette unité et fécondité, les supérieurs doivent être bénis et assistés d'une fécondité sainte et spirituelle, produisant et étendant la connaissance et l'amour de Dieu dans les âmes, en honneur et imitation des processions divines qui sont par amour et par connaissance.[64]

Conclusion

The Reformers objected to the Mass viewed as a work, another sacrifice in addition to Calvary. Bérulle turned to metaphysics to support his ideals surrounding both adoration and adherence in defense of the Mass and of the priest as sacrificer.

In terms of his defense of the priesthood, this meant an essentialist relation to Christ, one that appears to have been both a conversion of the inferior and a production by the superior.

Dupuy noted that for Bérulle, Christ's human actions became the actions of God. So, too, the priest's actions become those of Christ through a voluntarist spirituality emphasizing an affective union of the wills. Just as Dupuy noted that

---

[61] Blanchard, "La spiritualité christocentrique," 242–49.
[62] Gaston Rotureau, "États de Jésus," in *DSAM*, vol. 4, pt. 2 (1961), col. 1406.
[63] *OC, Discours de l'état et des grandeurs de Jésus* (1996), 385, *Mémorial*, 13.
[64] Ibid., 405–6, *Mémorial*, 33.

Bérulle viewed Christ's actions as not as important as his being, so the idea of the priest's being gained prominence. The spiritual technology of how the Oratorians were to accomplish this adherence and transfusion is the subject of the next chapter.

Chapter 17
The Vows of Servitude

Introduction

The notions of liberty, servitude, perfection, and vows came under scrutiny at the time of the Reform. Bérulle's vows of servitude were his attempt at a formation spirituality to bring priests into union and conformity with Christ and to achieve a kind of theopathic state. The following chapter highlights the debates, as well as the concepts Bérulle borrowed from a newly popularized *prisca theologia*, including theurgy, anagogy, and *sympatheia* in his system of spirituality for Oratorians based on vows of servitude.

The dynamic of relation, as Bérulle understood it, became the ideal behind of the vows of servitude.[1]

Background

Luther's Enslaved Will

Bérulle's answer to Luther's enslaved will, according to Vieillard-Baron, was to insist on the state of servitude in nature, grace, and in the hypostatic union. To honor Christ's servitude was to live in imitation of an ecstatic possession similar to that of Mary Magdalene.[2]

Dupuy noted that Bérulle's notions of servitude were based on the creature's dependence on continual creation. The vows of servitude for both Carmelite religious and Oratorian priests were serving Jesus and not the law, and represented a response as well to the Reformers' critique of the legalism of vows in general.[3]

---

[1]   *Subsistence*, 126. See *OP* 87 (1071), 905.
[2]   Jean-Louis Vieillard-Baron, "L'image de l'homme chez Descartes et chez le cardinal de Bérulle," *Revue philosophique de la France et de l'étranger* 182, no. 4 (Oct.–Dec. 1992): 415.
[3]   Dupuy, *Le Christ de Bérulle*, 54.

Calvin and Perfection

Calvin's goal, according to Fisk, was not to restore us to the changeable condition of Adam who was able not to sin, but to change the disposition of our nature by uniting our humanity to Christ. He quotes Calvin: "The original freedom was to be able not to sin; but ours is much greater, not to be able to sin."[4] This extraordinary confirmation in grace was a challenge that Bérulle met, we would argue, with a reinterpretation of the traditional states of perfection to emphasize how the priest, and the perfect in general, can maintain a stable state of holiness through a system of mental elevations, which had as their beginning the vows of servitude.

The Vows of Servitude

Confirmation in Grace and Covenant Theology

Protestant Reformers criticized vowed religious profession as being a kind of new baptism.[5] Bérulle avoided the idea of religious vows but did propose vows of servitude for both Oratorians and Carmelite nuns.

Bérulle's idea of a state of servitude was the basis for what Pourrat called his Christological spirituality.[6] Returning to the theme of liberty, his notion of rebirth in true liberty depended on servitude to God and Christ. The humanism of the Renaissance era, with its Stoic tendencies, gave a high regard to liberty, according to Pouliquen.[7] The themes of liberty, freewill, authority, and God's free and sovereign choice predominated in the Reform and beyond as well. Pouliquen noted that, while psychological liberty consisted in free choice, spiritual liberty, for Bérulle, depended on our acknowledgement of our dependence on God, our relation to Him, and our capacity to give ourselves to him and others, as we have

---

[4]   Calvin, *Institutes* (1960), 2.3.13; *CO* 30: 223: "Primam fuisse libertatem, posse non peccare: nostram multo maiorem, non posse peccare." Quoted in Philip Fisk, "Calvin's Metaphysics of Our Union with Christ," *International Journal of Systematic Theology* 11, no. 3 (July 2009): 324.

[5]   Dupuy, "Perfection," col. 1132. Dupuy referenced Confession d'Augsburg, art. 6, *De votis monachorum*, in Philip Melanchthon, *Confessio fidei exhibita…* (Witebergae: Rhau, 1530); Philipp Melanchthon, *Apologia confessionis* (n.p., 1541), 43.

[6]   P. Pourrat, *Christian Spirituality: Later Developments, From the Renaissance to Jansenism* (London: Burns, Oates and Washbourne Ltd., 1927), 333.

[7]   Tanguy Marie Pouliquen, *Renaître à la vraie liberté* (Toulouse: Éditions du Carmel, 2012), 7–12.

explored. This liberty was to be found in a relationship with the deified humanity of Christ, which could make us into the image of God, as we have also explored.[8]

Servitude and States

Aquinas had written on states of freedom or servitude, whether spiritual or civil. For Aquinas, spiritual servitude consists in being inclined to evil by habit or to good by the habit of justice. Man by nature is inclined to justice.[9] Bérulle, on the other hand, as detailed, regarded humanity as tending toward nothingness.

Morgain's Analysis of Bérulle's Political Theology and the Vows of Servitude

Morgain wrote on Bérulle's political theology not only in regard to his defense of the Church with the notion of the Mystical Body, but also in relation to the founding of the Oratory. Bérulle spoke of *homage* and *servitude* to Jesus and Mary, medieval expressions related to the submission of a vassal to a lord. These words, as well as the notions of kingship, dependence, and obedience, had their roots in the politics of his era, according to Morgain. Bérulle:

> Notre Congrégation ... reconnaît comme son Patron Jésus-Christ notre Seigneur. Mais son caractère particulier est qu'elle l'a choisi avec, en même temps, la très bienheureuse Marie toujours Vierge, sa Mère. C'est pourquoi, à la manière des courtisans qui viennent ensemble saluer leur Prince quotidiennement, qu'aucune journée ne se passe sans que nous nous présentions pour rendre hommage le plus humblement possible à Notre Seigneur Jésus-Christ.[10]

Bérulle wrote of three kinds of servitude: that of the essential servitude of all creatures (nature), that of servitude to Christ (grace), and a third kind to Jesus and Mary. Christ, sovereign over all humanity through the hypostatic union, reintroduced the City of God. Two perfect societies exist – that of the Trinity and that which the Word founds between humanity and the Trinity. One must honor Christ by a state of *anéantissement* and absolute dependence. All were to be bound in a relation of servitude.[11] Bérulle:

---

8   Ibid., 104–6.
9   Aquinas, *ST*, 2–2.183.
10 Bérulle in *OC, Conférences et fragments* (1995), piece dated November 11, 1611, 1, quoted in Morgain, *La théologie politique de Pierre de Bérulle*, 188–89. See 387 for Morgain's commentary.
11 Ibid., 202–13.

En ces deux sociétés, sont divinement fondées et établies toutes les sociétés du ciel et de la terre, de Dieu, des anges and des hommes, du temps et de l'éternité, car elles sont toutes établies, et pour figurer, comme des ombres et images, et pour adorer, comme servantes et tributaires, ces deux sociétés suprêmes et parfaites. Et toutes les sociétés malignes et illégitimes seront ruinées par la puissance de ses deux sociétés, et toutes celles qui seront légitimement établies en l'ordre de la grâce, de la nature et de la gloire, doivent tribute et hommage de servitude et de louange, et sont en état de relation, d'assujettissement et de dépendance à ces deux sociétés divines, de la très sainte Trinité et de l'Incarnation du Verbe.[12]

To refuse this relation of servitude was heresy, according to Bérulle.

Morgain held that with this schema, Bérulle was attempting to recover what he saw as a lost unity. Bérulle, writing on Protestantism:

Maudite hérésie qui a changé vos grandeurs en malheurs, votre gloire en ces opprobes, vos trophées en ces misères, vos triomphes en ces ruines. Funestre et infidèle hérésie qui, adultérant avec le sens humain et l'ambition des grands, a ruiné l'État et l'Église ensemble, qui, aux Français accoutumés à vaincre, leur apprend à être vaincus, et vaincus par eux-mêmes!…et naissant en la France au milieu d'une conjuration inflâme…rend les abois au milieu d'une conjuration prodigieuse, vouant ses glaives au sang des chrétiens, au saccagement de leurs villes, au sacrilege de leurs temples, aux ruines de l'État, à la desolation de l'Église et aux furies d'Énfer! …[13]

Cochois's Analysis of the Vows

In one of the most cogent summaries of Bérulle's project, Cochois wrote that in *Collationes congregationis nostrae*, Bérulle combined the Spanish devotion of slavery to Mary and Jesus, the *wesenmystique* of the Rheno-Flemish school, the mysticism of "aspiration" of the Franciscan School, and the theology of hierarchical mediation of Pseudo-Dionysius with the goal of putting in place for his Oratorians a *pati divina* so that God could operate in them, imprinting his states in the same way as the Thearchy radiates its perfections throughout the

[12] Ibid., 211, quoting Bérulle, *OC, Grandeurs* (1996), Discours 8, 335.
[13] Ibid., 213, quoting Bérulle, *Grandeurs, Dédicace au roi*, 18–19.

hierarchy.[14] As Brown noted, Oratorians could only become hierarchs, links in the redemptive chain, and capable of their mission if they participated in these vows of servitude.[15]

A Spirituality of Servitude

Cadoux on Oratorian Exemplarist Spirituality

Cadoux focused his study of Bérulle's exemplarism as based on the vows of servitude, the center of the spiritual program of the Oratorians.[16] Bérulle's early work showed the significant influence of the abstract school, which proposed direct contact with the essence of God without intermediary (including Christ), via a passivity that encompassed the senses, the intellect, and the will, and a self-annihilation that gained a complete absorption of the human will in the divine will, allowing for a permanent state of depersonalization. Cadoux called this an annihilation at the ontological level, characterized by a state of total servitude.[17] As of 1609, Bérulle began to see Christ as the perfect model of this servitude.[18]

Blanchard on the Christocentric Spirituality of the Oratorians

Blanchard treated the evolution of Bérulle's Christocentric sacerdotal spirituality, especially as found in his oral conferences.[19] Blanchard clarified how Bérulle's thought developed regarding the efficacy of the mysteries of the life of Christ in the life of the priest, and how it related to union with Christ. The souls of Oratorians must be tightly united with Christ through an interiorization of the interior actions of his soul and its mysteries. As Blanchard related, this concept of meditating on the states and mysteries later grew from being a simple intention or disposition into a continual operation of the soul. By rendering honor to Jesus at all times, from the first instant of his Incarnation, Oratorians could penetrate into a kind of lasting place within the interior of Jesus Christ.[20] For example,

---

[14] Paul Cochois, "Bérulle, initiateur mystique: les vœux de servitude," *École pratique des hautes études, section des sciences religieuses: Annuaire* (1958): 111–15.

[15] Roberta Brown, "Trinitarian Mechanisms: From Bérulle to Descartes," *Proceedings of the…Annual Meeting of the Western Society for French History* 12 (1984): 43.

[16] Cadoux, "Le Sacrement de l'Incarnation," 3.

[17] Ibid., 7–8.

[18] Cadoux, "Le Sacrement de l'Incarnation," 12.

[19] Blanchard, "La spiritualité christocentrique," 10–12.

[20] Ibid. See 20–47.

directing the Oratorians to meditate on Christ, Bérulle begins a meditation on the psychological state of Christ during His Passion, "O combien digne et estimable fut cette mémoire de la passion qu'eut l'âme du Christ dès ce premier instant qu'elle fut unie au corps."[21]

The Vows and Priesthood

Cochois on Priesthood and the Vows

Cochois wrote an expanded analysis of the vows in relation to Bérulle's ideal of sacerdotal life which is important to review. In order to re-establish the virtue and perfection of the priesthood, the origin of all holiness in the Church, Bérulle created a program of initiation.[22] His Oratorians were required to develop three dispositions in order to participate in the divine life: the removal of all obstacles to acting in conformity with grace, servitude and abnegation, and passivity. As Cochois wrote, they were to ratify through the vows their power, origin, and emanation in God, and their essential servitude through adoration and love so that the humanity of Christ would then recreate them and be the *lieu* of their divinization. As Cochois expressed it, quoting Bérulle, "à saisir qu'elle n'est possible pour nous, qui sommes 'creati in Christo Jesu,' qu'en cette humanité déifié et déifiante. Est le 'lieu' de notre divinisation. Pour 'renouveler par l'exercice de nos puissances le privilège de notre essence', il nous faut 'subsister' en elle."[23]

The vows would permit them to live the grace of their vocation. Christ alone is priest, and their role was to be his ministers by a special tie, conjoined to his ministry in a special manner, as already noted.[24] Bérulle wrote, "Nous ne sommes prêtres que pour autant que c'est lui qui l'est en nous. En aucune façon nous ne faisons nombre avec lui: 'Ipse sacerdos, nos ministri'."[25]

The vow to Jesus included the following language: "Je supplie l'âme sainte et déifiée de Jésus de daigner prendre par elle-même la puissance sur moi que je ne lui peux donner…et qu'elle me fasse être à elle et la servir non seulement par mes

---

[21] Ibid, 46, quoting Bérulle, Coll. 290 / March 6, 1612.

[22] Paul Cochois, "Les vœux de servitude et l'idéal de vie sacerdotal proposé par le Pére de Bérulle," *Oratoriana* 4 (Nov. 1961): 101. See *CB*, vol. 1, 118.

[23] Ibid., 103–9. See *CB*, vol. 3, 315, letter dated 1627, and *OP* 87.

[24] Ibid., 113. See *OP* 192, no. 2, col. 1270.

[25] Bérulle, Arch. De l'Oratoire, 1 bis, 12, 21, quoted in Cochois, "Les vœux de servitude," 113.

actions, mais encore par l'état et condition de mon être et de ma vie intérieure et extérieure."[26]

In becoming a slave, the priest could be a priest in his interior as well as exterior. According to Cochois, the ideal was that for one vowed in servitude, all activity became theandric, just as all acts of Christ were sacerdotal acts.[27]

Importantly, as Ocáriz, Seco, and Riestra noted, as a result of the influence of Pseudo-Dionysius, it had at one time become frequent for theologians to speak of the theandric actions of Jesus.[28] Arguably, Bérulle's emphasis on the Word Incarnate as Man-God, divinely human and humanly divine, pointed to a new kind of action.

The Vows and Mystical Possession

As Cochois explained, the particular affective mystical theology of the Rheno-Flemish School included the idea that one can raise oneself to God by the way of desire. Bérulle noted that his elevations were themselves prayers of desire. These prayers were not like Augustine's prayers of admiration but were, rather, technically specific. The formularies of the vows, which he later called elevations, were characterized by a double movement: the gift of self followed by the permission for Mary, Christ, or God to take mystical possession. As the purpose was to instill in Oratorians a permanent offering, they were encouraged to review their oblations daily.[29]

Bérulle's Christocentrism consisted in a transposition of Pseudo-Dionysius' idea of radiation by applying it to the deified humanity, as we have noted. Souls called to belong to the choirs of Jesus and Mary took on an eternal vocation as long as they maintained their dependence. Important to this study, Cochois

---

[26] Cochois, "Les vœux de servitude," 115. This quote was taken from the critical text of the vows of 1614 and 1615. Those that were included in the *Œuvres complètes* had been retouched in 1620 and 1622.

[27] Ibid., 115, 117.

[28] Ocáriz et al., *The Mystery of Jesus Christ*, 101. The authors referred to the error of Monoenergetism which spoke of "divine-human (theandric) actions of Jesus, in the sense of these actions not being regarded as divine and human but a new 'intermediary,' 'divine-human' type of action." See Pseudo-Dionysius, Epist. 4, 1072C, *CD* 161.7–10: "καὶ τὸ λοιπὸν οὐ κατὰ θεὸν τὰ θεῖα δπάσας, οὐ τὰ ἀνθρώπεια κατὰ ἄνθρωπον, ἀλλ' ἀνδρωθέντος θεοῦ, καινήν τινα τὴν θεανδρικὴν ἐνέργειαν ἡμῖν πεπολιτευμένος."

On another topic, the authors pointed to the error in which the adjectives of the divine nature are predicated of the concrete names of the human nature. It could be argued that this was an error into which Bérulle seems to have fallen in his ideal of Jesus as deified man. See 135.

[29] Cochois, "Bérulle et le pseudo-Denys," 187–88. See *Collationes*, 152–53.

asserted that in this program, Bérulle developed an idea of the psychological presence of the sacred humanity.[30]

Cochois also studied what he called Bérulle's Dionysian theology of priesthood in relation to his program of initiation.[31] A review of Cochois's analysis will be helpful in parsing Bérulle's ideals on how the priest is or should be a mediator.

Essential Servitude

In Bérulle's talks to his Oratorians, he urged them, in order to be fully priests, to be moved without ceasing by the Holy Spirit. The first step in this process was to ratify their radical dependence or "essential servitude" as creatures, with a passivity like Mary's as a slave to Christ as model. In Bérulle's system, however, Mary was not just a model, but also a mediator of mystical grace herself. Oratorians, as members of the choirs of Jesus and Mary, participated in relations with Jesus and the Father in a special way, changing their essential creaturely servitude into a mystical servitude. The Oratorians were to take vows of servitude in order to enter these choirs.[32]

In *Collationes*, Bérulle concentrated on the superiority of the priesthood to religious: that religious received their holiness from priests, and that priests were superior not only due to their powers, but also to their *science* of the things of God and their degree of divinization. The vows, then, were to elevate Oratorians to perfection through a mystical passivity, giving God power over the soul offered to him. In requiring this, Cochois noted, Bérulle associated the power of order closely to the holiness of the priest.[33]

Cadoux summarized the major and complex controversy that erupted over the vows of servitude, first due to Bérulle having required Carmels in France to make the vow to Mary a requirement. Cadoux summarized more recent scholarship than Yelle's regarding the incident involving a bad copy of the vow to Jesus which had been seized from a Bordeaux Carmel and which included the following language: "Je révère le dénuement que l'humanité de Jésus a fait de sa subsistence." This yielded Bérulle the charge of Nestorianism. The problem in this language is that the actions of Christ are not of his nature but of his person. Bérulle had actually written, "le dénuement que Jésus a de sa subsistence."

---

30 Ibid., 191–92 and 197–98.
31 Cochois, "Bérulle, hiérarque dionysien," 37: 314–18. This review follows the author's exposition closely.
32 Ibid., 314–15.
33 Ibid., 319–22.

However, the main point of the reproach, without regard to that particular error, had to do with a charge of Monophysitism and was addressed to Bérulle himself. The vows addressed a servitude to be given to Jesus Christ—to his deified humanity and humanized divinity. This formulary suggestsed that Bérulle misunderstood the communication of idioms, according to Cadoux.[34] The following excerpt from the formulary illustrates these concerns:

…je fais vœu à Dieu de servitude perpétuelle à Jésus-Christ, à son humanité déifiée et à sa divinité humanisée. Et par ainsi, en l'honneur de l'unité et du Fils avec le Père et le Saint-Esprit, et de l'union de ce même Fils avec cette nature humaine qui la prise et jointe à sa propre personne, j'unis et je lie mon être à Jésus et à son humanité déifiée par le lien de servitude perpétuelle; et je fais cette liaison de ma part, de toute ma puissance, et je le supplie de me donner plus de puissance pour me lier à lui d'une liaison plus grande et plus étroite, en l'honneur des liaisons saintes et sacrées qui'il veut avoir avec nous en la terre est aussi au ciel, en la vie de la grâce et de gloire. Je révére et adore la vie et l'anéantissement de la divinité en cette humanité, et la vie, la subsistance et la déification de cette humanité en la divinité, toutes les actions humainement divines et divinement humaines qui ont précédé et de cette vie nouvelle et mutuelle de l'Homme-Dieu en sa double essence éternelle et temporelle, divine et humaine. Et je lui dédie et consacre ma vie et mes actions de nature et de grâce, comme étant vie et actions d'un sein esclave pour jamais. Je révére le dénuement que l'humanité de Jésus a de sa subsistence propre et ordinaire pour être revêtue d'une subsistance autre, étrangère et ses actions ne sont plus d'elle, ni à elle proprement, mais sont de celui et à celui qui la soutient ainsi dénuée totalement et pour jamais de sa propre subsistence. Et en l'honneur de cela, je renonce à toute la puissance, autorité, propriété et liberté que j'ai de disposer de moi, de mon être, de toutes les conditions, circonstances et appartenances d'iceluy et de toutes mes actions, pour m'en démettre entièrement entre les mains de Jésus, et de son humanité sacrée, à son honneur et gloire, et pour l'accomplissement de tous ses vouloirs et pouvoirs sur moi. Je vous fais, ô Jésus, et à votre humanité déifiée, une oblation et donation entière,

---

[34] Cadoux, "Le Sacrement de l'Incarnation," 15–19. For discussions of the controversy, see Cochois, "Bérulle, initiateur mystique: les vœux de servitude et l'idéal de vie sacerdotal proposé par le Père de Bérulle"; Stéphane-Marie Morgain, "Pierre de Bérulle et le gouvernement des carmélites de France: histoire d'une querelle, 1583–1629" (PhD diss., Université de Fribourg, 1992). See also the subsequent publication of the book by Stéphane-Marie Morgain, *Pierre de Bérulle et les carmélites de France: la querelle du gouvernement, 1583–1629* (Paris: Éditions du Cerf, 1995).

absolue et irrévocable de tout ce que je suis par vous en l'être et en l'ordre de nature et de grâce, de tous ce qui en dépend, de toutes les actions naturelles, indifférentes et bonnes que j'opérerai à jamais, me référant tout, tout ce qui est en moi, et tout ce que je puis référer à l'hommage et honneur de votre humanité sacrée, que je prends et regarde désormais comme objet auquel après Dieu je fais relation de mon âme et de ma vie intérieure et extérieure et généralement de tout ce qui est mien.[35]

In 1621, the theological faculties of Louvain and Douai censured the vows of servitude. Lessius said the vows led to scruples and anxiety and contained doctrinal confusions, including the idea that they were somehow to be held as vows of religion.[36]

Whannou provided a cogent summary of the highly complex vows controversy, listing the *animadversiones* regarding thirteen propositions which were considered theologically erroneous, including the absurdity of a vow to never revoke a vow, servitude to Mary as a confused Mariology, and an aura of Nestorianism, Docetism, Monophysitism, and Monoenergism, among others.[37]

Influences

Prisca Theologia, *Theurgy, and Anagogy*

New to the fifteenth and sixteenth centuries, and opposed by Calvinists, was the renaissance of "intellectual magic, the Hermetic renaissance" as Hill termed it.[38]

The early Reformed Church had more of an affinity in the origins of its ideas, according to McGrath, with the Renaissance than with Lutherans: the younger Calvin was a humanist.[39] As a follower of the Florentine Academy, Bérulle had an interest in the Christian Platonism of the Renaissance which, this analysis suggests, was key to both his critique and his adoption of Calvinist ideals.

---

[35] Ibid.; see Bérulle, "Vœu de servitude à Jésus," 171–73.
[36] Williams, The French Oratorians and Absolutism, 153–58. See a critique of the vows issued by Carmelite monks under the name "Ami de Vérité," which included the opinion of Lessius: *Jésus. Maria. Advis salutaire du un certain qutriesme voeu de Religion, composé par un bon Ecclésiastique, et introduit dans un Ordre d'authorité propre et privée*, n.p., n.d.
[37] See *Subsistence*, 130–31 for a discussion of the complex debates.
[38] Hill, *The Collected Essays*, 293.
[39] McGrath, *The Intellectual Origins of the European Reformation*, 53–58, 180–81.

Neoplatonism, which had degenerated into theurgical practice with such philosophers as Iamblichus and Maximus, among others, according to Vacherot, served as the origin of the "idealist" doctrines of the mystics of the sixteenth century.[40] Whereas during the medieval period the influence of Neoplatonism was indirect, with Scholastic theology receiving ideas through the Arabs, Eastern theologians, and Pseudo-Dionysius, in the fifteenth century the Florentine Academy consulted the school directly.[41]

Collections of Orphic fragments were published in 1573 and 1588. The generally accepted opinion at the time was that religious truths were found in "ancient theology" (as previously discussed)—either from the Jews, usually considered from Moses via Egypt, or from other pre-Christian revelations. One predominant view was that an imperfect revelation came to the Greeks from Moses. Such thinkers as Justin and Clement of Alexandria assumed that Plato and his predecessors, Orpheus and Pythagoras, had visited Egypt and studied the writings of Moses (the Pentateuch) and had learned from Mosaically indoctrinated Egyptian priests. While in Egypt, they may have learned the Hermetic tradition. Most of the French asserted that Hermes followed Moses in time and in doctrine.[42]

During Bérulle's era, the Florentine Platonists were considered heroes for affirming the idea that ancient tradition and revelation were linked, as well as upholding the union between nature and grace. Bérulle accepted the already noted view that Hermes Trismegistus, for example, was first in the line of theologians who held to the truths of a primitive revelation which influenced Plato and Platonists.[43]

Dupuy's Defense

Dupuy argued that Bérulle's *vision en Dieu* consisted in adoration as a movement of the intelligence and will toward God. This spiritual attitude, Dupuy noted, was not a metaphysical theory of knowledge but, rather, one of faith. That said, one can detect in Bérulle's vision a turn to the *via eminentiae* of the Scholastics, according to Dupuy, arriving at the discernment that God is, and what he is, in

---

[40]   Étienne Vacherot, *Histoire critique de l'école d'Alexandrie*, vol. 3 (Paris: Ladrange, 1846), v–vii.

[41]   Ibid., 177–78.

[42]   D. P. Walker, *The Ancient Theology: Studies in Christian Platonism from the Fifteenth to the Eighteenth Century* (Ithaca, NY: Cornell University Press, 1972), 67–72, paraphrased.

[43]   Dagens, *Bérulle et les origines*, 18 and 23.

part. For Bérulle, this vision in God became possible in the Incarnate Word by communion with his Spirit, with Christ become the Divine Idea.[44]

Writing on the same topic thirty years later, Dupuy noted that the phrase "l'élévation de l'esprit vers Dieu" did not exactly characterize Christian prayer. He also noted that this phrase came from John Damascene and Evagrius of Pontus, who might have been influenced by Iamblichus.[45]

Bérulle wrote that although pagans elevated their thoughts to God, they lacked love. Dupuy insisted that Bérulle's elevations were a means to love God.[46] Bérulle, in his *vision en Dieu*, argued Dupuy, saw humankind, rather, as having already been oriented to God by our nature: "Noter notre néant, impuissance…néant au regard de l'être, c'est pourquoi Dieu nous crée; néant au regard de la grâce (et bien plus, péché, originel ou actuel ou éternel)….C'est pourquoi la justification est appelée création. Il y a seulement capacité à recevoir cette grâce, capacité imprimée de Dieu en la nature, mais non puissance à y atteindre."[47]

Dupuy declined to find any anagogical process in the Oratorians' meditation on Christ and his actions, as recommended by Bérulle. Dupuy insisted the opposite: that it was in discovering the dignity of the *esse* of Christ in their

---

[44] Michel Dupuy, "L'adoration d'après le cardinal de Bérulle," *École pratique des hautes études, Section des sciences religieuses: Annuaire* (1961): 130–32.

[45] Dupuy, "Bérulle et la grâce," 43. See John Damascene, *Exposition of the Orthodox Faith*, 3.24, in Philip Schaff and Henry Wace, *A Select Library of Nicene and Post-Nicene Fathers of the Christian Church,* Second Series, vol. 9, *St. Hilary of Poitiers, John of Damascus* (Grand Rapids, MI: Eerdmans, 1979), 70: "Prayer is an uprising of the mind to God or a petitioning of God for what is fitting…He appropriated to Himself our personality and took our impress on Himself, and became an ensample for us, and taught us to ask of God and strain towards Him, and guided us through His own holy mind in the way that leads up to God." In Greek, *De fide orthodoxa, PG*, 94, 1089D–1092A: "Προσευχή ἐστιν ἀνάβασις νοῦ πρὸς Θεὸν, ἢ αἴτησις τῶν προσηκόντων παρὰ Θεοῦ. …ἀλλὰ τὸ ἡμέτερον οἰκειούμενος πρόσωπον, καὶ τυπῶν ἐν ἑαυτῷ τὸ ἡμέτερον, καὶ ὑπογραμμὸς ἡμῖν γενόμενος, καὶ διδάσκων ἡμᾶς παρὰ Θεοῦ αἰτεῖν, καὶ πρὸς αὐτὸν ἀνατείνεσθαι, καὶ διὰ τοῦ ἁγίου αὐτοῦ νοῦ ὁδοποιῶν ἡμῖν τὴν πρὸς Θεὸν ἀνάβασιν."

See Evagrius, *De oratione*, no. 36, in John Eudes Bamburger and Evagrius, *The Praktikos [&] Chapters on Prayer* (Spencer, MA: Cistercian Publications, 1972), 60: "Prayer is an ascent of the spirit to God." In Greek, *PG*, 79, no. 35, 1173D: "Προσευχή ἐστιν ἀνάβασις νοῦ πρὸς Θεόν."

See Iamblichus, *De mysteriis*, 1, 12: "…the sacred names of the gods and other types of divine symbol that have the capacity of raising us up to the gods…" In Iamblichus and Emma C. Clarke, *Iamblichus on The Mysteries* (Atlanta, GA: Society of Biblical Literature, 2003), 53. In Greek, ibid., 52: "Ὅθεν δὴ καὶ ὀνόματα θεῶν ἱεροπρεπῆ καὶ τἆλλα θεῖα συνθήματα ἀναγωγὰ ὄντα πρὸς τοὺς θεοὺς συνάπτειν αὐτὰς δύναται."

[46] Dupuy, "Bérulle et la grâce," 43.

[47] Bérulle, *OC*, Migne ed., *OP* 107 A, quoted in Dupuy, "Bérulle et la grâce," 44.

meditations that Christ's actions were revealed.[48] Dupuy admitted, however, that Bérulle invited the Oratorians to review the actions of Christ as a means given to lift them to himself: "Ces bienfaits et opérations sont mis entre nos mains comme des moyens et des degrés pour nous conduire et nous élever à lui-même." Clarifying, Dupuy held that adoration for Bérulle was not in climbing by degrees but a simple regard.[49] Lastly, Dupuy admitted that the young Bérulle had an assurance that one could participate in the divine perfections, pointing to the following opuscule:[50]

> S'élever en la pensée de l'état de la gloire en laquelle il a plu à Dieu constituer ses saints, admirant fort la bonté de Dieu envers eux de ce qu'il lui a plu mettre sa gloire en la gloire de ses saints...
>
> L'ordre que j'y observerai sera de premièrement contempler cette perfection en Dieu, donnant lieu à l'esprit de s'étendre en cette vue et d'en recevoir tous les mouvements que la grâce de Dieu excitera en moi; secondement de voir la communication de celle perfection en ses saints; troisièmement de faire une application de celle perfection à mon âme ou par désir, ou par langueur ou par transformation.[51]

In his concluding remarks, Dupuy asked whether Bérulle's making of adoration into the recognition of ontological dependence constituted a climbing from effect to cause. He declined, noting that Bérulle's *vision en Dieu* avoided this because he held that all creatures, including ourselves and Christ, are already in God.[52]

Thompson's Critique

Thompson weighed in on what he saw as both positive and negative aspects of the French School. He saw its idea of God emanating in history as a "Christic sharing in the inner life and love of the Trinity." Among other positive aspects, he cited its reuniting of authority, learning, and holiness as a source for contemporary renewal, its accent on service and adoration, its acknowledgment of the reality of human depravity, as well as its balanced Mariology. Thompson also thought that it had some success in removing Dionysian influences by

---

[48] *BSA*, 225–26.
[49] *OP* 87, quoted in *BSA*, 228.
[50] *BSA*, 254, referencing *OP* 107. Dupuy also referenced Coll. 33 in which Bérulle urged the meditation on twelve divine perfections for each month, repeated daily.
[51] Bérulle, *OC* (1995), 430–31, Opuscule 162 (revised numeration). The word *transformation* was omitted from the Bourgoing edition. See footnote 431n2.
[52] *BSA*, 314–15.

focusing on the "Jesus-centered nature of Christianity and its ecclesial nature."[53] Most notably, however, he cited Schillebeeckx's concern that the school "dangerously" anchored the priesthood in the divinity of Jesus, making it cultic.[54]

The Cyrillian Priesthood

We now explore the influence of Cyril in greater detail. Cyril was influenced by both Gnosticism and Neoplatonism, and, with a backdrop of a "théurgisme cosmique," presented a concept of participation as dynamic and transfiguring, according to Garrigues, Le Guillou, and Riou. For Cyril, the work of Christ was most of all to compenetrate in his person both God and man, with Christ's humanity penetrated by divine power. This divinized humanity became a channel of divine energy for humanity overall. Cyril called priests those who are "…assumant en quelque sorte sa [Christ's] personne…"[55] a phrase that Bérulle echoed. This transmission of sacerdotal power was the divine power of the Holy Spirit and corresponded to *une sotériologie monoénergiste* in which the divinity alone is priest. It represented a theology of grace and ministry in which the divine nature is its own mediation and priesthood, and with an immediate presence of God in the energy of the Holy Spirit. This *économie de théurgisme descendant* required passivity on the part of priests. That said, the authors noted that this ideal of character was radical in affirming a "transmutation fondamentale de l'être par la participation directe au pouvoir incréé de la nature divine en Christ."[56] By the power of the Spirit, priests are *transmués*. They communicate with the nature of Christ through participation in the Spirit, giving their own nature a power and glory above the rest of humankind. As Cyril wrote: "Le Christ consacre les âpostres par une réelle sanctification en les faisant communier à sa propre nature par la participation de l'Esprit et en reforgeant en quelque sorte la nature humaine en une puissance et une gloire qui est au-dessus de l'homme."[57]

---

[53] Thompson, in Bérulle and Thompson, *Bérulle and the French School*, 87. See 84–88 for discussion.

[54] Ibid. See Schillebeeckx, *The Church with a Human Face*, 3 and 202–3.

[55] Garrigues et al., "Le caractère sacerdotal dans la tradition des Pères Grecs," 811–12, paraphrased. See Cyril of Alexandria, *In II Cor.*, PG, 74, 944D: "οἷον αὐτοῦ τὸ πρόσωπον ἀναλαβόντες Χριστοῦ."

[56] Ibid., 812–13.

[57] Ibid., 812–13. See Cyril, *In Joann.*, PG, 74, 712D: "Τελειοῖ δὲ δι' ἁγιασμοῦ τοῦ κατὰ ἀλήθειαν τῆς ἰδίας φύσεως κοινωνοὺς διὰ τῆς τοῦ Πνεύματος μετουσίας ἀναδεικνὺς, καὶ μεταχαλκεύων τρόπον τινὰ τὴν ἀνθρώπου φύσιν εἰς τὴν ὑπὲρ ἄνθρωπον δύναμίν τε καὶ δόξαν."

Iamblichan Anagogy

Iamblichus' ideals regarding anagogical theurgy are next reviewed in relation to Bérulle's vows of servitude to Jesus and Mary, and the elevations he urged for Oratorians.

According to Rorem, Iamblichus held a place of importance in the sacramental theology of the late Greek fathers, and had a major influence on late Neoplatonic theurgy as well. Instead of a purely rational contemplation as a way to divine union, he emphasized an anagogy based on *The Chaldean Oracles*, identifying Platonists' metaphysical process with the Chaldeans' theurgy. By linking *reditus* to "uplifting," Iamblichus changed it to become anagogical theurgy. Anagogy for Iamblichus involved union with the gods who are not called down. Rather, humans are elevated to the divine via the divine names and signs.[58]

Both Pseudo-Dionysius and Iamblichus held to the notion of a superior realm where no material aids were needed for worship, and their notions of uplifting or anagogy were also similar.[59] Iamblichus termed the uplifting influenced by the Chaldean Oracles' ceremonial uplifting of the soul the "hieratic uplifting among the Egyptians."[60]

This anagogy for Iamblichus had both soteriological and mystical significance: it summarized the gifts of the divine presence; was tied to union with the gods; and served to define ecstasy, whether through prayer, sacrifice, or theurgy in general.[61]

The goal of theurgy, then, was this "ascent by means of the summonings."[62] While a more detailed study would be needed to draw definite conclusions, a closer examination of Iamblichus' ideals surrounding theurgy and the theurgist himself yields some interesting parallels with Bérulle's ideals as well. First, Iamblichus rejected philosophy for theurgy because he believed the soul is weak.

---

[58] Paul Rorem, *Biblical and Liturgical Symbols within the Pseudo-Dionysian Synthesis* (Toronto: Pontifical Institute of Mediaeval Studies, 1984), 106–8. See Hans Lewy and Michel Tardieu, *Chaldean Oracles and Theurgy: Mysticism, Magic and Platonism in the Later Roman Empire,* new ed. (Paris: Institut d'Études Augustiniennes, 1978), 489.

[59] Ibid., 107. See *EH*, 5 501c 42f.

[60] Iamblichus, *De mysteriis*, 10.6.292.10: "τῆς παρ᾽ Αἰγυπτίοις ἱερατικῆς ἀναγωγῆς." Quoted in Rorem, *Biblical and Liturgical Symbols*, 107.

[61] Ibid., 107–8.

[62] Iamblichus, *De mysteriis*, 1.12.42.1: "ἡ διὰ τῶν κλήσεων ἄνοδος." Quoted in Rorem, *Biblical and Liturgical Symbols*, 108.

For Iamblichus, according to Feichtinger, theurgists were both human and god in that the gods acted through them, their souls become theurgic.[63]

According to Uždavinys, the perfection of the soul meant assimilation with the gods and their purity and essence—an object few attain. Those who do are separated from nature and perform rational, immaterial ritual in an immaterial level of cult. Their invocations would create a new life and power, pure and unchanging. In this, the soul's attitude must be passive and must recognize its own nothingness before God. Ultimately, as Uždavinys described it, when the mind of the theurgist is engaged through prayer, and by submitting to the divine will, the divine ray lifts the soul up to the heavens to join with the gods.[64]

The Berullian sacerdotal themes of elevation, separation, purity, essence, nothingness, passivity, emanation, and divine will, as already detailed, seem to contain, at least, echoes of this thought system.

The Philosophical Priesthood of Iamblichus

Leadbetter explored what he called the philosophical priesthood of Iamblichus. In the following description of Iamblichan anagogical theurgy and priesthood, echoes of Bérulle's rhetoric can be heard. For Iamblichus, knowledge lay in the "cosubsistence or mystical participation in the chain of being, a state acquired only by priests upon whom these countless divinities have bestowed their beneficence."[65] The gods are causes who lead souls toward their intelligible principle. They then become repositories of divine knowledge, superior to others. They become participants in gnosis, in the One beyond essence. They also become mediators. The divine operation in them does not involve their intellects, virtue, or wisdom, but is of the gods. This operation is activated through worship. There are two religious acts of the priest: divination and sacrifice, which is not to honor the gods but to avoid evil and to remove the influence of the soul's original guardian demon. Most evils come from the fact that matter is incapable of receiving divine causality in right proportion.

---

[63] Hans Feichtinger, "Οὐδένεια and *Humilitas*: Nature and Function of Humility in Iamblichus and Augustine," *Dionysius* 11 (Dec. 2003): 126–28. See Gregory Shaw, *Theurgy and the Soul: The Neoplatonism of Iamblichus* (University Park, PA: Pennsylvania State University Press, 1995), 51, 67. See also J. Rist, "Pseudo-Dionysius, Neoplatonism and the Weakness of the Soul," in *From Athens to Chartres: Neoplatonism and Medieval Thought*, ed. H. J. Westra (Leiden and New York: Brill, 1992), 144.

[64] Algis Uždavinys, *Philosophy and Theurgy in Late Antiquity* (San Rafael, CA: Sophia Perennis, 2010), 134–37, paraphrased.

[65] Lewis W. Leadbetter, "Aspects of the Philosophical Priesthood in Iamblichus' *De Mysteriis*," *Classical Bulletin* 47, no. 6 (April 1971): 90–91.

This "demonization of the cosmos," as McGinn termed it, had roots in both Hellenistic philosophy and religion.[66]

Again, further study is needed, but Berullian themes seemingly echoed in the Iamblichan priesthood include states, a knowledge superior to others, mediation, divine operation, and, notably, evil in relation to the soul.

Pseudo-Dionysius

Pseudo-Dionysius summarized the relationship between the Christian and Jewish scriptures with the following: "theurgy is the consummation of theology," or, as also translated, "the divine works are the consummation of the divine words."[67] Pseudo-Dionysius proposed a theurgic, two-termed structure, according to Garrigues, Le Guillou, and Riou. As they wrote, "…la Théarchie ou procession (indistinctement d'être et de grâce) de Dieu 'ad extra' et la Hiérarchie ou ordre des degrés, selon lesquels Dieu se communique à la creation."[68]

This Christology, with a Proclusian emanationist metaphysics, as they called it, placed Christ as head of the ecclesiastical hierarchy but retained his place beneath the angels in the celestial hierarchy.[69] The authors further explained that Pseudo-Dionysius's thearchic Monoenergism, as the foundation of sacerdotal ministry, reduced Christological mediation to a simple and necessary dialectical moment of emanation, but, at the same time, expanded it to include all acts of priesthood as occasions for thearchic power.[70] The double defect of this ontology,

---

[66] McGinn, *The Foundations of Mysticism*, 19–20.

[67] Pseudo-Dionysius, *EH* 3, 432B, quoted in Rorem, *Biblical and Liturgical Symbols*, 9. *CD*, "καὶ ἔστι τῆς θεολογίας ἡ θεουργία συγκεφαλαίωσις." See footnote 24.

[68] Garrigues et al., "Le caractère sacerdotal dans la tradition des Pères Grecs," 815. The authors noted that for Dionysius, Christ was "l'esprit très *théarchique* et suressentiel, principe, essence et puissance très théarchique de toute hiérarchie, de toute sainteté et de toute opération divine." See *EH*, 372A, *CD*, 63.12–64.2: "ὁ θεαρχικώτατος νοῦς καὶ ὑπερούσιος, ἡ πάσης ἱεραρχίας ἁγιαστείας τε καὶ θεουργίας ἀρχὴ καὶ οὐσία καὶ θεαρχικωτάτη δύναμις."

[69] Garrigues et al., "Le caractère sacerdotal dans la tradition des Pères Grecs," 815. See *CH*, 181C. *CD*, 23.10–14 (see ch. 13, n. 24): "Ὁρῶ γὰρ ὅτι καὶ αὐτὸς Ἰησοῦς ἡ τῶν ὑπερουρανίων οὐσιῶν ὑπερούσιος αἰτία πρὸς τὸ καθ᾽ ἡμᾶς ἀμεταβόλως ἐληλυθὼς οὐκ ἀποπηδᾷ τῆς ὑπ᾽ αὐτοῦ ταχθείσης τε καὶ αἱρεθείσης ἀνθρωποπρεποῦς εὐταξίας, ἀλλ᾽ εὐπειθῶς ὑποτάττεται ταῖς τοῦ πατρὸς καὶ θεοῦ δι᾽ ἀγγέλων διατυπώσεσιν."

[70] Ibid., 815–816. See *EH*, 504C: "…the sacraments of the synaxis and of the myron-ointment provide a perfecting knowledge and understanding of the divine workings and that it is through this that there is effected both the unifying uplifting toward the divinity and the most blessed communion with it." *CD*, "τῆς συνάξεως δὲ καὶ τῆς τοῦ μύρου τελετῆς τελειωτικῆς τῶν θεουργιῶν γνώσεως καὶ ἐπιστήμης, δι᾽ ἧς ἱερῶς ἡ πρὸς τὴν θεαρχίαν ἑνοποιὸς ἀναγωγὴ καὶ μακαριωτάτη κοινωνία τελεσιουργεῖται."

according to the authors, which conflated the orders of grace and ordination, was that the priest became both a manifestation of divine power (with an ontological superiority in the order of grace) and a passive instrument. Sacerdotal character became a mark of perfection.

This double error characterized Bérulle's spiritual theology of priesthood, as we have explored.

According to Miller, Pseudo-Dionysius transposed theurgy into a Christian context: the divine operations became activities of the Trinity, the initiator, Christ. The chorus of initiates (including all angels and contemplatives) were to dance around the Logos, receiving eternal life from "Christ's theurgic rays..."[71] Priests, according to Rorem, were guides to prepare laity to contemplate and participate in the sacraments.[72] So, too, Bérulle's Oratorians, as we have reviewed.

Taveau's Analysis

Taveau conducted an in-depth analysis of the foundational ideas of Bérulle's system—an affective theology of the Incarnate Word in which Jesus is both the means and the end: "Jésus-Christ seul est fin et moyen en la Croix et en l'Eucharistie. Là, nous devons nous lier à lui comme à notre fin, et user de lui comme d'un moyen."[73] While the ancients taught two worlds of the sensible and the intelligible, Christ encompasses both in Bérulle's system.[74] The ideas of God which should be studied, such as life, love, and holiness, are reproduced and honored by the Word Incarnate. Important to this study, the Son is the subsistent idea of God, the idea of resemblance himself.[75] As Bérulle wrote, "comme le Fils est l'image vive et l'idée parfaite de son Père en la divinité, il veut être en ce sien œuvre comme l'image vive et parfaite de soi-même."[76]

Taveau clarified the details of the kinds of mysteries upon which Bérulle's Oratorians were called to meditate, and how these mysteries gained them access to union with Christ. For Bérulle, the participation of creatures in resemblance, which is the Word, the Son of God, permits them not only to be, but to be images. By these images, Taveau wrote, one can climb to God, see his perfections, and make an act of religion. For example, "Ainsi en la terre nous devons voir le ciel, Dieu en nous, et le Créateur dedans les créatures; car aussi les a-t-il faites comme

---

71 Miller, *Measures of Wisdom*, 506, paraphrased. Miller quoted Pseudo-Dionysius, *CH*, 7, 2, 208C. *CD*, "τῶν θεουργικῶν αὐτοῦ φώτων."

72 Rorem, *Biblical and Liturgical Symbols*, 34. See Pseudo-Dionysius, *EH*, 505D 40 to 508A 1.

73 Taveau, *Le cardinal de Bérulle*, 72, citing *OC*, 1290, Migne ed.

74 Taveau, *Le cardinal de Bérulle*, 38. See *Œuvres de controverse*, 673; *Grandeurs*, 209.

75 Ibid., 39. See *Grandeurs*, 229–30.

76 *Grandeurs*, 229–30, quoted in Taveau, *Le cardinal de Bérulle*, 39.

autant de miroirs qui nous représentent ses grandeurs admirables, et comme autant de moyens qui nous conduisent à lui."[77] Taveau listed Bérulle's created symbols which point to the divine realities and have adoring functions under the categories of dogmatic, spiritual, and symbol mysteries.[78]

In this act of contemplating, one moves from *grâce commune* to *grâce éminente*.[79] Elevation for Bérulle was an attempt by the intelligence to seize a revealed truth, in order to receive a quality or impression:

> Élevons-nous donc à la contemplation de Dieu fait homme…recherchant beaucoup plus d'entrer par révérence et par amour en ses lumières, que par lumière en son amour, encore que nous désirions recovoir de lui l'une et l'autre qualité et impression, en la conduite de nos mouvements et affections vers un objet et un mystère d'amour et de lumière tout ensemble.[80]

Taveau called Bérulle's a mystical cosmography wherein, as Bérulle noted, Jesus is *un nouveau centre de l'univers*.[81]

Christ's State of Glory

The last state of Christ's life is that of his Resurrection, Ascension, and eternal life, or the state of glory. Bérulle's works on the glorious life were not published by Bourgoing, likely due to the fact that the fruits of this state are joy and impassibility, something that might have easily been associated with illuminism and quietism, according to McKay.[82]

We would argue that its censure might have been due to the possible ramifications of its association with the theology of priesthood.

Preckler asked what, then, is the participation of souls in this state of glory. He quoted Bérulle, noting that his thought was inspired by the liturgy:

> La conformité que nous devons avoir en nos dévotions à la conduite de l'Église nous représente, en ce temps, l'état de la vie nouvelle et glorieuse du Fils de Dieu, nous convie à prendre quelque pensée de vie (…) en ce

---

[77] Ibid., 39–41. See *OC*, 926.
[78] Ibid., 42–46.
[79] Ibid., 73–74. See Élévation vers sainte Madeleine, 573.
[80] *Grandeurs*, 159–60, quoted in Taveau, *Le cardinal de Bérulle*, 81.
[81] *Grandeurs*, 220, quoted in Taveau, *Le cardinal de Bérulle*, 96.
[82] TG, 276–77.

temps, il me semble que la perfection divine que nous devons considérer et adorer, soit la vie divine, la vie de Dieu en soi-même, puisque le mystère que l'Église propose qui est l'état de la vie ressuscitée du Fils de Dieu, a rapport à cette perfection...[83]

In this state, in which the Oratorian conforms himself to the impassability of the Son in glory, he would be incapable of sadness. As Bérulle insisted, "il faut que nous ôtions toutes ces sensibilités et nous conformer en quelque manière à l'impassibilité du Fils de Dieu en son état glorieux."[84] This impassability included a kind of death and great separation from all things:

> Or pour imiter sa résurrection, nous devons mourir et vivre, et mourir pour vivre, mourir à tout ce qui est de la terre pour vivre en Jésus-Christ. Nous devons encore nous conformer par grâce aux qualités de sa gloire; imiter: son amour par une prompte correspondance aux inspirations divines; subtilité par une abstraction et séparation des choses de la terre; impassibilité, domptant, par le moyen de la grâce de Dieu, nos passions avec telle puissance que si nous n'en avions point...[85]

In order to parse Bérulle's understanding of the relationship between priesthood and Christ's state of glory and impassability, a review is warranted of Pseudo-Dionysius' ideals as influenced by Proclus and others.

Sympatheia *and the Theopathic State*

Iamblichus held, according to Dodds, that salvation is obtained through ritual rather than reason.[86] This ritual was theurgy. Itter noted that scholars' knowledge of theurgic rites is limited, but that Dodds and Lewy attempted to explain their roots as demonstrated in Neoplatonic texts.[87]

Pseudo-Dionysius was strongly influenced by Proclus, as well as the Alexandrian School and the Cappadocians, according to Itter. Coulter, quoting

---

[83] Bérulle, Archives nationales M, 233, 73 A, quoted in Preckler, *Bérulle aujourd'hui*, 102.

[84] Ibid.

[85] *OC* (1995), *OP* 103, 292.

[86] E. R. Dodds, *The Greeks and the Irrational*, 7th printing (Berkeley: University of California Press, 1971), appendix 2, "Theurgy," 278. Cited in Andrew Itter, "Pseudo-Dionysian Soteriology and Its Transformation of Neoplatonism," *Colloquium Journal* 32 (May 2000): 76.

[87] Itter, "Pseudo-Dionysian Soteriology," 76. See Dodds, *The Greeks and the Irrational*, and Hans Lewy, *Chaldean Oracles and Theurgy* (Cairo: Imprimerie de l'Institut français d'archéologie orientale, 1956), 287.

and summarizing Dodd's commentary on Proclus, addressed the theurgic notion of *sympatheia*:

> A closely related notion [to that of cause and effect in Proclus], it seems, is that of "sympathy"… a bond of "shared feeling" between some object in the visible world and unseen reality. Because of this 'sympathy,' objects may have "receptivity" (*epitedeiotes*), i.e. "a capacity for the reception of a *synthema* or *symbolon*, a magical correspondence which links each material thing *entautha* with a particular spiritual principle or group of principle *ekei*." It is through a desire for identification with this *synthema*, and through it with the cause that matter, which otherwise possesses no *energeia*, i.e. a capacity to act on its own, reverts to its originative source.[88]

Through various incantations and material objects, the theurgist "set in motion a chain of sympathies running up…to the god he was trying to evoke."[89]

Pseudo-Dionysius used the term *theourgia* many times. Itter emphasized that it is important to take into account the difference both the Christian context and the Incarnation made in how *sympatheia* was understood. Pseudo-Dionysius wrote of his teacher Hierotheus, for example, who experienced "union through a 'shared feeling' with divine things."[90] Louth called this a "theopathic state," comparing it to a submission to the will of God such that one's own knowing is negated as God comes to live within.[91] This suffering with Christ is something experienced "through the potency of the sacraments."[92]

Christian vs. Neoplatonic Theurgy

Rorem noted a fundamental difference between Neoplatonic and Christian understandings of theurgy. Whereas for Iamblichus, theurgy was an objective

---

[88] J. A. Coulter, *The Literary Microcosm: Theories of Interpretation of the Later Neoplatonists* (Leiden: E. J. Brill, 1976), 55, quoted in Itter, "Pseudo-Dionysian Soteriology," 76. See 71 for Itter's discussion.

[89] Arthur Hilary Armstrong, *An Introduction to Ancient Philosophy*, 3rd ed. (London: Methuen, 1957), 202, quoted in Itter, "Pseudo-Dionysian Soteriology," 76.

[90] Itter, "Pseudo-Dionysian Soteriology, 78, quoting Pseudo-Dionysius, *DN*, 648B. *CD*, 134.2–4: "τῆς πρός αὐτά συμπαθείας, εἰ οὕτω χρὴ φάναι, πρὸς τὴν ἀδίδακτον αὐτῶν καὶ μυστικὴν ἀποτελεσθεὶς ἕνωσιν καὶ πίστιν."

[91] Ibid., 79, referencing Louth without attribution.

[92] Ibid., 79.

genitive "work of God," it became subjective in the Christian context, suggesting God's activity, including God's saving work and his divine acts in Christ.[93]

That said, Pseudo-Dionysius held to the idea that the priestly office enables the lifting up to Christ, as cited: "...we come closer to those beings who are superior to us. We imitate as much as we can their abiding, unwavering, and sacred constancy, and we thereby come to look up to the blessed and ultimately divine ray of Jesus himself."[94]

This passage is echoed in Bérulle's system of mystical initiation and elevations as the means to obtain grace. As Cochois summarized, the bond which priests have with Christ, the thearchic source, is made perfect through a mystical servitude by means of the elevations Bérulle proposed: "je m'élève et m'unie à cette nature (*humaine de Jésus*), et par elle au Verbe éternel, et par le Verbe au Père qui l'a engendré et nous l'a donné."[95] Importantly, this mystical union was characterized by psychological and ontological ecstasy, as already noted.[96]

Conclusion

The vows of servitude, as part of a program of formation for priests and the perfect, mirrored Calvin's confirmation in grace, associated with his definition of faith as firm and sure knowledge. An ontological self-annihilation, by means of the legalism of a vow, guaranteed priests' subjective holiness. A pseudo-juridical status, also a mirror of the Reformers' covenantal ideals, made vocation into an election and a personalist initiative rather than an ecclesial calling. An ontological ecstasy guaranteed a personalist grafting and moral authority proposed by the Reformers.

Bérulle's fascination with Pseudo-Dionysian theurgy was perhaps also in response to Calvin's *sursum corda* as a rejection of the Mass as work, dependent

---

[93] Rorem, *Biblical and Liturgical Symbols*, 14–15, quoted in Itter, "Pseudo-Dionysian Soteriology," 79–80.

[94] Pseudo-Dionysius, *EH*, 372B, in Pseudo-Dionysius, Luibhéid, and Rorem, *Pseudo-Dionysius: The Complete Works*, 196. *CD*, 64.8–11 (see ch. 15, n. 66): "ἐγγύτεροι μὲν αὐτοὶ γινόμεθα τῶν ὑπὲρ ἡμᾶς οὐσιῶν τῇ κατὰ δύναμιν ἀφομοιώσει τοῦ μονίμου τε καὶ ἀνεξαλλάκτου τῆς αὐτῶν ἱερᾶς ἱδρύσεως καὶ ταύτῃ πρὸς τὴν μακαρίαν Ἰησοῦ καὶ θεαρχικὴν αὐγὴν ἀναβλέψαντες."

[95] Cochois, "Bérulle, hiérarque dionysien," 37: 339. See Formulaires des vœux de servitude, 18, 2, 4th redaction, *Sermons et conférences du cardinal de Bérulle et du P. de Condren, et de M. Duval aux carmélites*, ms. des Archives de l'Oratoire (Montsoult). See explication of numeration, 316.

[96] Ibid., 37: 331.

on the priest. Cyril, clearly Pseudo-Dionysius's precursor in this current of thought, was also perhaps an influence in that Bérulle held that the priest assumes the person of Christ.

In this, the priest became a Reformist pastoral effigy himself, as we will now explore.

Chapter 18
The Pastoral Effigy

Introduction

Bérulle's notions surrounding the priest in relation to the person of Christ, and as visible image of Christ the head, are best understood within the context of the Reformation debates surrounding images.

Adherence to the will of God and union with Christ through servitude and mental elevations, combined with a monastic rigorism and a negative strain of Augustinian piety, does not tell the entire story of Bérulle's spiritual theology of priesthood.

At the heart of Bérulle's project is the notion of the priest as the visible image of Christ. This preoccupation with image was of serious concern to Reformers and Bérulle alike in terms of ecclesiology as well as pastoral identity, as this chapter will explore.

Embedded in this notion were deeper layers of ideals associated with conformity of the will and deiformity, in terms of both configuration and conformity to Christ, for both the laity and priests. Other ideas include likeness, as well as notions already explored, such as participation, contemplation, holiness and perfection, here treated in relation to image and likeness.

Icons, Effigies, and Efficacious Images

Koerner wrote, "By a strange logic of development, Lutherans replaced the saints' icons with effigies of themselves." The piety of pastors was publicly displayed on church walls.[1]

As is well known, the notion of image featured prominently in the Reformation. For example, Luther held the sacraments to be "visible words," a notion taken from St. Augustine, according to Koerner.[2] Calvin, too, held that

---

[1] Koerner, *The Reformation of the Image*, 388–89.
[2] Ibid., 43n32. See Augustine, *Visibile Verbum, Tractatus in Iohannis Evangelium* 80.3 (see *WA* 30.1: 223); Karl-Heinz Zur Mühlen, "Zur Rezeption der Augustinischen Sakramentsformel 'Accedit verbum ad elementum et fit sacramentum', in der Theologie Luthers," *Zeitschrift für Theologie und Kirche* 70 (1973): 50–76.

the images of baptism and communion were the only images permitted in church.[3]

Opposing image-breaking Calvinists were not only Roman Catholics, but also Lutherans, whose defense of images included their opinion that keeping images supported the idea that they themselves were more apostolic than the Romans.[4]

Calvinist Iconoclasm

Calvinist iconoclasts had a fear not just of idolatry but of the idols themselves, which were seen to have some kind of power, according to Kibbey.[5] As Calvinist anti-imagist controversialists insisted, believers were the "true and living images of God."[6] Referring to Calvin's above-referenced ideal of the living and iconic images of both baptism and the Lord's Supper,[7] Kibbey noted, "The idea of the living image emerged at the very heart, the very core, of Protestant sacramental theory, defining Protestantism as a religion that opposed false images, but not all images."[8] The Calvinist idea of real presence, she noted, focused on the Mystical Body. As she wrote, "The living images of the Protestant sacrament articulated a corporate theory of the image."[9] Bérulle would take up this debate, holding both laity and priests to be living images, but with priests as the image of Christ as head of the Mystical Body.

Important to this study, Houdard's treatment of the priest as representation of the Mystical Body underscored the Protestant rejection of the priest as false image. Calvin wrote: "bien qu'ils nous allèguent le temple, la prêtrise et toutes sortes d'autres masques, cela nous doit point émouvoir pour nous faire considérer qu'il y ait Eglise où il n'y apparaît point de Parole de Dieu."[10] In 1600,

---

[3]   Ibid., 43. See *Institutes*, 1.11.13. *Institution*: "Et encores que les dangers n'y fussent pas si apparens, si est-ce que quand ie considère à quell usage les temples sont dédiez et ordonnez, il me semble que c'est chose mal séante à leur saincteté qu'on y mette d'autres images que celles que Dieu a consacrée par sa parole, lesquelles ont sa vraye marque imprimée, l'enten le Baptesme et la saincte Cène du Seigneur..."

[4]   Ibid., 58.

[5]   Ann Kibbey, *Theory of the Image* (Bloomington: Indiana University Press, 2005). See discussion, 6–16.

[6]   Ibid., 10, quoting a French Protestant circular in Phyllis Crew, *Calvinist Preaching and Iconoclasm in the Netherlands, 1544–1569* (Cambridge: Cambridge University Press, 1978) 23.

[7]   Ibid., 10.

[8]   Ibid., 10.

[9]   Ibid., 15.

[10] Calvin, *Institution*, 4.2. Also quoted in Houdard, "Sacerdoce et direction spirituelle," 109.

Plessis-Morney followed, writing that *masques* were not substantial but exterior.[11]

Arguably, Bérulle would combine, in an echo of Luther, the emphasis on the pastor as pious effigy and apostolic purity based on adherence to the word with a reaction against Calvin's iconoclasm, defending the priest as the representative and image of Christ. This included an emphasis on a sacerdotal consecration based on the substantial holiness of Christ, and a piety higher than that of religious through adherence to the Spirit of Jesus.

Configuration and Conformity

The notion of image in relation to configuration and conformity was key to Bérulle's reform of the priesthood, as noted. That said, Bérulle's interpretation of likeness also became a central one in terms of each.

A distinction has been typically made between three kinds of likeness in the soul: that associated with sacramental character, which is legal and official; that of the natural image and likeness of God; and that of the likeness produced by grace, faith, hope, and charity.[12]

Understandably, if priests were to be the visible legal image of Christ on earth, they should reflect the likeness of Christ in the moral realm. But how?

The Priest as Imago Dei

The doctrine of image and likeness had a large place in the history of Eastern spirituality.[13] Danielou explored the ideals surrounding the sacerdotal ministry according to the Greek fathers. Of special interest is the relationship between the priesthood and image in Gregory Nazianzen, who wrote, "Le but (du sacerdoce)…consiste à maintenir…fortifier… restaurer…l'image de Dieu dans l'homme...de faire un dieu qui participe à la béatitude d'En-Haut..."[14]

---

[11]   Philippe de Mornay, *Traité de l'église*, 2nd ed. (La Rochelle, 1600), 65, quoted in Houdard, "Sacerdoce et direction spirituelle," 110n9.

[12]   Ryan, "Character." See Aquinas, *ST*, 3.63.3, ad 2, in *Summa theologiae*, 12.1: 35 (see ch. 13, n. 29).

[13]   J. Lemaitre, "Contemplation: La theoria phusikè," in *DSAM*, vol. 2, pt. 2 (1953), cols. 1828–29.

[14]   Gregory Nazianzen, *PG*, 35, 432B: "τῇ δὲ τὸ προκείμενον...τὸ κατ᾽ εἰκόνα...τηρῆσαι...χειραγωγῆσαι...ἀνασώσασθαι...Θεὸν ποιῆσαι, καὶ τῆς ἄνω μακαριότητος, τὸν τῆς ἄνω συντάξεως." Quoted in J. Danielou, "Le ministère sacerdotal chez les pères grecs," in *Études sur le sacrement de l'ordre* (Paris: Éd. du Cerf, 1957), 149–50.

In terms of the priest as a living image of God, Maximus presented the priesthood as a participation in the saving power of the hypostatic kenosis of the Son to reconcile the freedom of men with God, with the priest taking the place of the Son, who "prend sur la terre la place du Fils de Dieu, moyennant quoi, dit Maxime, Dieu ne cesse pas d'être vu corporellement…"[15]

In this brief quote can be seen outlines of Bérulle's notions as well, most especially the idea of hypostatic kenosis and imaging.

Most pertinent perhaps were the formal principles that Bérulle borrowed from the Neoplatonism of Pseudo-Dionysius, including, as Dupuy wrote, the fundamental relation between beings that is resemblance itself, and by which they become intelligible; the linking of causes and similitudes; and the knowing of creatures and their place on the scale of being by what they imitate and by their archetypes.[16] As Cochois noted, reversing the celestial hierarchies and placing Christ at the apex, Bérulle made Christ the archetype.[17]

Participation, Image, and Priesthood

Dupuy wrote that, just as religious may imitate a particular aspect of Christ, the priest, for Bérulle, in the image of the Word Incarnate, imitates the union of Christ's divinity and humanity.[18] Dupuy summarized Bérulle's conceptualization of the priesthood as something "essential" to the priest, the *all* of his spiritual life through the contemplation of the archetype of the hypostatic union.[19] Dupuy wrote:

> Parce que l'union hypostatique est une union essentielle, une union dans l'être, il importe que le sacerdoce qui l'honore soit dans la vie du prêtre essentiel, non pas seulement quelque chose dans sa vie, mais toute sa vie spirituelle. Il ne devrait pas être dans l'existence un simple accident, parce que l'Homme-Dieu n'est pas prêtre par accident, mais en raison de l'union substantielle de son humanité à sa divinité. Bien sûr, du point de vue de la nature humaine, les prêtres reçoivent le sacerdoce de la même manière

---

[15] Garrigues et al., "Le caractère sacerdotal dans la tradition des Pères Grecs," 820, quoting Maximus, *Lettre à l'évêque de Cydonie*, PG, 91, 604D. In Greek: "δείξας μάλα σαφῶς, δι᾽ ὧν ἀκίβδηλον τὴν πρὸς Θεὸν ἐκτήσατο μίμησιν, ὡς τὴν ἱερωσύνην ὁ Θεὸς ἐπὶ γῆς ἀνθ᾽ ἑαυτοῦ χειροτονήσας προὐβάλετο. Ἐφ᾽ ᾧτε καὶ σωματικῶς ὁρώμενος, καὶ τὰ αὐτοῦ μυστήρια τοῖς ὁρᾶν δυναμένοις μὴ διαλίπῃ φαινόμενα."

[16] See *BLS*, 151, as also cited in *État*, 63.

[17] See Cochois, "Bérulle et le pseudo-Denys," 198–99, as also cited in *État*, 63.

[18] *BLS*, 183.

[19] Ibid., 185.

qu'un accident qui inhère à la substance. Mais précisément ce n'est pas du seul point de vue de la nature humaine qu'on peut comprendre ce qu'est la vie spirituelle du prêtre. Il faut plutôt contempler l'archétype divin qui nous est offert par l'union hypostatique.[20]

The example the Oratorians must contemplate and follow is the abnegation and *anéantissement* of the Incarnate Word.[21] Echoing Orcibal, it is precisely here that we pass from metaphysics to holiness. Bérulle wrote that the priest must: "répandre odeur ni du péché, ni de soi-même, mais de Jésus-Christ…ce qui suppose une très grande perfection et une présence, vie et plénitude de Jésus en l'âme qui la remplit, la pénètre, la vivifie et répand par elle, comme par une chose qui lui est conjoint, la sainte odeur de sa présence, sainteté et vertu divine."[22]

Augustine and the Divine Ideas: Image and Emanation

In analyzing Bérulle's thought, Orcibal referenced Gilson's analysis of St. Augustine's notions regarding image and the divine ideas.[23] Notably, according to Orcibal, Bérulle took from an early ideal of Augustine (which Augustine later rejected for creation *ex nihilo*) something of the flavor of Mani's doctrine that God is light, and a corporeal substance.[24]

In Augustine's thought, as Gilson summarized, the Word is the perfect image of the Father who engenders him as the perfect likeness of himself. Matter becomes an imperfect image of the Word and his ideas via a conversion toward him.[25]

---

20 Ibid., 185.
21 Bérulle, Coll. 38, quoted in *BLS*, 170. See *OC, Collationes* (1995): "statu exinanitionis."
22 Bérulle, *Mémorial*, 21, quoted in *BLS*, 173.
23 Jean Orcibal, "Néo-platonisme et Jansénisme: Du 'De libertate' du Gibieuf à 'l'Augustinus'," *Analecta Gregoriana* 71 (1954): 34. See Étienne Gilson, *Introduction à l'étude de saint Augustin*, Librairie Philosophique (Paris: J. Vrin, 1929), 268–74; also referenced in Taveau, *Le cardinal de Bérulle*, 268–78, regarding exemplarism.
24 Augustine, *Sancti Aurelii Augustini Hipponensis episcopi Opera omnia*, bk. 4 (Paris: Migne, n. d.), 16, 31, quoted in Gilson, *Introduction à l'étude de saint Augustin*, 242: "sed quid mihi hoc proderat, putanti quod tu, Domine Deus veritas, corpus esses lucidum et immensum et ego frustum de illo corpore?"
25 Ibid., 260n1, quoting Augustine, *De Genesi ad litteram imperfectus liber*, ed. J. Zycha, Corpus Scriptorum Ecclesiasticorum Latinorum, vol. 28 (Vienna: Verlag der Österreichischen Akademie der Wissenschaften, 1894), 1, 4, 9; bk. 34, col. 249: "An cum primum fiebat informitas materiae sive spiritalis sive corporalis, non erat dicendum: *Dixit Deus fiat*…; sed tunc imitatur Verbi formam, semper atque incommutabiliter Patri cohaerentem, cum et ipsa pro sui generis conversione ad id quod vere ac semper est, id est ad creatorem suae substantiae, formam capit, et fit perfecta creatura…: fit autem Filii

It is clear that Bérulle's rhetoric follows, in some measure, the bright ideals of Augustine, as this study has detailed.

Forming an Image in the Christian and in the Priest

For Bérulle, as Le Lannou wrote, only through the destruction of all attachments and the establishment of oneself in Jesus Christ is there ultimate freedom. In this vacuum, God can, as Bérulle noted "former en moi une image vive" of himself.[26] This imaging is based on an emanationist exemplarism, and in terms of the priest, Bérulle described his representation of Christ as an emanation of the Son, who, in turn, is emanated from the Father.

> Et comme dans la Sainte Trinité le Fils est l'image du Père et le Père est le prototype et origine du Fils, aussi le Fils a voulu que, comme il est l'image du Père dans la terre, il y eût aussi des prêtres qui fussent l'image du Fils, d'autant que comme le Fils est émané du Père, aussi les prêtres sont émanés du Fils; et comme le Fils en terre représente le Père, aussi les prêtres représentent le Fils.[27]

For Bérulle, the order of the priesthood itself was founded by Christ as an image of himself in order to communicate the body of Christ to the Church. Bérulle:

> le premier ordre de l'Église, et ordre essential et absolument nécessaire à icelle, est l'ordre de la prêtrise, lequel a été institué immédiatement…du Fils de Dieu même.
>
> Et il [le Fils] l'a institué sur soi-même, c'est-à-dire sur l'état et le modèle de la prêtrise, comme un exemplaire et organe de sa prêtrise en la terre, comme une image de soi-même en ce bas monde.[28]

This imaging extended to the priests themselves as living images. Bérulle wrote, "Nous devons reproduire le Christ, en être l'image, une image qui vive et respire.

---

commemoratio, quod etiam Verbum est, eo quod scriptum est *Dixit Deus, fiat*; ut per id quod principium est, insinuet exordium creaturae existentis ab illo adhuc imperfectae; per id autem quod Verbum est, insinuet perfectionem creaturae revocatae ad eum, ut formaretur inhaerendo Creatori, et pro suo genere imitando formam sempiterne atque incommutabiliter inhaerentem Patri, a quo statim hoc est quod ille."

26   *OC, Grandeurs* (1996), 321, quoted in SM, 226–27.
27   *BLS, OR* 80, no. 6, 418.
28   Ibid., 281, *OR* 9, nos. 6 and 7.

Car le prêtre est l'image du Christ sur terre; et c'est lui que les pécheurs doivent venir trouver, pour puiser en lui la grâce, la vie et l'Esprit du Christ."[29]

A Spirituality of Image and Ecstasy

Just as Protestant pastors were depicted as pious icons, replacing the images of saints on the walls of churches, in some fashion, Bérulle's construction of a spiritual theology of priesthood paralleled this emphasis on image and love, already present in tradition.

Dagens noted that Bernard influenced Bérulle in how he interiorized the life of Christ in the spirit of St. Paul, in that for Bernard, holiness is forming Christ in us, conforming ourselves, transforming ourselves into His image. Christians become members of Christ who is exemplar, but also active principle.[30]

According to Lehninger, Bernard introduced a theology of deification by ecstatic love, borrowing the ideal of *excessus* (moving out of oneself toward God) from Maximus, as well as the idea of a lover becoming the image of the beloved, such that in the height of the ecstatic experience the distinction between the human being and God is nearly lost, with its own form disappearing (but not its essence). As Bernard wrote, "the substance remains, but in another form."[31] Bernard:

> When will flesh and blood, this vessel of clay, this earthly dwelling, grasp this? When will it experience this kind of love, so that the mind, drunk with divine love and forgetting itself, making itself like a broken vessel, throws itself wholly on God and clinging to God, becomes one with him in spirit and says, "My body and my heart have fainted, O God of my heart; God, my part in eternity"? I should call him blessed and holy to whom it is given to experience even for a single instant something which is rare indeed in this life. To lose yourself as though you did not exist and to have no sense of yourself, to be emptied out of yourself and almost annihilated, belongs to heavenly not to human love.[32]

---

29 Ibid., 364, *OR* 42, no. 2.
30 Dagens, *Bérulle et les origines*, 303, without citation.
31 Bernard of Clairvaux, *De diligendo Deo*, 10.28, Sources chrétiennes (Paris: Éditions du Cerf, 1993), 393.132; *Bernard: On Loving God*, trans. G. R. Evans (New York: Paulist, 1987), 196, quoted in Lehninger, "Luther and Theosis," 71: "Manebit quidem substantia, sed in alia forma…" See 65–71.
32 Bernard of Clairvaux, *De diligendo Deo*, 10.27, 393.128–30, 195, quoted in Lehninger, "Luther and Theosis," 68: "Caro et sanguis, vas luteum, terrena inhabitatio quando capit hoc? Quando huiuscemodi experitur affectum, ut divino debriatus amore animus, *oblitus*

Aquinas versus Augustine

A comparison, again, between Bérulle's ideals and those of Aquinas can aid us in parsing Bérulle's project. Writing on the doctrine of the image of God and its influence, Sullivan noted that Aquinas diverged from Augustinianism, with the move to Aristotelianism over Neoplatonism.[33] Sullivan wrote: "It would seem that the concept of image used by Augustine demands the presence of God, not simply as a principle of origin—much less would this demand be satisfied by the 'intentional' presence of God in the image itself—but requires the enduring presence of the exemplar as the term of the dynamic activity found in an image."[34]

For Aquinas, the image must be considered primarily according to acts ("in mente secundum actus,") for only by actual knowledge is the mental word produced in man ("cogitando interius verbum formamus"). The image is placed in the powers of the soul ("Ergo imago attenditur secundum potentias, et non secundum actus.").[35]

The concept of image according to Augustine, however, involved a relation of likeness, and a relation of origin from which likeness is derived. There must be a likeness in regards to a closeness in nature but also a relation to the exemplar as term of the dynamic tendency in the image. The exemplar is present in regards to the relation of origin and term. Therefore, efficient, exemplar, and final causality are involved.[36] So, too, for Bérulle, as he held to the ideal that to be a priest, one must attempt to participate in Christ at all times through acts of will in the service of the intellect, thus conforming to the image of Christ.

---

sui, factusque sibi ipsi tamquam vas perditum, totus pergat in Deum et, *adhaerens Deo, unus cum eo spiritus fiat* et dicat: *Defecit caro mea et cor meum; Deus cordis mei, et pars mea Deus in aeternum?* Beatum dixerim et sanctum, cui tale aliquid in hac mortali vita raro interdum, aut vel semel, et hoc ipsum raptim atque unius vix momenti spatio, experiri donatum est. Te enim quodammodo perdere, tamquam qui non sis, et omnino non sentire teipsum, et a *temetipso exinaniri,* et paene annullari, caelestis est conversationis, non humanae affectionis."

[33] John Edward Sullivan, *The Image of God: The Doctrine of St. Augustine and Its Influence* (Dubuque, IA: Priory Press, 1963), 204. This review follows the author's exposition closely.

[34] Ibid., 21.

[35] Ibid., 259. See *ST*, 1.93.6.

[36] Ibid., 21.

The Priesthood and Image

Aquinas held that the priest bears Christ's image in the sacrifice of the Mass. The priest and victim are also, in some measure, one.[37] The question remains regarding the interpretation of this representation and imaging for Bérulle.

Bérulle urged priests to make frequent prayers to conform to Christ in order to become this living image. Just as Christ is the image of the Father, so priests are to be the image of the Son on earth. Priests must pray to be transformed:

> Pour y entrer (dans cet état d'instrument conjoint au Fils de Dieu), il faut beaucoup traiter avec lui en l'oraison, nous conformer avec lui par les vertus intérieures et extérieures et faire en sorte que nous soyons une image vive de Jésus en la terre comme il est une image vive de son Père au ciel. C'est le propre du Fils d'être l'image de son Père...Ce doit être aussi une des conditions propres des prêtres d'être l'image du Fils de Dieu en la terre... Aimez-le et le priez de vous transformer en lui...[38]

The Spiritual Theology of Priesthood and Conformity: Similitude and Likeness

As already noted, Ozment questioned whether a young Luther might not have represented a synthesis between nominalism and mysticism. He was a devotee of medieval mysticism, a trained Ockhamist, had annotated Tauler and Biel, and edited *Theologia Deutsch*. Ozment opined, however, that Luther rejected the axiom of similitude as presented in both traditions respectively.[39]

How did Bérulle treat similitude?

Néantisme *and Image*

McKay explained Bérulle's thought on the mysteries of the life of Christ in relation to the soul's deification. The states and mysteries of the life of Christ were

---

[37] See Dennis Michael Ferrara, "Representation or Self-Effacement? The Axiom *in Persona Christi* in St. Thomas and the Magisterium," Theological Studies 55 (1994): 195–224. See 198, quoting Aquinas, *ST*, 3.83.1, ad 3. In *Summa theologiae*, 12.1: 271, here expanded, in Latin: "Ad tertium dicendum quod, per eandem rationem, etiam sacerdos gerit imaginem Christi, in cuius persona et virtute verba pronunciat ad consecrandum, ut ex supra dictis patet. Et ita quodammodo idem est sacerdos et hostia."

[38] Bérulle, 11 June 1617; *CB*, vol. 1, 241; also Letter 168, no. 3, col. 1503, quoted in Cochois, "Bérulle, hiérarque dionysien," 37: 330n34.

[39] Ozment, "Mysticism, Nominalism and Dissent," 91–92.

deified in the risen Christ.[40] She wrote, "Therefore the share in divine life which is communicated through the states of Christ imprints on souls His interior dispositions, simultaneously effecting and evoking likeness to him."[41] This is made possible by the substantial sanctification of the humanity and the deification of all the states.[42]

As demonstrated, Bérulle chose to focus on dispositions, the conformity of the will to God, and the soul's capacity to receive God; however, his particular *néantisme* denied the idea of likeness as fulfilling one's own nature.

To the contrary, just as Gibieuf held that it is only the relation of the quasi-*néant* of human *être* that allows rational creatures to be formed in the image and likeness of God,[43] so, too, did Bérulle.

Conclusion

To answer Luther's charge regarding false images and Calvin's insistence that all Christians were true images, Bérulle emphasized how believers and priests were true and living images. This formed the basis of his defense of the priest as a living and visible image of Christ the head, in which remains the enduring presence of the exemplar.

Luther's own vision of the minister as transparent (so that the image of Christ is present) was taken up in earnest by Bérulle in his kenotic spiritual theology. While Luther was reacting against the notion of the priest as representative of Christ in his person, Bérulle defended the same, absorbing this transparency, which, arguably, heightened an essentialist representationalism.

Bérulle absorbed Calvin's notion of the living image as particularly applicable to priests. In so doing, he underscored and strengthened his defense of the ideal of the priest as conjoint instrument, inflating the Thomistic notion of personal instrumentality.

This absorption and adaption of Reformist ideals increased the focus on the person of the priest and his personal power beyond the traditional ideals pertaining to either Western cultic representation or patristic metaphor or mysticism.

---

[40]   TG, 269. See *OP* 17, no. 2, col. 940.

[41]   Ibid., 269–70.

[42]   Ibid., 294.

[43]   Orcibal, "Néoplatonisme et Jansénisme," 38. See Guillaume Gibieuf, *De libertate Dei et creaturae libri duo* (Paris, 1630), 96, 269, 361–64, and 371–73.

Particularly, Bérulle's conflation of legal and official image with that produced by grace, faith, and charity (which is mirrored in his notions regarding configuration and conformity, and character and grace) further expanded an essentialist interpretation of sacerdotal image through the loss of the sense of the natural image, which he replaced with the concept of the *néant*.

The result was an iconoclastic spirituality, that is, one that destroyed the natural image of God in the priest, in favor of a kenotic spiritual theology that moved the psychological to the ontological and fused the images of the priest and Christ into one metaphysical, moral, and political entity.

Chapter 19
Conclusions

Introduction

Bérulle's attempt to renew the priesthood created a sea change in the spiritual theology of priesthood. His project's aim was to construct a new system of spiritual practices designed to create more educated and holy priests, a system which could be termed a "technology of the self," a term coined by de Certeau in his exploration of the idea that technologies of the self shape the psyche.[1]

This study indicates that Bérulle's sacerdotal program of spirituality, based on a complex spiritual theology of priesthood, with which he hoped to form new priests to meet the challenges of evangelization during the Counter-Reformation, represented just such a technology of the self.

This technology also represented a major turn in spirituality and in the spiritual theology of priesthood, a turn toward the self and the subjective, resulting in an inflated yet kenotic sacerdotal identity. These impulses served both the Church hierarchy's and the Jansenist agendas, and remained in place for centuries.

The Oratorians' turn toward a monastic high ascesis followed a reformist trend in the sacerdotal culture of the Post-Tridentine era. Bérulle's incorporation of them into his intense program of spiritual formation of priests, and Saint-Cyran and Jansen's use of the Oratory to promote their ends, created a sum greater than its parts in that it at once forged and spread a new sacerdotal spiritual theology.

These effects were related to distortions of key theological concepts affirmed by Trent, as scholars reviewed have noted. Bérulle took Trent's affirmation of indelible character and elevated it to include the ideas of quasi-substantial and quasi-hypostatic unions. He utilized Trent's affirmation of the Pseudo-Dionysian concept of a divinely-instituted hierarchy and affirmed the power of clerics as sole dispensers of grace. He expanded Trent's notion of the priest as the representative of Christ in the offering of the sacrifice of the Mass into the notion that the priest not only acts in the person of Christ at the Mass but, in fact,

---

[1] See Michel Foucault, "Technologies of the Self," in Michel Foucault and Luther H. Martin, *Technologies of the Self: A Seminar with Michel Foucault* (Amherst: University of Massachusetts Press, 1988), 16–49.

assumes the person of Christ at all times, a Cyrillian inheritance, but only through a required continuous moral effort.

This study now ends with a final exposition and synthesis of the many aspects of Bérulle's spiritual theology of priesthood reviewed and uncovered in this study.

Concluding Synthesis

As Rahner wrote, there is no mystical theology outside the body of theology. Just so, there is no spiritual theology of priesthood outside of the theology of priesthood, which, as this study has illustrated, is dependent upon a host of applied ideas taken from speculative mysticism and metaphysics as related to Christology, pneumatology, and the Trinity.

A renewed spiritual theology of priesthood will depend on a renewed theology of priesthood, in turn dependent on gains in other fields of theological and philosophical inquiry by scholars from a broad range of specializations, resolving longstanding questions pertaining to such doctrines as the Mass as sacrifice, the Mystical Body, and other ideas such as relation, causality, and grace, all of which came to the fore at the time of the Reformation.

Bérulle's spiritual theology of priesthood can only be fully understood when compared with others leading up to and following his era, so any conclusions are tentative. That said, this study, albeit preliminary, can serve as a basis for exploring other spiritual theologies of priesthood in that it illustrates the importance of understanding underlying philosophical ideals.

This study may also provide benchmarks for future lines of inquiry in the exploration of the history of the theology of priesthood in general. More specifically, it serves to highlight one attempt to describe the participated priesthood at a crucial moment in the history of the faith, and what, according to generally accepted traditional notions, the participated priesthood likely is not—that is, if doctrinal ambiguities, and Reformist and Counter-Reformist inheritances and aporias are taken into consideration.

This concluding chapter will review and summarize these notions, attempting to see them as a whole. First, a discussion is warranted of the field of aporetics and its importance in parsing Berullian themes.

Rescher's Work

One aim of this study is to provide scholars with a better view of understudied aspects of Bérulle's spiritual theology of priesthood, aspects which may continue to have a presence within current ideals, whether assumed in popular books on the priesthood or suggested in official documents. Rescher's work on aporetics points to some of the difficulties facing scholars working in any field and is particularly applicable to the discipline of the spiritual theology of priesthood, a discipline in which tradition may have uncritically retained and accepted as canonical certain syncretistic notions which had their genesis in Reformist or Counter-Reformist ideologies.

As Rescher wrote, "The root idea of aporetics lies in the combination of reductive quality control in situations where we have succumbed to the cognitive overcommitment of inconsistency and find ourselves having to salvage some part of what must be abandoned."[2]

As evidenced by Terrien's and Cancouët's analyses, there remain current complexes of ideas surrounding the priesthood which have been retained in some form, however naïvely, from the era under consideration. This study indicates that when disassembled into various free-standing theses, certain of these notions do not survive the light of accepted doctrine and tradition. Each combination of these notions could be considered what Rescher called an "apory" or "a group of individually plausible but collectively incompatible theses."[3]

This study has demonstrated that Bérulle took a number of plausible but incompatible theses available in his eclectic age and assembled them into a spiritual theology that, viewed in its entirety, contributed to an untenable overall theology of priesthood.

At the time of the Counter-Reformation in France, the Church faced extreme tensions, resulting in repeated wars and the final breakdown of the unity of Christendom. Bérulle attempted to defend the crown, the Church, and the priesthood by stretching numerous ideas to their maximum interpretation and limits in support of what became, arguably, a grandiose immanentism, one that affected Christology, the priesthood, and ecclesiology as well. As scholars have noted and this study has detailed, a number of these ideals may be described as Reformist and Counter-Reformist inheritances and aporias.

Rescher described this kind of exaggerated absorption, and how, over time, it can create a delayed crisis, something that could arguably be happening in the current moment:

> In addressing cognitive problems we seek to maximize our opportunities by pressing matters to the limits. We thus embark on speculations that not only reach, but also overreach, and thereby plunge into inconsistency.

---

[2]   Nicholas Rescher, *Aporetics: Rational Deliberation in the Face of Inconsistency* (Pittsburgh: University of Pittsburgh Press, 2009), ix.

[3]   Ibid., 1.

This process reflects a general—and understandable—tendency to hypertrophy that manifests itself in many areas as populations or organizations grow to a point that threatens their very viability.[4]

While Bérulle's attempt was a noble one, it began an ideological current that has lasted for centuries. Bérulle's ideals may have been expunged from published texts, but many survived to take root and flourish in the French School. The reason for the widespread acceptance of Bérulle's ideals may be an example of what Rescher would call "cognitive presumption," which is characterized as the acceptance that something is true because an authority has put it forward as such.[5]

Berullian Reformist Inheritances and Aporias

Bérulle's was a near-encyclopedic effort, framed in pious rhetoric, to address a myriad of Reformist and Counter-Reformist positions. He did so by means of a coordinated defense of concepts related to the Mass, the priesthood, and the Church. His own background as a polemicist gave him a unique perspective with which to reformulate, summarize, and apply already-proposed ideas put forward by others. By couching extraordinarily complex ideas, both orthodox and unorthodox, into phraseology accessible to the neophyte seminarian involved in an exalted spiritual formation, and easily passed on in pious sacerdotal literature, a robustness was created in his idea system.

These ideas have been dismissed as non-essential by systematic theologians, but embraced by others influenced themselves by the French School tradition. Still others, aware of the difficulties and cognizant of weaknesses in the tradition known to be influential in flavoring some church documents, have attempted to quietly reformulate these ideas in an attempt to modernize them, rooting out distortions where possible, as Glendon's attempt testifies.

A final summary of these Reformist and Counter-Reformist inheritances and aporias follows.

---

[4]   Ibid., 2.
[5]   Ibid., 18.

Trinitarian Mechanics

Bérulle's was a radical innovation in the spiritual theology of priesthood first and foremost because he attempted to frame a Trinitarian emanationism inside a syncretistic Christic personalism, with the priest's person emanating from that of Christ's person, in an essentialist relation, as well as in a quasi-hypostatic union with the Holy Spirit.

Christ became autotheotic, operating in time in the person of the priest as public person and visible head of the Church, not only during the administration of the sacraments, but at all times. In his efforts to reinforce the union of the person of the priest with the divine persons, Bérulle conflated the ideas of existence, subsistence, substance, person, and relation, notably approaching them from a personalist and moralistic viewpoint in which the idea of person as personality seemed to rise to the surface, seen as *néant*.

Conflating religion with the virtue of religion, Bérulle's priest not only was placed inside the adoration of Christ, but became himself the center of a rigorist ecclesial culture, made a necessary public agent of morality. A graced Trinitarian immensity, forgotten in the Counter-Reform, was replaced by a willed Christic immensity, accessible through heroic acts of the will, via a way of eminence reserved for the perfect and for the priest if perfected himself.

What was lost in this crucible of history was nothing less than the sensibilities of both Christian and ecclesial identities, once founded in the life of the Trinity. Trinitarian immensity, belonging to all humanity, was replaced with a kind of union with Christ as substance, restricted to the elect.

Speaking about Ockham's thought and the influence of nominalism, Paul Tillich offered the following:

> God has become an individual Himself. As such, He is separated from the other individuals, He looks at them and they look at Him. God is not in the center of everything any more, as He was in the Augustinian kind of thought, but He has been removed from this center into a special place distant from the things, just as man. I.e., God Himself has become an individual. The individual things have become independent. The substantial presence of God in all of them doesn't mean anything anymore, because that presupposes some kind of mystical realism. Therefore God has to know the things, so to speak, empirically, from outside. He is in our situation. As man approaches the world empirically, because he is not the center any more, he doesn't know anything immediately, he can only know empirically—so God knows everything empirically, but empirically not as before, by being in the center. God

Himself has ceased to be the center in which all reality is united. He is no more center. The whole thing is a pluralistic philosophy in which there are many individual beings, of which God is one, although the most important one. In this way the unity of the things in God has come to an end. Their individual separation has the consequence that they cannot participate in each other immediately because each of them participates in a universal. The one tree does not participate in the other as it did before, when mystical realism gave them the universal treehood as the space in which they participated in each other. Community, as we had it in the Augustinian type of thinking, is replaced by social relations, by society. We live today in the consequence of this nominalistic thinking, in a society in which we are related to each other in terms of cooperation and competition, but neither the one nor the other word means something of the type of participation.[6]

In Tillich's terms, for Bérulle's priest, God was no longer the center but rather Christ, and the priest was to participate in him as if by way of a universal christhood. The relation of the priest to the Trinity became, with Bérulle, a social relation between the priest and the society of the Trinity. The full exercise of the priest's sacramental power demanded the priest's willed cooperation and perfection in order to maintain this relation, a relation made first in and through Christ.

Rejection of the Mass as Sacrifice Becomes a Sacrificial and Kenotic Spirituality

The Lutheran rejection of the Mass as sacrifice, and the notion of sacrifice as that of praise and love, following Aquinas, was met by Bérulle with a spirituality for both laity and priests based on a kenotic Word Christology extended to the point of moral annihilation.

Influenced by a Lutheran architectonic of an Eckhartian-influenced imputed being and righteousness, along with a rejection of *habitus* theology, Bérulle's priest was forced to a required perfection of his high office by participating in an essentialist mysticism to maintain union with Christ. Luther's requirement that the minister be transparent to the image of Christ was mirrored in this kenotic spiritual theology.

---

[6] Paul Tillich, "The History of Christian Thought: Lectures in Church History," Lecture 28, Spring 1953, Union Theological Seminary, New York, verbatim class notes, http://www.religion-online.org/showchapter.asp?title=2310&C=2333.

Calvin's Metaphysics as Sacerdotal Spirituality

Calvin's and Calvinist ideals appear to have had considerable influence in Bérulle's spiritual theology of priesthood, themselves reactions against ideas Bérulle sought to defend with new emphases. "Putting on Christ," being "inside the person of Christ," "assuming the person of Christ"—these echoes of scriptures, the fathers, and Calvin's Christology were Bérulle's attempt to legitimate the priest's actions in the Mass and in the governance of the Church by equating subjective and objective holiness.

First, Calvin's insistence on the priesthood of Christ as begun in glory, along with an emphasis on adoration, became, in Bérulle's project, a focus on a theopathic state for priests which they could maintain through constant adoration and preoccupation with the mysteries of Christ in glory, effectuating similitude through an exemplar causality. This idea of assimilation as the cause of Christ's or the Spirit's dwelling in the soul, rather than the effect of Trinitarian indwelling, had ramifications in the conflation of configuration and conformity. Importantly, it conflated the ideas of substantial and affective unions.

Calvin's emphasis on the union of the two natures and his ideals of a quasi-personal relationship with the Holy Spirit and *unio mystica* were mirrored in Bérulle's sacerdotal spirituality with a constant meditation on Christ the God-Man to maintain election, as it were. A substantial formal holiness, based on a confused communication of idioms, formed the basis both of the priest's participation in the priesthood of Christ and of a quasi-hypostatic union with the Holy Spirit. In Bérulle's Stoic Christosyncretism, Christ became subsistence and substance of the Mystical Body and of the priest himself. By making the Incarnation into the fourth order of the universe, Bérulle placed the priest inside the hypostatic union itself.

The Scotist and Calvinist emphasis on relation, and the blurring of *ad intra* and *ad extra* operations, was taken up by Bérulle as he failed to distinguish between Trinitarian relations, the relation of the humanity to the divinity of Christ, and the believer's relation to Christ. Bérulle utilized this overextended notion of relation, absorbing a Calvinist emphasis on radical obedience and union, and creating a schema emphasizing an intense personalist and voluntarist union between the priest and Christ.

Calvin's emphasis on election, servitude, and covenantal relations was met by Bérulle with a system that conflated moral, psychological, juridical, and ontological categories. An ecclesial authority based on a conflation of procession and mission was given to the priest through an interiorized piety rather than an external office belonging first to the bishop. Vocation and office became internalized as the priest became a holy mediator of redemption and holiness through a willed unicity.

Elements of Non-Christian Priesthood

Added to these conflations was the adoption of two characteristics of non-Christian priesthood, blending magical and political power: a notion similar to the Iamblichan sacerdotal spirituality based on theurgical practice and to that of the ideal of the Roman public person, representative of the *respublica christiana*, public participant in the redemption of both the body politic and the Church. A Florentine intellectualist soteriology based on the divine formation of the intellectual power was also included in this schema to reinforce the priest's role in his own and the laity's salvation.

Cyrillian and Pseudo-Dionysian Priesthoods

Pseudo-Dionysian inheritances have been well-documented. Less well analyzed has been the influence of Cyril's thought overall, as well as his doctrine on the priesthood, a clear precursor to Pseudo-Dionysius. As with Cyril, Bérulle held that the priest assumes the person of Christ. His Oratorians' sacerdotal power was the power of the Holy Spirit but only in terms of the same Monoenergist soteriology in which Christ, as the sole priest, operates at all times.

That said, in response to Reformists' clear rejection of this soteriology, Bérulle developed a participation based on an intense voluntarism to maintain this power.

Other Aporias

Bérulle's nihilism was characterized by a radical rejection of univocity, in that hell is at the center of the soul rather than God, who must be reinserted by a willed unicity centered on person rather than being. The same nihilism included a radical rejection of the analogy of being through a generative exemplarism that made the priest a theandric conjoint instrument.

The rejection of both univocity and analogy of being required that the priest be a *néant* in order to cede place to Christ. This self-naughting was perhaps by way of ameliorating this grandiosity. Bérulle's annihilationism involved a Maximian transposition of a Stoic ideal into an ideal of the soul as receiving the Word Incarnate as a substitute for its own ego. At the same time, it reflected a Calvinist emphasis on a Word Christology at the expense of both the humanity of Christ and the humanity of the priest.

The influence of nominalism can be seen in Bérulle's spiritual theology: God is both the highest expression of the priestly self as visible image and head, and yet is transcendent and distant, as the priest must also be a kenotic vessel and immolated victim in order to become mediator of redemption, participating in the mediation of Christ at the level of being.

Another key nominalist influence, according to Bouyer, was the reduction of being to act. Rather, Bérulle's was a reduction of being to action. His priesthood was radically functional, making the priest a conjoint instrument, subject to an exaggerated exemplar causality in which all the actions of the priest become Christ's based on the erroneous notions of the divine person as a kind of quasi-formal cause and of an essentialist relation or union with one or more divine persons.

This study also indicates that Bérulle's spiritual theology of priesthood was more than a high ascesis modeled after the monk-priest of the patristic era, but rather a radical assumption of certain Neoplatonic notions regarding the relationship of being to contemplation placed in the service of a negative strain of Augustinian piety and Neostoic ethicism.

This study suggests that in Bérulle's era, as in other eras, a singular appropriation of classical and patristic notions, which had gained renewed interest, was a key characteristic. This influence appears to have been considerable and suggests that the tensions and dichotomies between what might be called the spiritual theology of priesthood of the historical Jesus and that of the Christ of faith may rest at the heart of current questions facing any renewal.

This study would also indicate that the current debates surrounding character involve a false dichotomy between the functional and the essential, a dichotomy which has its roots in ambiguities related to certain patristic currents in spirituality, the philosophical influences of middle Platonism, and a polemicized Scotism presented in Thomistic terms in the Christological debates of the sixteenth century, as noted by various authors.

The Transparent Public Person

Perhaps one of the strongest Reformist aporias involved the combining of the notion of public person with that of transparent image. Bérulle's reply to both Lutheran and Calvinist rejections of the priest as the image of Christ and mediator led to an iconoclastic representationalism in which the priest became both transparent and multi-hypostatic. Bérulle's priest was not only a public person and visible image of Christ the head, but also an efficacious sign, an agent of redemption, and a holy mediator of holiness.

Conclusion

Bérulle's Oratorian stood in the rubble of a war-torn France, at the dawn of the modern era, moving and having his being, as it were, inside a Stoic and Copernican Christ, a super-Renaissance God-Man, substance and subsistence of a priesthood under attack. Bérulle married a wide variety of mystical and ascetical ideals to give birth to a chimera—the modern priest.

Last, Bérulle's project followed a major turn in the theologizing of his era, toward an emphasis on movements of the soul and a polemicized positive theological method that has continued into the present, unaware of its own past trajectories.

Afterword
Toward a Renewed Spiritual Theology of Priesthood

Any contemplation of the priesthood of Christ can only bring us to the edge of one of the central mysteries of our faith. With this caveat in mind, the findings of this study suggest some avenues for exploration toward a renewed theology of priesthood. In terms of a renewed spiritual theology of priesthood, I would offer some closing remarks.

Bérulle's intuition of the importance of the Trinity was not misplaced. A renewal in the study of the Trinity in relation to the theology of the Mass and of the priesthood could bear much fruit. In addition, a renewed study of the many historical expressions of participated priesthood and sacerdotal spirituality could begin to bring to light alternative ways of conceptualizing participation in the priesthood of Christ beyond any narrowings or expansions which occurred in the eras of the Reformation and Counter-Reformation.

One question for exploration is how Christ is made present on the altar through Trinitarian action, made possible by the words of the priest. What might the role of the priest become in terms of presider at the Eucharist in the presence of the Trinity? Viewing sacrifice in Thomistic terms, as love and adoration, suggests the possibility of a vision of the sacerdotal identity of the Trinity itself as loving and life-giving in essence.

Next, study of the historical Jesus and his own Jewish sacerdotal spirituality could aid in expanding a vision of priesthood that is more in line with scriptures.

The ideal of a kind of way of eminence, a foretaste of the kingdom, characterized by a union of wills and various charismata in the service of the Church, is an ideal to build on in terms of renewal. Building on a relationship with Christ foremost as friend and exemplum, and with the Holy Spirit as comforter, could foster any renewal of the priesthood in terms of formation spiritualities and theologies freed from any immanentist grandiosity or rigorist ethicism.

The ideals of the priest as holy mediator, transparent image, and public person with a kenotic public spirituality have not served the Church well. Every priest is likely called to a vocation within a vocation, and any of a myriad of spiritualities which the Church offers. His public witness could best be nurtured if built upon his own God-given charisms.

In summary, Bérulle had a dream of a renewed priesthood in the service of the Church, society, and the coming of the kingdom. The dream continues.

Selected Bibliography

Editions of Bérulle's Complete Works

Les Œuvres de l'éminentissime et révérendissime P. cardinal de Bérulle...augmentées de divers opuscules de controverse et de piété, avec plusieurs lettres: et enrichies de sommaires et de tables. Edited by François Bourgoing. Paris: Antoine Estienne, 1644.

Les Œuvres de l'eminentissime et reverendissime Pierre Cardinal de Bérulle, instituteur, et premier Superieur General de la Congregation de l'Oratoire de Iesus-Christ nostre Seigneur: Augmentées de divers opuscules de controverse & de pieté, auec plusieurs lettres: et enrichies de sommaires & de tables. Paris: Chez Sebastien Huré, au Cœur-bon, et Frederic Leonard, à l'Escu de Venise, 1657.

Œuvres complètes de Bérulle, cardinal de l'Église romaine, fondateur et premier supérieur de l'Oratoire, augmentées de plusieurs opuscules inédits et d'un grand nombre de pièces recueillies dans divers ouvrages, disposés dans un ordre logique. Paris: Ateliers catholiques Migne, 1856.

Œuvres complètes. Reproduction de l'Édition Princeps. Montsoult: Maison d'Institution de l'Oratoire, 1960.

Œuvres complètes. Paris: Oratoire de Jésus–Les éditions du Cerf, 1995–2011.

Vol. 1   *Conférences et fragments.* Translated into French by Auguste Piedagnel. Edited by Michel Dupuy. With a preface by Jean Dujardin. Paris, 1995.

Vol. 2   *Collationes.* Latin text of *Conférences et fragments.* Edited by Michel Dupuy. Paris, 1995.

Vol. 3   *Œuvres de piété* (1–165). Edited by Michel Dupuy. Paris, 1995.

Vol. 4   *Œuvres de piété* (166–385). Edited by Michel Dupuy. Paris, 1996.

Vol. 6   *Courts traités: Bref discours de l'abnégation intérieure, Traité des énergumènes, Trois discours de controverse, Autres œuvres de controverses.* Edited by Michel Dupuy. Paris, 1997.

Vol. 7   *Discours de l'état et des grandeurs de Jésus.* With an introduction by Rémi Lescot. Edited by Michel Join-Lambert and Rémi Lescot. Paris, 1996.

Vol. 8   *Discours de l'état et des grandeurs de Jésus, Narré, Approbations, Élévations, Vie de Jésus, Mémorial de direction, Élévation vers sainte Marie-Madeleine.* Edited by Joseph Beaude, Blandine Delahaye, Michel Join-Lambert, and Rémi Lescot. Paris, 1996.

Bérulle's Other Works

Bérulle, Pierre de. *Collationes congregationis nostrae,* manuscrit latin 18210. Paris: Bibliothèque nationale.

———. *Mémorial de quelques points servans à la direction des Supérieurs en la Congrégation de l'Oratoire de Iesus.* Paris, 1632.

———, and Jean Dagens. *Correspondance du cardinal Pierre de Bérulle.* 3 vols. Paris: Desclée, de Brouwer, 1937–39.

———, and Olivier Piquand. *Discours de l'estat et des grandeurs de Jésus par l'union ineffable de la divinité avec l'humanité.* Paris: Siffre Fils et cie, 1865.

———, and William Thompson. *Bérulle and the French School: Selected Writings.* New York, NY, and Mahwah, NJ: Paulist Press, 1989.

Secondary Sources

Abel, Günter. *Stoizismus und frühe Neuzeit: zur Entstehungsgeschichte modernen Denkens im Felde von Ethik u. Politik.* Berlin and New York: De Gruyter, 1978.

Académie française. *Dictionnaire de l'Académie Française.* 1st ed. Paris: J. B. Coignard, 1694. http://artfl-project.uchicago.edu/content/dictionnaires-dautrefois.

———. *Dictionnaire de l'Académie Française.* 4th ed. Paris: chez la veuve de B. Brunet, 1762.

Alberigo, Giuseppe. "La 'réception' du concile de Trente par l'Église catholique romaine." *Irenikon* 58 (1985): 311–37.

Alcorta, J. I. *La teoría de los modos en Suárez.* Madrid: Consejo Superior de Investigaciones Cientificas, Instituto "Luis Vives" de Filosofía, 1949.

Amelote, Denis. *La vie du père Charles de Condren, second supérieur général de la Congrégation de l'Oratoire de Jésus.* Paris. 1643.

Angers, Julien-Eymard d'. "L'exemplarisme bérullien: les rapports du naturel et du surnaturel dans l'œuvre du cardinal de Bérulle." *Revue des sciences religieuses* 31 (1957): 122–39.

Aquinas, Thomas. *De potentia Dei.* In *Quaestiones disputatae de potentia Dei.* Translated by the English Dominican Fathers. Westminster, MD: Newman Press, 1952.

———. *Quaestiones disputatae de veritate.* Vol. 22 of *Sancti Thomae de Aquino opera omnia iussu Leonis XIII P. M. edita.* Vol. 1, fasc. 2, *QQ. 1–7.* Rome: Ad Sanctae Sabinae, 1970.

———. *Scriptum super Sententiis magistri Petri Lombardi.* Edited by Maria Fabianus Moos. Vols. 3 and 4. Paris: P. Lethielleux, 1933–47.

———. *Summa theologiae ad codices manuscriptos vaticanos exacta cum commentariis Thomae de Vio Caietani ordinis Praedicatorum S. R. E. cardinalis.* Vols. 4–12 of *Sancti Thomae Aquinatis doctoris angelici opera omnia iussu impensaque Leonis XIII P. M. edita.* Rome: Ex Typographia Polyglotta S. C. de Propaganda Fide, 1888–1906.

Árbouze, Marguerite d'. *Traité de l'oraison.* Paris, 1625.

Aristotle, Kenelm Foster, Silvester Humphries, and Ivo Thomas. *Aristotle's De anima: In the Version of William of Moerbeke and the Commentary of St. Thomas Aquinas*. London: s.n., 1951.

Armstrong, Arthur Hilary. *An Introduction to Ancient Philosophy*. 3rd edition. London: Methuen, 1957.

Auer, Johann, and Hugh M. Riley. *A General Doctrine of the Sacraments and the Mystery of the Eucharist*. Washington, D.C.: Catholic University of America Press, 1995. Originally published as Johann Auer and Joseph Ratzinger, *Allgemeine Sakramentenlehre und das Mysterium der Eucharistie*. Regensburg: Friedrich Pustet Verlag, 1971.

Aumann, Jordan, *Christian Spirituality in the Catholic Tradition*. San Francisco, CA: Ignatius Press, 1985.

Augustine. *De Genesi ad litteram imperfectus liber*. Edited by J. Zycha. Corpus Scriptorum Ecclesiasticorum Latinorum. Vol. 28. Vienna: Verlag der Österreichischen Akademie der Wissenschaften, 1894.

———. *Sancti Aurelii Augustini Hipponensis episcopi Opera omnia*. Paris: Migne, n. d.

———. *The Trinity*. Translated by Edmund Hill. Brooklyn, NY: New City Press, 1991.

——— and Almut Mutzenbecher. *Sancti Aurelii Augustini De diversis quaestionibus octoginta tribus, De octo Dulcitii quaestionibus*. Corpus Christianorum, Series Latina. Vol. 44a. Turnholt: Brepols, 1975.

Augustinus, Aurelius, and Johann Kreuzer. *De Trinitate: Bücher VIII–XI, XIV–XV, Anhang Buch V*. Hamburg: Felix Meiner Verlag, 2001.

Bacchi, L. F. *The Theology of Ordained Ministry in the Letters of Augustine of Hippo*. San Francisco: International Scholars Publications, 1998.

Balic, Charles. "Duns Scot." In *DSAM*. Vol. 3 (1957), cols. 1801–15.

Balthasar, Hans Urs von. "Don du Christ et sacrifice eucharistique." *Communio* 10, no. 3 (1985): 4–7.

———, John Kenneth Riches, and Brian McNeil. *The Glory of the Lord: A Theological Aesthetics.* Vol. 5, *The Realm of Metaphysics in the Modern Age.* Edinburgh: T. & T. Clark, 1991. Originally published as *Herrlichkeit: Eine theologische Ästhetik.* Einsiedeln: Joannes, 1961–69.

Bamburger, John Eudes, and Evagrius. *The Praktikos [&] Chapters on Prayer.* Spencer, MA: Cistercian Publications, 1972.

Bauer, Ferdinand Christian. *Die christliche Lehre von der Dreieinigkeit und Menschwerdung Gottes in ihrer geschichtlichen Entwicklung.* Vol. 3. Tübingen: C. F. Oslander, 1843.

Baumgartner, Charles. "Contemplation: conclusion générale." In *DSAM.* Vol. 2 (1953), col. 2171.

Beaude, Joseph. "Historicité et vie mystique: la vie de Jésus du cardinal de Bérulle." *Archives de Philosophie* 29 (1986): 571–82.

Beckwith, Roger. "The Calvinist Doctrine of the Trinity." *Churchman* 115, no. 4 (2001): 308–15.

Bellarmine, Robert. *De Controversiis Christianae Fidei.* Vol. 3. Naples, 1856–1858.

———. *Disputationes de Controversiis Christianae Fidei adversus hujus temporis Haereticos.* Ingolstadt, 1581–93.

———. *De Sacramento Ordinis Roberti Bellarmini.* In *Opera omnia.* Vol. 5. Edited by Justinus Fèvre. Paris: Ludovicum Vivès, 1870–74.

———. "The Fourteenth Precept: On the Sacrament of Orders." In *The Art of Dying Well,* trans. John Dalton, 99–106. London: Richardson and Son, 1847. Original published as *Ars bene moriendi,* 1619.

———. *Opera omnia.* Paris: Ludovicum Vives, 1870.

Bellemare, Robert. *Le sens de la créature dans la doctrine de Bérulle.* Paris: Desclée de Brouwer, 1959.

Benedict XVI. *Apostolic Letter: Proclaiming Saint John of Ávila, Diocesan Priest, a Doctor of the Universal Church.* Vatican City: Libreria Editrice Vaticana, 2012.

Berman, Harold. *Law and Revolution.* Vol. 2, *The Impact of the Protestant Reformations on the Western Legal Tradition.* Cambridge, MA: Harvard University Press, 2003.

Bernard of Clairvaux. *Bernard: On Loving God.* Translated by G. R. Evans. New York: Paulist, 1987.

———. *De diligendo Deo.* Sources chrétiennes. Paris: Éditions du Cerf, 1993.

Besse, Pierre de. *Royale prestrise, c'est à dire; des excellences; des qualités requises, & des choses defendues aux prêtres.* Paris, 1610.

Beveridge, Henry. "Preface." In John Calvin, *Institutes of the Christian Religion,* trans. Henry Beveridge. Peabody, MA: Hendrickson Publishers, 2008.

Bifet, Juan Esquerda. "Estado actual de la reflexión teológica sobre el sacerdocio." In José Capmany Casamitjana, *Teología del sacerdocio: orientaciones metodológicas.* Vol. 1, 155–225. Burgos: Ediciones Aldecoa, S.A., 1969.

———. *Teología de la espiritualidad sacerdotal.* Madrid: Editorial Católica, 1976.

———. *Teología del sacerdocio: historia de la espiritualidad sacerdotal.* Vol. 19. Burgos: Ediciones Aldecoa, S.A., 1985.

Billot, L. *De Verbo Incarnato.* 7th ed. Rome: Gregorianum, 1927.

Blanchard, Virgile. "La spiritualité christocentrique de Pierre de Bérulle dans les écrits des premières années de l'Oratoire de France: 1611–1615." PhD diss., Université d'Ottawa, 1978.

Boisset, Jean. *Sagesse et sainteté dans la pensée de Jean Calvin: essai sur l'humanisme du Réformateur français.* Paris: Presses Universitaires de France, 1959.

Bossy, John. "The Counter-Reformation and the People of Catholic Europe." *Past and Present* 47 (May 1970): 51–70.

Bourgoing, François. "Préface." In *OC*, Migne ed.

Bouwsma, William J. *A Usable Past: Essays in European Cultural History*. Berkeley and Los Angeles, CA: University of California Press, 1990.

———. *The Waning of the Renaissance: 1550–1640*. New Haven: Yale University Press, 2000.

Bouyer, Louis. *Orthodox Spirituality and Protestant and Anglican Spirituality*. Translated by Barbara Wall. London: Burns & Oates, 1969. The original published as *La spiritualité orthodoxe et la spiritualité protestante et anglicane*. Vol. 3, *Histoire de la spiritualité chrétienne*. Paris: Aubier, 1965.

———. *La vie de la liturgie: une critique constructive du mouvement liturgique*. Paris: Éditions du Cerf, 1956.

Bray, G. L. *The Doctrine of God*. Leicester: Inter Varsity Press, 1993.

Bremond, Henri. *A Literary History of Religious Thought in France from the Wars of Religion Down to Our Own Times*. Vol. 3, *The Triumph of Mysticism*. Translated by K. L. Montgomery (London: Society for Promoting Christian Knowledge, 1928–36). The 1936 edition has been cited in this study. Originally published as *Histoire littéraire du sentiment religieux en France depuis la fin de guerres de religion jusqu'a nos jours*. Vol. 3, *La conquête mystique: l'École française*. Paris: Bloud et Gay, 1921.

Broglie, V. de. *De gratia*. Unpublished manuscript.

Brown, Peter. "The Rise and the Function of the Holy Man." In *Society and the Holy in Late Antiquity*, 103–52. Berkeley and Los Angeles: University of California Press, 1982.

Brown, Roberta. "Trinitarian Mechanisms: From Bérulle to Descartes." In *Proceedings of the...Annual Meeting of the Western Society for French History* 12 (1984): 40–49.

Brunner, Peter. *Nikolaus von Amsdorf als Bischof von Naumburg: eine Untersuchung zur Gestalt des evangelischen Bischofamtes in der Reformationszeit*. Gütersloh: G. Mohn, 1961.

Burton-Christie, Douglas. "Introduction: Beginnings." In *Minding the Spirit: The Study of Christian Spirituality*, ed. Elizabeth Dreyer and Mark S. Burrows, xxi–xxvii. Baltimore, MD: Johns Hopkins University Press, 2005.

Butin, Philip Walker. *Revelation, Redemption and Response: Calvin's Trinitarian Understanding of the Divine-Human Relationship*. New York and Oxford: Oxford University Press, 1995.

Butler, C. *Western Mysticism*. London, 1922.

Buzzi, Franco. "La 'scolastica barocca' come risposta alla Riforma e ai tempi nuovi." In *Per il Cinquecento religioso italiano: clero, cultura, società: atti del Convegno internazionale di studi, Siena, 27–30 giugno 2001*, ed. Maurizio Sangalli, 65–96. Roma: Edizioni dell'Ateneo, 2003.

Cadoux, Richard. "Le Sacrement de l'Incarnation: l'exemplarisme dans *Les grandeurs de Jésus* du cardinal Pierre de Bérulle." Master's thesis, Université Catholique de Lyons, 1993.

Cajetan, Tommaso de Vio. *Commentaria*. In Thomas Aquinas, *Summa theologiae ad codices manuscriptos vaticanos exacta cum commentariis Thomae de Vio Caietani ordinis Praedicatorum S. R. E. cardinalis*. Vols. 4–12 of *Sancti Thomae Aquinatis doctoris angelici opera omnia iussu impensaque Leonis XIII P. M. edita*. Rome: Ex Typographia Polyglotta S. C. de Propaganda Fide, 1888–1906.

———. *De ente et essentia D. Thomae Aquinatis Commentaria*. N.p., n.d.

Calvin, John. *Christianae religionis institutio, totam fere pietatis summam, & quicquid est in doctrina salutis cognitu necessarium: complectens: omnibus pietatis studiosis lectu dignissimum opus, ac recens editum: Praefatio ad Christianissimum regem Franciae, qua hic ei liber pro confessione fidei offertur*. Basel: Thomam Platterum & Balthasarem Lasium, 1536.

———. "The Commentaries on the Epistles of Paul the Apostle to the Hebrews." In John Calvin, *The Comprehensive John Calvin Collection*. CD-ROM. Albany, OR: AGES Software, 1998.

———. *Commentary on a Harmony of the Evangelists, Matthew, Mark, and Luke*. N.p., n.d.

———. *Corpus Reformatorum*. Brunswick: C. A. Schwetschke, 1863–1900.

———. *Harmonia ex Euangelistis tribus composita, Matthaeo, Marco, & Luca*. Geneva: Apud Eustathium Vignon, 1582.

———. *Institutes of the Christian Religion*. Edited by John T. McNeill. Translated by Ford Lewis Battles. Philadelphia: Westminster Press, 1960.

———. *Institutes of the Christian Religion*. Translated by Henry Beveridge. Peabody, MA: Hendrickson Publishers, 2008. This edition was based on the 1845 English translation of Calvin's last Latin edition.

———. *Institution de la religion chrestienne: en laquelle est comprinse une somme de piété, et quasi tout ce qui est nécessaire à congnoistre en la doctrine de salut: Composée en latin par Iean Calvin, et translatée en françois, par luymesme: Avec la préface addressée au tres chrestien roy de France, Francoys premier de ce nom: par laquelle ce présent livre luy est offert pour confession de foy*. 1541.

———. *John Calvin's New Testament Commentaries*. Vol. 11, *The Epistles of Pa ul to the Galatians, Ephesians, Philippians, and Colossians*. Translated by T. H. L. Parker. Grand Rapids: Wm. B. Eerdmans Publishing Co., 1965.

———, and J. D. Benoit. *Institution de la religion chrestienne*. Paris: Vrin, 1957–60.

———, Joseph Haroutunian, and Louis Pettibone Smith. *Commentaries*. With an introduction by J. Haroutunian. Philadelphia, PA: Westminster Press, 1958.

———, David W. Torrance, and Thomas F. Torrance. *Commentaries*. Grand Rapids: Eerdmans, 1959.

Cancouët, M. "Traces de la théologie et de la pratique de l'École française à Vatican II et au-delà." *Bulletin de Saint-Sulpice* 6 (1980): 214–36.

Canfield, Benet. *Exercice de la volonté de Dieu*. In *La règle de perfection*. Paris, 1608.

———. *La règle de perfection*. Paris, 1608.

————. *La règle de perfection*. Paris: Presses universitaires de France, 1982.

Canlis, Julie. *Calvin's Ladder: A Spiritual Theology of Ascent and Ascension*. Grand Rapids, MI: W. B. Eerdmans Pub. Co., 2010.

Canons and Decrees of the Council of Trent. Translated by H. J. Schroeder. St. Louis, MO, and London: B. Herder Book Co., 1960.

Capestrano, San Juan de. *Speculum Claricorum*. Venetiis, 1580.

Johannes Capreolus, Johannes. *Defensiones theologicae divi Thomae Aquinatis*. Vol. 5. Tours, 1879.

Carmody, James M., and Thomas E. Clarke. *Word and Redeemer: Christology in the Fathers*. Glen Rock, NJ: Paulist Press, 1966.

Carraud, Vincent. "De l'état de néant à l'état anéanti: le système du néant de Bérulle." *Cahiers de philosophie de l'Université de Caen*, no. 43 (2007): 211–47.

————. "De la destruction: Métaphysique et idée du sacrifice selon Condren," *Archivo di filosofia* 76 (2008): 331–48.

Carré, M. H. *Realists and Nominalists*. London: Oxford University Press, 1946.

Castellani, A. *Liber sacerdotalis*. Venetiis, 1523.

Catholic Church. *Encyclical Letter (Mystici corporis Christi) of His Holiness Pius XII on the Mystical Body of Jesus Christ and Our Union with Christ Therein*. London: Catholic Truth Society, n.d.

———— and John Paul II. *Post-synodal Apostolic Exhortation Pastores Dabo Vobis of His Holiness John Paul II: To the Bishops, Clergy and Faithful on the Formation of Priests in the Circumstances of the Present Day*. Vatican City: Libreria Editrice Vaticana, 1992.

Cérisy, Habert de. *La vie de cardinal de Bérulle*. Paris: Sebastian Hure, 1646.

Certeau, Michel de. *The Mystic Fable*. Vol. 1, *The Sixteenth and Seventeenth Centuries*. Translated by Michael B. Smith. Chicago and London:

University of Chicago Press, 1992. Originally published as *La fable mystique, XVI–XVIIe siècle*. Paris: Éditions Gallimard, 1982.

———. "La réforme dans le catholicisme." In *Histoire spirituelle de la France: spiritualité du catholicisme en France et dans les pays de langue française, des origines à 1914*, 195–216. Paris: Beauchesne, 1964.

Chirico, Petro F. "The Divine Indwelling and Distinct Relations to the Indwelling Persons in Modern Theological Discussion." PhD diss., Rome: Pontificiae Universitatis Gregorianae, 1960.

Cistellini, Antonio. "Oratoire Philippin." In *DSAM*. Vol. 11 (1982), cols. 853–75.

Clichtove Josse. *De vita et moribus sacerdotum, singularem eorum dignitatem ostendens et quibus ornati esse debeant virtutibus explanans*. Paris: Simon de Colines, 1519.

Cochois, Paul. *Bérulle et l'école française*. Paris: Seuil, 1963.

———. "Bérulle et le pseudo-Denys." *Revue de l'histoire des religions* 159, no. 2 (1961): 173–204.

———. "Bérulle, hiérarque dionysien." *Revue d'ascétique et de mystique* 37 (1961): 314–53; 38 (1962): 354–75.

———. "Bérulle, initiateur mystique: les vœux de servitude." *École pratique des hautes études, section des sciences religieuses: Annuaire* (1958): 111–15.

———. "Bérulle, initiateur mystique: les vœux de servitude." PhD diss., Institut catholique de Paris, 1960.

———. "Les vœux de servitude et l'idéal de vie sacerdotal proposé par le Père de Bérulle." *Oratoriana* 4 (Nov. 1961): 101–18.

Cognet, Louis. "Bérulle et la théologie de l'Incarnation." *XVIIe siècle* 29 (Oct. 1955): 330–55.

———. *Introduction aux mystiques rhéno-flamands*. Paris: Desclée, 1968.
———. *Les origines de la spiritualité française au XVIIe siècle*. Paris: La Colombe, 1949.

———. *Post-Reformation Spirituality*. New York: Hawthorn Books, 1959. Originally published as *De la dévotion moderne à la spiritualité française*. Paris: Librairie Arthème Fayard, 1958.

———. *La spiritualité moderne (1500–1650)*. Paris: Aubier, 1966.

Collins, Ardis. *The Secular Is the Sacred: Platonism and Thomism in Marsilio Ficino*. The Hague: Martinus Mijhoff, 1974.

Condren, Charles de. *L'idée du sacerdoce et du sacrifice de Jésus-Christ*. Paris, 1697.

Confession d'Augsburg. *De votis monachorum*. In Philip Melanchthon, *Confessio fidei exhibita…* Witebergae: Rhau, 1530.

Congar, Yves M.-J. *A History of Theology*. Translated and edited by Hunter Guthrie. Garden City, NY: Doubleday, 1968. Based on the article "Théologie" appearing in *DTC*. Vol. 15, pt. 1 (1946), cols. 341–502.

"Contemplation." In *DSAM*. Vol. 2, pt. 2 (1950–52), cols. 1643–2193.

Copleston, Frederick. *The History of Philosophy: Late Medieval and Renaissance Philosophy*. Vol. 3, pt. 1. New York: Image Books, 1963.

Costello, Timothy. *Forming a Priestly Identity: Anthropology of Priestly Formation in the Documents of the VIII Synod of Bishops and the Apostolic Exhortation Pastores Dabo Vobis*. Roma: Editrice Pontificia Università Gregoriana, 2002.

Coulter, J. A. *The Literary Microcosm: Theories of Interpretation of the Later Neoplatonists*. Leiden: E. J. Brill, 1976.

Council of Trent – 1545–1563: Session 6 (January 1547). "Decree on Justification," ch. 7. In *The Christian Faith*. Edited by J. Neuner and J. Dupuis. Bangalore and New York, 2001.

Courtney, William J. *Covenant and Causality in Medieval Thought: Studies in Philosophy, Theology and Economic Practice*. London: Variorum, 1984.

Cranz, F. Edward. "Cusanus, Luther, and Mystical Tradition." In *The Pursuit of Holiness in Late Medieval and Renaissance Religion,* ed. Charles Trinkaus with Heiko A. Oberman. Leiden: E. J. Brill, 1974.

Crew, Phyllis. *Calvinist Preaching and Iconoclasm in the Netherlands, 1544–1569.* Cambridge: Cambridge University Press, 1978.

Croken, Robert C. *Luther's First Front: The Eucharist as Sacrifice.* Ottawa: University of Ottawa Press, 1990.

Cross, Richard. *Duns Scot.* New York and Oxford: Oxford University Press, 1999.

Cunningham, Francis L. B. *The Indwelling of the Trinity: A Historico-Doctrinal Study of the Theory of St. Aquinas.* Dubuque: Priory Press, 1955.

Daeschler, R. "Abnégation: II. Tradition patristique, médiévale, moderne." In *DSAM.* Vol. 1, cols. 73–101. Paris: Beauchesne, 1937.

Dagens, Jean. *Bérulle et les origines de la restauration catholique.* Bruges: Desclée de Brouwer, 1952.

———. "Notes bérulliennes…." In *Revue d'histoire ecclésiastique* 27 (1931): 318–52.

———. "Le XVIIe siècle, siècle de Saint Augustin." *Cahiers de l'association internationale des études françaises,* nos. 3–5 (1953): 31–38.

Daly, Robert J. "Robert Bellarmine and Post-Tridentine Eucharistic Theology." *Theological Studies* 61 (2000): 239–60.

Damascene, John. *Exposition of the Orthodox Faith.* In Philip Schaff and Henry Wace, *A Select Library of Nicene and Post-Nicene Fathers of the Christian Church,* Second Series. Vol. 9, *St. Hilary of Poitiers, John of Damascus.* Grand Rapids, MI: Eerdmans, 1979.

Danielou, J. "Le Ministère sacerdotal chez les pères grecs." In *Études sur le sacrement de l'ordre,* 147–65. Paris: Éd. du Cerf, 1957.

Delius, Hans-Ulrich. "Das Naumburger Bischofsexperiment und Martin Luther." In *Martin Luther und das Bischofsamt,* 131–40. Stuttgart: Calwer Verlag, 1990.

Denzinger, Heinrich, Peter Hünermann, and Helmut Hoping. *Enchiridion symbolorum definitionum et declarationum de rebus fidei et morum = Kompendium der Glaubensbekenntnisse und kirchlichen Lehrentscheidungen.* Freiburg, Basel, Wien: Herder, 2014.

Deville, Raymond. *L'école française de spiritualité.* Paris: Desclée de Brouwer, 2008.

Diepen, H.-M. "Le critique du baslisme selon Saint Thomas d'Aquin." *Revue thomiste* 50 (1950): 82–118 and 290–329.

———. "L'unique Seigneur Jésus-Christ." *Revue thomiste* 53 (1953) 28–81.

Dodds, E. R. *The Greeks and the Irrational.* 7th printing. Berkeley: University of California Press, 1971.

Dolan, George Edward. *The Distinction between the Episcopate and the Presbyterate according to the Thomistic Opinion.* Washington, DC: Catholic University of America Press, 1950.

Dolan, John. *History of the Reformation: A Conciliatory Assessment of Opposite Views.* New York: Desclee Company, 1965.

Dominicé, Max. *L'humanité de Jésus, d'après Calvin.* Cahors: A. Coueslant, 1933.

Donovan, Daniel. *What Are They Saying about the Ministerial Priesthood?* New York, NY, and Mahwah, NJ: Paulist Press, 1992.

Doolan, Gregory T. *Aquinas on the Divine Ideas as Exemplar Causes.* Washington, DC: Catholic University of America Press, 2008.

Doyle, William. *Jansenism: Catholic Resistance to Authority from the Reformation to the French Revolution.* New York: St. Martin's Press, 2000.

Dress, Walter. *Die Theologie Gersons: eine Untersuchung zur Verbindung von Nominalismus und Mystik im Spätmittelalter.* Gütersloh: C. Bertelsmann, 1931.

Driel, Edwin Chr. van. "The Logic of Assumption." In *Exploring Kenotic Christology: The Self-Emptying of God*, ed. C. Stephen Evans, 265–90. New York: Oxford University Press, 2006.

Dubé, Wilfrid. "Bérulle et les protestants, 1593–1610: contribution à l'étude de la controverse religieuse au début du 17e siècle." PhD diss., University of Paris, 1966.

Dulles, Avery. "Models for Ministerial Priesthood." *Origins* 20 (1990): 287.

Dupuy, Michel. "L'adoration d'après le cardinal de Bérulle." *École pratique des hautes études, Section des sciences religieuses: Annuaire* (1961): 129–32.

–––––. "Bérulle et la grâce." *XVIIe siècle* 43, no. 1 (1991): 39–50.

–––––. *Bérulle: une spiritualité de l'adoration*. Tournai, Belgium: Desclée & Co., 1964.

–––––. *Le Christ de Bérulle*. Paris: Desclée, 2001.

–––––. "Un guide de lecture pour Bérulle." *La Vie spirituelle* (April 1963): 462–75.

–––––. "Perfection, VI: 16e–17e siècles." In *DSAM*. Vol. 12, pt. 1 (1984), col. 1132.

–––––. "Le prêtre selon Duvergier de Hauranne, 1581–1643." In *L'image du prêtre dans la littérature classique, XVIIe–XVIIIe siècles: Actes du colloque organisé par le Centre "Michel Baude-Littérature et spiritualité" de l'Université de Metz, 20–21 novembre 1998*, ed. Danielle Pister, 53–60. Peter Lang Verlag, 2001.

–––––, and Pierre de Bérulle. *Bérulle et le sacerdoce: étude historique et doctrinale*. Paris: Lethielleux, 1969.

Duvergier de Hauranne, Jean (Saint-Cyran). *Lettres chrétiennes et spirituelles de messire Jean du Verger de Hauranne, abbé de S. Cyran*. Lyon: chés J. Bapt. Bourlier & Laur. Aubin, 1674.

Eckhart, Meister. *Book of Divine Consolation.* In Meister Eckhart, *Die deutschen und lateinischen Werke,* ed. Josef Quint. Deutsche Forschungsgemeinschaft. Stuttgart: Kohlhammer, 1936.

———. *Meister Eckhart: A Modern Translation.* Translated by R. B. Blakney. New York and London, 1941.

———. *Meister Eckhart: Die deutschen und lateinischen Werke herausgegeben im Auftrag der deutschen Forschungsgemeinschaft.* Vol. 3. Stuttgart/Berlin: Kohlhammer, 1936–.

———. "Sermon on the Eternal Birth." In *Late Medieval Mysticism,* ed. Ray C. Petry, 177–85. Library of Christian Classics. Vol. 13. Philadelphia: Westminster, 1957.

———, and Franz Pfeiffer. *Meister Eckhart.* Göttingen: Vandenhoeck & Ruprecht, 1906.

Edmonson, Stephen. *Calvin's Christology.* New York: Cambridge University Press, 2004.

Egan, Harvey D. *An Anthology of Christian Mysticism.* 2nd ed. Collegeville, MN: Liturgical Press, 1996.

Epictetus and William Abbott Oldfather. *The Discourses as Reported by Arrian, The Manual, and Fragments.* Vol. 1. Cambridge: Harvard University Press, 1946.

Étienne, J. *Spiritualisme érasmien et théologiens louvanistes: un changement de problématique au début du XVIe siècle.* Louvain: Publications universitaires de Louvain, 1956.

Evagrius, Antoine Guillaumont, and Claire Guillaumont. *Traité pratique ou le moine.* Paris: Éditions du Cerf, 1971.

Faider, Paul, and Paulus pseud? Pompilius. *Études sur Sénèque.* Gand: van Rysselberghe & Rombaut, 1921.

Farrelly, M. John. *The Trinity: Rediscovering the Central Christian Mystery.* Rowman & Littlefield Publishers, Inc., 2005.

Feichtinger, Hans. "Οὐδένεια and *Humilitas*: Nature and Function of Humility in Iamblichus and Augustine." *Dionysius* 11 (Dec. 2003): 123–60.

Ferrara, Dennis Michael. "Representation or Self-Effacement? The Axiom *in Persona Christi* in St. Thomas and the Magisterium." *Theological Studies* 55 (1994): 195–224.

Ferrari, Anne. *Figures de la contemplation: la "rhétorique divine" de Pierre de Bérulle*. Paris: Éditions du Cerf, 1997.

———. "La notion de sacrifice dans l'école française de spiritualité et à Port-Royal." In *Port-Royal et l'école française de spiritualité: Colloque organisé par la Société des Amis de Port-Royal (15–16 septembre 2006)*, ed. Helene Michon and Laurence Devillairs, 67–82. *Chroniques de Port-Royal*. Vol. 57. Paris: Bibliothèque Mazarine, 2007.

Fesko, John V. "Metaphysics and Justification in Sixteenth- and Seventeenth-Century Reformed Theology." *Calvin Theological Journal* 46 (2011): 29–47.

Festugière, A. J. *Contemplation et vie contemplative selon Platon*. 3rd ed. Paris: J. Vrin, 1967.

Ficino, Marsilio. *De Amore*. In Marsilio Ficino and Sears Reynolds, *Marsilio Ficino, Commentary on Plato's Symposium on Love*. 2nd ed. Dallas, TX: Spring Publications, 1985.

———. *Platonic Theology*. English translation by Michael J. B. Allen with John Warden. Latin text by James Hankins with William Bowen. 6 vols. Cambridge: Harvard University Press, 2001–6.

Filthaut, Theodor. *Die Kontroverse über die Mysterienlehre*. Warendorf: Schnell, 1947.

Fisk, Philip. "Calvin's Metaphysics of Our Union with Christ." *International Journal of Systematic Theology* 11, no. 3 (July 2009): 309–31.

Fontaine, Jean-Baptiste-Louis de Gonzague. Pseudonym Lascasas. *Le cardinal Pierre de Bérulle, devant la Champagne, son pays*. A. Berthelon, 1847.

Foucault, Michel. "Technologies of the Self." In Michel Foucault and Luther H. Martin, *Technologies of the Self: A Seminar with Michel Foucault*, 16–49. Amherst: University of Massachusetts Press, 1988.

Fuller, Ross. *The Brotherhood of the Common Life and Its Influence*. State University of New York Press, 1995.

Gadamer, Hans-Georg. *Truth and Method*. 2nd printing. New York: Seabury Press, 1975. Originally published as *Wahrheit und Methode*. Tübingen: J. C. B. Mohr, 1972.

Gallego Palomero, Juan José. *Sacerdocio y oficio sacerdotal en San Juan de Ávila*. Córdoba: Caja de Ahorros y Monte de Piedad de Córdoba, 1998.

Galliardi, Achilles, and Isabella Cristina Berinzaga. *Breve compendio di perfezione cristiana, e "vita di Isabella Berinzaga" per la prima volta pubblicata, con introduzione e note di Mario Bendisciolo*. Firenze: Libreria editrice fiorentina, 1952.

Galot, Jean. *La nature du caractère sacramentel: étude de théologie médiévale*. 2nd ed. Paris: Desclée de Brouwer, 1956–58.

———. *La personne du Christ: recherche ontologique*. Bruxelles: Duculot-Lethielleux, 1969.

———. *Who Is Christ: A Theology of the Incarnation*. Chicago: Franciscan Herald Press, 1980.

Galtier, P. *L'habitation en nous des trois personnes*. 2nd ed. Rome: Pont. Università Gregoriana, 1950.

Galy, Jean. *Le sacrifice dans l'école française*. Paris: Nouvelles Éditions Latines, 1951.

Gamaches, Philippe de. *Summa theologica*. Paris, 1627.

García Mateo, Rogelio. "Cristología sacerdotal en Juan de Ávila." *Estudios eclesiásticos* 86, no. 336 (2011): 81–102.

Garrigou-Lagrange, Réginald. *De Christo Salvatore*. Turin: R. Berruti, 1946.

———. "Le langage des spirituels comparé à celui des théologiens." *Supplément à la Vie spirituelle* 49 (Dec. 1, 1936): 257–76.

———. *Le Sauveur et son amour pour nous*. Paris: Éditions du Cerf, 1933.

Garrigues, J.-M., M.-J. Le Guillou, and A. Riou. "Le caractère sacerdotal dans la tradition des Pères Grecs." *Nouvelle revue théologique* 93 (1971): 801–20.

Gaudel, A. "Eminence: Méthode d'." In *DTC*. Vol. 4, pt. 2 (1911), col. 2428.

Gibieuf, Guillaume. *De libertate Dei et creaturae libri duo*. Paris, 1630.

Gilson, Étienne. *L'être et l'essence*. Paris: Vrin, 1948.

———. *History of Christian Philosophy in the Middle Ages*. New York: Random House, 1955.

———. *Introduction à l'étude de saint Augustin*. Librairie Philosophique. Paris: J. Vrin, 1929.

———. *Jean Duns Scot, Introduction à ses positions fondamentales*. Paris: Vrin, 1952.

———. *La liberté chez Descartes et la théologie*. Paris: Alcan, 1913.

Glendon, Lowell Martin. "Jean-Jacques Olier's View of the Spiritual Potential of Human Nature: A Presentation and an Evaluation." PhD diss., New York: Fordham University, 1983.

Graver, Margaret, "Epictetus." In *Stanford Encyclopedia of Philosophy*. Spring 2013 Edition. Edited by Edward N. Zalta. http://plato.stanford.edu /archives/spr2013/entries/epictetus.

Greenstock, David L. "Exemplar Causality and the Supernatural Order." *Thomist* 16, no. 1 (January 1953): 1–31.

Gregory the Great and George Demacopoulos. *The Book of Pastoral Rule*. Crestwood, NY: St. Vladimir's Seminary Press, 2007.

Guerra, Manuel. "Problemática del sacerdocio ministerial en las primeras comunidades cristianas." In José Capmany Casamitjana, *Teología del sacerdocio*. Vol. 1, *Orientaciones metodológicas,* 9–91. Burgos: Ediciones Aldecoa, S.A., 1969.

Gy, Pierre-Marie. *The Reception of Vatican II Liturgical Reforms in the Life of the Church.* Milwaukee, WI: Marquette University, 2003.

Hales, Alexander. *Summa Universae Theologiae.* N.p., n.d.

Hankey, Wayne J. "From St. Augustine and St. Pseudo-Dionysius to Olier and Bérulle's Spiritual Revolution: Patristic and Seventeenth-Century Foundations of the Relations between Church and State in Québec." *Laval théologique et philosophique* 63, no. 3 (Oct. 2007): 515–59.

———. "Philosophy as Way of Life for Christians? Iamblichan and Porphyrian Reflections on Religion, Virtue, and Philosophy in Thomas Aquinas." *Laval théologique et philosophique* 59, no. 2 (2003): 193–224.

Hankins, James. "Marsilio Ficino and the Religion of the Philosophers." *Rinascimento* 48 (2009): 101–21.

Hardon, John A. *The Catholic Catechism.* Garden City, NY: Doubleday, 1975.

Harnack, Adolf von. *Das Wesen des Christentums.* Leipzig, J. C. Hinrichs, 1902.

Haroutunian, J. "Introduction." In John Calvin, Joseph Haroutunian, and Louis Pettibone Smith, *Commentaries.* Philadelphia, PA: Westminster Press, 1958.

Harrison, Peter. "Philosophy and the Crisis of Religion." In *Cambridge Companion to Renaissance Philosophy,* 234–46. Cambridge: Cambridge University Press, 2007.

Hastings, Adrian. "Christ's Act of Existence." *Downside Review* 73 (1955): 139–59.

Hayen, André. "Deux théologiens: Jean Duns Scot et Thomas d'Aquin." *Revue philosophique de Louvain,* 3rd series, 51, no. 30 (1953).

Heck, Erich. *Der Begriff religio bei Thomas von Aquin; seine Bedeutung für unser heutiges Verständnis von Religion.* München: F. Schöningh, 1971.

Herbermann, Charles George, Edward A. Pace, Condé Bénoist Pallen, Thomas J. Shahan, John J. Wynne, and Andrew Alphonsus MacErlean. *Catholic Encyclopedia: An International Work of Reference on the Constitution, Doctrine, Discipline, and History of the Catholic Church.* New York: Robert Appleton Co, 1907–12. S.vv. "Actual Grace," "Character (In Catholic Theology)," "Charismata," "Priesthood," "Sanctifying Grace," and "The Oratory of Saint Philip Neri."

Herp, Hendrik. *Theologia mystica.* Vol. 1. Cologne: Melchior Novesanius, 1538.

———. *Theologiae mysticae libri tres.* Vol. 1. Cologne, 1611.

Hill, Christopher. *The Collected Essays of Christopher Hill.* Vol. 3, *People and Ideas in Seventeenth Century England.* Amherst: University of Massachusetts Press, 1986.

Holtzen, Thomas L. "Union with God and the Holy Spirit: A New Paradigm of Justification." PhD diss., Milwaukee, WI: Marquette University, 2002.

Hopfner, Theodor, and Jacques Paul Migne. *Patrologiae cursus completus / Patrologia Graeca: seu Bibliotheca universalis, integra, uniformis, commoda, oeconomica omnium ss. patrum, doctorum, scriptorumque ecclesiasticorum, sive latinorum, sive Graecorum, qui ab aevo apostolico ad aetatem Innocenti III (ann. 1216) pro Latinis et ad Photii tempora (ann. 863) pro Graecis floruerunt.* Paris: Migne, 1866.

Houdard, Sophie. "Sacerdoce et direction spirituelle: le prêtre et la représentation du corps mystique." In *L'image du prêtre dans la littérature classique, XVIIe–XVIIIe siècles: Actes du colloque organisé par le Centre "Michel Baude–Littérature et spiritualité" de l'Université de Metz, 20–21 novembre 1998,* ed. Danielle Pister, 109–20. Peter Lang Verlag, 2001.

Howells, Edward. "Relationality and Difference in the Mysticism of Pierre de Bérulle." *Harvard Theological Review* (April 1, 2009): 225–43.

Hudson, Nancy J. *Becoming God: The Doctrine of Theosis in Nicholas of Cusa.* Washington, DC: Catholic University of America Press, 2007.

Huijben, J. "Aux sources de la spiritualité française du XVIIe siècle." *Supplément à la Vie spirituelle* 25 (December 1930): 113–39; 26 (January 1931): 17–46; 26 (February 1931): 75–111; 27 (April 1931): 20–42; and 27 (May 1931): 94–122.

Hurtubise, Pierre. "Le prêtre tridentin: idéal et réalité." In *Homo religiosus: autour de Jean Delumeau*, 208–17. Paris: Fayard, 1997.

Iamblichus and Emma C. Clarke. *Iamblichus on The Mysteries*. Atlanta, GA: Society of Biblical Literature, 2003.

Idiart, P. "Prêtre païen et prêtre chrétien." In *Études sur le sacrement de l'ordre*, 325–70. Paris: Éditions du Cerf, 1957.

Idigoras, Ignacio Tellechea. "El clero tridentino: entre ideal y realidad." *Ricerche per la storia religiosa di Roma* 337 (1988): 11–26.

Itter, Andrew. "Pseudo-Dionysian Soteriology and Its Transformation of Neoplatonism." *Colloquium Journal* 32 (May 2000): 71–92.

Iturrioz, Daniel. *La definición del Concilio de Trento sobre la causalidad de los sacramentos*. Madrid: Ediciones FAX, 1951.

Iwand, Hans Joachim. *Nachgelassene Werke*. Vol. 5, *Luthers Theologie*. München: Chr. Kaiser, 1974.

Janz, Denis R. "Thomism." In *Oxford Encyclopedia of the Reformation*. Vol. 4, 151–54. New York and Oxford: Oxford University Press, 1996.

Jésus. Maria. Advis salutaire du un certain qutriesme voeu de Religion, composé par un bon Ecclésiastique, et introduit dans un Ordre d'authorité propre et privée, n.p., n.d.

Jetté, F. "État." In *DSAM*. Vol. 4, pt. 2, col. 1378. Paris: Beauchesne, 1961.
John of Avila. *Audi, Filia*. Translated and with an introduction by Joan Frances Gormley. New York: Paulist Press, 2006.

Jones, Cheslyn, Geoffrey Wainwright, and Edward Yarnold. *The Study of Spirituality*. New York: Oxford University Press, 1986.

Jones, Michael Keenan. "Toward a Christology of Christ the High Priest." PhD diss., Rome: Editrice Pontificia Università Gregoriana, 2006.

Jones, Rufus. *Some Exponents of Mystical Religion*. London, 1930.

Juan de Ávila. *Obras completas del Santo Maestro Juan de Ávila*, 6 vols. Madrid, Spain: Biblioteca de autores cristianos, 1970–71.

——— and Juan Esquerda Bifet. *Escritos sacerdotales*. Madrid, Spain: Biblioteca de autores cristianos, 2012.

Kenny, Anthony. *The Rise of Modern Philosophy: A New History of Western Philosophy*. Vol. 3. Oxford: Clarendon Press, 2006.

Kibbey, Ann. *Theory of the Image*. Bloomington: Indiana University Press, 2005.

Kilmartin, Edward J. *The Eucharist in the West: History and Theology*. Edited by Robert J. Daly. Collegeville: Liturgical Press, 1998.

Kinneer, Jack. "Calvin's Use of the Sursum Corda." *Roots of Reformed Worship* (November 1998): n.pp.

Klima, Gyula. "The Medieval Problem of Universals." In *Stanford Encyclopedia of Philosophy*, published Sept. 10, 2000, revised July 8, 2013. http://plato.stanford.edu/entries/universals-medieval/index.html. Pagination is from printed copy of online edition.

Knecht, Robert. *The French Religious Wars 1562–1598*. Oxford, UK: Osprey Publishing, 2002.

Koerner, Joseph Leo. *The Reformation of the Image*. Chicago, IL: University of Chicago Press, 2004.

Kolfhaus, Wilhelm. *Christusgemeinschaft bei Johannes Calvin*. Beiträge zur Geschichte und Lehre der Reformierten Kirche. Vol. 3. Neukirchen: Buchhandlung d. Erziehungsvereins, 1938.

Kraye, Jill Adrian. "Moral Philosophy." In *Cambridge History of Renaissance Philosophy*, ed. C. B. Schmitt, Quentin Skinner, Eckhard Kessler, and Jill Kraye, 303–86. Cambridge: Cambridge University Press, 1988.

Krumenacker, Yves. "Du prêtre tridentin au 'bon prêtre'." In *L'image du prêtre dans la littérature classique, XVIIe–XVIIIe siècles*, ed. Danielle Fister, 121–39. Frankfurt: Peter Lang, 2001.

–––––. *L'école française de spiritualité: des mystiques, des fondateurs, des courants et leurs interprètes*. Paris: Éditions du Cerf, 1998.

–––––. "Qu'est-ce qu'une école de spiritualité?" In *Port-Royal et l'école française de spiritualité: actes du colloque organisé par la société des amis de Port-Royal*, 11–23. Paris: Bibliothèque Mazarine, 2007.

Lacoste, Jean-Yves. *Encyclopedia of Christian Theology*. Vol. 1. 2nd ed. New York: Routledge, 2005.

Lathrop, Gordon. *The Pastor: A Spirituality*. Minneapolis: Fortress Press, 2006.

Latourette, Kenneth Scott. *A History of Christianity*. Vol. 1. New York: Harper & Row, 1975.

Laurentin, R. *Marie, l'Église et le sacerdoce: étude théologique*. Paris: Nouvelle editions latines, 1953.

Lauster, Jörg. "Marsilio Ficino as a Christian Thinker: Theological Aspects of His Platonism." In *Marsilio Ficino: His Theology, His Philosophy, His Legacy*, ed. Michael J. B. Allen, V. Rees, and Martin Davis, 45–69. Leiden: Brill, 2001.

Le Bachelet, X. "Bellarmin, François-Robert-Romulus." In *DSAM*. Vol. 2 (1905), cols. 560–78.

Le Brun, Jacques. "Le grand siècle de la spiritualité française et ses lendemains." In *Histoire spirituelle de la France: spiritualité du catholicisme en France et dans les pays de langue française, des origines à 1914*, 227–85. Paris: Beauchesne, 1964.

Le Jay, CL. *Speculum sacerdotii*. Parisiis, 1559.

Le Lannou, Jean-Michel. "Le 'sacrifice du moi' selon Bérulle." *Revue des sciences religieuses* 78, no. 2 (2004): 205–30.

Leadbetter, Lewis W. "Aspects of the Philosophical Priesthood in Iamblichus' *De Mysteriis*." *Classical Bulletin* 47, no. 6 (April 1971): 89–92.

Lecuyer, J. "La pérennité des mystères du Christ." *La Vie spirituelle* 87 (1952): 451–63.

Legrand, Hervé-Marie. "The 'Indelible' Character and the Theology of Ministry." *Concilium* 74 (1972): 54–62.

Lehninger, Paul. "Luther and Theosis: Deification in the Theology of Martin Luther." PhD diss., Milwaukee, WI: Marquette University, 1999.

Leinsle, Ulrich G. *Introduction to Scholastic Theology*. Translated by Michael J. Miller. Washington, DC: Catholic University of America Press, 2010.

Lemaitre, J. "Contemplation: La theoria phusikè." In *DSAM*. Vol. 2, pt. 2 (1953), cols. 1828–29.

Lemaitre, Nicole. "Le prêtre mis à part ou le triomphe d'une idéologie sacerdotale au XVIe siècle." *Revue d'histoire de l'Église de France* 85, no. 3 (1999): 275–89.

Lepin, Maurius. *L'idée du sacrifice de la messe d'après les théologiens depuis l'origine jusqu'à nos jours*. 2nd ed. Paris: Beauchesne, 1926.

Lewy, Hans. *Chaldean Oracles and Theurgy*. Cairo: Imprimerie de l'Institut français d'archéologie orientale, 1956.

———, and Michel Tardieu. *Chaldean Oracles and Theurgy: Mysticism, Magic and Platonism in the Later Roman Empire*. New ed. Paris: Institut d'Études Augustiniennes, 1978.

Lipsius, Justus. *De constantia libri duo, qui alloquium praecipuè continent in publicis malis*. N.p., n.d.

Lloumeau, Pére. *La vie spirituelle à l'école du Bienheureux G. de Montfort*. 3rd ed. Paris: Desclée, Lefebvre, 1913.

Lohr, Charles H. "Metaphysics." In *Cambridge History of Renaissance Philosophy*, ed. C. B. Schmitt, Quentin Skinner, Eckhard Kessler, and Jill Kraye, 537–638. Cambridge: Cambridge University Press, 1988.

Louth, Andrew. *The Origins of the Christian Mystical Tradition: From Plato to Pseudo-Dionysius*. Oxford: Oxford University Press, 2007.

Lowenich, W. von. *Luthers Theologia Crucis*. 2nd ed. Munich, 1954.

Lubac, Henri de. *Le mystère du surnaturel*. Paris: F. Aubier, Éditions Montaigne, 1965.

Ludolphe le Chartreux. *Vita Jesu Christi*. Vol. 5. Paris, 1878.

Luther, Martin. *Commentary on Galatians*. English translation. 1807.

———. *Luthers Werke: Kritische Gesammtausgabe*. Weimar: Hermann Böhlau, 1883–.

———. *Luther's Works*. American edition. Edited by Jaroslav Pelikan, Helmut T. Lehmann, and Christopher Boyd Brown. 75 vols. Philadelphia and St. Louis: Fortress Press, 1955–.

———. *Martin Luthers Werke: Kritische Gesammtausgabe, Abteilung Briefe*. Weimar: Hermann Böhlaus Nachfolger, 1930–85.

———. *Tischreden: (1531–1546)*. Weimar: Hermann Böhlau, 1912.

Mackenzie, Ross, and Christopher Kiesling. "Reformed and Roman Catholic Understandings of the Eucharist." *Journal of Ecumenical Studies* 13 (1976): 70–76.

Macleod, Donald. *Behold Your God*. Ross-shire, UK: Christian Focus Publications, 1991.

Magnard, Pierre. "L'Incarnation selon le cardinal de Bérulle." In *Port-Royal et l'école française de spiritualité: colloque de Port-Royal des Champs, 15–16 septembre, 2006: Chroniques de Port-Royal*, 109–16.

Mahieu, Léon. *Francisco Suárez: sa philosophie et les rapports qu'elle a avec sa théologie*. Paris: Desclée de Brouwer & Co., 1921.

Mahoney, Edward P. "Metaphysical Foundations of the Hierarchy of Being according to Some Late Medieval and Renaissance Philosophers." In *Philosophies of Existence: Ancient and Medieval*, ed. Parviz Morewedge, 165–257. New York: Fordham University Press, 1982.

Maldonat, Jean. "Discours inaugural de Maldonat." In J. M. Prat, *Maldonat et l'Université de Paris au XVIe siècle*. N.p., 1856.

Mancha, Jr., Louis A. "Aquinas, Suárez and Malebranche on Instrumental Causation and Premotion." *International Philosophical Quarterly* 52, no. 3 (Sept. 2012): 335–53.

Margerie, Bertrand de. *The Christian Trinity in History*. Studies in Historical Theology. Vol. 1. Translated by Edmund J. Fortman. Still River, MA: St. Bede's Publications, 1982.

Marion, Jean-Luc. "The Idea of God." In *Cambridge History of Seventeenth-Century Philosophy*. Vol. 1, ed. D. Garber and M. Ayers, 265–304. Cambridge: Cambridge University Press, 1998.

Maritain, Jacques. "À propos de l'école française." *Revue thomiste* (1971): 463–79.

———. "Apropos of the French School." In *Untrammeled Approaches*, trans. Bernard Doering, with a preface by Ernst R. Korn, a pseudonym for Heinz R. Schmitz, 424–41. Notre Dame, IN: University of Notre Dame Press, 1997. Originally published as "À propos de l'école française." *Revue thomiste* (1971): 463–79.

———. *Distinguer pour unir; ou, Les degrés du savoir*. 3rd ed. Paris: Desclée, de Brouwer et cie, 1932.

Martelet, Gustave. *Deux mille ans d'Église en question: théologie du sacerdoce*. Vol. 3, *Du schisme d'Occident à Vatican II*. Paris: Éditions du Cerf, 1990.

Massaut, Jean-Pierre. *Josse Clichtove, l'humanisme et la réforme du clergé*. 2 vols. Paris: Les Belles Lettres, 1968.

———. "Le XVIe siècle." In *Histoire spirituelle de la France: spiritualité du catholicisme en France et dans les pays de langue française, des origines à 1914*, 185–93. Paris: Beauchesne, 1964.

Mauss, Marcel. "A Category of the Human Mind: The Notion of the Person, the Notion of the Self." Translated by H. D. Halls. In *The Category of the Person: Anthropology, Philosophy, History*, ed. Michael Carrithers, Steven Collins, and Steven Lukes, 1–25. Cambridge: Cambridge University Press, 1985.

McClintock, John, and James Strong. "Pantheism." In *Cyclopaedia of Biblical, Theological, and Ecclesiastical Literature*, vol. 7, 616–64. New York: Harper & Brothers, 1894.

McGinn, Bernard. *The Foundations of Mysticism*. Vol. 1, *The Presence of God: A History of Western Christian Mysticism*. New York: Crossroad, 1991.

———. *The Harvest of Mysticism in Medieval Germany*. Vol. 4, *The Presence of God: A History of Western Christian Mysticism*. New York: Crossroad Publishing Company, 2005.

———. "The Letter and the Spirit: Spirituality as an Academic Discipline." In *Minding the Spirit: The Study of Christian Spirituality*, ed. Elizabeth Dreyer and Mark S. Burrows, 25–41. Baltimore, MD: Johns Hopkins University Press, 2005.

———. *The Mystical Thought of Meister Eckhart: The Man from Whom God Hid Nothing*. New York: Crossroad Publishing Company, 2001.

———. "Mysticism." In *Oxford Encyclopedia of the Reformation*. Vol. 3, 119–24. New York and Oxford: Oxford University Press, 1996.

———. *The Varieties of Vernacular Mysticism 1350–1550*. New York: Crossroad Publishing Company, 2012.

McGovern, Thomas. *Priestly Identity: A Study in the Theology of Priesthood*. Dublin: Four Courts Press, 2002.

McGrath, Alister E. *The Intellectual Origins of the European Reformation*. 2nd ed. Malden, MA: Blackwell Publishing, 2004.

————. *Iustitia Dei: A History of the Doctrine of Justification.* 2 vols. 2nd ed. Cambridge: Cambridge University Press, 1998.

————. *A Life of John Calvin: A Study in the Shaping of Western Culture.* Oxford, UK: Basil Blackwell, 1990.

————. *Reformation Thought: An Introduction.* Oxford, UK, and Cambridge, MA: Blackwell, 1993.

————. "Scholasticism." In *Oxford Encyclopedia of the Reformation.* Vol. 4, 17–20. New York and Oxford: Oxford University Press, 1996.

McGrath-Merkle, Clare. "Gregory the Great's Metaphor of the Physician of the Heart as a Model for Pastoral Identity." *Journal of Religion and Health* 50, no. 2 (June 2011): 374–88.

McKay, Mary Jane. "A Theology of Grace in the Works of Cardinal Pierre de Bérulle (1575–1629)." PhD diss., South Bend, IN: University of Notre Dame, 1992.

McLaughlin, R. Emmet. "Clergy." In *Oxford Encyclopedia of The Reformation.* Vol. 1, 363–66. New York and Oxford: Oxford University Press, 1996.

Mechtilde of Hackeborn, *Liber specialis gratiae* (Paris, 1877).

Meier, Georg August. *Die Lehre von der Trinität in ihrer historischen Entwickelung.* Hamburg: F. und A. Perthes, 1844.

Melanchthon, Philip. *Apologia confessionis.* N.p., 1541.

————. "The Apology of the Augsburg Confession." In *The Book of Concord: The Confessions of the Evangelical Church*, ed. Robert Kolb and Timothy J. Wengert, 27–107. Minneapolis: Fortress Press, 2000.

————. *Confessio fidei exhibita…* Witebergae: Rhau, 1530.

Mercer, Christia. "Platonism and Philosophical Humanism on the Continent." In *A Companion to Early Modern Philosophy*, ed. Steven Nadler, 25–44. Malden, MA: Blackwell Publishing, 2002.

Mersch, Émile. *Le corps mystique du Christ.* Vols. 2 and 3. 2nd ed. Paris: Bruxelles: 1936.

———. "Filii in Filio." *Nouvelle revue théologique* 65 (1938): 551–82, 681–702, 809–30.

———. *La théologie du corps mystique.* Vol. 2. 4th ed. Bruges: Desclée de Brouwer, 1954.

———. *The Whole Christ: The Historical Development of the Doctrine of the Mystical Body in the Scriptures and Tradition.* 2nd ed. Translated by John R. Kelly. Milwaukee: Bruce Publishing Company, 1938. Originally published as *Le Corps Mystique Du Christ.* Paris: Desclée de Brouwer, 1936.

Michel, A. "Hypostase." In *DTC.* Vol. 7 (1970), cols. 418–21.

———. "Ordre: Théologie du XVIe siècle." In *DTC.* Vol. 11 (1931), col. 1365.

———. "Trinité: La crise protestante." In *DTC.* Vol. 15, pt. 2 (1950), cols. 1766–68.

Milbank, John. "Liberality versus Liberalism." In *Religion and Political Thought,* ed. Michael Hoelzl and Graham Ward, 225–36. London and New York: Continuum International Publishing Group, 2006.

Milet, Jean. *God or Christ: The Excesses of Christocentricity.* New York: Crossroad Publishing Company, 1981.

Miller, James. *Measures of Wisdom: The Cosmic Dance in Classical and Christian Antiquity.* Toronto: University of Toronto Press, 1986.

Minton, Anne H. "The Figure of Christ in the Writings of Pierre de Bérulle (1575–1629)." PhD diss., New York University, UMI Dissertation Service, 1979.

———. "Pierre de Bérulle: The Search for Unity." In *The Roots of the Modern Christian Tradition,* 105–23. Kalamazoo, MI: Cistercian Publications, Inc., 1984.

————. "The Spirituality of Bérulle: A New Look." *Spirituality Today* 36, no. 3 (Fall 1984): 210–19.

Mojsisch, Burkhard. "Meister Eckhart." In *Stanford Encyclopedia of Philosophy*, published January 4, 2006, revised April 25, 2011. http://plato.stanford.edu/entries/meister-eckhart/#Bib.

Molien, A. "Bérulle." In *DSAM*. Vol. 1 (1937), cols. 1546–47.

————. *Le cardinal de Bérulle: histoire—doctrine—les meilleurs textes*. Paris: Beauchesne, 1947.

Molina, Antonio de. *Instruccion de sacerdotes*. Burgos, 1608.

Mols, Roger. "Saint Charles Borromée, pionnier de la pastorale moderne." *Nouvelle revue théologique* (1957): 600–622 and 715–47.

Moore, Edward. "Monophysitism and the Evolution of Theological Discourse in Christian Neoplatonism." In *Metaphysical Patterns in Platonism: Ancient, Medieval, Renaissance, and Modern Times*, ed. John F. Finamore and Robert M. Berchman, 133–46. International Society for Neoplatonic Studies. New Orleans: University Press of the South, Inc., 2007.

Morainvillier, Louis de. *Réponse à un libelle diffamatoire sous le nom de l'ami de la verité*. Paris: Estienne, 1622.

Morgain, Stéphane-Marie. "Pierre de Bérulle et le gouvernement des carmélites de France: histoire d'une querelle, 1583–1629." PhD diss., Université de Fribourg, 1992.

————. *Pierre de Bérulle et les carmélites de France: la querelle du gouvernement, 1583–1629*. Paris: Éditions du Cerf, 1995.
————. "La prêtrise selon Pierre de Bérulle: un état et une vie d'unité par intériorité et de société par son extériorité." *Société d'histoire religieuse de la France* 93, no. 1 (2007): 139–52.

————. *La théologie politique de Pierre de Bérulle, 1598–1629*. Paris: Publisud, 2001.

Mornay, Philippe de. *Traité de l'église*. 2nd ed. La Rochelle, 1600.

Mühlen, Karl-Heinz Zur. "Christology." In *Oxford Encyclopedia of the Reformation*. Vol. 1, 314–22. New York and Oxford: Oxford University Press, 1996.

———. "Zur Rezeption der Augustinischen Sakramentsformel 'Accedit verbum ad elementum et fit sacramentum', in der Theologie Luthers." *Zeitschrift für Theologie und Kirche* 70 (1973): 50–76.

Mülejans, Hans. "Publicus und privatus im römischen Recht und im älteren kanonischen Recht unter besonderer Berücksichtigung der Unterscheidung Ius publicum und Ius privatum." PhD diss., Munich: Max Hueber, 1961.

Muñoz, Luis, and Martin Boswood. *Vida y virtudes del venerable varon el P. maestro Iuan de Ávila ...: con algunos elogios de las virtudes, y vidas de algunos de sus mas principales discipulos*. Madrid: Imprenta Real, 1635.

Murray, John. "Systematic Theology." In *Collected Writings of John Murray*. Edinburgh: Banner of Truth, 1982.

Nacchianti, J. *Opera*. Vols. 1 and 2. Venice, 1564–67.

Nazario, J. P. *Commentarium in III partem*. N.p., 1620.

Neuner, J., and J. Dupuis, eds. "Decree on Justification." In *The Christian Faith*, 1932. Bangalore and New York, 2001.

Nicolas, Marie-Joseph. *Théotokos, le mystère de Marie*. Paris, 1965.

Novak, J. D. *Learning, Creating, and Using Knowledge: Concept Maps as Facilitative Tools for Schools and Corporations*. Mahwah, NJ: Lawrence Erlbaum & Associates, 1998.

Noye, Irénée. "Religion, Vertu de: II. École Bérullienne." In *DSAM*. Vol. 13 (1988), col. 316.

O'Brien, Elmer. "Current Theology: Ascetical and Mystical Theology, 1952–1953." *Theological Studies* 15, no. 2 (June 1954): 258–93.

O'Collins, Gerald, and Michael Keenan Jones. *Jesus Our Priest: A Christian Approach to the Priesthood of Christ.* Oxford: Oxford University Press, 2010.

O'Malley, J. "Diocesan and Religious Models of Religious Formation: Historical Perspectives." In Robert James Wister, *Priests: Identity and Ministry,* 54–70. Wilmington, DE: M. Glazier, 1990.

Ocáriz, F., L. F. Mateo Seco, and J. A. Riestra. *The Mystery of Jesus Christ.* Corrected reprint. Gateshead, England: Athenaeum Press Ltd., 2008. Originally published as *El misterio de Jesucristo: lecciones de cristología y soteriología.* Pamplona: Universidad de Navarra, 1991.

Ockham, Guilelmus de, and Philotheus Boehner. *Philosophical Writings: A Selection.* Reprint. London: Nelson, 1962.

Oestreich, Gerhard, Brigitta Oestreich, and H. G. Koenigsberger. *Neostoicism and the Early Modern State.* Translated by David McLintock. Cambridge: Cambridge University Press, 1982. Expanded from the original, Gerhard Oestreich, *Geist und Gestalt des frühmodernen Staates.* Berlin: Duncker & Humblot, 1969.

Olier, J. J. "Lettre 156." In *Lettres spirituelles de M. Olier.* Vol. 2, 83–85. Paris, 1862.

———. "Living Sacraments of Jesus Christ." In *Living for God in Christ Jesus.* An anthology of the writings of Olier published privately for the U.S. Province.

Orcibal, Jean. *Le cardinal de Bérulle: évolution d'une spiritualité.* Paris: Éditions du Cerf, 1965.

———. "Néoplatonisme et Jansénisme: du 'De Libertate' du Gibieuf à 'l'Augustinus'." *Analecta Gregoriana* 71 (1954): 33–52.

———. "Les œuvres de piété du cardinal de Bérulle: essai de classement des inédits et conjectures chronologiques." *Revue d'histoire ecclésiastique* 57 (1962): 813–62.

———. *Origines du jansénisme.* Vol. 2. Paris: Vrin, 1947.

―――. "Vers l'épanouissement du 17e siècle (1580–1600)." In *Histoire spirituelle de la France: spiritualité du catholicisme en France et dans les pays de langue française, des origines à 1914*, 217–26. Paris: Beauchesne, 1964.

Origen. *Commentarii in evangelium Joannis*. In *Origenes Werke*. Vol. 2, ed. E. Preuschen. Die griechischen christlichen Schriftsteller der ersten drei Jahrhunderte. Leipzig: Hinrichs, 1903.

―――. *Commentary on the Song of Songs*. In Deutsche Akademie der Wissenschaften zu Berlin, *Die griechischen christlichen Schriftsteller der ersten Jahrhunderte*, vol. 8. Berlin: Akademie-Verlag.

Osborne, Kenan B. *Priesthood: A History of the Ordained Ministry in the Roman Catholic Church*. New York: Paulist Press, 1989.

Ozment, Stephen. "Mysticism, Nominalism and Dissent." In *The Pursuit of Holiness in Late Medieval and Renaissance Religion*, ed. Charles Trinkaus with Heiko A. Oberman. Leiden: E. J. Brill, 1974.

Paul VI. *Decree on Priestly Training: Optatam Totius*. Boston, MA: St. Paul Editions, 1965.

Pépin, Jean. "Univers dionysien et univers augustinien." In *Aspects de la dialectique*, 179–224. Paris: Desclée de Brouwer, 1956.

Perautl, R. *De dignitate sacerdotali super omnes reges terrae*. N.p., n.d.

Pereira, José, and Robert Fastiggi. *The Mystical Theology of the Catholic Reformation: An Overview of Baroque Spirituality*. Lanham, MD: University Press of America, 2006.

Perl, Eric. "Methexis: Creation, Incarnation, Deification in Saint Maximus Confessor." PhD diss., New Haven, CT: Yale University, 1991.

Persich, Nicholas C. "The Priesthood of the Mystical Body." PhD diss., Rome: Pontificio Instituto Angelico; St. Louis: Society of the Congregation of the Missions, 1951.

Pétau, Denis. "De Trinitate." In *Dogmata theologica Dionysii Petavii e Societate Jesu*. Vol. 3. Paris: Ludovicum Vivès, 1865.

Pfeffer, J. *Directorium sacerdotale*. N.p., 1482.

Philo. *De Somniis*. Loeb Classical Library. Vol. 5. Cambridge: Harvard University Press, 1934.

Pico della Mirandola, Giovanni. *Commento sopra una canzone di Benivieni*. In Giovanni Pico della Mirandola and Sears Reynolds Jayne, *Commentary on a Canzone of Benivieni*. New York: P. Lang, 1984.

Pintard, J. "Caractère sacerdotal et fidélité." *Esprit et vie* 84 (1974): 161–70.

Piolanti, A. "De 'una persona mystica' quadam Jac. Nacchianti." *Euntes docete* 10 (1957): 236–43.

Plotinus, A. H. Armstrong, and Porphyrius Neoplatonicus. "On Nature and Contemplation and the One." In *Plotinus*. Vol. 3. London: William Heinemann, 1967.

Pohle, J. "Priesthood." In *Catholic Encyclopedia*. Vol. 12. New York: Robert Appleton Company, 1911. http://www.newadvent.org/cathen/12409a .htm.

———. "Sanctifying Grace." In *Catholic Encyclopedia*. Vol. 6. http:// www.newadvent.org/cathen/06701a.htm.

Pottier, Aloÿs. *Le P. Louis Lallemant et les grands spirituels de son temps: essai de théologie mystique comparée*. Paris: P. Téqui, 1929.

Pouliquen, Tanguy Marie. *Renaître à la vraie liberté*. Toulouse: Éditions du Carmel, 2012.

Pourrat, P. *Christian Spirituality: Later Developments, From the Renaissance to Jansenism*. London: Burns, Oates and Washbourne Ltd., 1927.

———. *Le sacerdoce: doctrine de l'école française*. Paris: Bloud and Gay, 1931.

———. *Theology of the Sacraments*. St. Louis, MO, and Freiburg: B. Herder, 1910. Originally published as *La théologie sacramentaire: étude de théologie positive*. Paris: Lecoffre, 1907.

Prat, Jean-Marie. *Recherches historiques et critiques sur la Compagnie de Jésus en France au temps du Coton.* Vol. 2. Lyon, 1876.

Preckler, Guillén F. *Bérulle aujourd'hui: 1575–1975: pour une spiritualité de l'humanité du Christ.* Paris: Beauchesne, 1978.

———. *"État" chez le cardinal de Bérulle: théologie et spiritualité des états bérulliens.* Rome: Università Gregoriana, 1974.

Pruett, Gordon E. "A Protestant Doctrine of the Eucharistic Presence." *Calvin Theological Journal* 10 (November 1975): 142–74.

Pseudo-Dionysius. *De Trinitate.* In *Theologica Dogmata*, ed. F. A. Zachariae. Paris, 1865.

———, Colm Luibhéid, and Paul Rorem. *Pseudo-Dionysius: The Complete Works.* New York: Paulist Press, 1987.

———, Beate Regina Suchla, Günter Heil, and Adolf Martin Ritter. *Corpus Dionysiacum.* Berlin: de Gruyter, 1990.

Quintin, J. *Speculum sacerdotii.* Parisiis, 1559.

Rada, Juan de. *Controversiae theologicae inter S. Thomam et Scotum super Tertium Sent.* Vol. 3. Rome, 1615.

Rahner, Hugo. "Die Gottesgeburt: Die Lehre der Kirchenväter von der Geburt Christi aus dem Herzen der Kirche und der Gläubigen." In *Symbole der Kirche*, 11–87. Salzburg: Müller, 1964.

Rahner, Karl. *The Practice of the Faith: A Handbook of Contemporary Spirituality.* New York: Crossroad Publishing Company, 1983. Originally published as *Praxis des Glaubens: geistliches Lesebuch,* ed. Karl Lehmann and Albert Raffelt. Zürich: Benziger, 1982.

Rayez, André. "Dons du Saint-Esprit: III. Période Moderne: Les Spirituels." In *DSAM.* Vol. 3 (1957), cols. 1604–10.

Renaudet, A. *Préréforme et humanisme, à Paris pendant les premières guerres d'Italie, 1494–1517.* Paris: E. Champion, 1916.

Rescher, Nicholas. *Aporetics: Rational Deliberation in the Face of Inconsistency.* Pittsburgh: University of Pittsburgh Press, 2009.

Rétif, André. "Trinité et Mission d'après Bérulle." *Neue Zeitschrift für Missionswissenschaft* 13 (1957): 1–8.

Reymond, Robert L. *John Calvin: His Life and Influence.* Ross-shire, UK: Christian Focus Publications, 2004.

———. *'What is God?' An Investigation of the Perfections of God's Nature.* Ross-shire, UK: Christian Focus Publications Ltd., 2007.

Rhee, Jung Suck. "A History of the Doctrine of Eternal Generation of the Son and Its Significance in the Trinitarianism." Master's thesis, Calvin Theological Seminary, 1989.

Richard, Lucien Joseph. *The Spirituality of John Calvin.* Atlanta: John Knox Press, 1974.

Rist, J. "Pseudo-Dionysius, Neoplatonism and the Weakness of the Soul." In *From Athens to Chartres: Neoplatonism and Medieval Thought*, ed. H. J. Westra, 135–61. Leiden and New York: Brill, 1992.

Ritchl, Albrecht. *A Critical History of the Christian Doctrine of Justification and Reconciliation.* Vol. 1. Translated by John S. Black. Edinburgh: Edmonston and Douglas, 1872.

Rorem, Paul. *Biblical and Liturgical Symbols within the Pseudo-Dionysian Synthesis.* Toronto: Pontifical Institute of Mediaeval Studies, 1984.

———. *Pseudo-Dionysius: A Commentary on the Texts and an Introduction to Their Influence.* New York: Oxford University Press, 1993.

Rotureau, Gaston. *Le cardinal de Bérulle: opuscules de piété.* Paris: Aubier, 1943.

———. "États de Jésus." In *DSAM.* Vol. 4, pt. 2 (1961), col. 1406.

Rousseau, O. "Sacerdoce et monachisme." In *Études sur le sacrement de l'ordre*, 213–31. Paris: Éditions du Cerf, 1957.

Rulla, Luigi M., Joyce Ridick, and Franco Imoda. *Anthropology of the Christian Vocation*. Vol. 1, *Interdisciplinary Bases*. Rome: Gregorian University Press, 1986. First published as *Antropologia della vocazione cristiana*. Casale Monferrato: Ed. Piemme di Pietro M. Rietti, 1985.

———. *Entering and Leaving Vocation: Intrapsychic Dynamics*. Rome: Gregorian University Press, 1976.

Ryan, Michael James. "Character (in Catholic Theology)." In *Catholic Encyclopedia*. Vol. 3, 2. New York: Robert Appleton Company, 1908. http://newadvent.org/cathen/0586a.htm.

Saint-Jean, Raymond. "Religion, Vertu de: I. Théologie Scolastique." In *DSAM*. Vol. 13, cols. 308–20. Paris: Beauchesne, 1988.

Sánchez Bella, Florencio. *La reforma del clero en San Juan de Ávila*. 3rd edition. Madrid: Ediciones Rialp, S.A., 1981.

Scheel, O. "Taulers Mystik und Luthers reformatorische Entdeckung." In *Festgabe D. J. Kaftan*, 298–318. Tübingen, 1920.

Schillebeeckx, Edward. *The Church with a Human Face: A New and Expanded Theology of Ministry*. Translated by John Bowden. New York: Crossroad, 1987. Originally published as *Pleidooi voor Mensen in de Kerk: Christelijke Identiteit en Ambten in de Kerk*. Baarn, Holland: Uitgeverij H. Nelissen BV, 1985.

Schneiders, Sandra. "The Study of Christian Spirituality: Contours and Dynamics of a Discipline." In *Minding the Spirit: The Study of Christian Spirituality*, ed. Elizabeth A. Dreyer and Mark S. Burrows. Baltimore, MD: The Johns Hopkins University Press, 1994.

Schürmann, Reiner, and Meister Eckhart. *Meister Eckhart, Mystic and Philosopher: Translations with Commentary*. Bloomington: Indiana University Press, 1978. Originally published as *Maître Eckhart ou la joie errante: Sermons allemands traduits et commentés*. Paris: Éditions Planète, 1972.

Scot, John Duns. *Opera omnia*. Vol. 26. Paris: Ludovicum Vivès, 1891.

———. *Opera omnia*. Edited by Luke Wadding. Lyons: Sumptibus Laurentii Durand, 1639.

Sebastian, Henry Bowden. "The Oratory of Saint Philip Neri." *Catholic Encyclopedia*. Vol. 11. New York: Robert Appleton Company, 1911. http://www.newadvent.org/cathen/11272a.htm.

Second Vatican Council. *Decree on the Ministry and Life of Priests, December 7, 1965 [Presbyterorum Ordinis]*. Washington, DC: National Catholic Welfare Conference, 1965.

Sedgwick, Alexander. *Jansenism in Seventeenth-Century France: Voices from the Wilderness*. Charlottesville: University of Virginia, 1977.

Sellier, Philippe. "La rhétorique de Saint-Cyran, 1." In *Les deux abbés de Saint-Cyran: Chroniques de Port-Royal, 1977–1978*, 39–54. Paris: Bibliothèque Mazarine.

Serracino-Inglott, Peter. "Ficino the Priest." In *Marsilio Ficino: His Theology, His Philosophy, His Legacy*, ed. Michael J. B. Allen, V. Rees, and Martin Davis, 1–14. Leiden: Brill, 2001.

Shaw, Gregory. *Theurgy and the Soul: The Neoplatonism of Iamblichus*. University Park, PA: Pennsylvania State University Press, 1995.

Sheldon, Henry C. *History of Christian Doctrine*. 2nd ed. New York: Harper & Bros., 1886.

Sheldrake, Philip. *New Westminster Dictionary of Christian Spirituality*. 1st American ed. Louisville, KY: Westminster Knox Press, 2005.

Shepherd, Norman. "The Imputation of Active Obedience." In *A Faith That is Never Alone: A Response to Westminster Seminary California*, ed. P. Andrew Sandlin, 249–78. La Grange, CA: Kerygma Press, 2007.

———. "Justification by Works in Reformed Theology." In *Backbone of the Bible: Covenant in Contemporary Perspective*, ed. P. Andrew Sandlin, 103–20. Nacogdoches, TX: Covenant Media Press, 2004.

Sloyan, Gerard S. *The Three Persons in One God*. Englewood Cliffs, NJ: Prentice-Hall, Inc., 1964.

Solano, J. "De Verbo Incarnato." In *Sacrae Theologiae Summa*. Vol. 3. 3rd ed. Madrid: Editorial Católica, 1953.

Soto, P. *Lectiones de institutione sacerdotum*. Dillingen, 1558.

Spade, P. V. *A Survey of Medieval Philosophy*. Version 2.0. 1985. http://www.pvspade.com/Logic/docs/Survey%202%20Interim.pdf.

Stein, Edith. *The Science of the Cross*. Washington, DC: ICS Publications, 2002. Originally published as *Kreuzzeswissenschaft, Studie über Joannes a Cruce*. Vol. 1, *Edith Steins Werke*. Freiburg im Breisgau: Herder, 1954.

Straubinger, Heinrich. *Religionsphilosophie mit Theodizee*. 2nd ed. Freiburg: Verlag Herder, 1949.

Strenski, Ivan. *Contesting Sacrifice: Religion, Nationalism, and Social Thought in France*. Chicago: University of Chicago Press, 2002.

Strohl, H. *Luther jusqu'en 1520*. New ed. Paris: Presses universitaires de France, 1962.

Suárez, Francisco. *Opera omnia*. Paris: Ludovicum Vivès, 1856–78.

Sullivan, John Edward. *The Image of God: The Doctrine of St. Augustine and Its Influence*. Dubuque, Iowa: Priory Press, 1963.

Tamburello, Dennis E. *Union with Christ: John Calvin and the Mysticism of St. Bernard*. Louisville, KY: Westminster John Knox Press, 1994.

Tan, Seng-Kong. "Calvin's Doctrine of Our Union with Christ." *Quodlibet Online Journal of Christian Theology and Philosophy* 5, no. 4 (Oct. 2003). http://www.quodlibet.net/ articles/tan-union.shtml#_edn3.

Taveau, Claude. *Le cardinal de Bérulle: maître de la vie spirituelle*. Paris: Desclée de Brouwer, 1933.

Terrien, Lawrence. "Living Sacraments: Some Reflections on Priesthood in Light of the French School and Documents of the Magisterium." *Bulletin de Saint-Sulpice* 31 (2005): 243–59.

Thayer, David D. "All or Nothing." Unpublished manuscript.

———. "Living the Life of a Prophet." Unpublished manuscript.

Théron, H. "Le théandrisme spirituel de Bérulle." *L'année théologique augustinienne* 12 (1952): 187–90.

Théry, Gabriel. "Edition critique des pièces relatives au procès d'Eckhart contenues dans le manuscrit 33b de la bibliothèque de Soest." *Archives d'histoire doctrinale et littéraire du moyen âge* 1 (1926–27): 129–268.

Thunberg, Lars. *Man and the Cosmos: The Vision of St. Maximus the Confessor.* Crestwood, NY: St. Vladimir's Seminary Press, 1985.

Tillich, Paul. "The History of Christian Thought: Lectures in Church History." Lecture 28 (Spring 1953), Union Theological Seminary, New York. Verbatim class notes. http://www.religion-online.org/showchapter .asp?title=2310&C=2333.

Trepanier, Lee. "The Protestant Revolution in Theology, Law, and Community." *First Principles,* ISI Web Journal. http://www.firstprinciplesjournal.com /articles.aspx?article=1503.

Trinterud, Leonard J. "The Origins of Puritanism." *Church History* 20 (March 1951): 37–57.

Tripp, D. H. "The Modern World: The Protestant Reformation." In *The Study of Spirituality*, ed. Cheslyn Jones, Geoffrey Wainwright, and Edward Yarnold, 342–46. New York: Oxford University Press, 1986.

Tritemio, J. *De vitae sacerdotalis institutione.* Maguntiae, 1494.

Tronson, Louis, Gilles Chaillot, Paul Cochois, and Irénée Noye. *Traité des saints ordres: 1676: comparé aux écrits authentiques de Jean-Jacques Olier (1657).* Paris: Procure de la Compagnie de Saint-Sulpice, 1984.

Trueman, Carl. "*Simul peccator et Justus*: Marin Luther and Justification." In *Justification in Perspective: Historical Developments and Contemporary Challenges*, ed. Bruce L. McCormack, 73–97. Grand Rapids, MI: Baker Academic, 2006.

Ubertino de Casale. *Arbor vitae crucifixae Jesu*. N.p., n.d.

Uždavinys, Algis. *Philosophy and Theurgy in Late Antiquity*. San Rafael, CA: Sophia Perennis, 2010.

Vacant, Alfred, E. Mangenot, and Emile Amann. *Dictionnaire de théologie catholique, contenant l'exposé des doctrines de la théologie catholique, leurs preuves et leur histoire*. Paris: Letouzey et Ané, 1899–1950. S.vv. "Bellarmin, François-Robert-Romulus," "Eminence. Méthode d'," "Ordre: Théologie du XVIe siècle," "Théologie," "Trinité," and "Trinité: La crise protestante."

Vacherot, Étienne. *Histoire critique de l'école d'Alexandrie*. Vol. 3. Paris: Ladrange, 1846.

Vair, Guillaume Du, and G. Michaut. *De la sainte philosophie: philosophie morale des stoïques*. Paris: J. Vrin, 1945.

Van Essche, Nicholas, Philippe Despont, Ch. de Mallery, and Veuve de Guillaume de La Nouë. *La perle évangelique: tresor incomparable de la sapience divine, nouvellement traduict de latin en francois par les PP. Ch. lez Paris*. Paris, 1602.

Van Manen, Max. *Phenomenology of Practice: Meaning-Giving Methods in Phenomenological Research and Writing*. London and New York: Routledge, Taylor & Francis Group, 2016.

Vázquez, Gabriel. *Commentariorum ac Disputationum in Primum Secundae Sancti Thomae Tomus secundus*. Lyon, 1631.

———. *Commentariorum et disputationum in Tertiam...* Ingolstadt, 1612.

———. "De Sacramento Ordinis." In *Commentaria et Disputationes in III Partem Sancti Thomae*, ed. novissima. Vol. 3. Lyon, 1631.

Venard, Marc. *Histoire du christianisme*. Vol. 8. Paris: Desclée-Fayard, 1995.

———. "Le prêtre en France au début du XVIIe siècle." *Bulletin de Saint-Sulpice* 6 (1980): 197–213.

Venema, Cornelius. "Calvin's Doctrine of the Imputation of Christ's Righteousness: Another Example of 'Calvin against the Calvinists'?" *Mid-Atlantic Journal of Theology* 20 (2009): 15–47.

Verbeke, Gerard. *The Presence of Stoicism in Medieval Thought*. Washington, DC: Catholic University of America Press, 1983.

Versaldi, G. "Priestly Celibacy from the Canonical and Psychological Points of View." In *Vatican II, Assessment and Perspectives: Twenty-five Years After (1962–1987)*. Vol. 3, ed. R. Latourelle, 131–57. Mahwah, NJ, 1989.

Vieillard-Baron, Jean-Louis. "L'image de l'homme chez Descartes et chez le cardinal de Bérulle." *Revue philosophique de la France et de l'étranger* 182, no. 4 (Oct.–Dec. 1992): 403–19.

Viller, Marcel, Charles Baumgartner, and André Rayez. *Dictionnaire de spiritualité: ascétique et mystique, doctrine et histoire*. Paris: G. Beauchesne et ses fils, 1932–95. S.vv. "Abnégation: II. Tradition patristique, médiévale, moderne," "Bellarmin, François-Robert-Romulus," "Bérulle," "Contemplation," "Contemplation: conclusion générale," "Contemplation: La theoria phusikè," "Dons du Saint-Esprit: III. Période Moderne: Les Spirituels," "Duns Scot," "État," "États de Jésus," "Hypostase," "Perfection," "Perfection, VI: 16e–17e siècles," "Religion, Vertu de," and "Religion, Vertu de: II. École Bérullienne."

Voet, Gisbert. *Selectae Disputationes Theologiae*. Pt. 1. N.p., 1648.

Vogel, C. "Le retour du presbytre au rang des laïcs." *Revue des sciences religieuses* (Jan. 1973): 56–122.

Walker, D. P. *The Ancient Theology: Studies in Christian Platonism from the Fifteenth to the Eighteenth Century*. Ithaca, NY: Cornell University Press, 1972.

Walsh, Eugene Aloysius. "The Priesthood in the Writings of the French School: Bérulle, de Condren, Olier." PhD diss., Washington, DC: Catholic University of America, 1949.

Warfield, Benjamin Breckenridge. *Calvin and Calvinism*. Grand Rapids, MI: Baker Book House, 1931. Reprint, 1981.

Weaver, Rebecca Harden. *Divine Grace and Human Agency: A Study of the Semi-Pelagian Controversy*. North American Patristic Society, Patristic Monograph Series 15. Macon, GA: Mercer University Press, 1996.

Weeks, Andrew. *German Mysticism*. Albany, NY: State University of New York, 1993.

Welch, Lawrence J. "Priestly Identity Reconsidered: A Reply to Susan Wood." *Worship* 70, no. 4 (July 1996): 307–18.

Wengert, Timothy J. *Priesthood, Pastors, Bishops: Public Ministry for the Reformation and Today*. Minneapolis, MN: Fortress Press, 2008.

Whannou, Charles A. *Subsistence chez Bérulle: essai historique et doctrinale sur la place et l'importance de la notion de "subsistence" dans la spiritualité bérullienne de la divinisation*. Porto-Novo, République du Bénin: Imprimerie Notre-Dame, 1993.

Wiles, Maurice. "Eternal Generation." *Journal of Theological Studies* 12 (October 1961): 284–91.

Wilhelm, J. "Charismata." In *Catholic Encyclopedia*. Vol. 3. http://www.newadvent.org/cathen/03588e.htm.

Williams, Charles E. *The French Oratorians and Absolutism, 1611–1641*. New York: Peter Lang, 1989.

Yelle, G. *Le mystère de la sainteté du Christ selon le cardinal Pierre de Bérulle*. Montréal: Université de Montréal, 1938.

Zanta, Léontine. *La renaissance du stoïcisme au XVIe siècle*. Paris: H. Champion, 1914.

Zwanepol, Klaas. "A Human God: Some Remarks on Luther's Christology," *Concordia Journal* 30, nos. 1–2 (Jan.–Apr. 2004): 40–53.

Clare McGrath-Merkle

Bérulle's Spiritual Theology of Priesthood

For Beth,
With deepest gratitude!
Clare

Studien zur systematischen Theologie, Ethik und Philosophie

Herausgegeben von
Thomas Marschler und Thomas Schärtl

Band 12